Call First! Many things change
from month to month: hours of opera-
tion, location, entertainment offered, facilities,
etc. Telephone area codes are listed next to the
city name.

Bars Many codes apply only a few nights a week -
for example **CW** (country/western), **D** (dancing), **L**
(leather), **E** (live entertainment), **K** (karaoke) or **18+**.
You should call the bar to verify what entertainment is
scheduled for which nights. Bars coded **BW** (beer/wine)
might not serve both.

Accommodations Most accommodations (especially
B&Bs) require advance reservations. It's a good idea to
request a brochure ahead of time, and to be clear about
deposit and cancellation policies when making reservations.

Restaurants All restaurants listed are gay-friendly; those
with mostly gay/lesbian clientele are coded **MW**. Cafes usually serve just pastries or sandwiches; if they serve hot food,
"full menu" is listed. "Cont'l" means European or French fare.
"American" menus range from steak & seafood to home-
style or hamburgers. If a variety of vegetarian entrees is
offered, "plenty veggie" is noted.

Gyms are workout facilities, not bathhouses. They're
mostly straight, unless coded **MW** or **MO**.

Men's Clubs include sex clubs, bathhouses, playspaces
and sex-oriented groups.

Cruisy Areas In larger cities (San Diego, for instance),
you're more likely to meet vice cops than partners
at public grounds. Try the local bar or bath-
house instead if you're bent on picking
up. To avoid entrapment, note the
Sodomy Laws on page 6.

TABLE OF CONTENTS

TABLE OF CONTENTS

G. M. Gatta

This is the 33rd edition of the **Damron Address Book** - which many know simply as "the guide" - the essential cheat-sheet for finding gay community since before Stonewall!

In many ways, Damron has documented the history of gay men in America. Browsing through old books, you can see how our communities and resources have changed and grown. Here at Damron, we hear the stories everyday, "how Damron's guide influenced my life."

We publish a variety of titles, each with their own personality. **Damron Accommodations** delivers all the details you want when choosing a bed-and-breakfast. **The Damron Road Atlas** gives you the maps you need when locating a business in a big city. And "the guide" gives you everything you need when exploring new territory - whether a bump-in-the-road or a metro city!

My job for the last seven years has been compiling fresh data to maintain Damron's position as the best seller in this competitive market of gay travel, newly-discovered by the "straight" publishing world. Huge conglomerates have entered the fray, trying to cash in on the gay market, but Damron's 33-year reputation with gay travellers has kept us on top.

After all, we are a gay-owned and gay-run company. Who else but a lesbian president, her gay brother and a staff of fags, dykes, fag hags, and a tranny-boy, could deliver the information that gay men rely on to explore North America? Our rapport with our gay "family" helps us maintain accurate, concise listings.

You be the judge of our success - does "the guide" give you what you need? I know you'll let me know what we've missed. Correspondence with you is why Damron is the leader in up-to-date gay travel information. New information and corrections submitted by our readers have been our bloodline! In fact, if you send us information that we haven't yet discovered, we'll include it in the next edition and you will receive a complimentary copy! What better way for us to say thanks for your expertise?

As your options for gay travel, and gay-oriented travel guides, increase, we're glad you've chosen to stay with "the guide" that's been an essential part of gay men's travels for decades.

THE DAMRON ADDRESS BOOK

is produced by

Publisher	**Damron Company**
President & Editor-in-Chief	**Gina M. Gatta**
Chief Financial Officer	**Edward Gatta, Jr.**
Vice President	**Mikal Shively**
Managing Editor	**Ian Philips**
Editors	**Drew K. Campbell** **Erika O'Connor**
Design & Layout	**Beth Rabena Carr**
Art Director	**Kathleen Pratt**
Advertising/Sales Director	**David Howley**
Account Executive	**Gillian Francis**
Comptroller	**Louise Mock**
In Memory of	**Bob Damron** **Dan Delbex**

Mail: PO Box 422458, San Francisco, CA 94142
Email: DamronCo@aol.com
Web: http://www.damron.com/
Fax: (415) 703-9049
Phone: (415) 255-0404
Copyright © 1997 Damron Company Inc.
Printed in Hong Kong

SODOMY LAWS

You may be shocked to see this word "up in lights" but we think you'll be more shocked to find out that in certain states you can be fined and even imprisoned for sodomy. So before you go, know your rights. And play safe.

STATES WITH HETEROSEXUAL & HOMOSEXUAL SODOMY LAWS:

Alabama	Arizona	Florida
Georgia	Idaho	Louisiana
Michigan	Massachusetts	Mississippi
North Carolina	Minnesota	Rhode Island
South Carolina	Utah	Virginia

STATES WITH HOMOSEXUAL SODOMY LAWS ONLY:

Arkansas	Kansas	Maryland
Missouri	Montana	Oklahoma
	Tennessee	

To get your state off this list, contact the National Gay & Lesbian Task Force at [202] 332-6483.

PLEASE READ THIS NOTICE ABOUT "CRUISY AREAS"

Certain locations are categorized as "Cruisy Areas." These areas include but are not limited to parks, rest stops, beaches, university campuses and other public facilities. Information regarding these areas is furnished to Damron by various sources and due to time and other constraints, Damron is unable to investigate these areas. Areas marked as "AYOR" (At Your Own Risk) may involve risk and the reader should proceed with caution. However, the absence of an AYOR rating does not guarantee the safety or security of any area. Therefore, Damron makes no warranty or representation as to the safety, security or status of those areas marked as cruisy areas. Damron urges readers to avoid sexual activity within Cruisy Areas. **MOST POLICE DEPTS. IN THE USA HAVE COPIES OF THE ADDRESS BOOK, BEWARE.**

NATIONAL RESOURCES

AIDS/HIV

National AIDS/HIV Hotlines
[800] 342-2437
[800] 243-7889 (TTY)
[800] 344-7432 (en español)

Sexual Health Information Line
[613] 563-2437 (Canada)

CANCER

Cancer Information Service
[800] 422-6237

HATE CRIMES

National Hate Crimes Hotline
[800] 347-4283

YOUTH SERVICES

Hetrick-Martin Institute
[212] 674-2400 (TTY)

LYRIC (Lavendar Youth Recreation/Information Center)
[415] 863-3636
[800] 246-7743 (outside San Francisco)

CHEMICAL DEPENDENCY

Pride Institute [800] 547-7433

LEGAL RIGHTS

Lambda Legal Defense Fund
[212] 995-8585 (New York City, NY)

National Gay/Lesbian Task Force
[202] 332-6483 (Washington, DC)
[202] 332-6219 (TTY)

TRAVEL

**International Gay Travel
Association (IGTA)**
[800] 448-8550

Enter the Damron

PROVINCETOWN

Enjoy the quaint New England charm of the award-winning Six Webster Place.

Sweepstakes Rules

Responsibility: Damron Company assumes no responsibility for any delay, loss or accident caused by fault or negligence of any hotel, transportation company or local operator rendering any part of tour services, nor for any damage or inconvenience caused by late air travel. Damron Company shall not be responsible for any expense caused by loss or damage of personal items including but not limited to luggage and its contents.

Deadline: Entries must be received by April 15, 1997

Prize: 4 nights lodging in Provincetown, Massachusetts. Airfare not included.

Drawing: Prize Winner will be determined by random drawing on April 20, 1997 from all entries received. Prize winners will be notified by mail and/or phone.

Eligibility: Open to anyone over 18 years of age, except employees of Damron Company, their affiliates and agencies or employees and agents for the resorts participating in these sweepstakes. Void where prohibited or restricted by law. All federal, state and local laws apply.

No purchase necessary. One entry per person. Complete entry form and mail to the Damron Company.

Sweepstakes

WIN!
4 NIGHTS

accommodations for two in the friendly coastal resort town of Provincetown.

Clip-and-mail this coupon

Entries must be received by April 15, 1997

☐ I'd be happy to accept a FREE Damron catalog

Name _____

Address _____

City _____

State/Zip _____

Phone _____

I hereby certify that I am 18 years of age or older, and I have read the rules and regulations governing this sweepstakes and comply.

Signature _____

complete and mail to: **The Damron Company**
PO Box 422458, San Francisco, CA 94142-2458

The most informative travel guide for lesbians-on-the-go, with overviews that give you the "inside story" on local lesbian hangouts and nightlife. Covers the U.S., Canada and the Caribbean with **over 4,500 listings** for lesbian-friendly bars, accommodations, and resources. Detailed listings note multi-racial clientele, wheelchair accessibility, and much more for women of all backgrounds and abilities. Plus special section on **Camping & RVs**, and year-long **calendars of women's Festivals & Events**, as well as commercial Tours & Adventures.

Only **$11.95**

To order, call **(800) 462-6654**

or turn forward one page to the Mail Order Form

Outside the U.S., call **(415) 255-0404**

Mail: Damron Mail Order
PO Box 422458,
San Francisco, CA 94142

*please include $5 shipping fee
plus $1 for each additional item*

The only lesbian & gay atlas is the perfect companion to the Address Book and the Women's Traveller! This attractive full-color guide features **more than 125 maps** with color-coded dots that pinpoint lesbian & gay bars, accommodatons and bookstores in **over 60 cities** and resorts in the U.S. and Canada.

Damron Road Atlas

Unmapped listings cover restaurants, cafés, gyms, travel agencies, publications and more. "Info boxes" detail major annual gay events, local tourist

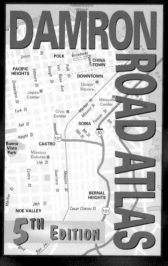

attractions, transit, weather, best views of the city, and directions from the airport.

Only **$14.95**

Ask for a FREE DAMRON CATALOG

of international lesbian & gay travel guides!

Damron Mail Order

item	qty	price
subtotal		
CA residents: 8.25% tax		
Shipping: $5 + $1 per additional item		
Overnight: add $15		
Total		

Payment

(no cash, COD or stamps)

☐ Check/Money Order   ☐ Mastercard

payable to Damron Company   ☐ Visa   ☐ Amex

Card # _____

Signature _____

Name _____

Address _____

City _____

State/Zip _____

Phone # _____

Allow 4-6 weeks for delivery • Packaged discreetly
Mail to: The Damron Company, PO Box 422458
San Francisco, CA 94142-2458   or call

[800] 462-6654   or   [415] 255-0404

Spartacus **$32.95**
(worldwide, for
men, 4 languages)

Odysseus **$25**
(worldwide, for
men & women)

San Francisco
Gay Escort
$10.95

Spartacus Spain
$19.95

Paris Scene,
London Scene
$11.95 each

Betty & Pansy's
Severe Queer Review
Please specify NY, DC,
or SF.   **$9.95** each

(800)
462-6654

International
Travel Guides

Colt
Calendar
(availability
limited)

$12

Best Guide
Amsterdam
$18.95

Gay Mexico
$21.95

G'Day Guide
(Australia accommodations)
$14.95

Damron Accommodations

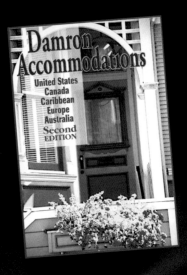

Now you'll always have a home away from home! The first and only **full-color guide** to gay-friendly B&Bs, inns, hotels and other accommodations in North America, Europe and Australia. Most listings include **color photographs** and a comprehensive description. Sophisticated travellers will appreciate the handy multiple **cross-referenced index**. Over 400 pages. Only **$18.95**

To order, call (800) 462-6654

or just turn back to the Damron Mail Order Section

The NAMES Project
AIDS Memorial
Quilt
1987-1997

**A tribute to the lives of those we have lost.
A celebration of the souls behind the statistics.
A way to teach youth about HIV.
A means of opening closed minds and
softening hard hearts.**

The NAMES Project displays the Quilt nearly 2,000 times
each year, in towns great and small, to help bring an end
to AIDS. You can help, too. Call or write us to find out
how you can remember a friend and remind a nation
that fighting AIDS is everyone's work.

How Many Names Will It Take?

THE NAMES PROJECT
FOUNDATION

310 Townsend Street, Suite 310 • San Francisco, CA 94107
415 • 882 • 5500 FAX 415 • 882 • 6200
http://www.aidsquilt.org

Sail Away!

• ADVance - Damron ADVenture Cruises

• RSVP

• Olivia

• Pied Piper

Call your ADVance - Damron cruise specialist at (713) 682-2650 or (800) 695-0880

http://www.advance-damron.com

ADVANCE·DAMRON
VACATIONS

1997 Damron Address Book

Somewhere Over the Rainbow is a Place Called San Francisco...

Put on your Ruby Slippers & Celebrate Pride '97 in San Francisco! June 28 & 29, 1997

Saturday & Sunday

Events all week before the Celebration!:
Films, culture, art, entertainment,
politics, and parties, parties, parties!

For information about the
Largest Pride Celebration
on this side of the Rainbow:

call 415/864-FREE Fax: 415/864-5889
email: sfpride@aol.com

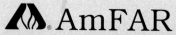

Your playground
just got bigger!

KEYWORD: OnQ
presented by the GLCF

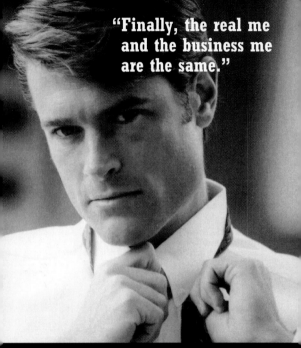

ALABAMA

Auburn (334)

BOOKSTORES & RETAIL SHOPS
Etc. 125 N. College St., 821-0080 (WC) noon-6pm, clsd Sun

Birmingham (205)

INFO LINES & SERVICES
AA Gay/Lesbian 933-8964, 8pm Wed, 11am Sat, 6pm Sun

▲ **Community Real Estate Referrals** (800) 346-5592, gay realtor at your service, n
rentals

Lambda Resource Center 205 32nd St. S., 326-8600, info line 6-10pm Mon-Sat

BARS
22nd Street Jazz Cafe 710 22nd St. S., 252-0407 (GF,F,E,S) clsd Sun-Tue

Club 21 117-1/2 21st St. N., 322-0469 (GF,D,MRC-AF,E,S) 10pm-4am Th-Sat

Mikatam 3719 3rd Ave. S. , 592-0790 (M,D,WC) 3pm-?, patio

Misconceptions Tavern 600 32nd St. S., 322-1210 (M,F,V)

The Quest Club 416 24th St. S., 251-4313 (MW,WC) 24hrs daily, DJ Th-Sun, patio

Southside Pub 2830 7th Ave. S., 324-0997 (GF,F) 3pm-midnight Sun-Wed, til
2am Thurs, til 3am Fri-Sat

RESTAURANTS & CAFES
Anthony's 2131 7th Ave. S., 324-1215 (WC) lunch 11am-2:30pm weekdays & dinner 5pm-11pm Mon-Sat, clsd Sun

Common Ground 838-2277/424-2286, coffeehouse for youthful gay men & lesbians, their peers and their role models

TRAVEL & TOUR OPERATORS
A World of Travel 2101 Civic Center Blvd., 458-8888/(800) 458-3597, 8am-8pm,
til 5pm Fri, 1pm-5pm Sun, clsd Sat

Exotic Travel 1406 17th St. S., 930-0911/(800) 414-7015 (IGTA) 7am-7pm, clsd
Sun

Village Travel 1929 Cahaba Rd., 870-4866/(800) 999-2899 (IGTA)

SPIRITUAL GROUPS
BCC (Birmingham Community Church) PO Box 130221, 35233, 933-7305, 7pm
Tue Bible study, 7pm Sat services, gospel singing 2nd Sat

Covenant MCC 5117 1st Ave. N., 599-3363, 11am & 7pm Sun

Integrity/Alabama PO Box 530785, 35253-0785, 871-1815, 6pm 4th Sun

PUBLICATIONS
Alabama Forum 205 S. 32nd St. Ste. 216, 328-9228, monthly

The Rainbow Pages PO Box 36784, 35236, 424-2286, business & organization
guide

EROTICA
Alabama Adult Books 901 5th Ave. N., 322-7323, 24hrs

Birmingham Adult Books 7610 1st Ave. N., 836-1580, 24hrs

The Downtown Bookstore 2731 8th Ave. N., 328-5525

Jupiter Theater 2500 7th Ave. S., 324-4552, large screen movies

Pleasure Books 7606 1st Ave. N., 836-7379

Top Hat Cinema 9221 Todd Dr., 833-8221

Dothan (334)

BARS

Chuckie Bee's 134-A Foster St., 794-0230 (MW,D,S) 9pm-6am Th-Sun

Huntsville (205)

INFO LINES & SERVICES

GALOP (Gay/Lesbian Org. of Professionals) PO Box 914, 35804, 517-6127, meets 4th Th

Pink Triangle Alliance 539-4235, 9am-9pm , resource & info line

ACCOMMODATIONS

The Fairmont 1906 Fairmont Rd., 35801, 534-1177 (M,SW,N) hot tub

BARS

Vieux Carre 1204 Posey, 534-5970 (MW,NH,D,E,WC) 7pm-2am, from 4pm Sun, karaoke Tue, country/western Wed, DJ Fri-Sat, shows Sun

BOOKSTORES & RETAIL SHOPS

Rainbow's Ltd. 4321 University Dr. Ste. 400-B, rear, 722-9220 (WC) 11am-9pm Mon-Sat, 1pm-6pm Sun, clsd Tue, lesbigay

SPIRITUAL GROUPS

MCC 3015 Sparkman Dr., NW, 851-6914, 11am & 6pm Sun, 7pm Wed

Mobile (334)

BARS

B-Bob's 6157 Airport Blvd. #201, 341-0102 (MW,D,YC,PC,WC) 5pm til ?

Gabriel's Downtown 55 S. Joachim St., 432-4900 (M,V,PC) 5pm - ?

Golden Rod 219 Conti, 433-9175 (M,PC) 9am-?, 24hrs wknds

Outer Limits 7 S. Joachim St., 433-3262 (MW,D,F,E,S,PC) 24hrs

Society Lounge 51 S. Conception, 433-9141 (★MW,D,S,PC,WC) noon-?

Zippers 215 Conti St., 433-7436 (M,NH,PC) 4pm-?

SPIRITUAL GROUPS

Cornerstone MCC 2201 Gov't St., 476-4621, 11am & 7pm Sun

Montgomery (334)

INFO LINES & SERVICES

BWMT (Black/White Men Together) PO Box 603, 36101, 284-2421, social/support group

ACCOMMODATIONS

Lattice Inn B&B 1414 S. Hull St., 832-9931/Fax: 264-0075 (GF,SW) full brkfst

BARS

Hojons 215 N. Court St., 269-9672 (MW,D,S) 8pm-?, til 2am Sat, clsd Sun-Mon

Jimmy Mac's 211 Lee St., 264-5933 (MW,D,PC) 7pm-2am

TRAVEL & TOUR OPERATORS

Alabama Bureau of Tourism & Travel PO Box 4309, 36103, 242-4169/(800) 252-2262

SPIRITUAL GROUPS

MCC 5290 Vaughn (Unitarian Church), 279-7894, 5:30pm Sun

Tuscaloosa (205

INFO LINES & SERVICES
Gay/Lesbian/Bisexual Alliance UA Ferguson Student Center, 3rd flr., 348-7210, self-help/rap groups

BARS
Michael's 2201 6th St., 758-9223 (MW,D,S) 6:30pm-?, clsd Sun

Rumors 5479 Jug Factory Rd. E., 752-0499 (S) 8pm-? Wed-Sat

BOOKSTORES & RETAIL SHOPS
Illusions 519 College Park, 349-5725, 11am-5:45pm

ALASKA

Anchorage (907

INFO LINES & SERVICES
AA Gay/Lesbian 1231 W. 27th Ave., 272-2312, 7pm Mon, Th, Fri & Sun

▲ **Anchorage Confidential Connection** 563-MEET, Meet hot local guys! Record, listen, respond to free ads. Use free code 9966.

Anchorage Gay/Lesbian Helpline PO Box 200070, 99520, 258-4777, 6-11pm Wed-Sun

The Berdache Society P.O. Box 92381, 99509-2381, transgender group

Gay Teens 3201 Turnigan St. (Unitarian Church), 688-3906, 4-6pm Sat

ACCOMMODATIONS
Arctic Feather B&B 211 W. Cook, 277-3862 (MW) 5 min. to downtown, nice view

▲ **Aurora Winds Resort B&B** 7501 Upper O'Malley, 346-2533/Fax: 346-3192 (GF) on the hillside above Anchorage on nearly 2 acres

Cheney Lake B&B 6333 Colgate Dr., 337-4391/Fax: 338-1023 (GF)

The Pink Whale 3627 Randolph St., 563-2684 (GF) self-serve kitchen, smokefree children welcome

BARS
Blue Moon 530 E. 5th Ave., 277-0441 (MW,D,S,WC) 2pm-2:30am, from 3pm wknds

O'Brady's Burgers & Brew 6901 E. Tudor Rd., 338-1080 (GF,F) 10am-midnight, some veggie

Raven 618 Gambell, 276-9672 (MW,NH,WC) 11am-2:30am

▲ **The Wave** 3103 Spenard Rd., 561-9283 (GF,D,S,V,WC) 6pm-2:30am, clsd Sun-Tue (seasonal), patio, also espresso bar upstairs

BOOKSTORES & RETAIL SHOPS
Cyrano's Bookstore & Cafe 413 'D' St., 274-2599 (F,S,BW,WC) 10am-10pm

TRAVEL & TOUR OPERATORS
Apollo 1207 West 47th Ave., 561-0661/(800) 770-0661 (IGTA)

Triangle Tours 733 W. 4th Ave. Ste. 817, 786-3707/(800) 779-3701 (IGTA)

SPIRITUAL GROUPS
Lamb of God MCC PO Box 142095, 258-5266, 11am & 7pm Sun, 7pm Wed

Unitarian Universalist Fellowship 3201 Turnigan St., 248-3737, 9am & 10:30am Sun

PUBLICATIONS
Anchorage Press 702 W. 32nd St. #203, 99503, 561-1737/Fax: 561-7777, alternative paper, arts & entertainment listings

▲ **Identity Northview** PO Box 200070, 99520, 258-4777/Fax: 248-2421, monthly, $3, also sponsors Fourth Fri Potluck & Anchorage Gay/Lesbian Helpline

EROTICA

French Quarter 4028 Mountain View, 276-9049

La Sex Shoppe/Ace's 305 W. Dimond Blvd., 522-1987, 24hrs

Swingers Books & Gifts 710 W. Northern Lights Blvd., 561-5039, 24hrs

Chugiak

INFO LINES & SERVICES

Alaskan Tpeople P.O. Box 670349, 99567-0349, transgender group

Fairbanks (907)

INFO LINES & SERVICES

Lesbian/Gay Info Line 458-8288, 5:30-8pm

ACCOMMODATIONS

Alta's B&B 5132 Haystack Mtn. Rd., 99708, 389-2582/457-0246 (MW) full brkfst, private/shared baths, log home above Chatanika River

Billie's Backpackers Hostel 2895 Mack Rd., 457-2034 (F) B&B, hostel and campsites

Crabtree Guest House 724 College Rd., 451-6501 (M) kitchens, shared baths, kids okay

Fairbanks Hotel 517 3rd Ave., Box Q, 99701, 456-6411/(888) 329-4685 (GF)

BARS

Palace Saloon Alaskaland, 456-5960 (GF,D,S) 7-10pm, til 3am Fri-Sat (seasonal), more gay after 11pm wknds

EROTICA

Fantasyland Video 1765 Richardson Hwy., 488-0879, 24hrs

Homer (907)

ACCOMMODATIONS

Island Watch B&B PO Box 1394, 99603, 235-2265 (GF,WC) full brkfst, kitchens, smokefree, kids okay, pets okay

TRAVEL & TOUR OPERATORS

Alaska Fishing Charters PO Box 2807, 99603, 235-6468/(800) 478-7777, deluxe cabin cruiser for big-game fishing (halibut)

Juneau (907)

RESTAURANTS & CAFES

Inn at the Summit Waterfront Cafe 455 S. Franklin St., 586-2050, 5-10pm, full bar

TRAVEL & TOUR OPERATORS

Alaska Tourism Marketing Council PO Box 110801, 99811, 465-2010, ask for vacation planner

Ketchikan (907)

ACCOMMODATIONS

Millar Street House PO Box 7281, 99901, 225-1258/(800) 287-1607 (GF) also kayak tours

Seward (907)

ACCOMMODATIONS
▲ **Sauerdough Lodging** 225 4th Ave., 224-8946 (GF)

ARIZONA

Bisbee (520)

BARS
St. Elmo's 36 Brewery Gulch Ave., 432-5578 (GF,E) 10am-1am, live bands Fri-Sat

Cottonwood (520)

ACCOMMODATIONS
Mustang B&B 4257 Mustang Dr., 646-5929 (MW) also one RV hookup, movie theater, full brkfst

Flagstaff (520)

INFO LINES & SERVICES
▲ **Community Real Estate Referrals** (800) 346-5592, gay realtor at your service, no rentals

ACCOMMODATIONS
Hotel Monte Vista 100 N. San Francisco St., 779-6971/(800) 545-3068 (GF,F) full bar, cafe, historic lodging circa 1927

BARS
Charlie's 23 N. Leroux, 779-1919 (GF,F,WC) noon-1am, Sun brunch, patio

The Depot 26 S. San Francisco St., 773-9550 (GF,D,E,WC) 3pm-1am, patio

Monte Vista Lounge 100 N. San Francisco St., 779-6971 (GF,E) 10am-1am, cafe from 6am

Kingman (520)

ACCOMMODATIONS

Kings Inn Best Western 2930 E. Andy Devine, 753-6101/(800) 528-1234 (GF,SW) non-smoking rooms available, bakery on premises

Mesa (602)

TRAVEL & TOUR OPERATORS

Executive Tour Associates PO Box 42151, 85274-2151, (800) 382-1113/898-0098 (IGTA)

EROTICA

▲ Castle Boutique 8315 E. Apache Trail, 986-6114, 24hrs

Phoenix (602)

INFO LINES & SERVICES

AA Lambda Club 2622 N. 16th St., 264-1341, 6pm, 8pm

Camelback Business & Professional Assoc. PO Box 2097, 85001, 225-8444

▲ Community Real Estate Referrals (800) 346-5592, gay realtor at your service, no rentals

Lesbian/Gay Community Switchboard 3136 N. 3rd Ave., 234-2752/Fax: 234-0873, 10am-10pm (volunteers permitting) info & referrals

▲ **Phoenix Confidential Connection** 252-3333, Meet hot local guys! Record, listen, respond to free ads. Use free code 9966.

Valley of the Sun Gay/Lesbian Center 3136 N. 3rd Ave., 265-7283, info & referrals

Valley One In Ten 3136 N. 3rd Ave., 264-5437, 7pm Wed, youth group, HIV peer education

Accommodations

Arizona Bed & Breakfast (800) 974-1474/274-1474, reservation service

▲ **Arizona Royal Villa Apts.** 1110 E. Turney Ave. #8, 266-6883 (MO,SW,N) jacuzzi, cont'l brkfst

▲ **Arizona Sunburst Inn** 6245 N. 12th Pl., 274-1474/(800) 974-1474 (MO,SW,N)

Arrowzona 'Private' Casitas PO Box 11253, Glendale, 85318, 561-1200/(800) 266-7829 (MW,IGTA) hot tub

Bed & Breakfast Inn Arizona PO Box 11253, Glendale, 85318, 561-0335/266-7829 (GF)

▲ **The Caritas B&B Network** Cave Creek, (800) CARITAS (227-4827), see ad in center National section

Larry's Bed & Breakfast 502 W. Claremont Ave., 249-2974 (M,SW,N) full brkfst; hot tub

Stewart's B&B 1319 E. Hayward, 861-2500/Fax: 861-0242 (M,L,N,WC)

Westways Resort P.O. Box 5550, Carefree, 488-1110 (MW,SW,IGTA)

Windsor Cottage B&B 62 W. Windsor, 264-6309 (MW,SW,N) patio, gay-owned/run

ARS

307 Lounge 222 E. Roosevelt, 252-0001 (M,NH,TG,F,S,WC) 6am-1am, Sun brunch

Ain't Nobody's Bizness 3031 E. Indian School #7, 224-9977 (MW,D,WC) 2pm-1am

Apollos 5749 N. 7th St., 277-9373 (M,NH,K) 8am-1am, diverse crowd

Cash Inn 2140 E. McDowell Rd., 244-9943 (MW,D,CW,WC) 6pm-1am, from 3pm Sun, clsd Mon-Tue

Charlie's 727 W. Camelback Rd., 265-0224 (M,D,CW,WC) noon-1am, Sun brunch & BBQ

Country Club Bar & Grill 4428 N. 7th Ave., 264-4553 (MW,D,CW,F,K,WC) 11am-1am

Cruisin' Central 1011 N. Central Ave., 253-3376 (M,S,OC,WC) 6am-1am, hustlers

Detour/Metro 4102 E. Thomas Rd., 224-9471 (M,NH,D,L,WC) 3pm-3am

The Eagle 4531 N. 7th St., 285-0833 (M,F) 3pm-1am, from 1pm Sun, sports pub

Foster's 4343 N. 7th Ave., 263-8313 (MW,D,L,YC,WC) 4pm-1am

Harley's 155 155 W. Camelback Rd., 274-8505 (MW,D) noon-1am, also The Cell in back (M,L)

J.C.'s Fun One Lounge 5542 N. 43rd Ave., Glendale, 939-0528 (MW,D,S,WC) 11am-1am

Johnny Mc's 138 W. Camelback Rd., 266-0875 (M,OC) 10am-1am

Marlys' 15615 N. Cave Creek Rd., 867-2463 (MW,NH,F,E) 3pm-1am

Nasty's 3108 E. McDowell Rd., 267-8707 (MW,D,WC) noon-1am, sports bar

Nu Towne 5002 E. Van Buren, 267-9959 (M,WC) 10am-1am, popular Sun & Tue

Options Restaurant & Media Bar 5111 N. 7th St., 263-5776 (MW,F,S,WC) 11am-1am, internet media lounge

Pookie's Cafe 4540 N. 7th St., 277-2121 (MW,E) noon-midnight, kitchen til 11pm, Sun brunch

The Pumphouse 4132 E. McDowell Rd., 275-3509 (M,NH) 1pm-1am

Trax 1724 E. McDowell, 254-0231 (M,D,A,L,YC,WC) 6am-1am, til 3am Fri-Sat

Winks 5707 N. 7th St., 265-9002 (★MW,F,E,S) 11am-1am

RESTAURANTS & CAFES

Alexi's 3550 N. Central, 279-0982, clsd Sun, patio, intercont'l, full bar

AZ-88 7535 E. Scottsdale Mall, 994-5576, 11am-11pm, some veggie

Azz Jazz 1906 E. Camelback Rd., 263-8482 (E,WC) 5-10pm, til 1am wknds, clsd Mon, Argentinian, full bar

Deceptions 5025 N. 7th Ave., 274-6275 (S,WC) 11am-1am, kitchen open til midnight, til 3am wknds

Eddie's Grill 4747 N. 7th St., 241-1188 (WC) lunch & dinner, clsd Sun, patio, some veggie, full bar

Katz's Deli 5144 N. Central, 277-8814, 7am-3pm, til 7:30pm Tue-Fri

Shorty'z 801 N. 1st St., 253-1985 (MW) 7am-3pm, patio

GYMS & HEALTH CLUBS

Beauvais Fitness Center 1301 E. University, 921-9551 (GF)

BOOKSTORES & RETAIL SHOPS

▲ **Obelisk the Bookstore** 24 W. Camelback Ste. A, 266-2665 (WC) 10am-10pm, noon-8pm Sun, lesbigay

Sexy Styles 2104 W. Camelback Rd., 242-2886, 11am-7pm, til 6pm Fri-Sat, clsd Sun, clothing & accessories for the MTF TG & drag communities

Tuff Stuff 1714 E. McDowell Rd., 254-9651, 10am-6pm, til 4pm Sat, clsd Sun-Mon, leather shop

▲ **Unique on Central** 4700 N. Central Ave. #105, 279-9691 (WC) 10am-8pm, cards & gifts

TRAVEL & TOUR OPERATORS

All About Destinations Gallery Three Plaza, 3819 N. 3rd St., (800) 375-2703/277-2703 (IGTA)

Arizona Office of Tourism 230-7733/(800) 842-8257

FirsTravel Ltd. 5150 N. 7th St., (800) 669-8885/265-0666 (IGTA)

TGI Travel Agency 5540 W. Glendale Ave. #A-102, Glendale, (800) 289-2172/939-1445 (IGTA)

SPIRITUAL GROUPS

Augustana Lutheran Church 2604 N. 14th St., 265-8400, 10:30am Sun

Casa de Cristo Evangelical Church 1029 E. Turney, 265-2831, 8:45am,10:30am & 6:30pm Sun

Community Church of Hope 502 W. Camelback (Ramada Inn), 234-2180, 10am Sun, independent Christian church & counseling center

Lutherans Concerned PO Box 7519, 85011, 870-3611

MCC Gentle Shepherd 5150 N. 16th St., 285-9020, 9am & 11am Sun

PUBLICATIONS

Echo Magazine PO Box 16630, 85011-6630, 266-0550, bi-weekly

Western Express PO Box 5317, 85010-5317, 254-1324, bi-weekly

MEN'S CLUBS
▲ **Chute** 1440 E. Indian School Rd., 234-1654 (L) 24hrs
▲ **Flex Complex** 1517 S. Black Canyon Hwy., 271-9011 (MO,SW,PC)

EROTICA
Adult Shoppe 111 S. 24th St., 306-1130, 24hrs
The Barn 5021 W. Indian School Rd., 245-3008, 24hrs
▲ **Castle Boutique** 300 E. Camelback, 266-3348, 24hrs, also 5501 E. Washington, 231-9837, 8802 N. Black Canyon Fwy, 995-1641
International Bookstore 3640 E. Thomas Rd., 955-2000, 24hrs
Pleasure Palace 1524 E. Van Buren, 262-9942, 24hrs

Scottsdale (602)

BARS
▲ **B.S. West** 7125 5th Ave. (pedestrian mall), 945-9028 (MW,D,V,WC) 1pm-1am, Sun BBQ
The Works 7223 E. 2nd St., 946-4141 (M,D,A,S,V,YC,WC) 10pm-3am Wed-Sat

RESTAURANTS & CAFES
Malee's 7131 E. Main, 947-6042, Thai

TRAVEL & TOUR OPERATORS
Dolphin Travel Services 10632-B N. Scottsdale Rd., (800) 847-2835/998-9191 (IGTA)
Welcome Aboard 7744 E. Northland Dr., 596-6787 (IGTA)

EROTICA
Zorba's Adult Book Shop 2924 N. Scottsdale Rd., 941-9891, 24hrs

Sedona (520)

ACCOMMODATIONS
Iris Garden Inn 390 Jordan Rd., 282-2552 (GF)
Sedona Artist Guest Suite PO Box 2130, 86335, 204-2966/Fax: 204-2966 (GF)
Straw Bale Inn at Montezuma's Well PO Box 406, Rimrook, 86335 (GF)

Tempe (602)

BOOKSTORES & RETAIL SHOPS
Changing Hands 414 S. Mill, 966-0203, 10am-9pm, til 10pm Fri-Sat, noon-5pm Sun, general, lesbigay section

SPIRITUAL GROUPS
Dignity/Integrity 2222 S. Price Rd., 222-8664, 6pm Sat, call for info, joint chapter of lesbigay Roman Catholics and Episcopalians

EROTICA
Modern World 1812 E. Apache, 967-9052, 24hrs

Tucson (520)

INFO LINES & SERVICES
AA Gay/Lesbian 624-4183, many meetings, call for info
▲ **Community Real Estate Referrals** (800) 346-5592, gay realtor at your service, no rentals

TORTUGA ROJA

BED & BREAKFAST

2800 EAST RIVER ROAD
TUCSON, ARIZONA 85718
(520) 577-6822 • (800) 467-6822

▲ **Tucson Confidential Connection** 770-1000, Meet hot local guys! Record, listen, respond to free ads. Use free code 9966.

Wingspan Community Center 422 N. 4th Ave., 624-1779, lesbigay & youth info, lesbigay AA, call for events

ACCOMMODATIONS

Casa Alegre B&B Inn 316 E. Speedway Blvd., 628-1800/628-5654 (GF,SW) hot tub, full brkfst, kids okay-inquire

Casa Tierra Adobe B&B Inn 11155 W. Calle Pima, 578-3058/Fax: 578-3058 (GF) patio, 30 min. outside Tucson, smokefree, kids 3+ okay

Catalina Park Inn 309 E. 1st St., 792-4541/(800) 792-4885 (GF) full brkfst, smokefree, kids 10+ okay, stylish environment of understated elegance & comfort

Elysian Grove Market B&B Inn 400 W. Simpson, 628-1522 (GF) kitchen in suite, full brkfst, renovated historic adobe building w/unusual & wonderful garden

Hacienda del Sol Guest Ranch Resort 5601 N. Hacienda del Sol Rd., 299-1501

Hampton Inn 6971 S. Tucson Blvd., 889-5789 (M,WC) cont'l brkfst, non-smoking rooms available, kids okay, pets okay

Hotel Congress 311 E. Congress, 622-8848/(800) 722-8848 (GF,F)

Montecito House PO Box 42352, 85733, 795-7592 (GF) cont'l brkfst, kids okay by arrangement

Natural B&B 3150 E. Presidio Rd., 881-4582/Fax: 326-1385 (M) massage available, smokefree, kids okay

Suncatcher B&B 105 N. Avenida Javelina, (800) 835-8012 (GF,SW,WC) full brkfst, hot tub, smokefree, kids okay, on 4 acres

▲ **Tortuga Roja B&B** 2800 E. River Rd., 577-6822/(800) 467-6822 (MW,SW,N,WC,IGTA) expanded con'tl brkfst, hot tub, smokefree, kids okay in cottage

BARS

Congress Tap Room (inside Hotel Congress), 622-8848 (GF,NH,D,A,E) 11am-1am, dance club from 9pm, theme nights

The Fineline 101 W. Drachman, 882-4953 (GF,D,18+) 6pm-1am, til 4am Fri-Sat

Graduate 23 W. University Ave., 622-9233 (M,D,S,WC) 11am-1am, cruisy, game room

Hours 3455 E. Grant, 327-3390 (★MW,NH,D,CW,WC) noon-1am

IBT's (It's About Time) 616 N. 4th Ave., 882-3053 (MW,D,S,WC) noon-1am

Stonewall Eagle 2921 1st Ave., 624-8805 (M,D,L,WC) noon-1am, Stonewall from 9pm, patio

Venture-N 1239 N. 6th Ave., 882-8224 (M,L,F) 6am-1am, from 10am Sun, patio

TRAVEL & TOUR OPERATORS

Arizona Travel Center 2502 E. Grant Rd., (800) 553-5471/323-3250 (IGTA)

SPIRITUAL GROUPS

Cornerstone Fellowship 2902 N. Geronimo, 622-4626, 10:30am Sun, 7pm Wed Bible Study

MCC 3269 N. Mountain Ave., 292-9151, 10:45am Sun, 7pm Wed

PUBLICATIONS

The Observer PO Box 50733, 85703, 622-7176, weekly

EROTICA

The Bookstore Southwest 5754 E. Speedway Blvd., 790-1550

Caesar's Bookstore 2540 N. Oracle Rd., 622-9479

Yuma (520)

EROTICA
Bargain Box 408 E. 16th St., 782-6742, 24hrs

ARKANSAS

Conway

INFO LINES & SERVICES
U of Central Arkansas Gay/Lesbian Student Union PO Box 7006, 72032

Crossett (501)

RESTAURANTS & CAFES
Pig Trail Cafe Rte. 16, east of Elkins, 643-3307 (★) 6am-9pm

Eureka Springs (501)

ACCOMMODATIONS
Arbour Glen Victorian Inn B&B 7 Lema, 253-9010/(800) 515-4536 (MW) full brkfst, kids okay, historic Victorian home, also guesthouse, jacuzzis, fireplaces

Cedarberry Cottage B&B 3 Kings Hwy., 253-6115/(800) 590-2424 (GF) full brkfst, kids okay

Cliff Cottage B&B Inn 42 Armstrong St., 253-7409/(800) 799-7409 (GF) suites & guestrooms in 1892 'Painted Lady', cruises, gourmet dinner, full brkfst

Crescent Dragonwagon's Dairy Hollow House 516 Spring St., (800) 562-8650/253-7444 (GF) hot tub, full brkfst

Dixie Cottage #2 Prospect, 253-7553 (GF,F,SW) camping April-Sept, restaurant open year-round

The Gardener's Cottage c/o 11 Singleton, 253-9111/(800) 833-3394 (GF) seasonal, private cottage on wooded site

Greenwood Hollow Ridge Rte 4, Box 155, 253-5283 (MW,WC) full brkfst, kitchen, private/shared baths, exclusively gay, on 5 quiet acres

▲ **Heart of the Hills** 5 Summit, 253-7468/253-7468 (GF) full brkfst, pets okay, kids okay, also reservation service, evening desserts, patio

Maple Leaf Inn 6 Kings Hwy., 253-6876/(800) 372-6542 (GF) full brkfst, hot tub, kids okay, restored Victorian

Morningstar Retreat Rte. 1 Box 653, 72632, 253-5995/(800) 298-5995 (GF)

Palace Hotel & Bath House 135 Spring St., 253-7474 (GF,WC) bath house open to all

Pond Mountain Lodge & Resort Rte. 1, Box 50, 72632, 253-5877/(800) 583-8043 (GF,SW,WC) full brkfst, smokefree, kids okay, mountain-top inn on 159 acres

Rock Cottage Gardens 10 Eugenia St., 253-8659/(800) 624-6646 (MW) full brkfst, hot tub

Singleton House B&B 11 Singleton, 253-9111/(800) 833-3394 (GF) full brkfst, kids okay, restored 1890's country Victorian home, near shops

The Woods 50 Wall St., 253-8281 (MW,WC) jacuzzis, kitchens

BARS
Celebrity Club 75 Prospect (Crescent Hotel), 253-9766 (GF,F,E,K) 6pm-1am Fri-Sat, also sports bar

Center Street Bar & Grille 10 Center St., 253-8102 (GF,D,F,E) 6pm-2am, kitchen open til 10pm Th-Mon, clsd Sun, Mexican, plenty veggie

Chelsea's Corner Cafe 10 Mountain St., 253-6723 (GF) 11am-2am, clsd Sun, patio

RESTAURANTS & CAFES
Ermilio's 26 White, 253-8806, 5-8:30pm, clsd Th, Italian, plenty veggie
The Plaza 55 S. Main, 253-8866, lunch & dinner, French

SPIRITUAL GROUPS
MCC of the Living Spring 17 Elk St. (Unitarian Church), 253-9337, 7pm Sun

Fayetteville (501)

INFO LINES & SERVICES
AA Live & Let Live Group 756-8367, 7pm Tue
BGLAD PO Box 2897, 72702
Gay/Lesbian Student Association University of Arkansas, AU517, 72701

BOOKSTORES & RETAIL SHOPS
Passages 200 W. Dickson, 442-5845, 10am-6pm, til 8pm Fri, 1-6pm Sun, new age/metaphysical

SPIRITUAL GROUPS
MCC of the Living Word 10571 N. Hwy. 265, 443-4278, 11am Sun

Fort Smith (501)

INFO LINES & SERVICES
WAGLTF (Western Arkansas Gay/Lesbian Task Force) PO Box 5824, 72913

BOOKSTORES & RETAIL SHOPS
Talisman 4119 Grand Ave., 782-7522, 11am-6pm

Helena (501)

ACCOMMODATIONS

Foxglove B&B 229 Beech, 338-9391/863-1926 (GF)

Hot Springs (501)

BARS

Our House Lounge & Restaurant 660 E. Grand Ave., 624-6868 (★MW,D,WC) 7pm-3am, shows monthly

Little Rock (501)

INFO LINES & SERVICES

AA Gay/Lesbian 3rd & Pulaski (Capitol View Methodist), 664-7303, 8pm Wed, 6pm Sun

AGLTF (Arkansas Gay/Lesbian Task Force) PO Box 45053, 72214

▲ **Community Real Estate Referrals** (800) 346-5592, gay realtor at your service, no rentals

Gay/Lesbian Task Force Switchboard PO Box 45053, 72214, (800) 448-8305 (in AR)/375-5504, 6:30-10:30pm, statewide crisis line & referrals

ACCOMMODATIONS

Little Rock Inn 601 Center St., 376-8301 (GF,SW,WC) full bar, kids okay, pets okay

BARS

Backstreet 1021 Jessie Rd. #Q, 664-2744 (MW,D,S,PC,WC) 9pm-?

Discovery III 1021 Jessie Rd., 664-4784 (★M,D,TG,S,PC,WC) from 9pm, clsd Sun-Wed

Michael's 601 Center St. (at Little Rock Inn), 376-8301 (MW,D,E,WC) 9pm-2am, 4-10pm Sun

RESTAURANTS & CAFES
Vino's Pizza 923 W. 7th St., 375-8466 (BW)

BOOKSTORES & RETAIL SHOPS
Twisted Entertainment 7201 Asher Ave., 568-4262, 11am-10pm, clsd Tue, gift shop

Wild Card 400 N. Bowman, 223-9071, 10am-8pm, 1-5pm Sun, novelties & gifts

TRAVEL & TOUR OPERATORS
Arkansas Department of Tourism One Capitol Mall, 72201, (800) 628-8725

Travel by Philip PO Box 250119, 72225-5119, 227-7690 (IGTA) specializes in gay motorcoach tours

SPIRITUAL GROUPS
MCC of the Rock 2017 Chandler, North Little Rock, 753-7075, 11am Sun, 7pm Wed

Unitarian Universalist Church 1818 Reservoir Rd., 255-1503 (WC) 11am Sun

PUBLICATIONS
Lesbian/Gay News Telegraph PO Box 14229-A, St. Louis MO, 63108, 664-6411/(800) 301-5468, covers AR,IL,KS,MO,TN

Triangle Rising PO Box 45053, 72214, 374-2681

Mabelvale   (501)

MEN'S CLUBS
NSN (Natural State Naturists) PO Box 755, 72103, 847-1918, non-sexual nudist society for men in AR

Texarkana   (501)

BARS
The Gig 201 East St. (Hwy. 71 S.), 773-6900 (M,D,S,PC) 8pm-5am, clsd Mon

Walcott   (501)

ACCOMMODATIONS
Double Tree Ranch PO Box 52, 72474, 236-7711

CALIFORNIA

Anaheim (714)

INFO LINES & SERVICES
▲ **Anaheim Confidential Connection** 539-7000, Meet hot local guys! Record, listen, respond to free ads. Use free code 9966.

▲ **Gay Connection** (900) 505-6339, talk and/or meet with other men from the area, at only 99 ¢ per minute

Gay/Lesbian Community Services Center 12832 Garden Grove Blvd. Ste. A, 534-0862, 10am-10pm, counseling, events, education

ACCOMMODATIONS
Country Comfort B&B 5104 E. Valencia Dr., Orange, 532-2802/Fax: 997-1921 (MW,SW,WC) full brkfst, hot tub, 7 mi. from Disneyland

Bakersfield (805)

INFO LINES & SERVICES
Friends PO Box 304, 93302, 323-7311, 6:30pm-11pm, support groups & community outreach

BARS
Casablanca Club 1030 20th St., 324-1384 (MW,NH,D) 7pm-2am

The Mint 1207 19th St., 325-4048 (GF,NH) 6am-2pm

The Place 3500 Wilson Rd., 835-0494 (MW,CW,WC) 11am-2am, from 6pm wknds

Town Casino Lounge 1813 'H' St. (Padre Hotel), 324-2594 (GF,E) 10am-2am, live piano Thur-Sun

SPIRITUAL GROUPS
MCC of the Harvest 2421 Alta Vista Dr., 327-3724, 7pm Sun

EROTICA
Deja Vu 1524 Golden State Hwy., 322-7300 (E)

Wildcat Books 2620 Chester Ave., 324-4243

Benicia (707)

ACCOMMODATIONS
Captain Walsh House 235 E. 'L' St., 747-5653/Fax: 747-6265 (GF,WC) gracious gothic charm, full brkfst

Berkeley (see East Bay)

Big Bear Lake (909)

ACCOMMODATIONS
Eagles' Nest 41675 Big Bear Rd., 866-6465 (GF,WC) 7 cottages,spa

Grey Squirrel Resort PO Box 1711-39372, 92315, 866-4335/Fax: 866-6271 (GF,SW) 18 private cabins

Hillcrest Lodge 40241 Big Bear Blvd. , 866-6040/(800) 843-4449 (GF,WC) suites, some non-smoking rooms, hot tub, fireplaces

▲ **Smoke Tree Resort** 40210 Big Bear Blvd. , 866-2415/(800) 352-8581 (GF,WC) B&B, cont'l brkfst, cabins, hot tub

RESTAURANTS & CAFES
Ché Faccia 607 Pine Knot Ave., 878-3222, 11am-10pm (seasonal), hours vary, Italian

Big Sur (408)

ACCOMMODATIONS
Lucia Lodge Hwy. 1, 667-2269/667-0161 (GF,IGTA) cabins, restaurant, store, ocean views

Bishop (619)

ACCOMMODATIONS
Starlite Motel 192 Short St., 873-4912 (GF,SW) 1 room available for pets

BOOKSTORES & RETAIL SHOPS
Spellbinder Books 124 N. Main, 873-4511 (WC) 9:30am-5:30pm, clsd Sun

Buena Park (714)

BARS
Ozz Supper Club 6231 Manchester Blvd., 522-1542 (MW,D,F,E,S) 6pm-2am, clsd Mon, American

Cambria (805)

ACCOMMODATIONS
The J. Patrick House 2990 Burton Dr., 927-3812/(800) 341-5258 (GF) authentic log cabin B&B, cont'l brkfst, wine, snacks, fireplaces

Carmel (408)

ACCOMMODATIONS
Happy Landing Inn PO Box 2619, 93921, 624-7917 (GF) Hansel & Gretel 1925 inn, full brkfst

Chico (916)

INFO LINES & SERVICES
Gay Hotline 893-3336/893-3338, hours vary

Stonewall Alliance Center 820 W. 7th St., 893-3338/893-3336, social 6pm-10pm Fri , Gay AA 7pm Tue, hotline

BARS
Rascal's 900 Cherry St., 893-0900 (MW,D) 6pm-2am

BOOKSTORES & RETAIL SHOPS
Travellin' Pages 1174 East Ave., 342-6931, hours vary, lesbigay section

Chula Vista (619)

EROTICA
▲ **F St. Bookstore** 1141 3rd Ave., 585-3314 (WC) 24hrs

Clearlake (707)

ACCOMMODATIONS
Blue Fish Cove Resort 10573 E. Hwy 20, Clearlake Oaks, 998-1769 (GF) lakeside resort cottages, boat facilities

Lake Vacations Reservations 1855 S. Main St., 263-7188, vacation-home rental service

Sea Breeze Resort 9595 Harbor Dr., Glenhaven, 998-3327/Fax: 998-3327 (MW,SW) RV hookups, cottages

Cloverdale (707)

ACCOMMODATIONS
Vintage Towers B&B 302 N. Main St., 894-4535 (GF) Queen Anne mansion, full brkfst

Concord (510)

EROTICA
Pleasant Hill Adult Books & Videos 2298 Monument, 676-2962

Corona del Mar (714)

TRAVEL & TOUR OPERATORS
New Directions Travel Company 2435 E. Coast Hwy., 675-5000/(800) 222-5531

Costa Mesa (714)

BARS
Lion's Den 719 W. 19th St., 645-3830 (MW,D,YC) 8pm-2am, from 6pm Sat, monthly live band

Metropolis 4255 Campus Dr., Irvine, 725-0300 (GF, D,F,18+) 7pm-2am, from 8pm Tue, call for events, Californian/sushi, 18+ Fri & Sun, lesbians/gay men Sun, dress code on wknds

Newport Station 1945 Placentia, 631-0031 (★MW,D,E,S,V,YC,WC) 9pm-2am Th-Sat

Tin Lizzie Saloon 752 St. Clair, 966-2029 (M,NH) noon-2am, from 2pm wknds

SPIRITUAL GROUPS
First MCC of Orange County 1259 Victoria St. (Unitarian Church), 548-2955, 7pm Sun

Cupertino (408)

BARS

Silver Fox 10095 Saich Wy., 255-3673 (M,NH,S,WC) 2pm-2am

Davis (916)

RESTAURANTS & CAFES

Cafe Roma 231 'E' St., 756-1615 (★WC) 7:30am-11pm, student hangout

East Bay (includes **Berkeley & Oakland**) (510)

INFO LINES & SERVICES

▲ **Community Real Estate Referrals** (800) 346-5592, gay realtor at your service, no rentals

▲ **East Bay Confidential Connection** 814-6699, Meet hot local guys! Record, listen, respond to free ads. Use free code 9966.

Gay/Lesbian/Bisexual/Transgender Switchboard (at the Pacific Center), Berkeley, 841-6224 (also TDD), 8-10pm Mon, Tue & Fri, 4-6pm Wed, info, referrals

Pacific Center 2712 Telegraph Ave., Berkeley, 548-8283, 10am-10pm, from noon Sat, 6pm-9pm Sun, support groups & counseling

ACCOMMODATIONS

Elmwood House 2609 College Ave., Berkeley, 540-5123/(800) 540-3050 (GF,IGTA)

BARS

Bench & Bar 120 11th St., Oakland, 444-2266 (★M,D,P,S,YC,WC) 3pm-2am, from 5pm Sat, Fri-Sun Latin nights

Cabel's Reef 2272 Telegraph Ave., Oakland, 451-3777 (M,D,MRC) noon-2am

Town & Country 2022 Telegraph Ave., Oakland, 444-4978 (M,NH,WC) 11am-2am

White Horse 6551 Telegraph Ave., Oakland, 652-3820 (MW,D,WC) 1pm-2am, from 3pm Mon-Tue, popular Fri night

RESTAURANTS & CAFES

Betty's To Go 1807 4th St., Berkeley, 548-9494, 6:30am-5pm, 8am-4pm Sun, sandwiches

Bison Brewery 2598 Telegraph at Parker, Berkeley, 841-7734 (BW,WC) 11am-1am, live music, sandwiches

Brick Hut 2512 San Pablo, Berkeley, 486-1124 (MW) 7:30am-2pm, 8:30am-3pm wknds, dinner 5:30pm-10pm Wed-Sat, popular for breakfast

Cafe Sorrento 2510 Channing, Berkeley, 548-8220 (MRC) 7am-7pm, 9am-4pm wknds, Italian

Cafe Strada corner of College & Bancroft, Berkeley, 843-5282 (★WC) students, great patio & white bianca mochas

The Edible Complex 5600 College, Oakland, 658-2172 (★) 7am-midnight, til 1am Fri-Sat, mostly students

Mama's Royale 4012 Broadway, Oakland, 547-7600 (★) 7am-3pm, from 8am wknds, come early for excellent weekend brunch

Mimosa Cafe 462 Santa Clara, Oakland, 465-2948, 11am-9pm, clsd Mon

BOOKSTORES & RETAIL SHOPS

Ancient Ways 4075 Telegraph Ave., Oakland, 653-3244, 11am-7pm, extensive occult supplies, classes, readings

Cody's 2454 Telegraph Ave., Berkeley, 845-7852, 10am-10pm, frequent readings & lectures, lesbigay section

Easy Going 1385 Shattuck (at Rose), Berkeley, 843-3533, 10am-7pm, til 6pm Sat, noon-6pm Sun, travel books & accessories, also 1617 Locust, Walnut Creek, 947-6660

Shambhala Booksellers 2482 Telegraph Ave., Berkeley, 848-8443 (WC) 10am-8pm, spiritual

TRAVEL & TOUR OPERATORS

New Venture Travel 404 22nd St., Oakland, 835-3800 (IGTA)

Travel By Design 3832 Piedmont Ave., Oakland, 653-6668

SPIRITUAL GROUPS

Albany Unified Methodist Church 980 Stannage Ave., Albany , 526-7346, 10am Sun

MCC New Life 1823 9th St., Berkeley, 843-9355 (WC) 12:30pm Sun

PUBLICATIONS

San Francisco Bay Times 288 7th St., San Francisco, 94103, (415) 626-8121 (★) bi-weekly, a 'must read' for Bay Area resources & personals

MEN'S CLUBS

▲ **Steamworks** 2107 4th St., Berkeley, 845-8992, 24hrs, call for recorded info, see ad in San Francisco section

EROTICA

Good Vibrations 2504 San Pablo, Berkeley, 841-8987, clean, well-lighted sex toy store, also mail order

Hollywood Adult Books 5686 Telegraph Ave., Oakland, 654-1169

L'Amour Shoppe 1801 Telegraph Ave., Oakland, 835-0381

L'Amour Shoppe 1905 San Pablo Ave., Oakland, 465-4216

Passion Flower 4 Yosemite Ave., Oakland, 601-7750, toys, leather, etc.

El Cajon (619)

EROTICA

▲ **F St. Bookstore** 158 E. Main, 447-0381, 24hrs

El Monte (818)

BARS

Infinities 2253 Tyler Ave., 575-9164 (W,D,MRC-L,WC) 4pm-2am, boys night Th

Escondido (619)

EROTICA

▲ **F St. Bookstore** 237 E. Grand Ave., 480-6031, 24hrs

Video Specialties 2322 S. Escondido Blvd., 745-6697, 24hrs

Eureka (707)

INFO LINES & SERVICES

Gay/Lesbian Alliance of Humboldt County PO Box 2368, 95502, 444-1061, info, call for events

ACCOMMODATIONS

Carter House Victorians 301 'L' St., 444-8062/(800) 404-1390 (GF,WC) enclave of 4 unique inns, full brkfst

BARS

Club Triangle (Club West) 535 5th St., 444-2582 (GF,D,A,18+,WC) 9pm-2am, gay Sun, also Star's Hamburgers, 8pm-11pm

Lost Coast Brewery Pub 617 4th St., 445-4480 (GF,F,BW,WC) 11am-2am

BOOKSTORES & RETAIL SHOPS
Booklegger 402 2nd St., 445-1344 (WC) lesbigay section

Fairfield (707)

INFO LINES & SERVICES
Solano County Gay/Lesbian Info Line PO Box 9, Vacaville, 95696, 448-1010, evenings call 449-0550, ask for Kristin or Kathy

Ferndale (707)

ACCOMMODATIONS
The Gingerbread Mansion Inn 400 Berding St., 786-4000/(800) 952-4136 (★GF) a grand lady in the Victorian village of Ferndale, afternoon tea, full brkfst

Fort Bragg (707)

ACCOMMODATIONS
Aslan House 24600 N. Hwy. 1, 964-2788/(800) 400-2189 (GF) cottages, hot tub, ideal place for romance & privacy on the Mendocino Coast, partial ocean view

Cleone Lodge Inn 24600 N. Hwy. 1, 964-2788/(800) 400-2189 (GF) country garden retreat on 9-1/2 acres, cottages, hot tub

Jug Handle Beach B&B 32980 Gibney Ln., 964-1415 (GF) full brkfst

BOOKSTORES & RETAIL SHOPS
Windsong Books & Records 324 N. Main, 964-2050, 10am-5:30pm, til 4pm Sun

Fremont (510)

INFO LINES & SERVICES
East Bay Network of Fremont PO Box 1238, 94538-0123

EROTICA
Cupid's Corner 34129 Fremont Blvd., 796-8697, men's dancewear, videos, CD-ROMS

L'Amour Shoppe 40555 Grimmer Blvd., 659-8161, 24hrs

Fresno (209)

INFO LINES & SERVICES
Community Link PO Box 4959, 93744, 266-5465, lesbigay support, also publishes Pink Pages

▲ Fresno Confidential Connection 271-9999, Meet hot local guys! Record, listen, respond to free ads. Use free code 9966.

GUS Inc. (Gay United Service) 1999 Tuolumne Ste. 625, 268-3541, 8am-5pm Mon-Fri, counseling, referrals

Serenity Fellowship AA 925 N. Fulton, 221-6907, various mtg. times, men's mtg 8pm Th

The Yosemite Chapter, Knights of Malta PO Box 4162, 93744, 496-4144, lesbigay leather group

BARS
El Sombrero 3848 E. Belmont Ave., 442-1818

▲ The Express 708 N. Blackstone, 233-1791 (★MW,D,E,V,WC) 5pm-2am, from 3pm Sun, 3 bars, cafe, patio

Hi-Ho Club 4538 E. Belmont Ave., 264-8283

Palace 4030 E. Belmont Ave., 264-8283 (W,NH,D,CW,S) 3pm-2am

Red Lantern 4618 E. Belmont Ave., 251-5898 (M,NH,WC) 2pm-2am

RESTAURANTS & CAFES
Cafe Express 708 N. Blackstone, 233-1791, 6pm-9pm, champagne brunch 10am-3pm Sun, clsd Mon, fine dining

Java Cafe 805 E. Olive, 237-5282 (★WC) 7am-11pm, til 12 Fri-Sat, bohemian

TRAVEL & TOUR OPERATORS
The Travel Address 6465 N. Blackstone Ave., (800) 800-9095 (IGTA)

SPIRITUAL GROUPS
Morrigan Tower Coven of Wyrd PO Box 7137, 93744-7137, monthly, co-gender

EROTICA
Only For You 1468 N. Van Ness Ave., 498-0284, noon-9pm, til 10pm Th-Sat, les-bigay

Wildcat Book Store 1535 Fresno St., 237-4525

Garberville (707)

ACCOMMODATIONS
Giant Redwoods RV & Camp PO Box 222, Myers Flat, 943-3198/Fax: 943-3359 (GF) campsites, RV, located off the Avenue of the Giants on the Eel River

Garden Grove (714)

INFO LINES & SERVICES
AA Gay/Lesbian 9872 Chapman Ave. #15 (Ash Inc.), 534-5820/537-9968, 6-10pm, clsd Fri, Sun

BARS
Frat House 8112 Garden Grove Blvd., 897-3431 (★MW,D,MRC,E,S,YC,WC) 9am-2am

Nick's 8284 Garden Grove Blvd., 537-1361 (M,NH,D,S,V,WC) 9pm-2am, 24hrs wknds

EROTICA
A-Z Bookstore 8192 Garden Grove Blvd., 534-9349, 24hrs wknds

Hip Pocket 12686 Garden Grove Blvd., 638-8595

▲ **Midnight Videos** 8745 Garden Grove Blvd., 534-9823

Party House 8751 Garden Grove Blvd., 534-9996

Video Rental & Preview Center 8743 Garden Grove Blvd., 534-9922

Glendale (818)

SPIRITUAL GROUPS
MCC Divine Redeemer 346 Riverdale Dr., 500-7124, 10:45am Sun, 7:30pm Wed

Grass Valley (916)

ACCOMMODATIONS
Murphy's Inn 318 Neal St., 273-6873 (GF,WC) no smoking, full brkfst

Gualala (707)

ACCOMMODATIONS
Starboard House 140 Starboard, 884-4808 (WC) vacation house, ocean views, hot tub

Half Moon Bay (415)

ACCOMMODATIONS

Mill Rose Inn 615 Mill St., 726-8750/(800) 900-7673 (GF) classic European elegance by the sea, hot tub, full brkfst

Hawthorne (310)

BARS

El Capitan 13825 S. Hawthorne, 675-3436 (MW,NH,BW) 4pm-2am, from noon Fri-Sun

Hayward (510)

BARS

I.J.'s Getaway 21859 Mission Blvd., 582-8078 (MW,D) noon-2am, til 4am Fri-Sat

Rumors 22554 Main St., 733-2334 (M,NH,WC) 10am-2am

Turf Club 22517 Mission Blvd., 881-9877 (MW,D,CW,E) 10am-2am, patio bar in summer

EROTICA

L'Amour Shoppe 22553 Main St., 886-7777

Healdsburg (707)

ACCOMMODATIONS

Camellia Inn 211 North St., 433-8182/(800) 727-8182 (GF,WC) full brkfst

Madrona Manor PO Box 818, 95448, 433-4231 (GF,F,SW,WC) full brkfst, elegant Victorian country inn

Twin Towers River Ranch 615 Bailhache, 433-4443 (GF) 1864 Victorian farmhouse on 5 acres, also vacation house

Hermosa Beach (310)

EROTICA

Tender Box 809 Pacific Coast Hwy., 318-2882

Huntington Beach (714)

INFO LINES & SERVICES

▲ **Huntington Beach Confidential Connection** 537-1000, Meet hot local guys! Record, listen, respond to free ads. Use free code 9966.

EROTICA

Paradise Specialties 7344 Center, 898-0400

Idyllwild (909)

ACCOMMODATIONS

The Pine Cove Inn 23481 Hwy. 243, 659-5033 (GF) full brkfst, fireplaces, on 3 wooded acres

Wilkum Inn B&B PO Box 1115, 92549, 659-8087/(800) 659-4086 (GF,WC) fireplaces, 1938 shingle-style inn, cabin available, cont'l brkfst

Imperial Beach (619)

EROTICA

Palm Avenue Books 1177 Palm Ave., 575-5081

Inglewood
(31C

BARS

Annex 835 S. La Brea, 671-7323 (M,NH) noon-2am

Caper Room 244 S. Market St., 677-0403 (M,MRC-AF) 11am-2am, from 4pm Sur

Lafayette

RESTAURANTS & CAFES

Java Jones 100 Lafayette Cir. #101 (MW,BW,WC) 9am-3pm, til 10pm Th-Sat, clsd Mon, brunch Sun

Laguna Beach
(714

INFO LINES & SERVICES

AA Gay/Lesbian 31872 Coast Hwy. (South Coast Medical Hospital), 499-7150, 8:30pm Fri

▲ **Community Real Estate Referrals** (800) 346-5592, gay realtor at your service, n rentals

Laguna Outreach 497-4237, educational/social group for Orange County, call fc details

ACCOMMODATIONS

Best Western Laguna Brisas Spa Hotel 1600 S. Coast Hwy., 497-7272/(800) 624-4442 (GF,SW,WC) in-room whirlpool spas, non-smoking rooms available, resort hotel

California Riviera 800 1400 S. Coast Hwy. Ste. 104, (800) 621-0500 (IGTA) exten sive reservation & accommodation services

Casa Laguna B&B Inn 2510 S. Coast Hwy., 494-2996/(800) 233-0449 (GF,SW) romantic mission-style inn & cottages overlooking the Pacific

▲ **The Coast Inn** 1401 S. Coast Hwy., 494-7588/(800) 653-2697 (MW,SW) oceanside accommodations w/ 2 bars & restaurant

Holiday Inn Laguna Beach 696 S. Coast Hwy., 494-1001 (GF,F,SW,WC)

Inn By The Sea 475 N. Coast Hwy., (800) 297-0007/497-6645 (GF,SW,WC) cont'l brkfst, hot tub

BARS

Boom Boom Room (at the Coast Inn), 494-7588 (★MW,D,E,S,V,YC,WC) 10am-2am

Little Shrimp 1305 S. Coast Hwy., 494-4111 (★MW,F,E,WC) opens 1pm, from 11am wknds, brunch Sun, patio

Main St. 1460 S. Coast Hwy., 494-0056 (M,E) noon-2am, piano bar

Newport Station (see Costa Mesa), 631-0031 (★MW,D,E,S,V,YC,WC) 9pm-2am Th-Sat

RESTAURANTS & CAFES

Cafe Zinc 350 Ocean Ave., 494-6302 (BW,WC) 7am-5:30pm, til 5pm Sun, also market, patio

Cafe Zoolu 860 Glenneyre, 494-6825 (WC) dinner

The Cottage 308 N. Coast Hwy., 494-3023, 7am-9:30pm, til 10:30 Sat-Sun

Dizz's As Is 2794 S. Coast Hwy., 494-5250, open 5:30pm, seating at 6pm, clsd Mon, patio

Leap of Faith 1440 Pacific Coast Hwy., 494-8595 (MW,E,BW) 6:30am-11pm, til midnight Fri-Sat, from 7:30am Sat-Sun, patio

TRAVEL & TOUR OPERATORS

Festive Tours 1220 N. Coast Hwy., 494-9966 (IGTA)

SPIRITUAL GROUPS
Christ Chapel of Laguna 976 S. Coast Hwy., 376-2099, 10am Sun, 7pm Wed
Evangelicals Concerned Laguna 451-3777, call for info, newsletter
Unitarian Universalist Fellowship 429 Cypress Dr., 497-4568/645-8597, 10:30am Sun

PUBLICATIONS
Orange County Blade PO Box 1538, 92652, 494-4898, monthly

EROTICA
Video Horizons 31674 Coast Hwy, 499-4519

Laguna Niguel (714)
SPIRITUAL GROUPS
S.D.A. Kinship PO Box 7320, 92677, 248-1299

Lake Tahoe (916)
ACCOMMODATIONS
▲ **Bavarian House B&B** PO Box 624507, 544-4411/(800) 431-4411 (MW) smokefree, exclusively gay/lesbian, open year round
BeachSide Inn & Suites 930 Park Ave., South Lake Tahoe, 544-2400/(800) 884-4920 (GF) walk to casinos & private beach access, outdoor spa & sauna
Inn Essence 865 Lake Tahoe Blvd., South Lake Tahoe, 577-0339/(800) 578-2463 (MW)

Ridgewood Inn 1341 Emerald Bay Rd., 541-8589/(800) 800-4640 (GF) hot tub, small country inn, quiet wooded setting

Secrets Honeymooners' Inn 924 Park Ave., South Lake Tahoe, 544-6767/(800) 441-6610 (GF) quiet, romantic adult-only inn, spas

Sierrawood Guest House PO Box 11194, 96155-0194, 577-6073/700-3802 (MW) romantic, cozy chalet

Silver Shadows Lodge 1251 Emerald Bay Rd., South Lake Tahoe, 541-3575/406-6478 (GF,SW) cont'l brkfst, 18 units

Tradewinds Motel 944 Friday (at Cedar), South Lake Tahoe, 544-6459/(800) 628-1829 (GF,SW) suite w/spas & fireplace available

BARS

Faces 270 Kingsbury Grade, Stateline NV, (702) 588-2333 (MW,D) 4pm-4am

RESTAURANTS & CAFES

Driftwood Cafe 4119 Laurel Ave., 544-6545 (WC) 7:30am-2pm

Lancaster (805)

INFO LINES & SERVICES

Antelope Valley Gay/Lesbian Alliance PO Box 2013, 93539, 942-2812

BARS

Back Door 1255 W. Ave. 'I', 945-2566 (MW,D) 6pm-2am

SPIRITUAL GROUPS

Antelope Valley Unitarian Universalist Fellowship 43843 N. Division St., 272-0530, 11am Sun

Sunrise MCC of the High Desert 45303 23rd St. W., 942-7076, 11am Sun

Long Beach (310)

INFO LINES & SERVICES

AA Gay/Lesbian (Atlantic Alano Club) 441 E. 1st St., 432-7476, hours vary

▲ **Community Real Estate Referrals** (800) 346-5592, gay realtor at your service, no rentals

Lesbian/Gay Center & Switchboard 2017 E. 4th St., 434-4455, 9am-10pm, 9am-6pm Sat, clsd Sun, info

▲ **Long Beach Confidential Connection** 421-9231, Meet hot local guys! Record, listen, respond to free ads. Use free code 9966.

South Bay Lesbian/Gay Community Organization PO Box 2777, Redondo Beach, 90278, 379-2850, support/education for Manhattan, Hermosa & Redondo Beaches, Torrance, Palos Verdes, El Segundo

ACCOMMODATIONS

Bed & Breakfast of California 3924 E. 14th St., 90804, (800) 383-3513 (GF) B&B reservation service of California

BARS

The Brit 1744 E. Broadway, 432-9742 (M,NH) 10am-2am

The Broadway 1100 E. Broadway, 432-3646 (M,NH) 10am-2am

The Bulldogs (The Crest) 5935 Cherry Ave., 423-6650 (MW) 2pm-2am

Club 5211 5211 N. Atlantic St., 428-5545 (M,NH,WC) 6am-2am, karaoke Wed

The Club 740 740 E. Broadway, 437-7705 (★M,D,MRC-L) 6pm-2am

Executive Suite 3428 E. Pacific Coast Hwy., 597-3884 (MW,D,WC) 8pm-2am, clsd Tue, more men Mon

The Falcon 1435 E. Broadway, 432-4146 (M,NH) 7am-2am

Floyd's 2913 E. Anaheim St. (entrance on Gladys St.), 433-9251 (MW,D,CW,WC) 6pm-2am, from 2pm Sun, clsd Mon, CW dance lessons Tue-Th

Inn Kahoots 1435 E. Broadway, 432-4146 (M,NH) noon-2am

Mineshaft 1720 E. Broadway, 436-2433 (★M,D,L,WC) 10am-2am

Pistons 2020 E. Artesia, 422-1928 (M,L) 6pm-2am, til 4am Fri-Sat, patio

Ripples 5101 E. Ocean, 433-0357 (★M,D,F,E,V,YC) noon-2am, patio

Silver Fox 411 Redondo (M,K,V) noon-2am, from 8am Sun, popular happy hour, karaoke 9pm Wed & Sun

Sweetwater Saloon 1201 E. Broadway, 432-7044 (M,NH) 6am-2am, popular days, cruisy

Whistle Stop 5873 Atlantic, 422-7927 (M,NH) 11am-2am, from 8am wknds

RESTAURANTS & CAFES

Birds of Paradise 1800 E. Broadway, 590-8773 (MW,E,WC) 10am-1am , cocktails, live piano Wed-Sun

Cha Cha Cha 762 8th, 436-3900 (WC) lunch & dinner

Egg Heaven 4358 E. 4th St., 433-9277, 7am-2pm, til 3pm Sat-Sun, American, some veggie

Madame JoJo 2941 Broadway, 439-3672 (★MW,BW,WC) 5pm-10pm, Mediterranean, some veggie

Original Pack Pantry 2104 E. Broadway, 434-0451 (MW) lunch & dinner, Mexican/American/Asian, some veggie

BOOKSTORES & RETAIL SHOPS

By The Book 2501 E. Broadway, 434-2220 (WC) 10am-10pm, til 6pm Sun, books, magazines, large gay section

Dodd's Bookstore 4818 E. 2nd St., 438-9948 (WC) 10am-10pm, noon-6pm Sun, strong gay section

Hot Stuff 2121 E. Broadway, 433-0692, 11am-7pm, til 5pm wknds, cards, gifts, toys, etc.

Out & About On Broadway 1724 E. Broadway, 436-9930, 12:30pm-10pm, noon-8pm Sun, clothing, videos, books

TRAVEL & TOUR OPERATORS

Touch of Travel 3918 Atlantic Ave., (800) 833-3387/427-2144 (IGTA)

SPIRITUAL GROUPS

Christ Chapel 3935 E. 10th St., 438-5303 (GF,WC) 10am & 6pm Sun, 7pm Wed, non-denominational

Dignity PO Box 15037, 90815, 984-8400 (MW) call for service times & location

Trinity Lutheran Church 759 Linden Ave., 437-4002 (WC) 10am Sun

PUBLICATIONS

Directory - Long Beach 4102 E. 7th St. #621, 434-7129, directory of gay & gay-supportive businesses, published Jan & July; also publishes Orange County directory

MEN'S CLUBS

▲ **1350 Club** 510 Anaheim St., Wilmington, 830-4784 (MO,V,PC) 24hrs

EROTICA

The Crypt on Broadway 1712 E. Broadway, 983-6560, leather, toys

CRUISY AREAS

Please Note: All cruisy areas for Long Beach have been removed by request of various lesbigay community organizations.

Los Angeles

Los Angeles is divided into 7 geographical areas:

- L.A. - Overview
- L.A. - West Hollywood
- L.A. - Hollywood
- L.A. - West L.A. & Santa Monica
- L.A. - Silverlake
- L.A. - Midtown
- L.A. - Valley

L.A. - Overview

Info Lines & Services

AA Gay/Lesbian (213) 936-4343/993-7400, call for meeting times & locations

Alcoholics Together Center 1773 Griffith Park Blvd., (213) 663-8882, call for mtg. times, open to groups on 12-step system

Asian/Pacific Lesbians/Gays West Hollywood PO Box 433 Ste. 109, 90096, (213) 980-7874, call for events, Asian/Pacific Islanders & friends

Bi-Social (Pansocial) Center & Bi-Line 7136 Matilija Ave., Van Nuys, (213) 873-3700/(818) 989-3700, 24hr hotline for bi, transgender & gay info & referrals

Black Gay/Lesbian Leadership Forum 1219 S. La Brea, 90019, (213) 964-7820, nat'l group, sponsors annual conference

The Celebration Theatre 7051-B Santa Monica Blvd., (213) 957-1884, lesbigay theater, call for more info

▲ **Community Real Estate Referrals** (800) 346-5592, gay realtor at your service, no rentals

▲ **Gay Connection** (900) 505-6339, talk and/or meet with other men from the area, at only 99 ¢ per minute

Gay/Lesbian Youth Talk Line (213) 993-7475, 7-10pm, clsd Sun, referrals & support for those 23 & under

IMRU Gay Radio KPFK LA 90.7 FM, (818) 985-2711, 10pm Sun, also 'This Way Out' 4:30pm Tue

International Gay Penpals PO Box 7304 Ste. 320, 91603

International Gay/Lesbian Archives USC, (310) 854-0271, by appt.

Los Angeles Gay/Lesbian Community Center 1625 N. Shrader, (213) 993-7400, 9am-10pm, til 6pm Sun, wide variety of services

MACT (Men of All Colors Together) Los Angeles 7985 Santa Monica Blvd. #109-136, West Hollywood, (213) 664-4716, 7:30pm Sat, call for further details

South Bay Lesbian/Gay Community Organization PO Box 2777, Redondo Beach, 90278, (310) 379-2850, support/education for Manhattan, Hermosa & Redondo Beaches, Torrance, Palos Verdes, El Segundo

Uptown Gay/Lesbian Alliance PO Box 65111, 90065, (213) 258-8842, monthly social 2pm-5pm 2nd Sun, also publishes newsletter

Accommodations

Bed & Breakfast of California 3924 E. 14th St., Long Beach, 90804, (310) 498-0552/(800) 383-3513, B&B reservation service of California

▲ **The Caritas B&B Network** (800) CARITAS (227-4827), see ad in center National section

Travel & Tour Operators

▲ **Bob Leech Autorental** (800) 635-1240, see ad in San Francisco section

SPIRITUAL GROUPS

Beth Chayim Chadashim 6000 W. Pico Blvd., (213) 931-7023, 8pm Fri

PUBLICATIONS

Community Yellow Pages 2305 Canyon Dr., 90068, (800) 745-5669/(213) 469-4454, annual survival guide to lesbigay southern CA

The Edge 6434 Santa Monica Blvd., Hollywood, 90038, (213) 962-6994

Frontiers 7985 Santa Monica Blvd. #109, 90046, (213) 848-2222, bi-weekly

Genre 7080 Hollywood Blvd. #1104, 90028, (213) 896-9778

Leather Journal 7985 Santa Monica Blvd. #109-368, 90046, (213) 656-5073

Nightlife 6363 Santa Monica Blvd., 90038, (213) 462-5400, bi-weekly

Pink Pages 2101 S. Standard Ste. C, , (800) 844-6574/(714) 241-7465, semi-annual directory for southern CA

L.A. - West Hollywood (310)

INFO LINES & SERVICES

▲ **West Hollywood Confidential Connection** 854-6666, Meet hot local guys! Record, listen, respond to free ads. Use free code 9966.

ACCOMMODATIONS

The Grove Guesthouse 1325 N. Orange Grove Ave., 876-7778/Fax: 876-3170 (MW,SW) hot tub, kitchens, 1-bdrm guest cottage

Holloway Motel 8465 Santa Monica Blvd., West Hollywood, (213) 654-2454/Fax: (310) 821-3680 (M,IGTA) centrally located to the gay community

▲ **Le Montrose Suite Hotel** 900 Hammond St., 855-1115/(800) 776-0666 (★GF,F,SW,WC,IGTA) rooftop patio & pool, gym, also full restaurant

Le Parc 733 N. West Knoll Dr., West Hollywood, 855-8888/578-4837 (★GF,F,SW,WC,IGTA) tennis courts

Le Reve 8822 Cynthia St., 854-1114/(800) 835-7997 (GF,SW,WC,IGTA)

Ma Maison Sofitel 8555 Beverly Blvd., 278-5444/(800) 521-7772 (GF,F,SW,WC)

Ramada West Hollywood 8585 Santa Monica Blvd., West Hollywood, 652-6400/(800) 845-8585 (GF,F,SW,WC,IGTA) modern art deco hotel & suites

San Vincente B&B Resort 845 San Vincente Blvd., West Hollywood, 854-6915/Fax: 289-5929 (M,SW,N) hot tub

BARS

7702 SM Club 7702 Santa Monica Blvd., West Hollywood, (213) 654-3336 (MW,NH,WC) 6am-2am, 24hrs wknds

7969 7969 Santa Monica Blvd., (213) 654-0280 (GF,TG,S) 9pm-2am, theme nights, leather-friendly

Axis 652 N. La Peer, 659-0471 (M,D,A,S,V,YC) 9pm-2am Wed-Sun, women only Fri

Checca Bar & Cafe 7323 Santa Monica Blvd., (213) 850-7471 (★MW,D,E) 11:30am-2am, theme nights, patio

The Circus 6655 Santa Monica Blvd., (213) 462-1291 (★M,D,S,V) 9pm-2am Tue & Fri

Comedy Store 8433 Sunset Blvd., (213) 656-6225 (GF) 8pm-1am, stand-up club, lesbigay comedy Sat in 'Belly Room'

E & P T-Dance 657 N. Robertson Blvd. (upstairs behind Axis), West Hollywood, 335-5412 (M,D) 7pm-2am Sun

Gold Coast 8228 Santa Monica Blvd., (213) 656-4879 (★M,NH) 11am-2am, from 10am Sat-Sun

Hunters 7511 Santa Monica Blvd., (213) 850-9428 (M,NH) 9am-2am, from 6am wknds, hustlers

REVOLVER · MICKY'S · MOTHER LODE · AXIS · ABC · CBS

BEVERLY CENTER · SUNSET STRIP · SPAGO · HOLLYWOOD BOWL · BILLBOARD LIVE

PARAMOUNT STUDIOS · LITTLE FRIDA'S · CAFFE LUNA

ARENA · RAGE

UNIVERSAL STUDIOS HOLLYWOOD · SUNSET PLAZA NUMBERS

HOUSE OF BLUES · HOLLYWOOD BOWL

PACIFIC DESIGN CENTER

...DEO DRIVE · SANTA MONICA BLVD. · PLANET HOLLYWOOD

Improvisation 8162 Melrose Ave., (213) 651-2583 (GF,F) stand-up comedy

La Plaza 739 N. La Brea Ave., (213) 939-0703 (M,D,MRC-L,S) 8pm-2am, shows nightly at 10:15 & midnight

Love Lounge 657 N. Robertson Blvd., 659-0471 (MW,D,A,E) 9pm-2am, theme nights, women only Sat

▲ **Micky's** 8857 Santa Monica Blvd., 657-1176 (★M,D,V,YC) noon-2am

Mother Lode 8944 Santa Monica Blvd., 659-9700 (★M,NH,WC) noon-2am

Numbers 8029 Sunset Blvd., (213) 656-6300 (★M,OC) 5pm-2am, hustlers

Rafters 7994 Santa Monica Blvd., (213) 654-0396 (M,D,CW,V) noon-2am

Rage 8911 Santa Monica Blvd., 652-7055 (★M,D,F,S,V,YC,WC) 1pm-2am, T-dance 5pm Sun, lunch daily

Revolver 8851 Santa Monica Blvd., 659-8851 (★M,A,V) 4pm-2am, til 4am Fri-Sat, from 2pm Sun

Spike 7746 Santa Monica Blvd., (213) 656-9343 (★M,L,WC) 1pm-2am, til 4am wknds, cruise bar, patio

Trunks 8809 Santa Monica Blvd., 652-1015 (M,NH,YC) 1pm-2am, sports video bar

Union 8210 Sunset Blvd., West Hollywood, (213) 654-1001, 8pm-2am

Viper Room 8852 Sunset Blvd., West Hollywood, 358-1880, 9pm-2am

RESTAURANTS & CAFES

The 442 Restaurant 442 N. Fairfax, (213) 651-4421 (WC) 6pm-10:30pm, clsd Sun, fresh healthy cuisine

The Abbey 692 N. Robertson, 289-8410 (MW,WC) 7am-3am, patio

Amigos 7953 Santa Monica Blvd., (213) 650-8517 (★WC) lunch & dinner, Mexican, some veggie

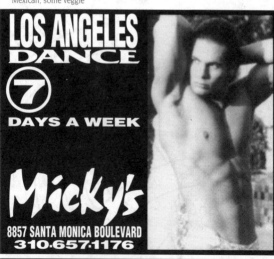

Baja Bud's 8575 Santa Monica Blvd., West Hollywood, 659-1911, 7am-10pm, til 11pm Fri-Sat, healthy Mexican

Benvenuto 8512 Santa Monica Blvd., West Hollywood, 659-8635, lunch, Mon-Fri, dinner 5:30-10:30pm, til 11pm Fri-Sat, patio, Italian

Bossa Nova 685 N. Robertson Blvd., West Hollywood, 657-5070, 11am-11pm, patio, Brazilian

Caffe Luna 7463 Melrose Ave., (213) 655-9177 (WC) 8am-3am, til 4am wknds, popular afterhours, Italian country food, some veggie

Canter's Deli 419 N. Fairfax, (213) 651-2030 (WC) 24hrs, hip afterhours, Jewish/American, some veggie

Club Cafe 8560 Santa Monica Blvd (in World's Gym), West Hollywood, 659-6630, 7am-9pm, til 6pm Sat, til 5pm Sun, salads & sandwiches

Crostini 846 N. La Cienega Blvd., West Hollywood, 652-8254, lunch & dinner, clsd Sun, Italian bistro

Daily Grind 8861 Santa Monica Blvd., 652-6040 (★MW,E) 8am-3am, from 10am wknds, coffeehouse

Figs 7929 Santa Monica Blvd., (213) 654-0780, dinner, Sun brunch, Californian, some veggie

French Quarter Market Place 7985 Santa Monica Blvd., (213) 654-0898 (★MW) 7am-midnight, til 3:30am Fri-Sat, American/cont'l, some veggie

The Greenery 8945 Santa Monica Blvd., 275-9518 (WC) 8am-1am, til 3am Fri-Sat, Californian, some veggie

The Heights Cafe 1118 N. Crescent Heights Blvd., (213) 650-9688 (MW,BYOB) 7am-11pm, 8pm-midnight Fri-Sat, til 9pm Sun, bistro, plenty veggie

Hoy's Wok 8163 Santa Monica Blvd., (213) 656-9002 (WC) noon-11pm, from 4pm Sun, Mandarin, plenty veggie

L'Orangerie 903 N. La Cienega Blvd., West Hollywood, 652-9770, lunch & dinner, clsd Mon, patio, haute French

La Masía 9077 Santa Monica Blvd., West Hollywood, 273-7066, Spanish/cont'l

Little Frida's Coffee House 8730 Santa Monica Blvd., West Hollywood, 854-5421, 8am-midnight, til 1am Fri-Sat, clsd Mon

Luna Park 655 N. Robertson, 652-0611 (WC) dinner, cabaret, cont'l/Mediterranean, some veggie

Mani's Bakery 519 S. Fairfax Ave., (213) 938-8800 (WC) 6:30am-11:45pm, 7:30am-1am wknds, coffee & dessert bar

Marix Tex Mex 1108 N. Flores, (213) 656-8800 (MW,WC) 11am-midnight, great margaritas

Mark's Restaurant 861 N. La Cienega Blvd., 652-5252, 6-10pm, upscale dining

Melrose Place 650 N. La Cienega Blvd., 657-2227 (E,WC) 5-11pm, cont'l/ Californian, some veggie, full bar

Nature Club Cafe 7174 Melrose Ave. (at Formosa), (213) 931-8994 (WC) noon-10pm, vegetarian, also elixir bar, yoga & massage

Paradise Grill 8745 Santa Monica Blvd., 659-6785 (MW,BW,WC) dinner, lunch & brunch wknds, patio

The Shed 8474 Melrose Ave., West Hollywood, (213) 655-6277, dinner, cont'l

Skewers 8939 Santa Monica Blvd., West Hollywood, 271-0555 (BW) 11am-2am, low-fat grill

Tango Grill 8807 Santa Monica Blvd., 659-3663 (MW,BW,WC) noon-11pm, some veggie

Tommy Tang's 7313 Melrose Ave., 937-5733 (★BW) noon-11pm, popular Tue nights w/ 'Club Glenda'

G·I·F·T·S

ALL KINDS OF GIFTS
FOR
ALL KINDS OF PEOPLE

Dorothy's Surrender

Trocadero 8280 Sunset Blvd., West Hollywood, (213) 656-7161, 6pm-3am, patio, full bar

Who's On Third Cafe 8369 W. 3rd St., (213) 651-2928, 8am-6pm, til 3pm Sun, American

Yukon Mining Co. 7328 Santa Monica Blvd., 851-8833 (★BW) 24hrs, champagne Sun brunch

GYMS & HEALTH CLUBS

Easton's Gym 8053 Beverly Blvd., (213) 651-3636 (GF)

World Gym-West Hollywood 8560 Santa Monica Blvd., West Hollywood, 659-6630 (F) also Club Cafe

BOOKSTORES & RETAIL SHOPS

A Different Light 8853 Santa Monica Blvd., West Hollywood, 854-6601 (★) 10am-midnight, lesbigay

▲ **Dorothy's Surrender** 7985 Santa Monica Blvd. #111, (213) 650-4111, 10am-11:30pm, cards, periodicals, T-shirts, gifts

International Male 9000 W. Santa Monica Blvd., 275-0285, 10am-9pm

NaNa 1228 3rd St., Santa Monica, 394-9690, 11am-9pm, til 11pm Fri-Sat, hip shoes & clothes, also NaNa outlet at 8737 W. 3rd St., (213) 653-1252

TRAVEL & TOUR OPERATORS

Cruise Holidays of Beverly Hills 224 S. Robertson, 652-8521

Embassy Travel 906 N. Harper Ave. Ste. B, (800) 227-6668/(213) 656-0743 (IGTA)

Friends Travel 322 Huntley Dr. Ste. 100, 652-9600/(800) GAY-0069

Gunderson Travel, Inc. 8543 Santa Monica Blvd. #8, (800) 872-8457/657-3944 (IGTA)

In Hollywood

Sauna
Jacuzzi
Sundeck
Video Lounge
Video in every room
Open 24 Hours

Weekly JO Party with
your favorite video stars

Melrose Baths
(213) 937-2122
7269 Melrose Ave
Hollywood, CA

It's not WHERE you do it
CONDOMS ARE FREE
It's HOW you do it

MasterCard

VISA

Melrose Baths

http://members.gnn.com/midtowne

1997 Damron Address Book

Magnum Select Travel Service 8500 Wilshire Blvd. Ste. 900, (800) 782-9429/652-7900 (IGTA)

SPIRITUAL GROUPS

West Hollywood Presbyterian Church 7350 Sunset Blvd., (213) 874-6646 (WC) 11am Sun

MEN'S CLUBS

▲ **Melrose Baths** 7269 Melrose Ave., 937-2122 (★MO,PC) 24hrs

EROTICA

▲ **Circus of Books** 8230 Santa Monica Blvd., (213) 656-6533, videos, erotica, toys

▲ **Drake's** 8932 Santa Monica Blvd., 289-8932, gifts, toys, videos, also at 7566 Melrose Ave. (213) 651-5600

Gauntlet 8720-1/2 Santa Monica Blvd., West Hollywood, 657-6677, noon-7pm, til 5pm Sun, body piercings

▲ **Pleasure Chest** 7733 Santa Monica Blvd., West Hollywood, (213) 650-1022

Skin Graffiti Tattoo 8722 Santa Monica Blvd. (upstairs), 358-0349, noon-7pm, til 4pm Sun, clsd Mon

L.A. - Hollywood (213)

INFO LINES & SERVICES

▲ **Community Real Estate Referrals** (800) 346-5592, gay realtor at your service, no rentals

ACCOMMODATIONS

▲ **Coral Sands Hotel** 1730 N. Western Ave., 467-5141 (M,SW) hot tub, sauna, weights

Hollywood Celebrity Hotel 1775 Orchid Ave., Hollywood, 850-6464/(800) 222-7017 (GF,IGTA) 1930s Art Deco hotel

Hollywood Metropolitan Hotel 5825 Sunset Blvd., Hollywood, 962-5800/(800) 962-5800 (GF) also full restaurant, American

BARS

Blacklite 1159 N. Western, 469-0211 (MW,NH) 6am-2am

Faultline 4216 Melrose, 660-0889 (★M,L,F,V) 2pm-2am, from 4pm Tue-Th, til 4am Fri-Sat, 'leather ethic observed,' patio, beer/soda bust 3-7pm Sun, also Faultline Store, 660-2952

Mugi 5221 Hollywood Blvd., 462-2039 (M,NH,MRC-A) 5pm-2am, clsd Mon

Probe 836 N. Highland Ave., (310) 281-6292 (★M,D) gay non-stop 9pm Sat through 10am Sun only, also '1970' (213) 669-1000 (MW,D,18+) 9pm Sun

Spotlight 1601 N. Cahuenga, 467-2425 (M,NH,WC) 6am-2am

Study 1723 N. Western, 464-9551 (★M,NH,MRC-AF) 11am-2am

Temple (call for location), 243-5221 (M,D,A) underground house Sat, call for events

Tempo 5520 Santa Monica Blvd., 466-1094 (M,D,MRC-L,E,S) from 8pm, from 6pm Sun, til 4am wknds

RESTAURANTS & CAFES

Hollywood Canteen 1006 Seward St., 465-0961, 11:30am-10pm, classic

Il Piccolino Trattoria 641 N. Highland Ave., 936-2996, lunch, dinner til midnight, clsd Mon

La Poubelle 5907 Franklin Ave., Hollywood, 465-0807 (WC) 6pm-midnight, French/Italian, some veggie

Prado 244 N. Larchmont Blvd., 467-3871 (WC) lunch & dinner

Quality 8030 W. 3rd St. (at Laurel), 658-5959 (WC) 8am-4pm, homestyle brkfst, some veggie

GYMS & HEALTH CLUBS
Gold's Gym 1016 N. Cole Ave., Hollywood, 462-7012

BOOKSTORES & RETAIL SHOPS
Archaic Idiot/Mondo Video 1724 N. Vermont, 953-8896, noon-10pm, vintage clothes, cult & lesbigay videos
▲ **Michael Design** 7510 Sunset Blvd #2, Hollywood, 650-0520, art

TRAVEL & TOUR OPERATORS
Jacqleen's Travel Service 6222 Fountain Ave. #314, 463-7404 (IGTA)

SPIRITUAL GROUPS
Dignity-LA PO Box 42040, 90042, 344-8064, 5:30pm Sun, Spanish Mass 3rd Sat

MEN'S CLUBS
▲ **Flex Complex** 4424 Melrose Ave., 663-5858 (MO,SW) 24hrs
▲ **Hollywood Spa** 1650 N. Ivar, 463-5169 (★MO,PC) 24hrs
MB Club 4550 Melrose Ave., 669-9899 (MO,PC)
The Zone 1037 N. Sycamore Ave., Hollywood, 464-8881 (MO,PC)

EROTICA
Highland Books 6775 Santa Monica Blvd., 463-0295
▲ **Le Sex Shoppe** 6315-1/2 Hollywood Blvd., 464-9435, 24hrs

ALWAYS OPEN-WE NEVER CLOSE
Call Today!
1-800-SPA-CLUB
The HOLLYWOOD Spa
TWO LOCATIONS!
1650 Ivar, Downtown Hollywood
5636 Vineland, North Hollywood

L.A. - West L.A. & Santa Monica (310)

INFO LINES & SERVICES
▲ **Community Real Estate Referrals** (800) 346-5592, gay realtor at your service, no rentals

ACCOMMODATIONS
Malibu Beach Inn 22878 Pacific Coast Hwy., 456-5428/(800) 462-6444 (GF,WC) on the ocean

The Mansion Inn 327 Washington Blvd., Venice, 821-2557/(800) 828-0688 (GF,WC) cont'l brkfst

Rose Avenue Beach House 55 Rose Ave., Venice, 396-2803 (GF) Victorian beach house 1 blk. from ocean & boardwalk

▲ **Seaview Inn at the Beach** 3400 Highland Ave., Manhattan Beach, 545-1504/Fax: 545-4052 (GF) ocean views, pool & courtyard

BARS
J.J.'s Pub 2692 S. La Cienega, 837-7443 (M,NH,WC) 11am-2am

Roosterfish 1302 Abbot Kinney Blvd., Venice, 392-2123 (★M,NH) 11am-2am, patio

Trilogy 2214 Stoner Ave., West Los Angeles, 477-2844 (GF,TG,F,S) opens 6pm, full bar, dinner theater w/drag waitresses/performers

RESTAURANTS & CAFES
The Local Yolk 3414 Highlands Ave., Manhattan Beach, 546-4407, 6:30am-2:30pm

Siamese Princess 8048 W. 3rd St., (213) 653-2643 (BW) 5:30-11pm, clsd Mon & Th, Thai, lunch weekdays

TRAVEL & TOUR OPERATORS
Atlas Travel Service 8923 S. Sepulveda Blvd., (800) 952-0120 (outside L.A.)/670-3574 (IGTA)

Firstworld Travel Express 1990 S. Bundy Dr. Ste. 175, (800) 366-0815/820-6868

SPIRITUAL GROUPS
MCC LA PO Box 46609, 90046, (213) 460-2911, 9am & 11:15am Sun, Spanish service 10am Sun

MEN'S CLUBS
Roman Holiday 12814 Venice Blvd., Mar Vista, 391-0200 (MO) 24hrs

L.A. - Silverlake (213)

INFO LINES & SERVICES
▲ **Community Real Estate Referrals** (800) 346-5592, gay realtor at your service, no rentals

▲ **Los Angeles Confidential Connection** 734-7822, Meet hot local guys! Record, listen, respond to free ads. Use free code 9966.

BARS
Cuffs 1941 Hyperion Ave., 660-2649 (★M,L) 4pm-2am

Detour 1087 Manzanita, 664-1189 (M,L)

Drag Strip 66 2500 Riverside Dr. (Rudolpho's), 969-2596 (★) queer dance club, call for events

Garage 4519 Santa Monica Blvd., East Hollywood, 683-3447 (M,D,E) 5pm-2am

Gauntlet II 4219 Santa Monica Blvd., 669-9472 (★M,L,WC) 2pm-2am, uniform bar

Houston's 2538 Hyperion Ave., 661-4233 (M,NH,F,E) 11am-2am, piano bar

Hyperion 2810 Hyperion Ave., 660-1503 (★M,D,MRC,S) 11:30am-2am, til 4am Sat

Joly's Two 4356 Sunset Blvd., 665-6810 (M,NH) 5pm-2am

Le Bar 2375 Glendale Blvd., 660-7595 (M,NH,MRC-L) 11am-2am

Little Joy 1477 W. Sunset Blvd., 250-3417 (M,NH,MRC-L,OC) 4pm-2am, from 11am wknds

Mr. Mike's 3172 Los Feliz Blvd., 669-9640 (M,E,OC) 11am-2am, piano bar Th-Sun

Silverlake Lounge 2906 Sunset Blvd., 663-9636 (M,NH,MRC-L,S) 10am-2am

RESTAURANTS & CAFES

Casita Del Campo 1920 Hyperion Ave., 662-4255 (★) 11am-10pm, Mexican, patio, also 'Plush Cabaret' Wed, call 969-2596 for details

Cha Cha Cha 656 N. Virgil (at Melrose), 664-7723 (MW,WC) 8am-10pm, til 11pm Fri-Sat, Caribbean, plenty veggie

The Cobalt Cantina 4326 Sunset Blvd., 953-9991 (★MW,WC) 11am-11pm, patio, Cal-Mex, some veggie, also full bar

The Crest Restaurant 3725 Sunset Blvd., 660-3645, 6am-11pm, diner/Greek

Da Giannino 2630 Hyperion Ave., 664-7979, lunch (Tue-Fri) & dinner, clsd Mon

El Conquistador 3701 Sunset Blvd., 666-5136, 5pm-11pm, from 11am wknds, Mexican

Rudolpho's 2500 Riverside Dr., 669-1226 (E) 8pm-2am, patio, salsa music & dancing lessons

Zen Restaurant 2609 Hyperion Ave., 665-2929/665-2930, 11:30am-2am, Japanese

GYMS & HEALTH CLUBS

Body Builders 2516 Hyperion Ave., 668-0802 (GF)

TRAVEL & TOUR OPERATORS

Burgan Travel 428 N. Azusa Ave., West Covina, (818) 915-8617

SPIRITUAL GROUPS

Holy Trinity Community Church 4209 Santa Monica Blvd., 662-9118, 10am Sun

MCC Silverlake 3621 Brunswick Ave., 665-8818, 1:30pm Sun

MEN'S CLUBS

▲ **Basic Plumbing** 1924 Hyperion Ave., 953-6731 (MO)

King of Hearts 1800 Hyperion Ave., 661-9417 (MO,PC) after hours

Night Hawk 1064 Myra Ave., 662-4726 (MO) 10pm-?, from 5pm Sun, clsd Mon-Wed

EROTICA

▲ **Circus of Books** 4001 Santa Monica Blvd., (213) 666-1304

L.A. - Midtown (213)

BARS

Jewel's Catch One Disco 4067 W. Pico Blvd., 734-8849 (★MW,D,A,MRC,WC) noon-2am, til 5am Fri-Sat

The Red Head 2218 E. 1st St., 263-2995 (MW,NH) 2pm-midnight, til 2am wknds

Score 107 W. 4th St., 625-7382 (M,NH,D,MRC-L) 10am-2am, 'Beer Bust' Sun

RESTAURANTS & CAFES

Atlas 3760 Wilshire Blvd., 380-8400 (D,WC) lunch & dinner except Sun, global, some veggie, also bar, 11am-2am

Sauna

Steam

Jacuzzi

Sundeck

Pool

Video Lounge

Open 24 Hrs

Private Video in every room

Weekly JO party featuring your favorite porn stars

NEW! 24 Hour Secured Parking Garage!

Midtowne Spa
(213) 680-1838
615 S. Kohler
Los Angeles, CA

It's not WHERE you do it
CONDOMS ARE FREE
It's HOW you do it

http://members.gnn.com/midtowne

Also visit us in Denver, New Orleans, Houston and Dallas!

VISA

MasterCard

MEN'S CLUBS

▲ **Midtowne Spa** 615 S. Kohler, 680-1838 (MO,SW,PC) 24hrs

L.A. - Valley (818)

INFO LINES & SERVICES

▲ **Community Real Estate Referrals** (800) 346-5592, gay realtor at your service, no rentals

▲ **San Fernando Valley Confidential Connection** 734-4848, Meet hot local guys! Record, listen, respond to free ads. Use free code 9966.

BARS

Apache Territory 11608 Ventura Blvd., Studio City, 506-0404 (★MW,D,S) 8pm-2am, til 4am Fri-Sat

The Bullet 10522 Burbank Blvd., North Hollywood, 760-9563 (M,L) noon-2am, til 4am Fri-Sat, patio

Driveshaft 13641 Victory Blvd., Van Nuys, 782-7199 (M,NH) 3pm-2am, from noon wknds, patio

Escapades 10437 Burbank Blvd., North Hollywood, 508-7008 (★MW,NH,S,WC) 1pm-2am

Gold 9 13625 Moorpark St., Sherman Oaks, 986-0285 (M,NH,OC) 11am-2am, from 7am Sat-Sun

Incognito Valley 7026 Reseda Blvd., Reseda, 996-2976 (★M,D,WC) noon-2am

Jox 10721 Burbank Blvd., North Hollywood, 760-9031 (M,NH,S) 4pm-2am, from noon wknds

Lodge 4923 Lankershim Blvd., North Hollywood, 769-7722 (★M,D,WC) noon-2am

Mag Lounge 5248 N. Van Nuys Blvd., Van Nuys, 981-6693 (★M,YC,WC) 11am-2am

Oasis 11916 Ventura Blvd., Studio City, 980-4811 (MW) 3pm-2am, piano bar

Oil Can Harry's 11502 Ventura Blvd., Studio City, 760-9749 (M,D,CW,E,S) 9pm-2am, from 7:30pm Tue, Th, clsd Sun

Queen Mary 12449 Ventura Blvd., Studio City, 506-5619 (★GF,S) 11am-2am, clsd Mon-Tue, shows wknds

Rawhide 10937 Burbank Blvd., North Hollywood, 760-9798 (★M,D,CW) 7pm-2am, from 2pm Sun, clsd Mon-Wed

RESTAURANTS & CAFES

Venture Inn 11938 Ventura Blvd., Studio City, 769-5400 (★MW,WC) lunch & dinner, champagne brunch Sun, cont'l, also full bar

Wellington's 4354 Lankershim Blvd., North Hollywood, 980-1430 (MW,E,WC) 11am-11pm, cont'l

GYMS & HEALTH CLUBS

Gold's Gym 6233 N. Laurel Canyon Blvd., North Hollywood, 506-4600

SPIRITUAL GROUPS

Christ Chapel of the Valley 5006 Vineland Ave., North Hollywood, 985-8977, 10am Sun, 7:30pm Wed, full gospel fellowship

MCC in the Valley 5730 Cahuenga Blvd., North Hollywood, 762-1133, 10am Sun

MEN'S CLUBS

▲ **The North Hollywood Spa** 5636 Vineland, 760-6969 (MO,PC) 24hrs

Roman Holiday 14435 Victory Blvd., Van Nuys (MO,SW) 24hrs

LE SEX SHOPPE

EROTICA
▲ **Le Sex Shoppe** 12323 Ventura Blvd., 760-9352, 24hrs
▲ **Le Sex Shoppe** 21625 Sherman Way, 992-9801, 24hrs
▲ **Le Sex Shoppe** 4539 Van Nuys Blvd., Sherman Oaks, 501-9609, 24hrs
▲ **Le Sex Shoppe** 4877 Lankershim Blvd., North Hollywood, 760-9529, 24hrs
  Stan's Video 7505 Foothill Blvd., Tujunga, 352-8735
  Video & Stuff 11612 Ventura Blvd., Studio City, 761-3162

Manhattan Beach (310)

ACCOMMODATIONS
▲ **Seaview Inn at the Beach** 3400 Highland Ave., 545-1504/Fax: 545-4052 (GF)
  ocean views, pool & courtyard

Marysville

CRUISY AREAS
  Ellis Lake (AYOR)
  River Front Park (AYOR)

Mendocino (707)

ACCOMMODATIONS
  Agate Cove Inn 11201 N. Lansing, 937-0551/(800) 527-3111 (GF) full brkfst, fireplaces
  Glendeven 8221 N. Hwy. 1, Little River, 937-0083 (GF) full brkfst, charming farmhouse on the coast
  McElroy's Inn 998 Main St., 937-1734/937-3105 (GF) located in the Village

Mendocino Coastal Reservations PO Box 1143, 95460, (800) 262-7801 (GF) 9am-6pm, call for available rentals

Seagull Inn 44594 Albion St., 937-5204 (GF,WC)

Stanford Inn by the Sea Coast Hwy. 1 & Comptche-Ukiah Rd., 937-5615 (GF,WC) full brkfst, fireplaces

RESTAURANTS & CAFES
The Cafe Beaujolais 961 Ukiah, 937-5614 (WC) dinner, California country food

BOOKSTORES & RETAIL SHOPS
Book Loft 45050 Main, 937-0890 (WC) 10am-6pm

Merced

CRUISY AREAS
Applegate Park off 'M' St. (AYOR)

Mission Viejo (714)

TRAVEL & TOUR OPERATORS
Sunrise Travel 23891 Via Fabricante #603, 837-0620

Modesto (209)

INFO LINES & SERVICES
AA Gay/Lesbian 1203 Tully Rd. Ste. B, 572-2970/531-2040 (MW) 8pm daily, 7pm Sun

▲ **Modesto Confidential Connection** 473-5959, Meet hot local guys! Record, listen, respond to free ads. Use free code 9966.

BARS
Brave Bull 701 S. 9th, 529-6712 (M,L) 7pm-2am, from 4pm Sun

The Mustang Club 413 N. 7th St., 577-9694 (MW,D,S) 4pm-2am, from 2pm Fri-Sun, open 30 years!

RESTAURANTS & CAFES
Espresso Caffe 3025 Mettenig Ave., 571-3337, 7am-11pm, til midnight Fri-Sat

BOOKSTORES & RETAIL SHOPS
Bookstore 2400 Coffee Rd., 521-0535 (WC) 10am-6pm, til 8:30pm Fri, til 5pm Sat, noon-5pm Sun

EROTICA
L'Amour Shoppe 1022 9th St., 521-7987

Liberty Adult Book Store 1030 Kansas Ave., 524-7603, 24hrs

Montebello

CRUISY AREAS
Legg Lake N. end (AYOR)

Monterey (408)

INFO LINES & SERVICES
AA Gay/Lesbian at the Little House in the Park, at Central & Forest, 373-3713, 8pm Th, also 10:30am Sat at Unitarian Church, Hwy. 1 @ Aguajito

ACCOMMODATIONS
Gosby House Inn 643 Lighthouse Ave., Pacific Grove, 375-1287 (GF,WC) full brkfst

Monterey Fireside Lodge 1131 10th St., 373-4172/(800) 722-2624 (GF) cont'l breakfast, hot tub, fireplaces

BARS
After Dark 214 Lighthouse Ave., 373-7828 (MW,D,V) 8pm-2am, patio

RESTAURANTS & CAFES
The Clock Garden Restaurant 565 Abrego, 375-6100 (WC) 11am-midnight, patio, American/cont'l

Napa (707)

ACCOMMODATIONS
Bed & Breakfast Inns of Napa (Napa County Visitors Bureau) 1310 Napa Town Center, 226-7459 (GF) 9am-5pm, call for extensive brochure

The Ink House B&B 1575 St. Helena Hwy., St. Helena, 963-3890 (GF) full brkfst, smokefree, Italianate Victorian, sunset wine

Willow Retreat 6517 Dry Creek Rd., 944-8173 (GF,SW,WC) hot tub, day use available

BOOKSTORES & RETAIL SHOPS
Ariadne Books 3780 Bel Aire Plaza, 253-9402, 10am-6pm, til 5pm Sat, clsd Sun, lesbigay section, also espresso bar

Nevada City (916)

RESTAURANTS & CAFES
Friar Tucks 111 N. Pine St., 265-9093 (WC) dinner nightly, American/fondue, bar

BOOKSTORES & RETAIL SHOPS
Nevada City Postal Company 228 Commercial St., 265-0576, 9am-6pm, til 5pm Sat, clsd Sun

Novato (415)

TRAVEL & TOUR OPERATORS
Dimensions in Travel, Inc. 2 Commercial Blvd., (800) 828-2962/883-3245x202

Oakland (see East Bay)

Oceanside (619)

INFO LINES & SERVICES
▲ **Oceanside Confidential Connection** 754-5555, Meet hot local guys! Record, listen, respond to free ads. Use free code 9966.

BARS
Capri Lounge 207 N. Tremont, 722-7284 (M,NH,WC) 10am-2am

RESTAURANTS & CAFES
Greystokes 1903 S. Coast Hwy., 757-2955 (MW,S)

EROTICA
▲ **Midnight Videos** 316 3rd St., 757-7832, 24hrs

Orange (714)

SPIRITUAL GROUPS
Calvary Open Door Tabernacle 608 W. Katella (Phil's Ballroom), 284-5775, 10:30am & 6:30pm Sun

Palm Springs (619)

INFO LINES & SERVICES
AA Gay/Lesbian 324-4880, call for mtg schedule

▲ **Community Real Estate Referrals** (800) 346-5592, gay realtor at your service, no rentals

Desert Business Association PO Box 773, 92263, 324-0178 (IGTA) lesbigay business association

▲ **Palm Springs Confidential Connection** 322-9200, Meet hot local guys! Record, listen, respond to free ads. Use free code 9966.

Palm Springs Lesbian/Gay Pride PO Box 861, Cathedral City, 92235, 322-8769, 24hr helpline

ACCOMMODATIONS

▲ **The 550** 550 Warm Sands Dr., 320-7144/(800) 669-0550 (MO,SW,N) hot tub, kitchens, videos, waterfall spa

▲ **Abbey West** 772 Prescott Cir., 320-4333/(800) 223-4073 (M,SW,IGTA) B&B, priv. patios, gym, hot tub

▲ **Alexander Resort Hotel** 598 Grenfall Rd., 327-6911/(800) 448-6197 (MO,SW,N) contemporary guesthouse, hot tub, cont'l brkfst

Aruba Hotel Suites 671 S. Riverside Dr., 325-8440/(800) 842-7822 (MW,SW,N,IGTA) gorgeous apartments on 2 levels, hot tub

▲ **The Atrium** 981 Camino Parocela, 322-2404/(800) 669-1069 (MO,SW,N,WC,IGTA) hot tub

Avanti Resort Hotel 715 San Lorenzo Rd., 325-9723/(800) 572-2779 (M,SW,N,IGTA) secluded resort, spa, mist system, hot tub, private baths, kitchen

Cabana Club Resort 970 Parocela Pl., 323-8842 (SW,N) Marilyn Monroe Suite, adult film channels

▲ **Camp Palm Springs** 722 San Lorenzo Rd., 322-2267/(800) 793-0063 (MO,SW,N,WC,IGTA) private baths, kitchens, spa

Hacienda en Sueño

Your House of Dreams

586 Warm Sands Drive
Palm Springs, California 92264
1-800-359-2007

INN
Exile
PALM SPRINGS
a man's resort

pools
jacuzzi
gymnasium
steam room
breakfast
luncheon
king sized beds
cooling mist
outdoor fireplace

clothing is
always optional

**545
Warm Sands Drive
Palm Springs
CA 92264**

phone:
619 327-6413

fax:
619 320 5745

brochure
reservations:
800 962 0186

Where the Sands are Warm & the Memories are Hot!

Palm Springs, California (near Los Angeles)

LARGEST GAY RESORT AREA IN THE WORLD

In a charming 50's style with all new king-size beds. 26 rooms, large swimming pool, Jacuzzi, natural sunbathing, private phones, TV's, private hot movie channels, 18 rooms with kitchens, 5 rooms with wood-burning fireplaces.

Rates Start At
$39.50

Warm Sands
V I L L A S
A PRIVATE MENS RESORT
SINCE 1933

555 Warm Sands Dr.
Palm Springs, California 92264
Phone: 619-323-3005 Fax: 619-323-4006

Reservations (USA): **800-357-5695**

With Over
4,000 Videos
to Choose From
We Have
the Largest
Selection of
Videos, Books
& Magazines
in the Desert.
50 Channel
Video Arcade
with 19' TV's.
Video Sales
Rentals

Lube,
Lotions,
Leather
Goods

PEREZ
VIDEO & BOOKS
(619) 321-5597
68-366 PEREZ RD., CATHEDRAL CITY, CA

PHOTO©DAVID MORGAN

For the best view in the Desert!

Desert Palms Inn
RESORT

Come visit the
Desert Palms Inn
and enjoy the
Desert's most famous
full-service Gay Resort!

▸ Incredible **HOT BOD POOL PARTIES** and **SPECIAL EVENTS!**

▸ All 29 beautiful rooms have **POOLSIDE VIEWS!**

▸ Indoor and outdoor dining at the fabulous **DP CAFE!**

▸ Cool off at the **DP POOLSIDE BAR!**

▸ Enjoy the sun around the **KEYHOLE POOL!**

(619) 324-3000
Reservations 1-800-801-8696
67580 E. Palm Canyon Dr.
Cathedral City, California 92234

▲ **Canyon Boys' Club Hotel** 960 N. Palm Canyon Dr., 322-4367/(800) 295-2582 (MO,BW,SW,N) hot tub, sauna/steam room, kitchens, private baths

Casa Rosa 589 Grenfall Rd., 322-4143/(800) 322-4151 (M) full brkfst, kitchens, hot tub, private patios, mist system

▲ **Cathedral City Boys' Club** 68-369 Sunsair Rd., Cathedral City, 324-1350/(800) 472-0836 (MO,SW,N) private men's resort, hot tub, steam room, free shuttle around town

▲ **Columns Resort** 537 Grenfall Rd., 325-0655/(800) 798-0655 (MO,SW,N,IGTA) studios, full brkfst, hot tub, kitchens, sauna, spa

The Coyote Inn 234 S. Patencio Rd., 322-9675/(800) 269-6830 (MO,SW,N,WC) patio, classic southwest inn, cont'l brkfst

▲ **Desert Hangout** 1466 N. Palm Canyon Dr., 320-5984/(800) 660-5066 (MO,SW,N) hot tub, spa, cont'l brkfst

▲ **Desert Palms Inn** 67-580 Hwy. 111, Cathedral City, 324-3000/(800) 801-8696 (MW,F,SW) huge courtyard, bar & restaurant on premises, American, some veggie

▲ **Desert Paradise Hotel** 615 Warm Sands Dr., 320-5650/(800) 342-7635 (outside CA) (MO,SW,N,IGTA) fresh fruit brkfst, hot tub

Desert Shadows 260 Chuckwalla, (800) 292-9298/325-6410 (GF,SW,N,WC) hot tub, naturist hotel, also restaurant

▲ **El Mirasol Villas** 525 Warm Sands Dr., 327-5913/(800) 327-2985 (MW,F,SW,N) private, hot tub

▲ **Hacienda en Sueño Resort** 586 Warm Sands Dr., 327-8111/(800) 359-2007 (★MO,SW,N,WC,IGTA) VCRs, hot tub

▲ **Harlow Club Hotel** 175 E. El Alameda, 323-3977/(800) 223-4073 (MO,SW,IGTA) lunch buffet, hot tub, gym

Hot Desert Knights 435 E. Avenida Olancha, (800) 256-7938/325-5456 (MO,SW,N) no smoking, gay naturist hotel, kitchens, patio

Ingleside Inn 200 W. Ramon Rd., 325-0046 (GF,SW,WC) hot tub, also a restaurant, French cont'l, cont'l brkfst

▲ **Inn Exile** 960 Camino Parocela, 327-6413/(800) 962-0186 (MO,F,SW,N,IGTA) resort, hot tub, gym

▲ **Inndulge Palm Springs** 601 Grenfall Rd., 327-1408/(800) 833-5675 (M,SW,N) hot tub, cont'l brkfst, afternoon wine & cheese

Inntimate 556 Warms Sands Dr., 778-8334/(800) 698-3846 (MO,SW,N) kitchens, serene & secluded gentlemanly inn

▲ **Inntrigue** 526 Warm Sands Dr., 323-7505/(800) 798-8781 (MO,SW,N) hot tub, intimate & secluded resort, kitchens, spa

Mira Loma Hotel 1420 N. Indian Canyon Dr., 320-1178 (MW,SW) cont'l brkfst, smokefree

▲ **Mirage** 574 Warm Sands Dr., (800) 669-1069/322-2404 (MO,N,WC) kitchens, private resort, waterfall, gym, hot tub

▲ **Sago Palms Resort** 595 Thornhill Rd., 323-0224/(800) 626-7246 (MO,SW,N) kitchens, fireplaces, intimate resort, patios, hot tub

Santiago Resort 650 San Lorenzo Rd., (800) 710-7729/322-1300 (MO,SW,N) hotel, expanded cont'l brkfst, hot tub

Smoke Tree Inn 1800 Smoke Tree Ln., 327-8355 (GF,SW,WC) secluded on 4-1/2 acres, hot tub

Triangle Inn 555 San Lorenzo Rd., 322-7993/(800) 732-7555 (MO,SW,N) hot tub, expanded cont'l brkfst

▲ **The Villa Hotel** 67-670 Carey Rd., Cathedral City, 328-7211/(800) 845-5265 (M,SW,IGTA) individual bungalows, sauna, hot tub, masseur, cont'l brkfst, kitchens

INNTRIGUE

A PRIVATE RESORT

We Have What You're Looking For!

- *Poolside studios & suites*
- Kitchens, private patios & fireplaces available.
- *Two sparkling clothes-optional pools and spas.*
- *Pool table • Continental breakfast*
- *Complimentary Gold's Gym Passes*
  ...and so much more

800-798-8781

526 Warm Sand's Dr., Palm Springs, CA 92264
619-323-7505 • FAX 619-323-1055

The NAMES Project Chapters

(USA)

California
Bay Area	415-863-1966
Inland Empire	909-784-2437
Long Beach	310-434-0021
Los Angeles	213-653-6263
Orange County	714-490-3880
Sacramento	916-484-5646
San Diego	619-492-8452
Ventura County	805-650-7382

Connecticut
Central Connecticut	203-369-9670

District of Columbia
National Capital Area	202-296-2637

Hawaii
Honolulu	808-948-1481

Iowa
Cedar Valley	319-266-7903

Illinois
Chicago	312-472-4460

Indiana
Indianapolis	317-920-1200

Louisiana
Louisiana Capital Area	504-753-0864

Massachusetts
Boston	617-262-6263

Maine
Maine	207-774-2198

Michigan
Detroit	313-337-5895
Thumb Area	810-982-6361

Minnesota
Twin Cities	612-373-2468

Missouri
St. Louis	314-995-4638

North Carolina
Charlotte	704-376-2637

New Jersey
New Jersey	908-739-4863

New Mexico
New Mexico	505-466-2211

New York
Buffalo	716-838-4860
Long Island	516-477-2447
New York City	212-226-2292
Syracuse	315-498-4940

Oklahoma
Tulsa	918-748-3111

Oregon
Portland	503-650-7032

Pennsylvania
Philadelphia	215-735-6263
Pittsburgh	412-343-9846
Susquehanna Valley	717-234-0629

Rhode Island
Rhode Island	401-847-7637

Texas
Dallas Metroplex	214-520-7397
Ft. Worth/Tarrant County	817-336-2637
Houston	713-526-2637

Utah
Salt Lake City	801-487-2323

Virginia
Central Virginia	804-346-8047

Washington
Seattle	206-285-2880

West Virginia
Upper Ohio Valley	304-242-9443

▲ **Vista Grande Villa** 574 Warm Sands Dr., 322-2404/(800) 669-1069 (MO,SW,N,IGTA) private men's resort, kitchens

▲ **Warm Sands Villas** 555 Warm Sands Dr., 323-3005/(800) 357-5695 (MO,SW,N,WC) hot tub

BARS

Backstreet Pub 72-695 Hwy. 111 #A-7, Palm Desert, 341-7966 (MW,NH,WC) 2pm-2am

▲ **Choices** 68-352 Perez Rd., Cathedral City, 321-1145 (★MW,D,E,V,WC) 7pm-2am, patio

Dates 67-670 Cary Rd.(at The Villa), Cathedral City, 328-7211 (M) 10am-midnight, patio, poolside bar, also cafe w/ brkfst & lunch

Iron Horse Saloon 36-650 Sun Air Plaza, Cathedral City, 770-7007 (MW,CW) 4pm-2am, patio

J.P.'s 1117 N. Palm Canyon, 778-5310 (M,D) 4pm-midnight

Poolside Bar (at the Desert Palms Inn), 324-5100 (M,F,E) 9am-2am, piano bar

Richard's 68-599 E. Palm Canyon Dr., Cathedral City, 321-2841 (MW,F,E,WC) 10am-2am, also restaurant for lunch & dinner, American

Streetbar 224 E. Arenas, 320-1266 (★M,NH,E,WC) 2pm-2am

Tool Shed 600 E. Sunny Dunes, 320-3299 (M,NH) 10am-2am, from 6am-4am wknds, call for events

Two Gloria's 2400 N. Palm Canyon Dr., 322-3224 (M,F,E,OC) 4am-2am, piano bar, also restaurant (MW)

The Wolf's Den 67-625 Hwy. 111, Cathedral City, 321-9688 (M,L) 8pm-2am, bears & big men welcome, leather shop, patio

RESTAURANTS & CAFES

Billy Reed's 1800 N. Palm Canyon Rd., 325-1946, American, some veggie, full bar, bakery

Bistro 111 70-065 Hwy. 111, Rancho Mirage, 328-5650, clsd Sun-Tue, seasonal, healthy American, some veggie

Donatello Ristorante Italiano 196 S. Indian Canyon, 778-5200 (BW) dinner, Italian, some veggie

El Gallito Mexican Restaurant 68820 Grove St., Cathedral City, 328-7794 (BW) Mexican

Elan Brasserie 415 N. Palm Canyon Dr., 323-5554 (S) lunch & dinner, Provençal/Mediterranean, full bar

Maria's Italian Cuisine 67-778 Hwy. 111, Cathedral City, 328-4378 (BW) 5:30-9:30pm dinner only, clsd Mon, Italian, plenty veggie

Mortimer's 2095 N. Indian Canyon, 320-4333 (E) lunch & dinner, California/French

Rainbow Cactus Cafe 212 S. Indian Canyon, 325-3868, 11am-2am, authentic Mexican, full bar

Red Tomato 68-784 Grove St. at Hwy. 111, Cathedral City, 328-7518 (BW,WC) pizza & pasta, plenty veggie

Robí 78-085 Avenida La Fonda, La Quinta, 564-0544 (E,BW,WC) dinner only, clsd Mon (seasonal April-Oct), cont'l, some veggie

Shame on the Moon 69-950 Frank Sinatra Dr., Rancho Mirage, 324-5515 (WC) 6pm-10:30pm, clsd Mon (summer only), cont'l, some veggie, also full bar, patio

Silas' on Palm Canyon 664 N. Palm Canyon Dr., 325-4776, clsd. Sun, full bar, continental, patio, intimate

The Wilde Goose 67-938 Hwy. 111, Cathedral City, 328-5775 (E) from 5:30pm, cont'l/wild game, some veggie, full bar

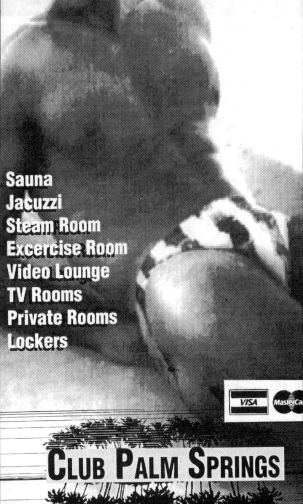

Sauna
Jacuzzi
Steam Room
Excercise Room
Video Lounge
TV Rooms
Private Rooms
Lockers

CLUB PALM SPRINGS

68-449 Perez Rd.
Cathedral City, CA • (619) 324-8588

GYMS & HEALTH CLUBS

Gold's Gym 40-70 Airport Center Dr., 322-4653 (GF) 6am-10pm, 8am-8pm Sat, 9am-5pm Sun

Palm Springs Athletic Club 543 S. Palm Canyon, 323-7722 (GF) 6am-11pm, til midnight Fri-Sat, til 9pm Sun

BOOKSTORES & RETAIL SHOPS

Between the Pages 214 E. Arenas Rd., Cathedral City, 320-7158, 11am-9pm, lesbigay, espresso bar

Bloomsbury Books 555 S. Sunrise Way, 325-3862, 11am-9pm, clsd Sun, lesbigay

Moonlighting 307 E. Arena, 323-8830, 6pm-2am, til 6am Th-Sun

TRAVEL & TOUR OPERATORS

Journey's Travel 42462 Bob Hope Dr. at Hwy. 111, Rancho Mirage, (800) 733-3646/340-4545

Las Palmas Travel 403 N. Palm Canyon Dr., (800) 776-6888/325-6311 (IGTA)

Rancho Mirage Travel 71-428 Hwy. 111, Rancho Mirage, (800) 369-1073/341-7888 (IGTA)

SPIRITUAL GROUPS

Christ Chapel of the Desert 4707 E. Sunny Dunes, 327-2795, 10am Sun

Integrity of the Desert 125 W. El Alameda, 322-2150, 4th Fri, call for location, lesbian/gay Episcopalians

Unity Church of Palm Springs 815 S. Camino Real, 11am Sun, 7:30pm Tue, also bookstore & classes

PUBLICATIONS

The Bottom Line 1243 N. Gene Autry Tr. Ste. 121-122, 323-0552, bi-weekly

Directory-Palm Springs 4102 E. 7th St. #621, Long Beach, 90804, 434-7129, annual directory of gay & gay-supportive businesses

Hijinx 15-685 Palm Dr. #36, Desert Hot Springs, 329-2421, free lesbigay guide to Palm Springs & desert resorts

Lifestyle Magazine PO Box 2803, Rancho Mirage, 92270, 321-2685

MEN'S CLUBS

▲ **Club Palm Springs** 68-449 Perez Rd. #1, Cathedral City, 324-8588 (★MO,V,PC) 24hrs, spa, exercise room, steam & sauna, hot tub, deck

▲ **The Gravel Pit** 68144 Summit, Cathedral City, 324-9771, 10pm-dawn Fri-Sat, 9pm-2am Sun

EROTICA

Black Moon Leather 68-449 Perez Rd. #7, Cathedral City, (800) 945-3284/770-2925, 3pm-midnight, til 2am wknds, also 67-625 Hwy. 111 location (inside 'Wolf's'), 9pm-midnight Wed-Sun

Hidden Joy Book Shop 68-424 Commercial, Cathedral City, 328-1694, 24hrs

▲ **Perez Books** 68-366 Perez Rd., Cathedral City, 321-5597, 24hrs, arcade

World Wide Book Store 68-300 Ramon Rd., 321-1313

Palmdale (805)

EROTICA

Sunshine Gifts 38519 Sierra Hwy., 265-0652, 24hrs

Palo Alto (415)

BOOKSTORES & RETAIL SHOPS

Books Inc. 157 Stanford Shopping Center, 321-0600, 9:30am-9pm, 10am-8 Sat, til 6pm Sun, general, lesbigay section

Stacey's Bookstore 219 University Ave., 326-0681, 9am-9pm, til 10pm Fri-Sat, 11am-6pm Sun, lesbigay section

Pasadena (818)

INFO LINES & SERVICES

Hugo Au Go-Go's Video Lending Library 126 W. Del Mar Blvd., (800) 543-8272, free video lending library for people w/ HIV/AIDS

▲ **Pasadena Confidential Connection** 576-0090, Meet hot local guys! Record, listen, respond to free ads. Use free code 9966.

BARS

Boulevard 3199 E. Foothill Blvd., 356-9304 (M,NH,E) 1pm-2am, piano bar Sun

Encounters 203 N. Sierra Madre Blvd., 792-3735 (MW,D,YC) 2pm-2am

Nardi's 665 E. Colorado Blvd., 449-3152 (M,NH,WC) 1pm-2am

RESTAURANTS & CAFES

La Risata 60 N. Raymond (at Union), 793-9000 (WC) lunch & dinner, Northern Italian, patio

Little Richy's 39 S. Fair Oaks Ave., 440-0306 (WC) 11am-10pm, clsd Mon, Latin American, some veggie

SPIRITUAL GROUPS

First Congregational United Church of Christ 464 E. Walnut, 795-0696, 10am Sun

Pescadero (415)

ACCOMMODATIONS
Oceanview Farms PO Box 538, 94060, 879-0698/642-9438 (MW) located on working horse breeding farm

Petaluma (707)

TRAVEL & TOUR OPERATORS
Sunquest Travel Co. 789 Hudis St., Rohnert Park, 588-8747, also business language school

Pismo Beach (805)

ACCOMMODATIONS
▲ **Palomar Inn** 1601 Shell Beach Rd., Shell Beach, 773-4207 (MW) close to nude beach, gay owned and operated

Placerville (209)

ACCOMMODATIONS
Rancho Cicada Retreat PO Box 225, Plymouth, 95669, 245-4841 (MW,SW,N) riverside retreat

Pleasant Hill (510)

EROTICA
Pleasant Hill Books 2298 Monument Blvd., 676-2962

Pomona (909)

INFO LINES & SERVICES
Gay/Lesbian Community Center Hotline 884-5447, 6:30pm-10pm

BARS
Alibi East 225 E. San Antonio Ave., 623-9422 (M,D,S) 10am-2am, til 4am Fri-Sat
Back Alley Bar (at Alibi East), 623-9422 (M) 9pm-3am Fri-Sat
BVD's/Dynasty Club 732 W. Holt Ave., 622-7502/622-1403 (M,D,S) 2pm-2am
Mary's 1047 E. 2nd St., 622-1971 (MW,D,F,WC) 2pm-2am
Robbie's 390 E. 2nd St. (at College Plaza), 620-4371 (MW,D,S) 6pm-2am, clsd Tue-Wed, call for events

RESTAURANTS & CAFES
Haven Coffeehouse & Gallery 296 W. 2nd St., 623-0538 (E) 11am-11pm, sandwiches & salads

EROTICA
Mustang Books 961 N. Central, Upland, 981-0227

Porterville

ACCOMMODATIONS
▲ **The Caritas B&B Network** (800) CARITAS (227-4827), see ad in center National section

Red Bluff

CRUISY AREAS
The Dog Island Park (AYOR) days
Park along the river (AYOR) early evenings

Redding (916)

BARS
Club 501 1244 California St. (enter rear), 243-7869 (MW,D,F,YC) 6pm-2am, from 4pm Sun

EROTICA
Hilltop Adult Bookstore 2131 Hilltop Dr. (behind Maytag store), 222-9542 (GF) 24hrs, videos

CRUISY AREAS
Clear Creek Rd. 4 mi. W. of old 99 (AYOR) summers
Lake Redding Park nr. boatramp, AYOR

Redondo Beach (310)

BARS
Dolphin 1995 Artesia Blvd., 318-3339 (M,NH,WC) 1pm-2am

Redwood City (415)

BARS
Shouts 2034 Broadway, 369-9651 (MW,NH,D,WC) 11am-2am

SPIRITUAL GROUPS
MCC of the Peninsula 2124 Brewster Ave. (Unitarian Church), 368-0188, 5pm Sun

EROTICA
Golden Gate Books 739 El Camino Real, 364-6913, 24hrs

Riverside (909)

INFO LINES & SERVICES
Great Outdoors Inland Empire Chapter PO Box 56586, San Bernardino, 627-3442, outdoor social group

BARS
Menagerie 3581 University Ave., 788-8000 (M,D,WC) 4pm-2am
VIP Club 3673 Merrill Ave., 784-2370 (MW,D,F,WC) 4pm-2am, til 3am Fri-Sat

SPIRITUAL GROUPS
St. Bride's PO Box 1132, 92501, 369-0992 (GF) 11am Sun, Celtic Catholic service

Russian River (707)

INFO LINES & SERVICES
▲ **Community Real Estate Referrals** (800) 346-5592, gay realtor at your service, no rentals
Country Inns of the Russian River PO Box 2416, Guerneville, 95446, (800) 927-4667, info & referrals for 6 inns
GLBA (Gay/Lesbian Business Association) 869-9000
Russian River Tourist Bureau (800) 253-8800, info

ACCOMMODATIONS
Applewood- An Estate Inn 13555 Hwy. 116 , Guerneville, 869-9093 (GF,F,SW,WC) 21+, full brkfst, no smoking
Avalon 4th & Mill St., Guerneville, 869-9566 (GF,SW)
The Chalet 864-4061 (GF) rental home on 1/4 acre sleeps 6, 4 min. to downtown Guerneville

HIGHLANDS RESORT

Cabins with fireplaces
Rooms, Camping and
Day use.
Swimming Pool and
Hot Tub.
Nude Sunbathing

Located a short walk
from town on 3 acres
of redwood trees and
beautiful gardens..

Open all year!

HIGHLANDS RESORT

P.O. Box 346/14000 Woodland Dr.
Guerneville, CA 95446
http://travel.org/HighlandsResort
(707) 869-0333 Fax (707) 869-0370

Faerie Ring Campground 16747 Armstrong Woods Rd., Guerneville, 869-2746/869-4122 (GF) on 14 acres, campsites, RV

Fern Falls PO Box 228, Cazadero, 632-6108/Fax: 632-6216 (MW) waterfall, hot tub

▲ **Fern Grove Inn** 16650 River Rd., Guerneville, 869-9083/(800) 347-9083 (GF,SW) cottages

▲ **Fife's Resort** PO Box 45, Guerneville, 95446, 869-0656/(800) 734-3371 (MW,SW,IGTA) cabins & 60-100 campsites, also bar (D,CW) also full restaurant, some veggie

Golden Apple Ranch 17575 Fitzpatrick Ln., Occidental, 874-3756 (GF,WC)

▲ **Highland Dell Inn** 21050 River Blvd., Monte Rio, 865-1759/(800) 767-1759 (GF,SW) full brkfst

▲ **Highlands Resort** 14000 Woodland Dr., Guerneville, 869-0333/Fax: 869-0370 (MW,SW,N) hot tub, cont'l brkfst

House of a Thousand Flowers 11 Mosswood Cir., Cazadero, 632-5571/Fax: 632-6215 (GF) full brkfst, country B&B

Huckleberry Springs Country Inn 8105 Old Beedle, Monte Rio, 865-2683/(800) 822-2683 (GF,SW,IGTA) dinner served, no smoking, private cottages, Japanese spa, videos, massage cottage

▲ **Jacques' Cottage at Russian River** 6471 Old Trenton Rd., Guerneville, 575-1033 (MW,SW,N) hot tub

The Mountain Lodge 16350 First St., Guerneville, 869-3722/Fax: 869-0556 (MW,SW,WC) apartments, hot tub

Paradise Cove Resort 14711 Armstrong Woods Rd., Guerneville, 869-2706 (MW,SW) hot tub, fireplaces, studio units, decks

Redwood Grove RV Park & Campground 16140 Neely Rd., Guerneville, 869-3670 (GF)

Rio Villa Beach Resort 20292 Hwy. 116, Monte Rio, 865-1143/Fax: 865-0115 (GF) cabins, on the river

Riverbend Campground & RV Park 11820 River Rd., Forestville, 887-7662 (GF,WC)

▲ **Russian River Resort/Triple 'R' Resort** 16390 4th St., Guerneville, 869-0691/(800) 417-3767 (MW,F,E,V,SW,N,WC) hot tub, cocktail lounge, full American restaurant, some veggie

Schoolhouse Canyon Park 12600 River Rd., 869-2311 (GF,SW) private beach, campground, RV sites

Villa Messina 316 Burgundy Rd., Healdsburg, 433-6655/Fax: 433-4515 (MW) in-room hot tubs, full brkfst

▲ **The Willows** 15905 River Rd., Guerneville, 869-2824/(800) 953-2828 (MW) old-fashioned country lodge & campgound

The Woods Resort 16881 Armstrong Woods Rd., Guerneville, 869-0111/479-6637 (M,SW,N) rooms & cabins, bar, cafe

BARS

Molly's Country Club 14120 Old Cazadero Rd., Guerneville, 869-0511 (MW,D,CW,F) 4pm-2am, from noon wknds, til midnight Sun-Th

Mr. T's Bullpen 16246 1st St., Guerneville, 869-3377 (M,NH)

Rainbow Cattle Co. 16220 River Rd., Guerneville, 869-0206 (M,NH) 6am-2am

RESTAURANTS & CAFES

Big Bertha's Burgers 16357 Main St., Guerneville, 869-2239 (BW) 11am-8pm

Breeze-Inn Barb-Q 15640 River Rd., Guerneville, 869-9208/869-9209 (★) take-out & delivery, some veggie

Burdon's 15405 River Rd., Guerneville, 869-2615 (MW,WC) call for hours, cont'l pasta, plenty veggie

Coffee Bazaar 14045 Armstrong Woods Rd., Guerneville, 869-9706, 7am-8pm, soups, salads & pastries

Flavors Unlimited 16450 Main St. (River Rd.), Guerneville, 869-0425, hours vary, custom-blended ice cream

Hiding Place 9605 Old River Rd., Forestville, 887-9506, 8am-9pm, homecooking, some veggie

International Café 10940 River Rd., Forestville, 887-4644 (WC) 6am-8pm, 8am-10pm wknds, cybercafe

Mill St. Grill (at Triple 'R' Resort), Guerneville, 869-0691 (MW,WC) American, some veggie, full bar, patio

River Inn Restaurant 16141 Main St., Guerneville, 869-0481 (WC) seasonal, local favorite, American

Sweet's River Grill 16251 Main St., Guerneville, 869-3383 (★BW) noon-9pm

BOOKSTORES & RETAIL SHOPS

Up the River 16212 Main St., Guerneville, 869-3167, cards, gifts, T-shirts & more

SPIRITUAL GROUPS

MCC of the Redwood Empire 14520 Armstrong Woods Rd. (Guerneville Community Church), Guerneville, 869-0552, noon Sun

CRUISY AREAS

The Nude Beach on Russian River at Wohler Bridge, Guerneville (AYOR)

Sacramento (916)

INFO LINES & SERVICES

▲ **Community Real Estate Referrals** (800) 346-5592, gay realtor at your service, no rentals

▲ **Gay Connection** (900) 505-6339, talk and/or meet with other men from the area, at only 99 ¢ per minute

Lambda Community Center 1931 'L' St., 442-0185/442-7960, 10am-7pm, youth groups plus many other groups

Men's Coming Out Group (at the Lambda Center), 442-0185, 5:30pm Mon

Northall Gay AA 2015 'J' St. #32, 454-1100, 8pm Wed

▲ **Sacramento Confidential Connection** 489-2300, Meet hot local guys! Record, listen, respond to free ads. Use free code 9966.

ACCOMMODATIONS

Hartley House B&B Inn 700 22nd St., 447-7829/(800) 831-5806 (GF) full brkfst, conference facilities

BARS

Bojangles 7042 Folsom Blvd., 382-9882

Faces 2000 'K' St., 448-7798 (M,D,CW,E,V,WC) 5pm-2am, from 1pm wknds

Joseph's Town & Country Bar 3514 Marconi, 483-1220 (MW,D,F,S) 4pm-2am, Italian

The Mercantile Saloon 1928 'L' St., 447-0792 (M,NH,WC) 10am-2am

Mirage 601 15th St., 444-3238 (MW,NH,WC) 6pm-2am

The Townhouse 1517 21st St., 441-5122 (M,NH,WC) 3pm-2am, from 10am wknds, dinner Fri-Sat, Sun brunch

The Western 2001 'K' St., 443-9831 (M,NH,WC) 6am-1:30am

Wreck Room 2513 Broadway, 456-1181 (M,L,WC) 5pm-2am, afterhours Fri-Sat, from 4pm Sun

RESTAURANTS & CAFES

Cafe Lambda (at the Lambda Center), 442-0185 (MW,E) 8pm-midnight Fri

Constant Cravings 6494 Broadway, 457-2233, 6am-8pm, clsd Sun

Ernesto's 1901 16th St., 441-5850, 11am-10pm, from 9am wknds, Mexican, full bar

Hamburger Mary's 1630 'J' St., 441-4340

Rick's Dessert Diner 2322 'K' St., 444-0969, 10am-midnight, til 1pm Sun-Mon

GYMS & HEALTH CLUBS

Valentis 921 11th St., 863-9629 (GF,SW) also juice bar

BOOKSTORES & RETAIL SHOPS

Films for Days 2300 'O' St., 448-3456, noon-10pm, til 11pm Fri-Sun, lesbigay titles

The Open Book 910 21st St., 498-1004/Fax: 498-1014, 9am-midnight, lesbigay bookstore & coffeehouse

TRAVEL & TOUR OPERATORS

Aladdin Travel 818 'K' St. Mall, (800) 655-0633 (in CA)/446-0633 (IGTA)

Mad About Travel 930 Bell Ave., (800) 856-0441/567-1958

The Sports Leisure Travel 9527-A Folsom Blvd., (800) 951-5556/361-2051 (IGTA)

SPIRITUAL GROUPS

Integrity 2620 Capital Ave., 394-1715, lesbigay Episcopalians

PUBLICATIONS

MGW (Mom Guess What) 1725 'L' St., 441-6397, bi-monthly

Outword 709 28th St., 329-9280

EROTICA

Adult Discount Center 1800 Del Paso Blvd., 920-8659

Goldies I 201 N. 12th St., 447-5860, 24hrs, also 2138 Del Paso Blvd. location, 922-0103

L'Amour Shoppe 2531 Broadway, 736-3467

CRUISY AREAS

American River Access off La Rivera Dr. nr. Howe Ave. & Watt Ave. (AYOR)

Beach & levee on American River at end of N. 10th St., off Richards Blvd. (AYOR)

Paradise Beach on American River (AYOR)

Vine St. btwn. N. 10th & Richards Blvd. (AYOR) by car only

Salinas (408)

EROTICA

L'Amour Shoppe 325 E. Alisal St., 758-9600

San Bernardino (909)

INFO LINES & SERVICES

AA Gay/Lesbian 825-4700, numerous mtgs for Inland Empire, call for times

Gay/Lesbian Community Center 1580 N. 'D' St. Ste. 7, 884-5447, 6:30pm-10pm, raps, counseling, library

Inland Empire Couples PO Box 3023, Rancho Cucamonga, 91729, 864-7883, call for mtg. times & location

Project Teen 335-2005, 7:30pm Tue, support group for lesbigay teens

▲ **San Bernardino Confidential Connection** 784-4000, Meet hot local guys! Record, listen, respond to free ads. Use free code 9966.

RESTAURANTS & CAFES
Green Carnation Coffeehouse 1580 N. 'D' St. Ste. 7, 384-1940 (MW) 6pm-midnight, clsd Sun

SPIRITUAL GROUPS
St. Aelred's Parish 1580 N. 'D' St. Ste. 5, 384-1940, 11am Sun, 7pm Wed

EROTICA
Bearfacts Book Store 1434 E. Baseline, 885-9176, 24hrs

San Clemente
CRUISY AREAS
San Onofre Beach State Park N. end of Camp Pendleton (N, AYOR)

San Diego   (619)
INFO LINES & SERVICES
AA Gay/Lesbian 1730 Monroe St., 298-8008, Live & Let Live Alano

▲ **Community Real Estate Referrals** (800) 346-5592, gay realtor at your service, no rentals

▲ **Gay Connection** (900) 505-6339, talk and/or meet with other men from the area, at only 99 c per minute

Gay/Lesbian Association of North County PO Box 2866, Vista, 92085, 945-2478, social/support group

Gay/Lesbian Info Line 294-4636, 24hrs

GMSD (Girth & Mirth San Diego) PO Box 86822, 92138-6822, 685-8822, 3rd Sat, social org. for heavyset men & their admirers

Lesbian/Gay Men's Community Center 3916 Normal St., 692-4297, 9am-10pm, resource information line, center

SAGE of California 282-1395, social 1st Wed, seniors' social group

▲ **San Diego Confidential Connection** 692-1200, Meet hot local guys! Record, listen, respond to free ads. Use free code 9966.

▲ **Turn Key Real Estate** 299-DEAN

ACCOMMODATIONS

▲ **Balboa Park Inn** 3402 Park Blvd., 298-0823/(800) 938-8181 (GF,WC,IGTA)

▲ **Banker's Hill B&B** 3315 2nd Ave., 260-0673/(800) 338-3748 (GF,SW)

The Beach Place 2158 Sunset Cliffs Blvd., 225-0746 (MW,N) 4 blks from beach, hot tub

The Blom House B&B 1372 Minden Dr., 467-0890 (GF)

▲ **The Caritas B&B Network** (800) CARITAS (227-4827), see ad in center National section

Carole's B&B Inn 3227 Grim Ave., 280-5258/Fax: 283-9558 (GF,SW) full brkfst

Clarke's Flamingo Lodge 1765 Union, 234-6787

Dmitri's B&B 931 21st St., 238-5547 (MW,SW,WC) smokefree, overlooks downtown, hot tub

Embassy Hotel 3645 Park Blvd., 269-3141

Friendship Hotel 3942 8th Ave., 298-9898 (GF)

Heritage Park B&B 2470 Heritage Park Row, 239-4738 (GF,WC) full brkfst

Hill House B&B 2504 'A' St., 239-4738

HILLCREST INN HOTEL

IN THE HEART OF HILLCREST

1-800-258-2280   (619) 293-7078
3754 FIFTH AVENUE
SAN DIEGO, CA 92103

▲ **Hillcrest Inn Hotel** 3754 5th Ave., 293-7078/(800) 258-2280 (MW,WC,IGTA)

Kasa Korbett 1526 Van Buren Ave., 291-3962 (MW,WC) smokefree, comfortable craftsman-designed B&B in Hillcrest, spa

Keating House 2331 2nd Ave., 239-8585/(800) 995-8644 (GF) Victorian B&B, full brkfst

Park Manor Suites 525 Spruce St., 291-0999/(800) 874-2649 (GF) 1926 hotel

Quince St. Trolley B&B PO Box 7654, 226-8454

Travelodge 2223 El Cajon Blvd., 296-2101 (GF,F,SW,WC)

Welcome Inn 1550 E. Washington St., 298-8251/Fax: 298-7333 (GF,WC)

BARS

Bourbon Street 4612 Park Blvd., 291-0173 (M,E) noon-2am, from 9am Sun brunch, piano & jazz, patio

Brass Rail 3796 5th Ave., 298-2233 (M,D,F,E,V,WC) 10am-2am

Caliph Lounge 3100 5th Ave., 298-9495 (M,P,E,OC) 11am-2am, piano bar

Chee Chee Club 929 Broadway, 234-4404 (M,NH) 6am-2am, hustlers

Cheers 1839 Adams, 298-3269 (M,NH) 10am-2am

▲ **David's Place** 3766 5th Ave., 294-8908 (MW,E,WC) 7am-midnight, til 3am wknds, non-profit coffeehouse for positive people & their friends, patio

Eagle 3040 North Park Wy., 295-8072 (M,L,WC) 4pm-2am

Flicks 1017 University Ave., 297-2056 (★M,V,YC) 2pm-2am

The Hole 2820 Lytton, 226-9019 (M) 2pm-2am

▲ **Kickers** 308 University Ave., 491-0400 (M,D,CW,WC) 7pm-2am

The Loft 3610 5th Ave., 296-6407 (M,NH,WC) 10am-2am

Matador 4633 Mission Blvd., Pacific Beach, 483-6943 (M,YC) noon-2am, beach bar

▲ **The No. 1 Fifth Ave. (no sign)** 3845 5th Ave., 299-1911 (M,P,V) noon-2am, patio

North Park Country Club 4046 30th St., 563-9051 (MW,NH,BW,WC) 1pm-2am

Numbers 3811 Park Blvd., 294-9005 (M,V,WC) noon-2am, patio

Pecs 2046 University Ave., 296-0889 (★M,D,V,YC) noon-2am, til 4am Fri-Sat

Redwing Bar & Grill 4012 30th St., 281-8700 (M,NH,F,WC) 10am-2am

Rich's 1051 University Ave., 295-2195 (★M,D,V,YC) open Th-Sun

S.R.O 1807 5th Ave., 232-1886 (M,NH,P,F,OC) 10am-2am

Shooterz 3815 30th St., 574-0744 (M,NH) noon-2am, sports & cruise bar

Waterloo Station 3968 5th Ave., 574-9329 (M,NH,BW) 11am-2am

Wolf's 3404 30th St., 291-3730 (M,L,BW) 6pm-4am, also erotic toy store

RESTAURANTS & CAFES

Bayou Bar & Grill 329 Market St., 696-8747, lunch & dinner, Sun champagne brunch, Creole/Cajun, also full bar

Big Kitchen 3003 Grape St., 234-5789 (WC) 7am-2pm, American, some veggie

Cafe Eleven 1440 University Ave., 260-8023 (WC) dinner, clsd Mon, country French, some veggie

Cafe Roma UCSD Price Carter #76, La Jolla, 450-2141, 7am-midnight

California Cuisine 1027 University Ave., 543-0790 (WC) 11am-10pm, 5pm-10:30pm Sat-Sun, clsd Mon, French/Italian, some veggie

City Deli 535 University Ave., 295-2747 (BW) 7am-midnight, til 2am Fri-Sat, NY deli, plenty veggie

Crest Cafe 425 Robinson, 295-2510 (WC) 7am-midnight, American, some veggie

CLUB SAN DIEGO

"Gives you what the others can't!"
"A Bath House for the Discriminating Man"

San Diego's Largest & Friendliest Spa offers you...

MULTI-STATION UNIVERSAL GYM • STEAM ROOM

52 PRIVATE ROOMS • TANNING BED • JACUZZI

300 LOCKERS • SNACKBAR • 2 VIDEO LOUNGES

SAUNA • 5 VIP SUITES • 17 TELEVISION ROOMS

**3955 Fourth Avenue
San Diego, CA
(619) 295-0850**

Unwind in the friendly atmosphere of our private men's club. We offer the very best in steam, sauna and jacuzzi facilities — 24 hours a day, every day of the year. Plus, low rates and specials on Mondays and Wednesdays.

VULCAN

Steam & Sauna

Facilities
▼ Steam Room
▼ Sauna Room
▼ Whirlpool
▼ Patio Sundeck
▼ Private Rooms
▼ Community Rooms
▼ Bunkroom
▼ Lockers
▼ Snack Machines
▼ Air Conditioning
▼ Four TV Lounges
▼ Security Boxes

**805 West Cedar Street
San Diego, CA 92101
(619) 238-1980**

▲ **Hamburger Mary's** 308 University Ave., 491-0400 (WC) 11am-10pm, from 8am wknds, American, some veggie, also full bar

Liaison 2202 4th Ave., 234-5540 (WC) dinner & Sun brunch, French country, prix fixe dinner

Pannikin 523 University Ave., 295-1600, 6am-11pm, til midnight wknds

GYMS & HEALTH CLUBS

Hillcrest Gym 142 University Ave., 299-7867 (MW)

BOOKSTORES & RETAIL SHOPS

Auntie Helen's 4028 30th St., 584-8438, 10am-5pm, clsd Sun-Mon, thrift shop benefits PWAs

Blue Door Bookstore 3823 5th Ave., 298-8610, 9am-9pm, large lesbigay section

Eclectic Pleasures 3825 5th Ave., 298-2260, 11am-9:30pm, til 8pm Sun, gifts, candles, incense

Groundworks Books UCSD Student Center 0323, La Jolla, 452-9625 (WC) 9am-7pm, 10am-6pm Fri-Sat, clsd Sun, alternative, lesbigay section

International Male 3964 5th Ave., 294-8600, 10am-9pm, 11am-8pm Sun

Moose Leather 2923 Upas St., 297-6935, noon-9pm, clsd Sun-Mon

▲ **Obelisk the Bookstore** 1029 University Ave., 297-4171 (WC) 11am-10pm, noon-8pm Sun, lesbigay

TRAVEL & TOUR OPERATORS

Firstworld Travel of Mission Gorge 7443 Mission Gorge Rd., 265-1916 (IGTA) contact Dennis

Hillcrest Travel 431 Robinson Ave., (800) 748-5502/291-0758 (IGTA)

Midas Travel 525 University Ave., 298-1160 (IGTA)

Sports Travel International Ltd. 4869 Santa Monica Ave. Ste. B, (800) 466-6004/225-9555 (IGTA)

Undersea Expeditions PO Box 9455, Pacific Beach, 92169, (800) 669-0310/270-2900 (IGTA) scuba trips worldwide

SPIRITUAL GROUPS

Anchor Ministries 3441 University Ave., 284-8654, 10am & 6pm Sun, non-denominational

Dignity 4190 Front St. (First Unitarian Universalist Church), Hillcrest, 645-8240, 6pm Sun

First Unitarian Universalist Church 4190 Front St., 298-9978, 10am (July-Aug); 9am & 11am (Sept-June)

Integrity/San Diego PO Box 34253, 92163-0801, 236-8176, call for mtg. times, lesbigay Episcopalians

MCC 4333 30th St., 280-4333, 9am & 11am Sun

Spirit Eagle MCC 2770 Glebe Rd., Lemon Grove, 447-4660, 6pm Sun

Yachad PO Box 3457, 92163, 492-8616, Jewish lesbian/gay/bisexual social group

PUBLICATIONS

Gay/Lesbian Times 3636 5th Ave. Ste. 101, 299-6397, weekly

Update 2801 4th Ave., 299-4104, weekly

MEN'S CLUBS

▲ **Club San Diego** 3955 4th Ave., 295-0850 (MO,PC) 24hrs

Dave's Club 4969 Santa Monica Ave., 224-9011 (MO,SW,PC) 24hrs

▲ **Mustang Spa** 2200 University Ave., 297-1661 (SW,PC) 24hrs

▲ **Vulcan Sauna** 805 W. Cedar St., 238-1980 (MO,PC) 24hrs

EROTICA

▲ **Cinema 'F'** 1202 University Ave., 298-0854 (PC) 24hrs

▲ **Condoms Plus** 1220 University Ave., 291-7400, 11am-midnight, til 2am Fri-Sat, 1-9pm Sun, safer sex gifts for men & women

The Crypt 1515 Washington, 692-9499, also 30th St. location, 284-4724

▲ **F St. Bookstore** 2004 University Ave., 298-2644, 24hrs

▲ **F St. Bookstore** 3112 Midway Dr., 221-0075, 24hrs

▲ **F St. Bookstore** 4626 Albuquerque, 581-0400, 24hrs

▲ **F St. Bookstore** 751 4th Ave., 236-0841, 24hrs

▲ **F St. Bookstore** 7865 Balboa Ave., Kearney Mesa, 292-8083, 24hrs

▲ **F St. Bookstore** 7998 Miramar Rd., 549-8014, 24hrs

Gemini Adult Books 5265 University Ave., 287-1402

▲ **Midnight Videos** 1407 University Ave., 299-7186, 24hrs

▲ **Midnight Videos** 3604 Midway Dr., 222-9973, 24hrs

▲ **Midnight Videos** 4792 El Cajon Blvd., 582-1997, 24hrs

▲ **Midnight Videos** 836 5th Ave., 237-9056, 24hrs

North Park Adult Video 4094 30th St., 284-4724, 24hrs

CRUISY AREAS

Torrey Pines Beach State Park ('Blacks Beach') half hr. walk from parking lot (AYOR)

SAN FRANCISCO

San Francisco is divided into 7 geographical areas:

S.F. - Overview (415)

INFO LINES & SERVICES

18th St. Services/Operation Concern 861-4898, 9am-7pm Mon-Fri, lesbigay AA mtgs. at 15th & Market, offices at 217 Church St.

AA Gay/Lesbian 621-1326

The Bay Area Bisexual Resource Line 703-7977, info & referrals

Brothers Network 973 Market St. #650, 356-8140, 1:30-3:30pm Tue, transgender support group

Cafe Chats 431-2228, informal chats at local cafes for young queer men (25 & under)

▲ **Community Real Estate Referrals** (800) 346-5592, gay realtor at your service, no rentals

ETVC PO Box 426486, 94142, (510) 549-2665, 8pm last Th, transgender group

Frameline 346 9th St., (800) 869-1996 (outside CA)/703-8650, lesbigay media arts foundation that sponsors the annual SF Internat'l Lesbian/Gay Film Festival each June

FTM International 5337 College Ave. #142, Oakland, 94618, (510) 287-2646, info & support for female-to-male transgendered people, newsletter & resource guide

▲ **Gay Connection** (900) 505-6339, talk and/or meet with other men from the area, at only 99 ¢ per minute

Gay & Lesbian Historical Society of Northern California PO Box 424280, 94142, 777-5455

Gay/Lesbian Sierrans 281-5666, outdoor group

Intersex Society PO Box 31791, 94131, support for physically intersexed (hermaphroditic) people

Lesbian/Gay Switchboard (510) 841-6224, 10am-10pm Mon-Fri, info, referrals, rap line

LGBA (Lesbian/Gay/Bisexual Alliance) SFSU Student Center #M-100-A, 1650 Holloway Ave., 338-1952

LINKS PO Box 420989, 94142, 703-7159 (TG) S/M play parties & calendar

LYRIC (Lavender Youth Recreation/Information Cntr) 127 Collingwood, (800) 246-7743/703-6150, support & social groups; also crisis counseling for lesbigay & transgendered youth under 24 at 863-3636 (hotline #)

▲ **San Francisco Confidential Connection** 247-2000, Meet hot local guys! Record, listen, respond to free ads. Use free code 9966.

San Francisco Gender Information 3637 Grand Ave. #C, Oakland, 94610, send $3 & SASE for listings of transgender resources in northern CA

TARC Transgender Support Group 187 Golden Gate Ave., 431-7476, 1-3pm Wed & Fri

Transgender Support Groups 50 Lech Walesa (Tom Waddell Clinic), 554-2940, 5-7:30 pm Tue, support groups & counseling for MTF & FTM transsexuals, low-cost TG health clinic

ACCOMMODATIONS

American Property Exchange 170 Page St., (800) 747-7784/863-8484, daily, weekly & monthly furnished rentals in San Francisco

▲ **The Caritas B&B Network** (800) CARITAS (227-4827), see ad in center National section

Mi Casa Su Casa (800) 215-2272/(510) 268-8534 (MW) international home exchange network

TRAVEL & TOUR OPERATORS

▲ **Bob Leech Autorental** (800) 325-1240, see ad in this section

My Favorite City (800) 605-1357/273-5812

SPIRITUAL GROUPS

Bay Area Pagan Assemblies (408) 559-4242

Berdache 281-9377, monthly, for gay men interested in spirituality

Dignity/San Francisco 1329 7th Ave., 94122, 681-2491, 5:30pm Sun, lesbigay Roman Catholic services

Evangelicals Concerned 621-3297, also in East Bay & San Jose

Hartford Street Zen Center 57 Hartford St., 863-2507

Lutherans Concerned 566 Vallejo St. #25, 94133-4033, 956-2069

Native American Two-Spirit Talking Circle 217 Church St. (18th St. Services office), 6:30pm Wed

Oasis/California 110 Julian Ave., 522-0222/(800) 419-0222, gay & lesbian ministry of the Episcopal Diocese of California

Reclaiming PO Box 14404, 94110, 929-9249, pagan infoline & network

Tel-a-Fairy 626-3369, events & message tape for Bay Area Radical Faeries

PUBLICATIONS

B.A.R. (Bay Area Reporter) 395 9th St., 94103, 861-5019, weekly

Big Ad PO Box 14725, 94114-4725, 626-6350, national publication for big men

Cuir Underground 3288 21st St. #19, 94110, 487-7622, bi-monthly, S/M newspaper w/ calendar of events, e-mail: cuirpaper@aol.com

Oblivion 519 Castro St. #24, 487-5498

▲ **Odyssey Magazine** 584 Castro St. #302, 94114, 621-6514, all the dish on SF's club scene

San Francisco Bay Times 288 7th St., 94103, 626-8121 (★) bi-weekly, a 'must read' for Bay Area resources & personals

▲ **San Francisco Frontiers** 2370 Market St. 2nd. flr, 94114, 487-6000, news

S.F. - Castro & Noe Valley (415)

INFO LINES & SERVICES

Castro Country Club 4058 18th St., 552-6102 (MW) 11am-midnight, til 1am Fri-Sat, from 10am Sun, alcohol & drug-free club

▲ **Community Real Estate Referrals** (800) 346-5592, gay realtor at your service, no rentals

Gay/Lesbian Outreach to Elders 1853 Market St., 626-7000, 10am-2pm

Harvey Milk Public Library 3555 16th St., 554-9445, call for hours

▲ **Herth Real Estate** 555 Castro St., 487-1204, gay-friendly realtors

24 HENRY

*An intimate guesthouse
located on a quiet, tree-lined street
in the Castro District
of San Francisco*

*24 Henry Street
San Francisco, CA 94114
1-800-900-5686 (415) 864-5686
Fax (415) 864-0286*

The Albion House Inn

"A Fine Example of San Francisco Hospitality"

On a foggy day, a cozy fireplace,
a grand piano, a fabulous breakfast,
and an affordable restaurant.
full breakfast included

(415) 621-0896 • 800-6 ALBION
Fax (415) 621-3811
135 Gough Street
San Francisco, CA 94102

ACCOMMODATIONS

▲ **24 Henry** 24 Henry St., 864-5686/(800) 900-5686 (M,IGTA) smokefree, one-bdrm apt. also available 1 blk from guesthouse

▲ **Albion House Inn** 135 Gough St., 621-0896/625-2466 (GF,F) smokefree, also a restaurant, grill

Anna's Three Bears 114 Divisadero St., 255-3167/(800) 428-8559 (GF,IGTA) rental apt. B&B

Beck's Motor Lodge 2222 Market St., 621-8212 (GF)

▲ **Black Stallion Inn** 635 Castro St., 863-0131 (MO,L)

▲ **Castillo Inn** 48 Henry St., 864-5111/(800) 865-5112

▲ **The Cumberland** 2264-A Market St., 255-3086/(800) 605-1357 (GF) full brkfst, private baths, guesthouse above the Castro

Dolores Park Inn 3641 17th St., 621-0482 (GF) hot tub, kitchens, fireplaces, smokefree, Italianate Victorian mansion

▲ **Inn on Castro** 321 Castro St., 861-0321 (MW) full brkfst

Le Grenier 347 Noe St., 864-4748 (MW) suite, cont'l brkfst

Lemon Tree Homestays PO Box 460424, 94146, 861-4045 (M) smokefree, European-style B&B

Noe's Nest 3973 23rd St., 821-0751/Fax: 821-0723 (GF, IGTA) kitchens, fireplace, exp. cont'l brkfst

▲ **Pension SF** 1668 Market St., 864-1271 (GF) also a restaurant

▲ **San Francisco Cottage** 224 Douglass St., 861-3220/Fax: 626-2633 (MW) cottage & studio apt

▲ **San Francisco Views - The Villa** 379 Collingwood St., 282-1367/(800) 358-0123 (MW,SW,WC)

INN ON CASTRO
321 castro st · san francisco
ca 94114 · (415) 861·0321

PENSION
SAN FRANCISCO
EUROPEAN STYLE HOTEL

N.Y. TIMES "BUDGET CHOICE-1993"

Pension San Francisco, a hotel with a distinctly European flavor, is pleased to offer accommodations featuring rooms at very low rates.

1668 MARKET STREET
SAN FRANCISCO, CA 94102
415-864-1271 (FAX) 415-861-8116

San francisco Cottage

phone [415] 861-3220
fax [415] 626-2633

Lovely garden studios with flowered courtyard, redwood deck, and terraced garden. Short stroll to Castro bars, cafés, shops. Private entrance, self-catering with full amenities.

Very special. Very romantic.

224 Douglass St., San Francisco, CA 94114

THE WILLOWS INN
A GREAT CASTRO LOCATION
BREAKFAST IN BED
710 14TH ST. SAN FRANCISCO, CA 94114
(415)431-4770

Terrace Place 584 Castro St. Ste. 112, 94114, 241-0425/Fax: 552-7454 (MW) guest suite

Travelodge Central 1707 Market St., 621-6775/(800) 578-7878 (GF) non-smoking rooms available

▲ **The Willows B&B Inn** 710 14th St., 431-4770/Fax: 431-5295 (M,IGTA)

BARS

Badlands 4121 18th St., 626-9320 (★M,NH,WC) 11:30am-2am

▲ **The Cafe** 2367 Market St., 861-3846 (★MW,D,YC) noon-2am, deck overlooking Castro & Market Sts.

Cafe du Nord 2170 Market St., 861-5016 (GF,F,E) 4pm-2am, live jazz, various theme nights

Castro Country Club 4058 18th St., 552-6102 (MW) 11am-midnight, til 11am Fri-Sat, from 10am Sun, alcohol & drug-free club

Daddy's 440 Castro St., 621-8732 (★M,NH,L) 9am-2am, from 6am Sat-Sun, very cruisy, Red Hanky beer bust Tue

The Detour 2348 Market St., 861-6053 (★M,NH,A) 2pm-2am, cruise bar

The Edge 4149 18th St., 863-4027 (M,NH,L) noon-2am, from 6am Fri-Sun

▲ **Harvey's** 500 Castro St., 431-4278 (MW,NH,E,WC) also a restaurant

Josie's Cabaret & Juice Joint 3583 16th St., 861-7933 (★MW,F,E,WC) call for events, live comedy, cabaret, great healthy American food, plenty veggie

Men's Room 3988 18th St., 861-1310 (M,NH) noon-2am

The Metro 3600 16th St., 703-9750 (M,YC) 2:30pm-2am, karaoke Tue, also Chinese restaurant

▲ **Midnight Sun** 4067 18th St., 861-4186 (M,V) noon-2am

The Mint 1942 Market St., 626-4726 (MW,F,K,V) 11am-2am, also a restaurant

Moby Dick's 4049 18th St. (M,NH,V)

Pendulum 4146 18th St., 863-4441 (★M,MRC-AF) 6am-2am

Phoenix 482 Castro St., 552-6827 (M,D) 1pm-2am

Pilsner Inn 225 Church St., 621-7058 (MW,NH) 6am-2am, patio

The Transfer 198 Church St., 861-7499 (M,NH) 11am-2am, from 6am wknds

Twin Peaks 401 Castro St., 864-9470 (M,OC,WC) noon-2am

Uncle Bert's Place 4086 18th St., 431-8616 (M,NH) 6am-2am, patio

Underworld 978-9448 (M) party info line

RESTAURANTS & CAFES

Amazing Grace 216 Church St., 626-6411 (WC) 11am-10pm, vegetarian

Anchor Oyster Bar 579 Castro St., 431-3990 (MW,BW) seafood, some veggie

Bad Man Jose's 4077 18th St., 861-1706, 11am-11pm, healthy Mexican, some veggie

Bagdad Cafe 2295 Market St., 621-4434 (MW) 24hrs, American, some veggie

Cafe Flore 2298 Market St., 621-8579 (★MW,F) 7:30am-11:30pm, til midnight Fri-Sat, great patio, American, some veggie

Caffe Luna Piena 558 Castro St., 621-2566 (MW) lunch & dinner, patio

China Court 599 Castro, 626-5358 (BW) 5pm-11pm, Chinese, some veggie

Chloe's Cafe 1399 Church St., Noe Valley, 648-4116 (★) 8am-3:30pm, til 4pm wknds, come early for the excellent weekend brunch

Counter Culture 2073 Market St., 621-7488, gourmet take-out, some veggie

Cove Cafe 434 Castro St., 626-0462 (MW,WC) 7am-10pm, American, some veggie

CONNECTIONS

HIV/AIDS Services
for Gay and Bisexual Men of Color

When you're ready to discover
what hot safer sex is; or talk
about risky sex, substance use,
or about being gay, bisexual or
transgendered, connect with us.

EAGLE WARRIOR

Native American AIDS Project

CUATES

Proyecto ContraSIDA Por Vida

UMOJA

Brothers Network

CONNECTIONS is confidential, one-on-one peer support focusing on HIV prevention. We invite gay and bisexual men of color to get connected.

Prevention Peer Counselors will meet with you in a safe and confidential space. We can also connect you to other agencies for things like housing, HIV testing, food, legal assistance, and treatment education/intervention.

We provide one-on-one peer counseling, support groups, social contact, emotional support, and referrals. Languages spoken: English and Spanish.

CONNECTIONS is a local program of the National Task Force on AIDS Prevention, 973 Market Street, Suite 600, San Francisco, CA, 94103. Phone 415-356-8114, fax 415-356-8103.

Eric's Chinese Restaurant 1500 Church St., Noe Valley, 282-0919 (★) 11am-9pm, some veggie

Hot 'N Hunky 4039 18th St., 621-6365 (MW) 11am-11pm, burgers, some veggie

It's Tops 1801 Market St., 431-6395, 7am-3pm, 8pm-3am, diner

Jumpin' Java 139 Noe St., 431-5282 (MW) 7am-10pm

Just Desserts 248 Church St., 626-5774 (MW) 7am-11pm, great patio

Little Italy 4109 24th St., 821-1515 (BW) dinner only, plenty veggie

M&L Market (May's) 691 14th St., 431-7044, great huge sandwiches, some veggie

Ma Tante Sumi 4243 18th St., 552-6663 (MW) cont'l cuisine w/ a Japanese accent

Orbit Room Cafe 1900 Market St., 252-9525 (BW) 7am-midnight, til 2am Fri-Sat, great view of Market St. & trolley cars

Patio Cafe 531 Castro St., 621-4140 (MW) enclosed patio dining

Pozole 2337 Market St., 626-2666 (MW,BW) Mexican specialties, some veggie

The Quarterdeck 718 14th St., 431-0253 (M,E,OC) 3pm-midnight, also piano bar

The Sausage Factory 517 Castro St., 626-1250 (MW) noon-1am, pizza & pasta, some veggie

Sparky's 242 Church St., 626-8666, 24hrs, diner, some veggie

▲ **Valentine's Cafe** 1793 Church St., Noe Valley, 285-2257, 6:30am-10pm, 8am-5pm wknds, brkfst, lunch, & take-out dinners, plenty veggie

Welcome Home 464 Castro St., 626-3600 (★MW,BW) 8am-11pm, homestyle, some veggie

UNDER ONE ROOF

THE SHOP FOR AIDS RELIEF

THE UNIQUE SHOP WHERE YOU CAN BUY

THE GIFT THAT GIVES TWICE

100% OF THE PROFITS FROM EVERY SALE

BENEFIT AIDS SERVICE AGENCIES

2362 MARKET ST. AT CASTRO

SAN FRANCISCO, CA 94114

TELEPHONE (415) 252-9430

Without Reservations 460 Castro St., 861-9510 (MW,WC) 7am-2am, diner, some veggie

Zuni Cafe 1658 Market St., 552-2522 (★) clsd Mon, upscale cont'l/Mediterranean, also full bar

GYMS & HEALTH CLUBS

▲ **City Athletic Club** 2500 Market St., 552-6680 (MO) day passes available

▲ **Market Street Gym** 2301 Market St., 626-4488 (MW) day passes available

Muscle System 2275 Market St., 863-4700 (★MO) day passes available

BOOKSTORES & RETAIL SHOPS

A Different Light 489 Castro St., 431-0891 (★) 10am-11pm, til midnight Fri-Sat, bookstore & queer information clearinghouse

Books Etc. 538 Castro St., 621-8631, 11am-10pm, til midnight Fri-Sat

Books Inc. 2275 Market St., 864-6777 (WC) 10am-11pm, til 10pm Sun, also located at San Francisco Internat'l Airport, North Terminal, 3315 California St., 221-3666

Botanica 1478 Church St. at 27th, Noe Valley, 285-0612, 11am-7pm, Afro-Caribbean religious articles

Does Your Mother Know? 4079 18th St., 864-3160, 10am-8pm, cards & T-shirts

Don't Panic 541 Castro St., 553-8989, 10am-10pm, T-shirts, gifts & more

The Gauntlet 2377 Market St., 431-3133, noon-7pm, piercing parlor, jewelry

Headlines 557 Castro, 626-8061, 10am-9pm, clothes, cards, novelties

Image Leather 2199 Market St., 621-7551, 9am-10pm, 11am-7pm Sun, custom leather clothing, accessories & toys

ARTIST : JEFF LEFEVER

MARKET STREET GYM
2301 MARKET STREET
SAN FRANCISCO CALIFORNIA 94114
415/626-4488
VISITORS WELCOME - DAY/WEEKLY USE AVAILABLE
MARKET AT NOE NEAR CASTRO MUNI

Just for Fun 3982 24th St., Noe Valley, 285-4068 (WC) 9am-9pm, til 7pm Sun, gift shop

Leather Zone 2352 Market St., 255-8585, 11am-7pm, new & used fetishwear, bear T-shirts

Rolo 2351 Market St., 431-4545, designer labels, also 450 Castro location, 626-7171

▲ **Under One Roof** 2362 Market St., 252-9430, 11am-7pm, 100% of sales are donated for AIDS relief

TRAVEL & TOUR OPERATORS

Cruisin' the Castro 550-8110 (IGTA) guided walking tour of the Castro

Now, Voyager 4406 18th St., (800) 255-6951/626-1169 (IGTA)

Passport to Leisure 2265 Market St., 621-8300/(800) 322-1204 (outside CA) (IGTA)

Victorian Home Walks 2226 15th St., 94114, 252-9485 (IGTA) custom-tailored walking tours w/ San Francisco resident

Winship Travel 2321 Market St., (800) 545-2557/863-2555 (IGTA) ask for Susan

SPIRITUAL GROUPS

Congregation Sha'ar Zahav 220 Danvers St., 861-6932, 8:15pm Fri, lesbian/gay synagogue

MCC of San Francisco 150 Eureka St., 863-4434, 9am, 11am & 7pm Sun

Most Holy Redeemer Church 100 Diamond St., 863-6259, 7:30am & 10am Sun, 5pm Sat (vigil mass), open & affirming Roman Catholic parish

MEN'S CLUBS

Club 1808 1808 Market St., 431-1931 (PC) J/O club

▲ **Eros** 2051 Market St., 864-3767, safer sex club

EROTICA

▲ **Jaguar** 4057 18th St., 863-4777

Le Salon 4126 18th St., 552-4213

The MMO (Mercury Mail Order) 4084 18th St., 621-1188, leather, toys & more

Rob Gallery 1925 Market St., 252-1198, 11am-7pm, leather, latex & artwork

S.F. - South of Market (415)

ACCOMMODATIONS

▲ **Black Stallion Inn** (see Castro section), 863-0131 (MO,L)

Victorian Hotel 54 4th St., 986-4400/(800) 227-3804 (GF) 1913 landmark, also restaurant, full bar

BARS

The Box 715 Harrison St., 647-8258 (★MW,D,MRC) Th only

Brain Wash 1122 Folsom St., 431-9274 (★GF,E,BW) 7:30am-midnight, til 1am Fri-Sat, laundromat & cafe

C.W. Saloon 917 Folsom St., 974-1585 (GF,NH) 10am-2am, theme nights

Club Universe 177 Townsend, 985-5241 (★MW,D,A) 9:30pm-7am Sat

Endup 401 6th St., 495-9550 (M,D,MRC) many different theme nights, esp. popular Sun mornings

Ginger's Too 43 6th St., 543-3622 (M,NH,F,OC) 10am-2am

Hole in the Wall Saloon 289 8th St. (at Folsom), 431-4695 (★M,NH) noon-2am, 'a nasty little biker bar'

Lone Star 1354 Harrison St., 863-9999 (M,L) noon-2am, patio, bear bar

JAGUAR
ADULT BOOKS

4057 EIGHTEENTH STREET
SAN FRANCISCO
415 · 863 · 4777

STUD

Conrad Hechter Photography

SAN FRANCISCO'S PREMIER DANCE CLUB
OPEN DAILY 5 PM
AFTERHOURS FRIDAY & SATURDAY
NINTH AT HARRISON • SAN FRANCISCO
Info • (415) 252-STUD

My Place 1225 Folsom St., 863-2329 (M,L) noon-2am, bear bar

Pleasuredome 177 Townsend (at 3rd St.), 255-6434x69 (M,D) Sun night dance club, call hotline for details

Rawhide II 280 7th St., 621-1197 (M,D,CW) noon-2am

San Francisco Eagle 398 12th St., 626-0880 (M,L) 4pm-2am, from 2pm Sat, from noon Sun, great 'beer bust' Sun, patio

▲ **The Stud** 399 9th St., 863-6623 (MW,D,YC) 5pm-2am, Boys' Night Wed

Twenty Tank Brewery 316 11th St., 255-9455 (GF,F) microbrewery

V-SF 278 11th St., 621-1530 (MW,D,E) 4pm-4am, clsd Mon, Latin dance party Sun

RESTAURANTS & CAFES

Bistro Roti 155 Steuart, 495-6500, lunch & dinner, country French, also full bar

Caribbean Zone 55 Natoma St., 541-9465, lunch & dinner, festive decor, cocktails, some veggie

Fringale 570 4th St., 543-0573 (WC) lunch & dinner, Mediterranean

Half Shell 64 Rausch Alley, 552-7677 (MW) lunch & dinner, seafood, some veggie

Hamburger Mary's 1582 Folsom St., 626-5767/626-1985 (WC) 10am-2am, clsd Mon, American, some veggie, full bar

Line Up 398 7th St., 861-2887 (MW) 11am-10pm, Mexican, some veggie, cocktails

Lulu 816 Folsom St., 495-5775 (WC) lunch & dinner, upscale Mediterranean, some veggie, also full bar

Slow Club 2501 Mariposa, 241-9390 (WC) 7am-2am, clsd Sun, also a full bar

Wa-Ha-Ka! 1489 Folsom, 861-1410 (BW) Mexican, plenty veggie

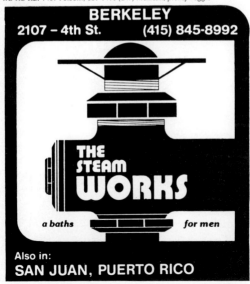

The Bear Store

**367 Ninth St.
(betw. Folsom
& Harrison)**

Every thing your parts desire.

mags
T-shirts
videos
books
sex toys
cards
novelties
belts...
**DADE/URSUS
FRAN FRISCH
BAD BEAR CLUB**
Mon-Sat 10:30-6

BOOKSTORES & RETAIL SHOPS

▲ **The Bear Store/Brush Creek Media** 367 9th St., 552-1506, toys, T-shirts, magazines & more for bears

Leather Etc. 1201 Folsom St., 864-7558, 10:30am-7pm, from 11am Sat

TRAVEL & TOUR OPERATORS

Above & Beyond Travel 330 Townsend, (800) 397-2681/284-1666 (IGTA)

Castro Travel Company 435 Brannan Ste. 214, (800) 861-0957/357-0957 (IGTA)

China Basin Travel Center 185 Berry St., 777-4747

MEN'S CLUBS

Blow Buddies 933 Harrison, 863-4323 (★MO,PC) call for hours

EROTICA

A Taste of Leather 317-A 10th St., (800) 367-0786/252-9166, noon-8pm

▲ **City Entertainment** 960 Folsom St., 543-2124, 24hrs wknds

▲ **Folsom Gulch** 947 Folsom, 495-6402, 24hrs wknds

Golden Gate Video #4 99 6th St., 495-5573

International Wavelength 2215-R Market St. Box 829, 94114, 864-6500, mail order Asian & Latin erotica

Mr. S Leather 310 7th St., 863-7764, 11am-7pm, noon-6pm Sun, erotic goods, leather & latex

Stormy Leather 1158 Howard St., 626-1672, noon-6pm, leather, latex, toys & magazines

CRUISY AREAS

Folsom St. btwn. 5th & 6th (AYOR) late

the *Essex*

✤ HOTEL ✤

With a European charm and tradition, the Essex is only one block from Polk Street. Close to shopping, bars, restaurants, theatres, and the City's gay life!

415-474-4664
Single $49

1-800-453-7739 USA

1-800-443-7739 CA

684 Ellis Street · San Francisco, CA · 94109

S.F. - Polk Street Area
(415)

ACCOMMODATIONS

Atherton Hotel 685 Ellis St., 474-5720/(800) 474-5720 (GF,F,IGTA)

▲ **Essex Hotel** 684 Ellis St., 474-4664/(800) 443-7739 (GF,WC)

Hotel Richelieu 1050 Van Ness Ave., 673-4711/(800) 227-3608 (GF,WC) gym, full bar, cont'l brkfst

▲ **Leland Hotel** 1315 Polk St., 441-5141/(800) 258-4458 (M,F,IGTA) kitchens, also Stardust Cafe'

The Lombard Hotel 1015 Geary St., 673-5232/(800) 777-3210 (GF,SW,WC)

▲ **Pensione International Hotel** 875 Post St., 775-3344/(800) 358-8123 (GF) cont'l brkfst, Victorian-styled B&B hotel

▲ **The Phoenix Hotel** 601 Eddy St., 776-1380/(800) 248-9466 (★GF,SW,IGTA) 1950s style motor lodge, also Caribbean restaurant, some veggie, full bar

BARS

The Cinch 1723 Polk St., 776-4162 (M,NH) 6am-2am

Gangway 841 Larkin St., 885-4441 (M,NH) 6am-2am

Giraffe Lounge 1131 Polk St., 474-1702 (M,V) 8am-2am

Kimo's 1351 Polk St., 885-4535 (M,NH,S,OC) 8am-2am, birthplace of the rainbow flag

Mother Lode 1002 Post St., 928-6006 (M,NH,S) 6am-2am, TS/TVs and their admirers

N' Touch 1548 Polk St., 441-8413 (M,NH,D,MRC-A,S) 3pm-2am, Karaoke Sun & Tue

Old Rick's Gold Room 939 Geary St., 441-9211 (M,NH) 6am-2am

In San Francisco, the perfect spot to lodge...

(lodge/loj' – to place between or into something; to be deposited or come to rest; to furnish with a dwelling place.)

...is the Leland.

1315 Polk Street
San Francisco, CA 94109
(415) 441-5141
Toll Free (800) 258-4458

the LELAND hotel

P.S. 1121 Polk St., 885-1448 (M,NH,OC) 6am-2am

Polk Gulch Saloon 1100 Polk St., 771-2022 (M,NH,OC) 6am-2am

Polk Rendezvous Bar 1303 Polk St., 673-7934 (M,NH,OC) 9am-2am

Q.T. 1312 Polk St., 885-1114 (M,NH) noon-2am, hustlers

Reflections 1160 Polk St., 771-6262 (M,NH) 6am-2am

The Swallow 1750 Polk St., 775-4152 (M,NH,E,OC) 10am-2am, piano bar

The Wooden Horse 622 Polk St., 771-8063 (M,NH,OC) 6am-2am

Yacht Club 2155 Polk St., 441-8381 (M,NH,OC) 10am-2am

RESTAURANTS & CAFES

Grubstake II 1525 Pine St., 673-8268 (MW,BW) 5pm-4am, 10am-4am wknds

Rendezvous Cafe 1760 Polk St., 292-4033, 7am-10pm, American, some veggie

Spuntino 524 Van Ness Ave., 861-7772 (BW) 7am-8pm, cont'l, also cafe & desserts

Stars Cafe 500 Van Ness Ave., 861-4344 (BW) lunch & dinner, New American

BOOKSTORES & RETAIL SHOPS

A Clean Well Lighted Place For Books 601 Van Ness Ave., 441-6670, 10am-11pm, general, lesbigay section

Hog On Ice 1630 Polk St., 771-7909, 10am-10pm, til 6pm Sat, novelties, books, CDs

TRAVEL & TOUR OPERATORS

Beyond the Bay 726 Polk St., 421-7721/(800) 542-1991 (IGTA)

Jackson Travel 1829 Polk St., 928-2500 (IGTA)

EROTICA

Century All-Male Theatre 816 Larkin St., 776-3045

▲ **Frenchy's** 1020 Geary St., 776-5940

Front Lyne Video 1259 Polk St., 931-9999

Le Salon Book Store 1118 Polk St., 673-4492

▲ **The Locker Roon Bookstore** 1038 Polk St., 775-9076

CRUISY AREAS

Polk St. btwn. Geary & California Sts. (AYOR) hustlers

S.F. - Downtown & North Beach (415)

INFO LINES & SERVICES

▲ **Community Real Estate Referrals** (800) 346-5592, gay realtor at your service, no rentals

ACCOMMODATIONS

▲ **The Abigail Hotel** 246 McAllister St., 861-9728/(800) 243-6510 (GF,IGTA) also 'Millennium' restaurant, Euro-Mediterranean, plenty veggie

Amsterdam Hotel 749 Taylor St., Nob Hill, 673-3277/(800) 637-3444 (GF) charming European-style hotel

The Andrews 624 Post St., (800) 926-3739/563-6877, also Italian restaurant

▲ **The Commodore International Hotel** 825 Sutter St., 923-6800/(800) 338-6848 (GF)

Dakota Hotel 606 Post St., 931-7475/Fax: 931-7486 (GF) near Union Square

Dockside Boat & Bed 77 Jack London Sq., Oakland, 94607, 444-5858/436-2574 (GF) houseboats w/ kitchen, private baths, cont'l brkfst

Hotel Griffon 155 Steuart St., 495-2100/(800) 321-2201 (WC) kitchens, fitness center, cont'l brkfst, also a restaurant, bistro/cont'l

The Hotel Rex 562 Sutter St., (800) 433-4434/433-4434 (GF) parking, full brkfst, full bar

Hotel Triton 342 Grant Ave., 394-0500/(800) 433-6611 (GF,WC,IGTA)

▲ **Hotel Vintage Court** 650 Bush St., 392-4666/(800) 654-1100 (GF,F,WC) home of world-famous 5-star Masa's restuarant, French

Howard Johnson Pickwick Hotel 85 5th St., 421-7500/(800) 227-3282 (GF)

Hyde Park Suites 2655 Hyde St. (at North Point), 771-0200/(800) 227-3608 (GF,IGTA) cont'l brkfst, kitchens, gym, sundeck

King George Hotel 334 Mason St., 781-5050/(800) 288-6005 (GF,F) also 'The Bread & Honey Tearoom' w/ morning & afternoon teas

Nob Hill Lambourne 725 Pine St., Nob Hill, 433-2287/(800) 274-8466 (GF) cont'l brkfst

Nob Hill Pensione 835 Hyde St., 885-2987/Fax: 921-1648 (GF) cont'l brkfst

The Pacific Bay Inn 520 Jones St., 673-0234/(800) 445-2631 (GF) also 'Dottie's True Blue Cafe'

▲ **Ramada Market St.** 1231 Market St. (800) 227-4747/626-8000 (GF,WC) serves full brkfst

▲ **Savoy Hotel** 580 Geary St., 441-2700/(800) 227-4223 (GF) cont'l brkfst, snacks, parking, also popular restaurant & bar

The York Hotel 940 Sutter St., 885-6800/(800) 808-9675 (GF,IGTA) boutique hotel, cont'l brkfst

BARS

Aunt Charlie's Lounge 133 Turk St., 441-2922 (GF,NH) 6am-2am

Company 1319 California St., 928-0677 (GF,NH) 1pm-2am

Affordable Elegance

HOTEL VINTAGE COURT

An Absolutely Fabulous place to stay in San Francisco for business or pleasure.

Absolutely the best location in San Francisco!

Close to everything from the Shops on Union Square, Restaurants of Chinatown and San Francisco's Theatre District. Only minutes to the Castro and SOMA Clubs.

107 Fabulous rooms offering comfortable and chic decor.

Continental Breakfast Daily. Complimentary wine served in our cozy lobby next to the fireplace.

Home of San Francisco's Number One rated restaurant,

Masa's
650 Bush Street • San Francisco, CA 94108

For Hotel Reservations or Information

Call (800)654-1100 • (415) 392-4666

Proud member of IGTA

SAVOY HOTEL

Elegant and romantic 83 room European-style boutique hotel.
Features feather beds, goose-down pillows, mini-bars,
and all the modern amenities in each room.

Complimentary sherry, tea and housemade cookies served daily.

Also featuring:
The Savoy Brasserie Restaurant
located in the hotel.

580 Geary Street
San Francisco, CA 94102
(415) 441-2700 • (800) 227-4223

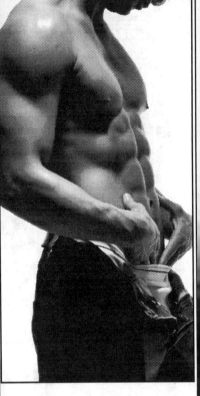

The Gate 1093 Pine St., 885-9871 (M,NH) 4pm-2am, 11am-2am wknds, Sun brunch

Ginger's Trois 246 Kearney St., 989-0282 (M,NH,P) 10am-10pm, piano bar

Hob Nob 700 Geary St., 771-9866 (M,NH) 6am-2am

RESTAURANTS & CAFES

Akimbo 116 Maiden Ln., 433-2288 (MW) lunch & dinner, clsd Sun

Basque Hotel & Restaurant uphill alley off Broadway between Columbus & Kearney, 788-9404 (BW)

Cafe Claude 7 Claude, 392-3505 (E) 8am-10pm, live jazz, as close to Paris as you can get in SF

Campo Santo 240 Columbus Ave., North Beach, 433-9623 (BW) lunch & dinner, from 5:30pm wknds, Mexican, some veggie, hip decor

China Moon Cafe 639 Post St., 775-4789, lunch & dinner, unique California nouvelle w/ Chinese accent, some veggie

US Restaurant 431 Columbus Ave., North Beach, 362-6251 (BW) 7am-9pm, clsd Sun-Mon, Italian food just like home

BOOKSTORES & RETAIL SHOPS

▲ **Billy Blue** 54 Geary (at Grant), (800) 772-BLUE

City Lights Bookstore 261 Columbus Ave., North Beach, 362-8193, 10am-midnight, historic beatnik bookstore, many progressive titles

PHOTO: CHAD CHRISTENSEN

The mens store GQ has called
"hip, discerning, distinctive...
and affordable."

BILLYBLUE
SAN FRANCISCO

54 Geary at Grant 800 772-BLUE (2583)

Validated Parking at Union Square Garage

EMAIL: billybl@aol.com
WEB: http://www.hia.com/hia/billyblue

TRAVEL & TOUR OPERATORS

Doin' It Right Tours & Travel 1 St. Francis Pl. Ste. 2106, (800) 936-3646/621-3576 (IGTA) Gay Travel Club meets 1st Wed

EROTICA

Campus Theater 220 Jones St., 673-3384

Circle J Video 369 Ellis St., 474-6995

Kearny Books & Video 1030 Kearny St., 391-9246, 24hrs

▲ **Nob Hill Theater** 729 Bush St., 781-9468, 24hrs

S.F. - Mission District (415)

INFO LINES & SERVICES

The Marsh 1062 Valencia (at 22nd St.), 641-0235, queer-positive theater

Theatre Rhinoceros 2926 16th St. (at So.Van Ness), 861-5079, lesbigay theater

ACCOMMODATIONS

▲ **Andora Inn** 2434 Mission, 282-0337/(800) 967-9219 (MW, IGTA) also a restaurant, expanded cont'l brkfst, parking, near Castro

▲ **The Inn San Francisco** 943 S. Van Ness Ave., 641-0188/(800) 359-0913 (GF,IGTA) Victorian mansion, full brkfst, hot tub, patio

BARS

Baby Judy's 527 Valencia (at the Casanova), 863-9328 (★M,D,E,WC) 9pm-1am Wed

El Rio 3158-A Mission St., 282-3325 (GF,NH,MRC-L,E) 3pm-2am, til midnight Mon, patio, popular Sun afternoons

Esta Noche 3079 16th St., 861-5757 (M,D,MRC-L,S) 2pm-2am, salsa & disco

Bed & Breakfast

Comfort and hospitality in a gracious
1872 twenty-seven room mansion.
Located near the Civic Center.
Antiques, fresh flowers, fireplaces and
private spas. Hot tub and sundeck.
Patio Garden. Telephones and television.
Parking. Major cards accepted.

THE INN SAN FRANCISCO
943 SOUTH VAN NESS AVENUE
SAN FRANCISCO, CA 94110
FAX (415) 641-1701

(415) 641-0188   (800) 359-0913

Phone Booth 1398 S. Van Ness Ave., 648-4683 (MW,NH) 10am-2am

RESTAURANTS & CAFES

Cafe Commons 3161 Mission St., 282-2928 (WC) 7am-7pm, sandwiches, plenty veggie, patio

Cafe Istanbul 525 Valencia St., 863-8854, 11am-midnight, Mediterranean, some veggie, authentic Turkish coffee, bellydancers Sat

Farleys 1315 18th St., Potrero Hill, 648-1545, 7am-10pm, from 8am wknds, coffeehouse

Just For You 1453 18th St., Potrero Hill, 647-3033 (★MW) 7am-3pm, American/Cajun, some veggie

Klein's Delicatessen 501 Connecticut St., Potrero Hill, 821-9149 (W,BW) 7am-7pm, sandwiches & salads, some veggie, patio

New Dawn Cafe 3174 16th St., 553-8888, 8am-3pm, hearty breakfasts, veggie

Pancho Villa 3071 16th St., 864-8840 (WC) 11am-10pm, best 'Mission-style' burritos in city, some veggie, also 'El Toro' at 18th & Valencia

Pauline's Pizza Pie 260 Valencia St., 552-2050 (★MW,BW) dinner only, clsd Sun-Mon

Picaro 3120 16th St., 431-4089, Spanish tapas bar

Radio Valencia 1199 Valencia St., 826-1199 (E,BW) 5pm-midnight, from noon Sat-Sun, artsy cafe, sandwiches & dessert

Ti-Couz 3108 16th St., 252-7373 (BW,WC) 11am-11pm, dinner & dessert crepes, plenty veggie

Val 21 995 Valencia St., 821-6622 (MW,WC) dinner, Sat-Sun brunch, eclectic Californian, some veggie

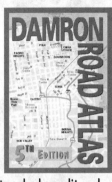

Valentine's

C A F E

GOURMET INTERNATIONAL VEGETERIAN CUISINE

FABULOUS DINNER AND WEEKEND BRUNCH!

Tuesday
6pm - 9:30pm

Wednesday & Thursday
11am - 2:30pm   6pm - 9:30pm

Friday
11am - 2:30pm   6pm - 10pm

Saturday & Sunday
8am - 3:30pm   6pm - 10pm

1793 Church St. @ 30th, SF
415.285.2257
Off the "J" Church & 24 Divisadero Lines

BOOKSTORES & RETAIL SHOPS

381 381 Guerrero St., 621-3830, 11am-6pm, til 7pm wknds, great kitsch, candles

Bernal Books 401 Cortland Ave., Bernal Hts., 550-0293, 10am-7pm, til 4pm Sun, clsd Mon, lesbigay section, community bookstore for Bernal Heights & beyond

Body Manipulations 3234 16th St., 621-0408, noon-6:30pm, til 7:30pm Fri-Sat, piercing (walk-in basis), jewelry

Leather Tongue Video 714 Valencia St., 552-2900, noon-11pm, great collection of camp, cult & obscure videos

Modern Times Bookstore 888 Valencia St., 282-9246 (WC) 11am-9pm, til 6pm Sun

SPIRITUAL GROUPS

The Episcopal Church of St. John the Evangelist 1661 15th St., 861-1436, mostly gay/lesbian parish, open to all

EROTICA

Good Vibrations 1210 Valencia St., 550-7399 (W) 11am-7pm, clean, well-lighted sex toy store, also mail order

▲ **Mission St. News** 2086 Mission St., 626-0309, 24hrs

S.F. - Haight, Fillmore & West (415)

ACCOMMODATIONS

▲ **Alamo Square Inn** 719 Scott St., 922-2055/(800) 345-9888 (GF) full brkfst, 1895 Queen Anne & 1896 Tudor Revival Victorian mansions

The Archbishops Mansion 1000 Fulton St., 563-7872/(800) 543-5820 (GF) one of San Francisco's grandest homes

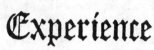

Auberge des Artistes 829 Fillmore, 776-2530/Fax: 441-8242 (GF) full brkfst, fireplaces, computer access

Bock's B&B 1448 Willard St., 664-6842/Fax: 664-1109 (GF,IGTA) restored 1906 Edwardian residence

Carl Street Unicorn House 156 Carl St., 753-5194 (GF) 1895 Victorian house

Casa Loma Hotel 610 Fillmore St., 552-7100 (GF) shared bath

▲ **The Chateau Tivoli** 1057 Steiner St., 776-5462/(800) 228-1647 (GF) historic San Francisco B&B

Gough Hayes Hotel 417 Gough St., 431-9131 (MW)

Holiday Lodge 1901 Van Ness Ave., Pacific Heights, 776-4469/(800) 367-8504 (GF,SW,IGTA)

Hotel Majestic 1500 Sutter St., Pacific Heights, 441-1100/869-8966 (GF,F,WC) Mediterranean restaurant, some veggie, one of SF's earliest grand hotels

Inn at the Opera 333 Fulton St., 863-8400/(800) 325-2708 (GF,F) also Mediterranean restaurant

Lombard Plaza Motel 2026 Lombard St., 921-2494/Fax: 921-5275 (GF)

▲ **The Mansions** 2220 Sacramento St., Pacific Heights, 929-9444/(800) 826-9398 (MW) full brkfst

Metro Hotel 319 Divisadero St., 861-5364 (GF,F)

Pension San Francisco 1668 Market St., 864-1271 (GF) cont'l brkfst

The Queen Anne Hotel 1590 Sutter St., Pacific Heights, 441-2828/(800) 227-3970 (★GF, IGTA) cont'l brkfst, fireplaces, beautifully restored 1890 landmark

Radisson Miyako Hotel 1625 Post St., Japantown, 922-3200/(800) 333-3333 (GF,WC) located in the heart of Japantown

**HISTORIC
VICTORIAN
MANSION**

*Alamo
Square
Inn*

**Beautiful hilltop views
Hearty breakfast and parking included
Owner-operated
719 Scott Street
San Francisco
415/922-2055 • 1-800-345-9888**

Stanyan Park Hotel 750 Stanyan St., 751-1000/Fax: 668-5454 (GF,WC) cont'l brkf-st, evening snacks, fireplaces

Bars

▲ **Alta Plaza** 2301 Fillmore, 922-1444 (★M,P) 4pm-2am, also restaurant, cont'l, some veggie

Hayes & Vine 377 Hayes St., 626-5301, 5pm-midnight, til 1am Fri-Sat, wine bar

The Lion Pub 2062 Divisadero St., 567-6565 (M,P) 3pm-2am

Marlena's 488 Hayes St., 864-6672 (MW,NH,WC) 10am-2am

Noc Noc 557 Haight St., 861-5811 (GF,BW) 5pm-2am

The Top 424 Haight St., 864-7386 (GF,D,A) call for events

Traxx 1437 Haight St., 864-4213 (M,NH,WC) noon-2am

Restaurants & Cafes

▲ **Alta Plaza** 2301 Fillmore, 922-1444, 5:30pm-10pm, cont'l, some veggie

Blue Muse 409 Gough St., 626-7505, 7:30am-11pm, cont'l, some veggie

Cafe Corbus (at the Muscle System), coffee bar & snacks

Cha Cha Cha's 1801 Haight St., 386-7670, 11:30am-11pm, Cuban/Cajun, excellent sangria, worth the long wait!

Charpe's Grill 131 Gough St., 621-6766 (WC) dinner nightly, American, some veggie, full bar

Geva's Caribbean 482 Hayes St., 863-1220 (MW,WC) dinner

Greens Fort Mason, 771-6222, dinner, Sun brunch, clsd Mon, gourmet prix fixe vegetarian

Ivy's 398 Hayes St., 626-3930, lunch & dinner, vegetarian

Kan Zaman 1793 Haight, 751-9656 (BW) noon-11:30pm, til 1:30am Fri-Sat, Mediterranean, some veggie, hookahs & tobacco available

Mad Magda's Russian Tearoom & Cafe 579 Hayes St., 864-7654 (★MW) eclectic crowd, magic garden, tarot & palm readers daily

Ya Halla 494 Haight St., 522-1509, lunch & dinner, Middle Eastern, plenty veggie

GYMS & HEALTH CLUBS
Muscle System 364 Hayes St., 863-4701 (MO)

BOOKSTORES & RETAIL SHOPS
La Riga 1391 Haight St., 552-1525, leather

Mainline Gifts 1928 Fillmore St., 563-4438, 10am-6pm, til 8pm Fri, from 11am Sun

Nomad 1881 Hayes St., 563-7771, noon-7pm, piercing (walk-in), jewelry

EROTICA
Romantasy 199 Moulton St., 673-3137, noon-7pm, books, videos, toys, clothing

CRUISY AREAS
Land's End (AYOR) inquire locally

San Gregorio

CRUISY AREAS
San Gregorio Beach 1 mi. N. of state beach (AYOR)

San Jose (408)

INFO LINES & SERVICES
AA Gay/Lesbian 297-3555, many mtgs, call for info

Billy DeFrank Lesbian/Gay Community Center 175 Stockton Ave., 293-2429, 3pm-9pm, from noon Sat, 9am-6pm Sun

Rainbow Gender Association PO Box 700730, 95170-0730, 984-4044, transgender group, recorded info

▲ **San Jose Confidential Connection** 532-3000, Meet hot local guys! Record, listen, respond to free ads. Use free code 9966.

BARS
641 Club 641 Stockton, 998-1144 (MW,D,MRC) 2pm-2am, from 11am wknds

Buck's 301 W. Stockton Ave., 286-1176 (MW,NH,D) noon-2am, from noon Fri til 2am Sun

Greg's Ballroom 551 W. Julian, 286-4388 (MW,D) noon-2am, leather night Th

Mac's Club 349 S. 1st St., 998-9535 (M,NH) 10am-2am

Renegades 393 Stockton, 275-9902 (M,NH,L) 11am-2am, patio

RESTAURANTS & CAFES
Cafe Leviticus 1445 The Alameda, 279-8877 (MW) 7am-midnight

El Faro 610 Coleman Ave., 294-1846, lunch & dinner, Sun champagne brunch 10am-3pm

Hamburger Mary's 170 W. St. John St., 947-1667 (WC) 11:30am-2am, from 9am wknds, American, some veggie, full bar

TRAVEL & TOUR OPERATORS
Yankee Clipper Travel 260 Saratoga Ave., Los Gatos, (800) 624-2664/354-6400 (IGTA) contact Jim

SPIRITUAL GROUPS
Hosanna Church of Praise 24 N. 5th St., 293-0708, 2pm Sun, charismatic pentecostal

Integrity El Camino 81 N. Second St., 377-4411, 2nd Tue, lesbigay Episcopalians

Just One Hour South of San Francisco (easy CalTrain access, too).

THE
WATERGARDEN
GAY AND BISEXUAL
MEN'S CLUB & BATHS

1010 THE ALAMEDA
SAN JOSE, CALIFORNIA
(408) 275-1215

OPEN 24 HOURS/7 DAYS A WEEK.
ONE TIME MEMBERSHIP AVAILABLE.
MEMBERSHIP REQUIRED
MUST BE 18 YEARS

MCC of San Jose 65 S. 7th St., 279-2711, 10:30am Sun

PUBLICATIONS
Out Now! 45 N. 1st St. #124, 991-1873, bi-weekly

MEN'S CLUBS
▲ **Watergarden** 1010 The Alameda, 275-1215 (PC) 24hrs

EROTICA
▲ **Leather Masters** 969 Park Ave., 293-7660, leather & fetish, clothes, toys, publications

San Leandro (510)
BARS
Bill's Eagle 14572 E. 14th, 357-7343 (MW,NH,D,E,WC) noon-2am

San Lorenzo (510)
SPIRITUAL GROUPS
MCC of Greater Hayward 100 Hacienda (Christ Lutheran Church), 481-9720, 12:30pm Sun

San Luis Obispo (805)
INFO LINES & SERVICES
GALA (Gay/Lesbian Alliance of the Central Coast) PO Box 3558, 93403, 541-4252, info & referrals, also newsletter

ACCOMMODATIONS
Adobe Inn 1473 Monterey St., 549-0321/Fax: 549-0383 (GF) full brkfst, kitchens

Casa De Amigas B&B 1202 8th St., Los Osos, 528-3701 (MW)

▲ **Palomar Inn** 1601 Shell Beach Rd., Shell Beach, 773-4207 (MW) close to nude beach, gay owned and operated

BARS

Breezes Pub & Grill 11560 Los Osos Valley Rd., Laguna Village #160, 544-8010 (MW,D,F,BW) 8pm-2am Wed-Sat, also a restaurant, Caribbean, some veggie

RESTAURANTS & CAFES

Linnea's Cafe 1110 Garden, 541-5888, til midnight, til 2am wknds, plenty veggie

BOOKSTORES & RETAIL SHOPS

Coalesce Bookstore & Garden Wedding Chapel 845 Main St., Morro Bay, 772-2880, 10am-5:30pm, 11am-4pm Sun, lesbigay section

Volumes of Pleasure 1016 Los Osos Valley Rd., Los Osos, 528-5565 (WC) 10am-6pm, clsd Sun, general, lesbigay section

SPIRITUAL GROUPS

MCC of the Central Coast 2333 Meadow Ln., 481-9376, 10:30am Sun

CRUISY AREAS

Diamond Cove W. of Pirates Cove & down a cliff (AYOR)

Morro Rock along Embarcadero, Morro Bay (AYOR) late

Pirates Cove Beach left turn off Avila (N,AYOR)

Pismo Dunes Grand Ave. to beach (AYOR)

San Mateo (415)

BARS

'B' Street 236 S. 'B' St., 348-4045 (MW,D,A,E,S,V,WC) hours vary

CRUISY AREAS
Coyote Point off US 101 btwn. San Mateo & Burlingame (AYOR) beach

San Rafael (415)

BARS
Aunt Ruby's 815 W. Francisco Blvd., 459-6079 (MW,D,WC) 4-11pm, 2pm-2am Fri-Sat, from noon Sun

San Ysidro (619)

EROTICA
▲ **F St. Bookstore** 4650 Border Village, 497-6042

Santa Ana (714)

SPIRITUAL GROUPS
Christ Chapel MCC 720 N. Spurgeon, 835-0722, 10am Sun

Santa Barbara (805)

INFO LINES & SERVICES
Gay/Lesbian Resource Center 126 E. Haley St. Ste. A-17, 963-3636, 10am-5pm Mon-Fri, social/educational & support services, youth groups

ACCOMMODATIONS
Glenborough Inn 1327 Bath St., 966-0589/(800) 962-0589 (MW) full brkfst, fireplaces
Ivanhoe Inn 1406 Castillo St., 963-8832/(800) 428-1787 (GF) expanded cont'l brkfst, kitchens

BARS
▲ **Chameleon Restaurant & Bar** 421 E. Cota, 965-9536 (MW,WC) 11am-2am, patio, Californian, plenty veggie
Club Oasis 224 Helena, 966-2464 (MW,D,E,WC) 4pm-2am, from 2pm wknds, piano bar
▲ **Fathom** 423 State St., 730-0022 (MW) call infoline for events, 882-2082
Gold Coast 30 W. Cota, 965-6701 (M,D,WC) 4pm-2am
Zelo's 630 State, 966-5792 (GF,D,F) 10pm-2am

RESTAURANTS & CAFES
Acacia 1212 Coast Village Rd., 969-8500 (WC) dinner, lunch wknds, modern American, full bar
Hot Spot Espresso Bar & Reservation Service 564-1637, 24hrs
Mousse Odile 18 E. Cota St., 962-5393, patio, French
Sojourner 134 E. Canon Perdido, 965-7922 (BW,WC) 11am-11pm, vegetarian

BOOKSTORES & RETAIL SHOPS
Chaucer's Books 3321 State St., 682-6787, 9am-9pm, til 10pm Fri-Sat, 10am-5pm Sun, general, lesbigay section
Choices Books & Espresso Bar 901 De La Vina St., 965-5477 (WC) 9am-9pm, 10am-6pm wknds
Earthling Books & Cafe 1137 State St., 965-0926, 9am-11pm, til midnight Fri-Sat, lesbigay

SPIRITUAL GROUPS
Integrity El Norte 1500 State St., 965-7419, 4th Sun, meets at Trinity Episcopal Church, lesbigay Episcopalians

CHAMELEON

Restaurant & Bar · Santa Barbara

Lunch / Dinner / Weekend Brunch / Cocktail Bar
Game Room / Banquet Facilities / Outdoor Patio

•

Atmosphere Provided by
World Of Magic
Santa Barbara's Queerest Store

•

421 East Cota Street, Santa Barbara, CA 93101
(805) 965-9536 / chamel421@aol.com

PUBLICATIONS
The Bulletin 126 E. Haley St. #A-17, 963-3636

EROTICA
For Adults Only 223 Anacupa, 963-9922, 24hrs

CRUISY AREAS
Cabrillo Beach E. of Wharf (AYOR)
East Beach (AYOR)
Padero Ln. Beach (AYOR) summers

Santa Clara (408)

BARS
Tynker's Damn 46 N. Saratoga, 243-4595 (M,D) 3pm-2am, 1pm-2am wknds

EROTICA
Borderline 36 N. Saratoga Ave., 241-2177, toys, videos
L'Amour Shoppe 2329 El Camino Real, 296-7076

Santa Cruz (408)

INFO LINES & SERVICES
AA Gay/Lesbian 457-2559, call for mtgs
Lesbian/Gay/Bisexual/Transgender Community Center 1328 Commerce Ln., 425-5422, noon-8pm, info, referrals, social/support groups, call for events

ACCOMMODATIONS
Battle Mountain B&B 105 Country Estates Terrace, 429-8687/Fax: 429-4132 (MW)

Chateau Victorian B&B Inn 118 1st St., 458-9458 (GF) expanded cont'l brkfst, fireplaces

BARS

Blue Lagoon 923 Pacific Ave., 423-7117 (MW,D,A,TG,S,V,WC) 4pm-2am

RESTAURANTS & CAFES

Costa Brava Taco Stand 505 Seabright, 423-8190, 11am-11pm

Crêpe Place 1134 Soquel Ave., 429-6994 (BW,WC) 11am-midnight, 10am-1am wknds, garden patio, plenty veggie

Saturn Cafe 1230 Mission, 429-8505, noon-midnight

GYMS & HEALTH CLUBS

Heartwood Spa Hot Tub & Sauna Garden 3150-A Mission Dr., 462-2192, noon-11pm, WO Sun night

BOOKSTORES & RETAIL SHOPS

Book Loft 1207 Soquel Ave., 429-1812, 10am-10pm, noon-6pm Sun, 10am-6pm Mon

Bookshop Santa Cruz 1520 Pacific Garden Mall, 423-0900 (WC) 9am-11pm, general, lesbigay section

Chimney Sweep Books 419 Cedar St., 458-1044, hours vary, mostly used, lesbigay section

TRAVEL & TOUR OPERATORS

Eco-Explorations PO Box 7944, 95061, 662-0652 (IGTA) lesbigay scuba & seakayaking trips

Pacific Harbor Travel 519 Seabright Ave., 427-5000/(800) 435-9463 (IGTA)

Santa Cruz Tours 95 Country Estates Ter., 429-8687/(800) 757-3891x7928, sightseeing, winetasting & artist studio tours

CRUISY AREAS

Laguna Creek Beach 7 mi. N. of town (AYOR)

Santa Maria (805)

INFO LINES & SERVICES

Gay/Lesbian Resource Center 2255 S. Broadway #4, 349-9947, info & referrals, also counseling services

RESTAURANTS & CAFES

Cafe Monet 1555 S. Broadway, 928-1912 (WC) 7am-7pm, til 10pm Wed & Fri, 9am-5pm Sun, men's night 7:30pm-9pm Wed

EROTICA

Book Adventure 306 S. Blosser Blvd., 928-7094

Santa Rosa (707)

INFO LINES & SERVICES

▲ **Santa Rosa Confidential Connection** 522-5001, Meet hot local guys! Record, listen, respond to free ads. Use free code 9966.

BARS

Santa Rosa Inn 4302 Santa Rosa Ave., 584-0345 (MW,D,E) noon-2am

RESTAURANTS & CAFES

Aroma Roasters 95 5th St. (Railroad Square), 576-7765, 7am-midnight, til 11pm wknds

BOOKSTORES & RETAIL SHOPS
North Light Books 95 5th St. (Historic Railroad Square), 579-9000, 9am-9pm, til 10pm Fri-Sat, 10pm-8pm Sun, strong lesbigay emphasis, also coffeehouse

Sawyer's News 733 4th St., 542-1311, 7am-9pm, til 10pm Fri-Sat

TRAVEL & TOUR OPERATORS
Santa Rosa Travel 542 Farmers Ln., 542-0943/(800) 227-1445

Sun Quest 1208 4th St., 573-8300/(800) 444-8300

SPIRITUAL GROUPS
1st Congregational Church of Christ 2000 Humboldt St., 546-0998, 10:30am Sun

Chapel of the Saints Sergius & Bacchus 200 5th St., 573-9463, 10am Sun

New Hope MCC 3632 Airway Dr., 526-4673, 12:15 Sun

PUBLICATIONS
We the People PO Box 8218, 95407, 573-8896, monthly

EROTICA
Santa Rosa Adult Books 3301 Santa Rosa Ave., 542-8248

Sausalito

CRUISY AREAS
Black Sand Beach off Lookout Rd.

Stockton (209)

BARS
Paradise 10100 N. Lower Sacramento Rd., 477-4724 (MW,D,E,S,YC) 6pm-2am, from 4pm wknds

EROTICA
Adult Books 332 N. California, 941-8607

Tustin (714)

BOOKSTORES & RETAIL SHOPS
A Different Drummer II 14131 Yorba St. Ste. 102, 731-0224/3632, opens 11am, clsd wknds, lesbigay

Ukiah (707)

INFO LINES & SERVICES
The Billy Club PO Box 1572, 95482, 462-0766, support network for gay/bi men

BARS
Sunset Grill 228 E. Perkins St., 463-0740 (GF,D) lunch & dinner, clsd Mon, Californian

CRUISY AREAS
Jensen's Truck Stop Lovers Ln. (AYOR) nights

Lake Mendocino at the overlook (AYOR) days only

Upland (909)

EROTICA
The Toy Box 1999 W. Arrow Rte., 920-1135, 24hrs

Vacaville (707)

INFO LINES & SERVICES
Solano County Gay/Lesbian Infoline PO Box 9, 95696, 448-1010/449-0550

Solano Lambda Men's Association (at Vacaville Book Company), 7pm-9pm, 2nd & 4th Tue

BOOKSTORES & RETAIL SHOPS
Vacaville Book Co. & Coffeehouse 315 Main St., 449-0550, 9am-6pm, til 9pm Fri, from 8am Sat, clsd Sun

SPIRITUAL GROUPS
St. Paul's United Methodist Church 101 West St., 448-5154, 10:30am Sun

Vallejo (707)

BARS
Nobody's Place 437 Virginia St., 645-7298 (MW,D,E,WC) 10am-2am, patio

The Q 412 Georgia St., 644-4584 (M,D,WC) noon-2am, from 4pm Mon-Wed

Venice (also see Los Angeles - West L.A.) (310)

ACCOMMODATIONS
Rose Avenue Beach House 55 Rose Ave., 396-2803 (GF)

Ventura (805)

INFO LINES & SERVICES
AA Gay/Lesbian 739 E. Main, 389-1444

Gay/Lesbian Community Center 1995 E. Main, 653-1979, 10am-4pm & 6:30pm-9pm(Mon-Th), clsd wknds

▲ **Ventura Confidential Connection** 581-0700, Meet hot local guys! Record, listen, respond to free ads. Use free code 9966.

BARS
Club Alternative 1644 E. Thompson Blvd., 653-6511, 2pm-2am, patio

Paddy McDermott's 577 E. Main St., 652-1071 (MW,D,K,S) 2pm-2am

SPIRITUAL GROUPS
MCC Ventura 1848 Poli (Church of Latter Day Saints), 643-0502, 6:30pm Sun

EROTICA
Three Star Adult News 359 E. Main St., 653-9068, 24hrs

CRUISY AREAS
Bates Beach btwn. Ventura & Santa Barbara, no motel

Emma Wood St. Beach

Victorville (619)

BARS
West Side 15 16868 Stoddard Wells Rd., 243-9600 (MW,BW) 2pm-2am

EROTICA
Oasis Adult Dept. Store 14949 Palmdale Rd., 241-0788

CRUISY AREAS
Pebble Beach Park (AYOR)

Visalia

CRUISY AREAS

Ave. 283 off Shirk Rd. by Fwy. 99 (AYOR) evenings
Mooney Grove Park (AYOR) days

Walnut Creek (510)

INFO LINES & SERVICES

AA Gay/Lesbian 1924 Trinity Ave. (St. Paul's Episc. Church), 939-4155, 8:30pm Fri, 5:30pm Sat at 193 Mayhew Wy.

BARS

D.J.'s 1535 Olympic Blvd., 930-0300 (MW,F,E,WC) 4pm-2am
J.R.'s 2520 Camino Diablo, 256-1200 (★MW,D,CW,WC) 5pm-2am, til 4am Fri-Sat
Twelve Twenty 1220 Pine St., 938-4550 (MW,D,WC) 4pm-2am from 3pm wknds

SPIRITUAL GROUPS

MCC Diablo Valley 1543 Sunnyvale (United Methodist Church), 283-2238, 1pm Sun

Whittier (310)

SPIRITUAL GROUPS

MCC Good Samaritan 11931 E. Washington Blvd., 696-6213, 10am Sun, 7:30pm Wed

Willits (707)

RESTAURANTS & CAFES

Tsunami 50 S. Main St., 459-4750, 9:30am-8pm, Japanese

BOOKSTORES & RETAIL SHOPS

Leaves of Grass 630 S. Main St., 459-3744, 10am-5:30pm, noon-5pm Sun, alternative bookstore

TRAVEL & TOUR OPERATORS

Skunk Train California Western 299 E. Commercial St., 459-5248, scenic train trips

CRUISY AREAS

Eel River 15 mi. N. of town, warm summer days

Yosemite Nat'l Park (209)

ACCOMMODATIONS

The Ahwahnee Hotel Yosemite Valley Floor, 252-4848 (GF,F,SW) incredibly dramatic & expensive grand fortress
The Homestead 41110 Rd. 600, Ahwahnee, 683-0495 (GF) cottages, full brkfs

COLORADO

Alamosa (719)

ACCOMMODATIONS
Cottonwood Inn 123 San Juan Ave., 589-3882/(800) 955-2623 (GF)

Aspen (970)

INFO LINES & SERVICES
Aspen Gay/Lesbian Community PO Box 3143, 81612, 925-9249, info/resources, outdoor activities, monthly events

ACCOMMODATIONS
Aspen Bed & Breakfast Lodge 311 W. Main, 925-7650/(800) 362-7736 (GF,SW)
Hotel Aspen 110 W. Main St., 925-3441/(800) 527-7369 (GF,SW,WC)
Hotel Lenado 200 S. Aspen St., 925-6246/(800) 321-3457 (GF)
Rising Star Guest Ranch (888) 429-7624 (MW,SW,IGTA) call for location
Sardy House 128 E. Main St., 920-2525/(800) 321-3457 (GF,SW) hot tub

BARS
Double Diamond 450 S. Galena, 920-6905 (GF,E,S) seasonal
Silver Nugget Hyman Ave. Mall, 925-8154 (GF,D,E,WC) 10pm-2am
The Tippler 535 E. Dean, 925-4977 (GF,D,F,E,WC) 11:30am-2am (seasonal), Italian

RESTAURANTS & CAFES
Syzygy 520 E. Hyman, 925-3700 (E,WC) 5pm-10pm, bar til 2am

BOOKSTORES & RETAIL SHOPS
Explore Booksellers & Bistro 221 E. Main, 925-5336 (F,WC) 10am-11pm, vegetarian menu

CRUISY AREAS
Hyman St. Mall (AYOR)

Boulder (303)

INFO LINES & SERVICES
▲ **Community Real Estate Referrals** (800) 346-5592, gay realtor at your service, no rentals
LBGT (Lesbian/Bisexual/Gay/Transgendered) Alliance University Memorial Center Rm. 28, Colo.Univ., 80309, 492-8567, events schedule & resource info

ACCOMMODATIONS
Boulder Victorian Historic B&B 1305 Pine St., 938-1300 (GF)
The Briar Rose 2151 Arapahoe Ave., 442-3007/Fax: 786-8440 (GF)

BARS
Boulder Blue Steel Aspen Plaza, 786-8860 (★GF,D,WC) 7pm-2am, clsd Mon
Marquee 1109 Walnut, 447-1803 (GF,D,S,WC) 7pm-2am
The Yard 2690 28th St. #C, 443-1987 (MW,D,WC) 4pm-2am, from 2pm wknds

RESTAURANTS & CAFES
Walnut Cafe 3073 Walnut, 447-2315 (★WC) 7am-11pm, til 3pm Sun-Mon, patio

BOOKSTORES & RETAIL SHOPS
Aria 2043 Broadway, 442-5694 (WC) 10am-6pm, noon-5pm Sun, cards, T-shirts, gifts

Left Hand Books 1825 Pearl St., 2nd flr., 443-8252, noon-9pm, 1pm-4pm Sun

Word Is Out 1731 15th St., 449-1415 (WC) 10am-6pm, noon-5pm Sun, clsd Mon, lesbigay section

TRAVEL & TOUR OPERATORS

Adventure Bound Expeditions 711 Walnut St., 449-0990, mountain tours & hiking excursions

SPIRITUAL GROUPS

Gay/Lesbian Concerned Catholics 904 14th St., 443-8383, monthly events

PUBLICATIONS

Colorado Community Directories PO Drawer 2270, 80306, 443-7768/Fax: 642-3122, extensive statewide resources

EROTICA

The News Stand 1720 15th St., 442-9515

Breckenridge (303)

ACCOMMODATIONS

Allaire Timbers Inn 9511 Hwy. 9, S. Main St., 453-7530/(800) 624-4904 (GF,WC) full brkfst, hot tub

The Bunkhouse Lodge PO Box 6, 80424, 453-6475 (MO,SW,N) full brkfst, hot tub, kitchens, also Bunkhouse Bar (M,NH,CW)

Colorado Springs (719)

INFO LINES & SERVICES

▲ **Community Real Estate Referrals** (800) 346-5592, gay realtor at your service, no rentals

Pikes Peak Gay/Lesbian Community Center Helpline PO Box 574, 80901, 471-4429, 6pm-9pm Mon-Fri, call for events

ACCOMMODATIONS

Pikes Peak Paradise PO Box 5760, 236 Pinecrest Rd., Woodland Park, 80866, 687-7112/(800) 354-0989 (GF) full brkfst, hot tub, mansion w/ view of Pikes Peak

BARS

Hide & Seek Complex 512 W. Colorado, 634-9303 (★MW,D,CW,F,S,YC,WC) 10:30am-2am, til 4am Fri-Sat, 4 bars & restaurant

Hour Glass Lounge 2748 Airport Rd., 471-2104 (GF,NH) 10am-2am

The Penthouse 1715 N. Academy, 597-3314 (M,NH,D,WC) 3pm-2am, til 4am Fri-Sat

True Colors 1865 N. Academy Blvd., 637-0773 (W,D,MRC,WC) 3pm-2am, clsd Sun-Tue

RESTAURANTS & CAFES

Art of Espresso 2021 W. Colorado Ave., 632-9306, 8am-10pm, til midnight Fri-Sat, til 6pm Sun, art gallery

Dale Street Cafe 115 E. Dale , 578-9898, 11am-9pm, clsd Sun, vegetarian menu

SPIRITUAL GROUPS

Pikes Peak MCC 730 N. Tejon (Unitarian Church), 634-3771, 5pm Sun

EROTICA

First Amendment Adult Bookstore 220 E. Fillmore, 630-7676

Crested Butte (303)

ACCOMMODATIONS

The Crested Beauty P.O. Box 1204, 81224, 349-1201 (WC)

Denver (303)

INFO LINES & SERVICES

AA Gay/Lesbian 322-4440, many meetings

Gay/Lesbian/Bisexual Community Center 1245 E. Colfax Ave. Ste. 125, 831-6268/837-1598 (WC) 10am-6pm Mon-Fri, extensive resources & support groups

Gender Identity Center 3715 W. 32nd Ave., 202-6466, resources & statewide support group for transgendered people

Girth & Mirth of the Rockies Box 2351, 80201, 784-5814, social group for big men & their admirers

Young Alive Group 860-1819, social/support group for ages 18-29, sponsored by MCC

ACCOMMODATIONS

Castle Marve 1572 Race St., 331-0621/926-2763 (GF) full brkfst, grand historic mansion

Elyria's Western Guest House 1655 E. 47th Ave., 291-0915/Fax: 296-9892 (MW) cont'l brkfst, hot tub, historic neighborhood

Mile Hi B&B 329-7827/513-7827 (M)

P.T. Barnum Estate 360 King St., 830-6758 (★GF) exp. cont'l brkfst, B&B on turn-of-the-century estate

The Queen Anne Inn 2147 Tremont Place, 296-6666 (GF) full brkfst,

The Spectacular View B&B Capital Hill, 830-6758 (GF,SW,WC) high-rise apartment

Stapleton Plaza Hotel 3333 Quebec St., 321-3500/(800) 950-6070 (GF,F,SW,WC) also full restaurant

▲ **Victoria Oaks Inn** 1575 Race St., 355-1818/662-6257 (GF) exp. cont'l brkfst, fireplaces

BARS

Adonis (Club America) NW corner of the Tivoli, 534-1777 (M,D,A) 9pm-2am Sun only

▲ **B.J.'s Carousel** 1380 S. Broadway, 777-9880 (★M,NH,S,WC) 10am-2am, patio, volleyball court, also full restaurant

Brick's 1600 E. 17th Ave., 377-5400 (M,NH,F,WC) 11am-2am, lunch daily

Charlie's 900 E. Colfax Ave., 839-8890 (★M,D,CW,WC) 10am-2am, also full restaurant, 11am-4pm

Club 22 22 Broadway, 733-2175 (MW,D)

Club Proteus 1669 Clarkson, 869-4637 (MW,D,V,WC) 9pm-2am, from 5pm Fri & Sun, patio

Club Synergy 3240 Larimer, 575-5680 (★W,D,A) 11pm-5am Th-Sat, til 3am Sun

Colfax Mining Co. 3014 E. Colfax Ave., 321-6627 (MW,NH,D,WC) 10am-2am

The Colorado Triangle 2036 Broadway, 293-9009 (M,L) 4pm-2am, from 1pm wknds

The Compound 145 Broadway, 722-7977 (M,NH) 7am-2am, from 8am Sun, also 'Basix' (M,D,A) 9pm-2am

Den 5110 W. Colfax Ave., 534-9526 (M,NH,F,WC) 10am-2am

GAY DENVER'S
PREMIER NIGHT CLUB

THE METRO EXPRESS CLUB

Denver • Colorado

Metro Video Bar
Patio Gardens
Express Dance Bar

The Mile High City's
HOTTEST PARTY

All Gay, All the Time

METRO EXPRESS • 314 E 13th Ave • 894-0668

Denver Detour 551 E. Colfax Ave., 861-1497 (★MW,D,E,WC) 11am-2am, lunch & dinner daily

The Elle 716 W. Colfax, 572-1710 (W,D,WC) 6pm-2am, 2pm-midnight Sun, clsd Mon-Tue, patio

Flavors 1700 Logan, 830-0535 (MW,D,E,WC) 10am-2am

Garbo's 116 E. 9th Ave., 837-8217 (M,P,E,WC) 11am-2am, live jazz & piano bar

The Grand Bar 538 E. 17th Ave., 839-5390 (MW,E,WC) 3pm-2am, upscale piano bar

Industry 1222 Glenarm Pl., 620-9554 (M,D) call for events

Maximilian's 2151 Lawrence St., 297-0015 (GF,D,MRC,YC) 9pm-2am Fri & Sat

▲ **Metro Express** 314 E. 13th Ave., 894-0668 (★MW,D,E,V,WC) 4pm-2am, from 2pm Sun, patio

Mike's 60 S. Broadway, 777-0193 (MW,D,WC) 2pm-2am

Mr. Bill's 1027 Broadway, 534-1759 (M,NH) 9am-2am

R&R Denver 4958 E. Colfax Ave., 320-9337 (M,NH) 9am-2am

Rock Island 1614 15th St., 572-7625 (GF,D,A,YC,WC) call for events

Snake Pit 608 E. 13th Ave, 831-1234 (★M,D,A,WC) 5pm-2am

Ye 'O Matchmaker Pub 1480 Humboldt, 839-9388 (MW,D,MRC,S) 10am-2am, also full restaurant, Mexican/American

RESTAURANTS & CAFES

Alfresco's 100 E. 9th (at Lincoln), 894-0600, lunch & dinner, Sun brunch, bar from 11am, great patio

Basil's Cafe 30 S. Broadway, 698-1413 (★BW,WC) lunch & dinner, clsd Sun, nouvelle Italian, plenty veggie

Blue Note Cafe 70 S. Broadway, 744-6774 (MW,E) 8am-10pm, til midnight Fri-Sat, clsd Mon

City Spirit 1434 Blake, 575-0022 (E,WC) 11am-midnight, full bar

Daily Planet Cafe 1560 Broadway, 894-8308 (S,WC) clsd wknds, full bar

Denver Sandwich Co. 1217 E. 9th Ave., 861-9762 (WC) 10:30am-9pm, noon-8pm Sun

Diced Onions 609 Corona St., 831-8353, 7am-3pm, 5pm-8pm Fri & Sat, clsd Mon, diner/deli

Footloose Cafe 104 S. Broadway, 722-3430 (MW,WC) 9am-10pm, til 5pm Sun, some veggie, also full bar

Java Creek 287 Columbine St., 377-8902 (E,WC) 7am-10pm, til 5pm Sun, coffeehouse

Las Margaritas 1066 Old S. Gaylord St., 777-0194 (WC) from 11am, bar til 2am

GYMS & HEALTH CLUBS

Broadway Bodyworks 160 S. Broadway, 722-4342 (GF,WC) 6am-9pm, 7am-6pm Sat, 10am-4pm Sun

BOOKSTORES & RETAIL SHOPS

Category Six 1029 E. 11th Ave., 832-6263, 10am-6pm, 11am-5pm wknds, lesbigay

Isis Bookstore 5701 E. Colfax Ave., 321-0867 (WC) 10am-7pm, til 6pm Fri-Sat, noon-5pm Sun, new age, metaphysical

Magazine City 200 E. 13th Ave., 861-8249, 8am-7pm, 10am-6pm wknds

Newsstand Cafe 630 E. 6th Ave., 777-6060 (★WC) 7am-10pm, til 4pm Sun

Tattered Cover Book Store 2955 E. 1st Ave., 322-7727/(800) 833-9327 (WC) 9:30am-9pm, 10am-6pm Sun, 4 flrs.

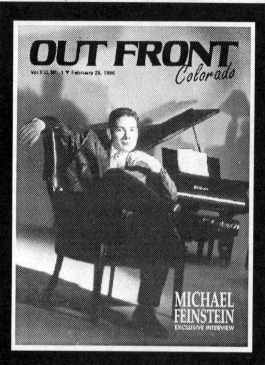

SUBSCRIBE TO
Colorado's Leading Gay & Lesbian Publication Since 1976

1 year $60
(25 issues)

303/778-7900

▲ **Thomas Floral & Adult Gifts** 1 Broadway Ste. 108 (at Ellsworth), 744-6400 (WC) 8:30am-6pm, til 5pm Sat, clsd Sun

Unique of Denver 2626 E. 12th, 355-0689, lesbigay gift shop

TRAVEL & TOUR OPERATORS

B.T.C. World Travel 2120 S. Holly Ste. 100, 691-9200

ColoradoTourism Board PO Box 38700, 80238, (800) 265-6723

Compass Travel 1001 16th St. Ste. A-150, 534-1292/(800) 747-1292 (IGTA)

Let's Talk Travel/Carlson Travel Network 1485 S. Colorado Blvd. #260, 759-1318/(800) 934-2506 (IGTA)

Lizard Head Expeditions 1280 Humboldt St #32, 820-2066/(800) 444-5238, mountaineering, canyoneering & other wilderness skills, tours in central Rocky Mountains & Utah canyon country

Metro Travel 90 Madison Ste. 101, 333-6777 (IGTA)

Travel 16th St. 535 16th St. #250, 595-0007/(800) 222-9229 (IGTA)

Travel Boy Company Ltd. 201 Steele St. Ste. 2-B, 333-4855/(800) 334-2285 (IGTA)

Travel Junction 5455 W. 38th Ave. Ste. C, 420-4646/(800) 444-8980 (IGTA)

SPIRITUAL GROUPS

Congregation Tikvat Shalom Box 6694, 80206, 331-2706, lesbigay Jewish fellowship

Dignity-Denver 1100 Fillmore (Capitol Hts. Presb. Church), 322-8485, 5pm Sun

Integrity 1280 Vine St. (St. Barnabas), 388-6469, 7pm Sun, lesbigay Episcopalians

MCC of the Rockies 980 Church St., 860-1819, 9am & 11am Sun

Pagan Rainbow Network PO Drawer E , 80218, 377-6283, 11am 3rd Sun, at Community Center

St. Paul's Church (Methodist) 1615 Ogden, 832-4929, 11am Sun , reconciling congregation

PUBLICATIONS

Fag Mag 3888 E. Mexico #200, 80210, 839-9100

▲ **Out Front** 244 Washington, 80203, 778-7900, bi-weekly

Quest/H. Magazine 430 S. Broadway, 722-5965, newspaper, bar guide

MEN'S CLUBS

Community Country Club 2151 Lawrence St., 297-2601 (MO,PC) 24hrs

Denver Swim Club 6923 E. Colfax Ave., 321-9399 (★MO,V,YC,SW,PC) 24hrs

▲ **Midtowne Spa** 2935 Zuni St., 458-8902 (MO,PC) 24hrs

EROTICA

The Crypt 131 Broadway, 733-3112, 10am-10pm, noon-8pm Sun, erotica, leather, etc.

Crypt Adult Entertainment 139 Broadway, 778-6584, 24hrs, all-male theaters & arcades

Heaven Sent Me 482 S. Broadway, 733-9000 (★WC) 10am-10pm, full line of erotic goods

Pleasure Entertainment Center 127 S. Broadway, 722-5852, 24hrs, other locations: 3250 W. Alameda, 934-2373 & 3490 W. Colfax, 825-6505

CRUISY AREAS

Cheesman Park nr. Pavilion (AYOR)

Durango   (303)

ACCOMMODATIONS

Leland House 721 2nd Ave., 385-1920/(800) 664-1920 (★GF) full brkfst

CRUISY AREAS

Main Mall days

Narrow Gauge Train Station (AYOR)

Estes Park   (970)

ACCOMMODATIONS

Distinctive Inns of Colorado PO Box 2061, 80517, 866-0621, great brochure

Sundance Cottages P.O. Box 4830, 80517, 586-3922 (GF,WC)

Fort Collins   (970)

INFO LINES & SERVICES

Gay/Lesbian/Bisexual Alliance Lory Student Ctr., LSU Box 206, 80523, 491-7232, call for ino

BARS

Nightingales 1437 E. Mulberry St., 493-0251 (★MW,D,S,V,WC) 4pm-2am, clsd Mon

TRAVEL & TOUR OPERATORS

Fort Collins Travel 333 W. Mountain Ave., 482-5555/(800) 288-7402

Never Summer Nordic PO Box 1983, 80522, 482-9411, yurts (tipi-like shelters) sleep 8-12 in Colorado Rockies, mountain-biking & skiing

Grand Junction (303)

BARS
Quincy's 609 Main St., 242-9633 (GF,NH,WC) gay after 8pm

CRUISY AREAS
Hawthorne & Lincoln Parks (AYOR) clsd midnight

Grand Lake (970)

ACCOMMODATIONS
Grandview Lodge 12429 Hwy. 34, 627-3914 (★GF) sundeck, hot tub

Greeley (970)

INFO LINES & SERVICES
Greeley Gay/Lesbian Alliance at U. of Northern Colorado, 351-2065, leave message for referrals

BARS
C Double R Bar 1822 9th St. Plaza, 353-0900 (MW,D,A,CW,WC) 4pm-2am, from 2pm Sun

CRUISY AREAS
Island Grove Park (AYOR)

Idaho Springs (303)

ACCOMMODATIONS
Glacier House B&B 603 Lake Rd., 567-0536 (MW) full brkfst, hot tub, home-style B&B

Keystone (970)

ACCOMMODATIONS
Tanrydoon 463 Vail Circle, 468-1956 (MW) full brkfst, magnificent mountain home

Pueblo (719)

INFO LINES & SERVICES
Pueblo After 2 PO Box 1602, 81002, 564-4004, social/educational network, newsletter

BARS
Pirate's Cove 409 N. Union, 542-9624 (MW,NH,WC) 2pm-2am, from 4pm Sun, clsd Mon

SPIRITUAL GROUPS
MCC Pueblo Bonforte & Liberty (Christ Cong. Church), 543-6460, 12:30pm Sun

CRUISY AREAS
Mineral Palace Park (AYOR)

Steamboat Springs (970)

ACCOMMODATIONS
Elk River Estates PO Box 5032, 80477-5032, 879-7556 (GF) full brkfst, suburban townhouse B&B

Vail (303)

RESTAURANTS & CAFES
Sweet Basil 193 E. Gore Creek Dr., 476-0125 (WC) lunch & dinner, full bar

Winter Park (970)

ACCOMMODATIONS
Silverado II 490 Kings Crossing Rd., 726-5753 (GF) condo ski resort

RESTAURANTS & CAFES
Silver Zephyr (at Silverado II), 726-8732 (WC) 5pm-10pm

Woodland Park

ACCOMMODATIONS
▲ **The Caritas B&B Network** (800) CARITAS (227-4827), see ad in center National section

CONNECTICUT

Bridgeport (203)

INFO LINES & SERVICES
▲ **Bridgeport Confidential Connection** 394-6222, Meet hot local guys! Record, listen, respond to free ads. Use free code 9966.
▲ **Community Real Estate Referrals** (800) 346-5592, gay realtor at your service, no rentals

RESTAURANTS & CAFES
Bloodroot Restaurant 85 Ferris St., 576-9168, clsd Mon, vegetarian

SPIRITUAL GROUPS
Church of the Celestial Ministries 384-1660/Fax: 331-1981, call for events

CRUISY AREAS
Bridgeport Country News Boston Post Rd. nr. Post Office (AYOR)
Main St. nr. downtown (AYOR) hustlers

Danbury (203)

BARS
Triangles Cafe 66 Sugar Hollow Rd. Rte. 7, 798-6996 (★MW,D,S) 5pm-2am, clsd Mon, patio

TRAVEL & TOUR OPERATORS
Aldis The Travel Planner 46 Mill Plain Rd., 778-9399/(800) 442-9386 (IGTA)

CRUISY AREAS
The Oldtown Dikes Pt. Park, E. side of Lake Candlewood (AYOR)

East Windsor (203)

RESTAURANTS & CAFES
The Eatery 297 S. Main St., 627-7094 (E,WC) lunch Mon-Fri, dinner nightly

Enfield (203)

EROTICA
Bookends 44 Enfield St. (Rte. 5), 745-3988

Groton (203)

EROTICA
▲ **Video Expo** 591 Rte. 12, 448-0787

Hamden (203)

TRAVEL & TOUR OPERATORS
Adler Travel 2323 Whitney Ave., 288-8100/(800) 598-2648 (IGTA)

Hammonasset

CRUISY AREAS
Hammonasset State Beach (AYOR)

Hartford

INFO LINES & SERVICES
AA Gay/Lesbian (see listing in 'Metroline' magazine), daily at Gay/Lesbian Community Center, call for info.
▲ **Community Real Estate Referrals** (800) 346-5592, gay realtor at your service, no rentals
Gay/Lesbian Community Center 1841 Broad St., 724-5542 (WC) 10am-10pm, wknd hours vary, also coffeehouse
Gay/Lesbian Guide Line 366-3734, 7pm-10pm Tue & Th, statewide info, referrals & support
▲ **Hartford Confidential Connection** 293-3969, Meet hot local guys! Record, listen, respond to free ads. Use free code 9966.
XX Club PO Box 387, 06141-0387, transsexual support group

ACCOMMODATIONS

The 1895 House B&B 97 Girard Ave., 232-0014 (GF) expanded cont'l brkfst, Victorian home

BARS

Chez Est 458 Wethersfield Ave., 525-3243 (★M,D) 3pm-2am, from noon wknds

Metro Club & Cafe 22 Union Pl., 549-8023 (★MW,D,F,S) 4pm-1am, til 2am Fri-Sat, from 3pm Sun, clsd Mon, patio

Nick's Cafe House 1943 Broad St., 956-1573 (MW,D) 4pm-1am, til 2am Fri-Sat, cafe & disco

The Sanctuary 2880 Main St., 724-1277 (M,D,V,YC,WC) 8pm-2am, from 6pm Sun, clsd Mon-Tue

Starlight Playhouse & Cabaret 1022 Main St., East Hartford, (860) 289-0789 (MW,F,WC) 4:30pm-1am Th (club), Fri-Sat (shows)

BOOKSTORES & RETAIL SHOPS

MetroStore 493 Farmington Ave., 231-8845, 8am-8pm, til 5:30pm Tue, Wed, Sat, clsd Sun, books, leather & more

Reader's Feast Bookstore Cafe 529 Farmington Ave., 232-3710 (E) 10am-9pm, til 10pm Fri-Sat, til 2:30pm Sun, progressive bookstore

Water Hole Custom Leather 982 Main St., East Hartford, 528-6195, clsd Mon

TRAVEL & TOUR OPERATORS

▲ **Damron Atlas World Travel** 653-2492/ (888) 907-9777

SPIRITUAL GROUPS

Congregation Am Segulah (800) 734-8524 in CT only, Shabbat services for lesbi-gay Jews

Dignity-Hartford 144 S. Quaker Ln. (Quaker Mtg. House), 522-7334, 6pm Sun

MCC 50 Bloomfield Ave. (meeting house), 724-4605, 7pm Sun

PUBLICATIONS

Metroline 846 Farmington Ave. Ste.6, W. Hartford, 06119, 570-0823

EROTICA

Aircraft Book & News 349 Main St., East Hartford, 569-2324

Danny's Adult World 35 W. Service Rd., 549-1896

Red Lantern Book Store 1247 Main St., East Hartford, 289-5000, clsd Sun

CRUISY AREAS

Constitution Plaza (AYOR)

The Dikes E. to W. Service Rd. of I-91 N. (AYOR) Riverside Park

Manchester (203)

EROTICA

▲ **Video Expo** 691 Main St., 649-0451

Meriden (203)

EROTICA

▲ **Video Expo** 1919 N. Broad St., 235-5512

CRUISY AREAS

Hubbard Park (AYOR)

New Britain (860)

TRAVEL & TOUR OPERATORS
Weber's Travel Services 24 Cedar St., 229-4846 (IGTA)

CRUISY AREAS
Walnut Hill Park Veteran's Monument (AYOR)

New Haven (203)

INFO LINES & SERVICES
▲ **Community Real Estate Referrals** (800) 346-5592, gay realtor at your service, no rentals

BARS
168 York St. Cafe 168 York St., 789-1915 (MW,WC) 2pm-1am, patio
The Bar 254 Crown St., 495-8924 (GF,D,WC) 4pm-1am, more gay Tue
DV8 148 York St., 865-6206 (MW,NH,D,WC) 4pm-1am

TRAVEL & TOUR OPERATORS
Plaza Travel Center 208 College St., 777-7334/(800) 887-7334 (IGTA)

SPIRITUAL GROUPS
Dignity P.O. Box 9362, 06533, 6:30pm Sun
MCC 34 Harrison St. (United Church), 389-6750, 11:30am & 4pm Sun

EROTICA
Fairmont Theatre 33 Main St., 467-3832
▲ **Video Expo** 754 Chapel St., 562-5867

CRUISY AREAS
Long Wharf Dr. parking lot (AYOR)

New London (203)

INFO LINES & SERVICES
New London People's Forum Affirming Lesbian/Gay Identity 76 Federal (St. James), 443-8855, 7:30pm Wed, educational/support group

BARS
Frank's Place 9 Tilley St., 443-8883 (MW,D,E,WC) 4pm-1am, til 2am Fri-Sat, patio
Heroes 33 Golden St., 442-4376 (MW,NH,D) 4pm-1am

CRUISY AREAS
Ocean Park Beach nr. boardwalk (AYOR)

New Milford

CRUISY AREAS
Lynn Deming Park (AYOR)

Norfolk (860)

ACCOMMODATIONS
Loon Meadow Farm 41 Loon Meadow Dr., 542-1776 (GF)
Manor House B&B 69 Maple Ave., 542-5690 (GF) 1898 Victorian Tudor estate

Norwalk (203)

INFO LINES & SERVICES
Triangle Community Center 25 Van Zant St., 853-0600, 7:30pm-9:30pm Mon-Fri, activities, newsletter

TRAVEL & TOUR OPERATORS
B.W. Travel 852-0200 (IGTA)

CRUISY AREAS
Cranbury Park on Grumman Ave. (AYOR)

Norwich (203)

INFO LINES & SERVICES
Info Line for Southeastern Connecticut 74 W. Main St., 886-0516, 8am-8pm Mon-Fri, info, referrals, crisis counseling

Pomfret

CRUISY AREAS
Frog Rock (AYOR)

Portland (203)

TRAVEL & TOUR OPERATORS
Brownstone Travel Agency 278 Main St., 342-3450/(800) 888-4169

Ridgefield

CRUISY AREAS
Riverside on Rte. 7 opp. Ridgefield Motor Inn (AYOR)

Stamford (203)

INFO LINES & SERVICES
Gay/Lesbian Guide Line PO Box 8185, 06905, 366-3734, 7pm-10pm Tue-Th, statewide referrals & crisis counseling
Thompson Realty 1845 Summer St., 324-1012, ask for Debbie

BARS
Art Bar 84 W. Park Pl., 973-0300 (GF,D,A) 9pm-1am, gay night Sun from 8pm

EROTICA
▲ **Video Expo** 59 Broad St., 353-3331

CRUISY AREAS
Cove Island Beach

Storrs (203)

INFO LINES & SERVICES
Bisexual/Gay/Lesbian Association Box U-8, 2110 Hillside Rd., Univ. of CT, 06268, 486-3679, 7:30pm Th

Wallingford (203)

BARS
Choices 8 North Turnpike Rd., 949-9380 (M,D,E) 7pm-1am

Waterbury (203)

BARS
The Brownstone 29 Leavenworth St., 597-1838 (MW,S,WC) 5pm-1am, clsd Mon

Maxie's Cafe 2627 Waterbury Rd., 574-1629 (MW,D,E) 6pm-1am, til 2am Fri-Sat, clsd Mon

SPIRITUAL GROUPS
Integrity/Waterbury Area 16 Church St. (St. John's), 754-3116, call for mtg times

CRUISY AREAS
Lakewood Ponds (AYOR)

West Haven (203)

ACCOMMODATIONS
Beach Club 295 Beach St., 937-8100 (MW,D,F,SW,WC) also bar, opens 4pm

Westport (203)

BARS
The Brook Cafe 919 Post Rd. E., 222-2233 (✶M,D,E,S,WC) 5pm-1am, til 2am Fri-Sat, 4pm-11pm Sun, patio

Wethersfield (203)

EROTICA
▲ **Video Expo** 1870 Berlin Turnpike, 257-8663

Willimantic (860)

EROTICA
Dan's Adult World 1110 Main St., 456-3780

Thread City Book & Novelty 503 Main St., 456-8131

DELAWARE

Bethany Beach

INFO LINES & SERVICES
▲ **Community Real Estate Referrals** (800) 346-5592, gay realtor at your service, no rentals

Bethany Village (302)

BARS
Nomad Village Rte. 1 (3 mi. N. in Tower Shores), 539-7581 (MW,NH) 10am-1am (seasonal), also Oasis (MW,D)

Dover (302)

INFO LINES & SERVICES
▲ **Community Real Estate Referrals** (800) 346-5592, gay realtor at your service, no rentals

BARS
Rumors 2206 N. DuPont Hwy., 678-8805 (✶MW,D,F,S,WC) 11am-2am, from 5pm Sun

TRAVEL & TOUR OPERATORS
Delaware Tourism Office PO Box 1401, 19903, (800) 441-8846

New Castle (302)

EROTICA
Discount Adult Books
174 S. DuPont Hwy., 328-4812

Rehoboth Beach (302)

INFO LINES & SERVICES
Camp Rehoboth 39-B Baltimore Ave., 227-5620, 10am-5pm, clsd wknds, info service for lesbigay businesses, also newsletter

▲ **Community Real Estate Referrals** (800) 346-5592, gay realtor at your service, no rentals

ACCOMMODATIONS
At Melissa's B&B 36 Delaware Ave., 227-7504/(800) 396-8090 (GF)

Beach House B&B 15 Hickman St., 227-7074/(800) 283-4667 (GF,SW)

Mallard Guest House 67 Lake Ave., 226-3448 (MW) also 60 Baltimore Ave.

▲ **The Rams Head** RD 2 Box 509, 226-9171 (MO,SW,N) hot tub, gym, openbar

Rehoboth Guest House 40 Maryland Ave., 227-4117 (MW) Victorian beach house

Renegade Restaurant & Lounge/Motel 4274 Hwy. 1, 227-4713 (★MW,D,F,SW,WC) dinner only, full bar, 10-acre resort

Sand in My Shoes Canal & 6th St., 226-2006/(800) 231-5856 (MW) sundeck, some kitchenettes

▲ **Shore Inn at Rehoboth** 703 Rehoboth Ave., 227-8487/(800) 597-8899 (M,SW) seasonal, hot tub

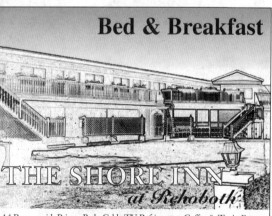

▲ **Silverlake** 133 Silver Lake Dr., Rehoboth, 226-2115/(800) 842-2115 (MW,IGTA) nr. Poodle Beach

BARS

Blue Moon 35 Baltimore Ave., 227-6515 (★MW) 4pm-2am, clsd Jan, dinner, Sun brunch

RESTAURANTS & CAFES

Back Porch Cafe 59 Rehoboth Ave., 227-3674 (WC) lunch & dinner, Sun brunch, seasonal

Celsius 50-C Wilmington Ave., 227-5767 (WC) 5:30pm-11pm, northern Italian & French

Iguana Grill 52 Baltimore Ave., 227-0948, 11am-1am, Southwestern, patio, full bar

Java Beach 59 Baltimore Ave., 227-8418, 7am-6pm, patio

La La Land 22 Wilmington Ave., 227-3887, 6pm-1am (seasonal), patio, full bar

Mano's Restaurant & Bar 10 Wilmington Ave., 227-6707, 5pm-10pm

Square One 37 Wilmington Ave., 227-1994 (MW) 5pm-1am (seasonal)

Sydney's Side Street Restaurant & Blues Place 25 Christian St., 227-1339 (E) 5pm-1am, from 11am Sun, clsd Mon-Tue, patio, full bar

Tijuana Taxi 207 Rehoboth Ave., 227-1986 (WC) 5pm-10pm, from noon wknds

The West Side Cafe 137 Rehoboth, 226-0888 (MW,WC) 6pm-1am, bar opens 5pm

GYMS & HEALTH CLUBS

Body Shop 401 N. Boardwalk, 226-0920 (MW) 8am-7pm

CRUISY AREAS
Cape Henlopen State Park Beach (AYOR)
Carpenter's Beach below S. end of Boardwalk at foot of Queen St. (AYOR)
Poodle Beach S. park of Boardwalk (AYOR)

Wilmington (302)

INFO LINES & SERVICES
▲ **Community Real Estate Referrals** (800) 346-5592, gay realtor at your service, no rentals
Gay AA at the Gay/Lesbian Alliance, 8pm Tue & Th
Gay/Lesbian Alliance of Delaware 601 Delaware Ave., 652-6776, 10am-9pm, til 7pm Sat, clsd Sun

BARS
814 Club 814 Shipley St., 657-5730 (MW,D) 5pm-1am
Everybody's 11 E. 4th St. (upstairs) (MW,D,MRC-AF,AYOR) opens 10pm Wed-Sat
Renaissance 107 W. 6th St., 652-9435 (★MW,D,F,E) 10am-2am, sandwiches served
Roam 913 Shipley St. (upstairs), 658-7626 (★MW,D,MRC-AF,YC) 5pm-1am

RESTAURANTS & CAFES
The Shipley Grill 913 Shipley St., 652-7797, lunch & dinner

SPIRITUAL GROUPS
More Light Hanouver Presb. Church (18th & Baynard), 764-1594, 1st & 3rd Sun, dinner 5:30pm & worship 6:45pm

CRUISY AREAS
8th St. btwn. Shipley & Tetnell
Brandywine Park Footbridge & Woods (AYOR)

DISTRICT OF COLUMBIA

Washington (202)

INFO LINES & SERVICES
Asians & Friends (202) 387-2742
BiCentrist Alliance PO Box 2254, 20013-2254, (202) 828-3065
▲ **Community Real Estate Referrals** (800) 346-5592, gay realtor at your service, no rentals
▲ **D.C. Confidential Connection** 408-7878, Meet hot local guys! Record, listen, respond to free ads. Use free code 9966.
Gay/Lesbian Hotline (Whitman-Walker Clinic), (202) 833-3234, 7pm-11pm
Gay/Lesbian Switchboard 628-4667/628-4669
Hola Gay 332-2192, 7pm-11pm Th, hotline en español
Latino/a Lesbian/Gay Organization (LLEGO) 703 'G' St. SE, 466-8240, 9am-6pm Mon-Fri, bi-monthly newsletter 'Noticias de LLEGO'
Lesbian/Gay Youth Helpline (at Sexual Minority Youth Assistance League), (202) 546-5911, 7pm-10pm M-F
Transgender Education Association PO Box 16036, Arlington VA, 22215, (301) 949-3822, social/support group for crossdressers & transsexuals
Triangle Club 2030 'P' St. NW, 659-8641, various 12-Step groups, see listings in 'The Washington Blade'

ACCOMMODATIONS

1836 California 1836 California St. NW, 462-6502/Fax: 265-0342 (GF) historic house (1900), sundeck

The Brenton 1708 16th St. NW, 332-5550/(800) 673-9042 (M,IGTA)

Capitol Hill Guest House 101 5th St. NE, 547-1050 (GF) Victorian rowhouse in historic Capitol Hill district

The Carlyle Suites 1731 New Hampshire Ave. NW, 234-3200/(800) 964-5377 (GF,F,WC) art deco hotel, Neon Cafe

The Embassy Inn 1627 16th St. NW, 234-7800/(800) 423-9111 (GF)

▲ **Kalorama Guest House at Kalorama Park** 1854 Mintwood Pl. NW, 667-6369/Fax: 319-1262 (GF,IGTA)

▲ **Kalorama Guest House at Woodley Park** 2700 Cathedral Ave. NW, 328-0860/Fax: 319-1262 (GF,IGTA)

The River Inn 924 25th St. NW (at 'K' St.), 337-7600/(800) 424-2741 (GF,WC) also 'Foggy Bottom Cafe'

Savoy Suites Hotel 2505 Wisconsin Ave. NW, Georgetown, 337-9700/(800) 944-5377 (GF,WC) Italian restaurant

The William Lewis House B&B 1309 'R' St. NW, 462-7574 (M) turn-of-the-century B&B

The Windsor Inn 1842 16th St. NW, 667-0300/(800) 423-9111 (GF)

BARS

The Annex (upstairs in Badlands bar), 296-0505 (M,S,V)

Bachelors Mill (downstairs in Back Door Pub), 544-1931 (MW,D,MRC-AF,S,WC) 8pm-2am, til 5am Fri-Sat, clsd Mon

Back Door Pub 1104 8th St. SE, 546-5979 (M,MRC-AF) 5pm-2am, til 3am Fri-Sat

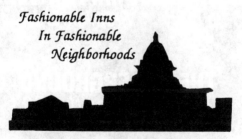

*Fashionable Inns
In Fashionable
Neighborhoods*

o *Walk to Dupont Circle, fashionable
clubs and restuarants, and the subway (Metro)*
o *Enjoy breakfast and evening aperitif*

THE KALORAMA GUEST HOUSES
Kalorama Park (202) 667-6369
Woodley Park (202) 328-0860

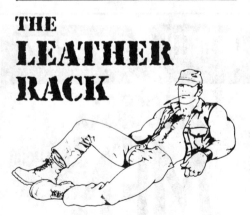

Badlands 1415 22nd St. NW, 296-0505 (M,D,V,YC,WC) 9pm-2am, til 5am Fri-Sat, clsd Mon & Wed

Bent 1344 'U' St. NW, 986-6364 (GF,D,V) 9pm-3am Fri-Sat

Cafe Escandalo 2122 'P' St., 822-8909 (MW,D,MRC-L) 4pm-2am, til 5am Fri & Sat, Tex/Mex restaurant

Chief Ike's Mambo Room 1725 Columbia Rd. NW, 332-2211 (GF,D) 4pm-2am

▲ **The Circle** 1629 Connecticut Ave. NW, 462-5575 (★M,D,S) 11am-2am, also "Dining on the Avenue" upstairs

▲ **D.C. Eagle** 639 New York Ave. NW, 347-6025 (★M,L,WC) 6pm-2am, from noon Fri-Sun, til 3am Fri-Sat

The Delta Elite Social Club 2734 10th St. NE, 529-0626

Diversité 1526 14th St. NW, 234-5740 (GF, D) Fri & Sun only

The Edge 56 'L' St. SE, 488-1200/488-1202 (M,F,V,WC) 9pm-close Mon-Thur, 10pm-5am Fri & Sat

El Faro 2411 18th St. NW, 387-6554 (MW, MRC-L,E) noon-2am, Mexican/El Salvadorean restaurant

▲ **Fireplace** 2161 'P' St. NW, 293-1293 (M,NH,V) 1pm-2am

Fraternity House 2122 'P' St. NW (rear entrance), 223-4917 (★M,D,V,YC) 4pm-2am, 8pm-5am wknds

▲ **Green Lantern** 1335 Green Court NW, 638-5133 (★M,V) 1pm-2am

▲ **J.R.'s Bar & Grill** 1519 17th St. NW, 328-0090 (★M,V,YC) 11am-2am, til 3am Fri-Sat, cruisy, hot cocktail hour

La Cage Aux Follies 18 'O' St. SE, 554-3615 (★M,S,V,YC) 7:30pm-2am, til 3am Fri-Sat, nude go-go boys

Larry's Lounge 1836 18th St. (at 'T' St. NW), 483-1483 (M,NH,F,WC) 5pm-midnight, til 2am Fri-Sat

Mr. Henry's Capitol Hill 601 Pennsylvania Ave. SE, 546-8412 (★GF,F,WC) full restaurant

Mr. P's 2147 'P' St. NW, 293-1064 (M,V) 3pm-2am

Nob Hill 1101 Kenyon NW, 797-1101 (M,D,MRC-AF,F,S) 5pm-2am, from 6pm wknds

Phase One 525 8th St. SE, 544-6831 (W,NH,D,WC) 7pm-2am, til 3am Fri-Sat

Remington's 639 Pennsylvania Ave. SE, 543-3113 (★M,D,CW,V,WC) 4pm-2am

Tavern Terrace 1629 Connecticut Ave. NW (at the Circle), 462-5575 (★MW,K,V,PC) 2pm-2am, til 3am Fri-Sat

Tracks 1111 First St. SE, 488-3320 (★MW,D,A,F,YC,WC) 9pm-4am

Trumpets 1603 17th St. NW, 232-4141 (★MW,P,WC) 4pm-2am, from 11am Sun (brunch), New American restaurant

▲ **The Underground** 1629 Connecticut Ave. NW (at The Circle bar), 462-5575 (★MW,E,S,V,YC) 9pm-2am

▲ **Wet** 56 'L' St. SE, 488-1200/488-1202 (M,F,V,WC) 7pm-2am Sun-Thur, til 3am Fri-Sat, go-go boys in showers

Ziegfields 1345 Half St. SE, 554-5141 (MW,D,A,E,WC) 8pm-3am Th-Sun, also 'Secrets' strip bar (entrance on 'O' St. SE)

RESTAURANTS & CAFES

Annie's Paramount Steak House 1609 17th St. NW, 232-0395 (★) opens 11am, 24hrs Fri-Sat, full bar

Arizona 1211 Connecticut Ave. NW, 785-1211 (D) 11:30am-9:30pm, Southwestern, plenty veggie, dance club Th-Sat til 2am, clsd Sun

1997 Damron Address Book

Armand's Chicago Pizza 4231 Wisconsin Ave. NW, 686-9450, 10am-11pm, til 1am Fri-Sat, full bar; also 226 Massachusetts Ave. NE, Capitol Hill, 547-6600; also full bar, also 226 Massachusetts Ave. NE, Capitol Hill, 547-6600

The Belmont Kitchen 2400 18th St. NW, 667-1200 (WC) clsd Mon, popular brunch plenty veggie, patio, also full bar

Cafe Berlin 322 Massachusetts Ave. NE, 543-7656, lunch & dinner, dinner only Sun, German

Cafe Japoné 2032 'P' St. NW, 223-1573 (MRC-A,E,K) 5:30pm-2am, Japanese, full bar, live jazz

Cafe Luna 1633 'P' St., 387-4005 (★MW,MRC) 11am-11pm

Gabriel 2121 'P' St. NW, 956-6690 (E,WC) 10:30am-midnight, Southwestern, full bar

Greenwood 1990 'K' St., 833-6572 (WC) lunch & dinner, clsd Sun, vegetarian/seafood, full bar

Guapo's 4515 Wisconsin Ave. NW, 686-3588 (WC) lunch & dinner, Mexican, full bar

Hanibal's Connecticut Ave. at 'Q' St. NW, 232-5100 (WC) 7am-10pm, til 11pm Fri-Sat, coffee, desserts

HIV+ Coffeehouse 2111 Florida Ave. NW (Friends Meeting House), 483-3310, 7:30pm-10:30pm Sat, HIV+ & friends

Howard's Grill 613 Pennsylvania Ave. SE, 543-2850 (MW,WC) 11am-2am, American, full bar

The Islander 1762 Columbia Rd. NW, 234-4955 (BYOB) noon-10pm, from 5pm Mon, clsd Sun, Caribbean

Lauriol Plaza 1801 18th St. NW, 387-0035, noon-midnight, Latin American

Pepper's 1527 17th St. NW, 328-8193 (WC) global American, full bar

Roxanne 2319 18th St. NW, 462-8330, 5pm-11pm, bar til 2am wknds, Tex/Mex, also Peyote Cafe

Sala Thai 2016 'P' St. NW, 872-1144, lunch & dinner

Skewers 1633 'P' St. NW, 387-7400 (★) noon-11pm, Middle Eastern, full bar

Straits of Malaya 1836 18th St. NW, 483-1483 (MW) lunch & dinner, Singaporean/Malaysian, rooftop patio, full bar

Trio 1537 17th St. NW, 232-6305 (WC) 7:30am-midnight, full bar

Trocadero Cafe 1914 Connecticut Ave. (Hotel Pullman), 797-2000 (WC) intimate French restaurant

Two Quail 320 Massachusetts Ave. NE, 543-8030 (★) lunch Mon-Fri & dinner nightly, New American, full bar

BOOKSTORES & RETAIL SHOPS

Earth Star Connection 1218 31st St. NW, 965-2989, 10am-7pm, Native American handcrafts, rock shop, crystals

Kramer Books & Afterwords 1517 Connecticut Ave. NW, 387-1400 (WC) opens 7:30am, 24hrs wknds, also cafe

Lambda Rising 1625 Connecticut Ave., 462-6969 (WC) 10am-midnight, lesbigay bookstore

The Map Store, Inc. 1636 'I' St. NW, 628-2608/(800) 544-2659, extensive maps & travel guides

Outlook 1706 Connecticut Ave. NW, 745-1469 (WC) 10am-10pm, til midnight Fri-Sat, cards, gifts, etc.

Vertigo Books 1337 Connecticut Ave. NW, 429-9272 (WC) 10am-7pm, noon-5pm Sun, global politics, literature, African-American emphasis

CREW CLUB

**We Have All The
Equiptment You
Need!
24 Hours A Day**

1321 14th Street NW
Washington DC 20005
(202) 319-1333
Lockers * Private Dressing Rooms* Movies
Pool Table * Tanning * Full Gym
Cable Cross * Hot Music
Hot 1/2 Price Night * Tuesday 8AM to Midnight
Photo ID Required

TRAVEL & TOUR OPERATORS

▲ **Kasper's Livery Service** 201 'I' St. Ste. 512, 554-2471/(800) 455-2471, limousine service serving DC, MD & VA

Passport Executive Travel 1025 Thomas Jefferson St. NW, 337-7718/(800) 222-9800 (IGTA)

Travel Escape 1725 'K' St. NW, 223-9354/(800) 223-4163 (IGTA)

Washington, DC Convention & Visitors Association 1212 New York Ave. NW, 789-7000

SPIRITUAL GROUPS

Bet Mishpachah 5 Thomas Cir. NW, 833-1638, 8:30pm Fri, lesbigay synagogue

Dignity Washington 1820 Connecticut Ave. NW (St. Margaret's Church), 387-4516, 4:30pm & 7:30pm Sun

Faith Temple (Evangelical) 1313 New York Ave. NW, 232-4911, 1pm Sun

Friends (Quaker) 2111 Florida Ave. NW (enter on Decatur), 483-3310, 9am, 10am, 11am Sun, 7pm Wed

Lambda Light-DC PO Box 7355, Silver Springs MD, 20907, (301) 961-1001, new age meditation group

MCC Washington 474 Ridge St. NW, 638-7373, 9am, 11am & 7pm Sun

More Light Presbyterians 400 'I' St. SW (Westminister Church), 484-7700, 7pm, 11am Sun

PUBLICATIONS

LLEGO Informacion 300 'I'St. NE, 4th flr., 544-0092, latino newsletter

▲ **MW/Metro Arts & Entertainment** 1649 Hobart St. NW, 20010, 588-5220

Washington Blade 1408 'U' St. NW, 2nd flr., 797-7000, weekly

MEN'S CLUBS
Club Washington 20 'O' St. SE (upstairs), 488-7317 (MO,PC) 24hrs
▲ **Crew Club** 1321 14th St. NW, 319-1333, 24 hrs
GHC (The Gloryhole) 24 'O' St. SE, 863-2770, 11am-3am, 24hrs Fri-Sat

EROTICA
Follies 24 'O' St. SE (upstairs), 484-0323, 24hrs
▲ **Leather Rack** 1723 Connecticut Ave. NW, 797-7401
▲ **Pleasure Place** 1710 Connecticut Ave. NW, 483-3297, leather, body jewelry

CRUISY AREAS
23rd & 'N' St. (AYOR)
Beach Drive in Rock Creek Park, above 16th St. (AYOR)
DuPont Circle (AYOR)

FLORIDA

Amelia Island (904)

ACCOMMODATIONS
The Amelia Island Williams House 103 S. 9th St., 277-2328

Boca Raton (407)

INFO LINES & SERVICES
▲ **Community Real Estate Referrals** (800) 346-5592, gay realtor at your service, no rentals

ACCOMMODATIONS
Floresta Historic B&B 755 Alamanda St., 391-1451 (MW,SW)

BARS
Choices 21073 Powerline Rd. 2nd flr., 482-2195 (M,D,E,V,WC) 3pm-2am, til 3am Fri-Sat

SPIRITUAL GROUPS
Church of Our Savior MCC 4770 Boca Raton Blvd. Ste. C, 998-0454 (WC) 10:30am & 7pm Sun

CRUISY AREAS
Spanish River Park

Bonita Springs (941)

TRAVEL & TOUR OPERATORS
Bonita Beach Travel 4365 Bonita Beach Rd. #124, (800) 856-4575/498-0877 (IGTA)

Bradenton (941)

EROTICA
C&J's Adult Center 4949 14th St. W, 755-9076

CRUISY AREAS
Coquina Beach

Cape Canaveral

CRUISY AREAS
Jetty Park & Beach (AYOR) days

Cape Coral (941)

RESTAURANTS & CAFES
Palate Pleasers 3512 Del Prado South, 945-6333

Clearwater (813)

INFO LINES & SERVICES
▲ **Community Real Estate Referrals** (800) 346-5592, gay realtor at your service, no rentals
Gay/Lesbian Referrral Service of Pinellas County 586-4297, 7pm-11pm, touch-tone service 24hrs

BARS
Lost & Found 5858 Roosevelt Blvd. (State Rd. 686), 539-8903 (M,S,WC) 4pm-2am, clsd Mon

Mango's 18425 US 19 N., 531-4431 (M,K,S,WC) 2pm-2am

Pro Shop Pub 840 Cleveland, 447-4259 (★M,NH) 11:30am-2am, from 1pm Sun

Cocoa Beach (407)

INFO LINES & SERVICES

▲ **Community Real Estate Referrals** (800) 346-5592, gay realtor at your service, no rentals

BARS

Blondies 5450 N. Atlantic Ave., 783-5339 (MW,NH,D,WC) 2pm-2am

RESTAURANTS & CAFES

Mango Tree 118 N. Atlantic Ave., 799-0513 (WC) opens 6pm, clsd Mon, fine dining

SPIRITUAL GROUPS

Breaking the Silence MCC 1261 Range Rd., Cocoa, 631-4524, 7pm Sun

Crescent City (904)

ACCOMMODATIONS

Crescent City Campground Rt 2 Box 25, 32112, 698-2020/(800) 634-3968 (GF,SW)

Daytona Beach (904)

INFO LINES & SERVICES

▲ **Community Real Estate Referrals** (800) 346-5592, gay realtor at your service, no rentals

Gracious Accommodations

"Beautifully appointed guest rooms… a romantic hideaway… impeccable service." - *Our World Magazine*

Antique-filled rooms, private baths, victorian soaking tubs (we supply the bubbles), full gourmet breakfasts, fresh flowers, fireplaces, bicycles. Close to beach, dining, night life.

The Coquina Inn B&B

544 S. Palmetto Ave. • Daytona Beach, FL 32114

904-254-4969 800-805-7533

email: coquina@travelbase.com

Lambda Center 320 Harvey Ave., 255-0280

Live & Let Live AA 1130-B Ridgewood Ave. (Easy Does It Club), 258-9407 (WC)

RESPECT, Inc. PO Box 5218, 32118, 257-7071, gay youth educational group, referrals

ACCOMMODATIONS

Buccaneer Motel 2301 N. Atlantic Ave., 253-9678/(800) 972-6056 (GF,SW,IGTA)

▲ **Coquina Inn** 544 S. Palmetto Ave., 254-4969/(800) 805-7533 (GF,SW,WC,IGTA)

The Villa 801 N. Peninsula Dr., 248-2020/Fax: 248-2020 (GF,SW,N,IGTA) historic Spanish mansion

BARS

7-69 Restaurant & Lounge 769 Alabama, 253-4361 (MW,NH,WC) 5pm-3am

Barndoor 615 Main St., 252-3776 (MW,NH,F) 11am-3am

The Barracks 952 Orange Ave., 254-3464 (★M,D,S,V,WC) 3pm-3am, from 4pm Sun (BBQ)

Beach Side Club 415 Main St., 252-5465 (★M,D,S) 2pm-3am, from noon wknds

RESTAURANTS & CAFES

Cafe Frappes 174 Beach St., 254-7999, patio

TRAVEL & TOUR OPERATORS

Monahan Travel Services 485 S. Nova Rd., Daytona, (800) 476-5876/677-4495 (IGTA)

SPIRITUAL GROUPS

Hope MCC 56 N. Halifax (Unitarian Church), 254-0993, 7pm Sun

CRUISY AREAS

Boardwalk & beach in front of sightseeing tower & bandshell (AYOR)

Dunedin (813)

BARS

1470 West 325 Main St., 736-5483 (MW,D,E,S,WC) 4pm-2am, from 8pm Mon

Fort Lauderdale (954)

INFO LINES & SERVICES

▲ **Community Real Estate Referrals** (800) 346-5592, gay realtor at your service, no rentals

▲ **Fort Lauderdale Confidential Connection** 497-3000, Meet hot local guys! Record, listen, respond to free ads. Use free code 9966.

Gay/Lesbian Community Center 1164 E. Oakland Park Blvd., 563-9500 (WC) 10am-10pm

Lambda South 1231 E. Las Olas Blvd., 761-9072 (WC) 12-step clubhouse

ACCOMMODATIONS

215 Guesthouse 215 SW 7th Ave., 527-4900 (M)

▲ **Admiral's Court** 21 Hendricks Isle, 462-5072/(800) 248-6669 (MW,SW,IGTA)

▲ **Big Ruby's Guest House** 908 NE 15th Ave., 523-7829 (MO,SW,N)

The Blue Dolphin 725 N. Birch Rd., 565-8437/(800) 893-2583 (MO,SW,IGTA)

Club Caribbean Resort 2851 N. Federal Hwy., 565-0402/Fax: 565-1565 (MW,SW,IGTA)

▲ **Edun House** 2733 Middle River Dr., 565-7775/(800) 479-1767 (M,SW,N) patio, cont'l brkfst

Kelly's Guesthouse 1909 SW 2nd St., 462-6035 (MO,SW,N)

- Rooms • Efficiencies
- Suites

Our centralized location on

scenic waterway is only a short walk

to beach or fashionable Las Olas Blvd.'s

shopping, dining and nightlife.

Two pools, BBQ, Refrigerator in

rooms. Friendly atmosphere

Call about our affordable rates.

800-248-6669

Admiral's Court
A Superior Resort On Scenic Waterfront
21 Hendrick's Isle, Ft. Lauderdale, FL 33301 • 954-462-5072 • FAX 954-763-8863

FT. LAUDERDALE

Big Ruby's

Tropical Key West Style Guesthouse in the Heart of Ft. Lauderdale

- Singles, doubles, and suites with private bath, cable/movie, TV-VCR and selection of tapes, Bahama fans, and refrigerator
- Large tropical pool with cascading waterfall
- Nude sundeck • Workout Area • Central to bars, clubs & beaches
- Affordable rates

(954) 523-7829
908 N.E. 15th Ave., Ft. Lauderdale, Fla. 33304

King Henry Arms Motel 543 Breakers Ave., 561-0039/(800) 205-5464 (MW,SW,IGTA)

La Casa del Mar 3003 Granada St., 467-2037/(800) 739-0009 (MW,SW,IGTA) exclusively lesbian & gay , non-cruisy

▲ **Midnight Sea** 3005 Alhambra St., 463-4827 (M,N) hot tub

Orton Terrace 606 Orton Ave., 566-5068/(800) 323-1142 (GF,SW,IGTA) apts & motel units

▲ **The Palms on Las Olas** 1760 E. Las Olas Blvd., 462-4178/(800) 550-7656 (MO,SW,IGTA)

Robindale Suites 709 Breakers Ave., 565-4123/(800) 342-7109 (GF,SW)

▲ **The Royal Palms Resort** 2901 Terramar, 564-6444/(800) 237-7256 (★MO,SW,IGTA)

Saint Sebastian Guest Suites 2835 Terramar, Fort Lauderdale Beach, 568-6161/(800) 425-8105 (MO,SW,IGTA) charming Bahamian style villa

▲ **Sea Eagle Guest House** 2609 NE 13 Court, 568-0292

BARS

825 825 E. Sunrise Blvd., 524-3333 (★ M,D,S) 1pm-2am

Adventures 303 SW 6th St., Pompano Beach, 782-9577 (MW,NH,F,WC) 2pm-2am

Boot's 901 SW 27th Ave., 792-9177 (M,CW,L,WC) noon-2am, til 3am Sat

Bus Stop 2203 S. Federal Hwy., 761-1782 (M,NH) noon-2am

Bushes 3038 N. Federal Hwy., 561-1724 (★M,NH,E,WC) 9am-2am, til 3am Sat

Club Caribbean 2851 N. Federal Hwy., 565-0402 (★M,D)

FORT LAUDERDALE BEACH

midnight sea

ART DECO GUESTHOUSE
The Nearest (60 yards) from Gay Beach
Calm & close to Nightlife
AC, fridge, cable TV, tel., jacuzzi, sundeck, breakfast, rentals
USA & CAN-1-800-910-2357
1-954-463-4827 / 3005 Alhambra Street
FORT LAUDERDALE, FL 33304 USA

SEA EAGLE
GUEST HOUSE

BEACH AND CENTRAL

GAY AND LEATHER
BARS LOCATION

POOL. SPA. BBQ. TV. VCR. GYM.
AC. KITCHEN. PARKING. TELEPHONE
CONT. BREAKFAST. PET OK.

2609. NORTHEAST. 13TH COURT
FT. LAUDERDALE. FLORIDA. 33308
(954) 568-0292 FAX. (954) 390-0904

Club Cathode Ray 1105 E. Las Olas Blvd., 462-8611 (★M,V) 2pm-2am, til 3am Sat

Club Electra 1600 SE 15th Ave., 764-8447 (MW,D,S) call for events

▲ **Copa** 624 SE 28th St., 463-1507 (MW,D,E,V,YC) 9pm-4am

Cubby Hole 823 N. Federal Hwy., 728-9001 (M,NH,L,WC) noon-2am, til 3am Sat

Eagle 1951 Powerline Rd. (NW 9th Ave.), 462-6380 (★M,L,WC) 2pm-2am

End Up 3521 W. Broward Blvd., 584-9301 (M,D) 9pm-4am

Everglades Bar 1931 S. Federal Hwy., 462-9165 (M,NH,WC) 9am-2am, from noon Sun

Gold Coast Bar & Grill 2471 E. Commercial, 492-9222 (M,K,S) 2pm-2am

Grotto 1914 E. Oakland Park Blvd., 563-0721 (M,NH,S) noon-2am, Sat TV/TG night

Hideaway 2022 NE 18th St., 566-8622 (M,V) 9am-2am, from 2pm Sun & Mon

I-beam 3045 N. Federal Hwy., 561-2424 (M,D,V) 4pm-2am

Johnny's 1116 W. Broward Blvd., 522-5931 (M,NH,S) 11am-2am, from noon Sun

Jungle 545 S. Federal Hwy., 832-9550 (M,V)

Lefty's 710 N. Federal Hwy. (entrance in rear), 764-2752 (★M,NH,S) 8am-2am

Our Placehouse 1608 E. Commercial Blvd., 771-0001 (W,NH,E) 4pm-2am, from 2pm Sun

Ramrod 1508 NE 4th Ave., 763-8219 (M,L) 3pm-2am, uniform dress code, patio

Side Street 1753 N. Andrews Ave., 525-2007 (M,V) 2pm-2am, karaoke Th-Fri

Stanley's 626 S. Federal Hwy., 523-9769 (M,S) 9pm-2am, til 3am Sat

▲ **The Stud** 1000 State Rd. 84, 525-7883 (M,D,S) 5pm-2am, from 2pm Sun

Tropic's Cabaret & Restaurant 2004 Wilton Dr., 537-6000 (M,NH,D,WC) 4pm-2am

RESTAURANTS & CAFES

Chardee's 2209 Wilton Dr., 563-1800 (MW,P,E,WC) 5pm-2am, full bar

Courtyard Cafe 2211 Wilton Dr., 564-9365, 7am-4pm, til 2pm wkds

Dalt's Grill 1245 N. Federal, 565-2333, cont'l

The Deck 401 N. Atlantic (Bahama Hotel), 467-7315, oceanfront cafe, cont'l

Galeria G'Vannis: The Boulevard Dining Gallery 625 E. Las Olas Blvd., 524-5246 (E,WC) Italian, full bar

Legends Cafe 1560 NE 4th Ave. (Wilton Manors Dr.), 467-2233 (MW,BYOB,WC) 6pm-10pm, clsd Mon

Lester's Diner 250 State Rd. 84, 525-5641 (★) 24hrs, more gay late nights

Sukothai 1930 E. Sunrise Blvd., 764-0148 (★) Thai

Victor Victoria's 2345 Wilton Dr., 563-6296 (E,WC) 6pm-2am, Italian, full bar

Victoria Park 900 NE 20th Ave., 764-6868 (BW) dinner only, call for reservations

Wild Cactus Cafe 303 SW 6th St., Pomano Beach, 784-1445, 5:30pm-11pm, clsd Sun & Mon, Tex-Mex

BOOKSTORES & RETAIL SHOPS

Audace 813 E. Las Olas Blvd., 522-7503, from 10am, from noon Sun

Fallen Angel 3045 N. Federal Hwy., 563-5230, opens 11am, leather, cards, toys

Hot Spots 5100 NE 12th Ave., 928-1862, bar guide, weekly

J. Miles Clothing 1023 E. Las Olas Blvd., 462-2710

TRAVEL & TOUR OPERATORS
Tom Rosenblatt Travel 927-8697/(800) 877-8389 (IGTA)
Up, Up & Away 701 E. Broward Blvd., 523-4944/(800) 234-0841 (IGTA)

SPIRITUAL GROUPS
Congregation Etz Chaim 3970 NW 21st. Ave., 714-9232, 8:30pm Fri, gay/lesbian synagogue
Dignity Fort Lauderdale 330 SW 27th St. (at MCC location), 463-4528, 2nd & 4th Sun
Sunshine Cathedral MCC 330 SW 27th St., 462-2004 (WC) 8:30am, 10am, 11:30am, 7pm Sun

PUBLICATIONS
Scoop Magazine 2219 Wilton Dr., 561-9707

MEN'S CLUBS
▲ **Club Fort Lauderdale** 400 W. Broward Blvd., 525-3344 (MO,SW,PC) full gym
Clubhouse II 2650 E. Oakland Park Blvd., 566-6750 (MO,V,PC) 24hrs, full gym

EROTICA
▲ **Catalog X** 850 NE 13th St., 524-5050, 10am-9pm, noon-6pm Sun, free catalog
Fetish Factory 821 N. Federal Hwy., 462-0032, 11am-7pm, noon-6pm Sun
Jaybird's Toybox (at Copa's bar), 791-8655
Omni Book & Video 3224 W. Broward Blvd., 584-6825, 24hrs
Secrets 4509 N. Pine Island Rd., Sunrise, 748-5855

CRUISY AREAS
Holiday Park (AYOR)

COPA

2800 S. FEDERAL HWY • FT. LAUDERDALE, FL • (954) 463-1507
Winner of WAVE Magazine's "Best Gay Bar in South Florida"

Fort Myers (941)

INFO LINES & SERVICES
▲ **Community Real Estate Referrals** (800) 346-5592, gay realtor at your service, no rentals

Gay Switchboard PO Box 546, 33902, 332-2272, 8am-11pm, also publishes 'Support-line' newsletter

BARS
Attitudes 1605 Hedry St., 332-3504 (M,D,WC) 3pm-2am

Bottom Line 3090 Evans Ave., 337-7292 (MW,D,V,S,WC) 3pm-2am

Office Pub 3704 Grove, 936-3212 (M,NH,BW) noon-2am

RESTAURANTS & CAFES
Oasis 2222 McGregor Blvd., 334-1566 (BW,WC)

The Velvet Turtle 1404 Cape Coral Pkwy., 549-9000 (WC) 5am-9pm, clsd Sun

SPIRITUAL GROUPS
St. John the Apostle MCC 2209 Unity, 278-5181 (WC) 10am & 7pm Sun, 7pm Wed

CRUISY AREAS
Bunche Beach John Morris Pkwy. (AYOR) south end of beach

Fort Walton Beach (904)

BARS
Frankly Scarlett 223 Hwy. 98 E., 664-2966 (MW,D,S,WC) 8pm-2am, til 4am wknds

Gainesville (352)

INFO LINES & SERVICES
▲ **Community Real Estate Referrals** (800) 346-5592, gay realtor at your service, no rentals

Gay Switchboard 332-0700, volunteers 6pm-11pm, 24hr touchtone service

Lesbian/Gay/Bisexual Student Union (U of FL) PO Box 118505, 32611-8505, 392-1665 x310, several weekly mtgs.

BARS
Ambush Room (at Melody Club), 376-3772 (★M,CW) 4pm-2am

Melody Club 4130 NW 6th St., 376-3772 (★MW,D,S,WC) 8pm-2am, clsd Sun & Mon, small side bar 'Ambush' open 4pm daily, also 'Fishbowl Bar' from 1pm daily

The Oz 7118 W. University Ave., 332-2553 (MW,D,WC) 5pm-2am, 11am-11pm Sun, patio

The University Club 18 E. University Ave., 378-6814 (MW,D,S,WC) 5pm-2am, til 4am Fri-Sat, til 11pm Sun, patio

TRAVEL & TOUR OPERATORS
Destinations PO Box 15321, 32604, 373-3233 (IGTA) publishes resource directory to Gainesville area

SPIRITUAL GROUPS
Trinity MCC 11604 SW Archer Rd., 495-3378 (WC) 10:15am Sun

CRUISY AREAS
Bivens Arm Nature Park (AYOR)

Hallandale (305)

ACCOMMODATIONS
Club Atlantic Resort 2080 S. Ocean Dr., 458-6666/(800) 645-8666 (GF,SW,WC)

Holiday (813)

SPIRITUAL GROUPS
Spirit of Life MCC 4810 Mile Stretch Dr., 942-8616 (WC) 10:30am Sun, 7:30pm Wed

Hollywood (305)

INFO LINES & SERVICES
▲ **Community Real Estate Referrals** (800) 346-5592, gay realtor at your service, no rentals

ACCOMMODATIONS
Maison Harrison Guesthouse 1504 Harrison, 922-7319, spa

BARS
Zachary's 2217 N.Federal Hwy., 920-5479 (W,NH) 4pm-2am, from 11am wknds

EROTICA
Hollywood Book & Video 1235 S. State Rd. 7, 981-2164, 24hrs

CRUISY AREAS
Young Circle

Inverness

ACCOMMODATIONS
▲ **The Caritas B&B Network** (800) CARITAS (227-4827), see ad in center National section

Jacksonville (904)

INFO LINES & SERVICES
▲ **Community Real Estate Referrals** (800) 346-5592, gay realtor at your service, no rentals
Gay/Lesbian Information & Referral System 396-8044

BARS
Boot Rack Saloon 4751 Lenox Ave., 384-7090 (M,CW) 2pm-2am, patio
Eagle 1402-6 San Marco Blvd., 396-8551 (M,L,F,WC) patio
Edgewater Junction 1261 King St., 388-3434 (M,NH,F,BW) 2pm-2am
Exile 616 Park St., 354-2025 (M,NH,S,BW) 3pm-2am, from 5pm wknds, patio
HMS 1702 E. 8th St., 353-9200 (M,NH,BW) 2pm-2am, patio
In Touch Tavern 10957 Atlantic Blvd., 642-7506 (MW,NH,BW,WC) noon-2am, from 3pm Sun
The Metro 2929 Plum St., 388-8719 (MW,NH,D,S,WC) 4pm-2am, clsd Mon, patio
My Little Dude/Jo's Place 2952 Roosevelt Blvd., 388-9503 (W,D,S,WC) 4pm-2am
Park Place Lounge 2712 Park St., 389-6616 (M,NH,WC) noon-2am
Tackee's 1746 Talleyrand, 355-1700 (M) 3pm-2am, patio
Third Dimension 711 Edison Ave., 353-6316 (M,D,A,E,S,WC) 3pm-2am, from 5pm wknds

BOOKSTORES & RETAIL SHOPS
Otherside of the Rainbow 2709 Park St., 389-5515 (WC) 11am-7pm, clsd Sun, pride gift store

SPIRITUAL GROUPS
St. Luke's MCC 1140 S. McDuff Ave., 389-7726, 10am & 6pm Sun

PUBLICATIONS
The Last Word PO Box 60582, 32236, 384-6514/(800) 677-0772

MEN'S CLUBS
Club Jacksonville 1939 Hendricks Ave., 398-7451 (SW,PC) 24hrs

Jacksonville Beach (904)

INFO LINES & SERVICES
▲ **Community Real Estate Referrals** (800) 346-5592, gay realtor at your service, no rentals

BARS
Bo's Coral Reef 201 5th Ave. N., 246-9874 (MW,D,E,S) 2pm-2am

CRUISY AREAS
5th Ave. Beach & S. to Boardwalk

Jasper (904)

ACCOMMODATIONS
The Swan Lake B&B 238 Rte. 129, 792-2771 (MW,SW,N)

Key West (305)

INFO LINES & SERVICES
▲ **Community Real Estate Referrals** (800) 346-5592, gay realtor at your service, no rentals

Gay AA 296-8654, call for times & locations

Helpline 296-4357, gay-friendly referrals & assistance

▲ **Key West Business Guild** PO Box 1208, 33041, 294-4603/(800) 535-7797 (IGTA)

ACCOMMODATIONS
The 1004 Eaton 1004 Eaton St., 296-8132/(800) 352-4414 (MW,SW,N) restored 1880s Conch house

Alexander Palms Court 715 South St., 296-6413/(800) 858-1943 (GF,SW)

Alexander's Guest House 1118 Fleming St., 294-9919/(800) 654-9919 (M,SW,N,IGTA)

▲ **Andrew's Inn** Zero Whalton Lane, 294-7730/Fax: 294-0021 (★MW,SW,WC) elegantly restored rooms & garden cottages

The Artist House 534 Eaton St., 296-3977/(800) 593-7898 (GF) Victorian guesthouse

Atlantic Shores Resort 510 South St., 296-2491/(800) 526-3559 (GF,F,SW,IGTA) also 3 bars

Author's of Key West 725 White St., 294-7381/(800) 898-6909 (GF,SW)

Banana's Foster Bed 537 Caroline St., 294-9061/(800) 653-4888 (GF,SW,WC) historic Conch house B&B

▲ **Big Ruby's Guesthouse** 409 Appelrouth Ln., 296-2323/477-7829 (M,SW,N,WC,IGTA) evening wine service, full brkfst

▲ **Blue Parrot Inn** 916 Elizabeth St., 296-0033/(800) 231-2473 (GF,SW,N)

express yourself

key west

key west

you're among friends

for free directory & assistance
call the key west business guild
800.535.7797 or 305.294.4603

▲ **The Brass Key Guesthouse** 412 Frances St., 296-4719/(800) 932-9119 (★M,SW,WC,IGTA) luxury guesthouse, spa, full brkfst

▲ **Chelsea House** 707 Truman Ave., 296-2211/(800) 845-8859 (GF,SW,N,WC,IGTA)

Coconut Grove Guesthouse 817 Flemming St, 296-5107/(800) 262-6055 (M,SW,N,IGTA) 2 Victorian mansions

▲ **Colours - The Guest Mansion** 410 Fleming St., 294-6977/(800) 277-4825 (★MW,SW,IGTA) complimentary sunset cocktails

▲ **Coral Tree** 822 Fleming, 296-2131/(800) 362-7477 (MO) upscale suites

The Cuban Club Suites 1102-A Duval St., 296-0465/(800) 432-4849 (GF,IGTA) award-winning historic hotel overlooking Duval St.

▲ **Curry House** 806 Fleming St., 294-6777/(800) 633-7439 (★MO,SW,N,IGTA) hot tub

Cypress House 601 Caroline, 294-6969/(800) 525-2488 (★MO,SW,N)

▲ **Duval House** 815 Duval St., 294-1666/(800) 223-8825 (★GF,SW,IGTA)

Duval Suites 724 Duval St., 293-6600/(800) 648-3780 (MW,N)

Early House 507 Simonton St., 296-0214

Eaton Lodge 511 Eaton St., 292-2170/(800) 294-2170 (GF,SW) 1886 mansion & conch house, hot tub

▲ **Equator** 816 Fleming St., 294-7775 (MO)

Garden House 329 Elizabeth St., 296-5368/(800) 695-6453

Heron House 512 Simonton St., 294-9227/937-5656

Incentra Carriage House Inn 729 Whitehead St., 296-5565/(800) 636-7432 (GF,SW,WC) 3 houses surrounding lush garden & pool

▲ **Island House for Men** 1129 Flemming St, 294-6284/(800) 890-6284 (★MO,F,SW,N,IGTA) sauna, gym

▲ **Key Lodge Motel** 1004 Duval St., 296-9750/(800) 458-1296 (★GF,SW)

La Casa de Luces 422 Amelia St., 296-3993/(800) 432-4849 (GF,WC,IGTA) early 1900s Conch house

La Terraza/La Te Da 1125 Duval St., 296-6706/(800) 528-3320 (★MW,SW,IGTA) tropical setting, gourmet restaurant, 2 bars, Sun T-dance

▲ **Lighthouse Court** 902 Whitehead St., 294-9588 (MO,SW,N,IGTA) tropical poolside restaurant & bar

▲ **Lime House Inn** 219 Elizabeth St., 296-2978/(800) 374-4242 (MO,SW,N) hot tub

Mangrove House 623 Southard St., 294-1866/(800) 294-1866 (MO,SW,N) fully restored 'Eyebrow' house

Marquesa Hotel 600 Fleming St., 292-1919/(800) 869-4631 (GF,SW,WC) also 'Cafe Marquesa' 6pm-11pm, full bar

Merlinn Guesthouse 811 Simonton St., 296-3336/(800) 642-4753 (GF,WC) full brkfst

The Mermaid and the Alligator 729 Truman Ave., 294-1894/(800) 773-1894 (GF,SW,N) full brkfst

▲ **Newton Street Station** 1414 Newton St., 294-4288/(800) 248-2457 (MO,SW,N)

▲ **Oasis Guest House** 822/823 Fleming St, 296-2131/(800) 362-7477 (★MO,SW,N,IGTA)

Pegasus International 501 Southard, 294-9323/(800) 397-8148 (GF,F,SW)

Pier House Resort & Caribbean Spa 1 Duval St., 296-4600/(800) 327-8340 (GF,SW) private beach, restaurants, bars, spa, fitness center

DUVAL HOUSE

Escape…To our Historic Inn with breezy tropical gardens in the heart of Old Town…all welcome.

815 Duval St./Key West, FL 33040
(305) 294-1666 • 800-22-DUVAL

LIGHTHOUSE COURT

At Historic Key West Lighthouse, an exquisitely relaxed compound of cottages, rooms, suites and apartments, nestled in over a half-acre of sundecks and tropical gardens. Just a block from Duval Street Bars, Restaurants and Shops. Heated pool, jacuzzi, Health Club, Cafe and Bar, across from Hemingway's House at 902 Whitehead, Key West, FL 33040/(305) 294-9588

Pilot House Guest House 414 Simonton St., 294-8719/(800) 648-3780 (MW,SW,N) 19th century Victorian in Old Town

▲ **The Pines Guest House** 521 United St., 296-7467/(800) 282-7463 (★M,SW,N,IGTA)

▲ **The Sea Isle Resort** 915 Windosr Lane, 294-5188/(800) 995-4786 (★M,SW,N,IGTA) large private courtyard, gym, sundeck

Seascape 420 Olivia, 296-7776/(800) 765-6438 (GF,SW) restored 1889 inn in heart of Old Town

▲ **Simonton Court Historic Inn & Cottages** 320 Simonton St., 294-6386/(800) 944-2687 (★MW,SW,IGTA) 23 unit compound built in 1880s, 3 pools

Tropical Inn 812 Duval St., 294-9977 (GF,SW) hot tub

Watson House 525 Simonton St., 294-6712/(800) 621-9405 (GF,SW)

William Anthony House 613 Caroline St., 294-2887/(800) 613-2276 (GF,SW,WC) complimentary brkfst & social hour

The William House 1317 Duval St., 294-8233/(800) 848-1317 (GF) turn-of-the-century guesthouse, spa

BARS

801 Bar 801 Duval St., 294-4737 (★M,NH,E) 11am-4am, also Dan's Bar from 9pm (M,L)

Bourbon Street Pub 730 Duval St., 296-1992 (MW,E,V,WC) noon-4am

Club International 900 Simonton St., 296-9230 (W,NH,V) 1pm-4am

▲ **Copa** 623 Duval St., 296-8522 (★M,D,E,S,V,YC) patio

Donnie's 618 Duval St. (rear), 294-5620 (GF,NH,WC) 24 hrs

Numbers 1029 Truman, 296-0333 (M,NH,D,S) 2pm-4am

Key West's Hottest New Men's Resort

• Central
• Attentive
• Comfortable
• Tropical
• Lavish

800-278-4552

816-18 Fleming St. Key West, FL 33040 • 305-294-7775

The Sea Isle!

In the Center of Gay Key West

- Great Location…3 Blocks to Duval
- Free Breakfast and Weekend Cocktails
- Deluxe Rooms, A/C, Color TV, Frig and Private Bathrooms
- Large Pool and Great Gym
- Lots of Sunning Space
- Clothing Optional
- Big Towels
- Fun People
- Super Staff
- Private Parking

Sea Isle

Call for Reservations
800-995-4786 • 305-294-5188

915 Windsor Lane • Key West, FL 33040

More than a Guesthouse…

Paradise!

Secluded
Rendezvous

SIMONTON COURT
The Island Resort
Historic Inn *&* Cottages

Quiet. Romantic.
A block from Duval Street
in Key West.

For more information call:
1-800-944-2687

epoch: (ep'e.k) 1. The Beginning of a new and important period in the history of anything.
2. A period of time considered in terms of noteworthy and characteristic events, Developments, Persons, Ect.
3. A point in time or precise date; Now rare, the time at which observations are made, as of the position of planets or stars.

623 Duval Street, Key West Fl. 33040

*In the Copa Memorial Bldg.

305.296.8521 tel
305.296.6640 fax
keepluvn@web2000.net

One Saloon 524 Duval St. (enter on Appelrouth Ln.), 296-8118 (★M,D,WC) 10pm-4am, 3 bars, patio

RESTAURANTS & CAFES

Antonia's 615 Duval St., 294-6565 (★) 6pm-11pm, Northern Italian

B.O.'s Fish Wagon corner of Duval & Fleming, 294-9272 (★) lunch, seafood & eat it

Cafe des Artistes 1007 Simonton St., 294-7100, 6pm-11pm, tropical French, full bar

Croissants de France 816 Duval St., 294-2624 (MW,BW) 7:30am-4pm, French pastries, crepes, gallettes, patio

Dim Sum 613-1/2 Duval St., 294-6230 (BW) clsd Tue, Pan-Asian, sake cocktails

Duffy's Steak & Lobster House 600 Truman Ave., 296-4900, 11am-11pm, also full bar

Dynasty 918 Duval St., 294-2943 (BW) 5:30pm-10pm, Chinese

La Trattoria Venezia 524 Duval St., 296-1075 (MW) Italian, also full bar

Lobos 611 1/2 Duval St., 296-5303 (BW) 11am-6pm,clsd wknds

Louie's Backyard 700 Waddell Ave., 294-1061 (★) lunch & dinner, bar 11:30am-2am, fine dining

Mango's 700 Duval St., 292-4606 (WC) 11am-2am, Internat'l, full bar

Palm Grill 1029 Southard St., 296-1744

Pancho & Lefty's Southwestern Cafe 632 Olivia St., 294-8212, 5pm-10:30pm, clsd Tue, Mexican

The Quay 10 Duval St., 294-4446, gourmet

Rooftop Cafe 310 Front St., 294-2042 (E) American/Caribbean, cocktails

Savannah 915 Duval St., 296-6700 (★MW,BW) dinner nightly, Southern home cooking, garden bar

South Beach Seafood & Raw Bar 1405 Duval St., 294-2727, 7am-10pm

The Twisted Noodle 628 Duval St., 296-6670, 5pm-10:30pm, Italian

Yo Sake 722 Duval St., 294-2288 (BW) 6pm-11pm, Japanese & sushi bar

GYMS & HEALTH CLUBS

Club Body Tech 1075 Duval St., 292-9683 (MW) 6am-11pm, 9am-10pm wknds, full gym, sauna, massage therapy available

Pro Fitness 1111 12th St., 294-1865, 6am-9pm, from 9am-7pm Sat & 11am-5pm Sun

BOOKSTORES & RETAIL SHOPS

Aloegenetic 524 Front St., (800) 445-2563

Blue Heron Books 538 Truman Ave., 296-3508, 10am-10pm, til 9pm Sun, lesbi-gay section

Caroline St. Books & Cafe 800 Caroline St., 294-3931 (WC) 10am-10pm, also coffe bar

Fast Buck Freddie's 500 Duval St., 294-2007, 11am-7pm, clothing, gifts

Key West Island Books 513 Fleming St., 294-2904, 10am-6pm, new & used rare books

Lldo 532 Duval St., 294-5300, 10am-7pm, til 10pm Th-Sat, 11am-7pm Sun, clothing & gifts

Star Gazers 425-A Front St., 296-1186/(800) 291-1186, 10am-10pm, new age, metaphysical

TRAVEL & TOUR OPERATORS

Clione PO Box 1874, 33040, 296-1433, topsail schooner

Escape Cruises Key West Bight marina, 296-4608, 3-hr reef trip & sunset cruise on 'SS Sunshine'

Hans Ebensten Travel 513 Fleming St., 294-8174

IGTA (International Gay Travel Association) PO Box 4974, 33041, 296-6673/(800) 448-8550, active organization for lesbian/gay travel industry

Regency Travel 1075 Duval St. #19, 294-0175/(800) 374-2784 (IGTA)

SPIRITUAL GROUPS

MCC Key West 1215 Petronia St., 294-8912 (WC) 9:30am & 11am Sun

PUBLICATIONS

Southern Exposure 819 Peacock Plaza Ste. 575, 33041, 294-6303, monthly

EROTICA

Alligator News & Books 716 Duval St., 294-4004, 24hrs

Key West Videos 528 Duval St., 292-4113, 24hrs

Leather Masters 418-A Appelrouth Ln., 292-5051, custom leather & more

CRUISY AREAS

'Dick Dock' pier at end of Reynolds St. (AYOR)

Duval St. (AYOR) Queens for days!

Fleming St. (AYOR) Queens for nights!

Ft. Zachary Taylor Beach (AYOR)

Lake Worth (407)

BARS

Inn Exile 6 S. 'J' St., 582-4144 (M,K,V) 3pm-2am, til midnight Sun

K & E's 29 S. Dixie Hwy., 533-6020 (MW,F) 11am-2am, from 2pm wknds

EROTICA
Harold Video 4266 Lake Worth Rd., 964-2470

Lakeland (941)

INFO LINES & SERVICES
PGLA (Polk Gay/Lesbian Alliance) PO Box 8221, 33802-8221, 644-0085

ACCOMMODATIONS
Sunset Motel & RV Resort 2301 New Tampa Hwy., 683-6464 (GF,SW,WC) motels, apts, RV hookups & private home on 3 acres

BARS
Dockside 3770 Hwy. 92 E., 665-2590 (MW,D,E,WC) 4pm-2am
Roy's Green Parrot 1030 E. Main St., 683-6021 (★M,D,S,BW) 4pm-2am, til midnight Sun

Madeira Beach (813)

INFO LINES & SERVICES
▲ **Community Real Estate Referrals** (800) 346-5592, gay realtor at your service, no rentals

BARS
Surf & Sand Lounge/Back Room Bar 14601 Gulf Blvd., 391-2680 (M,NH,WC) 8am-2am, beach access

Melbourne (407)

BARS
Loading Zone 4910 Stack Blvd., 727-3383, 8pm-2am, clsd Mon
Saturday's Lounge 4060 W. New Haven Ave. , 724-1510 (★MW,D,S) 2pm-2am

CRUISY AREAS
Canova Beach (AYOR) nights
Melbourne Harbor Marina (AYOR)

Miami (see also Miami Beach/South Beach) (305)

INFO LINES & SERVICES
▲ **Community Real Estate Referrals** (800) 346-5592, gay realtor at your service, no rentals
Gay/Lesbian/Bisexual Hotline of Greater Miami 759-3661
Lambda Dade AA 573-9608 (WC) 8:30pm daily, call for other mtg. times
Lesbian/Gay/Bisexual Community Center 1335 Alton Rd., 531-3666, 6pm-9pm, clsd Sun-Mon
South Beach Business Guild 234-7224, maps & info
Switchboard of Miami 358-4357, 24hrs, gay-friendly info & referrals for Dade County

ACCOMMODATIONS
▲ **Island House** 715 82nd St., 864-2422/(800) 382-2422 (M,N,IGTA)

BARS
821 821 Lincoln Rd., 534-0887 (GF,NH,D) 3pm-4am
The Boardwalk 17008 Collins Ave., 949-4119 (★M,S) 7am-5am, 7am-5am
Cheers 2490 SW 17th Ave., Coconut Grove, 857-0041 (★W,D,E,WC) 9pm-3am, clsd Mon-Tue

Comedy Zone 1121 Washington Ave., 672-4788 (GF,E) Tue gay night, call for events

Loading Zone 1426-A Alton Rd., 531-5623 (M,L) 10pm-3am, til 5am Fri-Sat

Swirl 1049 Washington Ave., 534-2060 (MW,D) call for events

RESTAURANTS & CAFES

11th Street Diner 11th & Washington, 534-6373, til midnight, 24hrs on wknds, full bar

Cafe Atlantico 429 Espanola Wy., 672-1168, 6pm-midnight, bar til 3am, New World tapas

Palace Bar & Grill 1200 Ocean Dr., 531-9077, 8am-2am, American, full bar

Piola 637 Washington Ave., 531-7787, 6pm-2am, pasta & thin crust pizza, full bar

Sushi Rock Cafe 1351 Collins Ave., 532-2133, sushi & rock n' roll, full bar

TRAVEL & TOUR OPERATORS

▲ **Colours Destinations** 255 W. 24th St., Miami Beach, 532-9341/(800) 277-4825

SPIRITUAL GROUPS

Christ MCC 7701 SW 76th Ave., 284-1040, 9:30am & 7pm Sun

Grace MCC 10390 NE 2nd Ave., Miami Shores, 758-6822, 11:30am Sun

MCC 2100 Washington Ave., 759-1015, 11am Sun

PUBLICATIONS

TWN (The Weekly News) 901 NE 79th St., 757-6333

MEN'S CLUBS

▲ **Club Body Center Miami** 2991 Coral Wy., 448-2214 (★MO,SW,PC) 24hrs

CRUISY AREAS

Alice Wainwright Park (AYOR)

Bearcut Beach (AYOR)

Biscayne Beach (AYOR) hitchhikers

Hanover Beach Park (AYOR)

Matheson Hammock Beach on Old Cutler Rd. (AYOR)

Miami Beach/South Beach (305)

INFO LINES & SERVICES

▲ **Community Real Estate Referrals** (800) 346-5592, gay realtor at your service, no rentals

▲ **Miami Beach Confidential Connection** 999-9200, Meet hot local guys! Record, listen, respond to free ads. Use free code 9966.

ACCOMMODATIONS

Abbey Hotel 300 21st St., Miami Beach, 531-0031/Fax: 672-1663 (GF) studios with kitchens

The Bayliss 504 14th St., Miami Beach, 534-0010 (MW) art deco hotel

Bohemia Gardens 825 Michigan Ave., 758-3902/(800) 472-4102 (GF) hot tub

Chelsea Hotel 944 Washington Ave., 534-4069 (GF)

Collins Plaza 318 20th St., Miami Beach, 532-0849 (GF) hotel

▲ **The Colours - The Mantell Guest Inn** 255 W. 24th St., 538-1821/(800) 277-4825 (MW,SW,IGTA) several art deco hotels & apts available, complimentary cocktail hour

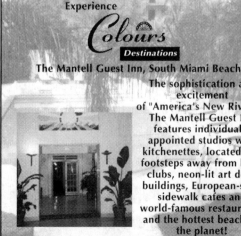

A TROPICAL DECO GUESTHOUSE FOR MEN IN *Fabulous* SOUTH BEACH

*S*pectacular heated pool with lap lane and jacuzzi

*T*ropical grotto with secluded, romantic hot tub

*C*lothing optional

*C*ompletely non-smoking

NORMANDY SOUTH

(305) 674-1197

Fax (305) 532-9771

European Guesthouse 721 Michigan Ave., 673-6665/Fax: 672-7442 (MW,IGTA) full brkfst, hot tub

Fountainbleu Hilton Resort & Spa 4441 Collins Ave., Miami Beach, 538-2000/(800) 445-8667 (GF,SW,WC)

Hotel Impala 1228 Collins Ave., 673-2021/(800) 646-7252 (GF,WC) luxury hotel near beach

▲ **Island House** 715 82nd St., 864-2422/(800) 382-2422 (M,N,IGTA) South, Mid, & North Beach locations, guesthouse, villas

▲ **Jefferson House** 1018 Jefferson, 534-5247/Fax: 534-5247 ★51 (GF,IGTA) newly renovated B&B, tropical garden

Kenmore Hotel 1050 Washington Ave., Miami Beach, 531-4199 (GF,SW)

Lily Guesthouse 835 Collins Ave., Miami Beach, 535-9900 (MW) studios, suites, sundeck

Lord Balfour 350 Ocean Dr., Miami Beach, 673-0401/(800) 501-0401 (GF)

Marlin Hotel 1200 Collins Ave., Miami Beach, 673-8770/(800) 688-7678 (GF,WC) upscale

▲ **Normandy South** 2474 Prairie Ave., 674-1197/Fax: 532-9771 (MO,SW,N,IGTA) Out & About Editor's Choice Award winner for extraordinary level of service & value

Park Washington 1020 Washington, Miami Beach, 532-1930 (GF,SW)

Penguin Hotel & Bar 1418 Ocean Dr., 534-9334/(800) 235-3296 (MW) cafe/juice bar

The Shelborne Beach Resort 1801 Collins Ave., Miami, 531-1271/(800) 327-8757 (★GF,SW) terrace cafe, poolside bar

Shore Club Resort 1901 Collins Ave., Miami Beach, 534-3443/(800) 327-8330

South Beach Central (800) 538-3616 (IGTA) hotel reservations, vacation rentals

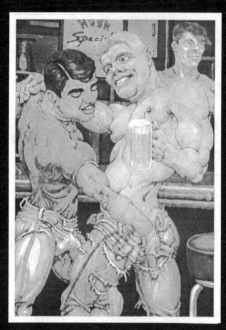

¡caliente!

around the clock ★

HOMBRE
south beach

925 Washington Ave.
Miami Beach, Florida 33139

305-538-7883
fax   305-672-0192
http://www.hombreweb.com

South Beach Destinations 666-0163/(800) 443-8224, reservation service

South Beach Hotel 236 21st St., Miami Beach, 531-3464 (GF,F) historic art deco hotel w/24hr cafe

▲ **South Florida Hotel Network** 1688 Meridian Ave., 538-3616/(800) 538-3616

Villa Paradiso Guesthouse 1415 Collins Ave., 532-0616/Fax: 667-0074 (GF)

The Winterhaven 1400 Ocean Dr., 531-5571/(800) 395-2322 (GF,F,IGTA) classic example of deco architecture

BARS

Bash 655 Washington Ave., 538-2274 (GF,D) 10pm-5am, clsd Mon, patio

Club Ozone 6620 Red Rd. (SW 57th Ave.), 667-2888 (★MO,D) 9:30pm-5am, patio

El Carol 930 SW Le Jeune Rd., 448-9148 (M,NH) 11am-5am

▲ **Hombre** 925 Washington Ave., 538-7883 (M,WC) 8am-5am, cruise bar

Kremlin 727 Lincoln Rd., Miami Beach, 673-3150 (M,D,S) 10am-4am, clsd Sun-Wed

Miami Eagle 1252 Corral Wy., 860-0056 (MO,PC,WC) 5pm-3am, from 9pm Fri-Sat

On the Waterfront 3615 NW South River Dr., 635-5500 (★MW,D,MRC,E,K,V) call for events

Salvation 1771 West Ave., Miami Beach, 673-6508 (MW,D,A) call for events

Splash 5922 S. Dixie Hwy., 662-8779 (M,D,V) 4pm-2am, clsd Mon

Sugar's 17060 W. Dixie, 940-9887 (M,NH,D,V,WC) 3pm-6am

Twist 1057 Washington Ave., 538-9478 (★M,D,WC) 1pm-5am

The Warsaw 1450 Collins Ave., 531-4555 (M,D,E,V) 9:30pm-5am Wed-Sun, clsd Mon-Tue & Th, progressive music

THE JEFFERSON HOUSE

BED & BREAKFAST

Located in the heart of Deco South Beach. Relax in the casual elegance that prevails. Bright and comfortable air conditioned rooms all have private baths. Enjoy breakfast each morning on our deck overlooking a tropical swim spa. Just a short walk to the beach, bars and restaurants. Come and visit with us, you'll love it!

Send for Brochure:
1018 Jefferson Avenue, Miami Beach, FL. 33139
or Call: (305) 534-5247

Westend 942 Lincoln Rd., 538-9378 (M,NH) noon-5am

RESTAURANTS & CAFES

A Fish Called Avalon 700 Ocean Dr., 532-1727 (★WC) 6pm-11pm, full bar

Bang 1516 Washington, 531-2361 (★) internat'l, full bar

Beehive 630 Lincoln Rd., 538-7484, noon-midnight, pizza & pasta, patio

El Rancho Grande 1626 Pennsylvania Ave., 673-0480, Mexican

The Front Porch 1420 Ocean Dr., 531-8300, 8am-midnight, healthy home cooking, full bar

Jams Tavern & Grill 1331 Washington, 532-6700, 11am-5am, full bar

Jeffrey's 1629 Michigan Ave., Miami Beach, 673-0690 (★) 6pm-11pm, from 5pm Sun, clsd Mon, bistro

Larios on the Beach 820 Ocean Dr., 532-9577, 11am-midnight, til 2am Fri-Sat, Cuban

Lucky Cheng's 1412 Ocean Dr., 672-1505 (★S) 6pm-midnight, full bar

Lulu's 1053 Washington, 532-6147 (★WC) 11am-2am, Southern homecooking, full bar

News Cafe 800 Ocean Dr., 538-6397 (★) 24hrs, healthy sandwiches

Norma's on the Beach 646 Lincoln Ave., 532-2809 (★) opens 4pm, clsd Mon, New World Caribbean, full bar

Oak Feed 2911 Grand Ave. , Coconut Grove, 446-9036, 11am-10pm, sushi & vegetarian

Pacific Time 915 Lincoln Rd., 534-5979 (BW) lunch & dinner weekdays, Pan-Pacific

The Strand 671 Washington Ave., Miami, 532-2340 (WC) 6pm-2am, full bar

Wolfie's Jewish Deli 2038 Collins Ave. (at 21st), 538-6626, 24hrs, 24hrs, gourmet deli

GYMS & HEALTH CLUBS

Club Body Tech 1253 Washington Ave., Miami Beach, 674-8222 (★GF)

BOOKSTORES & RETAIL SHOPS

The 9th Chakra 817 Lincoln Rd., 538-0671, clsd Mon, metaphysical books, supplies, gifts

GW's 720 Lincoln Rd. Mall, 534-4763, 11am-10pm, til 8pm Sun, lesbigay emporium

Lambda Passages Bookstore 7545 Biscayne Blvd., 754-6900, 11am-9pm, noon-6pm Sun, gay/lesbian/feminist bookstore

Whittal & Schon 1319 Washington, 538-2606, 11am-9pm, til midnight Fri-Sat, funky clothes

WOW Boutique 3415 Main Hwy., Coconut Grove, 443-6824, club clothes

TRAVEL & TOUR OPERATORS

Amazon Tours & Cruises 8700 W. Flagler Ste. 190, (800) 423-2791 (IGTA)

▲ **Connections Tours** 169 Lincoln Rd. #302, Miami Beach, 673-3153/(800) 688-8463 (IGTA)

Professional Travel Management 195 SW 15th Rd. Ste. 403, 858-5522/(800) 568-4064 (IGTA)

Vision Travel: Carlson Travel Network 2222 Ponce de Leon Blvd., 444-8484/(800) 654-4544

TOURS • HOTELS • TRANSPORTATION • TICKETS

CONNECTIONS Tours

Designer Trips to

FLORIDA

Experience It!

RESERVATIONS: (305) 673-3153
800-OUT-TIME (688-8463) • FAX: (305) 673-6501
E-MAIL: connectfl@aol.com • IGTA Member λ

▲ **Z-Max Travel** (800) TO-GO-GAY (IGTA) hotel reservations, tours & events, call for special bar admissions

PUBLICATIONS
Wire 1638 Euclid Ave., 33139, 538-3111, weekly, guide to South Beach

EROTICA
Biscayne Books & Video 11711 Biscayne Blvd., 891-3475, 24hrs
Cloverleaf Book & Video 14907 NW 7th Ave., 681-2001, 24hrs
Happy Books 9514 S. Dixie Hwy., 670-9203, 24hrs
Le Jeune Road Books 928 SW 42nd Ave., 443-1913, 24hrs
Perrine Books & Video 18093 S. Dixie Hwy., 233-3913
Pleasure Emporium 1019 5th St., Miami, 673-3311

CRUISY AREAS
Flamingo Park (AYOR) after midnight
The Gay Beach 12th & Ocean (AYOR)

Naples (941)

INFO LINES & SERVICES
▲ **Community Real Estate Referrals** (800) 346-5592, gay realtor at your service, no rentals
Lesbian/Gay AA 262-6535, several mtgs.

ACCOMMODATIONS
Festive Flamingo 455-8833 (MW,SW)

BARS
The Galley 509 3rd St. S., 262-2808 (MW,NH,F) 4pm-2am, from 1pm Sun

RESTAURANTS & CAFES
Cafe Flamingo 536 9th St. N., 262-8181 (MW) 8am-2pm

BOOKSTORES & RETAIL SHOPS
Book Nook 824 5th Ave. S., 262-4740 (WC) 8am-7pm
Lavender's 5600 Trail Blvd. #4, 594-9499, 11am-7pm, til 4pm Sat, clsd Sun & Mon, lesbigay book store & pride shop

CRUISY AREAS
Beach 18th Ave. S. (AYOR)
Lowdermilk Park Gulf Shore Blvd. N. (AYOR)
Vanderbilt Beach S. of the Ritz (AYOR)

Ocala (352)

BARS
Connection 3331 S. Pine Ave. (US 441), 620-2511 (MW,NH,WC) 3pm-2am

BOOKSTORES & RETAIL SHOPS
Barnes & Noble 3500 SW College Rd., 620-9195, lesbigay section

EROTICA
Secrets of Ocala 815 N. Magnolia Ave., 622-3858

Orlando (407)

INFO LINES & SERVICES

▲ **Community Real Estate Referrals** (800) 346-5592, gay realtor at your service, no rentals

Family Values WPRK 91.5 FM, 7pm Wed, lesbigay radio from Rollins College

Gay/Lesbian Community Center 714 E. Colonial Dr., 425-4527, 11am-9pm, noon-5pm Sat, clsd Sun

Gay/Lesbian Community Services of Central Florida 843-4297, 24hr touchtone helpline, extensive referrals

Metropolitan Business Association PO Box 568041, 32856, 420-2182, 6:30pm 1st Th, at the Radisson Hotel

▲ **Orlando Confidential Connection** 354-3005, Meet hot local guys! Record, listen, respond to free ads. Use free code 9966.

ACCOMMODATIONS

The A Veranda B&B 115 N. Summerlin Ave., 849-0321/(800) 420-6822 (GF,WC) hot tub

The Garden Cottage B&B 1309 E. Washington Ave., 894-5395/Fax: 894-3809 (★MW,WC) 1920s private cottage

Lakeview PO Box 689, 32802, 843-6671 (M) hot tub

▲ **Parliament House Motor Inn** 410 N. Orange Blossom Trail, 425-7571 (★MW,D,F,E,S,YC,SW) from 8pm, 5 bars on premises

Rick's B&B P.O. Box 22318, Lake Buena Vista, 32830, 396-7751 (MW,SW) full brkfst, patio

BARS

The Cactus Club 1300 N. Mills Ave., 894-3041 (M,P) 3pm-2am, patio

City Lights Cabaret (at The Complex), 422-6826 (★MW,D,S) noon-2am

The Club 578 N. Orange Ave., 426-0005 (★MW,D,E,S,V,18+) call for events

The Complex 3400 S. Orange Blossom Tr., 422-6826 (MW,D,WC) noon-2am, various bars, gym, video store

Copper Rocket 106 Lake Ave., Maitland, 645-0069 (MW,F,BW,WC) 11:30am-2am, from 4pm wknds, micro brews, internet access

The Edge 100 W. Livingston St., 839-4331 (GF,D) call for events

Faces 4910 Edgewater Dr., 291-7571 (★W,D,E,WC) 4pm-2am

Full Moon Saloon 500 N. Orange Blossom Tr., 648-8725 (M,CW,L) noon-2am, patio

Hank's 5026 Edgewater Dr., 291-2399 (M,NH,BW,WC) noon-2am, patio

Mannequins Paradise Island at Disney World (★GF,D) very straight except some gays on Employee Night, Th

Orlando Eagle (at The Complex), 843-6334 (M,L) 4pm-2am

Phoenix 7124 Aloma Ave., Winter Park, 678-9220 (MW,E,S) 4pm-2am

Secrets 745 Bennett Rd., 898-5603 (GF,D,S) 10pm-4am, clsd Mon-Thur

Southern Nights 375 S. Bumby Ave., 898-0424 (M,D,S,WC) 4pm-2am, patio

Stable (at Parliament House), 425-7571 (M,CW) 8pm-2am

Uncle Walt's Backstage 5454 International Dr., 351-4866 (GF,F,S,WC) 4pm-2am, piano bar & cabaret

Will's Pub 1820-50 N. Mills Ave., 898-5070 (GF,NH,F,BW,WC) 4pm-2am

Wyldes (at The Complex), 857-1609 (★M) 2:30pm-2am

RESTAURANTS & CAFES

Dug Out Diner (at Parliament House), 425-7571x711 (MW) 24hrs

Moorefields 123 S. Orange Ave., 872-6960 (★MW,BW,WC) lunch & dinner, clsd Sun-Mon

Thorton Park Cafe 900 E. Washington, 425-0033 (BW,WC) 11am-10pm, seafood/Italian, patio

White Wolf Cafe & Antique Shop 1829 N. Orange Ave., 895-5590 (E,BW,WC) 10am-midnight, clsd Sun, salads & sandwiches

BOOKSTORES & RETAIL SHOPS

Alobar 709 W. Smith St., 841-3050 (WC) 10am-9pm, noon-5pm Sun, books, music

Out & About Books 930 N. Mills Ave., 896-0204, 10am-8pm, noon-6pm Sun, lesbigay bookstore

Rainbow City 934 N. Mills Ave., 898-6096, lesbigay giftshop

TRAVEL & TOUR OPERATORS

Odyssey 334 E. Michigan St., 841-8686/(800) 327-4441 (IGTA)

SPIRITUAL GROUPS

Integrity/Central Florida PO Box 530031, 32853, 332-2743

Joy MCC 2351 S. Ferncreek Ave, 894-1081 (WC) 9:15am & 11am, 7:30pm Wed

PUBLICATIONS

The Triangle PO Box 533446, 32853, 425-4527, monthly

Watermark PO Box 533655, 32853-3655, 481-2243/Fax: 481-2246

MEN'S CLUBS

▲ **Club Orlando** 450 E. Compton St., 425-5005 (PC)

New Image Fitness Center (at The Complex), 420-9890 (MO,PC) 24hrs, sauna, steam & weights

EROTICA

Absolute Leather 3400 S. Orange Blossom Tr., 843-8168/(800) 447-4820 (WC) noon-9pm, til midnight Th-Sat

Fairvilla Video 1740 N. Orange Blossom Tr., 425-5352

The Leather Closet 498 N. Orange Blossom Tr., 649-2011 (WC) noon-2am

Midnight News (at Parliament House), 425-7571, 9pm-2am

CRUISY AREAS

Lake Eola (AYOR)

Palm Beach Gardens (407)

TRAVEL & TOUR OPERATORS

Vagabond Travels 601 Northlake Blvd., 848-0648/(800) 226-3830 (IGTA)

Panama City (904)

BARS

Bottoms Up 14896 Front Beach Rd., 233-7151 (GF,NH,F) 10am-4am

Fiesta Room 110 Harrison Ave., 784-9285 (★MW,D,S,WC) 8pm-3am

La Royale Lounge & Liquor Store 100 Harrison, 784-9311 (★MW,NH,WC) 3pm-3am, courtyard

CRUISY AREAS

Phillip's Inlet County Beach 1/2 mi. W. of Ramsgate Harbor (AYOR)

Pembroke Pines (305)

RESTAURANTS & CAFES
Blue Goose Cafe 1491 N. Palm Ave., 436-8677 (BW) from 5:30pm, clsd Mon, pasta/steak/seafood

Pensacola (904)

INFO LINES & SERVICES
AA Gay/Lesbian 415 N. Alcaniz (MCC location), 433-8528, 8pm Fri
▲ **Community Real Estate Referrals** (800) 346-5592, gay realtor at your service, no rentals

ACCOMMODATIONS
Noble Manor B&B 110 W. Strong St., 434-9544 (GF) hot tub

BARS
Numbers Pub 200 S. Alcaniz, 438-9004 (M,D,E,WC) 3pm-3am
Red Carpet 937 Warrington Rd., 453-9918 (W,D,E) 3pm-3am, patio
Red Garter 1 W. Main St., 433-9292 (MW,D,S,WC) 5pm-3am, from 3pm wknds
Round-up 706 E. Gregory, 433-8482 (★M,NH,V,WC) 2pm-3am

RESTAURANTS & CAFES
The Secret Cafe 23 S. Palafox Pl., 444-9020 (E) 10am-6pm, noon-midnight Fri & Sat, clsd Sun-Mon, coffeehouse & gallery

BOOKSTORES & RETAIL SHOPS
Silver Chord Bookstore 10901 Lillian Hwy., 453-6652 (WC) 10am-6pm, clsd Mon, metaphysical, lesbigay section

SPIRITUAL GROUPS
Holy Cross MCC 415 N. Alcaniz, 433-8528, 11am Sun, 7pm Wed

Plantation (305)

EROTICA
Adult World 1971 SW 40th Ave., 587-9750, 24hrs

Pompano Beach (954)

INFO LINES & SERVICES
The Eden Society PO Box 1692, 33061-1692, 316-8470, transgender group, newsletter

Port Richey (813)

BARS
BT's 7737 Grand Blvd., 841-7900 (MW,D,S,WC) 6pm-2am

Port St. Lucie (407)

BARS
Bourbon St. Cabaret & Cafe 2727 SE Morningside Blvd., 335-8608 (★MW,F,E,WC) 4pm-2am, steak & seafood, patio

Sarasota (941)

INFO LINES & SERVICES
▲ **Community Real Estate Referrals** (800) 346-5592, gay realtor at your service, no rentals

Friends Group (Gay AA) 2080 Ringling Blvd. #302, 951-6810, 8pm Mon & Wed, also 8pm Fri at 538 Payne Pkwy

ACCOMMODATIONS

Normandy Inn 400 N. Tamiami Tr., 366-8979/(800) 282-8050 (GF)

Vera's Place 3913 Chapel Dr., 351-3171 (MO,SW,N,WC)

BARS

Bumpers (Club X) 1927 Ringling Blvd., 951-0335 (GF,D) 9pm -2:30am, more gay Th-Sun

HG Rooster's 1256 Old Stickney Pt. Rd., 346-3000 (M,NH,S) 3pm-2am

Ricky J's 1330 Martin Luther King Jr. Wy., 953-5945 (★M,D,F,E,V,WC) 4pm-2am, patio

BOOKSTORES & RETAIL SHOPS

Charlie's 1341 Main St., 953-4688, 9am-10pm, til 5pm Sun, books, magazines, cards

TRAVEL & TOUR OPERATORS

Galaxsea Cruises 6584 Superior, 921-3456/(800) 633-5159 (IGTA)

SPIRITUAL GROUPS

Church of the Trinity MCC 7225 N. Lockwood Ridge Rd., 355-0847 (WC) 10am Sun

Suncoast Cathedral MCC 3276 Venice Ave., 484-7068

CRUISY AREAS

North Lido Beach (AYOR)

Satellite Beach (407)

EROTICA

Space Age Books & Temptations 63 Ocean Blvd., 773-7660

Sebastian (407)

ACCOMMODATIONS

The Pink Lady Inn 1309 Louisiana Ave., 589-1345 (W,SW)

South Beach (see **Miami Beach/South Beach**)

St. Petersburg (813)

INFO LINES & SERVICES

▲ **Community Real Estate Referrals** (800) 346-5592, gay realtor at your service, no rentals

Gay Information Line (The Line) 586-4297, volunteers 7pm-11pm

ACCOMMODATIONS

Bay Gables B&B and Garden 136 4th Ave. NE, 822-8855/(800) 822-8803 (GF) extended cont'l brkfst

Frog Pond Guesthouse 145 29th Ave. N., 823-7407 (GF)

Sea Oats & Dunes 12625 Sunshine Lane, Treasure Island, 367-7568/Fax: 397-4157 (GF,SW) directly on the Gulf of Mexico

BARS

Bedrox 8000 W. Gulf Blvd., Treasure Island, 367-1724 (★MW,D,F,E,WC) 10am-2am, 4 bars, on the beach

D.T.'s 2612 Central Ave., 327-8204 (M,NH,WC) 2pm-2am

Golden Arrow 10604 Gandy Blvd., 577-7774 (M,NH,WC) 1pm-2am

The Hideaway 8302 4th St. N., 570-9025 (W,NH,WC) 2pm-2am

The New Connection 3100 3rd Ave. N., 321-2112 (MW,NH,D,WC) 11am-2am

Sharp A's 4918 22nd Ave. S., Gulfport, 327-4897 (★MW,D,WC) 3pm-2am

RESTAURANTS & CAFES
Beaux Arts 7711 60th St. N., 328-0702 (MW) noon-5pm

BOOKSTORES & RETAIL SHOPS
Affinity Books 2435 Ninth St. N., 823-3662 (WC) 10am-6pm, til 8pm Th, noon-5pm Sun

Brigit Books 3434 4th St. N., 522-5775, 10am-8pm, til 6pm Fri-Sat, 1pm-5pm Sun

P.S. 111 2nd Ave. NE, 823-2937, 10am-6pm, cards & gifts

SPIRITUAL GROUPS
King of Peace MCC 3150 5th Ave. N., 323-5857 (WC) 10am

EROTICA
4th St. Books & Video 1427 4th St. S., 821-8824

CRUISY AREAS
Pass-a-Grille Beach below 8th St. (AYOR)

St. Petersburg Beach (813)

INFO LINES & SERVICES
▲ **Community Real Estate Referrals** (800) 346-5592, gay realtor at your service, no rentals

ACCOMMODATIONS
Pass-A-Grille Beach Motel 709 Gulfway Blvd., 367-4726 (GF,SW) apartment available

Tallahassee (904)

BARS
Brothers Bar 926 W. Tharpe St., 386-2399 (MW,D,S,V,18+,WC) 4pm-2am

Club Park Ave. 115 E. Park Ave., 599-9143 (★GF,E,S,V,YC) 10pm-2am, more gay wknds, mostly African Amerian Sun

RESTAURANTS & CAFES
The Village Inn 2690 N. Monroe St., 385-2903 (★) dinner

BOOKSTORES & RETAIL SHOPS
Rubyfruit Books 666 W. Tennessee St. #4, 222-2627 (WC) 10:30am-6:30pm, til 8pm Th, clsd Sun, alternative bookstore, gay titles

TRAVEL & TOUR OPERATORS
Florida Division of Tourism 487-1421

SPIRITUAL GROUPS
Integrity Big Bend PO Box 10731, 32302, 224-4661, 7:30pm Wed

CRUISY AREAS
Lost Lake Spring Hill Rd. (AYOR)

Tampa (813)

INFO LINES & SERVICES

▲ **Community Real Estate Referrals** (800) 346-5592, gay realtor at your service, no rentals

Gay Information Line (The Line) 586-4297

▲ **Tampa Confidential Connection** 626-6020, Meet hot local guys! Record, listen, respond to free ads. Use free code 9966.

University of South Florida Gay/Lesbian/Bisexual CTR 2466, 4202 E. Fowler Ave., 974-4297

ACCOMMODATIONS

▲ **Gram's Place B&B & Artist Retreat** 3109 N. Ola Ave., 221-0596/Fax: 221-0596 (MW,P,BYOB,N) artists' retreat & music lover's paradise named in honor of Gram Parsons

▲ **Ruskin House B&B** 120 Dickman Dr. SW, Ruskin, 645-3842 (GF) 1910 multi-story home, 30 min. S. of Tampa & 30 min. N. of Sarasota

BARS

2606 2606 N. Armenia Ave., 875-6993 (★M,L,WC) 3pm-3am, also leather shop opens after 9pm

Angel's Lounge 4502 Dale Mabry Hwy. S., 831-9980 (M,NH,S,WC) 3pm-3am

The Annex 2408 W. Kennedy Blvd., 254-4188 (M,NH,WC) noon-3am

Cherokee Club 1320 9th Ave., 2nd flr., Ybor City, 247-9966 (W,D,E) 9pm-3am, Fri & Sat only, call for events

City Side 3810 Neptune St., 254-6466 (MW,NH,P) noon-3am, patio

The Cove Lounge 3703 Henderson Blvd., 875-3290 (M,NH,E,S) noon-3am

Eden 913 Franklin (GF,D,YC) late night rave crowd

Howard Avenue Station 3003 N. Howard Ave., 254-7194 (★M,D) 8pm-3am

Impulse Channelside Village 302 S. Nebraska Ave., 223-2780 (M,D,V,YC,WC) 3pm-3am, patio, Sunday T-dance

Keith's Lounge 14905 N. Nebraska, 971-3576 (M,NH) 1pm-3am

Northside Lounge 9002 N. Florida Ave., 931-3396 (M,NH) noon-3am

Rascal's 105 W. Martin Luther King Blvd., 237-8883 (MW,NH,D,WC) 4pm-3am, from noon Sun, full restaurant

Tracks Tampa 1430 E. 7th Ave., 247-2711 (★M,D,S,V,YC,WC) 9pm-3am, clsd Wed & Sun

Tremors 15212 N. Nebraska Ave., 977-3433 (GF,D,A,S) 9pm-3am

Gyms & Health Clubs

Metro Flex Fitness 2511 Swann Ave., 876-3539

Bookstores & Retail Shops

Tomes & Treasures 202 S. Howard Ave., 251-9368, 11am-8pm, 1pm-6pm Sun, lesbigay bookstore

Spiritual Groups

MCC 408 Cayuga St., 239-1951

Publications

Encounter 1222 S. Dale Mabry Hwy. #913, 877-7913

Gazette PO Box 2650, Brandon, 33509-2650, 689-7566

Southern Exposure PO Box 8092, 33674, gay men's naturist group

Stonewall 3225 S. Madill #220, 832-2878, monthly

Men's Clubs

Club Tampa 215 N. 11th St., 223-5181 (★MO,F,PC) 24hrs

Erotica

Buddies Video 4322 W. Crest Ave., 876-8083, 24hrs

Playhouse Theatre 4421 Hubert N., 873-9235, 24hrs

Cruisy Areas

Ben T. Davis Beach Campbell Causeway (AYOR)

Titusville

Cruisy Areas

Playalinda Beach (AYOR)

Venice   (941)

Info Lines & Services

▲ **Community Real Estate Referrals** (800) 346-5592, gay realtor at your service, no rentals

Erotica

Fawlty Video 1800 S. Tamiami Tr., 497-1797

Cruisy Areas

Casperson Beach walk 1/2 mi. S. (AYOR)

West Palm Beach (407)

INFO LINES & SERVICES

▲ **Community Real Estate Referrals** (800) 346-5592, gay realtor at your service, no rentals

ACCOMMODATIONS

Hibiscus House B&B 501 30th St., 863-5633/(800) 203-4927 (MW,SW,IGTA) complimentary sunset cocktails

West Palm Beach B&B 419 32nd St. Old Northwood, 848-4064/(800) 736-4064 (M,SW,IGTA) relaxing & fun place to kick off your sandals

BARS

5101 Bar 5101 S. Dixie Hwy., 585-2379 (M,NH,WC) 7am-3am, til 4am Fri-Sat, noon-3am Sun

B.G.'s Bar 5700 S. Dixie Hwy., 533-3800 (M,NH,K,S) 7am-3am, from noon Sun

Dakota Lounge 3051 Broadway, 863-5863 (M,NH) 9am-11pm, clsd Mon-Tue

Enigma 109 N. Olive Ave., 832-5040 (MW,D,A,18+) 9pm-3am, clsd Mon-Tue

▲ **H.G. Rooster's** 823 Belvedere Rd., 832-9119 (★M,NH,WC) 3pm-3am, til 4am Fri-Sat

Heartbreaker 2677 Forrest Hill Blvd., 966-1590 (★MW,D,E,K,S,V,YC) 10pm-5am Wed-Sun, Chatters lounge open 5pm daily

▲ **Kozlow's** 6205 Georgia Ave., 533-5355 (★M,NH,CW,YC,PC,WC) noon-2am, patio

Leather & Spurs WPB 5004 S. Dixie Hwy., 547-1020 (M,L,F,BW) 4pm-3am, clsd Mon-Wed

H. G. ROOSTERS
Here And There

SARASOTA
1256 Old Stickney Pt. Rd.
Siesta Key, Sarasota
(813) 346-3000

WEST PALM BEACH
823 Belvedere Road
West Palm Beach
(407) 832-9119

RESTAURANTS & CAFES

Antonio's South 3001 S. Congress Ave., Palm Springs, 965-0707 (BW) dinner, southern Italian

Down Dixie Grill 3815 S. Dixie Hwy., 832-4959, dinner & lunch Mon-Fri

Respectable Street Cafe 518 Clematis St., 832-9999 (E) lunch & dinner

BOOKSTORES & RETAIL SHOPS

Changing Times Bookstore 911 Village Blvd. Ste. 806, 640-0496, 10am-7pm, noon-5pm Sun

Eurotique 3109 45th St. #300, 684-2302, 11am-7pm Mon-Fri, 12pm-6pm Sat, PVC, leather, books, videos

TRAVEL & TOUR OPERATORS

▲ **Damron Atlas World Travel** 205 N. Federal Hwy., 533-5272

PUBLICATIONS

Community Voice PO Box 17975, 33416, 471-1528, monthly

CRUISY AREAS

MacArthur Park Beach (AYOR)

Winter Park

INFO LINES & SERVICES

▲ **Community Real Estate Referrals** (800) 346-5592, gay realtor at your service, no rentals

CRUISY AREAS

Cady Way street bordering Ward Memorial Park (AYOR)

GEORGIA

Athens (706)

INFO LINES & SERVICES

LGBSU (Lesbian/Gay/Bisexual Student Union) Memorial Hall Rm. 213, 549-9368, 7pm Mon

BARS

Boneshakers 433 E. Hancock Ave., 543-1555 (MW,D,A,18+,WC) 7pm-2am, clsd Sun, CW Th

Forty Watt Club 285 W. Washington St., 549-7871 (GF,A,E,WC) theme nights

Georgia Bar 159 N. Clayton, 546-9884 (GF,WC) 4pm-2am, clsd Sun

The Globe 199 N. Lumpkin, 353-4721 (GF) 4pm-2am, clsd Sun, 30 single-malt scotches

RESTAURANTS & CAFES

The Athens Coffeehouse 105 College Ave., 369-8802 (WC) 9am-midnight, til 2am Th-Sat

The Bluebird 493 E. Clayton, 549-3663 (WC) 8am-9pm, popular Sun brunch

Espresso Royale Cafe 297 E. Broad St., 613-7449, 7am-midnight, from 8am wknds, best coffee in Athens

The Grit 199 Prince Ave., 543-6592 (WC) 10am-11pm, great Sun brunch

BOOKSTORES & RETAIL SHOPS

Barnett's Newsstand 147 College Ave., 353-0530, 8am-10pm

CRUISY AREAS

College Square Clayton & College Sts. (AYOR)

Atlanta (404)

INFO LINES & SERVICES

AALGA (African-American Lesbian/Gay Alliance) PO Box 50374, 30302, 239-8184, 4pm 1st Sun, social/political group

AEGIS (American Educational Gender Information Service) P.O. Box 33724, Decatur, 33003-0724, 939-0244, transgender info & helpline

▲ **Atlanta Confidential Connection** 870-8830, Meet hot local guys! Record, listen, respond to free ads. Use free code 9966.

Atlanta Gay Center 71 12th St. NE, 876-5372, 1pm-5pm Mon-Fri, social services center

Atlanta Gender Exploration P.O. Box 77562, 30357, transgender group

▲ **Community Real Estate Referrals** (800) 346-5592, gay realtor at your service, no rentals

Galano AA 585 Dutch Valley, 881-9188, lesbigay club

Gay Graffiti WRFG 89.3 FM, 523-8989, 7pm Th, lesbigay radio program

Gay Helpline 892-0661, 6pm-11pm, info & counseling

Greater Atlanta Business Coalition 377-4258

ACCOMMODATIONS

▲ **The Academy B&B** Alpharetta, (770) 667-0793 (MO,SW,N) full brkfst, limo service

▲ **Alternative Accommodations** (800) 209-9408 (IGTA)

▲ **The Caritas B&B Network** (800) CARITAS (227-4827), see ad in center National section

"May I take your bag sir..."

The World's Only Bed & Breakfast With Uniformed Military & Police Personnel As Your Hosts...

The Academy Training Center, long famous for providing prison, police and military experiences has now opened The Academy Bed & Breakfast. Guests have their choice of accommodations ranging from our elegant, antique furnished suites to barracks guest rooms to our infamous fully equipped prison cell block. Situated on 16 wooded acres north of Atlanta, our amenities include heated swimming pool, weight and billiard rooms, padded cell & private limousine service.

11770 Haynes Bridge Rd
Suite 205-366-DG
Alpharetta, GA 30201
(770) 667-0793

We Accept Visa, Master Card & American Express

Colony Square Hotel 118 14th St., 892-6000

Hello B&B 892-8111 (M) B&B in a private home

Magnolia Station B&B 1020 Edgewood Ave. NE, 523-3923 (M,SW)

▲ **Midtown Manor** 811 Piedmont Ave. NE, 872-5846/(800) 724-4381 (MW) Victorian guesthouse

The River's Edge 2311 Pulliam Mill Rd., Dewy Rose, (706) 213-8081 (MO,SW,WC) cabins, camping, RV

Sheraton Colony Square Hotel 188 14th St., 892-6000 (GF,F) full bar, gym

Triangle Pointe Rte. 4 Box 242, Dahlonega, 30533, (706) 867-6029 (MW) full brkfst, hot tub

Upper Echelons 1845 Branch Valley Dr., Roswell, 30076, (770) 642-1313 (SW) luxury penthouse in downtown Atlanta

Bars

Armory 836 Juniper St. NE, 881-9280 (★M,D,V,YC,WC) 4pm-4am, 3 bars

Atlanta Eagle 306 Ponce de Leon Ave. NE, 873-2453 (★M,D,L) 5pm-4am, S/M fetish bar, also 'Mohawk' leather store

▲ **Backstreet** 845 Peachtree St. NE, 873-1986 (★M,D,S,V,YC) 24hrs, 3 flrs

Blake's 227 10th St., 892-5786 (M,NH,F,S) 3pm-3am, from 1pm Sun

Buddies 2345 Cheshire Bridge Rd., 634-5895 (M,NH) 2pm-4am

Buddies Midtown 239 Ponce de Leon, 872-2655 (MW,WC) 3pm-4am, sports bar

▲ **Bulldog & Co.** 893 Peachtree St. NE, 872-3025 (★M,D,V) 2pm-4am, cruise bar

Burkhart's Pub 1492-F Piedmont Rd. (Ansley Sq. Shopping Center), 872-4403 (MW,NH,WC) 4pm-4am, from 2pm wknds

**ATLANTA'S FINEST ONCE LIVED HERE...
NOW THEY DO AGAIN...HERE'S WHY:**

- Authentic Victorian manor
- Private Phones & Color TV
- Close to public transportation
- Centrally located
- Off-street parking
- Laundry facilities

LOCATED IN THE HEART OF ATLANTA'S GAY DISTRICT

(800) 724-4381   (404) 872-5846

811 Piedmont Avenue N.E. • Atlanta, GA 30308

E.S.S.O. 489 Courtland St., 872-3776 (GF,D,F,WC) noon-?, rooftop deck, nouvelle, some veggie

Guys & Dolls 2788 E. Ponce de Leon Ave., Decatur, 377-2956 (GF,F,S,WC) 11:30am-4am, from 7pm Sat, from 4pm Sun, stripper bar, more gay Tue & Sun

Heretic 2069 Cheshire Bridge Rd., 325-3061 (M,D,L,F) 9am-4am, from noon wknds, 3 bars, patio, call for theme nights, also 'Heretic Leathers' toy shop

Hoedowns 1890 Cheshire Bridge Rd., 874-0980 (★M,D,CW,S,WC) 5pm-3am, from 2pm wknds

Karats 511 Peachtree St., 872-9777, 7pm-3am, clsd Mon-Tue

Kaya 1068 Peachtree St., 874-4460 (MW,D,MRC-AF,F,E,S) noon-midnight, til 4am Fri, from 5pm Sat-Sun, patio, American, some veggie

Le Buzz 585 Franklin Rd., Marietta, (770) 424-1337 (MW,NH) noon-2am

The Limit 735 Ralph McGill, 523-1535 (M,W,D,S,WC) 5pm-4am, from 2pm wknds

Loretta's 708 Spring St. NW, 874-8125 (GF,NH,D,MRC-AF,S,WC) 6pm-4am

Martini Club 1140 Crescent Ave., 873-0794 (GF,WC) 4pm-2am

The Metro 1080 Peachtree St., 874-9869 (M,D,S,V) 3pm-3am

Model T 699 Ponce de Leon, 872-2209 (MW,NH,S,WC) noon-4am

Moreland Tavern 1196 Moreland Ave. SE, 622-4650 (MW,NH,F,WC) 11am-4am, patio

New Order Lounge 1544 Piedmont Rd. NE, 874-8247 (M,NH,WC) 2pm-2am

Opus I 1086 Alco St. NE, 634-6478 (M,NH,WC) 9pm-4am

The Otherside of Atlanta 1924 Piedmont Rd., 875-5238 (★MW,D,CW,F,E,S,V) 6pm-4am, patio

Phoenix 567 Ponce de Leon, 892-7871 (M,NH,CW) 9am-4am, patio

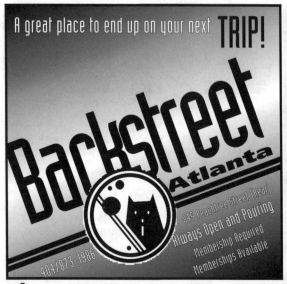

Revolution-Midtown 1492 Piedmont (Ansley Sq. Shopping Cntr.), 874-8455 (W,D,S,WC) 11am-2am, from 4pm Tue & Sat, from noon Sun, clsd Mon, deck

Scandals 1510-G Piedmont Rd. NE (Ansley Sq. Shopping Ctr.), 875-5957 (★M,NH,WC) noon-4am

Sol 917 Peachtree St., 815-8070 (GF,D,S) call for events

Transfer 931 Monroe Dr., 872-5200 (★M,D,WC) 4pm-4am

RESTAURANTS & CAFES

Bridgetown Grill 689 Peachtree (across from Fox Theater), 873-5361 (★) noon-11pm, funky Caribbean, some veggie, also Lil' 5 Points location 653-0110

Chow 1026-1/2 N. Highland Ave., 872-0869 (★WC) lunch & dinner, popular Sun brunch, contemporary American, some veggie

Cowtippers 1600 Piedmont Ave. NE, 874-3469 (TG) 11:30am-11pm

Dunk N' Dine (aka Drunk N' Dyke) 2276 Cheshire Bridge Rd., 636-0197 (★) 24hrs, downscale diner, queens abound

Eat Your Vegetables 438 Moreland Ave., 523-2671 (WC) lunch & dinner, Sun brunch, mostly veggie

Einstein's 1077 Juniper, 876-7925, noon-1am, American, full bar

The Flying Biscuit Cafe 1655 McLendon Ave., 687-8888 (BW,WC) 8:30am-10pm, clsd Mon, healthy brkfst all day, plenty veggie

Intermezzo 1845 Peachtree Rd. NE, 355-0411, 8am-2am, 9am-3am Fri-Sat, classy cafe, also full bar

Little 5 Points, Moreland & Euclid Ave. S. of Ponce de Leon Ave., hip & funky area w/ too many restaurants & shops to list

Majestic Diner 1031 Ponce de Leon (near N. Highland), 875-0276 (★) 24hrs, diner right from the '50s, cantankerous waitresses included

Murphy's 997 Virginia Ave., 872-0904 (★WC) 7am-10pm, til midnight Fri-Sat, fresh eclectic, plenty veggie, best brunch in town

R. Thomas 1812 Peachtree Rd. NE, 872-2942 (★BW,WC) 24hrs, healthy Californian/juice bar, plenty veggie

Veni Vidi Vici 41 14th St., 875-8424, lunch & dinner, upscale Italian, some veggie

GYMS & HEALTH CLUBS

Boot Camp 1544 Piedmont Ave. #105, 876-8686 (GF)

The Fitness Factory 500 Amsterdam, 815-7900 (★GF)

Mid-City Fitness Center 2201 Faulkner Rd., 321-6507 (MW)

BOOKSTORES & RETAIL SHOPS

Bill Hallman's 1054 N. Highland Ave., 876-6055, noon-1pm, til 6pm Sun-Tue, hip designer fashions

▲ **The Boy Next Door** 1447 Piedmont Ave. NE, 873-2664, 11am-7pm

▲ **Brushstrokes** 1510-J Piedmont Ave. NE, 876-6567, 10am-10pm, noon-9pm Sun, lesbigay variety store

Charis Books & More 1189 Euclid St., 524-0304 (WC) 10:30am-6:30pm, til 8pm Wed, til 10pm Fri-Sat, noon-6pm Sun, lesbigay bookstore

Condomart 632 N. Highland Ave. NE, 875-5665 (WC) 11am-11pm, noon-7pm Sun

Maddix 1034 N. Highland, 892-9337 (WC) 11am-10pm, til 7pm Sun, artful gifts

Malepak 549 Amsterdam Ave., 892-8004, 11am-7pm, 1pm-6pm Sun-Tue, swimwear, etc.

▲ **Outwrite Books** 991 Piedmont Ave., 607-0082 (WC) 11am-10pm, til midnight Fri-Sat, lesbigay bookstore, also cafe

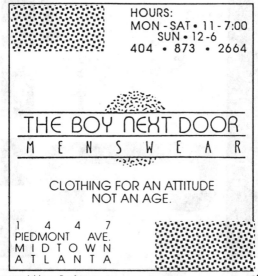

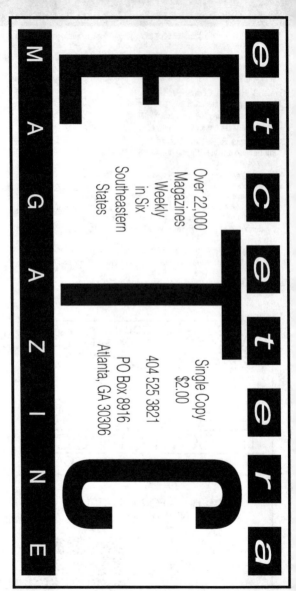

Oxford Books 2345 Peachtree, 364-2700, 9am-midnight, til 2am Fri-Sat, also cafe

TRAVEL & TOUR OPERATORS

Conventional Travel 1658 Lavista Rd. NE, 315-0107/(800) 747-7107 (IGTA)

Esquire Travel Service 3433 Havalyn Ln., 457-6696/(800) 786-6402

Hotlanta River Expo PO Box 8375, 30306, 874-3976, annual raft race & pageant

Midtown Travel Consultants 1830 Monroe Dr. Ste. F, 872-8308/(800) 548-8904 (IGTA)

Real Travel NE Plaza #1030, 3375 Buford Hwy, 872-8308/(800) 551-4202 (IGTA)

Travel Affair 1205 Johnson Ferry Rd. #116, Marietta, 977-6824/(800) 332-3417 (IGTA)

Trips Unlimited 1004 Virginia Ave. NE, 872-8747/(800) 275-8747

SPIRITUAL GROUPS

All Saints MCC 575 Boulevard SE, 622-1154 (WC) 7pm Sun

Congregation Bet Haverim 701 W. Howard Ave., Decatur, (770) 642-3467, 8pm Fri, 7:30pm 2nd Fri, lesbigay synagogue

First MCC of Atlanta 1379 Tullie Rd. NE, 325-4143 (WC) 9am, 11am & 7:30pm Sun, 7:30pm Wed

Integrity Atlanta 2089 Ponce de Leon (church), (770) 642-3183, 6:30pm 2nd & 4th Sun

Presbyterians for Lesbian/Gay Concerns PO Box 8362, 30306, 373-5830

PUBLICATIONS

Atlanta Community Yellow Pages 1888 Emery St. Ste. 220, 30318, 350-6720/(800) 849-0406, annual

▲ **ETC Magazine** PO Box 8916, 30306, 525-3821, weekly, bar & restaurant guide
  Southern Voice 1095 Zenolite Rd., 30306, 876-1819, weekly
  Venus Magazine P.O. Box 89238, 30312, 622-8069

Erotica
The Poster Hut 2175 Cheshire Bridge Rd., 633-7491
Starship 2275 Cheshire Bridge Rd., 320-9101, leather & more, 5 locations in Atlanta

Cruisy Areas
Tara Theatre Cheshire Bridge Rd. (AYOR)

Augusta (706)

Bars
Walton Way Station 1632 Walton Wy., 733-2603 (MW,D,S) 9pm-3am, clsd Sun

Spiritual Groups
MCC 609 Charton Dr., 722-6454 (WC) 7pm Sun

Cruisy Areas
Ft. Gordon PX (AYOR)

Bowden (706)

Bars
Rainbow Pub 1174 Hwy 166, 258-7766, 8:30pm til ?, clsd Mon-Wed

Restaurants & Cafes
Scandals
110 City Hall Ave., 258-7771, 11am-10pm, from 5pm Fri-Sat, clsd Sun, pizza

Carrollton (770)

Bookstores & Retail Shops
Blue Moon Gifts 113 Newnan St., 836-0014, 11am-6:30pm, clsd Sun

Cruisy Areas
Lake Carroll Rec. Area (AYOR)

Columbus (706)

Erotica
Foxes Cinema 3009 Victory Dr., 689-2211

Cruisy Areas
Broadway uptown (AYOR)
Callaway Gardens & Showers at Robin Lake Beach (AYOR)

Dalton (706)

Accommodations
Hurricane Mountain B&B 1058 Franklin Hill Rd., 673-6828 (MO,WC)

Macon (912)

Bars
Cherry St. Pub 425 Cherry St., 755-1400 (M,S)
Topaz 695 Riverside Dr., 750-7669 (MW,D,S,WC) 5pm-2am, clsd Sun

Cruisy Areas
Central City Park (AYOR)

Mountain City (706)

ACCOMMODATIONS
The York House York House Rd., 746-2068 (GF) 1896 historic country inn

Savannah (912)

INFO LINES & SERVICES
▲ **Community Real Estate Referrals** (800) 346-5592, gay realtor at your service, no rentals

First City Network, Inc. 335 Tatnall St., 236-2489, info & events line, social group

ACCOMMODATIONS
912 Barnard Victorian B&B 912 Barnard, 234-9121 (MW,N) fireplaces, hot tub, no smoking

BARS
Club One 1 Jefferson St., 232-0200 (MW,D,F,S) 5pm-3am

Faces II 17 Lincoln St., 233-3520 (M,NH,F) 11am-3am, patio

CRUISY AREAS
Monterey Square Bull St. (AYOR)

Tybee Island Beaches (AYOR)

Valdosta (912)

BARS
Club Paradise 2100 W. Hill Ave. (exit 4 I-95), 242-9609 (★MW,D,S) 9pm-2am, clsd Sun-Mon, patio

HAWAII

HAWAII (BIG ISLAND)

Captain Cook (808)

ACCOMMODATIONS
Hale Aloha Guest Ranch 84-4780 Mamalahoa Hwy, Captain Cook, 328-8955/(800) 897-3188 (GF,N) hot tub, workout equipment, expanded cont'l brkfst

▲ **RBR Farms** P.O. Box 930, Captain Cook, 96704, 328-9212/(800) 328-9212 (★MW,SW,N, IGTA) hot tub, full brkfst, on working macadamia nut & coffee plantation

Samurai House RR1 Box 359, Captain Cook, 328-9210 (★GF,WC) hot tub, traditional house brought from Japan

Honokaa (808)

ACCOMMODATIONS
Paauhau Plantation Inn P.O. Box 1375, Honokaa, 96727, 775-7222/(800) 789-7614 (GF) B&B w/cottages

Kailua-Kona (808)

ACCOMMODATIONS
Dolores Bed & Breakfast 77-6704 Kilohana, Kailua-Kona, 329-8778 (GF) full brkfst, ocean views

▲ **Hale Kipa 'O Pele** P.O. Box 5252, Kailua-Kona, 96745, 329-8676/(800) 528-2456 (MW,IGTA) hot tub, plantation-style B&B

▲ **Royal Kona Resort** 75-5852 Alii Dr., Kailua-Kona, 329-3111/(800) 774-5662 (GF,SW) overlooking Kailua Bay, private beach

BARS

▲ **Mask Bar & Grill** 75-5660 Kopiko St., Kailua-Kona, 329-8558 (★MW,NH,D,E,K) 6pm-2am, only gay & lesbian bar on the island

TRAVEL & TOUR OPERATORS

Ecoscapes 75-5626 Kuakini Hwy. Ste.1, Kailua-Kona, 329-7116/(800) 949-3483 (IGTA)

Rainbow Tours 87-3203 Road Guava, Captain Cook, 328-6406

CRUISY AREAS

Kahaluu Beach Park Kailua-Kona (AYOR)

Nude Beach 5 mi S. of Airport, Kailua-Kona (AYOR)

Kamuela (808)

BOOKSTORES & RETAIL SHOPS

▲ **The Art of Ray Helgeson** P.O. Box 383628, Waikoloa, 96738, 334-3330

Pahoa (808)

ACCOMMODATIONS

Huliaule'a B&B PO Box 1030, Pahoa, 96778, 965-9175 (MW)

Kalani Honua Seaside Retreat RR2 Box 4500, Beach Rd., Pahoa, 96778, 965-7828/(800) 800-6886 (GF,F,SW,IGTA)

Lava Tree Guest Farm PO Box 881, Pahoa, 96778-0881, 965-7325, renovated plantation home on working Macadamia farm

We put the 'Big' in "Big Island"

With 452 spacious guest rooms spread among 11 oceanfront acres, the Royal Kona Resort is the Kona Coast's premier full-service destination. We're set within walking distance of a sparkling gay beach and exciting gay nightlife, along with all of Kailua-Kona's shopping and fine dining.

Need more? Our gay-friendly staff strives to ensure your stay is truly unforgettable, and our exclusive Rest Assured Policy guarantees our gay clientele the best value in fine accommodations and complete satisfaction. Experience the Royal Kona Resort... and enjoy **big** service in a big way.

For Reservations Call:
800-774-KONA

Royal Kona Resort
FORMERLY THE KONA HILTON

Pamalu RR 2 Box 4023, Pahoa, 96778, 965-0830 (GF,SW) country retreat on 5 secluded acres

PUBLICATIONS

Outspoken PO Box 601, Pahoa, 96778, 982-7617, newsletter printed 6 times a year

Volcano Village (808)

ACCOMMODATIONS

Hale Ohia Cottages P.O. Box 758, Volcano Village, 96785, (808) 967-7986/(800) 455-3803 (GF,WC,IGTA)

KAUAI

Anahola (808)

ACCOMMODATIONS

▲ **Mahina Kai Bed & Breakfast** P.O. Box 699, Anahola, 96703, 822-9451/(800) 337-1134 (★MW,SW) country villa overlooking Anahola Bay, hot tub

CRUISY AREAS

Donkey Beach Anahola (AYOR) Rt. 56 at dirt road S. of 12 mile marker, nude beach, follow winding pat

Lydgate Park off Rte. 56, Anahola (AYOR)

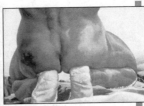

Hanalei (808)

INFO LINES & SERVICES
▲ **Community Real Estate Referrals** Hanalei, (800) 346-5592, gay realtor at your service, no rentals

ACCOMMODATIONS
Hale Maha PO Box 1438, Hanalei, 96714, 826-4447

BARS
Tahiti Nui Kuhio Hwy., Hanalei, 826-6277 (GF,F,E,WC) luau Fri, more gay Fri-Sat

Kalaheo (808)

INFO LINES & SERVICES
▲ **Community Real Estate Referrals** Kalaheo, (800) 346-5592, gay realtor at your service, no rentals

ACCOMMODATIONS
Black Bamboo Guest House 3829 Waha Rd., Kalaheo, 332-7518/(800) 527-7789 (★MW,SW,WC,IGTA) plantation-style house

Kapaa (808)

ACCOMMODATIONS
▲ **Aloha Kauai B&B** 156 Lihau St., Kapaa, 822-6966/(800) 262-4652 (MW,SW,WC) full brkfst
▲ **Hale Kahawai** 185 Kahawai Pl., Wailua, 822-1031 (MW) mountain views, hot tub

HALE KAHAWAI
BED & BREAKFAST
Accommodations on Kauai

Luxurious island home. Minutes to beaches, waterfalls and hiking trails.
Complimentary tropical breakfast.

(808) 822-1031
185 Kahawai Place, Kapa'a, Kauai, HI 96746
FAX: (808) 823-8220

Aloha Kauai

BED & BREAKFAST
156 Lihau, Street
Kapaa, Kauai, Hawaii 96746
Mainland Reservations: 1-800-262-4652
Locally (808) 822-6966

Above the lazy Wailua River in a quiet, garden surround, there is a place called Aloha Kauai. Here Hawaii speaks in the soft murmur of wind chimes, the sweet smell of tropical flowers and the shimmery water of the pool. Five minutes from Kapaa town beaches and 15 minutes to Donkey Beach, Aloha Kauai is not only a BED AND BREAKFAST alternative to hotel accommodations, it is a hideaway conveniently located within minutes of restaurants, shops and scenic attractions.

Situated in the path of the seven ancient heiau (Hawaiian temples) that stretch from the mouth of the Wailua River to the top of Mount Wai'ale'ale, Aloha Kauai is up the road from spectacular Opaekaa Falls and close to hiking trails and fishing spots. You can hike through the forests of Sleeping Giant, wander nearby Keahua Arboretum or enjoy freshwater fishing at the Wailua Reservoir.

Aloha Kauai's expansive living room with South Pacific decor is the perfect place to relax at day's end with refreshments served daily from 5 o'clock. Three delightful bedrooms, one with a private entry, and a charming pool house are available.

If you can appreciate seclusion and privacy, then let us show you a little Hawaiian hospitality with the personal service you deserve. We're pleased with what we have to offer you and can accommodate any special needs to make your stay here at Aloha Kauai the best ever in Hawaii.

For reservations, call toll free 1-800-262-4652 from the mainland U.S. Locally (808) 822-6966.

▲ **Kauai Coconut Beach Resort** PO Box 830, Kapaa, 96746, 822-3455/(800) 222-5642 (GF,SW) oceanfront resort, tennis, nightly luau

▲ **Mala Lani** 5711 Lokelani Blvd., Kapaa, 823-0422 (MW,IGTA)

Mohala Ke Ola B&B Retreat 5663 Ohelo Rd., Kapaa, 823-6398 (GF,SW)

Ola Hou Guest Retreat 332 Aina Loli Pl., Kapa'a, 823-0109/(800) 772-4567 (MW,SW) vacation rental

Royal Drive Cottages 147 Royal Dr., Wailua, 822-2321 (MW) private garden cottages, kitchenettes

BARS

Sideout 4-1330 Kuhio Hwy., 822-0082 (★GF,E,WC) noon-1:30am, bands Tue, Th & wknds

Kilauea (808)

ACCOMMODATIONS

Kai Mana P.O. Box 612, Kilauea, 96754, 828-1280/(800) 837-1782 (GF) Shakti Gawain's paradise home

Kalihiwai Jungle Home P.O. Box 717, Kilauea, 96754, 828-1626 (MW,N,WC) clifftop rental home, nr. beaches

▲ **Pali Kai** P.O. Box 450, Kilauea, 96754, 828-6691 (★MW) hilltop B&B w/ oceanview, hot tub

CRUISY AREAS

Secret Beach (inquire locally), Kilauea (AYOR)

Do It Naturally...
on Kauai At the full-service
Kauai Coconut Beach Resort, we offer
our gay guests easy access to it all.
Discover exciting gay nightlife within
walking distance, and explore all of
the natural wonders of Hawaii's
beautiful "Garden Isle" from
our central island location.

With spectacular, ocean-
front surroundings, newly-
redecorated guest rooms
and an exclusive Rest
Assured Policy which
guarantees our gay
clientele the best
value in fine accom-
modations and comp-
lete satisfaction, we
provide the ideal,
gay-friendly setting
to do it naturally...
on Kauai.

For Reservations Call:
800-22-ALOHA

Kauai Coconut Beach Resort
COCONUT PLANTATION

MAUI

Haiku (808)

ACCOMMODATIONS

Golden Bamboo Ranch 1205 Kaupakalua, Haiku, 572-7824/(800) 344-1238 (MW,IGTA) 7-acre estate w/ ocean views, cottages

Halfway to Hana House P.O. Box 675, Haiku, Maui, 96708, 572-1176 (GF) private studio w/ ocean view

Kailua Maui Gardens SR Box 9, Haiku, 572-9726/(800) 258-8588 (GF,SW,N,WC,IGTA) also suites, hot tub

Hana (808)

ACCOMMODATIONS

▲ **Blair's Original Hana Plantation Houses** 2957 Kala Kaua Ave., Honolulu, 96713, 248-7868/(800) 228-4262 (★M,SW,IGTA) tropical cottages & houses

Hana Alii Holidays Hana, 248-7742/(800) 548-0478, accommodations reservations service

Napualani O'Hana P.O. Box 118, Hana, 96713, 248-8935 (GF,WC) 2 full units, lanai, ocean & mtn views

Kahului (808)

TRAVEL & TOUR OPERATORS

Fodor's Island Travel 415 Dairy Rd. #E-201, Kahului, 875-7000 (IGTA)

PALI KAI

Bed and breakfast hide-away on Kauai's spectacular North Shore

P. O. Box 450, Kilauea, HI 96754 • 808-828-6691

Kihei (808)

ACCOMMODATIONS

▲ **Anfora's Dreams** Box 74030, Los Angeles CA, 90004, (213) 737-0731 (M,SW) rental condo nr. ocean, hot tub

Jack & Tom's Maui Condos P.O. Box 365, Kihei, 96753, 874-1048/(800) 800-8608

Ko'a Kai Rentals Box 1969, Kihei, 96753, 879-6058 (GF,SW) inexpensive rentals

Koa Lagoon 800 S. Kihei Rd., Kihei, 879-3002/(800) 367-8030 (GF,SW,WC) ocean-front suites, 5 night min.

Royal Hawaiian Accommodations PO Box 424, Puunene, 96784, (800) 285-1522, deluxe oceanfront accommodations

Triple Lei B&B PO Box 593, Kihei, 96753, 874-8645/(800) 871-8645 (M,SW,N) near nude beach

CRUISY AREAS

Kalama Park (AYOR)

Kula (808)

ACCOMMODATIONS

Camp Kula - Maui B&B P.O. Box 111, Kula, 96790, 878-2528 (★MW,WC) on the slopes of Mt. Haleakala, HIV+ welcome

Lahaina (808)

INFO LINES & SERVICES

AA Gay/Lesbian Lahaina, 244-9673, 8pm Wed, 7:30am Sun

▲ **Community Real Estate Referrals** Lahaina, (800) 346-5592, gay realtor at your service, no rentals

ACCOMMODATIONS

Kahana Beach Condominium Hotel 4221 Lower Honoapiilani Rd., Lahaina, 669-8611/(800) 222-5642 (GF) oceanfront studios & one-bdrm suites, kitchenettes, private lanai

▲ **The Royal Lahaina Resort** 2780 Kekaa Dr., Lahaina, 661-3611/(800) 447-6925 (GF,SW,WC) full service resort, world-class tennis courts & golf courses

BOOKSTORES & RETAIL SHOPS

Skin Deep Tattoo 626 Front St., Lahaina, 661-8531, 10am-10pm, til 7pm Sun, custom tattooing, adult toys, Harley-Davidson T-shirts

TRAVEL & TOUR OPERATORS

Maui Magical Weddings (800) 779-1320, traditional & non-traditional committment ceremonies in secluded Maui locations

Maui Surfing School PO Box 424, Puunene, 96784, 875-0625/(800) 659-1866, lessons for beginners, cowards & non-swimmers, 'surf-aris' for advanced

Royal Hawaiian Weddings PO Box 424, Puunene, 96784, 875-0625/(800) 659-1866 (IGTA) specializes in scenic gay weddings

CRUISY AREAS

Front St. along Beach Walk (AYOR)

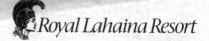

Makawao (808)

TRAVEL & TOUR OPERATORS
Maui Network 572-9555/(800) 367-5221, condo reservation service
Personal Maui 572-1589/(800) 326-5336, guide & driver for tours of the hidden Maui

Makena

CRUISY AREAS
Makena Nude Beach (AYOR)

Paia (808)

ACCOMMODATIONS
Huelo Point Flower Farm PO Box 1195, Paia, 96779, 572-1850 (GF,SW) cont'l brkfst, vacation rental, oceanfront estate

Wailea (808)

ACCOMMODATIONS
Coconuts Wailea, (800) 289-1522 (MW,SW,WC) hot tub

Wailuku (808)

BARS
Hamburger Mary's 2010 Main Str., Wailuku, 244-7776 (★MW,D,V) 10am-2am, kitchen open til 10pm, American, plenty veggie

RESTAURANTS & CAFES
Cafe Kup A Kuppa 79 Church St., Wailuku, 244-0500 (WC) 7am-4pm, 8am-1pm Sat, clsd Sun

MOLOKAI

Kaunakakai (808)

ACCOMMODATIONS
Kainehe HC-01 Box 751-Pukoo, Kaunakakai, 96748, 558-8207 (GF) fruit brkfst, on the water
Molokai Beachfront Escapes P.O. Box 248, Hana, 96713, 248-7868/(800) 228-4262 (GF,IGTA) beachfront units

OAHU

Aiea (808)

EROTICA
C 'n' N Liquor Aiea Shopping Ctr., Aiea, 487-2944
Suzie's Aiea Shopping Ctr., 2nd flr., 486-3103, 24hrs

Honolulu (808)

INFO LINES & SERVICES
▲ **Community Real Estate Referrals** Honolulu, (800) 346-5592, gay realtor at your service, no rentals
Gay/Lesbian AA 277 Ohua (Waikiki Health Ctr.), Honolulu, 946-1438, 8pm daily
Gay/Lesbian Community Center 1566 Wilder Ave. (YWCA), Honolulu, 951-7000, 9am-5pm Mon-Fri, info & referrals

ACCOMMODATIONS

Bed & Breakfast Honolulu (Statewide) 3242 Kaohinani Dr., Honolulu, 595-7533/(800) 288-4666 (GF) represents 350 locations on all islands, clientele & ownership vary (most gay-friendly)

Bed & Breakfast in Manoa Valley 2651 Terrace Dr., Honolulu, 988-6333 (GF) spectacular views

▲ **Blair's Original Hana Plantation Houses** 2957 Kala Kaua Ave., Honolulu, 96713, 248-7868/(800) 228-4262 (★M,SW,IGTA) tropical cottages & houses

The Coconut Plaza 450 Lewers St., Honolulu, 923-8828/(800) 882-9696 (GF,SW,WC) nr. beach

▲ **Hotel Honolulu** 376 Kaiolu St., Honolulu, 926-2766/(800) 426-2766 (★M,IGTA)

Pleasant Holiday Isle Hotel 270 Lewers St., Honolulu, 923-0777/(800) 222-5642 (GF,SW) 1 blk from the world-famous Waikiki beach

Waikiki Vacation Condos 1860 Ala Moana Blvd. #108, Honolulu, 946-9371/(800) 543-5663, furnished one & two-bdrm units, reservation service

BARS

▲ **Club Michaelangelo** 444 Hobron Ln. #P-8, Honolulu, 951-0008 (MW,D,K) 4pm-2am

Fusion Waikiki 2260 Kuhio Ave., 3rd flr., Honolulu, 924-2422 (★MW,D,A,TG,S) 10pm-4am, from 8pm wknds

Hula's Bar & Lei Stand 2103 Kuhio Ave., Honolulu, 923-0669 (★MW,D,E,V,YC) 10am-2am

Trixx 2109 Kuhio Ave., Honolulu, 923-0669 (MW,D,WC) 5pm-2am, from 3pm Sun (barbecue), also 'Treats' deli & the 'Fruit Bar' from 10am

Windows 444 Hobron Ln., Waikiki, Honolulu, 946-4442 (MW,E,WC) 11am-2am, lunch & Sun brunch

Restaurants & Cafes

Banana's 2139 Kuhio Ave. #125, Waikiki, Honolulu, 922-6262 (MW,WC) 5pm-2am, clsd Mon, Thai, also full bar

Cafe Sistina 1314 S. King St., Honolulu, 596-0061 (WC) lunch Mon-Fri, dinner nightly, northern Italian, some veggie, also full bar

Caffe Aczione 1684 Kalakaua Ave., Honolulu, 941-9552 (BYOB) 9am-midnight, til 2am Fri-Sat, til 10pm Sun, Italian, some veggie

Caffe Guccinni 2139 Kuhio Ave., Waikiki, Honolulu, 922-5287, 4pm-10:30pm, Italian, some veggie, also full bar

Crepe Fever/Mocha Java Ward Center, Honolulu, 591-9023, 8am-9pm, til 4pm Sun, plenty veggie

The Jungle 311 Lewers St., Honolulu, 922-7808 (D,E,WC) pasta, full bar

Keo's Thai 1200 Ala Moana Blvd., Honolulu, 533-0533 (★) dinner, also 1486 S. King St., 947-9988

La Provence 2139 Kuhio Ave., Honolulu, 924-6696, 4:30-10:30pm, clsd Mon, country French

Pieces of Eight 250 Lewers St., Waikiki, Honolulu, 923-6646 (WC) 5pm-11pm, steak & seafood, also full bar

Singha Thai 1910 Ala Moana, 941-2898 (E) 11am-11pm

Bookstores & Retail Shops

▲ Douglas Simonson-Artists Studio Honolulu, 737-6275, call for an appt.

Eighty Percent Straight 2139 Kuhio Ave., 2nd flr., Waikiki, Honolulu, 923-9996, 10am-midnight, lesbigay clothing, books, cards, etc.

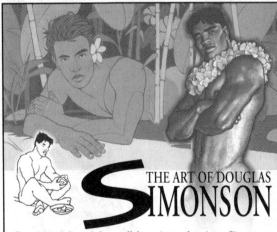

THE ART OF DOUGLAS SIMONSON

Send $5.00 for catalog; call for private showings. Simonson, 4614 Kilauea Avenue, Suite 330-D, Honolulu Hawaii 96816. Phone/fax: (808) 737-6275. Internet Gallery: http://www.pixi.com/~simonson/. E-mail: simonson@pixi.com.

TRAVEL & TOUR OPERATORS

Bird of Paradise Travel PO Box 4157, Honolulu, 96812-4157, 735-9103 (IGTA)

Hawaii Visitors Bureau 2270 Kalakaua Ave. #801, Honolulu, 923-1811

Island Pride Taxi & Tour 3151 Monsarrat Ave. #402, Honolulu, 732-6518 (IGTA)

▲ **Leis of Hawaii** (888) 534-7644, personalized Hawaiian greeting service, complete w/ fresh flower leis

▲ **Pacific Ocean Holidays** PO Box 88245, Honolulu, 96830, 923-2400/(800) 735-6600 (IGTA) also publishes semi-annual 'Pocket Guide to Hawaii'

Travel Travel 320 Ward Ave. Ste. 204, Honolulu, 596-0336 (IGTA)

SPIRITUAL GROUPS

Dignity Honolulu 539 Kapahulu Ave. (St. Mark's Church), Honolulu, 536-5536, 7:30pm Sun

Ke Annenue O Ke Aloha MCC 1212 University Ave. (Church of the Crossroads), Honolulu, 942-1027, 7pm Sun, also 11am at Cafe Valentino, 2139 Kuhio Ave.

Unitarian Universalists for Lesbian/Gay Concerns (Interweave) 2500 Pali Hwy., Honolulu, 595-4047 (WC) 10:15am Sun

Unity Church of Hawaii 3608 Diamond Head Cir., 735-4436 (WC) 7:30pm, 9am & 11am Sun

PUBLICATIONS

Island Lifestyle Magazine P.O. Box 11840, Honolulu, 96828, 737-6400, monthly; inquire about resource/travel guide

MEN'S CLUBS

▲ **Koko Pacific** 2139 Kuhio Ave., Waikiki, Honolulu, 923-1852 (★MO,PC) 24hrs

EROTICA
Diamond Head Video 870 Kapahulu Ave., Honolulu, 735-6066, also 25 Kaneohe Bay Dr., Kailau, 254-6066

Risque II Theatre 39 N. Hotel St. (upstairs), Honolulu, 531-7318, 24hrs

CRUISY AREAS
Ala Moana Beach Park nr. Waikiki Yacht Club, Honolulu (AYOR)

Diamond Head bushes above hwy. & below light house (AYOR)

Queens Surf Beach Kapiolani Park (AYOR)

Kailua

CRUISY AREAS
Kailua Beach Park (AYOR)

Kona Market Place (AYOR)

Kaneohe (808)

ACCOMMODATIONS
Windward Oahu B&B 46-251 Ikiiki, Kaneohe, 235-1124/(800) 235-1151 (MW,SW,IGTA) overlooks the bay

IDAHO

Boise (208)

INFO LINES & SERVICES
AA Gay/Lesbian 23rd & Woodlawn (First Cong. Church), (208) 344-6611, 8pm Sun & Tue

Community Center PO Box 323, 83701, 336-3870, 7pm-10pm

BARS
8th Street Balcony Pub 150 N. 8th St., 336-1313 (GF,NH,F,E) 2pm-midnight, til 2am Th-Sat

Emerald City Club 415 S. 9th, 342-5446 (MW,D,S) 10am-2:30am

The Papa's Club 96 1108 Front St., 333-0074 (M,NH) 2pm-2am, patio

Partners 2210 Main St., 331-3551 (MW,D,E,WC) 2pm-2am

RESTAURANTS & CAFES
The Flicks & Rick's Café American 646 Fulton St., 342-4288 (BW,MRC,E,WC) opens 4:30pm, from noon wknds, patio

BOOKSTORES & RETAIL SHOPS
Blue Unicorn 1809 W. State St., 345-9390 (WC) 10am-9pm, 11am-5pm Sun, self-help w/women's & gay/lesbian section

TRAVEL & TOUR OPERATORS
Idaho Travel Council 700 W. State St., (800) 635-7820

SPIRITUAL GROUPS
MCC 408 N. Garden St., 342-6764, 5:45pm Sun

PUBLICATIONS
Diversity PO Box 323, 83701, 323-0805, monthly

CRUISY AREAS
Ann Morrison Park nr. baseball fields (AYOR)

Caldwell (208)

Erotica
Adult Book Store 716 Arthur, 454-2422

Coeur D'Alene (208)

Accommodations
The Clark House on Hayden Lake 4550 S. Hayden Lake Rd., 772-3470/(800) 765-4593 (★GF,WC) mansion on 12-acre estate

Idaho Falls

Cruisy Areas
Riverside Dr. & The Loop opposite the hospital (AYOR)
Snake River Falls (AYOR)

Lava Hot Springs (208)

Accommodations
Lava Hot Springs Inn 5 Portneuf Ave., 776-5830 (GF, WC) full brkfst, hot tub

Cruisy Areas
Hot Pools (AYOR)

Lewiston

Info Lines & Services
Lewiston Lesbian/Gay Society PO Box 2054, 83501, meets 1st & 3rd Tue

Moscow (208)

Info Lines & Services
Inland Northwest PO Box 8135, 83843, 882-8034, 1st Mon
University of Idaho Gay/Lesbian/Bisexual Group 885-2691

Bookstores & Retail Shops
Bookpeople 512 S. Main, 882-7957, 9am-8pm

Pocatello (208)

Bars
Continental Bistro 140 S. Main St., 233-4433 (GF,F) 11am-1am, clsd Sun, northern Italian, patio

Bookstores & Retail Shops
The Silver Fox 143 S. 2nd St.43 S. 2nd St., 234-2477 (MW,NH,S,WC) 11am-10pm, clsd Sun

Erotica
Pegasus Book Store 246 W. Center, 232-6493

Cruisy Areas
Ross Park (AYOR)

Sand Point

Cruisy Areas
Cedar St. Bridge (AYOR)

Stanley (208)

ACCOMMODATIONS
Las Tejanas B&B 3610 Rampart St., Boise, 83704, 376-6077 (MW) May-Sept, natural hot tub, full brkfst

Twin Falls

CRUISY AREAS
City Park (AYOR)
Rockcreek Park (AYOR) days

ILLINOIS

Alton (618)

BARS
Alton Metro 602 Belle, 465-8687 (M,D,S,WC) 4pm-1:30am

PUBLICATIONS
TWISL (This Week In St. Louis) PO Box 8068, 62002, 465-9370

Aurora (284)

EROTICA
Denmark Book Store 1300 US Hwy. 30, 898-9838, 24hrs

Bellville (618)

BARS
Char Pei Lounge 400 Mascoutah Ave. , 236-0810 (MW,D,WC) 6pm-2am, from noon Sun

Bloomington (309)

BARS
Bistro 316 N. Main St., 829-2278 (MW,D,WC) 4pm-1am, from 8pm Sat, from 6pm Sun

BOOKSTORES & RETAIL SHOPS
Once Upon a Time (O.U.T) 311 N. Main, 828-3998, 1pm-8pm,10am-8pm Sat, noon-5pm Sun, clsd Mon, lesbigay

EROTICA
Risques 1506 N. Main, 827-9279, 24hrs

CRUISY AREAS
Jefferson St. (AYOR) nights, by courthouse square

Blue Island (708)

BARS
Clubhouse Players 13126 S. Western, 389-6688 (MW,D,WC) 8pm-2am, til 3am Fri-Sat

Calumet City (708)

BARS
Are You Crazy 48 154th Pl., 862-4605 (M) 7pm-2am
Intrigue 582 State Line Rd., 868-5240 (W,D,WC) 6pm-2am, 7pm-3am Sat, 2pm-2am Sun
Mr. B's 606 State Line Rd., 862-1221 (★M,D) 2pm-2am, til 3am Wed, Fri-Sat

Patch 201 155th St., 891-9854 (W,NH) 3pm-2am, til 3am Sat, 6pm-2am Sun, clsd Mon

Pour House 103 155th Pl., 891-3980 (M,D) 8pm-2am, til 3am Wed, Fri-Sat

CRUISY AREAS

Shabonna Woods & Sandridge Forest Preserves (AYOR)

Carbondale (618)

INFO LINES & SERVICES

AA Lesbian/Gay 549-4633

Gay/Lesbian/Bisexuals & Friends at Southern Illinois University, 453-5151

Champaign/Urbana (217)

INFO LINES & SERVICES

▲ **Community Real Estate Referrals** (800) 346-5592, gay realtor at your service, no rentals

People for Lesbian/Gay/Bisexual Concerns of Illinois (at University of Illinois), 333-1187, 6pm Tue, student group

BARS

Chester Street 63 Chester St., 356-5607 (GF,D,WC) 5pm-1am, 'Trash Disco' Tue

BOOKSTORES & RETAIL SHOPS

Horizon Book Store 1115-1/2 W. Oregon, 328-2988, 10am-6pm, clsd Sun

Jane Addams Book Shop 208 N. Neil, 356-2555, 10am-5pm, noon-4pm Sun, antiquarian bookstore

EROTICA

Holiday Video Arcade 213 S. Neil St., 351-8897

Illini Video Arcade 33 E. Springfield Ave., 359-8529

CHICAGO

Chicago is divided into 5 geographical areas:

Chicago - Overview

Chicago - Near North

Chicago - North Side

Chicago - New Town

Chicago - South Side

Chicago - Overview (312)

INFO LINES & SERVICES

AA Gay/Lesbian-Newtown Al-Anon Club 4407 N. Clark, 271-6822 (WC) 3pm-11pm, fom 8:30am wknds

▲ **Community Real Estate Referrals** (800) 346-5592, gay realtor at your service, no rentals

Gay/Lesbian South Asians (SANGAT) PO Box 268463, 60626

Gerber/Hart Library & Archives 3352 N. Paulina St., 883-3003, 6pm-9pm Mon & Th, noon-4pm wknds, lesbigay resource center

Horizons Community Services 961 W. Montana, 472-6469, 9am-10pm Mon-Th, til 5pm Fri

Leather Archives & Musuem 5007 N. Clark St., 275-1570, 4pm-midnight Sat or appt.

Lesbian/Gay Helpline 929-4357, 6pm-10pm

Lesbigay Radio WCBR 92.7 FM, 506-1521, 8am-noon Sun

ACCOMMODATIONS

▲ **Caritas B&B Network** (800) CARITAS (227-4827), see ad in center National Section

BOOKSTORES & RETAIL SHOPS

Barbara's Bookstore 1350 N. Wells St., 642-5044 (WC) 9am-10pm, 10am-9pm Sun, women's/lesbigay; also 3130 N. Broadway, 477-0411; also Oak Park (708) 848-9140

TRAVEL & TOUR OPERATORS

The Concierge Exclusif 75 E. Walker Dr. Ste.3600, 849-3604, personalized assistance for visitors

Illinois Tourist Information Center 310 S. Michigan Ste. 108, (800) 822-0292

SPIRITUAL GROUPS

Congregation or Chadash 656 W. Barry (2nd Unitarian Church), 248-9456, 8pm Fri, Shabbat services & monthly activities

Dignity Chicago 3344 N. Broadway, 296-0780, 7pm Sun

PUBLICATIONS

The Alternative Phone Book 425 W. Surf St. #114 , 472-6319, directory of local businesses

Gay Chicago 3121 N. Broadway, 327-7271, weekly

▲ **Outlines/Nightlines** 1115 W. Belmont Ave. #2-D, 871-7610, monthly

Windy City Times 325 W. Huron Ste.510, 397-0020, weekly

Chicago - Near North (312)

INFO LINES & SERVICES

▲ **Community Real Estate Referrals** (800) 346-5592, gay realtor at your service, no rentals

ACCOMMODATIONS

Cass Hotel 640 N. Wabash Ave., 787-4030/(800) 227-7850 (GF,F) full bar

Old Town Bed & Breakfast 440-9268 (GF) patio

BARS

Artful Dodger 1734 W. Wabansia, 227-6859 (GF,D) 5pm-2am, from 8pm Sat, clsd Sun

Baton Show Lounge 436 N. Clark St., 644-5269 (MW,S,WC) 8pm-4am Wed-Sun

Cairo 720 N. Wells, 266-6620 (GF,D,V,WC) 8pm-4am, 9am-5pm Sat, clsd Sun-Mon, more gay Sat

The Crowbar 1543 N. Kingsbury, 243-4800 (★GF,D) 10pm-4am, clsd Mon-Tue, more gay Sun

The Generator 306 N. Halsted, 243-8889 (MW,D,A,MRC-AF,WC) 9pm-4am, clsd Mon-Tue

▲ **Gentry** 712 N. Rush St., 664-1033 (★M,E,V) 1pm-2am

Ka-Boom 747 N. Green, River North, 243-4800 (GF,D) from 9pm, clsd Sun-Wed

Second Story Bar 157 E. Ohio St., 923-9536 (M,NH) noon-2am, from 3pm wknds

Vinyl 1615 N. Clybourn, 587-8469 (GF,F,E) opens 5:30pm

RESTAURANTS & CAFES

Fireplace Inn 1448 N. Wells St., 664-5264 (MW) 4:30pm-midnight, from 11am wknds(summer), BBQ, full bar

Iggy's 700 N. Milwaukee, River North, 829-4449, dinner nightly, til 4am Th-Sat, Italian, full bar

Urbis Orbis Coffeehouse 1934 W. North Ave., 252-4446, 9am-midnight, lesbigay periodicals

Travel & Tour Operators

C.R.C. Travel 2121 N. Clybourn, 525-3800/(800) 874-7701 (IGTA)

Envoy Travel 740 N. Rush St., 787-2400/(800) 443-6869 (IGTA)

River North Travel 432 N. Clark St., 527-2269 (IGTA)

Travel With Us, Ltd. 919 N. Michigan Ave. #3102, 944-2244/(800) 775-0919 (IGTA)

Spiritual Groups

Presbyterians for Lesbian/Gay Concerns 600 W. Fullerton Pkwy. (Lincoln Park Preb.), 784-2635, 11am Sun (10am summers), 'More Light' congregation

Erotica

Bijou Theatre 1349 N. Wells St., 943-5397, 24hrs

Leslie's Adult Books 738 N. Clark St., 751-9672, 24hrs

Chicago - North Side   (312)

Info Lines & Services

▲ **Community Real Estate Referrals** (800) 346-5592, gay realtor at your service, no rentals

Bars

Big Chicks 5024 N. Sheridan, 728-5511 (MW,NH,WC) noon-2am

Charmer's Lounge 1502 W. Jarvis, 465-2811 (M,NH) 4pm-2am, from noon Sun

Chicago Eagle 5015 N. Clark St., 728-0050 (MW,L,WC) 8pm-4am

Clark's on Clark 5001 N. Clark St., 728-2373 (★M,NH) 4pm-4am

Different Strokes 4923 N. Clark St., 989-1958 (M,NH) noon-2am, til 3am Sat

El Gato Negro 1461 W. Irving Park, 472-9353 (GF,TG,MRC-L)

Granville Anvil 1137 W. Granville, 973-0006 (M,NH) 11am-2am

Legacy 3042 W. Irving Park Rd., 588-9405 (M,NH) 8pm-4am, til 5am Sat

Lost & Found 3058 W.Irving Park Rd., 463-9617 (W,NH) 7pm-2am, from 4pm wknds, clsd Mon

Madrigal's 5316 N. Clark St., 334-3033 (MW,F,E) 5pm-2am

Numbers 6406 N. Clark St., 743-5772 (★M,D) 4pm-4am, patio

Off the Line 1829 W. Montrose, 528-3253 (W,NH) 5pm-2am, from 3pm wknds

Touché 6412 N. Clark St., 465-7400 (★M,L) 5pm-4am, from 3pm wknds

Traveler's Rest 1138 W. Granville Ave., 262-4225 (M,NH) 10am-2am, from 7am Sat

Restaurants & Cafes

Fireside 5739 N. Ravenswood, 878-5942 (WC) 11am-4am, full bar, patio

Tendino's 5335 N. Sheridan, 275-8100 (WC) 11am-11pm, pizzeria, also full bar

Bookstores & Retail Shops

Gay Mart 3457 N. Halsted St., 929-4272, open 11am

KOPI: A Traveler's Cafe 5317 N. Clark St., 989-5674 (E) 8am-11pm

Men's Clubs

Man's Country 5017 N. Clark St., 878-2069 (MO,PC) 24hrs

Man's World 4862 N. Clark St., 728-0400 (MO,PC) 24hrs

EROTICA
Howard Street Book Store 7614 N. Ashland, 465-9431, 24hrs

Chicago - New Town (312)

INFO LINES & SERVICES
▲ **Community Real Estate Referrals** (800) 346-5592, gay realtor at your service, no rentals

ACCOMMODATIONS
City Suites Hotel 933 W. Belmont, 404-3400/(800) 248-9108 (GF,IGTA)
Park Brompton Inn 528 W. Brompton Pl., 404-3499/(800) 727-5108 (GF)
Surf Hotel 555 W. Surf St., 528-8400/(800) 787-3108 (GF) 1920s hotel
▲ **Villa Toscana Guesthouse** 3447 N. Halstead St., 404-2643/(800) 684-5755 (MW) full brkfst

BARS
Annex 3 3160 N. Clark St., 327-5969 (MW,V,WC) noon-2am, til 3am Sat
Beat Kitchen 2100 W. Belmont, 281-4444 (GF,F,E) noon-2am
Berlin 954 W. Belmont, 348-4975 (★MW,D,S,WC) opening time varies, closes 4am
Buck's Saloon 3439 N. Halsted St., 525-1125 (M) 10am-2am, patio
Buddies Restaurant & Bar 3301 N. Clark St., 477-4066 (MW) 7am-2am, from 9am Sun
Charlie's Chicago 3726 N. Broadway, 871-8887 (M,D,CW) noon-4am
Closet 3325 N. Broadway St., 477-8533 (★MW,V) 2pm-4am, from noon wknds
Cocktail 3359 Halsted St., 477-1420 (MW,V,WC) 4pm-2am, from 2pm wknds

Villa Toscana
Guest House

A European Style B&B
in the Heart of Gay Chicago

7 Rooms
Air Conditioning
Private Phone Lines
Cable TV
Expanded Continental Breakfast
Parking Available
Rooms from $70

3447 N. Halsted St. • Chicago, IL 60657
1-800-684-5755

Dandy's Piano Bar 3729 N. Halsted St., 525-1200 (MW,NH) noon-2am

Dram Shop 3040 N. Broadway, 525-9885 (GF,NH) 7am-2am

▲ **Gentry** 3320 N. Halsted, 348-1053 (MW,S) 4pm-2am

Little Jim's 3501 N. Halsted St., 871-6116 (★M,NH) 9am-4am, til 5am Sat, from 11am Sun

Lucky Horseshoe 3169 N. Halsted St., 404-3169 (M,S) 2pm-2am, from noon wknds, patio

Manhandler 1948 N. Halsted St., 871-3339 (★M,CW,L) noon-4am, patio

Manhole 3458 N. Halsted St., 975-9244 (★M,D,L,V) 9pm-4am

The North End 3733 N. Halsted St., 477-7999 (M,NH) 3pm-2am, from 2pm wknds

Roscoe's 3354-3356 N. Halsted St., 281-3355 (★MW,NH,D,F,V) 2pm-2am, noon-3am Sat, patio

Sidetrack 3349 N. Halsted St., 477-9189 (★M,V,WC) 3pm-2:30am

Smart Bar/Cabaret Metro 3730 N. Clark St., 549-4140 (GF,D,E) 9:30pm-4am

Spin 3200 N. Halsted, 327-7711 (M,D,V) 4pm-2am

Vortex
3631 N. Halsted, 975-6622 (MW,D,A,E,V,WC) 9pm-4am, clsd Sun-Mon

RESTAURANTS & CAFES

Angelina Ristorante 3561 Broadway, 935-5933, 5:30pm-11pm, Sun brunch, Italian

Ann Sather's 929 W. Belmont Ave., 348-2378 (★) 7am-10pm, til midnight Fri-Sat

Cornelia's 750 Cornelia Ave., 248-8333 (WC) clsd Mon, dinner nightly, full bar

RAM

BOOKSTORE

Chicago's Biggest and Best Backroom!

3511 N Halsted * 525-9528

Mike's Broadway Cafe 3805 N. Broadway, 404-2205 (MW,WC) 7am-10pm, 24hrs Fri-Sat

The Pepper 3441 N. Sheffield, 665-7377 (MW) 6pm-2am, clsd Mon, supper club

Perk 3322 N. Halsted, 549-9900 (MW,WC) noon-1am

The Raw Bar & Grill 3720 N. Clark St., 348-7291, 5pm-2am, seafood

Scenes Coffee House & Dramatist Bookstore 3168 N. Clark St., 525-1007, 9:30am-midnight

GYMS & HEALTH CLUBS

▲ **The Bodyshop** 3246 N. Halsted St. (at the Unicorn), 248-7717 (MO) 6am-10pm

Chicago Sweat Shop 3215 N. Broadway, 871-2789, gay owned & run

BOOKSTORES & RETAIL SHOPS

▲ **People Like Us** 1115 W. Belmont, 248-6363, 10am-9pm, Chicago's only exclusively lesbigay bookstore

Unabridged Books 3251 N. Broadway St., 883-9119 (WC) 10am-10pm, til 8pm wknds

We're Everywhere 3434 N. Halsted St., 404-0590, noon-7pm

SPIRITUAL GROUPS

MCC Good Shepherd 615 W. Wellington Ave., 262-0099, 7pm Sun

MEN'S CLUBS

▲ **Unicorn Club** 3246 N. Halsted St., 929-6080 (MO,PC) 24hrs

EROTICA

Male Hide Leathers 2816 N. Lincoln Ave., 929-0069, noon-8pm, til midnight Fri-Sat, clsd Mon

HIDEAWAY II

The Hottest Club In Chicago's Western Suburbs!

(ONLY 10 MINUTES FROM OAK BROOK)

Relax In Our Intimate Lounge

or...

WORK UP A SWEAT

IN OUR

HEART POUNDING VIDEO DANCE BAR

HOME OF THE

MONDAY NIGHT PARTY

HOT MEN! HOT MUSIC! COOL DRINK PRICES

4 PLAY GRAPHICS 312 275 0459

7301 W. Roosevelt Rd. (2 Blks. West Of Harlem Ave.)
Forest Park, IL 708-771-4459
OPEN DAILY AT 3 PM

▲ **Ram Bookstore** 3511-1/2 N. Halsted St., 525-9528, 10am-6am

CRUISY AREAS
Belmont Rocks S. of Belmont at lake (AYOR)

Chicago - South Side (312)

INFO LINES & SERVICES
▲ **Community Real Estate Referrals** (800) 346-5592, gay realtor at your service, no rentals

BARS
Escapades 6301 S. Harlem, 229-0886 (M,D,V) 10pm-4am, til 5am Sat
Inn Exile 5758 W. 65th St., 582-3510 (M,D,V,WC) 6pm-2am, from noon Sun
Jeffery Pub/Disco 7041 S. Jeffery, 363-8555 (M,D,MRC,WC) 11am-4am

EROTICA
A&B Adult Books 6159 S. Cicero, 284-0938

Decatur (402)

EROTICA
Emporium 2015 N. 22nd St, 362-0105, 24hrs

Elgin (847)

INFO LINES & SERVICES
Fox Valley Gay Association PO Box 393, 60120, 392-6882, 7pm-10pm Mon-Fri, info & referrals

Elk Grove Village (847)

BARS
Hunters 1932 E. Higgins, 439-8840 (★M,D,V) 4pm-4am

Evanston

ACCOMMODATIONS
▲ **The Caritas B&B Network** (800) CARITAS (227-4827), see ad in center National section

CRUISY AREAS
Triangular Park Sheridan & Church (AYOR)

Forest Park (296)

BARS
▲ **Hideaway II** 7301 W. Roosevelt Rd., 771-4459 (M,D,S,V,WC) 3pm-2am, til 3am Fri-Sat
Nut Bush 7201 Franklin, 366-5117 (M,D,V) 3pm-2am Mon, til 3am Fri-Sat

Franklin Park (708)

BARS
Temptations 10235 W. Grand Ave., 455-0008 (★W,D,TG,E,V) 4pm-4am, 3pm-2am Sun

Galesburg

CRUISY AREAS
Storey Lake Park (AYOR)

Granite City (618)

BARS

Club Zips 3145 W. Chain of Rocks Rd., 797-0700 (★MW,E,V) 6pm-2am, outdoor complex

Hinsdale (708)

SPIRITUAL GROUPS

MCC Holy Covenant 17 W. Maple (Unitarian Church), 325-8488 (WC) 6pm Sun

Joliet (815)

BARS

Maneuvers 118 E. Jefferson, 727-7069 (MW,D) 8pm-2am, til 3am Fri-Sat, patio

Kankakee

CRUISY AREAS

Kankakee River State Park Rte. 102 (AYOR) across from main entrance, Dan Uze Area

LaGrange

CRUISY AREAS

Airie Crown Forest Preserve (AYOR) summers

Lansing (708)

RESTAURANTS & CAFES

Outriggers 2352 172nd St., 418-0202 (★E,WC) 11am-11pm, seafood, also comedy club

Lincolnwood (708)

TRAVEL & TOUR OPERATORS

Edward's Travel Advisors 7301 N. Lincoln Ave. #215, 677-4420/(800) 541-5158 (IGTA)

Marseille

CRUISY AREAS

Illinois State Park (AYOR) summers

Naperville (708)

TRAVEL & TOUR OPERATORS

Classic Travel 1271 E. Ogden Ave. #123, 963-3030/(800) 932-5789 (IGTA)

Nauvoo (217)

ACCOMMODATIONS

▲ **The Caritas B&B Network** (800) CARITAS (227-4827), see ad in center National section

Ed-Harri-Mere B&B 290 N. Page St., 453-2796 (GF)

Oak Park (708)

BOOKSTORES & RETAIL SHOPS

The Left Bank Bookstall 104 S. Oak Park Ave., 383-4700, 10am-8pm Mon-Th, til 9pm Fri-Sat, noon-5pm Sun

The Pride Agenda 1109 Westgate, 524-8429 (WC) 11am-7pm, til 8pm Th-Fri, 11am-5pm wknds

Ottawa

CRUISY AREAS
Starved Rock State Park (AYOR)

Peoria (309)

BARS
D.J.'s Timeout 703 SW Adams, 674-5902 (MW,D,WC) 1pm-1am
Quench Room 631 W. Main, 676-1079 (MW,NH,WC) 5pm-1am, from 1pm wknds
Red Fox Den 800 N. Knoxville Ave., 674-8013 (MW,D,F,E) 9pm-4am

PUBLICATIONS
The Alternative Times PO Box 5661, 61601, 688-1930

EROTICA
The Green Door 2610 W. Farmington Rd., 674-4337
Swingers World 335 SW Adams, 676-9275, 24hrs

Quincy (217)

INFO LINES & SERVICES
AA Gay/Lesbian 124-1/2 N. 5th (MCC), 224-2800

BARS
Irene's Cabaret 124 N. 5th St., 222-6292 (MW,D,S,WC) 9pm-1am, from 7pm Fri-Sat, clsd Mon

SPIRITUAL GROUPS
MCC 124-1/2 N. 5th , 224-2800, 6pm Sun

EROTICA SHOPS
Chelsea Books 5000 Gardner Expwy., 224-7000

Rock Island (309)

BARS
Augie's 313 20th St., 788-7389 (W,NH) 6am-3am, from 10am Sun
J.R.'s 325 20th St., 786-9411 (MW,D,S,WC) 3pm-3am, from noon Sun
Madison Square 319 20th St., 786-9400 (MW,D,S) 4pm-3am

BOOKSTORES & RETAIL SHOPS
All Kinds of People 1806 2nd Ave., 788-2567 (F,WC) 10am-11pm, alternative books & bistro

EROTICA
Centenial Video Center 309 20th St., 794-1682

Rockford (815)

BARS
Office 513 E. State St., 965-0344 (★MW,D,S,V) 5pm-2am, noon-midnight Sun

RESTAURANTS & CAFES
Cafe Esperanto 107 N. Main, 968-0123, noon-1am, 7pm-midnight Sun, gallery
Lucernes 845 N. Church St., 968-2665 (WC) 5pm-11pm, clsd Mon
Maria's 828 Cunningham, 968-6781 (WC) 5pm-9pm, clsd Sun-Mon

Schiller Park

CRUISY AREAS
Schiller Park Woods E. of River Rd. (AYOR)

Springfield (217)

INFO LINES & SERVICES
Brother To Brother PO Box 4681, 62708, support group for gay & bisexual men

BARS
New Dimensions 3036 Peoria Rd., 753-9268 (M,D) 8pm-3am Th-Sat

The Smokey's Den 411 E. Washington, 522-0301 (MW,D) 6pm-1am, til 3am Fri-Sat

The Station House 306 E. Washington, 525-0438 (GF,NH) 7am-1am, from noon Sun

SPIRITUAL GROUPS
MCC Faith Eternal 304 W. Allen, 525-9597, 10am & 6pm Sun

EROTICA
Expo I Books 300 N. 5th St., 544-5145

CRUISY AREAS
Lake Springfield (AYOR)

Sterling

INFO LINES & SERVICES
IAWIA (I Am What I Am) PO Box 1314, 61081, support group for northwest IL, meetings & newsletter

Waukegan (708)

TRAVEL & TOUR OPERATORS
Carlson Travel Network/Cray's Travel 410 S. Greenbay Rd., 623-4722 (IGTA)

CRUISY AREAS
Illinois Beach State Park trails & bird sanctuary (AYOR)

Wood River

CRUISY AREAS
Belk Park (AYOR)

INDIANA

Anderson

CRUISY AREAS
Meridian Plaza Jackson & Main Sts. (AYOR) late

Bloomington (812)

INFO LINES & SERVICES
Bloomington Gay/Lesbian/Bisexual Switchboard 855-5688, irregular volunteer hours, recorded info 24hrs

The Indiana Youth Group (800) 347-8336

Outreach Memorial Hall East #127, 855-3849, 6:30pm 2nd & 4th Tue, Support/discussion groups; call switchboard for hours & locations

ACCOMMODATIONS
Burr House 210 E. Chestnut St., 828-7686 (GF) full breakfast

BARS
The Bullwinkle's 201 S. College St., 334-3232 (MW,D,S) 7pm-3am, clsd Sun, more men Tues

The Other Bar 414 S. Walnut, 332-0033 (MW,NH,WC) 4pm-3am, clsd Sun, more women Tue & Th, patio

RESTAURANTS & CAFES
Village Deli 409 E. Kirkwood, 336-2303 (MW) 7am-9pm, some veggie

BOOKSTORES & RETAIL SHOPS
Athena Gallery 108 E. Kirkwood, 339-0734 (WC) 11am-6pm, til 8:00pm Fri-Sat, til 4pm Sun

SPIRITUAL GROUPS
Integrity Bloomington 400 E. Kirkwood Ave. (Trinity Episcopal Church), 336-4466 (WC) 7:30pm 2nd Wed

EROTICA
College Ave. Bookstore (Doc Johnson's) 1013 N. College Ave., 332-5160, 24hrs

Clarksville (812)

EROTICA
Theatair X 4505 Hwy. 131, 282-6976

Columbus

CRUISY AREAS
Mill Race Park (AYOR)

Crown Point

CRUISY AREAS
Lake Country Fairgrounds west side of lake & parking lot (AYOR)

Elkhart (219)

INFO LINES & SERVICES
Switchboard Concern 293-8671 (crisis only), 24hrs

SPIRITUAL GROUPS
Unitarian Universalist Fellowship 1732 Garden, 264-6525 (WC) 10:30am Sun

CRUISY AREAS
Elliott Park (AYOR)
Main Street (AYOR)
Oxbow Park (AYOR)

Evansville (812)

INFO LINES & SERVICES
Tri-State Alliance PO Box 2901, 47728, 474-4853, info, monthly social group, newsletter

BOOKSTORES & RETAIL SHOPS
A.A. Michael Books 1541 S. Green River Rd., 479-8979 (WC)

EROTICA
Studio Art Theatre 2113 W. Franklin St., 423-5508

CRUISY AREAS
The Levee (AYOR)
The Mesker Park (AYOR)
The Sunset Park (AYOR)

Fort Wayne (219)

INFO LINES & SERVICES
Gay/Lesbian AA (at Up the Stairs Community Center), 744-1199, 7:30pm Tue & Sat, 4:30pm Sun, call for complete schedule
Up the Stairs Community Center 3426 Broadway, 744-1199, helpline 7pm-10pm, til midnight Fri-Sat, 6:30pm-9pm Sun, space for various groups

BARS
After Dark 231 Pearl St., 424-6130 (MW,D,S,WC) 6pm-3:30am, clsd Sun
Downtown On The Landing 110 W. Columbia St., 420-1615 (MW,D) 7pm-3am, clsd Sun-Tue
Riff Raff's 2809 W. Main St., 436-4166 (M,NH,F,WC) 4pm-3am, clsd Sun

SPIRITUAL GROUPS
New World Church & Outreach Center 222 E. Leigh, 456-6570 (WC) 11am Sun
Open Door Chapel (at Up the Stairs Community Center), 744-1199, 7pm Sun

CRUISY AREAS
Foster Park nr. picnic shelters (AYOR)
Pearl St. from Harrison to Ewing (AYOR)

Gary

CRUISY AREAS
Marquette Park W. section at Holman & State (AYOR)
Miller Beach Line Ave. (AYOR)

Hammond (219)

RESTAURANTS & CAFES
Phil Smidt & Son 1205 N. Calumet Ave., 659-0025, lunch & dinner, full bar

MEN'S CLUBS
Sibley Court Yard Inn 629 Sibley, 933-9604 (PC) 24hrs, accommodations available

CRUISY AREAS
State St. & Sibley Blvd. btwn. Hohman & State Line Ave., (AYOR)

Indianapolis (317)

INFO LINES & SERVICES
AA Gay/Lesbian 632-7864
▲ **Community Real Estate Referrals** (800) 346-5592, gay realtor at your service, no rentals
Fellowship Indianapolis PO Box 2331, 46206-2331, 326-4614, social & support groups for lesbians/gay men
Gay/Lesbian Hotline PO Box 2152, 46206, 630-4297, 7pm-11pm daily, resources, crisis counseling
Men of All Color Together PO Box 88784, 46208, call Gay/Lesbian Switchboard for info

BARS

501 Tavern 501 N. College Ave., 632-2100 (★M,L,) 3pm-3am, clsd Sun, CW Tue, HiNRG Fri-Sat, also leather shop

Betty Boop's Lounge 637 Massachusetts Ave., 637-2310 (GF,NH,F) 10am-midnight, til 3am wknds, clsd Sun

Brothers Bar & Grill Inc. 822 N. Illinois St., 636-1020 (MW,E,WC) 11am-midnight, 4pm-1am wknds, also a restaurant, American

Club Cabaret 151 E. 14th St., 767-1707 (MW,D,S,WC) 8pm-3am, clsd Sun, call for events, patio

Illusions 1456 E. Washington, 266-0535 (MW,D,S) 7am-3am, clsd Sun

Jimmy's Bar & Restaurant 924 N. Pennsylvania St., 638-9039 (★M,NH,F,E) 5pm-3am, Continental

The Metro 707 Massachusetts, 639-6022 (MW,D,F,WC) 4pm-3am, noon-12:30am Sun, patio, full restaurant

Our Place 231 E. 16th St., 638-8138 (★M,D,L,WC) 4pm-3am, clsd Sun, patio

The Ten 1218 N. Pennsylvania St. (entrance in rear), 638-5802 (★W,D,S,WC) 6pm-3am, clsd Sun, CW Mon

Tomorrow's 2301 N. Meridian, 925-1710 (MW,D,F,S,WC) 5pm-3am, til 12:30am Sun, dinner nightly, Chinese American

The Varsity 1517 N. Pennsylvania St., 635-9998 (M,NH,F) 10am-3am, noon-midnight Sun, American

The Vogue 6259 N. College Ave., 259-7029 (GF,D,A,E) 9pm-1am, more gay Sun

RESTAURANTS & CAFES

Aesop's Tables 631-0055 (BW,WC) 11am-9pm, til 10pm Fri-Sat, authentic Mediterranean

Coffee Zone 137 E. Ohio St., 684-0432 (MW) 6:30am-6pm, clsd wknds

The Iron Skillet 2489 W. 30th St., 923-6353

BOOKSTORES & RETAIL SHOPS

Borders Book Shop 5612 Castleton Corner Ln., 849-8660, 9am-10pm, 11am-6pm Sun

▲ **Dreams & Swords** 6503 Ferguson St., 253-9966/(800) 937-2706, 10am-6pm, 10:30am-5pm Sat, noon-5pm Sun, feminist bookstore w/men's section

Indy News 121 S. Pennsylvania, 632-7680, 6am-7pm, til 6pm wknds

Just Cards 145 E. Ohio St., 638-1170 (WC) 9am-5:30pm, clsd Sun

Southside News 8063 Madison Ave., 887-1020, 6am-8pm, til 6pm Sun

TRAVEL & TOUR OPERATORS

Ross & Babcock Travel 832 Broad Ripple Ave., 259-4194/(800) 229-4194 (IGTA)

UniWorld Travel 1010 E. 86th St. #65E, 573-4919/(800) 573-4919

SPIRITUAL GROUPS

Jesus MCC 3620 N. Franklin Rd. (church), 895-4934 (WC) 6pm Sun

PUBLICATIONS

▲ **The Indiana Word** 225 E. North St. Tower 1 Ste. 2800, 579-3075, monthly

▲ **Out & About Indiana** 133 W. Market St. #105, 923-8550

A SOCIAL CLUB FOR GAY MEN

4120 N. Keystone Avenue
Indianapolis, IN 46205-2843
(317) 547-9210

▽ *One Day or Annual Memberships*
▽ *Suites-Video Rooms-Lockers*
▽ *Tanning-Gifts & Novelties*
▽ *Nautilus™ & Universal™ Machines*
▽ *Steam-Sauna-Air Conditioning*
▽ *In/Out Privileges-Outdoor Patio*
▽ *Free Parking*
▽ *Giant Screen Movie Room*
▽ *Telephones-Security Boxes*
▽ *Close to Indy's Nightlife*
▽ *Open 24 Hours*

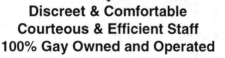

**Discreet & Comfortable
Courteous & Efficient Staff
100% Gay Owned and Operated**

We Gladly Accept Visa, Mastercard or American Express

MEN'S CLUBS
▲ **Club Indianapolis** 620 N. Capitol Ave., 635-5796 (MO,SW,PC) 24hrs
▲ **The Works** 4120 N. Keystone Ave., 547-9210 (MO,PC) 24hrs

Kokomo

CRUISY AREAS
Foster Park nr. tennis courts (AYOR)
Highland Park nr. 'Old Ben' (AYOR)

Lafayette   (317)

BARS
The Sportsman 644 Main St., 742-6321 (MW,NH,D) 9am-3am, from 5pm Sat, clsd Sun

BOOKSTORES & RETAIL SHOPS
The Fantasy 119 N. River Rd., W. Lafayette, 743-5042; noon-4am, 4pm-1am Sun, bookstore & videos

SPIRITUAL GROUPS
Dignity-Lafayette PO Box 4665, 47903, 742-1926, 7:30pm Wed, at Morton Community Center

EROTICA
Fantasy East 2320 Concord Rd., 474-2417

CRUISY AREAS
Happy Hollow Park W. Lafayette (AYOR)

Leroy

CRUISY AREAS
Stoney Run Park (AYOR)

Logansport

CRUISY AREAS
Spencer Park nr. tennis courts & trails along Eel River (AYOR)

Madison

CRUISY AREAS
Clifty St. Park btwn. Poplar & Oak groves (AYOR)
Third St. btwn. Broadway fountain & Mulberry (AYOR)
Vaughn Dr. along river (AYOR)

Merrillville

CRUISY AREAS
Deep River Park County Line Rd. Old 30 (AYOR)

Mishawaka

CRUISY AREAS
The Country Marketplace 100 Center & Univ. Park Malls (AYOR)

Monroe City   (812)

TRAVEL & TOUR OPERATORS
The Travel Club City Centre, Box 128, 47557, 743-2919, international membership-only non-profit travel club

Muncie (317)

INFO LINES & SERVICES
Live & Let Live AA 300 S. Madison (at Grace Church), 284-3331 (WC) 7:30pm Mon

BARS
Carriage House 1100 Kilgore, 282-7411 (GF,NH,F,WC) 3 flrs., food served, steak/seafood, gay-owned/run

Mark III Tap Room 107 E. Main St., 282-8273 (MW,D) 11am-3am, clsd Sun

CRUISY AREAS
Ball State U (AYOR)

New Carlisle

ACCOMMODATIONS
▲ **The Caritas B&B Network** (800) CARITAS (227-4827), see ad in center National section

Osceola (219)

EROTICA
Pleasureland Museum 5614 Ash Rd., 674-6260

Peru

CRUISY AREAS
Mississinewa Lake Rec. Area btwn. points 4 & 5 on 'Lost Sister Trail' (AYOR)

Richmond (317)

INFO LINES & SERVICES
Earlham Lesbian/Bisexual/Gay Peoples Union Box E-565 Earlham College, 47373

BARS
Coachman 911 E. Main St., 966-2835 (MW,D,A,WC) 6pm-3am, clsd Sun

South Bend (219)

INFO LINES & SERVICES
▲ **Community Real Estate Referrals** (800) 346-5592, gay realtor at your service, no rentals

Community Resource Center Helpline 232-2522, 8am-5pm, limited lesbigay info, also 24hr crisis hotline

ACCOMMODATIONS
Kamm's Island Inn 700 Lincoln Wy. W., Mishawaka, 256-1501/(800) 955-5266 (GF,SW,WC)

BARS
Sea Horse II Cabaret 1902 Western Ave., 237-9139 (MW,S,D,WC) 8pm-3am, clsd Sun

Starz Bar & Restaurant 1505 S. Kendall St., 288-7827 (M,D,S,YC,WC) 9pm-3am, clsd Sun

Truman's The 100 Center, Mishawaka, 259-2282 (★MW,D,F,SW) 5pm-3am, til midnight Sun, piano bar Fri-Sat, also café, patio

BOOKSTORES & RETAIL SHOPS
Little Professor Book Center Martins Ironwood Plaza North, 277-4488, 9am-9pm, 10am-5pm wknds

EROTICA
Pleasureland Museum 114 W. Mishawaka Ave., 259-6776, also 819 Michigan St. location, 288-9797

CRUISY AREAS
East Race Area (AYOR)

Potawatami Park (AYOR)

Terre Haute (812)

INFO LINES & SERVICES
Gay/Lesbian/Bisexual Terre Haute Info Line 237-6916, extensive touchtone directory of resources, bars & more

Heartland Care Center 237-7886

IYG-Terre Haute 231-6829, local chapter of statewide youth group, 21 years and under

BARS
Hightowers 13th at Chestnut, 232-3443 (GF,D,A,MRC) 8pm-3am

R-Place 684 Lafayette Ave., 232-9119 (MW,D,E) 8pm-3am, clsd Sun-Mon

CRUISY AREAS
City Park S. 1st Ave. (AYOR)

Valparaiso

CRUISY AREAS
Court House (AYOR)

Vincennes

CRUISY AREAS
George Rodgers Clark Memorial Park (AYOR)

Greg Park (AYOR)

The Circle Patrick Henry Dr. (AYOR)

Whiting (219)

RESTAURANTS & CAFES
Vogel's 1250 Indianapolis Blvd., 659-1250

Young America

CRUISY AREAS
Lion's Park 2-1/4 miles W. of Indiana State Rd. 18 (AYOR)

IOWA

Ames (515)

INFO LINES & SERVICES
Gay/Lesbian Alliance Iowa State University, 39 Memorial Union, , 50011, 294-2104, 10am-4pm, meets 7:30pm Wed in rm. 245

Help Central 232-0000, 9am-5pm, community info service, some lesbigay referrals

RESTAURANTS & CAFES
Lucallen's 400 Main St., 232-8484, 11am-11pm, Italian, full bar
Pizza Kitchen 120 Hayward, 292-1710 (MW,BW) 11am-10pm

EROTICA
Pleasure Palace Adult Books 117 Kellogg, 232-7717, 24hrs

Bettendorf (319)

ACCOMMODATIONS
Travelers Motel 433 14th St., 355-0285, XXX motel

Boone

CRUISY AREAS
McHose Park (AYOR)
Roadside Park 1 mi. W. on US 30 (AYOR)

Burlington (319)

BARS
Steve's Place 852 Washington, 752-9109 (GF,NH,WC) 9am-2am

Cedar Rapids (319)

INFO LINES & SERVICES
Gay/Lesbian Resource Center PO Box 1643, 52406, 366-2055, 6pm-9pm Mon, support group 1st & 3rd Wed

BARS
Rockafellas 2739 6th St SW, 399-1623 (MW,D) 3pm-2am, from 5pm wknds
Side Saddle Saloon 525 'H' St. SW, 362-2226 (MW,D,CW,S,WC) 5pm-2am, 2 bars (one smoke-free), dance lessons Mon & Th 8:30pm

CRUISY AREAS
Ellis Park (AYOR)
Shaver Park (AYOR)

Council Bluffs (712)

EROTICA
Adult Emporium 3216 1st Ave., 328-2673, 24hrs

Davenport (319)

BOOKSTORES & RETAIL SHOPS
Crystal Rainbow 1615 Washington St., 323-1050, 10am-5:30pm, clsd Sun

SPIRITUAL GROUPS
MCC Quad Cities 3707 Eastern Ave., 2:30pm Sun

EROTICA
TR Video 3727 Hickory Grove Rd., 386-7914, 24hrs

CRUISY AREAS
Credit Island Park W. end (AYOR) daytime
Le Clair Park on riverfront from Main to Ripley (AYOR) late

Decorah

BOOKSTORES & RETAIL SHOPS
Phil's Fun Stuff P.O. Box 431, 52101-0431, rainbow & AIDS awareness flags

Des Moines (515)

INFO LINES & SERVICES

▲ **Community Real Estate Referrals** (800) 346-5592, gay realtor at your service, no rentals

GLRC (Gay/Lesbian Resource Center) 522 11th St., 281-0634 (24hr info), youth groups, many other meetings

Iowa Bareskins Box 266, 50301, gay men's naturist (nudist) group

Out-Reach PO Box 70044, 50311, social/support group

ACCOMMODATIONS

Kingman House 2920 Kingman Blvd., 279-7312 (MW,WC) full brkfst, turn-of-the-century B&B

Racoon River Resort 2920 Kingman Blvd., 279-7312 (MW,F,N,WC) on the river, available for large groups

BARS

Blazing Saddles 416 E. 5th St., 246-1299 (★M,L,WC) 2pm-2am, from noon wknds

Garden 112 SE 4th St., 243-3965 (★MW,D,S) 5pm-2am, from 7pm Mon-Wed

Our Place Lounge 424 E. Locust, 243-9626 (MW,D,S,WC) 5pm-2am

Shooters Lounge 515 E. 6th, 245-9126 (MW,NH,WC) noon-2am

RESTAURANTS & CAFES

Chat Noir Cafe 644 18th St., 244-1353 (WC) 10am-11pm, clsd Sun-Mon

BOOKSTORES & RETAIL SHOPS

Borders Bookshop 1821 22nd St., West Des Moines, 223-1620

TRAVEL & TOUR OPERATORS

Iowa Division of Tourism 200 E. Grand Ave., (800) 345-4692

PUBLICATIONS

Outword PO Box 7008, 50309, 281-0634

Pen PO Box 1693, 50306, 265-3214

EROTICA

Axiom 412-1/2 E. 5th St., 246-0414, tattoos, piercings

Bachelors Library 2020 E. Euclid, 266-7992, 24hrs

Gallery Book Store 1114 Walnut St., 244-2916, 24hrs

CRUISY AREAS

Gay Loop 8th St. btwn. Crocker & Center (AYOR)

River Road off 2nd Ave. S. of freeway (AYOR)

Dubuque (319)

EROTICA

Gentleman's Bookstore 306 Main St., 556-9313

CRUISY AREAS

2nd St. Ice Harbor area (AYOR)

Julien Dubuque Monument Park (AYOR)

Fort Dodge (515)

EROTICA

Mini Cinema 15 N. 5th St., 955-9756

Grinnell (515)

INFO LINES & SERVICES
Stonewall Resource Center Grinnell College Box U-5, 50112, 269-3327, also quarterly newsletter

Iowa City (319)

INFO LINES & SERVICES
AA Gay/Lesbian 338-9111

Gay/Lesbian/Bisexual People's Union c/o SAC/IMU University of Iowa, 52242, 335-3251, also publishes 'Gay Hawkeye' newsletter

BARS
6:20 Club 620 S. Madison St., 354-2494 (★MW,D,YC,WC) 9pm-2am, clsd Sun-Tue

BOOKSTORES & RETAIL SHOPS
Alternatives 323 E. Market St., 337-4124 (WC) 10am-6pm, clsd Sun

Prairie Lights Bookstore 15 S. Dubuque St., 337-2681 (WC) 9am-9pm, til 5pm wknds

EROTICA
Just A Bit Different 116 E. 9th St., Coralville, 338-7978

Pleasure Palace Adult Books 315 Kirkwood Ave., 351-9444, 24hrs

Mason City

INFO LINES & SERVICES
GLNCI (Gays/Lesbians of North Central Iowa) Box 51, 50401

Newton (515)

ACCOMMODATIONS
La Corsette Maison Inn 629 1st Ave. E., 792-6833 (GF) upscale B&B w/ 4-star restaurant

Pella

MEN'S CLUBS
B Off RR 3 Box 225, 50219, write for info

Sioux City (712)

BARS
3 Cheers 414 20th St., 255-8005 (MW,NH,D,E,S,WC) 9am-2am

Kings & Queens 417 Nebraska St., 252-4167 (MW,D) 7pm-2am

Waterloo (319)

INFO LINES & SERVICES
Access PO Box 1682, 50704, 232-6805, weekly info & support, newsletter

BARS
The Bar Ltd. 903 Sycamore, 232-0543 (MW,D,S,WC) 7pm-2am

RESTAURANTS & CAFES
Joe's Country Grill 4117 University, Cedar Falls, 277-8785, 11am-11pm, 24hrs wknds

EROTICA
Danish Book World III 1507 Laporte Rd., 234-9340, 24hrs

KANSAS

Blue Rapids

CRUISY AREAS
Roadside Park 1 mi. E. on US 77 (AYOR)

Dodge City

CRUISY AREAS
Rest Stop 7 mi. E. on US 56 (AYOR) late

Fort Scott-Pleasanton

CRUISY AREAS
Rest Stop 20 mi. N. on US 69 (AYOR)

Hays (913)

INFO LINES & SERVICES
Western Kansas Gay/Lesbian Services Ft. Hayes Univ., 600 Park St., 67701, 628-5514

Junction City (913)

INFO LINES & SERVICES
JC Teddy Bears P.O. Box 744, 66441, 223-0850, call for events, social club for bears, cubs & their admirers

BARS
Revolutions 902 W. 7th St., 238-6374

Kansas City (see Kansas City, MISSOURI)

Kensington

CRUISY AREAS
Rest Stop on Hwy. 36 (AYOR)

Lawrence (913)

INFO LINES & SERVICES
Decca Center AA Support & Counseling 841-4138, info on Gay/Lesbian AA
GLOSK (Gay/Lesbian Services of Kansas) University of Kansas Box 13 KS Union, 66045, 864-3091, recorded info

BARS
Club Hideaway 106 N. Park, 841-4966
Jazzhaus 926-1/2 Massachusetts, 749-3320 (GF,E) 4pm-2am
Teller's Restaurant & Bar 746 Massachusetts Ave., 843-4111 (GF,E,WC) 11am-2am, 'Gay Family Night' Tue

BOOKSTORES & RETAIL SHOPS
Terra Nova Books & Cafe 920 Massachusetts St., 832-8300 (WC) 10am-9pm, til 10pm Fri-Sat, noon-6pm Sun, progressive, lesbigay section

CRUISY AREAS
Memorial Drive (AYOR)
Riverwall Park (AYOR)

Luray

CRUISY AREAS
Rest Stop at intersection of Hwys. 18 & 281 (AYOR)

Manhattan

CRUISY AREAS
Rest Stop on I-70, 10 mi. E. of Junction City (AYOR)

McPherson

CRUISY AREAS
Rest Stop on Rte. 135, 5 mi. N. (AYOR)

Norton

CRUISY AREAS
Rest Stop Hicks Park, 8 mi. SW on Hwy. 383 (AYOR)

Olathe

CRUISY AREAS
Cedar Lake off K-7 Hwy. (AYOR)

Osborne

CRUISY AREAS
Rest Stop at Hwys. 24 & 281 (AYOR)

Parsons

CRUISY AREAS
Rest Stop S. on Hwy. 59 (AYOR)

Salina

CRUISY AREAS
Oakdale Park (AYOR) late

Topeka (913)

INFO LINES & SERVICES
AA Gay/Lesbian 2425 SE Indiana Ave. (MCC), call Gay Rap Telephone for info
▲ **Community Real Estate Referrals** (800) 346-5592, gay realtor at your service, no rentals
Gay Rap Telephone PO Box 223, 66601, 233-6558, 8pm-midnight Wed-Sun

BARS
Classics 601 SW 8th, 233-5153 (MW,D,E) 4pm-2am, from noon Sun
Lyz 1009 S. Kansas Ave., 234-0482 (M) 1pm-2am, patio

BOOKSTORES & RETAIL SHOPS
Town Crier Books 1301 SW Gage Blvd. Ste. 120, 272-5060, 9am-9pm, noon-6pm Sun

TRAVEL & TOUR OPERATORS
Kansas Travel & Tourism Department (800) 252-6727

SPIRITUAL GROUPS
MCC Topeka 2425 SE Indiana Ave., 232-6196, 10am & 6pm Sun

Wichita (316)

INFO LINES & SERVICES
Gay/Lesbian Outreach 267-1852

Transitions 265-6657, monthly parties for lesbigay youth 18-21

Wichita Gay Info Line PO Box 16782, 67216, 269-0913, 6-10pm

Wichita Gay/Lesbian Community Center 111 N. Spruce, 262-3991, 6-10pm, clsd Sun-Tue, call for hours

ACCOMMODATIONS
Apartments by Appointments 1257 N. Broadway, 265-4323 (GF) unique apt. rentals, day, week or month

BARS
Our Fantasy 3201 S. Hillside, 682-5494 (MW,D,S,SW,WC) 8pm-2am Wed-Sun, also South Forty (CW), from 4pm

R&R Brass Rail 2828 E. 31st St. S., 685-9890 (MW,D,CW,F,S,WC) noon-2am

Sidestreet Saloon 1106 S. Pattie, 267-0324 (MW,NH) 2pm-2am

The T-Room 1507 E. Pawnee, 262-9327 (MW,NH) 3pm-2am, from noon wknds

RESTAURANTS & CAFES
The Harbor (at Our Fantasy bar), 682-5494 (MW) 8pm-4am, clsd Mon-Tue

The Lassen 155 N. Market St., 263-2777, lunch & dinner, clsd Sun

The Upper Crust 7038 E. Lincoln, 683-8088, lunch only, clsd wknds, homestyle

BOOKSTORES & RETAIL SHOPS
Mother's 3100 E. 31st St.S., 686-8116, noon-10pm, til 1am Fri-Sat, lesbigay

Visionz & Dreamz 2717 E. Central, 685-4404 (WC) 11am-7pm, noon-6pm Sun, clsd Mon, lesbigay bookstore

SPIRITUAL GROUPS
1st Metropolitan Community Church 156 S. Kansas Ave. , 267-1852, 10:30am & 6:30pm Sun

PUBLICATIONS
▲ **Liberty Press** PO Box 16315, 67216, 262-8289

Personally Speaking PO Box 16782, 67216-0782

EROTICA
Adult Entree 220 E. 21st St., 832-1816, 24hrs

Plato's Bookstore 1306 E. Harry, 269-9036, 24hrs

T.B. 1515 S. Oliver, 688-5343, 24hrs, 24 hrs

CRUISY AREAS
Boston Park on Herman Hill (AYOR)

Island Park (AYOR) days

KENTUCKY

Ashland

CRUISY AREAS
Central Park (AYOR)

Bowling Green

CRUISY AREAS
Lampkin Park off Morgan Town Rd. (AYOR)

Campbellsville

CRUISY AREAS
Cardinal Park Hwy. 68 (AYOR)
Green River Dam Hwy. 55 below Dam (AYOR)

Covington (606)

BARS
Rosie's Tavern 643 Bakewell St., 291-9707 (GF) 3pm-1am, from 1pm wknds

CRUISY AREAS
Madison btwn. 5th & 7th (AYOR)

Henderson

CRUISY AREAS
Audubon St. Park (AYOR) summers

Lexington (606)

INFO LINES & SERVICES
▲ **Community Real Estate Referrals** (800) 346-5592, gay realtor at your service, no rentals

BARS
The Bar Complex 224 E. Main St., 255-1551 (★MW,D,A,S,YC,WC) 4pm-1am, til 3:30am Fri-Sat, clsd Sun
Club 141 141 W. Vine St., 233-4262 (MW,D,S,WC) 8:30am-1am, til 3am Sat, clsd Sun-Mon
Crossings 117 N. Limestone St., 233-7266 (M,L,WC) 4pm-1am, clsd Sun, also 'The Rack Leather Shop', inside from 8pm
Joe's Bar & Cafe 120 S. Upper St., 252-7946 (MW,WC) 5pm-1am, open for lunch 11am-2pm, dinner nightly

RESTAURANTS & CAFES
Alfalfa 557 S. Limestone, 253-0014 (E) 11am-9pm, til 5pm Mon, 10am-2pm Sun, plenty veggie, healthy multi-ethnic, folk music Fri-Sat

BOOKSTORES & RETAIL SHOPS
Joseph-Beth 3199 Nicholasville Rd., 271-5330, 9am-10pm, 11am-6pm Sun

TRAVEL & TOUR OPERATORS
Pegasus Travel Inc. 245 Lexington Ave, 253-1644/(800) 228-4337 (IGTA)

SPIRITUAL GROUPS
Lexington MCC 134 Church St., 271-1407 (WC) 11:30am Sun
Pagan Forum PO Box 24203, 40524, 268-1640, 7:30pm every other Fri

PUBLICATIONS
GLSO (Gay/Lesbian) News PO Box 11471, 40575, monthly, calendar
The Kentucky Word 225 E. N. St. Tower 1 Ste. 2800, Indianapolis IN, 46204, (317) 579-3075, monthly

EROTICA
The New Bookstore 942 Winchester Rd., 252-2093, 24hrs

CRUISY AREAS
Jacobson Park (AYOR)
Woodland Park (AYOR)

Louisville (502)

INFO LINES & SERVICES

▲ **Community Real Estate Referrals** (800) 346-5592, gay realtor at your service, no rentals

Gay/Lesbian Hotline PO Box 2796, 40202, 897-2475/454-7613, 6pm-10pm, info for lesbigay AA

Louisville Gender Society PO Box 5458, 40255-0458, 966-8701, TS/TV group

Louisville Youth Group (800) 347-8336, 24hrs recorded info, live 7pm-10pm Th-Sun

(MACT) Men of All Colors Together PO Box 1838, 40201, 366-2949, 1st Sat of month

The Williams-Nichols Institute PO Box 4264, 40204, 636-0935, 6pm-9pm, lesbigay archives, library, referrals

BARS

Connection Complex 120 S. Floyd St., 585-5752 (★MW,D,F,E,S,V,WC) 8pm-4am, clsd Mon (restaurant from 6pm Wed-Sun)

Magnolia's 1398 S. 2nd St., 637-9052 (GF,YC) 11am-4am

Main Exchange 117 W. Main St., 584-8230 (W,D,CW,S) 5pm-2am, 7pm-4am Fri-Sat, clsd Mon

Murphy's Place 306 E. Main St., 587-8717 (M,NH,WC) 11am-4am, popular Tue

Score 252 E. Market St., 561-1043 (M) 9pm-4am, clsd Sun-Mon, sports bar, patio

Sparks 104 W. Main St., 587-8566 (MW,D,A,E,WC) 10pm-4am

Teddy Bears 1148 Garvin Pl., 589-2619 (M,NH) 11am-4am, from 1pm Sun

Tryangles 209 S. Preston St., 583-6395 (M,D,WC) 4pm-4am, from 1pm Sun

The Upstairs 306 E. Main St. (Murphy's Place), 587-1432 (MW,D) 9pm-4am, clsd Mon

BOOKSTORES & RETAIL SHOPS

Carmichael's 1295 Bardstown Rd., 456-6950, 10am-10pm, 11am-6pm Sun

Hawley Cooke Books 3042 Bardstown Rd., 456-6660, 9am-9:30pm, 11am-6pm Sun, also 27 Shelbyville Rd. Plaza, 893-0133

SPIRITUAL GROUPS

Dignity 1432 Highland Ave. (Triniity Church), 473-1408, 7pm 2nd & 4th Sun

MCC Louisville 4222 Bank St., 775-6636 (WC) 11am Sun

Phoenix Rising PO Box 2093, 40259, 636-2161, lesbigay pagans

PUBLICATIONS

The Kentucky Word 225 E. N. St. Tower 1 Ste 2800, Indianapolis IN, 46204, (317) 579-3075, monthly

▲ **The Letter** PO Box 3882, 40201, 772-7570, monthly

EROTICA

4600 Books 4600 Dixie Hwy., 449-1443

Arcade Adult Bookstore 2822 7th St., 637-8388

Blue Movies, Inc. 244 W. Jefferson St., 585-4627, 24hrs

Showboat Adult Bookstore 3524 57th St., 361-0007

CRUISY AREAS

James Taylor Park by riverfront (AYOR)

Owensboro (502)

INFO LINES & SERVICES
Owensboro Gay Alliance 685-5246

CRUISY AREAS
Smothers Park (AYOR) nights

Paducah (502)

INFO LINES & SERVICES
▲ **Community Real Estate Referrals** (800) 346-5592, gay realtor at your service, no rentals

BARS
Club DV8 1200 N. 8th St., 443-2545 (MW,D,S) 8pm-3am, clsd Sun, beer garden
Moby Dick 500 Broadway, 442-9076 (MW,D,S,WC) 5pm-3am, from 7pm Sat, clsd Sun

SPIRITUAL GROUPS
MCC of Paducah Ritz Hotel, 6th Floor, (22nd & Broadway), 898-2581 (WC) 11am & 7pm Sun

Prestonburg

CRUISY AREAS
Jenny Wiley St. Park (AYOR)

Radcliff

CRUISY AREAS
Radcliff City Park (AYOR)

Somerset (606)

INFO LINES & SERVICES
Cumberland Cares 678-5814, 4pm 1st Sat , lesbigay social & support for south-central & southeastern KY

LOUISIANA

Alexandria (318)

BARS
Unique Bar 3117 Masonic Dr., 448-0555 (★M,D) 7pm-2am, clsd Sun-Mon

TRAVEL & TOUR OPERATORS
Over the Rainbeaux Travel 1706 Pierce Rd., 442-0540

Baton Rouge (504)

INFO LINES & SERVICES
AA Gay/Lesbian 924-0030, 7pm Mon, 8pm Th, 9pm Sat, call for locations

ACCOMMODATIONS
Brentwood House P.O. Box 40872, 70835-0872, 924-4989 (M) 100+ yr old B&B

BARS
Argon 2160 Highland Rd., 336-4900 (★MW,D,A,YC) 9pm-2am Wed-Sat
George's Place 860 St. Louis, 387-9798 (★M,NH,WC) 3pm-2am, clsd Sun
Hideaway 7367 Exchange Pl., 923-3632 (W,NH,D,WC) 8pm-2am Wed-Sat

Mirror Lounge 111 3rd St., 387-9797 (MW,D,S,WC) 3pm-2am, from 6pm Sat, clsd Sun

Traditions 2183 Highland Rd., 344-9291 (MW,D,A,18+,WC) 9pm-2am, clsd Sun-Tue

RESTAURANTS & CAFES

Third Street Tavern & Deli 140 N. 3rd St., 336-4281 (MW,WC) 5pm-midnight, clsd Mon

BOOKSTORES & RETAIL SHOPS

Hibiscus Book Store 635 Main St., 387-4264, 11am-6pm, from noon wknds, lesbigay

TRAVEL & TOUR OPERATORS

Out & About Travel 11528 Old Hammond Hwy. Ste. 610, 272-7448

Trips Unlimited 10249 Cashel Ave., 927-7191/(800) 256-9661, gay-owned/run

SPIRITUAL GROUPS

Church of Mercavah PO Box 66703, 70896, 665-7815 (MW) 3pm Sun, interfaith, call for location

Dignity PO Box 4181, 70821, 383-6010

Joie de Vivre MCC 333 E. Chimes St., 383-0450, 11am Sun

PUBLICATIONS

Voices Magazine Licorice Unicorn Press, PO Box 66703, 70896, 665-7815, offbeat articles on everything, original artwork & writings

Gretna (504)

BARS

Cheers 1711 Hancock, 367-0149 (GF,NH) 10am-3am

Houma (504)

INFO LINES & SERVICES

▲ **Community Real Estate Referrals** (800) 346-5592, gay realtor at your service, no rentals

BARS

The Cha Cha Palace 1709 Havers, 868-0007 (GF,D,E) 9pm-?

Kixx 112 N. Hollywood, 876-9587 (MW,D,WC) 6pm-2am, clsd Sun-Mon

Lafayette (318)

INFO LINES & SERVICES

AA Gay/Lesbian 234-7814, call for locations

BARS

Frank's Bar 1807 Jefferson, 235-9217 (M,NH,WC) 2pm-2am, noon-midnight Sun

The Girl's Gym 408 Maurice St., 234-6688 (W,D,WC) 8pm-2am, from 5pm-midnight Sun, clsd Mon

Images 524 W. Jefferson, 233-0070 (MW,D,F,S,WC) 9pm-2am, clsd Mon-Tue

CRUISY AREAS

Garrand Park (AYOR)

Lake Charles (318)

BARS

Crystal's 112 W. Broad St., 433-5457 (MW,D,CW,F,S,WC) 9pm-2am, clsd Sun-Tue

SPIRITUAL GROUPS
MCC Lake Charles 510 Broad St., 436-0921, 11am Sun

Monroe (318)

BARS
Hot Shotz 110 Catalpa St., 388-3262 (MW,D,S,V) from 9pm, clsd Sun-Mon

CRUISY AREAS
Forsyth Park (AYOR)
Monroe Boat Dock & Picnic Area (AYOR)

New Orleans (504)

INFO LINES & SERVICES
AA Lambda Center 2106 Decatur, 947-0548, noon daily, call for meeting times
Gay/Lesbian Business Association 940 Royal #350, 271-0631, mtg. 2nd Tue, call for further details
Gulf Area Gender Alliance PO Box 56836, 70156, 833-3046, 2nd Sat
Lesbian/Gay Community Center 816 N. Rampart, 522-1103 (WC) noon-6pm Mon-Fri
Men of Color PO Box 57694, 70157-7694, 482-5341, 'Mantalk' bi-weekly Sat

ACCOMMODATIONS
A Private Garden 1718 Philip St., 523-1776 (MW) 2 private apts., enclosed garden, hot tub
▲ **Alternative Accommodations / Tande Reservations** 828 Royal St. #233, 529-2915/(800) 209-9408

Andrew Jackson Hotel 919 Royal St., 561-5881/(800) 654-0224 (GF) historic inn

The B&W Courtyards B&B 2425 Chartres St., 949-5313/(800) 585-5731 (GF)

Big D's Bed & Breakfast 704 Franklin Ave., 945-8049 (MW)

▲ **The Big Easy Guest House** 2633 Dauphine St., 943-3717 (MW) 8 blocks from French Quarter

▲ **The Biscuit Palace** 730 Dumaine, 525-9949 (GF) in the French Quarter

▲ **Bon Maison Guest House** 835 Bourbon St., 561-8498 (★GF) 3 studio apts., 2 suites

Bourbon Orleans Hotel Bourbon & Orleans, 523-2222/(800) 521-5338 (★GF)

▲ **Bourgoyne Guest House** 839 Bourbon St., 524-3621/525-3983 (★MW) 1830s Creole mansion, courtyard

▲ **Caritas B&B Network** (800) CARITAS (227-4827), see ad in center National Section

Casa de Marigny Creole Guest Cottages 818 Frenchman St., 948-3875 (MW,SW)

Chartres St. House 2517 Chartres, 945-2339 (MW,SW) handsome 1850's home, patio

The Chimes B&B Constantinople at Coliseum, 488-4640/(800) 729-4640 (GF) suites & rms in an 1876 home

Deja Vu Guest House 1835 N. Rampart St., 945-5912/(800) 238-1577 (M) individual Creole cottages

Faubourg Guest House 1703 Second St., 895-2004 (MW) 1860s Greek Revival

Fourteen Twelve Thalia - A B&B 1412 Thalia, 522-0453 (GF) one-bdrm apt in the Lower Garden District

▲ **French Quarter B&B** 1132 Ursuline, 525-3390 (MW,SW) priv. bath, full bkfst

BOURGOYNE
GUEST · HOUSE

Old World Charm
in the heart of the French Quarter.

Antiques • Charming courtyard
Private Baths • Kitchens

839 BOURBON

NEW ORLEANS, LA. 70116
(504) 525-3983 OR 524-3621

▲ **French Quarter Reservation Service** 940 Royal St. Ste. 263, 523-1246/(800) 523-9091 (IGTA)

▲ **French Quarter Suites** 1119 N. Rampart, 524-7725 / (800) 457-2253 (GF) pool, hot tub

▲ **The Frenchmen Hotel** 417 Frenchman St., 948-2166/(800) 831-1781 (★MW,SW,WC) 1860's creole townhouses, spa

The Greenhouse 1212 Magazine St., 561-8400/(800) 966-1303 (MW,SW)

Hotel de la Monnaie 405 Esplanade Ave., 947-0009 (GF,WC,IGTA) all-suite hotel

Lafitte Guest House 1003 Bourbon St., 581-2678/(800) 331-7971 (★GF) elegant French manor house

▲ **Lamothe House** 621 Esplanade, 947-1161/1(800) 367-5858

Lions Inn 2517 Chartres St., 945-2339 (MW,SW) handsome 1850s home

▲ **Macarty Park Guesthouse** 3820 Burgundy St., 943-4994/(800) 521-2790 (MW,SW,IGTA) rms & cottages just 5 minutes from the French Quarter

▲ **Maison Burgundy** 1860 Rue Burgundy, 948-2355/(800) 863-8813 (GF,SW) suites, hot tub

Maison Dauphine 2460 Dauphine St., 943-0861 (M) nr. French Quarter

▲ **Marigny Guest House** 621 Esplanade, (800) 367-5858

Mazant St. Guest House 906 Mazant, 944-2662 (GF)

The McKendrick-Breaux House 1474 Magazine St., 586-1700 (GF)

Mentone B&B 1437 Pauger St., 943-3019 (GF) suite in Victorian home

New Orleans Guest House 1118 Ursulines St., 566-1177/(800) 562-1177 (GF) 1848 Creole cottage, courtyard

Parkview Guest House 726 Frenchman St., 945-7875/(800) 749-4640 (MW)

Go for a splash in our refreshing heated pool. Enjoy beautiful cottages and rooms with color cable TV, phone, private baths, gym and continental breakfast. Just 5 minutes from the French Quarter. All this from only $59.

MACARTY PARK GUEST HOUSE

3820 Burgundy Street
New Orleans, LA 70117
504-943-4994 • 800-521-2790

▲ **Pauger Guest Suites** 1750 N. Rampart St., 944-2601/(800) 484-8334 x9834 (M) nr. French Quarter

Rainbow House 2311-15 N. Rampart St., 943-5805 (MW) walking distance to French Quarter, also apts

Rathbone Inn 1227 Esplanande Ave., 947-2100/(800) 947-2101 (IGTA) 1850s Greek Revival mansion

▲ **Renaissance Realty** (800) 238-1577, fully equipped rental properties

Rober House Condos 822 Ursuline St., 529-4663 (MW,SW,IGTA) courtyard

The Robert Gordy House 2630 Bell St., 486-9424/(800) 889-7359

Royal Barracks Guest House 717 Barracks St., 529-7269 (GF) jacuzzi, priv. patios

▲ **Rue Royal Inn** 1006 Royal St., 524-3900/(800) 776-3901 (GF, IGTA) 1830s Creole townhouse

St. Charles Guest House 1748 Prytania St., 523-6556 (GF,SW) little pensione-style guest house

▲ **St. Peter Guest House** 1005 St. Peter, 524-9232/(800) 535-7815 (GF) historic location, authentically appointed

Sun Oak B&B 2020 Burgundy St., 945-0322 (MW) Greek Revival Creole cottage, circa 1836, w/ gardens

▲ **Ursuline Guest House** 708 Ursuline St, 525-8509/(800) 654-2351 (★M,IGTA) hot tub, evening socials w/wine

Vieux Carre Rentals 841 Bourbon, 525-3983 (GF) 1 & 2-bdrm apts

YOUR INN IN THE FRENCH QUARTER

Ursuline Guest House

708 Rue des Ursulines
New Orleans, Louisiana 70116
(800) 654-2351 / (504) 525-8509

European Inns in

the French Quarter

"Lamothe House is one of a handful of fine French Quarter Hotels that have retained the ambience of an era gone by."
—Country Inns, Lodges and Discount Hotels of the South

800-367-5858 • FAX: 504-943-6536
LAMOTHE HOUSE
621 Esplanade, French Quarter, LA 70116 • 504-947-1161

Marigny Guest House

Handsomely restored 1860 Home with contemporary comfort, attentive service, complimentary continental breakfast, parking on premises.

800-367-5858
Fax: 504-943-6536

621 Esplanade, New Orleans LA 70116 • (504) 944-9700

NATIONAL
SECTION

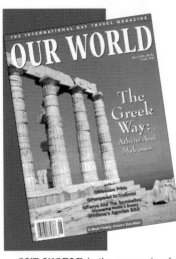

Looking for Dorothy?

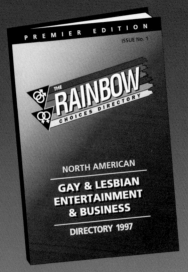

PREMIER EDITION
ISSUE No. 1

THE RAINBOW
CHOICES DIRECTORY

NORTH AMERICAN

GAY & LESBIAN
ENTERTAINMENT
& BUSINESS

DIRECTORY 1997

Find her in the Rainbow!

The Rainbow Choices Directory is your lesbian and gay entertainment &
business source which will reach more than a quarter of a million
lesbian and gay shoppers. Don't miss out on this exciting opportunity!

Book your ad today!
(416) 762-1320
Fax (416) 762-3600

Nightsweats & T-cells♥

If

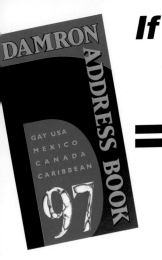 =

Then

 =

The Gay Companion to New York
For info Call (212) 627-0165

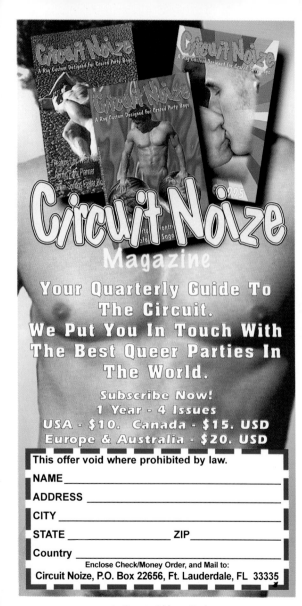

Here, There, and Everywhere Queer

With information about area bars, bookstores, lodgings and more in over 65 different gay-friendly destinations in the U.S., Canada and the U.S. Virgin Islands, a Columbia FunMap® is the perfect pocket-sized, gay travel companion.

Choose Any Four FunMaps® for $6.00 or a FunMap® TravelPak of all available maps for only $16.00. (*Check maps from list below. Then copy this page and send it to Columbia FunMap®, 118 East 28 Street #308, New York, NY 10016, or call us at 212-447-7877.*)

1997 Damron Address Book

BE AT HOME
WHEREVER YOU GO

• NEW YORK • CHICAGO • LOS ANGELES • AND POINTS BETWEEN •

Isn't it nice to know you can stay with friends! Caritas offers bed & breakfast accommodations in gay homes throughout America for the most discriminating traveler as well as for the budget-minded. Each host is carefully screened and inspected by Caritas. You can expect a gracious welcome from a host who is knowledgeable about their area and eager to make your stay in their home an enjoyable one. For a complete list of hosts, or information on becoming a host, contact Caritas toll free at:

1-800-CARITAS
THERE'S NO PLACE LIKE HOME
C A R I T A S

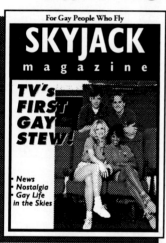

800-FLY-GAYS

NATIONWIDE

LOWEST AIRFARES

ALL AIRLINES

7 DAYS

MEMBER IGTA

FRAMELINE

presents

the 21st
san francisco
international
lesbian & gay
film festival

JUNE 13-22, 1997

For ticket information contact: Frameline 346 Ninth Street
San Francisco, CA 94103 tel: [415] 703-8650 fax: [415] 861-1404
e-mail: frameline@aol.com web site: www.frameline.org

the new Parade

New Orleans'
LARGEST & **#1**
Gay Dance Club

New Look
New Feeling
New DJs

Entrance @ 803 St. Ann
corner of Bourbon Street
located above the Bourbon Pub

*Simply,
the place to be!*

for info call
504 529 2107

BARS

Angles 2301 N. Causeway, Metairie, 834-7979 (MW,NH,D,WC) 4pm-4am

Another Corner 2601 Royal St., 945-7006 (M,NH) 11am-?

Big Daddy's 2513 Royal, 948-6288 (MW,NH,WC) 24hrs

▲ **Bourbon Pub** 801 Bourbon St., 529-2107 (★M,V,YC) 24hrs, cruise bar, 'hot numbers'

Buckaroo's 718 N. Rampart, 566-7559 (M,NH,TG) 3pm-?, drag queens & transsexuals

Buffa's 1001 Esplanade, 945-9373 (GF,NH,F) 11am-3am

Bus Stop 542 N. Rampart, 522-3372 (M,NH,F) 3pm-3am, from noon wknds

▲ **Cafe Lafitte in Exile/The Corral** 901 Bourbon St., 522-8397 (★M,V) 24hrs

Charlene's 940 Elysian Fields, 945-9328 (W,NH,D) 5pm-?, from 2pm Fri-Sun, clsd Mon, B&B accommodations available

Copper Top 706 Franklin Ave., 948-2300 (MW,WC) 24hrs, Cajun & CW

Corner Pocket 940 St. Louis, 568-9829 (★M,S) 24hrs, hustlers

Country Club 634 Lousia St., 945-0742 (MW,E,SW) 10am-11pm

The Double Play 439 Dauphine, 523-4517 (GF,NH) 24hrs

Footloose 700 N. Rampart, 524-7654 (MW,D,TG) 24hrs, shows on wknds

The Four Seasons 3229 N. Causeway, Metairie, 832-0659 (MW,NH,D) 3pm-4am

The Friendly Bar 2801 Chartres St., 943-8929 (MW,NH,WC) 11am-3am

The Full Moon 424 Destrehan, Harvey, 341-4396 (M,D,L) 7pm-? Wed-Sun

Golden Lantern 1239 Royal St., 529-2860 (M,NH) 24hrs

▲ **Good Friends Bar/Queen's Head Pub** 740 Dauphine, 566-7191 (★GF,P,WC) 24hrs, good cocktails, also 'Queens Head Pub', 6pm-3am Wed-Sun (M,NH)

M.R.B./Mr. B's on the Patio 515 St. Philip, 586-0644 (MW,NH,S) 24hrs

The Mint 504 Esplanade, 525-2000 (★MW,P,E,WC) noon-3am

Oz 800 Bourbon St., 593-9491 (M,D,YC,WC) 24hrs

▲ **Parade** (above Bourbon Pub), 529-2107 (★M,D) 'the place to dance'

Phoenix 941 Elysian Fields, 945-9264 (★M,NH,L) 24hrs, 'Men's Room' open 9pm-5am, cruise room

▲ **Rawhide 2010** 740 Burgundy, 525-8106 (★M,NH,CW,L) 24hrs

The Roundup 819 St. Louis, 561-8340 (M,CW,WC) 24hrs

Rubyfruit Jungle 640 Frenchmen, 947-4000 (MW,D,A,E,WC) 4pm-?, from 1pm wknds

T.T.'s 820 N. Rampart, 523-9521 (M,NH,E,OC) 11am-3am, hustlers

Wolfendale's 834 N. Rampart, 524-5749 (M,D,MRC-AF) 5pm-6am, patio

Xis 1302 Allo St., Marrero, 340-0049 (MW,NH,D,WC) 5pm-?

RESTAURANTS & CAFES

Cafe Istanbul 534 Frenchmen (upstairs), 944-4180 (E) clsd Tue, Turkish cuisine

Cafe Sbisa 1011 Decatur, 522-5565, dinner & Sun brunch, French Creole, patio

Clover Grill 900 Bourbon St., 523-0904 (★) 24hrs, diner fare

Feelings Cafe 2600 Chartres St., 945-2222 (E) dinner nightly, Fri lunch, Sun brunch, Creole, also piano bar wknds

Fiorella's Cafe 45 French Market Pl., 528-9566, dinner, Sun brunch, homestyle

Gram's Cafe Creole 533 Toulouse, 524-1479 (WC) 11:30am-?

Jack Sprat 3240 S. Carrollton, 486-2200, 11am-10pm, noon-5pm Sun, healthy vegetarian

La Peniche 1940 Dauphine St., 943-1460, 24hrs

Since 1952
Daddy of 'em all
Cafe Lafitte in Exile
The Corral
901 Bourbon Street
522-8397

Always Snappy Casual
Good Friends Bar
Queen's Head Pub
740 Dauphine Street
566-7191

Leather Levi & More
Rawhide 2010
740 Burgundy Street
525-8106

A Traveler's Dream

Lucky Cheng's 720 St. Louis, 529-2045

Mama Rosa 616 N. Rampart, 523-5546, 11am-10pm, clsd Mon, Italian

Mona Lisa 1212 Royal St., 522-6746, 11am-11pm, Italian, some veggie

Old Dog New Trick Cafe 307 Exchange Alley, 522-4569 (WC) 11am-9pm, vegetarian

Olivier's 911 Decatur St., 525-7734 (WC) 10am-10pm, Creole

Petunia's 817 St. Louis, 522-6440 (★) 8am-midnight, Cajun & Creole

PJ's 634 Frenchmen St., 949-2292 (★WC) 7pm-midnight

Poppy's Grill 717 St. Peter, 524-3287 (WC) 24hrs, diner

Quarter Scene 900 Dumaine, 522-6533, 24hrs, clsd Tue, homecooking, some veggie

Sammy's Seafood 627 Bourbon St., 525-8442, 11am-midnight, Creole/Cajun

Sebastian's 538 St. Philip, 524-2041

St. Ann's Cafe & Deli 800 Dauphine, 529-4421 (★MW,WC) 24hrs, American, some veggie

Vera Cruz 1141 Decatur St., 561-8081 (WC) noon-11pm, clsd Mon-Tue, Mexican

Whole Foods 3135 Esplanade Ave., 943-1626, 9am-9pm, healthy/veggi deli

BOOKSTORES & RETAIL SHOPS

Alternatives 902 Bourbon St., 524-5222, 11am-9pm, til 11pm Fri & Sat, clsd Tue & Wed, lesbigay

Bookstar 414 N. Peters (WC) 10am-11pm, til 8pm Sun

Faubourg Marigny Bookstore 600 Frenchmen St., 943-9875 (WC) 10am-8pm, til 6pm wknds, lesbigay

Gay Mart 808 Rampart St., 523-6005, noon-7pm

Sauna

Steam

3 Jacuzzi's

Mazes

Video Lounge

Open 24 Hrs

*Private Video
in every room*

*Weekly JO party
featuring hot
hunks and stars!*

*Close to
Bourbon
Street*

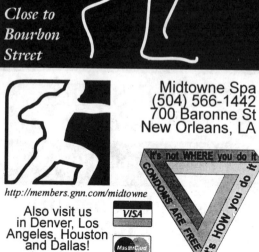

Midtowne Spa
(504) 566-1442
700 Baronne St
New Orleans, LA

http://members.gnn.com/midtowne

Also visit us
in Denver, Los
Angeles, Houston
and Dallas!

VISA

MasterCard

It's not WHERE you do it
CONDOMS ARE FREE
It's HOW you do it

Postmark New Orleans 631 Toulouse St., 529-2052/(800) 285-4247

Rings of Desire 1128 Decatur St., 2nd flr., 524-6147, 11am-7pm, piercing studio

Sidney's News Stand 917 Decatur, 524-6872, 8am-9pm, general magazine store w/ lesbigay titles

TRAVEL & TOUR OPERATORS

Alternative Tours & Travel 3003 Chartres, 949-5917/(800) 576-0238 (IGTA)

Avalon Travel Advisors 1206 Magazine, 70151, 561-8400/(800) 966-1303 (IGTA)

Community Travel 612 N. Rampart, 552-2913/(800) 811-5028 (IGTA)

Louisiana Office of Tourism (800) 334-8626

▲ **Old Quarter Livery** 3328 Marigny, 945-3796, limosine & tour service

Uptown Travel & Tours 4001 Toulouse St. Ste. 101, 488-9993/(800) 566-9312 (IGTA)

SPIRITUAL GROUPS

Integrity 1339 Jackson Ave. (Trinity Episcopal Church), 944-5346, 3rd Tue

Vieux Carre MCC 1128 St. Roch, 945-5390, 11am Sun

PUBLICATIONS

▲ **Ambush** PO Box 71291, 70171-1291, 522-8049, bi-weekly

Impact PO Box 52079, 70152, 944-6722, bi-monthly

The Second Stone PO Box 8340, 70182, 891-7555, nat'l paper for lesbigay Christians

MEN'S CLUBS

▲ **The Club New Orleans** 515 Toulouse St., 581-2402 (★MO,PC) 24hrs

▲ **Midtowne Spa** 700 Baronne St., 566-1442 (★MO,V) 24hrs

EROTICA

Airline Bookstore 1404 26th St., Kenner, 468-2931, 24hrs

Gargoyle's 1205 Decatur St., 529-4387, 11am-7pm, til10pm Fri-Sat, leather/fetish store

Panda Bear 415 Bourbon St., 529-3593 (WC)

Second Skin Leather 521 St. Philip St., 561-8167, noon-10pm, til 6pm Sun, also Above & Below piercing studio upstairs

CRUISY AREAS

Belle Promenade (AYOR)

Capitol Lakes Capitol Lakes & adjacent area (AYOR)

Riverwalk (AYOR) very interesting

Shreveport (318)

BARS

Central Station 1025 Marshall, 222-2216 (★MW,D,CW,S,WC) 4pm-4am, til midnight Sun

Korner Lounge 800 Louisana, 222-9796 (M,NH) 5pm-2am, clsd Sun

Outrageous 1309 Centenary Blvd., 221-7596 (MW,F,V) 2pm-2am, clsd Sun, patio, ladies night Tue

EROTICA

Fun Shop 1601 Marshall, 226-1308

MAINE

Auburn

CRUISY AREAS
West Pitch Park at Great Falls Plaza (AYOR)

Augusta (207)

BARS
P.J.'s 80 Water St., 623-4041 (★MW,D) 7pm-1am Tue-Sat

Bangor (207)

INFO LINES & SERVICES
AA Gay/Lesbian 126 Union (Unitarian Church), 7:30 Th

TRAVEL & TOUR OPERATORS
Dignity Bangor 300 Union St., 6pm 2nd & 4th Sun

CRUISY AREAS
Valley Avenue Park along river bank (AYOR)

Bar Harbor (207)

ACCOMMODATIONS
Manor House Inn 106 West St., 288-3759 (GF) May-Nov, full brkfst

Bath (207)

ACCOMMODATIONS
The Galen C. Moses House 1009 Washington St., 442-8771, full bkfst, gay-owned/run

Bethel (207)

ACCOMMODATIONS
Speckled Mountain Ranch RR 2, Box 717, 04217, 836-2908 (GF) horse farm

Biddeford

INFO LINES & SERVICES
Out for Good P.O. Box 727, 04005

Brunswick (207)

ACCOMMODATIONS
The Vicarage by the Sea B&B Rte. 1 Box 368-B, S. Harpswell, 04079, 833-5480 (GF,WC) full bkfst

BOOKSTORES & RETAIL SHOPS
Gulf of Maine Books 134 Maine St., 729-5083, 9:30am-5pm, clsd Sun

Camden (207)

INFO LINES & SERVICES
Mid Coast Maine Gay Men's Helpline 863-2728, 6pm-9pm Mon-Fri, also gay youth info, covers Rockland, Rockport, Belfast & Vinalhaven

ACCOMMODATIONS
The Old Massachusetts Homestead Campground PO Box 5 Rte. 1, Lincolnville Beach, 04849, 789-5135 (GF,SW) May-Nov

Caribou (207)

Info Lines & Services
Gay/Lesbian Phoneline 398 S. Main St., 498-2088, hours vary
Northern Lambda Nord PO Box 990, 04736, social & networking for northern ME and western Brunswick

Accommodations
The Westman House PO Box 1231, 04736, 896-5726 (★MW,F)

Corea Harbor (207)

Accommodations
The Black Duck Inn on Corea Harbor P.O. Box 39, 04624, 963-2689 (GF) full brkfst, restored farmhouse

Dexter (207)

Accommodations
Brewster Inn 37 Zions Hill, 924-3130 (GF)

Kennebunk (207)

Accommodations
Arundel Meadows Inn Rte. 1, Arundel, 985-3770 (GF)

Kennebunkport (207)

Info Lines & Services
▲ **Community Real Estate Referrals** (800) 346-5592, gay realtor at your service, no rentals

Accommodations
The Colony Hotel Ocean Ave & Kings Hwy., 967-3331/(800) 552-2363 (GF,F,SW) oceanfront property
White Barn Inn 37 Beach St., 967-2321 (GF,F)

Restaurants & Cafes
Bartley's Dockside by the bridge, 967-5050 (WC) 11am-10pm

Kittery (207)

Erotica
▲ **Video Expo** Rte. 236, 439-6285

Lewiston (207)

Info Lines & Services
Bates Gay/Lesbian/Straight Alliance Hirasawa Lounge, Chase Hall, Bates College, 786-6255, 8:30pm Sun

Bars
The Sportsman's Club 2 Bates St., 784-2251 (★MW,D) 8pm-1am, from 7pm Sun

Erotica
Paris Book Store 297 Lisbon St., 783-6677

Lincolnville Beach (207)

Accommodations
Sign of the Owl B&B RR 2 Box 85, 338-4669 (GF) full brkfst

Lovell (207)

ACCOMMODATIONS

The Stone Wall B&B RR1, Box 26, 04051, 925-1080/(800) 413-1080 (MW,IGTA) full bkfst

Naples (207)

ACCOMMODATIONS

Lambs Mill Inn Box 676 Lamb's Mill Rd., 693-6253 (GF,IGTA) full bkfst

Ogunquit (207)

INFO LINES & SERVICES

▲ **Community Real Estate Referrals** (800) 346-5592, gay realtor at your service, no rentals

ACCOMMODATIONS

Admiral's Inn 70 S. Main St., 646-7093 (GF,SW)

The Clipper Ship B&B Box 236, 03907, 646-9735 (GF)

The Gazebo Rte. 1, 646-3733 (GF,SW)

The Inn at Tall Chimney 94 Main St., 646-8974 (MW) April-Nov

The Inn at Two Village Square PO Box 864, 03907, 646-5779 (M) seasonal

Leisure Inn PO Box 2113, 03907, 646-2737 (GF) seasonal

Moon Over Maine Berwick Rd., 646-6666/(800) 851-6837 (GF)

The Ogunquit House 7 Kings Hwy., 646-2967 (★MW)

Old Village Inn 30 Main St., 646-7088 (GF,F)

Rockmere Lodge 40 Stearns Rd., 646-2985 (GF)

The Seasons Hotel 178 US Rte. 1, 646-6041/(800) 639-8508 (GF) seasonal

Yellow Monkey Guest Houses/Hotel 168 Main St., 646-9056 (MW) seasonal

BARS

The Club 13 Main St., 646-6655 (★M,D,F,V) open April-Oct, 9pm-1am, from 4pm Sun

RESTAURANTS & CAFES

Arrows Berrick Rd. (1.8 mi. W. of Center), 361-1100, 6pm-9pm Tue-Sun, clsd Dec-May

Clay Hill Farm Agamenticus Rd. (2 mile W. of Rte. 1), 646-2272, also piano bar

Front Porch Cafe Ogunquit Sq., 646-3976, Mexican/American, full bar

Grey Gull Inn 321 Webhannet Dr., Wells, 646-7501, New England fine dining

Johnathan's Bourne Ln., 646-4777 (WC) 5pm-9pm, full bar

Poor Richard's Tavern Perkins Cove at Shore Rd. & Pine Hill, 646-4722, 5:30pm-9:30pm, full bar, seasonal

CRUISY AREAS

Ogunquit Beach 200 yards N. of beach entrance (AYOR)

Orono (207)

INFO LINES & SERVICES

Wilde-Stein Club, Univ. of Maine Sutton Lounge, Memorial Union, 581-1731, 6pm Th (Sept-May)

ACCOMMODATIONS

Maine Wilderness Lake Island 866-4547 (MW) cabins

Pembroke (207)

ACCOMMODATIONS

Yellow Birch Farm RR 1 Box 248A, 04666, 726-5807 (W) B&B on working farm, daily & weekly rates; also cottage

Portland (207)

INFO LINES & SERVICES

▲ **Community Real Estate Referrals** (800) 346-5592, gay realtor at your service, no rentals

Gays in Sobriety 32 Thomas St. (Williston W. Church), 774-4060, 6:30pm Sun, 8pm Th

Outright 155 Brackett St., 774-4357, Fri 7:30pm, youth support group

Queer Alliance Univ. of Maine, The Power's House, 874-6596

ACCOMMODATIONS

The Inn at St. John 939 Congress St., 773-6481/(800) 636-9127 (GF) unique historic inn

The Pomegranate Inn 49 Neal St., 772-1066/(800) 356-0408 (GF) upscale B&B

BARS

The Blackstones 6 Pine St., 775-2885 (M,NH,WC) 4pm-1am

Raoul's Roadside Attraction 865 Forest Ave., 773-6886 (G,F,E) 11:30am-1am

Sisters 45 Danforth St., 774-1505 (W,D) 4pm-1am, from 6pm Sat, clsd Mon-Tue

Underground 3 Spring St., 773-3315 (★MW,D,S) 4pm-1am

Zootz 31 Forest Ave., 773-8187 (GF,D,A,E) 9pm-1am

RESTAURANTS & CAFES

Cafe Always 47 Middle St., 774-9399, dinner Tue-Sat

Katahdin 106 Spring St., 774-1740, 5pm-10pm, clsd Sun

Street & Co. 33 Wharf St., 775-0887 (★BW,WC) 5:30pm-9:30pm, Til 10pm Fri-Sat, seafood

Walter's Cafe 15 Exchange St., 871-9258, 11am-9pm

Westside 58 Pine St., 773-8223 (BW,WC) lunch & dinner, clsd Mon, Maine game & seafood

Woodford's Cafe 129 Spring St., 772-1374 (WC) 11am-10pm, til 1pm Fri-Sat, clsd Mon

BOOKSTORES & RETAIL SHOPS

Communiques 3 Moulton St., 773-5181, 10am-7pm, til 9pm (summer), cards, gifts, clothing

Drop Me A Line 611 Congress St., 773-5547, 10am-6pm, til 7pm Th-Fri, noon-5pm Sun

TRAVEL & TOUR OPERATORS

Adventure Travel 2 Elsie Wy., Scarborough, 885-5060 (IGTA)

Bob's Airport Livery 25 Alton St., 773-5135, shuttle & tour service, also covers Ogunquit

Maine Publicity Bureau (800) 533-9595

SPIRITUAL GROUPS

Circle of Hope MCC 156 High St., 773-0119, 4pm Sat

Congregaton Bet Ha'am 879-0028, gay-friendly synagogue

Integrity/Dignity 143 State St. (Church Chapel), 646-2820, 6pm 3rd Sun

Community Pride Reporter

P. O. Box 178
Saco, Maine 04072
207/282-4311

*Proudly serving the lesbian, gay,
bisexual and transgender community
of Maine and New Hampshire*

The Community Pride Reporter serves as a source of local,
state, national, and international news, information, ideas, and
opinions. We serve the lesbian, gay, bisexual, and
transgendered people of Maine, and the seacoast of
Portsmouth, New Hampshire, providing a forum whereby
increased awareness and acceptance of the rich diversity
among us will revitalize, actualize, and strengthen our
community.

SUBSCRIPTION FORM

_____ Yes, I wish to support COMMUNITY PRIDE REPORTER with my
subscription.
        I will receive 12 issues for $25.00 (more if you can, less if you can't) mailed in a
plain envelope.*
_____ I wish to support COMMUNITY PRIDE REPORTER with an additional
        donation of $_____.

NAME: _____

ADDRESS: _____

_____

PHONE #: _____

Please make checks payable to Community Pride Reporter & send to P. O. Box 178,
Saco, Maine 04072.
*We acknowledge the varying degrees to which members of our community are out,
and we respect their choice.

PUBLICATIONS
▲ **Community Pride Reporter** P.O. Box 178, 282-4311

EROTICA
▲ **Video Expo** 666 Congress St., 774-1377

Rockport (207)

ACCOMMODATIONS
Guesthouse 378 Commercial St., 236-9069 (MW) apt rental

Sebago Lake (207)

ACCOMMODATIONS
Maine-ly For You RR2 Box 745, Harrison, 583-6980 (GF)

Tennants Harbor (207)

ACCOMMODATIONS
Eastwind Inn PO Box 149, 04860, 372-6366 (GF,F)

Waterville (207)

INFO LINES & SERVICES
Colby College Bi/Lesbian/Gay Community Bridge Room, 872-4149, 7:30pm Mon

EROTICA
Priscilla's Book Store 18 Water St., 873-2774, clsd Sun
Treasure Chest 5 Sanger, 873-7411

York Harbor (207)

ACCOMMODATIONS
Canterbury House 432 York St., 363-3505 (GF)

MARYLAND

Annapolis (410)

ACCOMMODATIONS
Bed & Breakfast of Maryland 269-6232/(800) 736-4667 (GF) accommodations service
William Page Inn 8 Martin St., 626-1506/(800) 364-4160 (GF) renovated 1908 home

RESTAURANTS & CAFES
Grattis Cafe 47 State Circle, 267-0902, 9am-8pm, from 11am Sat, clsd Sun

EROTICA
20/20 Books 2020 West St., 266-0514

Baltimore (410)

INFO LINES & SERVICES
AA Gay/Lesbian 433-4843
▲ **Community Real Estate Referrals** (800) 346-5592, gay realtor at your service, no rentals
Gay/Lesbian Community Center 241 W. Chase St., 837-5445, 10am-4pm, clsd Sat & Sun
Gay/Lesbian Switchboard 837-8888/837-8529 (TDD), 7pm-10pm
PACT (People of all Colors Together) PO Box 33186, 21218, 323-4720

Transgender Support Group at the Center

ACCOMMODATIONS

Abacrombie Badger B&B 58 W. Biddle St., 244-7227 (GF)

▲ **Alternative Accommodations** (800) 209-9408

Biltmore Suites 205 W. Madison St., 728-6550/(800) 868-5064 (GF)

Chez Claire B&B 17 W. Chase St., 685-4666 (MW) 4-story townhouse

Mr. Mole B&B 1601 Bolton St., 728-1179 (★GF) suites on Bolton Hill

BARS

Allegro 1101 Cathedral St., 837-3906 (M,D) 6pm-2am, from 4pm Sun

Baltimore Eagle 2022 N. Charles St. (enter on 21st), 823-2453 (★M,L,WC) 6pm-2am

Central Station 1001 N. Charles St., 752-7133 (★MW,NH,F,V) 11:30am-2am, American

Club Atlantis 615 Fallsway, 727-9099 (M,D,S) 9pm-2am, from 4pm Sun, clsd Mon

Club Bunns 608 W. Lexington St., 234-2866 (MW,D,MRC-AF) 5pm-2am

Club Mardi Gras 228 Park Ave., 625-9818 (M,NH,WC) 4pm-2am, from noon Th-Fri

Club Seventeen Twenty-Two 1722 N. Charles St., 727-7431 (M,D,BYOB) 1:30am-5am Thur-Sun

Coconuts Cafe 311 W. Madison, 383-6064 (W,D,WC) 11am-2am, from 4pm wknds, clsd Mon

The Drinkery 203 W. Read St., 669-9820 (MW,NH) 11am-2am

The Gallery Studio Restaurant 1735 Maryland Ave., 539-6965 (MW) 1pm-2am, dinner nightly, American

Hepburn's 504 S. Haven St., 276-9310 (MW,D) 7pm-2am, from 4pm wknds, clsd Mon-Tue

Hippo 1 W. Eager St., 547-0069 (★MW,D,TG,K,V,WC) 3pm-2am, 3 bars

Leon's 870 Park Ave., 539-4850 (M,NH,WC) 11:30am-2am

Lynn's of Baltimore 774 Washington Blvd., 727-8924 (M,NH) 6pm-1am, from 11am Sat, clsd Sun

Orpheus 1001 E. Pratt St., 276-5599 (GF,D,18+) call for events

Randy's Sportsman's Bar 412 Park Ave., 727-8935 (M,NH) 6am-2am

Senator Bar 614 N. Howard St., 727-9620 (M,NH) 9am-2am

Stagecoach 1003 N. Charles St., 547-0107 (MW,D,CW,WC) 4pm-2am, rooftop cafe, Tex/Mex

Unicorn 2218 Boston St., 342-8344 (★M,NH,S,OC) 4pm-2am, from 2pm wknds

RESTAURANTS & CAFES

Cafe Diana 3215 N. Charles St., 889-1319 (★) 11am-11pm, American

Cafe Hon 1009 W. 36th St., 243-1230 (WC) 8am-10pm, clsd Sun, American

City Diner 911 Charles St., 547-2489, full bar

Donna's Coffee Bar 2 W. Madison, 385-0180 (BW)

Great American Melting Pot (GAMPY's) 904 N. Charles St., 837-9797 (MW,WC) 11:30am-2am, til 3am Fri-Sat

Guiseppe's 3215 N. Charles, 467-1177, pizza & pasta

Gypsy Cafe 1103 Hollins St., 625-9310, 11am-1am, til 3pm Sun

Louie's The Bookstore Cafe 518 N. Charles, 962-1224 (E,WC)

M. Gettier 505 S. Broadway, 732-1151 (WC) dinner nightly, clsd Sun, modern French

Mencken's Cultured Pearl Cafe 1114 Hollins St., 837-1947 (WC) Mexican

Metropol Cafe & Art Gallery 1713 N. Charles St., 385-3018, 6pm-11pm, 10am-6pm Sun, clsd Mon

Mount Vernon Stable & Saloon 909 N. Charles St., 685-7427, lunch & dinner, bar 11:30am-2am

Spike & Charlie's Restaurant & Wine Bar 1225 Cathedral St., 752-8144 (E) lunch, dinner & Sun brunch, clsd Mon

BOOKSTORES & RETAIL SHOPS

Adrian's Book Cafe 714 S. Broadway, Fells Point, 732-1048, 8am-8pm, til 11pm Fri-Sat, from 11am wknds, new & used, some gay titles

Lambda Rising 241 W. Chase St., 234-0069, 10am-10pm

TRAVEL & TOUR OPERATORS

Maryland Office of Tourism (800) 543-1036

Mt. Royal Travel Inc. 1303 N. Charles St., 685-6633/(800) 767-6925 (IGTA)

Safe Harbors Travel 25 South St., 547-6565/(800) 344-5656 (IGTA)

SPIRITUAL GROUPS

MCC 3401 Old York Rd., 889-6363, 10:30am Sun

PUBLICATIONS

The Baltimore Alternative PO Box 2351, 21203, 235-3401, monthly

The Baltimore Gay Paper PO Box 22575, 21203, 837-7748

Gay Community Yellow Pages-Baltimore 547-0380

EROTICA

Big Top Books 429 E. Baltimore, 547-2495

Center News 205 W. Fayette St., 727-9544

Leather Underground 136 W. Read St., 528-0991, 11am-7pm, til 8pm Fri, 10am-6am Sat, clsd Sun

Beltsville (301)

INFO LINES & SERVICES

▲ **Community Real Estate Referrals** (800) 346-5592, gay realtor at your service, no rentals

TRAVEL & TOUR OPERATORS

Your Travel Agent in Beltsville 10440 Baltimore Blvd., 937-0966/(800) 872-8537 (IGTA)

College Park

INFO LINES & SERVICES

▲ **Community Real Estate Referrals** (800) 346-5592, gay realtor at your service, no rentals

Columbia

INFO LINES & SERVICES

Gay/Lesbian Community of Howard County PO Box 2115, 21045, mail access only, multi-interest social group

Cumberland (301)

ACCOMMODATIONS

Red Lamp Post 849 Braddock Rd., 777-3262 (MW,F) dinner optional

Frederick (301)

RESTAURANTS & CAFES
The Frederick Coffee Co. & Cafe 100 East St., 698-0039, 8am-7pm, til 9pm Fri-Sat, 9am-6pm Sun

Greenbelt

INFO LINES & SERVICES
▲ **Community Real Estate Referrals** (800) 346-5592, gay realtor at your service, no rentals

CRUISY AREAS
Greenbelt Park (AYOR)

Hagerstown

CRUISY AREAS
S. Potomac St. & Summit St. (AYOR)

Hyattsville

INFO LINES & SERVICES
▲ **Community Real Estate Referrals** (800) 346-5592, gay realtor at your service, no rentals

Laurel (301)

INFO LINES & SERVICES
▲ **Community Real Estate Referrals** (800) 346-5592, gay realtor at your service, no rentals
Gay People Of Laurel PO Box 25, 20725

EROTICA
Route I News Agency 106 Washington Blvd., 725-9671, 24hrs

Parkton (410)

ACCOMMODATIONS
Hidden Valley Farm B&B 1419 Mt. Carmel Rd. (30 min. N. of Baltimore), 329-8084 (MW)

Potomac

INFO LINES & SERVICES
▲ **Community Real Estate Referrals** (800) 346-5592, gay realtor at your service, no rentals

Rockville (301)

INFO LINES & SERVICES
▲ **Community Real Estate Referrals** (800) 346-5592, gay realtor at your service, no rentals

TRAVEL & TOUR OPERATORS
▲ **Damron Atlas World Travel** 984-9060/(800) 357-4190

SPIRITUAL GROUPS
MCC of Rockville 15817 Barnesville Rd., 20849, 601-9112, 9am & 10:30am Sun

Salisbury (410)

EROTICA
Salisbury News Agency 616 S. Salisbury Blvd., 543-4469

CRUISY AREAS
Salisbury City Park (AYOR)

Silver Spring (301)

INFO LINES & SERVICES
▲ **Community Real Estate Referrals** (800) 346-5592, gay realtor at your service, no rentals

GLASS (Gay/Lesbian Assoc. of Silver Spring) PO Box 8518, 20907, 588-7330

TRAVEL & TOUR OPERATORS
Central Travel of Silver Spring 8609 2nd Ave., 589-9440 (IGTA)

Travel Central 8209 Fenton St., 587-4000/(800) 783-4000

EROTICA
Max Wonder 9421 Georgia Ave., 942-4196

Smith Island (203)

ACCOMMODATIONS
Smith Island Get-A-Way P.O. Box 187, Westport, (203) 579-9400 (GF) apt. rental in secluded a community accessible only by boat

MASSACHUSETTS

Amherst (413)

ACCOMMODATIONS
Ivy House B&B I Sunset Ct., 549-7554 (GF)

BOOKSTORES & RETAIL SHOPS
Food For Thought 106 N. Pleasant St., 253-5432 (WC) 10am-6pm, til 8pm Wed-Fri, noon-5pm Sun, progressive bookstore

TRAVEL & TOUR OPERATORS
Adventura Travel 233 N. Pleasant St., 549-1256

SPIRITUAL GROUPS
Integrity/Western MA Grace Church Chapel, Boltwood Ave., 532-5060, 7pm last Sun

Barre (508)

ACCOMMODATIONS
Jenkins House B&B Inn Scenic Rte.122 at Barre Common, 355-6444/(800) 378-7373 (GF)

Boston (617)

INFO LINES & SERVICES
BAGLY (Boston Alliance of Gay/Lesbian Youth) PO Box 814, 02103, (800) 422-2459/399-7337, support services for lesbigay youth 22 & under

Bisexual Resource Center 29 Stanhope St. 3rd flr, 424-9595

Black Gay Men's Group 566 Columbus Ave. (Harriet Tubman House), 536-8610

▲ **Community Real Estate Referrals** (800) 346-5592, gay realtor at your service, no rentals

Entre Nous, Inc. PO Box 984, 02103, men's & women's leather group

Gay/ Lesbian Helpline 267-9001, 4:30pm-11pm, 6pm-10pm wknds

International Foundation for Gender Education P.O. Box 367, Wayland, 01778, 894-8370, 4:30pm-11pm, 6pm-10pm wknds

Lesbian Al-Anon (at the Women's Center), 354-8807, 6:30pm Wed

Tiffany Club of New England P.O. Box 2283, Woburn, 01888, 891-9325, transgender hotline Tue night

ACCOMMODATIONS

463 Beacon St. Guest House 463 Beacon St., 536-1302 (★GF,IGTA)

Amsterdammerje PO Box 865, 02103, 471-8454 (MW) full brkfst, Euro-American B&B

▲ **The Caritas B&B Network** (800) CARITAS (227-4827), see ad in center National section

▲ **Chandler Inn** 26 Chandler St., 482-3450/(800) 842-3450 (★GF,IGTA)

Holworthy Place 102 Holworthy St., Cambridge, 864-7042 (GF) full brkfst

▲ **Oasis Guest House** 22 Edgerly Rd., 267-2262 (★M,IGTA)

Thoreau's Walden B&B 2 Concord Rd., 259-1899 (GF)

BARS

The Avalon 15 Lansdowne St., 262-2424 (★M,D,YC) 9pm-2am Sun only

The Bar 99 St. Botolph St., 266-3030 (MW,NH,F) 5pm-1am, from noon Sun

The Bolt 174 Lincoln, 695-1475 (MW,D,F,S,WC) 11am-2am, lunch daily

Boston Eagle 520 Tremont St., 542-4494 (★M,NH,L) 3pm-2am, from noon Sun

▲ **Boston Ramrod** 1254 Boylston St., 266-2986 (★M,L,F,S,V,YC,WC) noon-2am

BOSTON

Two Townhouses In The Heart Of Boston ♥ Telephones ♥ Color TV's ♥ Central Air ♥ Outdoor Decks ♥ Private & Shared Baths ♥ Continental Breakfast & Evening Snacks ♥ Close To All Major Sights & Nightlife ♥ Reasonable Rates ($59-$89 Per Night) ♥ MC, V & Amex

For More Information, Call, Write or Fax Us At:

OASIS GUEST HOUSE

O·A·S·I·S GUEST HOUSE B·O·S·T·O·N

22 Edgerly Road, Boston, MA 02115
617-267-2262 / Fax: 267-1920

Buzz 67 Stuart St., 267-8969 (★MW,D) 10pm Sat only

Campus/Man-Ray 21 Brookline, Cambridge, 864-0400 (GF,D,A,YC) 9pm-1am, clsd Mon-Tue, gay night Th

Chaps 27 Huntington Ave., 266-7778 (★M,D,V,WC) noon-2am, Wed Latino night

▲ **Club Cafe** 209 Columbus, 536-0966 (★MW,E,V,WC) 2pm-2am, from 11:30am Sun, also a restaurant

▲ **Fritz** (at the Chandler Inn), 482-3450 (★M, NH) noon-2am

Heaven/Hombre 7 Lansdowne St., 421-9595 (MW,D) 10pm-2am Wed & Sun

Jacques' 79 Broadway, 426-8902 (M,S) 11am-midnight, drag bar, drag bar

Luxor 69 Church, 423-6969 (M,F,V) 4pm-1am, also 'Jox' sports bar & 'Mario's' Italian restaurant

Napoleon Club 52 Piedmont, 338-7547 (M,D,OC) 5pm-2am

One Nineteen Merrimac 119 Merrimac St., 367-0713 (M,NH,L,WC) 10:30am-2am

Paradise 180 Massachusetts Ave., Cambridge, 864-4130 (★M,D,S,V,WC) 4pm-2am

Playland 21 Essex, 338-7254 (M) 8pm-2am, from noon Sun, hustlers

Quest 1270 Boylston St., 424-7747 (★MW,D,V) 9pm-2am, clsd Sun, roof deck

RESTAURANTS & CAFES

Art Zone Cafe 150 Kneeland St., 695-0087 (MW,WC) 11am-4pm, til 4am Th, 24hrs Fri-Sat, Southern BBQ, plenty veggie

The Blue Wave 142 Berkeley St., 424-6711/424-6664 (MW) noon-11pm, til 5pm Sun

The Casa Romero 30 Gloucester St., 536-4341, 5pm-10pm, til 11pm wknds

RAMROD

NEW ENGLAND'S #1 LEATHER & DENIM BAR
RAMROD 1254 BOYLSTON BOSTON 266-2986

The Icarus 3 Appleton St., 426-1790, dinner & Sun brunch, clsd Sun (summers)

Rabia's 73 Salem St., 227-6637 (WC) lunch & dinner, fine Italian

Regalia Restaurant & Wine Bar 480 Columbus Ave., 236-5252, dinner nightly, Sun brunch, tapas & American

Ristorante Lucia 415 Hanover St., 367-2353, great North End pasta

Roberto's at Cafe Amalfi 8 Westland Ave., 536-6396 (E) dinner & Sun brunch, full bar

GYMS & HEALTH CLUBS

Metropolitan Health Club 209 Columbus, 536-3006 (GF) 6pm-11pm, 9am-9pm wknds

Mike's Gym 560 Harrison Ave., 338-6210 (★) gay owned/run

BOOKSTORES & RETAIL SHOPS

Designs for Living 52 Queensberry St., 536-6150, 7am-9pm, cafe

Glad Day Books 673 Boylston St., 267-3010, 9:30am-10pm, til 11pm Fri-Sat, noon-9pm Sun, lesbigay

Globe Corner 1 School St., (800) 358-6013, also 49 Palmer St., Cambridge

Trident Booksellers & Cafe 338 Newbury St., 267-8688 (WC) 9am-mid

Unicorn Books 1210 Massachusetts Ave., Arlington, 646-3680, 10am-9pm, til 5pm wknds, spiritual titles

Waterstone's Booksellers 26 Exeter, 859-7300 (WC) 9am-11pm

▲ **We Think The World of You** 540 Tremont St., 423-1965 (★) open daily, lesbigay

The Wordsworth 30 Brattle St., Cambridge, 354-5201, 9am-11pm, 10am-10pm Sun

TRAVEL & TOUR OPERATORS

The 5 Star Travel 164 Newbury St., 536-1999/(800) 359-1999 (IGTA)

Alyson Adventures P.O. Box 181223, 02118, 353-0595/(800) 825-9766 (IGTA) active travel & tours

The Friend in Travel 5230 Washington St., W. Roxbury, 327-8600/(800) 597-8267 (IGTA)

Gibb Travel 673 Boylston St., 353-0595/(800) 541-9949 (IGTA)

Just Right Reservations 18 Piedmont St., 423-3550, covers Boston, NYC & P-town

Massachusetts Office of Tourism 100 Cambridge St., 13th flr., (800) 447-6277

Omega International Travel 99 Summer St., 737-8511/(800) 727-0599 (IGTA)

Travel Management 160 Commonwealth Ave., 424-1908/(800) 532-0055

SPIRITUAL GROUPS

Am Tikva PO Box 11, Cambridge, 02238, 926-2536, lesbigay Jewish group

Dignity Beacon Hill (St. John's Evangelist Church), 421-1915, 5:30pm Sun

Ecumenical Catholic Church 35 Bowdin St., 227-5794, 5:30pm Sun

Integrity 12 Quincy Ave. (Christ Church), Quincy, 773-0310, last Fri

MCC 131 Cambridge St. (Old West Church), 288-8029, 7pm Sun

PUBLICATIONS

Bay Windows 1523 Washington St., 266-6670

Gay Community News 29 Stanhope St, 262-6969

The Guide PO Box 990593, 02199, 266-8557, monthly

In 398 Columbus Ave. Ste. 283, 426-8246, weekly

Let's Go Harvard Student Agencies, Cambridge, travel info for lesbigay youths

MEN'S CLUBS
▲ **Safari Club** 90 Wareham St. 2nd flr., 292-0011 (MO) 24hrs

EROTICA
Art I & II Cinemas 204 Tremont, 482-4661
Innovations in Leather 1254 Boylston St. (at Ramrod Bar), 536-1546, 10pm-1am, clsd Mon-Wed
Marquis de Sade 73 Berkeley St., 426-2120
▲ **Video Expo** 1258 Boylston St., 859-8911

Brockton

CRUISY AREAS
N. end of WT Field Park trails (AYOR)

Charlemont (413)

ACCOMMODATIONS
The Inn at Charlemont Rt. 2, Mohawk Trail, 339-5796, (GF,F)

Chelsea (617)

BARS
Club 9-11 9-11 Williams St., 884-9533 (MW,NH,D,WC) 4pm-1am

Chicopee (413)

BARS
Eclipse 13 View St., 534-3065 (MW,NH,D) 7pm-2am, clsd Mon-Wed
Our Hide-away 16 Bolduc Ln., 534-6426, 6pm-2am, clsd Mon, outdoor volleyball

Dedham (617)

EROTICA
▲ **Video Expo** 520 Providence Hwy. (Rte. 1), 320-9377

Dennis

CRUISY AREAS
Fresh Pond Conservation Area Rte. 134 at Fresh Pond (AYOR)
West Dennis Beach (AYOR)

Fairhaven (508)

EROTICA
▲ **Video Expo** 991-8191

Fitchburg (508)

BARS
The Country Lounge 860 Ashby State Rd., 345-6703 (MW,D) 7pm-1am

Gloucester (508)

BOOKSTORES
The Bookstore 61 Main St., 281-1548

Greenfield (413)

BOOKSTORES & RETAIL SHOPS
World Eye Bookshop 60 Federal St., 772-2186, open 9am, from noon Sun

Hyannis (508)

INFO LINES & SERVICES
Gay/Lesbian AA 775-7060, 6pm Sun

ACCOMMODATIONS
Gull Cottage 10 Old Church St., Yarmouth Port, 362-8747 (MW,WC)

BARS
Duval Street Station 477 Yarmouth Rd., 775-9835 (★MW,D,F,E,WC) 6pm-1am,
Cape Cod's largest gay complex

Ipswich

CRUISY AREAS
Crane's Beach 1/2 mi. to the right (AYOR)

Lawrence

CRUISY AREAS
The Common nr. Haverhill St. (AYOR)

Lenox (413)

ACCOMMODATIONS
Summer Hill Farm 830 East St., 442-2057 (GF,WC)
Walker House 64 Walker St., 637-1271/(800) 235-3098 (GF,WC)

Lowell (508)

EROTICA
Tower News 101 Gorham St., 452-8693

CRUISY AREAS
Moody St. (AYOR)

Lynn (617)

BARS
Fran's Place 776 Washington, 598-5618 (MW,NH,D,WC) 1pm-2am
Joseph 191 Oxford St., 599-9483 (MW,D,V,WC) 5pm-2am

Marblehead (508)

INFO LINES & SERVICES
North Shore Gay/Lesbian Alliance Box 806, 01945, 745-3848

TRAVEL & TOUR OPERATORS
Around the World Travel Townhouse Square, 631-8620/(800) 733-4337

Martha's Vineyard (508)

ACCOMMODATIONS
Captain Dexter House of Edgartown 35 Pease's Point Way, Box 2798, 627-7289
(GF) 1843 home of sea captain
Martha's Place B&B 114 Main St., 693-0253 (MW,WC)
Webb's Camping Area RFD 3 Box 100, 693-0233 (GF) May-Sept

TRAVEL & TOUR OPERATORS
Martha's Vineyard Steamship Authority 540-2022, ferries from Boston

Methuen (508)

BARS

Xposure 280 Merrimack St., 685-9911 (GF,D) 9pm-2am Fri, til 1am Sat only

Milton

CRUISY AREAS

Blue Hills Wampatuck Rd. trails & parking lot (AYOR)

Nantucket (508)

INFO LINES & SERVICES

▲ **Community Real Estate Referrals** (800) 346-5592, gay realtor at your service, no rentals

ACCOMMODATIONS

House of Orange 25 Orange St., 228-9287 (GF) open May-Oct, old captain's home

CRUISY AREAS

Dunes W. of Surfside (AYOR)

New Bedford (508)

BARS

Le Place 20 Kenyon St., 992-8156 (★MW,D) 2pm-2am, from noon-1am Sat

Puzzles 428 N. Front St., 991-2306 (MW,D,F,WC) 4pm-2am, local fish menu & Sun brunch from 11am

Newbury (508)

ACCOMMODATIONS

46 High Road B&B 46 High Rd., 462-4664 (GF)

Northampton (413)

INFO LINES & SERVICES

Community Pride Line 585-0683

▲ **Community Real Estate Referrals** (800) 346-5592, gay realtor at your service, no rentals

East Coast FTM Group P.O. Box 60585 Florence Sta., 01060, 584-7616, support group for FTM transgendered people & their partners only, contact Bet Power

Gay/Bi Men's Support Group 585-5819

Lesbian/Gay Business Guild PO Box 593, 01061, 585-8839

Out & About Cable TV Channel 2, 9pm Mon

ACCOMMODATIONS

Corner Porches Baptist Corner Rd., Ashfield, 628-4592 (GF) full brkfst, 30 min. from Northampton

Old Red Schoolhouse 67 Park St., 01060, 584-1228 (W)

BARS

Club Metro 492 Pleasant St., 582-9898 (GF,D,A,S) Wed gay night

The Grotto 25 West St., 586-6900 (MW,D,F,E) 5pm-1am

Iron Horse 20 Center St., 584-0610 (GF,F,E) 8:30pm-?

Pearl Street Cafe 10 Pearl St., 584-7810 (MW,D) 9pm-1am Wed & Sat only

RESTAURANTS & CAFES

Bela 68 Masonic St., 586-8011 (WC) noon-8pm, til 10pm Th-Sat, clsd Sun-Mon

Curtis & Schwartz 116 Main St., 586-3278, 7:30am-3pm
Green Street Cafe 64 Green St., 586-5650, lunch & dinner
Haymarket Cafe 15 Amber Ln., 586-9969, 9am-midnight, clsd Mon
Paul & Elizabeth's 150 Main St., 584-4832 (BW,WC) seafood
Squire's Smoke & Game Club Rte. 9, Williamsburg, 268-7222 (★WC) from 5pm Wed-Sun

BOOKSTORES & RETAIL SHOPS
Pride & Joy 20 Crafts Ave., 585-0683, 11am-6pm, til 8pm Th, from noon-5pm Sun

TRAVEL AGENTS
Adventura Travel 122 Main St., 584-9441

Northborough (508)

BOOKSTORES & RETAIL SHOPS
▲ **Airborn for Men** 15 Belmont St. (Rte. 9), 366-3807, military-themed & casual clothes, erotica

Pittsfield

CRUISY AREAS
Berkshire Athenaeum (AYOR)
Burbank Park on Onota Lake (AYOR)

Provincetown (508)

INFO LINES & SERVICES
▲ **Community Real Estate Referrals** (800) 346-5592, gay realtor at your service, no rentals

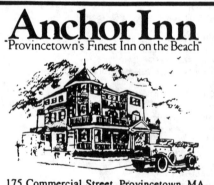

Provincetown Business Guild 115 Bradford St., 02657, 487-2313/(800) 637-8696 (IGTA)

ACCOMMODATIONS

A Tall Ship 452 Commercial St., 487-2247 (GF) beach house

▲ **Admiral's Landing Guest House** 158 Bradford St., 487-9665 (M,IGTA) seasonal

Ampersand Guesthouse 6 Cottage St., 487-0959 (MW)

▲ **Anchor Inn Guest House** 175 Commercial St., 487-0432/(800) 858-2657 (★MW) private beach

Angel's Landing 353-355 Commercial St., 487-1600 (MW) seasonal

Asheton House 3 Cook St., 487-9966 (GF)

Beachfront Realty 145 Commercial St., 487-1397, vacation rentals & housing

▲ **Beaconlite Inn** 12 Winthrop St., 487-9603 (★MW)

Benchmark Inn & Annex 6-8 Dyer St., 487-7440/(888) 487-7440 (MW,SW)

The Blue Beacon 8 Bradford St., 487-0516 (GF)

▲ **The Boatslip Beach Club** 161 Commercial St., 487-1669/(800) 451-7547 (★MW,F,SW) seasonal, seafood

Bradford Gardens Inn 178 Bradford St., 487-1616/(800) 432-2334 (★W)

Bradford House & Motel 41 Bradford St., 487-0173 (MW)

▲ **The Brass Key Guesthouse** 9 Court St., 487-9005/(800) 842-9858 (★M,SW,WC,IGTA)

The Buoy 97 Bradford St., 487-3082 (MW)

Burch House 116 Bradford St., 487-9170 (M) seasonal

The Captain & His Ship 164 Commercial St., 487-1850/(800) 400-2278 (★M) seasonal

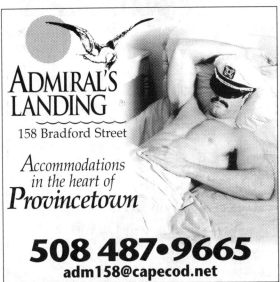

Provincetown's
Premiere Waterfront Resort

- Quality Waterfront Accommodations
With Private Baths • In-Room Telephones • Free Parking

- New England's Largest Outdoor Tea Dance

- Restaurant

- Open April Through October

THE
BOATSLIP
BEACH CLUB AT PROVINCETOWN

The Boatsllip Beach Club • 161 Commercial Street
P.O. Box 393 • Provincetown, MA 02657
Reservations or Brochure
(800) 451-SLIP (7547)
(508) 487-1669 • FAX (508) 487-6021

Captain Lysander's Inn 96 Commercial St., 487-2253 (GF)

▲ **Captain's House** 350-A Commercial St., 487-9353/(800) 458-8885 (M)

▲ **Carl's Guest House** 68 Bradford St., 487-1650/(800) 348-2275 (MO,N)

Chancellor Inn 17 Center St., 487-9423 (M)

▲ **Chicago House** 6 Winslow St., 487-0537 (M)

The Claredon House 118 Bradford St., 487-1645 (GF)

Coat of Arms 7 Johnson St., 487-0816 (★M) seasonal

Commons Guesthouse & Bistro 386 Commercial St., 487-7800/(800) 487-0784 (GF)

Crown & Anchor 247 Commercial St., 487-1430 (MW,F,E,SW)

Dexter's Inn 6 Conwell St., 487-1911 (W)

The Dunes Motel & Apartments PO Box 361, 02657, 487-1956 (MW) seasonal

▲ **Elephant Walk Inn** 156 Bradford St., 487-2543/(800) 889-9255 (★MW)

▲ **Elliot House** 6 Gosnold St., 487-4029 (MW)

Elm Guest House 9 Johnson St., 487-0793 (M) seasonal

▲ **Fairbanks Inn** 90 Bradford St., 487-0386/(800) 324-7265 (★MW,IGTA)

Four Bays 166 Commercial St., 487-0859/(800) 414-2297 (MW)

Gabriel's Guestrooms & Apartments 104 Bradford St., 487-3232/(800) 969-2643 (★W,IGTA)

Gifford House Inn & Dance Club 9-11 Carver St., 487-0688/(800) 434-0130 (M) seasonal

Grand View Inn 4 Conant St., 487-9193 (MW)

Hargood House at Bayshore 493 Commercial St., 487-9133 (GF)

Haven House 12 Carver St., 487-3031 (M,SW)

The
Captain's House
in
Provincetown

GUESTS

350A Commercial Street • MA 02657
508-487-9353

1-800-457-8885

*Private and Shared Baths • Cable
Color TV • Private Patio • Center of
Town • Immaculate Accommodations*

Chicago House

An Original Provincetown *Guest House*

Private Baths • Apartments
Continental Breakfast
Center of Town • Quiet Side Street
Parking • Airport Pickup

1-800 SEE-PTOWN

6 Winslow Street
Provincetown MA 02657

YEAR ROUND

Randy Godfrey, Innkeeper

Heritage House 7 Center St., 487-3692 (★MW)

Holiday Inn of Provincetown Rte. 6-A Box 392, 02657, 487-1711/(800) 422-4224 (GF,SW,WC,IGTA) harbor-view restaurant

The Inn at Cook Street 7 Cook St., 487-3894/(888) 266-5655 (GF) intimate & quiet

The Inn at the Egg 1944 Rte. 6-A, Brewster, 896-3123/(800) 259-8235 (GF) 20 min. from Provincetown

Ireland House 18 Pearl St., 487-7132/(800) 474-7434 (MW)

John Randall House 140 Bradford St., 487-3533 (MW)

▲ **Lamplighter Inn** 26 Bradford St., 487-2529 (MW)

Land's End Inn 22 Commercial St., 487-0706 (MW)

Lotus Guest House 296 Commercial St., 487-4644 (MW) seasonal

Mayflower Apartments 6 Bangs St., 487-1916 (GF)

▲ **Monument House** 129 Bradford St., 487-9664 (MW,IGTA) seasonal

Normandy House 184 Bradford St., 487-1197 (MW)

Pilgrim House 336 Commercial St., 487-6424 (W) also full restaurant & bar

Provincetown Inn 1 Commercial St., 487-9500 (GF,SW,WC)

▲ **Provincetown Reservations System** 293 Commercial St. #5, 487-2400/(800) 648-0364 (IGTA)

▲ **The Ranch** 198 Commercial St., 487-1542 (MO)

Red Inn 15 Commercial St., 487-0050 (MW) elegant waterfront dinner & lodging

Renaissance Apartments 48 Commercial St., 487-4600 (MW) seasonal

▲ **Revere Guesthouse** 14 Court St., 487-2292 (MW)

Roomers 8 Carver St., 487-3532 (M) seasonal

Spend the night with us.

The Lamplighter Inn

(800) 263-6574 or (508) 487-2529
26 Bradford Street • Provincetown, MA 02657

- Charmingly appointed guest rooms
- King, Queen & Full Size Beds
- Free Off-Street Parking
- Water Views
- Private sun deck
- Color/cable TV
- **Open all year**

Your Hosts: Steve Vittum & Brent Lawyer

Special Low Rates
May, June, Sept., Oct.

ELEPHANT WALK INN

800-889-WALK

Distinctive, Affordable Accommodations
Private Baths • TVs • Fridges • Parking
Sundeck • Breakfast • Optional A/C
Brochure

156 Bradford St. • Provincetown, MA 02657
(508) 487-2543   (800) 889-9255

Rose & Crown Guest House 158 Commercial St., 487-3332 (MW)

Sandbars 570 Shore Rd., 02657, 487-1290 (MW) all oceanfront rooms, private beach

▲ **Sandpiper Beach House** 165 Comerical St., 487-1928/(800) 354-8628 (★MW,IGTA)

Sea Drift Inn 80 Bradford St., 487-3686 (MO)

Shamrock Motel, Cottages & Apartments 49 Bradford St., 487-1133 (GF,SW) seasonal

Shiremax Inn 5 Tremont St., 487-1233 (M)

▲ **Six Webster Place** 6 Webster Pl., 487-2266/(800) 693-2783 (★MW,WC)

Somerset House 378 Commercial St., 487-0383 (★GF) seasonal

South Hollow Vineyards Rte. 6-A, North Truro, 487-6200 (GF) seasonal

Sunset Inn 142 Bradford St., 487-9810 (MW) seasonal

Swanberry Inn 8 Johnson St., 487-4242/(800) 847-7926 (MW)

Three Peaks 210 Bradford St., 487-1717/(800) 286-1715 (MW,IGTA)

Trade Winds 12 Johnson St., 487-0138 (M)

Tucker Inn 12 Center St., 487-0381 (GF) seasonal

Victoria House 5 Standish St., 487-4455 (MW)

Watermark Inn Guest House 603 Commercial St., 487-2506 (GF)

Watership Inn 7 Winthrop, 487-0094/(800) 330-9413 (★MW)

▲ **West End Inn** 44 Commercial St., 487-9555/(800) 559-1220 (M) seasonal

Westwinds Guest House 28 Commercial St., 487-1841 (MW,SW) seasonal

White Wind Inn 174 Commercial St., 487-1526 (MW)

Windsor Court 15 Cottage St., 487-2620 (MW,SW) hot tub, kitchens

BARS

Atlantic House Hotel 4 Masonic Pl. (The Big Room), 487-3821 (★M,D) 9pm-1am

Back Room (at Crown & Anchor accommodations), 487-1430 (★MW,D,E,YC) 10:30pm-1am, seasonal

Back Street Bar (at Gifford House), 487-0688 (M,D,E) seasonal

▲ **The Boatslip Beach Club** (at Boatslip Accommodations), 487-1669 (★MW,F,YC) popular T-dance 3pm daily, seasonal, seafood

Governor Bradford 312 Commercial St., 487-9618 (GF,FS) 11am-1am, check schedule for "Space Pussy" performance times

The Iguana Grill 135 Bradford St., 487-8800 (M,S,V) 9am-1am, restaurant from 5pm, Mexican

The Little Bar (at the Atlantic House Hotel), 487-3821 (M,NH) from noon daily

Pied Piper 193-A Commercial St., 487-1527 (★W,D) noon-1am

Rooster Bar (at the Crown & Anchor accommodations), 487-1430 (MW,NH,F,V) 6pm-1am

Town House 291 Commercial St., 487-0292 (★MW,F,E,OC) 11am-1am

Vault (downstairs at Crown & Anchor) (MO,L) from 7pm

Vixen 336 Commercial St., 487-6424 (W,D,S) 11am-1am

Zax 67 Shank Painter Rd., 487-3122 (MW,D,F)

RESTAURANTS & CAFES

Cafe Express 214 Commercial St., 487-3382 (WC) 9am-2am, vegetarian

Dodie's Diner 401-1/2 Commercial St., 487-3868, 8am-10pm

Dodie's Pizza 333 Commercial St., 487-3388 (★) 9am-2am

The Flagship 463 Commercial St., 487-4200 (E)

44 COMMERCIAL ST PROVINCETOWN MASSACHUSETTS 02657

508.487.9555 800.559.1220

WEST END INN

Franco's 133 Bradford St., 487-3178 (★MW) lunch & dinner, Luigi's upstairs, Italian

Front Street Restaurant 230 Commercial St., 487-9715 (MW) 6pm-10:30pm, til 1am bar, seasonal

Gallerani's 133 Commercial St., 487-4433 (★MW,BW) 8am-2pm, 6am-10:30pm Th-Mon

Landmark Inn Restaurant 404 Commercial St., 487-9319 (MW) dinner nightly 5:30pm-10pm, seasonal

Lobster Pot 321 Commercial St., 487-0842 (WC) noon-10pm

Mews 429 Commercial St., 487-1500 (★WC) lunch & dinner, seasonal

Napi's 7 Freeman St., 487-1145 (WC) internat'l/seafood

Post Office Cafe Cabaret 303 Commercial St. (upstairs), 487-3892 (MW,E) 8am-midnight (breakfast til 3pm)

Pucci's Harborside 539 Commercial St., 487-1964 (★WC) seasonal

Sal's Place 99 Commercial St., 487-1279 (★)

Sebastian's Long & Narrow 177 Commercial St., 487-3286 (WC) 11am-10pm

Spiritus 190 Commercial St., 487-2808 (★) 11am-2am, great espresso shakes & late night hangout for a slice

GYMS & HEALTH CLUBS

The Mussel Beach 33 Bradford St., 487-0001 (MW) 6am-9pm

The Provincetown Gym Inc. 170 Commercial St., 487-2776 (MW)

BOOKSTORES & RETAIL SHOPS

Don't Panic 192 Commercial St., 487-1280, lesbigay gifts

Far Side of the Wind 389 Commercial St., 487-3963 (WC) 11am-11pm, til 5pm off-season

Now, Voyager 357 Commercial St., 487-0848, 11am-11pm, til 5pm off season, lesbigay

Pride's 182 Commercial St., 487-1127, 10am-11pm (in-season), lesbigay gifts

Provincetown Bookshop 246 Commercial St., 487-0964, 10am-11pm, til 5pm off-season

TRAVEL & TOUR OPERATORS

All Provincetown 487-9000/(800) 786-9699, rental hotline

Cape Air Barnstable Municipal Airport, 771-6944/(800) 352-0714 (IGTA)

Portuguese Princess Whale Watch Shank Painter Rd., McMillan Wharf, 487-2651 (WC)

▲ **RSVP-Town Reservations** PO Box 614, 02657, 487-1883/(800) 677-8696 (IGTA)

Your Way Travel 145 Commercial St., 487-2992 (IGTA)

SPIRITUAL GROUPS

Dignity 1 Commercial St. (Provincetown Inn), 487-9500, 10:30am mass Sun (May-Oct)

PUBLICATIONS

In 398 Columbus Ave., Boston, 426-8246

Provincetown Banner PO Box 1978, 02657, 487-7400

▲ **Provincetown Magazine** 14 Center St., 02657, 487-1000, weekly

CRUISY AREAS

Herring Cove Beach (AYOR)

Randolph (508)

BARS

Randolph Country Club 44 Mazeo Dr. (Rte. 139), 961-2414 (★MW,D,E,V,SW,WC) 2pm-2am, (10am summer), volleyball

Sandwich

CRUISY AREAS

West side of Sandy Nook Beach (AYOR)

Springfield (413)

INFO LINES & SERVICES

Gay/Lesbian Info Service PO Box 80891, 01138, 731-5403

BARS

David's 397 Dwight St., 734-0566 (MW,D,YC,WC) 8pm-2am, clsd Sun-Mon

Just Friends 23 Hampden St., 781-5878 (MW,D,V,WC) 11am-2am, 3 flrs.

Pub 382 Dwight, 734-8123 (MW,NH,D,F,S,WC) 11am-2am, dinner Fri-Sun & Sun brunch

Quarry at the Pub, 734-8123 (M,L) 9pm-2am

TRAVEL & TOUR OPERATORS

A&D Travel 30 Main St., West Springfield, 737-5706/(800) 737-5712 (IGTA)

EROTICA

▲ **Video Expo** 486 Bridge St., 747-9812

Stoneham

CRUISY AREAS
Sheep's Fold Conservation Area Rte. 93 exit 33 (AYOR)

Sturbridge (508)

RESTAURANTS & CAFES
The Casual Cafe 538 Main St., 347-2281 (BYOB,WC) 5pm-10pm, clsd Sun-Mon, Italian/Japanese

Vineyard Haven (508)

ACCOMMODATIONS
Captain Dexter House of Vineyard Haven 100 Main St., Box 2457, 02568, 693-6564 (GF) 1843 home of sea captain

Waltham (617)

BOOKSTORES & RETAIL SHOPS
Synchronicity Transgender Bookstore 123 Moody St., 899-2212, over 100 TG titles

EROTICA
▲ **Video Expo** 465 Moody St., 894-5063

Ware (413)

ACCOMMODATIONS
The Wildwood Inn 121 Church St., 967-7798 (GF,WC)

Watertown

CRUISY AREAS
Bird Sanctuary near VFW Hall along the Charles River,   (AYOR)

Weymouth (617)

EROTICA
▲ **Video Expo** 138 Bridge St., 335-0446

Williamstown (413)

ACCOMMODATIONS
River Bend Farm B&B 643 Simonds Rd., 458-3121 (GF) seasonal

Worcester (508)

INFO LINES & SERVICES
AA Gay/Lesbian 752-9000
Gay/Lesbian Youth Group PO Box 592, Westside Stn., 01602, 755-0005, 24hrs

BARS
A-MEN 21-23 Foster St., 754-7742 (MW,D,A) clsd Mon-Tue
Club 241 241 Southbridge, 755-9311 (★MW,D,S,WC) 6pm-2am, from 2pm wknds, clsd Mon-Wed, rooftop deck
MB Lounge 282 Main St., 799-4521 (M,L,WC) 6pm-2am

GYMS & HEALTH CLUBS
Midtown Athletic Club 22 Front St. 2nd flr., 798-9703, 8am-8pm

SPIRITUAL GROUPS
Morning Star MCC 231 Main St., 892-4320 (WC) 11:15am Sun

MICHIGAN

Ann Arbor (313)

INFO LINES & SERVICES

▲ **Community Real Estate Referrals** (800) 346-5592, gay realtor at your service, no rentals

Gay/Lesbian Open House 518 E. Washington St., 665-0606, 8:45pm Mon, social group

Lesbian/Gay AA 482-5700

Lesbian/Gay Male/Bisexual Programs Office 3116 Michigan Union, 530 S. State St., 763-4186, 9am-5pm

Ozone House 608 N. Main St., 662-2222, 6:30pm Tue, lesbigay youth support group for ages 12-20

ACCOMMODATIONS

Judy's Place 906 Edgewood Pl., 662-4812 (GF) full brkfst

BARS

The Ark 637-1/2 S. Main St., 761-1451 (GF) concert house

\'aut\ Bar 315 Braun Ct., 994-3677 (MW,F,WC) 4pm-2am, from 11am Sun(brunch), patio, American/Mexican, pronounced 'out'

Blind Pig 208 S. 1st St. , 996-8555 (GF,NH,E,WC) 3pm-2am

Club Fabulous 763-4186 (MW) monthly chem-free dances during school year

Flame Bar 115 W. Washington St., 662-9680 (★M,NH) 7:30pm-2am

LesBiGay Happy Hour/Social At Dominick's 812 Monroe St. (at Tappan Ave.), 7pm-9pm Fri

The Nectarine 516 E. Liberty, 994-5835 (MW,D,V,YC) 9pm-2am Tue & Fri only

RESTAURANTS & CAFES

The Earle 121 W. Washington, 994-0211 (BW,WC) 6pm-10pm, til midnight Fri-Sat, clsd summer Sun, French/Italian, French/Italian

Sweet Lorraines 303 Detroit St., 665-0700 (WC) 11am-10pm, til midnight Fri-Sat, Modern American, full bar, patio

BOOKSTORES & RETAIL SHOPS

Borders Book Shop 303 S. State St., 668-7652, 9am-9pm, 11am-6pm Sun

Common Language 215 S. 4th Ave., 663-0036 (WC) open daily, lesbigay

Crazy Wisdom Books 206 N. 4th Ave., 665-2757, 10am-6pm, from noon Sun, holistic metaphysical

Webster's 2607 Plymouth Rd., 662-6150, 8am-11pm

TRAVEL & TOUR OPERATORS

Horizons Travel 475 Market Pl., 663-3434/(800) 878-7477 (IGTA)

SPIRITUAL GROUPS

Huron Valley MCC 1001 Green Rd., 434-1452, 2pm Sun

Atwood (616)

ACCOMMODATIONS

Stelle Wunderschönes 12410 Entrim Dr., 599-2847 (MW) full brkfst, cedar log home w/ lake views

Battle Creek (616)

BARS

Partners 910 North Ave., 964-7276 (MW,D,WC) 6pm-2am

Belleville (313)

BARS

Granny's Place 9800 Haggerty Rd., 699-8862 (MW,F,S,WC) 11am-2am, from 4pm wknds

Detroit (313)

INFO LINES & SERVICES

Affirmations Lesbian/Gay Community Center 195 W. 9-Mile Rd. Ste. 106, Ferndale, (810) 398-7105, 1pm-6pm, 9am-2pm Sat

▲ **Community Real Estate Referrals** (800) 346-5592, gay realtor at your service, no rentals

Lesbian/Gay Switchboard (810) 398-4297, 4:30pm-11pm, clsd Sat

Men of Color Motivational Group 8850 Woodward (church), 496-0158, 7pm Tue

Motor City Business Forum (810) 546-9347, 2nd Tue, business/social group mtg.

BARS

Adams Apple 18931 W. Warren, 336-2080 (M,NH,WC) 3pm-2am

Back Pocket 8832 Greenfield Rd., 272-8374 (★M,F) 6pm-2am, til 4am Wed & Sat

Backstage/Footlights 214 W. 6th St., Royal Oak, (810) 546-0526 (MW,F,E,WC) 4pm-2am, from 11am wknds, til 4am Fri-Sat, patio, patio, American

Backstreet 15606 Joy, 272-8959 (★M,D,YC,WC) 8pm-2am Wed & Sat

The Body Shop 22061 Woodward Ave., Ferndale, (810) 398-1940 (MW,D,F,WC) 4pm-2am, from 5pm Sat, from 2pm Sun

Chains 6228 Michigan, 897-3650 (★MO,L) 6pm-2am

Club Gold Coast 2971 E. 7-Mile Rd., 366-6135 (★M,D,S,WC) 7pm-2am

The Deck 14901 E. Jefferson, 822-1991 (M,NH,S) 4pm-2am, from 6:30pm Mon

Detroit Eagle 1501 Holden, 873-6969 (★M,D,CW,L,WC) 8pm-2am, from 5pm Fri, clsd Mon-Tue

The Edge 12322 Conant, 891-3343 (M,D,S) 4pm-2am, from 2pm wknds, patio

Gigi's 16920 W. Warren (rear entrance), 584-6525 (M,D,TG,K,S) noon-2am, from 2pm wknds

Hayloft Saloon 8070 Greenfield Rd., 581-8913 (M,OC,WC) 3pm-2am

Male Box 3537 E. 7-Mile Rd., 892-5420 (M,NH,D) 2pm-2am

Menjo's 928 W. McNichols, 863-3934 (★M,D,V,YC) noon-2am, from 1pm wknds

Number's 17518 Woodward, 868-9145 (M,V,YC) 8pm-4am

Off Broadway East 12215 Harper St., 521-0920 (M,D,YC) 9pm-2am

The Other Side 16801 Plymouth, 836-2324 (M,NH,F,WC) noon-2am

The Rainbow Room 6640 E. 8-Mile Rd., 891-1020 (MW,D,S) 7pm-2am, from noon Sun

Silent Legacy 1641 Middlebelt Rd., Inkster, 729-8980 (MW,D,S)

Stingers Lounge 19404 Sherwood, 892-1765 (MW) 4pm-2am

Sugarbakers 3800 E. 8-Mile Rd., 892-5203 (W,F) 6pm-2am, sports bar & grill

Tiffany's 17436 Woodward, 883-7162 (★M,D,CW) 6pm-2am, Wed-Sat, from 3pm Sun

Woodward Cocktail Lounge 6426 Woodward Ave., 872-0166 (★MW,F,WC) 8am-2am, from noon Sun, rear entrance after 3pm

Zippers 6221 E. Davison, 892-8120 (★MW,D,MRC-AF,E,S,WC) opens 9pm, from 8pm Sun

RESTAURANTS & CAFES

Como's 22812 Woodward, Ferndale, (810) 548-5005 (WC) 11am-2am, til 4am Fri-Sat, from 2pm wknds, American/Italian, full bar

Golden Star 22828 Woodward Ave., Ferndale, (810) 545-0994, open til1am wknds, Chinese

La Dolce Vita 17546 Woodward Ave., 865-0331 (MW,WC) 4pm-2am, 11am-midnight Sun, clsd Mon-Tue, Italian, patio

Lavender Moon Cafe 205 W. 9-Mile Rd., Ferndale, (810) 398-6666 (E,WC) 11am-11pm, til 2am Fri-Sat, from noon Sun, clsd Mon

Rhinoceros 265 Riopelle, 259-2208 (E) 11:30am-2am, American, jazz club

Sweet Lorraines 29101 Greenfield Rd., Southfield, (810) 559-5985 (WC) 11am-10pm, til mid Fri-Sat, modern American

Vivio's 2460 Market St., 393-1711, 7am-9pm, clsd Sun, American/Italian

BOOKSTORES & RETAIL SHOPS

Chosen Books 120 W. 4th St., Royal Oak, (810) 543-5758 (WC) noon-10pm, lesbi-gay

The Dressing Room 42371 Garfield Rd., Clinton Township, (810) 286-0412, cross-dressing boutique

TRAVEL & TOUR OPERATORS

Royal International Travel Services, Inc. 31455 South Field Rd., Birmingham, 644-1600/(800) 521-1600 (IGTA)

SPIRITUAL GROUPS

Dignity-Detroit 6th & Porter St. (Most Holy Trinity), (313) 961-4818, 6pm Sun

Divine Peace MCC 23839 John R, (810) 544-8335, 10am Sun & 7pm1st &3rd Sun only

Integrity 960 E. Jefferson Ave. (church), 259-6688, 7:30pm 3rd Fri

MCC of Detroit Pinecrest & Dreyton (church), Ferndale, (810) 399-7741, 10am & 7pm Sun

PUBLICATIONS

Between the Lines 33523 8-Mile Rd. Ste. 185-A3, Livonia, 48152, (810) 615-7003, covers southeastern MI

▲ **Cruise Magazine** 660 Livernois, Ferndale, (810) 545-9040

Metra PO Box 71844, Madison Heights, 48071, (810) 543-3500, covers IN, IL, MI, OH, PA, WI & Ontario, Canada

MEN'S CLUBS

TNT Health Club Complex 13333 W. 8-Mile Rd. (rear entrance), 341-5322 (★MO,PC) 24hrs

EROTICA

Fifth Wheel Adult Books 225 S. Shafer, 842-6720

Noir Leather 415 S. Main, Royal Oak, (810) 541-3979 (WC) 11am-8pm, 1pm-5pm Sun

Uptown Book Store 16541 Woodward Ave., 869-9477

Escanaba (906)

BARS

Club Xpress 904 Ludington St., 789-0140 (MW,D,WC) 8pm-2am, from 6pm Fri-Sat, clsd Sun-Tue

Flint (810)

BARS

Club Triangle 2101 S. Dort, 767-7552 (MW,D,18+) 4pm-2am

Merry Inn 2402 N. Franklin St., 234-9481 (★MW,NH,MRC,18+) 1pm-2am

State Bar 2512 S. Dort Hwy., 767-7050 (★MW,D,S,WC) 4pm-2am, from 1pm wknds

SPIRITUAL GROUPS

Redeemer MCC of Flint 1665 N. Chevrolet Ave., 238-6700 (WC) 11am Sun

Gaylord (517)

ACCOMMODATIONS

Heritage House B&B 521 E. Main St., 732-1199 (GF) full brkfst

Grand Rapids (616)

INFO LINES & SERVICES

▲ **Community Real Estate Referrals** (800) 346-5592, gay realtor at your service, no rentals

Lesbian/Gay Network 909 Cherry SE, 458-3511, 6pm-10pm, clsd wknds, info & referrals, AA meetings

BARS

The Apartment 33 Sheldon, 451-0815 (M,NH,WC) 11am-2am, from 1pm Sun

The Cell 76 S. Division St., 454-4499 (M,D,L,WC) 7am-2am, from noon wknds

The Club 67 67 S. Division Ave., 454-8003 (★MW,D,S,WC) 4pm-2am

Diversions 10 Fountain St. NW, 451-3800 (MW,D,F,V,WC) 11am-2am, from 8pm wknds, American

Reptile House 242-9955 (GF,E,18+) call for events

Taylors 8 Ionia SW, 454-4422 (MW,D,F,WC) 11am-2am, til 4am Fri-Sat, from 6pm Sun, burgers & soups

RESTAURANTS & CAFES

Cherie Inn 969 Cherry St., 458-0588 (WC) 8am-3pm, clsd Mon

BOOKSTORES & RETAIL SHOPS

Earth & Sky 6 Jefferson SE, 458-3520 (WC) 11am-7pm, clsd Sun, feminist

Sons & Daughters 962 Cherry SE, 459-8877, noon-midnight, from 10am wknds, lesbigay bookstore & coffeehouse

TRAVEL & TOUR OPERATORS

Vacation Depot 907 Cherry SE, 454-4339 (IGTA) ask for Karen

SPIRITUAL GROUPS

Dignity 1850 Hall St., 454-9779, 7:30 Wed

Reconciliation MCC 300 Graceland NE, 364-7633, 10am Sun

MEN'S CLUBS

Diplomat Health Club 2324 S. Division Ave., 452-3754 (PC) 24hrs

EROTICA
Cini-Mini I 1358 Plainfield NE, 454-2444, also Cini-Mini II at 415 Bridge St. NW, 454-7531

Kalamazoo (616)

INFO LINES & SERVICES
AA Gay/Lesbian 247 W. Level St., 343-2711, 8pm Tue
Alliance for Lesbian/Gay Support PO Box 226, Student Service Bldg., 49008, 387-2123, 2pm Sun (Kiba Room)
Kalamazoo Lesbian/Gay Resource Line 345-7878, 7pm-10pm, info & referrals

BARS
Brother's Bar 209 Stockbridge, 345-1960 (MW,D,PC,S) 4pm-2am, patio
Zoo 906 Portage St., 342-8888 (M,D) 4pm-2am,18+ Sun-Tue

BOOKSTORES & RETAIL SHOPS
Pandora's Books for Open Minds 226 W. Lovell St., 388-5656 (WC) 11am-7pm, til 6pm Fri-Sat, clsd Sun-Mon, feminist/lesbigay
Triangle World 551 Portage St., 373-4005 (WC) noon-10pm, clsd Mon, lesbigay

SPIRITUAL GROUPS
Phoenix Community Church 1758 N. 10th St. (Peoples Church), 381-3222 (WC) 6pm Sun

Lansing (517)

INFO LINES & SERVICES
AA Gay/Lesbian 1118 S. Harrison St. (United Ministries), E. Lansing, 321-8781
Lansing Lesbian/Gay Hotline PO Box 6565, E. Lansing, 48826, 332-3200, 7pm-10pm Mon-Fri, 2pm-5pm Sun, info & referrals
Michigan Alliance for Lesbian/Gay Youth Service 484-0946, statewide network for sexual minority youth

ACCOMMODATIONS
▲ **The Caritas B&B Network** (800) CARITAS (227-4827), see ad in center National section

BARS
Club 505 505 Shiawassee, 374-6312 (W,D) 4pm-2am
Esquire 1250 Turner, 487-5338 (M,NH,F,OC,WC) noon-2am
Paradise 224 S. Washington Square, 484-2399 (M,D,S,YC) 9pm-2am, clsd Mon

BOOKSTORES & RETAIL SHOPS
Community News Center 418 Frandor Shopping Center, 351-7562 (WC) 9am-9pm, til 7pm Sun
Real World Emporium 1214-16 Turner St., 485-2665 (WC) noon-8pm, clsd Mon, also cafe

SPIRITUAL GROUPS
Dignity 327 M.A.C (St. John's Parish), E. Lansing, 48826, 8pm Tue
Ecclesia 3020 S. Washington Ave. (church), 48826, 7pm Sun

Marquette (906)

BOOKSTORES & RETAIL SHOPS
Sweet Violets 413 N. 3rd St., 228-3307, 10am-6pm, clsd Sun

CRUISY AREAS
Presque Isle Point (AYOR)

Shinas Park - Picnic Rocks (AYOR)

Midland (517)

ACCOMMODATIONS
Jay's B&B 4429 Bay City Rd., 496-2498 (GF) deck

TRAVEL & TOUR OPERATORS
Travel Together PO Box 1453, 48641, 835-3452/(800) 433-5442

Mount Clemens (810)

BARS
Mirage 27 N. Walnut, 954-1919 (MW,D) 4pm-2am, from 2pm wknds

Mount Pleasant

CRUISY AREAS
Chipwater Park (AYOR) summers

Muskegon (616)

SPIRITUAL GROUPS
Muskegon MCC Christ Community Church, Spring Lake, 861-5275, 6pm Sun

Petoskey

CRUISY AREAS
Rotary Point opp. Holiday Inn (AYOR)

Pontiac (810)

BARS
Club Flamingo 352 Oakland Ave., 253-0430 (MW,D,K,S,WC) 2pm-2am

CRUISY AREAS
Dog Run Clarkston (AYOR)

Port Huron (810)

BARS
Seekers 3301 24th St., 985-9349 (MW,D) 4pm-2am, from 2pm Th-Sun

CRUISY AREAS
Lighthouse Beach (AYOR)
Pine Grove Park (AYOR)

Saginaw (517)

BARS
Bambi's 1742 E. Genessee, 752-9179 (MW,D,S) 7pm-2am
Heidelberg 411 S. Franklin, 771-9508 (M,OC,WC) 4pm-2am, from noon wknds

Saugatuck (616)

ACCOMMODATIONS
Camp It Rte. 6635 118th Ave., Fennville, 543-4335 (MW) seasonal
Douglas Dunes Resort PO Box 369, Douglas, 49406, 857-1401 (M,F,SW,IGTA) motel, cottages
Grandma's House B&B 2135 Blue Star Hwy., 543-4706 (MW) Victorian country estate

Hillby Thatch Cottages 1438 & 1440 71st, Glenn, 864-3553 (GF) 15 min. from Saugatuck

The Kirby House PO Box 1174, 49406, 857-2904 (GF,SW) Queen Anne Victorian manor

The Lighthouse Motel P.O. Box 759, 49406, 857-2271 (GF,SW,WC)

Moore's Creek Inn 820 Holland St., 857-2411/(800) 838-5864 (GF) old-fashioned farmhouse

The New Richmond Guest House 3037 57th St., 561-2591 (MW) full brkfst

The Newnham SunCatcher Inn 131 Griffith, 857-4249 (GF,SW) full brkfst

BARS

Douglas Disco (at Douglas Dunes resort), 857-1401 (M,D) 2 bars

RESTAURANTS & CAFES

Cafe Sir Douglas (at Douglas Dunes resort), 857-1401 (MW) 5pm-10pm, til 11pm Fri-Sat, clsd Tue-Wed, cont'l

Loaf & Mug 236 Culver St., 857-2974, 8am-3pm, til 8pm Fri-Sat

Pumpernickel's 202 Butler St., 857-1196, 8am-4pm, sandwiches, fresh breads

Restaurant Toulouse 248 Culver St., 857-1561 (WC) lunch & dinner, country French

Uncommon Grounds 123 Hoffman, 857-3333, coffee & juice bar

BOOKSTORES & RETAIL SHOPS

Hoopdee Scootee 133 Mason, 857-4141, 10am-9pm, til 6pm Sun, til 5pm winter, clothing, gifts

CRUISY AREAS

Beach Oral Beach (AYOR) walk north

Park on Water St. (AYOR)

St. Clair (810)

ACCOMMODATIONS

William Hopkins Manor 613 N. Riverside Ave., 329-0188 (GF) full brkfst

Traverse City (616)

INFO LINES & SERVICES

Friends North PO Box 562, 49685, 946-1804, social group, newsletter

ACCOMMODATIONS

The Interlochen 2275 M-137, P.O. Box 194, Interlochen, 49643, 276-9291 (GF,WC) seasonal

Neahtawanta Inn 1308 Neathawanta Rd., 223-7315 (GF) sauna

BARS

The Side Traxx Nite Club 520 Franklin, 935-1666 (MW,D,S,WC) 6pm-2am, from 2pm wknds

BOOKSTORES & RETAIL SHOPS

The Bookie Joint 120 S. Union St., 946-8862, 10am-6pm, clsd Sun, used books

CRUISY AREAS

Bryant Park (AYOR)

Westend Beach (AYOR)

Troy

INFO LINES & SERVICES
▲ **Community Real Estate Referrals** (800) 346-5592, gay realtor at your service, no rentals

Westland

CRUISY AREAS
Wm. P. Holliday Park (AYOR) summers

Ypsilanti   (313)

SPIRITUAL GROUPS
Tree of Life MCC 218 N. Adams St. (1st Congregational Church), 485-3922, 6pm Sun & Wed

EROTICA
The Magazine Rack 515 West Cross, 482-6944

MINNESOTA

Anoka   (612)

EROTICA SHOPS
Adult Book Store 6710 Hwy. 10, 427-2113

Bemidji   (218)

ACCOMMODATIONS
Meadowgrove Inn 13661 Powerdam Rd. NE, 751-9654 (GF,F) full brkfst, rural hideaway

CRUISY AREAS
Diamond Point Park (AYOR) summers
Library Park (AYOR)

Duluth   (218)

INFO LINES & SERVICES
Northland Gay Men's Center 8 N. 2nd Ave. E. Ste. 309, 722-8585

ACCOMMODATIONS
Stanford Inn B&B 1415 E. Superior St., 724-3044 (GF) full brkfst

GYMS & HEALTH CLUBS
Duluth Sauna 18 N. 1st Ave. E., 726-1388 (★GF) men only downstairs

BOOKSTORES & RETAIL SHOPS
At Sara's Table 728 E. Superior St., 723-8569 (WC) 8am-6pm, cafe

CRUISY AREAS
Leif Ericsson Park (AYOR)
Park Point Beach (AYOR) summers

Hastings   (612)

ACCOMMODATIONS
Thorwood & Rosewood Inns 315 Pine St., 437-3297 (GF) full brkfst

Hill City (218)

ACCOMMODATIONS

Northwoods Retreat 5749 Mt. Ash Dr., 697-8119 (MW,WC) cabins

Hinckley (612)

ACCOMMODATIONS

Dakota Lodge B&B Rte. 3, Box 178, 384-6052 (GF,WC) full brkfst, hot tub

Kenyon (507)

ACCOMMODATIONS

Dancing Winds Farm 6863 Country 12 Blvd., 789-6606 (MW) B&B & working dairy farm, tentsites, work exchange

Mankato (507)

INFO LINES & SERVICES

Mankato State U. Lesbigay Center 389-5131

RESTAURANTS & CAFES

The Coffee Hag 329 N. Riverfront, 387-5533 (E,WC) 9am-11pm, 11am-6pm Sun, clsd Mon

Minneapolis/St. Paul (612)

INFO LINES & SERVICES

▲ **Community Real Estate Referrals** , St. Paul, (800) 346-5592, gay realtor at your service, no rentals

District 202 2524 Nicollet Ave. S., St. Paul, 871-5559, 3pm-11pm, 3pm-1am Fri, noon-1am Sat, clsd Sun & Tue, resource center for lesbigay youth

Fresh Fruit KFAI 90.3 FM, Minneapolis, 341-0980, 7pm-8pm Th, gay radio program

Gay/Lesbian Community Action Council 310 E. 38th St., Minneapolis, 822-0127/(800) 800-0350, 9am-5pm Mon-Fri

Gay/Lesbian Helpline 822-8661/(800) 800-0907(in-state), noon-mid, from 4pm Sat, clsd Sun & holidays, covers IA,MN,NE,ND,SD,WI

GLEAM (Gay/Lesbian Elders Active in MN) 1505 Park Ave., Minneapolis, 721-8913, 1pm 2nd Sun

Green & Yellow TV Cable Channel 6, St. Paul, 11pm Th, gay news hour

Lambda AA 874-7430

Quatrefoil Library 1619 Dayton Ave., St. Paul, 641-0969, 7pm-9pm Mon-Th, 1pm-4pm wknds, lesbigay library & resource center

U of MN Gay/Lesbian/Bi/Transexual Groups 230 Coffman Memorial Library, Minneapolis, 626-2344, 4:30pm Wed

ACCOMMODATIONS

Abbotts Como Villa B&B 1371 W. Nebraska Ave., St. Paul, 647-0471 (MW) full brkfst wknds

Be Yourself Executive Inn - Twin Cities 1093 Snelling Ave. S., St. Paul, 698-3571 (M,N)

▲ **The Caritas B&B Network** (800) CARITAS (227-4827), see ad in center National section

Eagle Cove B&B W 4387 120th Ave., Maiden Rock WI, (715) 448-4302/(800) 467-0279 (GF,WC) country retreat, expanded cont'l brkfst

Garden Gate B&B 925 Goodrich Ave., St. Paul, 227-8430/(800) 967-2703 (GF)

▲ **Hotel Amsterdam** 828 Hennepin Ave., Minneapolis, 288-0459/(800) 649-9500 (MW)

Nan's Bed & Breakfast 2304 Freemont Ave. S., Minneapolis, 377-5118/(800) 214-5118 (GF) family home w/ guestrooms

BARS

19 Bar 19 W. 15th St., Minneapolis, 871-5553 (M,NH,BW,WC) 3pm-1am, from 1pm wknds

Brass Rail 422 Hennepin Ave., Minneapolis, 333-3016 (★M,K,V,WC) noon-1am

Bryant Lake Bowl 1810 W. Lake Bowl, Minneapolis, 825-3737 (GF,WC) 8am-2am, bar, theatre, restaurant & bowling alley

Checkers 1066 E. 7th St., St. Paul, 776-7915 (M,D,S,WC) 6pm-1am

Club Metro 733 Pierce Butler Rte., St. Paul, 489-0002 (★W,D,TG,F,E,WC) 3pm-1am

Gay 90s 408 Hennepin Ave., Minneapolis, 333-7755 (★MW,D,E,S,WC) 8am-1am (dinner nightly 5pm-9pm), 5 bar complex, erotica store

Innuendo 510 N. Robert St., St. Paul, 224-8996 (MW,NH,WC) 4pm-1am

Over the Rainbow 249 W. 7th St., St. Paul, 228-7180 (MW,D,K,S) 3pm-1am, from noon wknds

Rumours 490 N. Robert St., St. Paul, 224-0703 (★MW,D,F,E,WC) 4pm-1am, from noon wknds

The Saloon 830 Hennepin Ave., Minneapolis, 332-0835 (★M,D,F,WC) 9am-1am, til 3am Fri-Sun

The Times Bar & Cafe 1036 Nicollet Ave., Minneapolis, 333-2762 (MW,E,WC) 11am-1am

Town House 1415 University Ave., St. Paul, 646-7087 (★MW,D,CW) 2pm-1am, from noon wknds

RESTAURANTS & CAFES

Cafe Wyrd 1600 W. Lake St., Minneapolis, 827-5810 (MW) 7am-midnight

Cafe Zev 1362 LaSalle Ave., Minneapolis, 874-8477 (E)

La Covina 1570 Selby Ave., St. Paul, 645-5288 (WC) Mexican

Ruby's Cafe 1614 Harmon Pl., Minneapolis, 338-2089 (★MW) 7am-2pm, from 8am Sun

Rudolph's Bar-B-Que 1933 Lyndale, Minneapolis, 871-8969 (WC) 11am-midnight

The Safari 1424 Nicollet Ave., Minneapolis, 872-6375, 7am-10pm, from 8am Sat, from 9am Sun, Egyptian

Susan's Coffeehouse & Deli 2399 University Ave., Minneapolis, 644-7906, 7am-5:30pm, 9am-4pm Sat, clsd Sun

Vintage Joe's 1008 Marquette Ave., Minneapolis, 371-9882 (WC) 6am-midnight, 8am-2am Sat

GYMS & HEALTH CLUBS

Body Quest 245 N. Aldrich Ave. N., Minneapolis, 377-7222 (GF)

BOOKSTORES & RETAIL SHOPS

▲ **A Brother's Touch** 2327 Hennepin Ave., Minneapolis, 377-6279 (WC) 11am-9pm, til 5pm wknds, til 7pm Mon-Tue, lesbigay bookstore

Amazon Bookstore 1612 Harmon Pl., Minneapolis, 338-6560, 10am-9pm, til 7pm Fri, til 5pm wknds

Borders Bookshop 3001 Hennepin S. (Calhoun Square), Minneapolis, 825-0336

Magus Books 1316 SE 4th St., Minneapolis, 379-7669, noon-8pm, til 5pm wknds

The Rainbow Road 109 W. Grant, Minneapolis, 872-8448, 10am-10pm, lesbigay retail & video

TRAVEL & TOUR OPERATORS

All Airlines Travel 111 E. Kellogg Blvd. #225, St. Paul, 222-2210/(800) 832-0304 (IGTA)

Partners In Travel, Ltd. 825 Nicollet Mall, Minneapolis, 338-0004/(800) 333-3177 (IGTA)

The Travel Company 2800 University Ave. SE, Minneapolis, 379-9000/(800) 328-9131 (IGTA)

Travel Quest 245 Aldrich Ave. N, Minneapolis, 377-7700/(800) 373-7244 (IGTA)

SPIRITUAL GROUPS

Dignity Twin Cities Prospect Park Unitarian Methodist (Malcom & Orwin), Minneapolis, 827-3103, 7:30pm 2nd & 4th Fri

Integrity (Twin Cities) 317 17th Ave. SE (Univ. Episcopal Ctr.), Minneapolis, 331-3552, 7pm 1st Fri

Lutherans Concerned 100 N. Oxford, Minneapolis, 224-3371 (WC) 7:30pm 3rd Fri

MCC - All God's Children 3100 Park Ave., Minneapolis, 824-2673 (WC) 10am & 7pm Sun, 7pm Wed

Shir Tikvah 5000 Girard Ave., Minneapolis, 822-1440 (WC) 10am 1st Sat, then every Fri 8pm, lesbigay Jews

PUBLICATIONS

Focus Point 401 N. 3rd St. # 480, Minneapolis, 288-9000, weekly

Lavender Lifestyles 2344 Nicollet Ave. Ste 130, Minneapolis, 871-2237

Q Monthly 10 S. 5th St. #200, Minneapolis, 321-7300

EROTICA

▲ **Broadway Bookstore** 901 Hennepin Ave., Minneapolis, 338-7303, 24hrs

Fantasy House 81 S. 10th St., Minneapolis, 333-6313 (WC)

Panorama Video 1201 E. Lake St., Minneapolis, 721-5620, also 822 W. Lake St. 825-1979 & 2300 Hennepin Ave. S. 377-8883

CRUISY AREAS

East Lake Calhoun Blvd. at 33rd St., Minneapolis (AYOR) gay beach

Rochester (507)

INFO LINES & SERVICES

Gay/Lesbian Community Service PO Box 454, 55903, 281-3265, 5pm-7pm Mon & Wed

CRUISY AREAS

Eastwood Park (AYOR)

Soldiers Field Park (AYOR)

Rushford (507)

ACCOMMODATIONS

Windswept Inn 2070 N. Mill St., 864-2545 (GF)

St. Peter (507)

ACCOMMODATIONS

Park Row B&B 525 W. Park Row, 931-2495 (GF)

Two Harbors (218)

ACCOMMODATIONS
Star Harbor Resort 1098 Hwy. 61 E., 834-3796, cabins on Lake Superior

Wolverton (218)

RESTAURANTS & CAFES
District 31 Victoria's 995-2000 (BW) 5:30pm-9:30pm, clsd Sun, reservations required

MISSISSIPPI

Biloxi (601)

INFO LINES & SERVICES
▲ **Community Real Estate Referrals** (800) 346-5592, gay realtor at your service, no rentals

Gay/Lesbian Community Center 308 Caillavet St., 396-3333, 1pm-9pm, from 5pm Sun-Wed

BARS
Joey's 1708 Beach Blvd. (Hwy. 90), 435-5639 (MW,D,E) 9pm-2am, til 5am Fri-Sat, clsd Mon

EROTICA
The Adult Bookstore 1620 Pass Rd., 435-2802, clsd Sun
Adult Theatre 222 Iberville Dr., 435-5625
Adult Video Arcade 1854 Beach Blvd., 388-4212, 24 hrs
Satellite News 1632 Pass Rd., 432-8229, clsd Sun

CRUISY AREAS
Beach Hwy. btwn. Biloxi & Gulfport (AYOR)
Gulf Coast Beach btwn. Holiday Inn & Coliseum (AYOR)

Brookhaven

CRUISY AREAS
By-pass btwn I-55 & US Hwy. 51 south frontage Rd. of US Hwy. 84 (AYOR)

Florence (601)

INFO LINES & SERVICES
Aurora Transgender Support for Central MS PO Box 1306, 39073, 373-8610 x60/845-1328

Gulfport

INFO LINES & SERVICES
▲ **Community Real Estate Referrals** (800) 346-5592, gay realtor at your service, no rentals

Hattiesburg (601)

BARS
The Courtyard 107 E. Front St., 545-2714 (MW,D,F,E) hours vary

Holly Springs (601)

ACCOMMODATIONS
Somerset Cottage 310 S. Cedar Hills Rd., 252-4513 (GF)

Jackson (601)

INFO LINES & SERVICES

Gay/Lesbian Community Switchboard PO Box 7737, 39284, 373-8610/435-2398, 6pm-11pm, switchboard for many organizations, monthly publication

Lambda AA 4872 N. State St. (Unitarian Church), 373-8610 x55, 6:30pm Mon & Wed, 8pm Sat

Mississippi Gay/Lesbian Alliance Inc. Drawer 8457, 39284, 371-3019, also contact for AIDS project and MS monthly publications

Prime Timers 1521 W. Highland Dr., 373-8610-8-1 x49, monthly mtgs, social group for gay men over 30

BARS

Club City Lights 200 N. Mill St., 353-0059 (MW,D,MRC-AF,S,BW,BYOB) 10pm-? Wed, Fri-Sun

Jack's Construction Site (JC's) 425 N. Mart Plaza, 362-3108 (MW,NH,BW,BYOB) 5pm-?, from 2pm Sun

SPIRITUAL GROUPS

Affirmation PO Box 4362, 39296, 373-8610 x46, United Methodist gays & lesbians

Integrity Mississippi PO Box 68314, 39286, 373-8610 x47

MCC of the Rainbow 5565 Robinson Rd. Ext., Ste L, 992-6227/373-8610 x45, 11:30am Sun

Safe Harbor Family Church 2147 Henry Hill Dr. #203, 373-8610, 6pm Sun, 7pm Wed study, non-denominational, social events, support groups

St. Stephen's Community Church 4872 N. State St., 939-7181, 5pm 1st & 3rd Sun

PUBLICATIONS

Mississippi Voice PO Box 7737, 39284, 373-8610 x39

EROTICA

Terry Road Books 1449 Terry Rd., 353-9156, 24 hrs

CRUISY AREAS

Smith Park (AYOR)

Meridian (601)

BARS

Crossroads Rte. 1, Box 170, Enterprise, 39330, 655-8415 (MW,D,F,S,V,WC) 6pm-1am Fri, til 6am Sat

Olie Mae's at Crossroads, Enterprise, 655-8415 (GF,WC) 6pm-1am

Oxford

CRUISY AREAS

The Grove (AYOR)

Sardis Lake Beach (AYOR)

Pascagoula

CRUISY AREAS

Beach Park (AYOR)

Vicksburg (601)

EROTICA
Hill City News & Novelty 1214 Washington St., 638-4435

MISSOURI

Branson (417)

ACCOMMODATIONS
Pine Wood B&B P.O. Box 572, 779-5514 (GF) full breakfast, hot tub

Cape Girardeau (314)

BARS
Independence Place 5 S. Henderson St., 334-2939 (MW,D,TG,S) 8:30pm-1:30am, from 7:30pm Fri-Sat, clsd Sun

Columbia (573)

INFO LINES & SERVICES
Gay Men's Radio (This Way Out) KOPN 89.5 FM, 874-5676, 6pm Mon
Gay/Lesbian Helpline 449-4477, info & referrals
Triangle Coalition A02 Brady Commons UMC, 65211, 882-4427, meets 7pm Th

BARS
Contacts 514 E. Broadway, 443-0281 (MW,NH,D,E) 5pm-1:30am, from 8pm Sat, clsd Sun
Styx Inc. 3111 Old 63 South, , 499-1828 (MW,D) 3pm-1:30am, clsd Sun, patio,CW Tue

RESTAURANTS & CAFES
Ernie's Cafe 1005 E. Walnut, 874-7804, 6am-8pm, breakfast anytime

SPIRITUAL GROUPS
Christ the King Agape Church 515 Hickman Ave., 443-5316, 10:45am Sun & 6:30pm Wed
United Covenant Church PO Box 7152, 65205, 449-7194 (WC) 10am Sun, non-denominational

EROTICA
Eclectics 1122-A Wilkes Blvd., 443-0873
Midwest Adult Book Store 101 E. Walnut St., 442-6622

CRUISY AREAS
Cosmopolitan Park (AYOR)

Jefferson City (573)

ACCOMMODATIONS
Jefferson Victorian B&B 801 W. High St., 635-7196 (GF)

Joplin (417)

BARS
Partners 720 Main St., 781-6453 (MW,NH,D,CW) 2 bars

CRUISY AREAS
McClellan Park (AYOR)

Kansas City (816)

INFO LINES & SERVICES

▲ **Community Real Estate Referrals** (800) 346-5592, gay realtor at your service, no rentals

Gay Talk Crisis Line 931-4470, 6pm-midnight

Live & Let Live AA 4243 Walnut St., 531-9668, many mtgs

Unicorn Theatre 3820 Main, 531-3033, contemporary American theater

ACCOMMODATIONS

▲ **The Caritas B&B Network** (800) CARITAS (227-4827), see ad in center National section

Doanleigh Wallagh Inn 217 E. 37th St., 753-2667 (GF)

The Inn The Park 3610 Gillham Rd., 931-0797/(800) 708-6748 (GF,SW) full brkfst

BARS

Buddies 3715 Main St., 561-2600 (M,NH) 6am-3am

Cabaret 5024 Main St., 753-6504 (M,D,F,YC,WC) 6pm-3am, from 3pm Sun, clsd Mon

Dixie Bell Saloon 1922 Main St., 471-2424 (★M,L,E,WC) 11am-3am, also leather shop

The Edge 323 W. 8th (in the Lucas Place Bldg.), 221-8900 (MW,D,A,E,YC,WC)

The Fox 7520 Shawnee Mission Pkwy., Overland Park, 384-0369 (GF,NH) noon-2am, from 6pm Sat, clsd Sun, more gay in eves

Mari's Saloon & Grill 1809 Grand Blvd., 283-0511 (MW,D,F,V,WC) 5pm-10pm, from 11am Sun

Missie B's 805 W. 39th St., 561-0625 (M,NH,S) 11am-3am

Other Side 3611 Broadway, 931-0501 (M,NH,F,WC) 3:30pm-1:30am, clsd Sun

Sidekicks 3707 Main St., 931-1430 (M,D,CW,WC) 2pm-3am, clsd Sun

Soakie's 1308 Main St., 221-6060 (M,D,MRC-AF,F) 9am-1:30am, til 3am Fri-Sat, from 11am Sun

Ted's Bar & Grill 529 Walnut, 472-0569 (GF,NH,CW,F) 7am-1:30am, 11am-midnight Sun, lunch dailyz

View on the Hill 204 Orchard, Kansas City, KS , (913) 371-9370 (M,NH,WC) 4pm-2am, from noon wknds

The Vineyard 1108 Grand Ave., 421-1082 (M,S) 7am-1am

RESTAURANTS & CAFES

City Seen 1111 Main St., 472-8833 (WC) 11am-7pm

Classic Cup Cafe 301 W. 47th St., 753-1840 (WC) 7am-midnight, til 1am Fri-Sat

The Corner Restaurant 4059 Broadway, 931-6630 (BW,WC) 7am-9pm, til 2am wknds, American

Metropolis 303 Westport Rd., 753-1550 (MW,F,WC) lunch & dinner, clsd Sun

Otto's Malt Shop 3903 Wyoming, 11am-midnight, 24hrs wknds

BOOKSTORES & RETAIL SHOPS

Larry's Gifts & Cards 205 Westport Rd., 753-4757, 10am-7pm, til 5pm Sun

SPIRITUAL GROUPS

MCC of Johnson County 12510 W. 62nd Terrace #106, Shawnee KS, 66216, (913) 631-1184, 10:30am Sun & 7:30pm Wed

Spirit of Hope MCC 3801 Wyandotte, 931-0750, 10:15am Sun, 7:15pm Wed

PUBLICATIONS

Current News 809 W. 39th St. Ste. 1, 561-2679, weekly

News Telegraph P.O. Box 10085, 64171, 561-6266/(800) 303-5468

MEN'S CLUBS
1823 Club 1823 Wyandotte (MO,PC) 24hrs

EROTICA
Adrianne's Book Store 3314 Troust, 561-8996

Erotic City 8401 E. Truman Rd., 252-3370, 24hrs

Extremus 4037 Broadway, 756-1142, noon-8pm, clsd Sun, body piercing

Hollywood at Home 9063 Metcalf, Overland Park, 649-9666

Ray's Video & Newstand 3235 Main St., 753-7692, 24hrs

CRUISY AREAS
Country Club Plaza (AYOR)

Loose Park (AYOR) oh really!

Moberly

CRUISY AREAS
Reed St. (AYOR) nights

Rothwell (AYOR)

Noel (417)

ACCOMMODATIONS
Sycamore Landing Drawer H, Hwy 59 South, 475-6460, open May-Sept, campsites & canoe rental

Springfield (417)

INFO LINES & SERVICES
AA Gay/Lesbian SMS University @ Ecumenical Ctr (National off Cherry), 862-9264, 6pm Sat

BARS
The Gallery 424 N. Boonville, 865-1266 (MW) 1pm-1:30am, clsd Sun

Martha's Vineyard 219 W. Olive St., 864-4572 (M,NH,18+) 4pm-1:30am, from 2pm Sat, clsd Sun

RESTAURANTS & CAFES
Black Forest Inn 2185 S. Campbell, 882-6767, 3pm-11pm

EROTICA
Bolivar Road News 4030 N. Bolivar Rd., 833-3354

Sunshine News & Arcade 3537 W. Sunshine, 831-2298

CRUISY AREAS
Phelps Grove Park (AYOR)

St. Joseph (816)

BARS
Avis' Lounge 705 Esmond St., 364-9748 (MW,NH,D,WC) 5pm-1:30am, clsd Sun

CRUISY AREAS
Small Park downtown (AYOR)

St. Louis (314)

INFO LINES & SERVICES

The Center 2256 S. Grand Ave., 771-7995, lesbigay/transgendered community center

▲ **Community Real Estate Referrals** (800) 346-5592, gay realtor at your service, no rentals

Gay/Lesbian Hotline PO Box 23227, 63156, 367-0084, 6pm-10pm

PACT (People of All Colors Together) PO Box 775402, 63177, 995-4683/997-9897, mtgs 2nd Th

St. Louis Gender Foundation 997-9897, transgender info

Steps Alano Club 1935-A Park Ave., 436-1858

ACCOMMODATIONS

▲ **A St. Louis Guesthouse** 1032-38 Allen Ave., 773-1016 (MW) in historic Soulard district

Brewers House B&B 1829 Lami St., 771-1542 (MW) Civil War vintage B&B

▲ **The Caritas B&B Network** (800) CARITAS (227-4827), see ad in center National section

Napoleon's Retreat B&B 1815 Lafayette Ave., 772-6979 (MW) restored 1880s townhouse

BARS

Atlantis 3954 Central, 753-0112 (GF,D,A) 9pm-3am Wed-Sat, gay Th

Bacchus 6 S. Sarah, 531-1109 (M,E,WC) 5pm-1:30am, clsd Sun

Char Pei Lounge 400 Mascoutah Ave., Belleville IL, (618) 236-0810 (MW,D) 6pm-2am

A St. Louis Guesthouse

Located in Historic Soulard
Next Door To Clementines

Accommodations With Phone, Private Bath and Hot Tub in Courtyard

1032-38 Allen Ave.
St. Louis, MO 6310
(314) 773-1016

Clementine's 2001 Menard, 664-7869 (★M,L,F,WC) 10am-1:30am, from 11am wknds, til midnight Sun

The Complex 3511 Chouteau, 772-2645 (★M,D,F,E,WC) multiple bars

Drake Bar 3502 Papin St., 865-1400 (MW,E,WC) 5pm-1:30am, clsd Sun

Faces Complex 130 4th, E. St. Louis IL, (618) 271-7410 (M,D,L,E,S) 3pm-6am, 3 levels

Front Page 2330 Menard, 664-2939 (M,S,OC) 8am-1:30am, clsd Sun, drag bar

Grey Fox Pub 3503 Spring, 772-2150 (M,NH,TG) 1pm-1:30am, clsd Sun

Hyperspace 1014 Locust, 421-0003 (MW,E) 10pm-3am, clsd Th, 18+ Fri only

Loading Zone 16 S. Euclid, 361-4119 (★MW,V,WC)

Magnolia's 5 S. Vandeventer, 652-6500 (★M,MRC-AF,F,S,WC) 6pm-3am

Zippers 3145 W. Chain of Rocks Rd., Granite City IL, (618) 797-0700 (MW,D,S) 6:30pm-1am

RESTAURANTS & CAFES

Cafe Balaban 405 N. Euclid Ave., 361-8085 (★WC) wonderful Sun brunch

Duff's 392 N. Euclid Ave., 361-0522 (WC) clsd Mon, full bar

Einstein Bagels 2 N. Euclid Ave., 361-2020

Majestic Bar & Restaurant 4900 Laclede, 361-2011, 6am-1:30am

On Broadway Bistro 5300 N. Broadway, 421-0087 (WC) 11am-3am

Redel's 310 Debaliviere, 367-7005 (WC) hours vary

Sunshine Inn 8-1/2 S. Euclid Ave., 367-1413, 11:30am-9pm, fom 10:30am Sun, clsd Mon, vegetarian

BOOKSTORES & RETAIL SHOPS

Boxer's 310 N. Euclid Ave., 454-0209, 11am-6pm, 1pm-5pm Sun, men's underwear

Cheap Trx 3211 S. Grand, 664-4011, noon-8pm, til 6pm Sun, body piercing

Daily Planet News 243 N. Euclid Ave., 367-1333, 7am-8:30m

Friends & Luvers 3550 Gravois, 771-9405, 10am-10pm, noon-7pm Sun, novelties, videos and dating service

Heffalump's 387 N. Euclid Ave., 361-0544, 11am-8pm, til 10pm Fri-sat, noon-5pm Sun, gifts

Left Bank Books 399 N. Euclid Ave., 367-6731, 10am-10pm, 11am-5pm Sun, lesbian, feminist & gay titles

Our World Too 11 S. Vandeventer, 533-5322, 10am-9:30pm, noon-8pm Sun, lesbigay bookstore

Pages, Video & More 10 N. Euclid Ave., 361-3420, 9am-8pm, til 5pm Sun

TRAVEL & TOUR OPERATORS

Dynamic Travel 7750 Clayton Rd. Ste.105, 781-8400/(800) 237-4083 (IGTA)

Lafayette Square Travel Co. 1801 Lafayette Ave., 776-8747/(800) 727-1480 (IGTA)

Patrik Travel 22 N. Euclid Ave. Ste. 101, 367-1468/(800) 678-8747 (IGTA)

SPIRITUAL GROUPS

Agape Church 2026 Lafayette, 664-3588, 10:45am Sun, 6:30pm Wed

Dignity St. Louis 6400 Minnesota Ave., 997-9897 x63, 7:30pm Sun

MCC Living Faith 6501 Wydown, Clayton, 926-6387, 5pm Sun

MCC of Greater St. Louis 1120 Dolman, 231-9100, 9:30am & 11am Sun, 5:30 pm Sat

Trinity Episcopal Church 600 N. Euclid Ave., 361-4655, 8am & 10:30am Sun

PUBLICATIONS
The Lesbian/Gay News-Telegraph PO Box 14229-A, 63178, 664-6411

MEN'S CLUBS
▲ **Club St. Louis** 2625 Samuel Shepard Dr., 533-3666 (MO,PC,SW) 24hrs

CRUISY AREAS
Forest Park trails & Confederate Cir. (AYOR)
Shaw Gardens Missouri Botanical Garden (AYOR)

MONTANA

Billings (406)

INFO LINES & SERVICES
AA Gay/Lesbian (at MCC location), 245-7066, 8pm Sat

BARS
Monte Carlo N.29th & 1st Ave., 259-3393 (GF,NH) 10am-2am

RESTAURANTS & CAFES
Stella's Kitchen & Bakery 110 N. 29th St., 248-3060, 6am-3pm, bakery til 6pm, clsd Sun

BOOKSTORES & RETAIL SHOPS
Barjon's 2718 3rd Ave. N., 252-4398, 9:30am-5:30pm, clsd Sun

SPIRITUAL GROUPS
MCC Family of God 645 Howard St., 245-7066, 11am Sun & 7pm Wed, also 'Gospel Sing' 7pm 4th Sat

EROTICA
The Adult Shop 2702 Minnesota Ave., 245-4293
Big Sky Books 1203 1st Ave. N., 259-0051

Boulder (406)

ACCOMMODATIONS
Boulder Hot Springs Hotel & Retreat PO Box 930, 59632, 225-4339 (★GF,F,WC) irregular hours, spirituality/recovery, call for info

Bozeman (406)

INFO LINES & SERVICES
Lambda Alliance of Gay Men/Lesbians/Bisexuals PO Box 51, Strand Union Bldg., MSU, 59717, 994-4551

ACCOMMODATIONS
Gallatin Gateway Inn 76405 Gallatin Rd., 763-4672/(800) 676-3522 (GF,F,SW,WC) dinner nightly, Sun brunch

RESTAURANTS & CAFES
Spanish Peaks Brewery 120 N. 19th St., 585-2296, 11am-2am

EROTICA
Ms. Kitty's Adult Store 12 N. Wilson, 586-6989

Butte (406)

BARS
M&M Bar & Cafe 9 N. Main St., 723-7612, 24hrs, bar til 2am

RESTAURANTS & CAFES
Matt's Place Montana & Rowe Rds., 782-8049, 11:30am-7pm, clsd Sun-Mon, classic soda fountain diner
Pekin Noodle Parlor 117 S. Main, 2nd flr., 782-2217, 5pm-9pm, clsd Tue
Pork Chop John's 8 W. Mercury, 782-0812, 11am-9:30pm, clsd Sun
Uptown Cafe 47 E. Broadway, 723-4735, lunch & dinner, clsd Sun

EROTICA
Rocky Adult Book Store 121 W. Broadway, 723-7218

Corwin Springs (406)

RESTAURANTS & CAFES
The Ranch Kitchen Hwy. 89, 848-7891, lunch & dinner (seasonal)

Great Falls (406)

SPIRITUAL GROUPS
MCC Shepherd of the Plains 1505 17th Ave. SW, 771-1070, 11am Sun, 7pm Wed

EROTICA
Studio 209 209 4th St. S., 771-7266

CRUISY AREAS
Gibson Park (AYOR)

Helena (406)

INFO LINES & SERVICES
PRIDE P.O. Box 775, 59624, 442-9322/(800) 610-9322 (in MT), social contacts & newsletter

TRAVEL & TOUR OPERATORS
Travel Montana Dept. of Commerce, (800) 541-1447

Kalispell

CRUISY AREAS
Woodland Park (AYOR)

Missoula (406)

INFO LINES & SERVICES
AA Gay/Lesbian KC Hall 312 E. Pine, 523-7799, 9:30pm Wed
Lambda Alliance (U of MT) PO Box 7611, 59807, 243-5922

ACCOMMODATIONS
Foxglove Cottage B&B 2331 Gilbert Ave., 543-2927 (GF, SW) gay owned & run

BARS
Amvets Club 225 Ryman, 543-9174 (GF,D) noon-2am, more gay after 8pm

RESTAURANTS & CAFES
Black Dog Cafe 138 W. Broadway, 542-1138 (BYOB,WC) lunch & dinner, dinner only Sat, clsd Sun
Heidelhaus/Red Baron Casino 2620 Brooks, 543-3200 (WC) 6am-11pm, til midnight wknds, casino 24hrs

BOOKSTORES & RETAIL SHOPS
Freddy's Feed & Read 1221 Helen Ave., 549-2127, 7:30am-8pm, 9am-7pm Sat, 10am-5pm Sun

Second Thought 529 S. Higgins, 549-2790 (WC) 6:30am-10pm, bookstore & cafe

University Center Bookstore Campus Drive (U of MT), 243-4921, 8am-6pm, from 10am Sat, clsd Sun, gender studies section

EROTICA
Fantasy for Adults Only 210 E. Main St., 543-7760, also 2611 Brooks Ave., 543-7510

CRUISY AREAS
McCormick Park W. side of Orange St. Bridge (AYOR)

Ovando (406)

ACCOMMODATIONS
Lake Upsata Guest Ranch PO Box 6, 59854, 793-5890 (GF,F)

Ronan (406)

ACCOMMODATIONS
North Crow Vacation Ranch 2360 North Crow Rd., 676-5169 (MW,N) hot tub

NEBRASKA

Grand Island (308)

ACCOMMODATIONS
Midtown Holiday inn 2503 S. Locust , 384-1330 (GF,WC) "Images Pink Cadillac Lounge" on premises

EROTICA
Exclusively Yours Shop 216 N. Locust , 381-6984
K & L Market 2007 E. Hwy 30, 382-0910

CRUISY AREAS
Ashley Park (AYOR)
Pier Park (AYOR)

Kearney (308)

INFO LINES & SERVICES
Gay & Lesbian Association of Greater NE P.O. Box 2401, 68848, 472-3249, monthly social, support & newsletter

CRUISY AREAS
Harmon Park nr. rock garden & stage area (AYOR)

Lincoln (402)

INFO LINES & SERVICES
AA Gay/Lesbian 63rd & 'A' (Unitarian Church), 438-5214, 7:30pm Th

Lambda Business Association P.O. Box 6341, 68506, 483-6183, 3pm 4th Sun

SAGE PO Box 22043, 68542-2043, social/support & info for older members of the community

UNL Gay & Lesbian Student Assn. Nebraska Student Union Rm. 234, 472-5644, noon-6pm, meetings 7pm Tue during school year

Youth Talkline 473-7932, 7pm-midnight Fri-Sat, lesbigay info & referrals for age 23 & under

BARS
Panic 200 S. 18th St., 435-8764 (MW,D,S,V,WC) 4pm-1am, from 1pm wknds

The Q 226 S. 9th, 475-2269 (MW,D,E,K) 8pm-1am, from 5pm Fri, clsd Mon-Tue, 18+ Tue, CW Wed

BOOKSTORES & RETAIL SHOPS
Avant Card 1323 'O' St., 476-1918, 10am-7pm

TRAVEL & TOUR OPERATORS
Good Life Tour & Travel 8200 Fletcher Ave., 467-3900/(800) 233-0404
Nebraska Travel & Tourism PO Box 94666, 68509, (800) 228-4307

EROTICA
Adult Books & Cinema X 921 'O' St., 435-9323, 24hrs

CRUISY AREAS
15th St. from 'A' St. to State Capitol (AYOR)
Antelope, Pioneer & Van Dorn Parks (AYOR)

Norfork

CRUISY AREAS
Ta-Ha-Zooka Park (AYOR)

Omaha (402)

INFO LINES & SERVICES
AA Gay/Lesbian 345-9916 (AA#)
Gay/Lesbian Information & Referral Line 558-5303
HGRA (Heartland Gay Rodeo Association) P.O. Box 3354, 68103, 344-3103, contact Dan
L.E.O. (Leather Engineers of Omaha) P.O. Box 8181, educational & social group for gay men interested in leather-S/M
OPC (Omaha Players Club) PO Box 34463, 68134, 451-7987, 2pm 2nd Sat, S/M education & play group, pansexual mtgs
River City Gender Alliance P.O. Box 680, Council Bluffs IA, 51502, 398-1255, 7pm 1st Sat (at Hawthorne Suites), for CD's,TS & enquiring, all orientations, also newsletter

BARS
The Chesterfield 1901 Leavenworth St., 345-6889 (W,F,S,WC) 3pm-1am
CR Babe's 1951 St. Mary's Ave., 344-2310 (MW,K,S)
D.C.'s Saloon 610 S. 14th St., 344-3103 (MW,D,CW,L,E,S,WC) 3pm-1am, from 2pm wknds
Diamond Bar 712 S. 16th St., 342-9595 (M,NH,WC) 9am-1am, from noon Sun
Gilligan's Bar 1823 Leavenworth St., 449-9147 (MW,NH,F,K) 2pm-1am, til 4am Fri-Sat
The Infield 1401 Jackson, 346-3030 (MW,NH) 4pm-1am
The Max 1417 Jackson, 346-4110 (★MW,D,S,V,WC) 4 bars
The New Run 1715 Leavenworth St., 449-8703 (M,D,S,WC) 2pm-1am, til 4am Fri-Sat, volleyball court

RESTAURANTS & CAFES
French Cafe 1017 Howard St., 341-3547, lunch & dinner, brunch Sun
Neon Goose Cafe/Bar 1012 S. 10th, 341-2063 (WC) lunch & dinner, clsd Mon

BOOKSTORES & RETAIL SHOPS
New Realities 1026 Howard St., 342-1863 (WC) 11am-10pm, til 6pm Sun, progressive

TRAVEL & TOUR OPERATORS
  Regency Travel 10730 Pacific St., 393-0585/(800) 393-5482 (IGTA)

SPIRITUAL GROUPS
  Lutherans Concerned 453-7137, call for time & location
  MCC of Omaha 819 S. 22nd St., 345-2563, 9am & 10:30am Sun

PUBLICATIONS
  New Voice PO Box 3512, 68103, 556-9907, monthly

CRUISY AREAS
  Benson Park (AYOR)
  Carter Lake (AYOR)
  Hanscom Park (AYOR)

NEVADA

Carson City

INFO LINES & SERVICES
  ▲ **Community Real Estate Referrals** (800) 346-5592, gay realtor at your service, no rentals
  NV AIDS Hotline 505 E. King St. #304, (800) 842-2437, community info & resources, 8am-10pm

CRUISY AREAS
  Mills Park N. end (AYOR)

Elko

CRUISY AREAS
  Elko City Park (AYOR)

Lake Tahoe (702)

ACCOMMODATIONS
  Haus Bavaria P.O. Box 3308, 89450, 831-6122/(800) 731-6222 (GF) full brkfst
  Lakeside B&B Box 1756, Crystal Bay, 89402, 831-8281 (M) full brkfst, sauna, near great skiing

BARS
  Faces 270 Kingsbury Grade, 588-2333 (MW,D) 4pm-4am

Las Vegas (702)

INFO LINES & SERVICES
  Alcoholics Together 953 E. Sahara Ste. 233 (entrance on State St.), 737-0035, 12:15pm & 8pm, noon wknds, 9pm Tue
  Black Jack Bears P.O. Box 29307, 89126, 225-4513
  ▲ **Community Real Estate Referrals** (800) 346-5592, gay realtor at your service, no rentals
  Gay/Lesbian Community Ctr. 912 E. Sahara Ln., 733-9800, 10am-8pm, til 5pm wknds
  Latino Pyramid PO Box 545, 89125, 733-0570, men's social club

ACCOMMODATIONS
  Las Vegas Private B&B 384-1129 (M,SW,N) hot tub & sauna
  Oasis Guest House 662 Rolling Green Dr., 369-1396 (MW,SW)
  Secret Garden B&B 3670 Happy Ln., 451-3231 (MW,SW,N) full brkfst

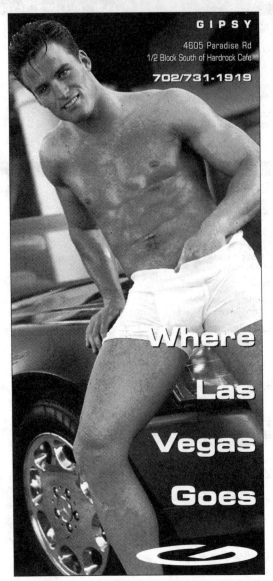

GIPSY

4605 Paradise Rd
1/2 Block South of Hardrock Cafe

702/731-1919

Where

Las

Vegas

Goes

BARS

Angles 4633 Paradise Rd., 791-0100/733-9677 (M,NH,V,WC) 24hrs

Backdoor 1415 E. Charleston, 385-2018 (MW,NH,D,WC) 24hrs

Backstreet 5012 S. Arville St. (Mosco Park), 876-1844 (MW,D,CW,WC) 24hrs

Badlands Saloon 953 E. Sahara Ste. 22-B, 792-9262 (M,NH,D,CW,WC) 24hrs

Buffalo 4640 Paradise Rd., 733-8355 (★M,L,V,WC) 24hrs

Choices 1729 E. Charleston, 382-4791 (M,NH,S,WC) 24hrs

Flex 4371 W. Charleston, 385-3539 (M,D)

▲ **Gipsy** 4605 Paradise Rd., 731-1919/796-8793 (★M,D,S)

Goodtimes 1775 E. Tropicana (Liberace Plaza), 736-9494 (M,D,E,WC) 24hrs

The Las Vegas Eagle 3430 E. Tropicana, 458-8662 (M,L) 24hrs, DJ Wed & Fri

Snick's Place 1402 S. 4th St., 385-9298 (M,NH,WC) 24hrs

RESTAURANTS & CAFES

Coyote Cafe (at MGM Grand), 891-7349 (WC) the original Santa Fe chef, 8:30am-11pm

Cyber City Cafe Flamingo & Maryland, 732-2001, Internet cafe

Garlic Café 3650 S. Decatur Blvd., 221-0266, dinner, lunch Mon-Fri

New York, New York 6370 Windy St., 896-1993 (MW,E,WC) 5pm-midnight

GYMS & HEALTH CLUBS

Great Shape 6020 W. Flamingo Rd. #8, 221-0275

BOOKSTORES & RETAIL SHOPS

Alternatives 3507 S. Maryland Pkwy. #2, 696-1885, books, t-shirts & videos, 11am-9pm

Cat O'Nine Tails Boutique 1717 S.Decatur Blvd. @ Fantastic Indoor Swap Meet, 258-9754, contemporary evening wear, TV/TS friendly, 10am-6pm Fri-Sun

Get Booked 4643 S.Paradise, 737-7780, 10am-midnight, til 2am Fri-Sat, lesbigay bookstore

Lock, Stock & Leather 4640 Paradise Rd. #10, 796-9801, bearwear & leather, 3pm-10pm, noon-2am Fri-Sat, from 4pm Sun

TRAVEL & TOUR OPERATORS

Cruise One 5030 Paradise Dr. Ste. B-101, 256-8082/(800) 200-3012 (IGTA)

Dazey Travel Service 4511 W. Sahara Ave., 876-8470

Gala Tours at A to Z Bargain Travel 3133 S. Industrial Rd., 369-8671 (IGTA)

Good Times Travel 624 N. Rainbow, 878-8900/(800) 638-1066 (IGTA)

Players Express Vacations 105 E. Reno Ave. Ste 6, 736-7011/(800) 237-7555

SPIRITUAL GROUPS

Christ Church Episcopal 2000 Maryland Pkwy., 735-7655, 8am,10am & 6pm Sun, 10am & 6pm Wed

Dignity/ Las Vegas 912 E. Sahara Ave (G&L Comm.Ctr.), 369-8127x344, 6pm Sat

God's Word Fellowship 1121 Almond Tree Ln. (Comm. Counseling Ctr.), 222-7814 (pager), Bible study, TS/TV welcome, 7pm Th

MCC of Las Vegas 2727 Civic Center Dr., 369-4380, 11:30am Sun

Unitarian Universalist Congregation 2200 W. Mesquite (Masonic Temple), 894-8911, 11am Sun

Valley Outreach Synagogue 436-4900 (GF) 8pm 1st Fri, call for location & events

PUBLICATIONS

Las Vegas Bugle PO Box 14580, 89132, 369-6260, monthly

Night Beat 3135 S. Industrial Rd. #204, 734-7223, lesbigay classified ads

EROTICA

Industrial Road Adult Books 3463 Industrial Rd., 734-7667, 24hrs

Price Video 4640 Paradise Rd. Ste.11, 734-1342

Pure Pleasure Book & Video 3177 S. Highland, Las Vegas, 369-8044, 24hrs

Tattoos R Us 320 E. Charleston, Ste. E, 387-6969, piercing & tattoo studio

Video West 5785 W. Tropicana, 248-7055, gay owned & run

CRUISY AREAS

Boulder Beach Lake Mead (AYOR)

Fantasy Park Washington btwn. Bruce & Las Vegas (AYOR)

Sunset Park (AYOR)

Reno   (702)

INFO LINES & SERVICES

▲ **Community Real Estate Referrals** (800) 346-5592, gay realtor at your service, no rentals

Knights of Malta, Western Chapter PO Box 7726, 89510, men's leather/levi club

Silver Dollar Court PO Box 6581, 89513, social group

BARS

1099 Club 1099 S. Virginia, 329-1099 (★MW,NH,S,V,WC) 24hrs wknds

Five Star Saloon 132 West St., 329-2878 (M,D,WC) 24hrs

The Quest 210 Commercial Row, 333-2808 (M,D,S) noon-5am, 24hrs Fri-Sat

Shouts 145 Hillcrest St., 829-7667 (GF,NH,WC) 10am-2am

Visions 340 Kietzke Ln., 786-5455 (★M,D,E,YC) noon-4am, 24hrs Fri-Sun, Glitter Palace gift shop wknds

BOOKSTORES & RETAIL SHOPS

Grapevine Books 1450 S. Wells Ave., 786-4869 (WC) lesbigay, 10am-6pm, til 8pm Fri-Sat, til 4pm Sun

TRAVEL & TOUR OPERATORS

Deluxe Travel 102 California Ave., 686-700 (IGTA)

SPIRITUAL GROUPS

MCC of the Sierras 3405 Gulling Rd. (Temple Sinai), 829-8602, 5pm Sun

MEN'S CLUBS

Steve's 1030 W. 2nd St., 323-8770 (MO,PC) 24hrs, spa

EROTICA

The Chocolate Walrus Grove & Wrondell, 825-2267 (★) 10:30am-6:30pm Fri, til 5pm Sat, clsd Sun

Fantasy Faire 1298 S. Virginia, 323-6969, 11am-7pm, til 8pm Fri-Sat, noon-4pm Sun, fetish, leather

Suzie's 195 Keitzke, 786-8557, 24 hrs

CRUISY AREAS

Idlewild Park (AYOR)

Sparks   (702)

INFO LINES & SERVICES

Silver State Leather Association PO Box 50762, 89435, 331-7059

Stateline (702)

ACCOMMODATIONS

BeachSide Inn & Suites 930 Park Ave., South Lake Tahoe CA, (916) 544-2400/(800) 884-4920 (GF) walk to casinos & private beach access, outdoor spa & sauna

Secret Honeymooners Inn 924 Park Ave., South Lake Tahoe CA, (916) 544-6767/(800) 441-6610 (GF) quiet, romanitc adult-only inn, spas

Tradewinds Motel 944 Friday (at Cedar), South Lake Tahoe CA, (916) 544-6459/(800) 628-1829 (GF,SW) suite w/spa & firelpace available

Virginia City

CRUISY AREAS

Union St. behind Pipers Opera House (AYOR) nights

NEW HAMPSHIRE

Bath Village (603)

ACCOMMODATIONS

Evergreen B&B Rte. 302, 747-3947 (MO) full brkfst, hot tub, camping avail., 1822 Federal home

Bridgewater (603)

ACCOMMODATIONS

The Inn on Newfound Lake 1030 Mayhew Trpk. Rte. 3-A, 744-9111/(800) 745-7990 (GF,F,SW) American restaurant, full bar

Centre Harbor (603)

ACCOMMODATIONS

Red Hill Inn RFD #1, Box 99M, 279-7001/(800) 573-3445 (GF,WC,IGTA) restored country inn & restaurant

Chocorua (603)

ACCOMMODATIONS

Mount Chocorua View House Rt. 16, 323-8350 (GF) 10 mi. S. of N. Conway

CRUISY AREAS

Scenic Rest Area on left of Rte 16 N (AYOR)

Colebrook (603)

ACCOMMODATIONS

Columbia Hills B&B P.O. Box 258, 03576, 237-5550 (MO) full brkfst, hot tub

Concord (603)

INFO LINES & SERVICES

Gay Info Line 224-1686, 6pm-8pm, clsd Tue & wknds, 24hr recorded info

TRAVEL & TOUR OPERATORS

Travel & Tourism Office PO Box 1856, 03302-1856, 271-2666

SPIRITUAL GROUPS

Spirit of the Mountain 177 N. Main (1st Congregational Church), 225-5491, 5pm 2nd & 4th Sun

PUBLICATIONS
Breathing Space PO Box 816, 03302

Conway

CRUISY AREAS
Dugway Scenic Rest Stop Still Rd. (AYOR)

Dover (603)

ACCOMMODATIONS
Payne's Hill B&B 141 Henry Law Ave., 742-4139 (W)

Durham (603)

INFO LINES & SERVICES
The UNH Alliance UNH, M.U.B., 03824, 862-4522, 7:30pm Mon

Franconia (603)

ACCOMMODATIONS
Blanche's B & B 351 Easton Valley Rd., 823-7061 (GF) full brkfst

Bungay Jar B&B PO Box 15, Easton Valley Rd., 823-7775 (GF,WC) balconies, saunas

Foxglove, A Country Inn Rte. 117 at Lovers Ln., Sugar Hill, 823-8840 (GF,F) full brkfst

The Horse & Hound Inn 205 Wells Rd., 823-5501 (GF) restaurant open for dinner except Tue, clsd April & Nov

Raynor's Motor Lodge Main St. (Rtes. 142 & 18), 823-9586 (GF,SW)

Glen (603)

ACCOMMODATIONS
Will's Inn Rte 302, 383-6757 (GF,SW)

Hampton

CRUISY AREAS
Hampton Beach (AYOR) summers

Jackson (603)

ACCOMMODATIONS
Wildcat Inn & Tavern Rte. 16A, 383-4245/383-6456 (GF) restaurant 6pm-9pm, tavern 3pm-midnight wknds

Keene (603)

BOOKSTORES
Oasis 45 Central Square, 352-5355, 10am-9pm, 11am-6pm Sun

Manchester (603)

BARS
Club Merri-Mac 201 Merrimack, 623-9362 (★MW,D,PC) 2pm-1:30am
Front Runner/Manchester Civic Club 22 Fir St., 623-6477 (★MW,D,TG,E,PC) 3pm-1:30am
Sporters 361 Pine St., 668-9014 (M,NH,D) 5pm-1am, from 3pm Sun

CRUISY AREAS
Weston Observatory Park Reservoir Rd. (AYOR)

Nashua

CRUISY AREAS
Main St. around City Hall (AYOR)

North Conway

CRUISY AREAS
Schouler Park (AYOR)

Portsmouth (603)

INFO LINES & SERVICES
▲ **Community Real Estate Referrals** (800) 346-5592, gay realtor at your service, no rentals

TRAVEL & TOUR OPERATORS
Worldwise Travel Co. Inc. 477 State St., 430-9060/(800) 874-9473 (IGTA)

EROTICA
Peter's Place Rte 1 Bypass N, 436-9622

CRUISY AREAS
Hilton Park Dover Rte. Rd. (AYOR)
Pierce Island dock area (AYOR)

NEW JERSEY

Asbury Park/Ocean Grove (908)

INFO LINES & SERVICES
▲ **Community Real Estate Referrals** (800) 346-5592, gay realtor at your service, no rentals
Gay/Lesbian Community Center 515 Cookman Ave., 774-1809/775-4429, 2pm-7pm Sat & various evenings, call for events

BARS
Down the Street 230 Cookman Ave., Asbury Park, 988-2163 (★M,D,S,V,WC) 2pm-2am (seasonal), beach crowd, volleyball

RESTAURANTS & CAFES
Raspberry Cafe 16 Main Ave., 988-0833, breakfast & lunch
The Talking Bird 224 Cookman, 775-9708, lunch & dinner, til 4am Fri-Sat

CRUISY AREAS
Boardwalk nr. Convention Hall (AYOR)

Atlantic City (609)

INFO LINES & SERVICES
▲ **Community Real Estate Referrals** (800) 346-5592, gay realtor at your service, no rentals

ACCOMMODATIONS
▲ **Ocean House** 127 S. Ocean Ave., 345-8203 (MO,N) turn-of-the-century house, once a convent & now a guesthouse exclusively for gay men
The Rose Cottage 161 S. Westminster Ave., 345-8196 (MW)
▲ **Surfside Hotel & Resort** 18 S. Mt. Vernon Ave., 347-0808 (MW,F) sundeck, restaurant in summer

OCEAN HOUSE
127 South Ocean Avenue
Atlantic City, NJ 08401
609-345-8203

A 100+ year old Queen Ann home that has been accommodating men exclusively since 1964. Central, beach block, everything of interest within walking distance: casinos, bars, restaurants, beach and boardwalk. Parking on premises, large sun porch, T/VCR lounge, refrigerator. Clothing optional. Intimate atmosphere. Brochure on request.

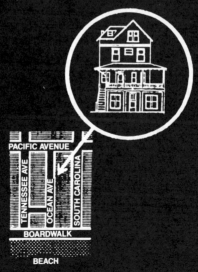

Bars

Brass Rail Bar & Grill 12 S. Mt. Vernon Ave., 348-0192 (★MW,NH,F,E,S) 24hrs

Reflections 181 S. South Carolina Ave., 348-1115 (MW,NH,D,V,WC) 24hrs

Rendezvous 137 S. New York Ave., 347-8539 (M,S,WC) 4pm-2am

▲ **Studio Six Video Dance Club** (upstairs at Brass Rail), 348-3310 (★MW,D,E,V) 10pm-6am

Travel & Tour Operators

New Jersey Division of Travel & Tourism (800) 537-7397

Schreve Lazar Travel (at Bally's Park Place Casino Hotel, Boardwalk & Park Place), 348-1189/(800) 322-8280 (IGTA)

Erotica

Atlantic City News 101 S. Martin Luther King Jr. Blvd., 344-9444, 24hrs

Cruisy Areas

Beach opposite Claridge's (AYOR)

Belmar

Cruisy Areas

Belmar Beach btwn. 2nd & 3rd (AYOR)

Berlin
(609)

Erotica

Red Baron Adult Books 310 Rte. 73 S., 767-1525, 24hrs

Boonton
(201)

Bars

Locomotion 202 Myrtle Ave., 263-4000 (MW,D,F) boys' night Th, opens 8pm Wed-Sat

Bricktown
(908)

Erotica Shops

Adult Book Store 2148 State Hwy. 88 E., 295-0166

Cherry Hill
(609)

Info Lines & Services

▲ **Community Real Estate Referrals** (800) 346-5592, gay realtor at your service, no rentals

Spiritual Groups

Unitarian Universalist Church 401 N. Kings Hwy., 667-3618, 10:15am Sun

Cruisy Areas

Cooper River Park behind Hyatt (AYOR)

Collingwood
(609)

Erotica

Adult Book Barn Rte. 130 & Richey Ave., 854-4566

Denville
(201)

Bookstores & Retail Shops

Perrin & Treggett, Booksellers 3130 Rte. 10 W., Denville Commons, 328-8811/(800) 770-8811, 10am-9pm, til 6pm Sat, noon-5pm Sun

EROTICA
Video Emporium 3049 Rte. 10, 361-9440

Egg Harbor City (609)

EROTICA
United Video Adult World 25 White Horse Park, 965-1110

Elizabeth

INFO LINES & SERVICES
▲ **Community Real Estate Referrals** (800) 346-5592, gay realtor at your service, no rentals

Florence (609)

EROTICA
Florence Book Store Rte. 103 S., 4 mi S. of Rte. 206, 499-9853

Hazlet (908)

TRAVEL & TOUR OPERATORS
Galaxy Travel 3048 Rte. 35 (K-Mart shopping ctr.), 219-9600/(800) 331-7245, IGTA

Highland Park (908)

BOOKSTORES & RETAIL SHOPS
All About Books 409 Raritan Ave., 247-8744, 9:30am-6pm, 11am-5pm Sun

Hoboken (201)

INFO LINES & SERVICES
▲ **Community Real Estate Referrals** (800) 346-5592, gay realtor at your service, no rentals

BARS
Excalibur 1000 Jefferson St., 795-1023 (★MW,D,E,S,WC) 9pm-3am, clsd Mon-Wed

RESTAURANTS & CAFES
Maxwell's 1039 Washington St., 656-9632 (M,D,E,WC) 5pm-2am, til 3am Fri-Sat, Italian

Howell (908)

EROTICA SHOPS
Adult Book Store 2043 US Hwy. 9, 363-9680

Jersey City

INFO LINES & SERVICES
▲ **Community Real Estate Referrals** (800) 346-5592, gay realtor at your service, no rentals

ACCOMMODATIONS
▲ **The Caritas B&B Network** (800) CARITAS (227-4827), see ad in center National section

CRUISY AREAS
Journal Square (AYOR)

Lambertville (609)

EROTICA
Joy's Books 103 Springbrook Ave., 397-2907

Long Branch

CRUISY AREAS
W. end of Boardwalk (AYOR)

Lyndhurst (201)

BARS
Aldo's 749 Marin Ave., 460-9824 (GF,D) 9pm-2am

Maplewood (201)

SPIRITUAL GROUPS
Dignity Metro New Jersey 550 Ridgewood Rd. (St. George's Episcopal Church), 857-4040, 8pm 1st & 3rd Tue

Montclair (201)

INFO LINES & SERVICES
Crossroads Real Estate Referral Network PO Box 1708, 07042, (800) 442-9735, non-profit lesbigay realtor referrals

BOOKSTORES & RETAIL SHOPS
Cohen's 635 Bloomfield Ave., 744-2399, 6am-8pm, til 2pm Sun, magazines & cafe
Dressing for Pleasure 590 Valley Rd., 746-5466, noon-6pm, til 8pm Th-Fri, from 10am Sat, clsd Sun-Mon, leather, latex, lingerie

Morris Plains (201)

TRAVEL & TOUR OPERATORS
Frankel Travel 60 E. Hanover Ave., 455-1111/(800) 445-6433 (IGTA)

Morristown (201)

INFO LINES & SERVICES
GAAMC Gay/Lesbian Youth in NJ Helpline 21 Normandy Hgts. Rd., 285-1595, 7:30-10:30pm, mtgs Sat 1:30pm-4:30pm (call for location)
Gay Activist in Morris County 285-1595, 7:30pm-10:30pm, meet 8:30pm Mon at 21 Normandy Hts. Rd.

New Brunswick (908)

INFO LINES & SERVICES
Latinos Unidos (at Pride Center), 846-2232
Lesbian/Gay Men of New Brunswick 109 Nichol Ave. (Quaker Meeting House), 247-0515, 8pm 2nd & 4th Tue
Pride Center of New Jersey 211 Livingston Ave., 846-2232, 7pm-10pm, 11am-1pm Tue, clsd wknds
Rutgers Univ. Lesbian/Gay/Bisexual Peer-Counseling 932-7886, 7pm-11pm Tue & Fri, call for details

RESTAURANTS & CAFES
The Frog and the Peach 29 Dennis St., 846-3216 (WC) 11:30am-11pm, til 1am Th-Sat
J. August Cafe 100 Jersey Ave., 545-4646 (MW) 9am-3pm Tue-Fri, 6pm-11pm Fri-Sat

Stage Left 5 Livingston Ave., 828-4444 (★MW,WC) 5:30pm-2am, from 4:30pm Sun

SPIRITUAL GROUPS

Dignity/New Brunswick 109 Nichol Ave. (Friends Mtg. House), 254-7942, 7:30pm Fri

MCC Christ the Liberator 40 Davidson Rd. (St. Michael's Chapel), Piscataway, 846-8227, 6:30pm Sun

CRUISY AREAS

Johnson Park parking lot & trails along river (AYOR) Highlands Park

Newark (201)

BARS

First Choice 533 Ferry St., 465-1944 (MW,D,MRC-AF) 8pm-2am, til 3am Th-Sat

Murphy's Tavern 59 Edison Pl., 622-9176 (MW,D,MRC-AF,WC) 11:30am-2am, lunch daily

SPIRITUAL GROUPS

Oasis 621-8151, Tue pm, call for info, lesbigay ministry of the Episcopal Church

CRUISY AREAS

Ferry St. Iron bound area (AYOR)

Oak Ridge (201)

BARS

Yacht Club 5190 Berkshire Valley Rd. (5 mi. off of Rte. 15), 697-9780 (★MW,D,V,WC) 7pm-3am, from 2pm Sun, Sun BBQ

Orange (908)

INFO LINES & SERVICES

▲ **Community Real Estate Referrals** (800) 346-5592, gay realtor at your service, no rentals

Intergroup AA 668-1882, 24hrs info & referrals

CRUISY AREAS

Big Rock at South Mtn. Reservation (AYOR)

Perth Amboy (908)

BARS

The Other Half Convery Blvd. (Rte. 35) & Kennedy, 826-8877 (★ M,D) 9pm-2am, til 3am Fri-Sat

Plainfield (908)

INFO LINES & SERVICES

▲ **Community Real Estate Referrals** (800) 346-5592, gay realtor at your service, no rentals

ACCOMMODATIONS

▲ **Caritas B&B Network** (800) CARITAS (227-4827)

Pillars 922 Central Ave., 753-0922/(800) 372-7378 (GF) Georgian/Victorian mansion

Princeton (609)

INFO LINES & SERVICES
▲ **Community Real Estate Referrals** (800) 346-5592, gay realtor at your service, no rentals

TRAVEL & TOUR OPERATORS
Edwards Travel Service 8 S. Tulane St., 924-4443/(800) 669-9692

Rahway

CRUISY AREAS
Rahway River Park (AYOR)

Red Bank (908)

INFO LINES & SERVICES
Monmouth Ocean Transgender Group P.O. Box 8243, 07701, 219-9094, mtgs/support

BOOKSTORES & RETAIL SHOPS
Earth Spirit 16 W. Front St., 842-3855, 10am-6pm, til 8pm Fri, noon-5pm Sun

River Edge (201)

BARS
Feathers 77 Kinder Kamack Rd., 342-6410 (★ M,D,K,S,V,YC,WC) 9pm-2am, til 3am Sat

Rocky Hill (609)

TRAVEL & TOUR OPERATORS
Travel Registry, Inc. 127 Washington St., 921-6900/(800) 346-6901 (IGTA)

Roselle (908)

ACCOMMODATIONS
Graywood Manor 139 W. 4th Ave., 245-5323 (MO,L,SW)

MEN'S CLUBS
Pump It Up c/o Mirza Inc. 139 W. 4th Ave., 245-5323, call for events; also monthly publication

Rosemont (609)

RESTAURANTS
The Cafe 88 Kingwood - Stockton Rd., 397-4097 (BYOB) 8am-3pm, dinner from 5pm Wed-Sat, clsd Mon

Sandy Hook

CRUISY AREAS
Nude Beach nr. Gunnison Park - South end (AYOR)

Sayreville (908)

BARS
Colosseum Rte. 9 & Rte. 35 N., 316-0670 (MW,D,S) 9pm-3am, from 4pm Sun

Seaside Heights

CRUISY AREAS
Franklin Ave. & Boardwalk (AYOR) summers only

Somerset (908)

BARS
▲ **The Den** 700 Hamilton St., 545-7329 (★ MW,D,MRC,S,V,18+,WC) 8pm-2am, from 7pm Sat, from 5pm Sun

Toms River

INFO LINES & SERVICES
▲ **Community Real Estate Referrals** (800) 346-5592, gay realtor at your service, no rentals

Trenton (609)

BARS
Buddies Pub 677 S. Broad St., 989-8566 (MW,D) 5pm-2am, from 6pm Sat-Sun
Center House Pub 499 Center St., 599-9558 (MW,NH) 4pm-2am, from 7pm wknds, patio

CRUISY AREAS
Clinton & State St. (AYOR)

Union City (201)

BARS
Nite Lite 509 22nd St., 863-9515 (MW,D,S) 8pm-3am Wed-Sun

West Paterson

CRUISY AREAS
Homo Beach river btwn. Union Blvd. & Little Falls (AYOR)

Woodbury (609)

INFO LINES & SERVICES
Rainbow Place 1103 N. Broad, 848-2455, info line & community center

NEW MEXICO

Albuquerque (505)

INFO LINES & SERVICES
AA Gay/Lesbian 266-1900 (WC)
Alternative Erotic Lifestyles 345-6484, pansexual S/M group
Common Bond Community Center 4013 Silver St. SE, 266-8041, 6pm-9pm
▲ **Community Real Estate Referrals** (800) 346-5592, gay realtor at your service, no rentals
Naked and Not Ashamed c/o Don Shrader 1810 Silver SE #B, 87106, 843-6595, 7pm Th, nudist conversation group
New Mexico Outdoors PO Box 26836, 87125, 822-1093, active lesbigay outdoors group
Sand'ía Leatherman 8900 Central SE, 275-1616, 7pm Sun at Cuffs (The Ranch)

ACCOMMODATIONS

Dave's B&B P.O. Box 27214, 87125, 247-8312 (M,WC) Southwestern home located close to river

Hacienda Antigua Retreat 6708 Tierra Dr. NW, 345-5399/(800) 484-2385x9954 (GF,SW) full brkfst

Hateful Missy & Granny Butch's Boudoir 29 Jara Millo Loop, Vequita, 243-7063/(800) 397-2482 (MW)

Mountain View PO Box 30123, 87190, 296-7277 (W,WC)

Nuevo Dia 11110 San Rafael Ave. NE, 856-7910, hot tub

Rio Grande House 3100 Rio Grande Blvd NW, 345-0120 (GF) adobe house nr. Old Town

Tara Cotta 3118 Rio Grande Blvd. NW, 344-9443 (GF,N) patio

W.E. Mauger Estate 701 Roma Ave. NW, 242-8755 (GF) full brkfst, intimate Queen Anne house

BARS

▲ **Albuquerque Mining Co. (AMC)** 7209 Central Ave NE, 255-4022 (M,D,YC,WC) noon-2am, til midnight Sun

Albuquerque Social Club 4021 Central Ave. NE (rear alley), 255-0887 (★MW,D,CW,PC) noon-2am, til midnight Sun

Club 414 414 Old Santa Fe Tr., 986-9971 (M) 4pm-2am

▲ **Foxes Lounge** 8521 Central Ave. NE, 255-3060 (M,D,S,WC) 10am-2am, noon-midnight Sun

Kingsize at the Zone 2nd & Central, 343-5196 (GF,D,A) 9pm Tue

Legends West 6132 4th St. NW, 343-9793 (MW,D) 4pm-2am, from 6pm Sat, noon-midnight Sun, clsd Mon

The Pulse 4100 Central SE, 255-3334 (M,D) 4pm-2am, til midnight Sun

▲ **The Ranch** 8900 Central SE, 275-1616 (M,D,CW,WC) 11am-2am, til midnight Sun, Cuffs leather bar inside

RESTAURANTS & CAFES

Cafe Intermezzo 3513 Central NE, 265-2556, 10am-11pm, til midnight Fri-Sat

Chef du Jour 119 San Pasquale SW, 247-8998 (WC) 11am-2pm, clsd wknds

Chianti's 5210 San Mateo NE, 881-1967 (BW) 11am-9pm, from noon wknds, Italian

Double Rainbow 3416 Central SE, 255-6633 (WC) 6:30am-midnight

BOOKSTORES & RETAIL SHOPS

In Crowd 3106 Central SE, 268-3750, 10am-6pm, noon-4pm Sun, lesbigay art

Newsland Books 2112 Central Ave SE, 242-0694, 8am-9pm

Page One 11018 Montgomery NE, 294-2026/(800) 521-4122, 7am-11:30pm

Sisters and Brothers Bookstore 4011 Silver Ave. SE, 266-7317, 9:30am-8pm, lesbigay

TRAVEL & TOUR OPERATORS

All World Travel 1930 Juan Tabo NE Ste. D, 294-5031/(800) 725-0695

The Travel Scene 2424 Juan Tabo Blvd. NE, 292-4343/(800) 658-5779

SPIRITUAL GROUPS

Dignity New Mexico 1815 Los Lomas, 880-9031, 7pm 1st Sun

Emmanuel MCC 341 Dallas NE, 268-0599, 10am Sun

First Unitarian Church 3701 Carlisle NE, 884-1801, 9:30am & 11am Sun

MCC 2404 San Mateo Pl. NE, 881-9088, 10am Sun

PUBLICATIONS
Out! Magazine PO Box 27237, 87125, 243-2540, monthly
▲ **Rainbow** PO Box 4326, 87196-4326, 255-1634

EROTICA
The Leather Shoppe 4217 Central Ave. NE, 266-6690
Mr. Peepers 4300 Edith Blvd. NE, 343-8063, 24hrs
Pussycat III 4012 Cental Ave. NE, 268-1631

CRUISY AREAS
Silver Ave W. of Washington St. (AYOR)

Clovis (505)

INFO LINES & SERVICES
Clovis-Portales Common Bond PO Box 663, 88101, 356-2656, lesbigay social/support line

CRUISY AREAS
Main St. btwn. 2nd & 7th (AYOR)

Galisteo (505)

ACCOMMODATIONS
Galisteo Inn HC75 Box 4, 466-4000 (GF,F,SW,WC) 23 mi. SE of Santa Fe

Hobbs (505)

EROTICA
Stateline Adult Book Store 6100 W. Carlsbad Hwy., 393-3616

Las Cruces (505)

INFO LINES & SERVICES
AA Gay/Lesbian 527-1803
Southwest Gay Men's Association P.O. Box 168, Mesilla, 88046, 522-3675

BOOKSTORES & RETAIL SHOPS
Spirit Winds Gifts 2260 Locust St., 521-0222, 7:30am-8pm, til 2pm Sun

TRAVEL & TOUR OPERATORS
Uniglobe Above & Beyond Travel 2225 E. Lohman Ste. A, 527-0200/(800) 578-5888 (IGTA)

SPIRITUAL GROUPS
Holy Family Parish 1701 E. Missouri (Church), 522-7119, 5:30pm Sat, inclusive Evangelical Anglican Church
Koinonia 521-1490, 7:30pm Th, lesbigay group for people of all religious traditions

Pecos (505)

ACCOMMODATIONS
Wilderness Inn PO Box 1177, 87552, 757-6694 (GF,WC)

Ruidoso (505)

ACCOMMODATIONS
Sierra Mesa Lodge P.O. Box 463, Alto, 88312, 336-4515 (GF)

Santa Fe

(505)

Info Lines & Services

AA Gay/Lesbian 1915 Rosina St. (Friendship Circle), 982-8932

▲ **Community Real Estate Referrals** (800) 346-5592, gay realtor at your service, no rentals

Pantheos PO Box 9543, 87504, personal network for gay & bi pagan men

Accommodations

Casa Torreon 1613 Calle Torreon, 982-6815 (GF) adobe guesthouse w/ kitchen

Four Kachinas Inn 512 Webber St., 982-2550/(800) 397-2564 (GF,WC) clsd Jan

Hummingbird Ranch Rte. 10, Box 111, 87501, 471-2921 (GF)

▲ **Inn of the Turquoise Bear** 342 E. Buena Vista St., 983-0798/(800) 396-4104 (MW) hot tub

Marriott Residence Inn 1698 Galisteo St., 988-7300/(800) 331-3131 (GF,SW,WC) suites

Open Sky B&B Rte.2, Box 918, 471-3475/(800) 244-3475 (GF,WC)

Triangle Inn PO Box 3235, 87501-0235, 455-3375 (MW,WC) 9 casitas

Restaurants & Cafes

Cafe Pasqual's 121 Don Gaspar, 983-9340 (WC) 7am-10:30pm

Dave's Not Here 1115 Hickock St., Santa Fe, 983-7060, 11am-10pm, clsd Sun, New Mexican

Paul's 72 Marcy St., 982-8738 (BW,WC) dinner

SantaCafe 231 Washington Ave., 984-1788 (WC) lunch & dinner, Southwestern/Asian

Tecolote Cafe 1203 Cerrillos Rd., 988-1362 (★) 7am-2pm, clsd Mon, great breakfasts

Vanessie of Santa Fe 434 W. San Francisco, 982-9966 (★) 5:30pm-10:30pm (bar til 1am), steak house, piano bar

BOOKSTORES & RETAIL SHOPS
The Ark 133 Romero St., 988-3709, 10am-8pm, til 5pm wknds

Downtown Subscription 376 Garcia St., 983-3085, 7:30am-7pm, til 9pm Fri-Sat, newsstand & coffee shop

Galisteo News 201 Galisteo St., 984-1316 (F) 7am-7pm, til 9pm Fri-Sat, gay periodicals & coffee shop

TRAVEL & TOUR OPERATORS
Earth Walks 988-4157, guided tour of American Southwest & Mexico

Taos (505)

ACCOMMODATIONS
The Ruby Slipper PO Box 2069, 87571, 758-0613 (MW) full brkfst

RESTAURANTS & CAFES
Wild & Natural Cafe 812-B Paseo del Pueblo Norte, 751-0480 (WC) 7am-9pm, clsd Sun, vegetarian

Thoreau (505)

ACCOMMODATIONS
White Eagle Retreat HC62 Box 5114, 862-7769 (GF,F,WC) full brkfst

NEW YORK

Adirondack Mtns. (518)

INFO LINES & SERVICES
Adirondack GABLE PO Box 990, Saranac Lake, 12983, 359-7358, local contact for area

ACCOMMODATIONS
The Doctor's Inn Trudeau Rd., RR1, Box 375, Saranac Lake, 12983, 891-3464/(800) 552-2627 (GF,IGTA)

Stony Water B&B RR1 Box 69, Elizabethtown, 12932, 873-9125/(800) 995-7295 (GF,SW,WC) full brkfst

Albany (518)

INFO LINES & SERVICES
▲ **Community Real Estate Referrals** (800) 346-5592, gay realtor at your service, no rentals

Gay AA (at Community Center), 7:30pm Sun

Homo Radio WRPI 91.5 FM, 276-6248, noon-2:30pm Sun

Lesbian/Gay Community Center 332 Hudson Ave., 462-6138, 7pm-10pm, til 11pm Fri-Sat, from 1pm Sun, 24hr directory

Lesbian/Gay/Bisexual Young People's Meeting (at the Community Center), 7:30pm Th

TGIC (Transgenderists Independence Club) PO Box 13604, 12212-3604, 436-4513, volunteers 8-10pm Th, social group meets weekly

Two Rivers Outdoor Club 449-0758

BARS
Cafe Hollywood 275 Lark St., 472-9043 (GF,NH,V) 3pm-3am

JD's Playhouse 519 Central Ave., 446-1407 (MW,NH,D) 4pm-4am, clsd Mon

Longhorns 90 Central Ave., 462-4862 (M.NH) 4pm-4am

Oh Bar 304 Lark St., 463-9004 (M,NH,MRC,V) 2pm-2am

Power Company 238 Washington Ave., 465-2556 (MW,D,WC) 2pm-2am, til 4am wknds

Waterworks Pub 76 Central Ave., 465-9079 (M,D,E) 4pm-4am, garden bar

RESTAURANTS & CAFES
Cafe Lulu 288 Lark St., 436-5660 (BW) 11am-midnight, til 1am Fri-Sat

Debbie's Kitchen 290 Lark St., 463-3829, 10am-9pm, 11am-6pm Sat, clsd Sun

Donnie's Cafe 75 75 Central Ave., 436-0378, 7am-3pm, from 3am wknds

El Loco Mexican Cafe 465 Madison Ave., 436-1855, clsd Mon

Mother Earth 217 Western Ave., 434-0944 (BYOB,WC) 11am-11pm, Gay/Bi/Lesbian Club Night 4th Mon, vegetarian

Yono's 289 Hamilton St., 436-7747, 4:30-10pm, clsd Sun, Indonesian/cont'l

BOOKSTORES & RETAIL SHOPS
Romeo's 299 Lark St., 434-4014, 11am-9pm, noon-5pm Sun

Video Central 37 Central Ave., 463-4153, 10am-10pm, lesbigay books & magazines

TRAVEL & TOUR OPERATORS
Atlas Travel Center Inc. 1545 Central Ave., 464-0271 (IGTA)

FreedomTravel 212 Clifton Country Mall, 371-3720

Spiritual Groups
Integrity 498 Clinton Ave. at Robbins St. (Grace & Holy Innocents Church), 465-1112, 6pm Sun

MCC of the Hudson Valley 275 State St. (Emmanuel Baptist Church), 785-7941 (WC) 1pm Sun

Publications
Community PO Box 131, 12201, 462-6138

Erotica
Savage Leather & Gifts 88 Central Ave., 434-2324, 11am-9pm, til midnight Fri-Sat, clsd Sun-Mon

Cruisy Areas
Empire State Plaza (AYOR)

Lark, State & Willet Sts. nr. Washington Park (AYOR)

Angelica (716)

Accommodations
Jones Pond Campground 9835 Old State Rd., 567-8100 (MO,SW,N) May-Oct 15

Annandale On Hudson (914)

Info Lines & Services
Bard Bisexual/Lesbian/Gay Alliance Bard College, 12504, 758-6822 (general switchboard), active during school year

Binghamton (607)

Info Lines & Services
AA Gay/Lesbian 183 Riverside Dr. (Unitarian Church), 722-5983, 7pm Wed & Sat

Gay/Lesbian/Bi Resource Line 729-1921, 7:30pm-9:30pm Wed

Lesbian/Gay/Bisexual Union 777-2202, mtgs 8pm Tue

Accommodations
Hillside Campgrounds PO Box 726, 13902, (717) 756-2007 (★MO,D,SW,N) campground nr. Scranton PA, disco Fri-Sat, cabins & trailers

Serenity Farms c/o Mirza Inc. 139 W. 4th Ave., Roselle NJ, 07203, (607) 656-4659 (MO,L) B&B, camping

Bars
Risky Business 201 State St., 723-1507 (★M,D,V,WC) 9pm-1am, from 5pm Th-Fri, til 3am Fri-Sat

Squiggy's 34 Chenango St., 722-2299 (MW,D) 5pm-1am, til 3am Fri-Sat, from 8pm Sun

Restaurants & Cafes
Kara's Kafe 585 Main St., Johnson City, 797-8567 (E,WC) clsd Sun, full bar

Lost Dog Cafe 60 Main St., 771-6063 (★MW,E) 11am-11pm, til 4am Fri-Sat

Spiritual Groups
Affirmation (United Methodist) 83 Main St., 775-3986, 7pm Sun

Publications
Amethyst PO Box 728 Westview Stn., 13905-0728, 723-5790, monthly

Men's Clubs
FFA-Binghamton c/o Mirza Inc. 139 W. 4th Ave., Roselle NJ, 07203, 656-4659/(908) 245-5323, private fisting parties monthly

Pump It Up c/o Mirza Inc. 139 W. 4th Ave., Roselle NJ, 07203, 656-4659/(908) 245-5323, demos; also monthly publication

EROTICA
Allie's Bookstore 140 Washington, 724-8659

North Street Bookshop 17 Washington Ave. Endicott, 785-1588

CRUISY AREAS
Oneida Campground (AYOR)

Buffalo (716)

INFO LINES & SERVICES
▲ **Community Real Estate Referrals** (800) 346-5592, gay realtor at your service, no rentals

Gay/Lesbian Community Network 239 Lexington Ave., 883-4750, 7-10pm Fri

Gay/Lesbian Youth Services 190 Franklin St., 14202, 855-0221, 6:30-9pm Mon-Tue, Th-Fri

Lesbian/Gay/Bisexual Alliance 362 Student Union SUNY-Buffalo, Amherst, 14260, 645-3063

BARS
Buddies 31 Johnson Park, 855-1313 (MW,D,E,WC) 1pm-4am

Cathode Ray 26 Allen St., 884-3615 (M,NH,V,WC) 1pm-4am

Club Marcella 150 Theatre Pl., 847-6850 (MW,D,S,WC) 10pm-4am, from 4pm Fri, clsd Mon

Lavender Door 32 Tonawanda St., 874-1220 (W,NH,WC) 6pm-4am, from 4pm Fri, clsd Mon

Metroplex 729 Main St., 856-5630 (MW,D,A,18+) 10pm-4am, clsd Mon

Mickey's 44 Allen St., 886-9367 (GF,NH) 10am-4am

Stagedoor 20 Allen St., 886-9323 (M,NH,E,K,OC) 5pm-4am, piano bar & patio

Tiffany's 490 Pearl St., 854-4840 (MW,D,F,E) 11am-2am, til 6am Fri-Sat, patio

Underground 274 Delaware Ave., 855-1040 (M,D) 4pm-4am, from noon wknds

BOOKSTORES & RETAIL SHOPS
Talking Leaves 3158 Main St., 837-8554, 10am-6pm, til 8pm Wed-Th, clsd Sun

Village Green Bookstore 765-A Elmwood Ave., 884-1200 (WC) 9am-11pm, til midnight Fri-Sat

TRAVEL & TOUR OPERATORS
Destinations Unlimited 130 Theater Pl., 855-1955/(800) 528-8877 (IGTA)

Earth Travelers, Inc. 683 Dick Rd., 685-2900/(800) 321-2901 (IGTA)

SPIRITUAL GROUPS
Dignity PO Box 75, 14205, 833-8995

Integrity 16 Linwood Ave. (Church of the Ascension), 884-6362

PUBLICATIONS
Volumé PO Box 106 Westside Stn., 14213, 885-4580, monthly, covers Buffalo, Rochester, & Southern Ontario, Canada

MEN'S CLUBS
▲ **Fort Erie Steambath** (see listing in Ft. Erie, OT)

New Morgan Sauna 655 Main St., 852-2153 (MO,PC) 24hrs

EROTICA
Village Books & News 3102 Delaware Ave., Kenmore, 877-5027, 24hrs

ISLAND PROPERTIES

REAL ESTATE & MANAGEMENT CORP.
LICENSED REAL ESTATE BROKER

RENTALS
WEEKLY • MONTHLY • SEASONAL

SALES
MORTGAGES
APPRAISALS
PROPERTY MGMT.

P.O. Box 5272
37 Fire Island Blvd.
Fire Island Pines, NY 11782

(516) 597-6900

*The Largest and Most Successful
Gay Owned and Gay Operated
Agency in the Pines*

Canaseraga (607)

ACCOMMODATIONS
Fairwise Llama Farm 1320 Rte.70, 545-6247 (MW) full brkfst, located btw. Letchworth & Stony Brook Parks

Catskill Mtns.

INFO LINES & SERVICES
▲ **Community Real Estate Referrals** (800) 346-5592, gay realtor at your service, no rentals

ACCOMMODATIONS
Bradstan Country Hotel P.O. Box 312, White Lake, 12786, (914) 583-4114 (GF) also piano bar & cabaret, 9pm-1am Fri-Sun

Palenville House B&B P.O. 465, Palenville, 12463, (518) 678-5649 (GF) full brkfst

Point Lookout Mountain Inn Rte. 23 Box 33, East Windham, 12439, (518) 734-3381 (GF,F) close to Ski Windham & Hunter Mountain

River Run B&B Main St., Box D-4, Fleischmanns, 12430, (914) 254-4884 (GF,IGTA) full brkfst, Queen Anne Victorian

Stonewall Acres Box 556, Rock Hill, 12775, (914) 791-9474/(800) 336-4208 (GF,WS) full brkfst, hot tub, guesthouse & 2 cottages

RESTAURANTS & CAFES
Catskill Rose Rte. 212, Mt. Tremper, (914) 688-7100, from 5pm Wed-Sun, full bar, patio

Cooperstown (607)

ACCOMMODATIONS
Toad Hall B&B RD1 Box 120, Fly Creek, 13337, 547-5774 (GF)

Tryon Inn 124 Main St., Cherry Valley, 264-3790 (GF,F) French/American

Cuba (716)

ACCOMMODATIONS
Rocking Duck Inn 28 Genesee Pkwy., 968-3335 (GF) full breakfast, also Aunt Minnie's Tavern

Elmira (607)

ACCOMMODATIONS
Rufus Tanner House B&B 60 Sagetown Rd., Pine City, 732-0213 (GF) full brkfst, hot tub

BARS
Bodyshop 425-27 Railroad Ave., 733-6609 (MW,D,MRC,S) 4pm-1:30am, from 2pm Fri-Sat, patio

The David 511 Railroad Ave., 733-2592 (✱MW,D,YC) 4pm-1am, from 7pm wknds

EROTICA
Deluxe Books 123 Lake St., 734-9656

Fire Island (see also **Long Island**) (516)

INFO LINES & SERVICES
AA Gay/Lesbian (at the Fire House), Cherry Grove, 654-1150

▲ **Community Real Estate Referrals** (800) 346-5592, gay realtor at your service, no rentals

Accommodations

Belvedere Hotel Box 26, Cherry Grove, 11782, 597-6448 (MO,SW,WC)

Boatel Pines/Dunes Yacht Club, Harbor Walk, 11782, 597-6500 (MW,SW)

Carousel Guest House Holly Walk, Cherry Grove, 597-6612 (M)

Cherry Grove Beach Hotel Main & Ocean, Cherry Grove, 597-6600 (M,SW,N,WC)
4 bars on premises

Dune Point PO Box 78, Cherry Grove, 11782, 597-6261 (★MW,WC)

Holly House Box 96, Cherry Grove, 597-6911 (MW) seasonal

▲ **Island Properties** 37 Fire Island Blvd., 11782, 597-6900, weekly, monthly, & seasonal rentals; also properties for sale

Pines Place P.O. Box 5309, Fire Island Pines, 11782, 597-6162 (★M) several locations available

Sea Crest Lewis Walk, Cherry Grove, 597-6849 (MW)

Bars

Cherry's Cherry Grove, 597-6820 (★M,E) noon-4am (seasonal)

Ice Palace (at Cherry Grove Beach Hotel), 597-6600 (MW,D,S,YC,WC) hours vary

The Island Club Fire Island Blvd. (above Pines Pizza), 597-6001 (M,D,E) 6pm-4am

Loft 36 Fire Island Blvd., 597-6720 (M) seasonal

Pavillion Fire Island Blvd., 597-6131 (★MW,D) 4pm-6am, seasonal, popular T-dance & AM dancing, also Yacht Club restaurant opens at noon

Restaurants & Cafes

Michael's Dock Walk, Cherry Grove, 597-6555, 24hrs Sat

Top of the Bay Dock Walk at Bay Walk, Cherry Grove, 597-6699 (★MW) 7pm-midnight, seasonal

CRUISY AREAS
Anywhere & Everywhere esp. bushes btwn Cherry Grove & W. end of Pines (AYOR)

Glen Falls (518)

BARS
Club M 70 South St., 798-9809 (MW,D,WC) noon-4am

CRUISY AREAS
Aviation Mall trails in woods behind the mall (AYOR)
City Park downtown (AYOR)

Greenwood Lake (914)

BARS
The Quarter Deck Jersey Ave. (1/2 mile S. of The Village Light), 477-2070 (MW,NH) 6pm-2am Th-Sun, from noon Sun

Highland (914)

BARS
Prime Time Rte. 9 W., 691-8550 (M,D) 9pm-4am, clsd Mon-Wed

Hudson Valley (see also **Kingston, New Paltz, Poughkeepsie & Stone Ridge**)

PUBLICATIONS
▲ **In The Life** PO Box 921, Wappingers Falls, 12590-0921, (914) 227-7456, monthly

Ithaca (607)

INFO LINES & SERVICES
AA Gay/Lesbian 201 E. Green St. (Mental Health Serv. Bldg.), 273-1541, 5:30pm Sun
Ithaca Gay/Lesbian Activities Board (IGLAB) PO Box 6634, 14851, 273-1505, 3rd Tue, ph# is for Common Ground bar; sponsors events including 'Finger Lake Gay/Lesbian Picnic'
LesBiGay Info Line (Cornell University), 255-6482, noon-4pm Mon-Fri, touch-tone info & referrals

ACCOMMODATIONS
Pleasant Grove B&B 168 Pleasant Grove Rd., 387-5420/(800) 398-3963 (GF) above Cayuga Lake, sundeck

BARS
Common Ground 1230 Danby Rd., 273-1505 (★MW,D,YC,WC) 4pm-1:30am, clsd Mon

RESTAURANTS & CAFES
ABC Cafe 308 Stewart Ave., 277-4770 (BW) lunch & dinner, wknd brunch, clsd Mon, vegetarian

BOOKSTORES & RETAIL SHOPS
Borealis Bookstore, Inc. 111 N. Aurora St., 272-7752 (WC) 10am-9pm, noon-5pm Sun, independent alternative w/ lesbigay sections

CRUISY AREAS
Reservoir at Upper Six Mile Creek at Van Etten Dam Waterfalls (AYOR)

Jamestown (716)

Info Lines & Services
10% Network 1255 Pendergast Ave. (Unitarian Church), 484-7285/664-5556, 7pm 3rd Sat, lesbigay social group

Bars
Nite Spot 201 Windsor (MW,D,S) 7pm-2am

Sneakers 100 Harrison, 484-8816 (MW,D,WC) 2pm-2am

Kingston (914)

Info Lines & Services
Coalition for Lesbigay Youth 255-7123

Ulster County Gay/Lesbian Alliance PO Box 3785, 12401, 626-3203, info & events line

Lake George (518)

Accommodations
King Hendrick Motel Lake George Rd. (Rte. 9), 792-0418 (GF,SW) also cabin available

Lake Placid (518)

Restaurants & Cafes
Artists' Cafe 1 Main St., 523-9493 (BW) 8am-10pm, steak & seafood

Dakota Cafe 124 Main St., 523-2337, steak & seafood

Cruisy Areas
Cooperas Pond Trail off E. side of Rte. 86 at junction of Rtes. 86 & 7 (AYOR)

Long Island (516)

Info Lines & Services
▲ **Community Real Estate Referrals** (800) 346-5592, gay realtor at your service, no rentals

EEGO (East End Gay Organization) PO Box 87, Southampton, 11968, 324-3699

GLIB (Gay Men & Lesbians in Brookhaven) PO Box 203, Brookhaven, 11719, 286-6867

Middle Earth Hotline 2740 Martin Ave., Bellmore, 679-1111, 24hrs, crisis & referral counseling, esp. for youth

Pride for Youth Coffeehouse 170 Fulton St., Farmingdale, 679-9000, 7:30pm-11:30pm Fri

Accommodations
132 North Main 132 N. Main, East Hampton, 324-2246

Centennial House 13 Woods Lane, East Hampton, 324-9414 (GF,SW)

Cozy Cabins Motel Box 848, Montauk Hwy., East Hampton, 11975, 537-1160 (MW) seasonal

Econo Lodge - MacArthur Airport 3055 Veterans Memorial Hwy., Ronkonkoma, 588-6800/(800) 553-2666 (GF)

EconoLodge - Smithtown/Hauppauge 755 Rte. 347, Smithtown, 724-9000/(800) 553-2666 (GF)

Gandalf House P.O. Box 385, Laurel, 11948, 298-4769 (GF)

Sag Harbor B&B 125 Mt. Misery Dr., Sag Harbor, 725-5945 (MW,WC)

Summit Motor Inn 501 E. Main St., Bayshore, 666-6000 (GF)

BARS

Blanche 47-2 Boundary Ave., South Farmingdale, 694-6906 (M,NH,E) 4pm-4am

Bunk House 192 N. Main St., Montauk Hwy., Sayville, 567-2865 (★M,D,S,WC) 8pm-4am, from 5pm Sun

Chameleon 40-20 Long Beach Rd., Long Beach, 889-4083 (★MW,D) 9pm-4am, clsd Mon-Wed

Club Swamp Montauk Hwy. at E. Gate Rd., Wainscott, 537-3332 (M,D,F,YC,WC) 6pm-4am, daily during summer, clsd Tue-Wed

Libations 3547 Merrick Rd., Seaford, 679-8820 (MW,NH) 3pm-4am

The Long Island Eagle 94 N. Clinton Ave., Bay Shore, 968-2750 (M,NH,L) 9pm-4am

Pal Joey's 2457 Jerusalem Ave., North Bellmore, 785-9301 (M,NH,WC) 4pm-4am

Silver Lining 175 Cherry Ln., Floral Park, 354-9641 (MW,D,E,S,V,YC,WC) 9pm-4am Wed-Sun

St. Mark's Place 65-50 Jericho Pkwy., Commack, 499-2244 (MW,D,WC) 4pm-4am

Thunders 1017 E. Jericho Trnpk., Huntington Station, 423-5241 (MW,E) clsd Mon

RESTAURANTS & CAFES

Bayman's Katch 220 Montauk Hwy., Sayville, 589-9744, 4pm-2am, clsd Tue

TRAVEL & TOUR OPERATORS

All Continent Tours Inc. 250 Hempstead Ave., Malverne, (800) 553-0009 (IGTA)

SPIRITUAL GROUPS

Dignity-Nassau County PO Box 48, East Meadow, 11554, 781-6225, 8pm 2nd & 4th Sat

Dignity-Suffolk County Box 621-P, Bay Shore, 11706, 654-5367, 2nd & last Sun

CRUISY AREAS

Beach at end of Two Mile Hollow Rd. go left, East Hampton (AYOR)

Fowle Beach go right, Southampton (AYOR)

Jones Beach field #6 (AYOR)

Nanuet (914)

TRAVEL & TOUR OPERATORS

Edlen Travel Inc. 161 S. Middletown Rd., 624-2100/(800) 624-2315 (IGTA)

Naples (716)

ACCOMMODATIONS

Landmark Retreat 6006 Rte. 21, 396-2383 (GF,WC)

New Paltz (914)

ACCOMMODATIONS

Churchill Farm 39 Canaan Rd., 255-7291 (GF) full brkfst

Ujjala B&B 2 Forest Glen, 255-6360 (GF) body therapy avaliable

BOOKSTORES & RETAIL SHOPS

The Painted Word 36 Main St., 256-0825 (WC) 10am-10pm, til 6pm Sun-Mon, lesbigay

TRAVEL & TOUR OPERATORS

New Paltz Travel Center, Inc. 7 Cherry Hill Center, 255-7706 (IGTA)

Your Home Away From Home

The Lesbian and Gay Community Services Center/New York

▼ **400 lesbian and gay organizations hold their meetings at the Center.**

▼ **5,000 people visit the Center each week.**

Come and enjoy our dances, our sexuality and health workshops, 12 step meetings, our readings, exhibits, library and lectures, our garden to rest your feet after a day of sightseeing and more!

LESBIAN AND GAY COMMUNITY SERVICES CENTER

208 West 13th Street, Greenwich Village

(14th Street stop on the 1,2 and 3 subway lines)

(212) 620-7310

Visit the Center's Web site at
http://www.panix.com/~dhuppert/gay/center

Please add my name to the Center mailing list.

Name: _____

Address: _____

_____

Telephone: _____

Mail to: The Center, 208 W. 13th Street, New York, NY 10011-7799

NEW YORK CITY

New York City is divided into 8 geographical areas:

N.Y.C. - Overview

N.Y.C. - Greenwich Village & Chelsea

N.Y.C. - Midtown

N.Y.C. - Uptown

N.Y.C. - Brooklyn

N.Y.C. - Queens

N.Y.C. - Bronx

N.Y.C. - Staten Island

N.Y.C. - Overview (212)

INFO LINES & SERVICES

AA Gay/Lesbian Intergroup 647-1680, many mtgs. at Lesbian/Gay Community Center

Asians & Friends of NY (at Lesbian/Gay Community Center), 8pm 3rd Sat

Bisexual Gay/Lesbian Youth of NY (at Lesbian/Gay Community Center), 3:30pm Sat

Bisexual Network 459-4784, recorded info on variety of social & political groups

▲ **Community Real Estate Referrals** (800) 346-5592, gay realtor at your service, no rentals

Eulenspiegel Society Box 2783, Grand Central Sta., 10163, 388-7022, 7:30pm Tue & Wed, pansexual S/M group, also publishes 'Prometheus'

GGALA (Greek Gay/Lesbian Association) (at Lesbian/Gay Community Center), 8pm 2nd & 4th Th

Girth & Mirth Club of NY (at the Center), 699-7735, 7pm 3rd Sat

Hetrick-Martin Institute 2 Astor Pl., 674-2400, extensive services for lesbigay youth; also publishes 'You Are Not Alone' resource directory

Identity House 39 W. 14th St. Ste. 205, 243-8181, walk-in 6pm-10pm Sun-Tue, peer-counseling, info & referrals

Just Couples (at Lesbian/Gay Community Center), 3:30pm 1st Sun

Kambal Sa Lusog (at Lesbian/Gay Community Center), Philippinas/os lesbians/gays/bisexuals

Legal Clinic (at Lesbian/Gay Community Center), 6:30pm Tue, drop-in, free consultation

▲ **Lesbian/Gay Community Services Center** 208 W. 13th St., 620-7310 (WC) 9am-11pm

Men of All Colors Together (at the Center), 330-7678, 8pm Fri

Metropolitan Gender Network 561 Hudson St. #45, 10014, (718) 461-9050, call for free information

NY CyberQueers (at Lesbian/Gay Community Center), 7pm 3rd Th, lesbigay & transgendered 'computer pros'

Party Talk Manhattan Cable Ch. 35, 9pm Th & 11pm Sun, club reviews

SAGE: Senior Action in a Gay Environment (at Lesbian/Gay Community Center), 741-2247

SALGA (South Asian Lesbian/Gay Association) (at Lesbian/Gay Community Center), 3:30pm 2nd Sat

Twenty Something (at Lesbian/Gay Community Center), 8pm 1st & 3rd Tue , social alternative to bars/clubs for lesbigays in late teens, 20s & early 30s

Village Playwrights (at the Center), 596-9905, 6-8pm Tue

ACCOMMODATIONS

Aaah! Bed & Breakfast PO Box 2093, 10108, 246-4000/(800) 362-8585 (GF) reservations agency

▲ **The Caritas B&B Network** Soho, (800) CARITAS (227-4827), see ad in center National section

▲ **New York Reservation Center** PO Box 2646, 11969, 977-3512 (MW,IGTA)

SPIRITUAL GROUPS

Axios (at Lesbian/Gay Community Center), 805-1952, 8pm 2nd Fri, Eastern & Orthodox Christians

Buddhist Lesbians/Gays: Maitri Dorje (at Lesbian/Gay Community Center), 6pm 2nd Tue

Congregation Beth Simchat Torah 57 Bethune St., 929-9498 (WC) 8:30pm Fri, lesbian/gay synagogue

Dignity 110 Christopher St., 627-6488

Evangelicals Concerned c/o Dr. Ralph Blair 311 E. 72nd St. #1G, 10021, 517-3171

Gay/Lesbian Yeshiva Day School Alumni (at Lesbian/Gay Community Center), 8:30pm 4th Th

Integrity NYC 691-7181

MCC of New York 446 W. 36th St., 629-7440, 10am & 7pm Sun

Meditation for Gays/Lesbians/Bisexuals (at Lesbian/Gay Community Center), 8pm 1st & 3rd Wed

Radical Faeries Info Line (718) 625-4505

If you want to pick him up...

then you'll have to pick us up.

The Gay Companion to New York For info Call (212) 627-0165

Society of Friends (Quakers) 15 Rutherford Pl. (Meeting House), 777-8866, 9:30am & 11am Sun

PUBLICATIONS

Colorlife 301 Cathedral Park Wy. Box 287, 10026, 222-9794, focuses on lesbians/gays of color

Gayellow Pages Box 533 Village Stn., 10014-0533, 674-0120, annual guidebook, national & regional editions

▲ **Homo Xtra** 19 W. 21st St., Ste 504, 627-0747, weekly complete party paper

Lesbian & Gay New York 225 Lafayette St. #1103, 343-7200

Manhattan Spirit 242 W. 30th St. 5th flr., 268-0454, monthly

New York Native/Stonewall News PO Box 1475 Church St. Stn., 627-2120, weekly

▲ **Next** 121 Varick St. 3rd flr., 226-6556, the scoop on New York's nightlife

PM PO Box 430, Babylon, 11702, (516) 587-8669, monthly

MEN'S CLUBS

FFA-NY c/o Mirza Inc. 139 W. 4th Ave., Roselle NJ, 07203, (908) 245-5323/(607) 656-4659, private fisting parties last Sat

Pump It Up c/o Mirza Inc. 139 W. 4th Ave., Roselle NJ, 07203, (908) 245-5323/(607) 656-4659, demos; also monthly publication

N.Y.C. - Greenwich Village & Chelsea (212)

INFO LINES & SERVICES

▲ **Community Real Estate Referrals** (800) 346-5592, gay realtor at your service, no rentals

M.A.N. 496A Hudson #133, 535-3914, gay men's group for non-sexual nudism

ACCOMMODATIONS

Abingdon B&B 13 8th Ave. (at W. 12th), 243-5384 (MW) smokefree

▲ **The Caritas B&B Network** (800) CARITAS (227-4827), see ad in center National section

Chelsea Inn 46 W. 17th St., 645-8989 (GF)

Chelsea Mews Guest House 344 W. 15th St., 255-9174 (M)

▲ **Chelsea Pines Inn** 317 W. 14th St., 929-1023 (★MW,IGTA)

▲ **Colonial House Inn** 318 W. 22nd St., 243-9669/(800) 689-3779 (M,IGTA)

Holiday Inn 138 Lafayette St., 966-8898 (GF,F)

Home Sweet Home 243-6496, hospitality & home exchanges

▲ **Incentra Village House** 32 8th Ave., 206-0007 (MW)

BARS

The Bar 68 2nd Ave. (4th St.), 674-9714 (M,NH,WC) 4pm-4am

Barracuda 275 W. 22nd St. (8th Ave), 645-8613 (M,E) 4pm-4am

Boots & Saddle 76 Christopher St., 929-9684 (M,NH,L) 8am-4am, noon-4pm Sun

The Break 232 8th Ave. (22nd St.), 627-0072 (★M,V) 2pm-4am

Champs 17 W. 19th St., 633-1717 (★M,D,S) 4pm-4am

Crow Bar 339 E. 10th St., 420-0670 (MW,S) 9pm-4am

Dick's Bar 192 2nd Ave. (12th St.), 475-2071 (M,V) 2pm-4am

The Dugout 185 Christopher St., 242-9113 (M,NH,WC) 4pm-2am, from noon Fri-Sun, Sun brunch, sports bar

CELEBRATING GAY PRIDE INTO THE 21ST CENTURY

THE MONSTER NEW YORK CITY

80 Grove St. • NY NY • (212) 924-3558

Duplex 61 Christopher St., 255-5438 (GF,E) 4pm-4am, piano bar & cabaret from 9pm

The Eagle 142 11th Ave. (at 21st), 691-8451 (★M,L,V,WC) 10pm-4am

Eighty Eights 228 W. 10th St., 924-0088 (GF,WC) 4pm-4am, piano bar & cabaret; also Sun brunch

Five Oaks 49 Grove St., 243-8885 (GF,F,E) 5pm-4am

Hanger Bar 115 Christopher St., 627-2044 (M,NH) 3pm-4am

Julius 159 W. 10th St., 929-9672 (M,NH,F) 8am-4am

Keller's 384 West St., 243-1907 (M,NH,MRC-AF) 1pm-4am

King 579 6th Ave., 366-5464 (M,D) 4pm-4am

Limelight 47 W. 20th St., 807-7850 (★M,D,A) Lick-It Wed

▲ **The Lure** 409 W. 13th, 741-3919 (★M,L) 8pm-4am, from 6pm Sun

Marie's Crisis 59 Grove St., 243-9323 (★MW,E) 5pm-3am

Meow Mix 269 E. Houston St., 254-1434 (★W,D,E) clsd Mon

Mike's Club Cafe 400 W. 14th St. (at 9th), 691-6606 (M,NH,F,E) 2pm-4am

▲ **The Monster** 80 Grove St., 924-3557 (★MW,D,F,E) 4pm-4am

Nuts & Bolts Lounge 101 7th Ave. S. (Grove), 620-4000 (M,E,K) 2pm-4am

Pieces 8 Christopher St. (6th Ave), 929-9291 (M,NH) 2pm-4am

Rawhide 212 8th Ave. (21st), 242-9332 (M,CW,WC) 8am-4am

Rome 290 8th Ave (24th St), 242-6969 (M,S)

Roxy 515 W. 18th St., 645-5156 (★M,D,A,S) rollerskating 8pm-2am Tue, dance floor Sat 11pm

Ruby Fruit Bar & Grill 531 Hudson St., 929-3343 (W,F) 3pm-4am

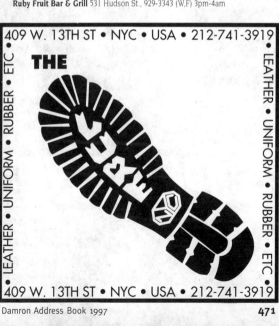

LEATHER • UNIFORM • RUBBER • ETC

409 W. 13TH ST • NYC • USA • 212-741-3919

THE LURE

PHOTO: DREW TAL MODEL: DARRYN TAYLOR

Saint-At-Large 674-8541 (★M,D) 4 huge parties a year: White Party in Feb, Black Party in Mar, Halloween, New Year's

Sneakers 392 West St., 242-9830 (M,NH,MRC,WC)

Sound Factory (SFB) 12 W. 21st St., 206-7770 (★M,D) 11pm Fri

Spike Bar 120 11th Ave. (20th St.), 243-9688 (M,L,WC) leather, military, western, fetish, dress code

▲ **Splash** 50 W. 17th St., 691-0073 (M,V,S,YC,WC) 4pm-4am

Stonewall Inn 53 Christopher St., 463-0950 (M,WC) 4pm-4am

Tunnel Bar 116 1st Ave. (7th St.), 777-9232 (★M,NH,YC) 2pm-4am

Two Potato 143 Christopher St., 255-0286 (M,NH,MRC-AF) noon-4am

Ty's 114 Christopher St., 741-9641 (M) 1pm-4am

Uncle Charlie's 56 Greenwich Ave., 255-8787 (★M,V,YC) 3pm-3am

Wonder Bar 505 E. 6th St. (Ave. A), 777-9105 (MW,NH,V) 8pm-4am

RESTAURANTS & CAFES

Black Sheep 344 W. 11th St., 242-1010 (M)

Brunetta's 190 1st Ave. (11th), 228-4030 (★MW) Italian

Chelsea Bistro & Bar 358 W. 23rd St. (9th Ave), 727-2026, trendy French

Circa 103 2nd Ave. (E. 6th St.), 977-4120 (★WC) open late

Claire 156 7th Ave. (19th St.), 255-1955

Cola's 148 8th Ave., 633-8020 (★) Italian

▲ **Community Bar & Grill** 216 7th Ave (22nd St), 242-7900 (E)

Empire Diner 210 10th Ave. (22nd St.), 243-2736, 24hrs

BRUNCH
Community
BAR & GRILL
GARDEN

216 Seventh Avenue (22-23)
New York City   212-242-7900

LIVE DJ

MEET YOUR NEW BROKER

WALL STREET SAUNA
ONE MAIDEN LANE
NEW YORK, NEW YORK 10038

WEEKDAYS 11AM-8PM
SATURDAYS 12PM-6PM
CLOSED SUN
OPEN TO THE PUBLIC

First 87 1st Ave (6th St.), 674-3823, late dining, hip crowd

Florent 69 Gansevoort St., 989-5779 (★) 24hrs, French diner

Food Bar 149 8th Ave. (17th St.), 243-2020 (★M)

Global 33 93 2nd Ave. (5th), 477-8427, 5pm-midnight, Int'l tapas

Lucky Cheung's 24 1st Ave. (2nd St), 473-0515 (★)

Orbit Cafe 46 Bedford St. (7th), 463-8717 (WC) lunch & dinner, gospel brunch noon-5pm Sun, bar noon-2am, til 4am Fri-Sat, midscale American w/ Latin accent

Restivo 209 7th Ave.(22nd St), 366-4133, intimate ambiance, gay-owned

Sazerac House Bar & Grill 533 Hudson, 989-0313, noon-midnight, Cajun

Sung Tieng 343 Bleecker St. (10th St.), 929-7800/924-8314 (★) delivery

Universal Grill 44 Bedford St., 989-5621 (★MW) lunch, dinner & Sun brunch

The Viceroy 160 8th Ave. (18th St.), 633-8484 (★) full bar

GYMS & HEALTH CLUBS

American Fitness Center 128 8th Ave., 627-0065 (★M)

Archives Gym 666 Greenwich Ave., 366-3725

Better Bodies 22 W. 19th St., 929-6789 (MW)

▲ **Chelsea Gym** 267 W. 17th St., 255-1150 (MO,PC)

David Barton Gym 552 6th Ave., 727-0004 (MW)

BOOKSTORES & RETAIL SHOPS

A Different Light 151 W. 19th St., 989-4850/(800) 343-4002, 11am-11pm, lesbigay bookstore & cafe

Alternate Card & Gift Shop 85 Christopher St., 645-8966, noon-11pm

Week $25   17th & 8th Avenue

Day $10

Beautiful Body Strong
Strong Mind Beautiful
Beautiful Body Strong
Strong Mind Beautiful
Beautiful Body Strong

CHELSEA GYM
Mind Beautiful

255-1150

Manhattan

west side club

27 West 20th Street 2nd floor
Chelsea, New York City

*A Hard Man
is Good
to Find*

24 Hours

**Private
Membership**

Photo: Jake Sorenlino

For info: 212•691•2700

1997 Damron Address Book

Bleecker Street Books 350 Bleecker St., 10am-midnight

Don't Panic 98 Christopher St., 989-7888

Greetings 45 Christopher St., 242-0424, 11am-10pm

Oscar Wilde Memorial Bookshop 15 Christopher St., 255-8097, 11:30am-9pm, lesbigay

The Rainbows & Triangles 192 8th Ave., 627-2166, 11am-9pm

Soho Books 351 W. Broadway, 226-3395, 10am-midnight

TRAVEL & TOUR OPERATORS

Empress Travel 224 W. 4th St 2nd Fl., 206-6900/(800) 429-6969 (IGTA)

Islander's Kennedy Travel 183 W. 10th St., 242-3222/(800) 988-1181 (IGTA) also Queens location: 267-10 Hillside Ave., Floral Park, (800)237-7433

Wilderness Bridges 427 Washington St., 802-9086, lesbigay outdoor adventures

MEN'S CLUBS

J's Hangout 675 Hudson St., 242-9292 (M,BYOB)

▲ **Wall Street Sauna** 1 Maiden Ln. (11th flr.), 233-8900 (★MO)

▲ **West Side Club** 27 W. 20th St., 691-2700, 24hrs

EROTICA

▲ **Ann St. Entertainment Center** 21 Ann St., 267-9760

▲ **Christopher St. Book Shop** 500 Hudson St., 463-0657, 24hrs, see ad in center National Section

Eros Cinema 732 8th Ave., 221-2450

Gay Pleasures 546 Hudson St., 255-5756

Leather Man 111 Christopher St., 243-5339

Damron online ◄

www.damron.com ◄

aol keyword: Damron ◄

UNICORN

ALL-MALE EROTICA

VIDEOS • MAGAZINES • TOYS • ETC.
VIDEO ARCADE w/PRIVATE BOOTHS
"Your Source in Chelsea"
277-C West 22ND Street
BETWEEN 7TH & 8TH AVENUES
(212) 924-2921

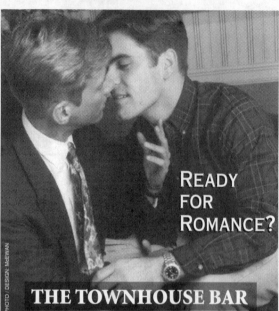

Noose 261 W. 19th St., 807-1789, clsd Mon
Pleasure Chest 156 7th Ave S., 242-2158
▲ **Unicorn Bookstore** 277-C W. 22nd St., 924-2921

N.Y.C. - Midtown (212)

ACCOMMODATIONS

▲ **The Caritas B&B Network** (800) CARITAS (227-4827), see ad in center National section
Central Park South B&B 586-0652 (MW,WC)
Hotel Beverly 125 E. 50th St., 753-2700/(800) 223-0945 (GF,F,IGTA)
Park Central Hotel 870 7th Ave. at 56th St., 247-8000/(800) 346-1359 (GF,F,WC)

BARS

Bump 218 W. 47th St, 869-6103 (★M,D) 11pm-4am Sun
Buster's 129 Lexington Ave. (at 29th), 684-8832 (MW,NH,TG) noon-4am
Cafe Con Leche 124 W. 43rd St., 819-0377 (★M,D,A,MRC-L) 10pm Sun
Cat's Bar 232 W. 48th, 245-5245 (M,NH) 10am-4am, hustlers
Cleo's Saloon 656 9th Ave. (46 St.), 307-1503 (M,NH) 8am-4am
Don't Tell Mama 343 W.46th St., 757-0788 (★GF,E,YC) 4pm-4am
Edelweiss 580 11th Ave. (43rd St), 629-1021 (★GF,D,TG,S) 4pm-4am
G.H. Club 353 E.53rd St., 223-9752 (M,F,OC) 4pm-1am, til 2am Fri-Sat, piano bar
Sally's 2 252 W. 43rd St. (Hotel Carter), 944-6000x212 (M,S,WC) 4pm-4am
Savoy 335 W. 41st St., 560-9635 (M)
South Dakota 405 3rd Ave. (29 St.), 684-8376 (M,NH,WC) 3pm-4am

America's Only Spa Designed Exclusively for Men

Now Open 24 hours •7 days a week
Massage available by appointment 24 hours

Body Wraps•Facials•Salt Glo Scrubs
Roman Steam Room• Sauna•Hairstyling
Cybex and Cardio-vascular Equipment

Day and Evening Memberships Available
227 East 56th St. NYC 212-754-0227

Grab it and Hold on

In the Heart of Manhattan's Upper-East Side

Temporary membership available to out-of-town men with proper I.D.

east side club

227 E. 56 Street, New York (212) PL3-2222

PHOTO / DESIGN: MCEWAN

Stella's 266 W.47th St. (8th Ave), 974-0973 (M,S) noon-4am

Twilo 530 W.27th St. (10th Ave), 268-1600 (GF,D,E) 11pm Fri & Sat

The Web 40 E. 58th St., 308-1546 (M,D,MRC-AF) 4pm-4am

RESTAURANTS & CAFES

Cafe Un Deux Trois 123 W. 44th St., 354-4148 (★) noon-midnight, bistro

Good Diner 554 42nd St. (at 11th Ave.), 967-2661, 24hrs

Mangia e Bevi 800 9th Ave (53rd St), 956-3976, Italian

Revolution 611 9th Ave. (43rd St), 489--8451, trendy video dining

Rice & Beans 744 9th Ave (50th St), 265-4444, Latin/Brazilian

▲ **Townhouse Restaurant** 206 E. 58th (at 3rd), 826-6241 (★MW,E) lunch & dinner, Sun brunch, late on wknds

GYMS & HEALTH CLUBS

▲ **Spa 227** 227 E. 56th St., 754-0227 (MO) 24hrs

TRAVEL & TOUR OPERATORS

Our Family Abroad 459-1800/(800) 999-5500 (IGTA)

Pied Piper Travel 330 W. 42nd St. Ste. 1601, 239-2412/(800) 874-7312 (IGTA)

Stevens Travel Management 432 Park Ave. S., 9th flr., 696-4300/(800) 275-7400 (IGTA)

MEN'S CLUBS

▲ **East Side Club** 227 E. 56th St., 6th flr., 753-2222 (★MO,PC) 24hrs

EROTICA

Eros I Cinema 732 8th Ave., 221-2450

Gaiety Burlesk 201 W. 46th St., 221-8868

Les Hommes
BOOK SHOP

217 West
80th Street
2nd Floor
NYC, NY
between
Broadway
and
Amsterdam Ave.

Video Screening Room
Private Screening Booths
The Latest Releases
Extensive Video Rental Libray
Magazines, Videos, Toys etc.

"THE" All-Male Uptown Book Store

Image: Tom Fuller © Champion Design: Grayscale

N.Y.C. - Uptown (212)

INFO LINES & SERVICES

▲ **Community Real Estate Referrals** (800) 346-5592, gay realtor at your service, no rentals

ACCOMMODATIONS

Malibu Studios Hotel 2688 Broadway, 222-2954/(800) 647-2227 (GF)

New York B&B 134 W. 119th St., 666-0559 (GF)

BARS

Brandy's Piano Bar 235 E. 84th St., 650-1944 (M,WC) 4pm-4am

. **Bridge Bar** 309 E.60th St., 233-9104, 4pm-4am

Candle Bar 309 Amsterdam (74th St.), 874-9155 (★M,NH) 2pm-4am

Joe L's 4488 Broadway (192nd), 567-8555 (M,S) clsd Mon-Tue

Pegasus 119 E.60th St., 888-4702 (M,E) piano bar

▲ **Regents** 317 E.53rd St., 593-3091 (M,F,E) noon-4am, Italian

Tool Box 1748 2nd Ave. (91st St.), 427-3106 (M,S) 7pm-4am

The Work's 428 Columbus (81st St.), 799-7365 (★M,V,YC) 2pm-4am, great Sun beer bust

EROTICA

Come Again 353 E. 53rd St., 308-9394, clsd Sun

▲ **Les Hommes Book Shop** 217 W. 80th St. 2nd Fl (Broadway)

N.Y.C. - Brooklyn (718)

INFO LINES & SERVICES

Foot Friends PO Box 150790, 11215, 832-3952, 8pm last Mon at The Lure bar

BARS

Carry Nation 363 5th Ave, Park Slope (MW,NH) 5pm-3am, from 11am wknds

One Hot Spot 1 Front St., 852-0139 (MW,D,E,MRC,WC) 9pm-3am, clsd Sun-Tue, from 6pm Th

The Roost 309 7th Ave., 788-9793 (GF,NH) noon-2am

Spectrum 802 64th St., 238-8213 (★MW,D,E,S) 9pm-4am, clsd Mon-Tue

RESTAURANTS & CAFES

Kokobar Cybercafe & Bookstore 59 Lafayette Ave. (at Fulton), 243-9040 (WC) 7am-10pm, 10am-11pm Sat, til 10pm Sun

BOOKSTORES & RETAIL SHOPS

Community Book Store 143 7th Ave., 783-3075, 10am-9pm

TRAVEL & TOUR OPERATORS

Avalon Travel 9421 3rd Ave., 833-5500 (IGTA)

Deville Travel Service 7818 3rd Ave., 680-2700 (IGTA)

J. Bette Travel 4809 Ave. 'N' #279, 241-3872 (IGTA)

N.Y.C. - Queens (718)

INFO LINES & SERVICES

▲ **Community Real Estate Referrals** (800) 346-5592, gay realtor at your service, no rentals

Q-GLU (Queens Gay/Lesbians United) PO Box 4669, 11104, 1st Tue

ACCOMMODATIONS
▲ **The Caritas B&B Network** (800) CARITAS (227-4827), see ad in center National section

BARS
BS East 113-24 Queens Blvd., Forest Hills, 263-0300 (M,NH,S,V,WC) 5pm-4am

Bum Bum 63-14 Roosevelt, 651-4145 (M,NH,MRC,L) 5pm-2am Fri-Sun

Friends Tavern 78-11 Roosevelt Ave., Jackson Hts., 397-7256 (M,NH,MRC-L) 2pm-4am

Krash 34-48 Steinway St., Astoria, 366-2934 (MW,D,MRC)

Love Boat 77-02 Broadway, Elmhurst, 429-8670 (M,NH,MRC-L,S) unconfirmed '97

Lucho's Club 38-19 69th St., Woodside, 899-9320 (M;MRC,L) 9pm-2am, clsd Mon-Tue

Magic Touch 73-13 37th Ave., Jackson Hts., 429-8605 (★M,D,S) 3pm-4am

Music Box 40-08 74th St., 429-9356 (M,MRC,L) 4pm-4am

Stella's 12-21 Jackson Ave., Long Island City, 392-2132 (MW,S) 11pm-4am

MEN'S CLUBS
Northern Men's Sauna 3365 Fairington St., Flushing, 359-9817 (MO,PC)

N.Y.C. - Staten Island (718)

INFO LINES & SERVICES
Lambda Associates of Staten Island PO Box 665, Staten Island, 10305, 876-8786

BARS
Legacy (Club Taboo) 23 Sands St. (Bay St.), Stapleton, 816-0713 (MW,D) 9pm-4am

Sand Castle 86 Mills Ave., 447-9365 (★MW,D,S,WC) 9am-4am

Niagara Falls (718)

INFO LINES & SERVICES
GALS (Gay/Lesbian Support) P.O. Box 1464, 14302, mtg 2nd Sat

ACCOMMODATIONS
Old Niagara House B&B 610 4th St., 285-9408 (GF)

BARS
Club Alternate 492 19th St. (Ferry) (M,D) inquire locally

EROTICA
Horizon Books 8601 Niagara Falls Blvd.

Nineteen St. Books & News 641 19th St., 284-2214, 24hrs

Nyack (914)

BARS
Barz 327 Rte. 9 W., 353-4444 (MW,D,WC) 6pm-4am, from 2pm Sat, from 1pm Sun, clsd Mon

Coven Cafe 162 Main St., 358-9829 (GF,F,WC) noon-midnight, til 2am Fri-Sat, Sun brunch, clsd Mon, Wed men's night

BOOKSTORES & RETAIL SHOPS
New Spirit Books & Beyond 128 Main St., 353-2126, noon-7pm, clsd Mon

Orange County (914)

INFO LINES & SERVICES
Orange County Gay/Lesbian Alliance PO Box 1557, Greenwood Lake, 10925, 782-1525, 7:30pm Tue

RESTAURANTS & CAFES
Folderol II Rte. 284, Westtown, 726-3822 (E,WC) noon-3pm & 5pm-9pm, til 11pm Fri-Sat, 3pm-9pm Sun, clsd Mon

Owego (607)

TRAVEL & TOUR OPERATORS
Tioga Travel 189 Main St., 687-4144 (IGTA)

Plattsburg (518)

BARS
Blair's Tavern 30 Marion St., 561-9071 (MW,D)

CRUISY AREAS
Triple A Video Margaret St., exit 39 off Interstate 87 (AYOR)

Port Chester (914)

BARS
Sandy's Old Homestead 325 N. Main St., 939-0758 (GF,F,WC) 8am-4am

Poughkeepsie (914)

INFO LINES & SERVICES
▲ **Community Real Estate Referrals** (800) 346-5592, gay realtor at your service, no rentals
Poughkeepsie GALA (Gay/Lesbian Association) PO Box 289, Hughsonville, 12537, 431-6756, 7:30pm Tue

BARS
Congress 411 Main St., 486-9068 (MW,NH,WC) 3pm-4am, from 8pm Sun

TRAVEL & TOUR OPERATORS
Community Travel Connections 30 Griffen St., 227-4059/(800) 930-3011 (IGTA)

SPIRITUAL GROUPS
Dignity-Integrity 15 Brandy St. (Christ Church), 724-3209, 8pm 3rd Fri

EROTICA
Hamilton Book & Video 216 N. Hamilton St., 473-1776

Rochester (716)

INFO LINES & SERVICES
AA Gay/Lesbian 232-6720
▲ **Community Real Estate Referrals** (800) 346-5592, gay realtor at your service, no rentals
Finger Lakes Gay/Lesbian Social Group Box 941, Geneva, 14456, 536-7753, 1st Fri & 3rd Tue, ask for Sam Edwards
Gay Alliance 179 Atlantic Ave., 244-8640, 1pm-9pm, til 6pm Fri

BARS
Anthony's 522 Main St. E., 325-1350 (MW,NH) noon-2am
Atlantis 10-12 S. Washington St., 423-9748 (M,D) call for events

Avenue Pub 522 Monroe Ave., 244-4960 (★M,NH,D) 4pm-2am

Bachelor Forum 670 University Ave., 271-6930 (M,L) 1pm-2am, from 3pm wknds

Chena's 145 E. Main St., 232-7240 (W,NH,F,WC) 11am-2am

Club Marcella 123 Liberty Pole Wy., 454-5963 (MW,D,S) clsd Mon-Tue

Common Grounds 139 State St., 262-2650 (MW,NH) 11am-2am

Freakazoid 169 N. Chestnut St., 987-0000 (GF,D,A) call for events

Muther's 40 S.Union, 325-6216 (MW,F) 3pm-2am, patio

Tara 153 Liberty Pole Wy., 232-4719 (★MW,NH,E) noon-2am

Restaurants & Cafes

Little Theatre Cafe 240 East Ave., 258-0412 (★E,WC) 6pm-10pm, from noon wknds, til midnight Fri-Sat

Slice of Life 742 South Ave., 271-8010, 11:30am-8pm, 10am-2pm Sun, clsd Mon-Tue, vegetarian

Triphammer Grill 60 Browns Race, 262-2700, lunch & dinner, clsd Sun-Mon (dinner), patio

Bookstores & Retail Shops

Borders 1000 Hylan, 292-5900, cafe

The Pride Connection 728 South Ave., 242-7840, 10am-9pm, noon-6pm Sun

Rochester Custom Leathers 274 N. Goodman St., 442-2323/(800) 836-9047 (★) 11am-9pm, also lesbigay magazines & videos

Village Green Books 766 Monroe Ave., 461-5380, 6am-11pm, also 1954 West Ridge Rd. location

Travel & Tour Operators

DePrez Travel 145 Rue De Ville, 442-8900 (IGTA) ask for Ray Breslin

Great Expectations 1649 Monroe Ave., 244-8430/(800) 836-8110 (IGTA)

Park Ave. Travel 25 Buckingham St., 256-3080 (IGTA)

Spiritual Groups

Dignity/Integrity 17 S. Fitzhugh (St. Luke's/St. Simon's Church), 262-2170, 5pm Sun

More Light Presbyterian 4 Meigs St., 271-6513 (WC) 10:30am Sun

Nayim PO Box 18053, 14618, 473-6459/442-3363, lesbigay Jews

Open Arms MCC 875 E. Main St., 271-8478 (WC) 10:30am Sun

Publications

Empty Closet 127 Atlantic Ave., 244-9030, monthly

Men's Clubs

Rochester Spa & Body Club 109 Liberty Pole Wy., 454-1074 (PC) 24hrs

Erotica

Clinton Book Mart 115 N. Clinton, 325-9322, 24hrs

Dundalk News 561 State St., 325-2248, 24hrs

Saratoga Springs (518)

Bookstores & Retail Shops

Nahani 482 Broadway, 587-4322 (WC) 10am-6pm, noon-5pm Sun

Cruisy Areas

Congress Park summers (AYOR) after dusk

Schenectady (518)

ACCOMMODATIONS

Widow Kendall B&B 10 N. Ferry St., (800) 244-0925 (GF) gourmet brkfst

BARS

Blythewood 50 N. Jay St., 382-9755 (M,NH,WC) 9pm-4am

Clinton St. Pub 159 Clinton St., 382-9173 (MW,NH) noon-4am

Seneca Falls (315)

ACCOMMODATIONS

Guion House 32 Cayuga St., 568-8129 (GF) full brkfst

Spring Valley (914)

BARS

Electric Dreams 302 N. Main St., 362-4063 (MW,D)

Stone Ridge (914)

ACCOMMODATIONS

Inn at Stone Ridge Rte. 209, 687-0736 (GF,F)

Syracuse (315)

INFO LINES & SERVICES

AA Gay/Lesbian 463-5011

Gay/Lesbian Conference Hotline 422-5732

Pride Community Center P.O.Box 6608, 13217, 446-4436, newsletter

Syracuse Peace Council 924 Burnet Ave., 472-5478, also houses the Front Room Bookstore, lesbigay, call for hours

ACCOMMODATIONS

John Milton Inn Carrier Circle, Exit 35, 463-8555/(800) 352-1061 (GF)

BARS

Armory Pub 400 S. Clinton, 471-9059 (M,D,WC) 8am-2am

Mr. T's 218 N. Franklin St., 471-9026 (★M,NH,D) 3pm-2am, noon-2am Sun

My Bar 205 N. West St., 471-9279 (W,D,F,E) 10am-2am, til 4am Fri-Sat, patio

Ryan's Someplace Else 408-410 Pearl St., 471-9499 (★M,D,V,WC) 8pm-2am, from noon Sun, clsd Mon-Wed

Trexx 319 N. Clinton St., 474-6408 (M,D,S,WC) 8pm-2am, til 4am Fri-Sat, clsd Mon-Wed

RESTAURANTS & CAFES

Happy Endings 317 S. Clinton St., 475-1853 (E,WC) 8am-11pm, 10am-2am Fri-Sat, 6pm-11pm Sun, lunch & coffeehouse

Tu Tu Venue 731 Jay St., 475-8888 (★MW) 4pm-1am, clsd Sun

BOOKSTORES & RETAIL SHOPS

My Sister's Words 304 N. McBride St., 428-0227, 10am-6pm, til 8pm Th-Fri, clsd Sun (except Dec)

SPIRITUAL GROUPS

MCC of Ray of Hope 326 Montgomery St., 471-6618 (WC) 6pm Sun

PUBLICATIONS

Pink Paper PO Box 6462, 13217, 476-5186

EROTICA
Boulevard Books 2576 Erie Blvd. E., 446-1595, 24hrs
The City News 3713 Brewerton Rd., 454-0629, 24hrs

CRUISY AREAS
Thunder Park pink triangle rock (AYOR)

Troy (518)

EROTICA
Cinema Art Show World 289 River St., 274-7708
▲ **Video Expo** 516 River St., 272-7577

Utica (315)

INFO LINES & SERVICES
▲ **Community Real Estate Referrals** (800) 346-5592, gay realtor at your service, no rentals

Greater Utica Lambda Fellowship PO Box 122, 13505

BARS
Carmen D's 812 Charlotte St., 735-3964 (MW,NH) 4pm-2am,from 8pm Sat, clsd Sun

Options 1724 W. Oriskany, 724-9231 (MW,D) 5pm-2am, clsd Mon-Tue

That Place 216 Bleecker St., 724-1446 (★M,D,L,YC,WC) 8pm-2am, from 4pm Fri

Wappingers Falls (914)

PUBLICATIONS
▲ **In The Life** PO Box 921, 12590-0921, 227-7456, monthly

White Plains (914)

INFO LINES & SERVICES
The Loft 200 Hamilton Ave., 948-4922, switchboard 1pm-4pm, 7pm-10pm, lesbi-gay community center

BARS
Stutz 202 Westchester Ave., 761-3100 (★M,D,S) 5pm-4am, from 8pm wknds

Woodstock (914)

ACCOMMODATIONS
Woodstock Inn 38 Tannery Brook Rd., 679-8211 (GF,SW,WC)

BOOKSTORES & RETAIL SHOPS
Golden Notebook 29 Tinker St., 679-8000 (WC) 10:30am-7pm, til 9pm (summers)

Yonkers (914)

BARS
Harlee's 590 Nepperham Ave., 965-6900 (MW,D) 10pm-4am

NORTH CAROLINA

Asheville (704)

INFO LINES & SERVICES

CLOSER (Community Liaison for Support, Education & Reform) PO Box 2911, 28802, 277-7815, 7:30pm Tue (at All Souls Episcopal Church), social/support group

▲ **Community Real Estate Referrals** (800) 346-5592, gay realtor at your service, no rentals

Lambda AA 254-8539, 8pm Fri at All Souls Church, Biltmore Village

Mountain Buffs P.O. Box 5001, 28813, gay men's naturist club

OutFit 277-7815, 1st & 3rd Sat, lesbigay youth support group

Phoenix P.O. Box 18332, 28814, transgender support group, counseling & referrals available

ACCOMMODATIONS

Apple Wood Manor Inn 62 Cumberland Cir., 254-2244 (GF) full brkfst

The Bird's Nest 41 Oak Park Rd., 252-2381 (MW) comfortable & quiet B&B

The Gate House P.O. Box 85, 28711, 669-0507 (GF) large rental bungalow

The Inn on Montford 296 Montford Ave., 254-9569/(800) 254-9569 (GF) full brkfst, English cottage

May Tree Guesthouse 16 Oak Park Rd., 254-7266

Mountain Laurel B&B 139 Lee Dotson Rd., Fairview, 628-9903 (MW) full brkfst, secluded mountain cove, 25 miles from Asheville

Trails End Guesthouse 31 Floyd Dr., 274-3111

BARS

The Barber Shop/Hairspray Cafe 38 N. French Broad Ave., 258-2027 (MW,D,E,PC) 7pm-2am, also 'Club Metropolis' from 10pm Th-Sat

O'Henry's 59 Haywood St., 254-1891 (MW,NH,D,PC) 1pm-2am, from 11am Sat

Scandals 11 Grove St., 252-2838 (MW,D,A,S,WC) 10pm-3am, clsd Sun-Wed, 18+ Th, also 'Getaways' Lounge (V)

RESTAURANTS & CAFES

Grove Street Cafe 11 Grove St., 255-0010, 6pm-1am Wed-Sat, outside deck, summer T-dance & BBQ 2-8pm Sun, full bar

Laughing Seed Cafe 40 Wall St., 252-3445 (BW,WC) 11:30am-9pm, til 10pm Th-Sat, clsd Sun, patio, vegetarian/vegan

Laurey's 67 Biltmore Ave., 252-1500 (★WC) 10am-6pm, til 4pm Sat, clsd Sun, delicious salads & cookies, dinners to go

BOOKSTORES & RETAIL SHOPS

Downtown Books & News 67 N. Lexington Ave., 253-8654, 8am-6pm, from 6am Sun, used books & new magazines

The Goddess Store 382 Montford Ave., 258-3102 (WC) noon-6pm, clsd Sun-Mon

Malaprop's Bookstore & Cafe 61 Haywood St., 254-6734/(800) 441-9829 (E) 9am-8pm, til 10pm Fri-Sat, noon-6pm Sun, readings & performances

Rainbow's End 10 N. Spruce St., 285-0005, 10am-8pm, lesbigay

TRAVEL & TOUR OPERATORS

Blue Ridge Travel 102 Cherry St., Black Mountain, 669-8681/(800) 948-3430, books lesbigay tours & cruises

Journeys, Inc. 8 Biltmore Ave., Pack Plaza, 232-0800/(800) 256-8235 (IGTA)

Kaleidoscope Travel 120 Merrimon Ave., 253-7777/(800) 964-2001

SPIRITUAL GROUPS

The Cathedral of All Souls Biltmore Village, 274-2681 (WC) 8am, 9am, 11am Sun & noon Wed

ManSpirit 99 Beech Glen Rd., Mars Hill, 689-5515, 1st Sat, gay men seeking to expand spiritual awareness & deepen connection w/ the earth

MCC of Asheville 1 Edwin Pl. (Unitarian Universalist Church), 259-3055 (WC) 6:20pm Sun

Unitarian Universalist Church of Asheville 1 Edwin Pl., 254-6001 (WC) 9am & 11am Sun (10am Sun during summer)

PUBLICATIONS

Community Connections PO Box 18088, 28814, 285-8861/285-9390, monthly

CRUISY AREAS

The Cage blk around federal bldg. (AYOR)

Bat Cave (704)

ACCOMMODATIONS

Old Mill B&B Hwy 74, Box 252, 28710, 625-4256 (GF) full brkfst

Blowing Rock (704)

ACCOMMODATIONS

Stone Pillar B&B 144 Pine St., 295-4141 (GF,WC) full brkfst, historic 1920s house

Boone (704)

SPIRITUAL GROUPS

MCC of the High Country P.O. Box 504, 28607, 963-8582, 7pm Sun

Chapel Hill (see also **Durham** & **Raleigh** listings) (919)

INFO LINES & SERVICES

B-GLAD (Bisexuals, Gay Men, Lesbians & Allies for Diversity) Box 39, Carolina Union CB#5210, 27599, 962-4401, call for events

▲ **Community Real Estate Referrals** (800) 346-5592, gay realtor at your service, no rentals

RESTAURANTS & CAFES

Crooks Corner 610 Franklin St., 929-7643 (WC) 6pm-10:30pm, Sun brunch, Southern cooking, full bar

Weathervane Cafe Eastgate Shopping Center, 929-9466 (WC) lunch & dinner, Sun brunch, New American, patio, full bar

BOOKSTORES & RETAIL SHOPS

Internationalist Books 405 W. Franklin St., 942-1740, 10am-8pm, til 6pm Sun, progressive/alternative, readings, 'Movie Night' Fri

SPIRITUAL GROUPS

Community Church (Unitarian Universalist) 106 Purefoy Rd., 942-2050, 11am Sun

Jewish Gay/Lesbian/Bisexual Student Group 942-4057, call for info

Charlotte (704)

INFO LINES & SERVICES

AA Gay/Lesbian 3200 Park Rd. (St. Luke's Lutheran Church), 332-4387, 8pm Tue

Carolina Bear Lodge P.O. Box 37103, 28237, 529-2891, social group for bears & their admirers

Charlotte Business Guild P.O. Box 35445, 28235-5445, 565-5075, networking group for lesbigay professionals

▲ **Community Real Estate Referrals** (800) 346-5592, gay realtor at your service, no rentals

Gay/Lesbian Switchboard 535-6277, 6:30-10:30pm, info, referrals, crisis counseling

MACT (Men of All Colors Together) PO Box 29061, 28229-9061, 375-6477, 3rd Sat, active social organization

Prime Timers - Charlotte P.O. Box 11202, 28220-1202, 561-2257, 5pm 2nd Sun, social group for mature gay & bisexual men 40 & over

ACCOMMODATIONS

601 Poplar Street B&B 601 N. Poplar St., 358-1464

BARS

1800 West City View 1800 W. Morehead St., 333-9769 (MW,D,MRC-AF,S,PC,WC) 10pm-4am Th-Sun

Brass Rail 3707 Wilkinson Blvd., 399-8413 (★M,NH,L,PC,WC) 5pm-2:30am, from 3pm Sun

Chaser's 3217 The Plaza, 339-0500 (MW,D,S,V,PC,WC) 5pm-2am, from 3pm Sun

Liaisons 316 Rensselaer Ave., 376-1617 (★MW,NH,PC) 4pm-1am

Mythos 300 N. College St., 375-8765 (★GF,D,A,S,PC,WC) 10pm-3am, til 4am wknds, more gay Wed-Th

Oleen's Lounge 1831 S. Blvd., 373-9604 (★MW,D,S,WC) 8pm-2am, from 3pm Sun

Scorpio's Lounge 2301 Freedom Dr., 373-9124 (★MW,D,S,V,PC,WC) 9pm-3:30am, clsd Mon, CW Tue

RESTAURANTS & CAFES

300 East 300 East Blvd., 332-6507, 11am-11pm, New American, some veggie also full bar

521 Cafe 521 N. College, 377-9100 (WC) lunch Tue-Fri, dinner nightly, Italian

Dikadees Front Porch 4329 E. Independence Blvd., 537-3873 (WC) 11am-10pm, til 11pm Fri-Sat, American, full bar

Dilworth Diner 1608 E. Blvd., 333-0137 (WC) 7am-10pm, til 11pm Fri-Sat, 11am-5pm Sun

El Gringo Grill & Cantina 3735 Monroe Rd., 347-4241, lunch Mon-Fri, dinner daily, Mexican, full bar

Lupie's Cafe 2718 Monroe Rd., 374-1232, 11am-11pm, from noon Sat, home-style

BOOKSTORES & RETAIL SHOPS

Paper Skyscraper 330 East Blvd., 333-7130 (WC) 10am-6pm, til 9pm Fri, noon-5pm Sun, books & gifts

Rising Moon Books & Beyond 316 East Blvd., 332-7473 (WC) 10am-6pm, lesbigay & multicultural books

Urban Evolution 1329 East Blvd., 332-8644, 11am-9pm, 1pm-6pm Sun, clothing & more

White Rabbit Books 834 Central Ave.; 377-4067, 11am-9pm, 1-6pm Sun, lesbi-gay, gifts

Travel & Tour Operators
Damron Atlas World Travel/Pink Fairy Travel 1409 East Blvd. Ste 6-A, 28203, 332-5545/(800) 243-3477 (IGTA)

Spiritual Groups
Lutherans Concerned 1900 The Plaza (Holy Trinity Church), 651-4328, 1st Sun

MCC Charlotte 4037 E. Independence Blvd. #300, 563-5810, 10:45am & 7:30pm Sun

New Life MCC 234 N. Sharon Amity Rd. (Unitarian Church), (910) 784-0723, 7pm Sun

Publications
▲ **The Front Page** PO Box 27928, Raleigh , 27611, 829-0181

In Unison PO Box 8024, Columbia SC, 29202, (803) 771-0804

Q Notes PO Box 221841, 28222, (704) 531-9988/531-1361

Erotica
Independence News 3205 The Plaza, 332-8430

Cruisy Areas
Park on Eastway & Shamrock Dr. (AYOR)

Plaza Road (AYOR)

Durham (see also **Chapel Hill** & **Raleigh** listings) (919)

Info Lines & Services
▲ **Community Real Estate Referrals** (800) 346-5592, gay realtor at your service, no rentals

MACT (Men of All Colors Together) Triangle PO Box 3411, 27702, 490-0653, monthly mtgs.

Outright - Triangle Lesbian/Gay Youth PO Box 3203, 27715, 286-2396/(800) 879-2300, 6pm-9pm info & referrals, 2pm Sat mtg.

Steps, Traditions & Promises AA 2109 N. Duke (Christ Lutheran), 286-9499, 7:30pm Tue

Bars
Boxers 5504 Chapel Hill Blvd, 489-7678 (M,A,P,V,YC) from 5pm

Power Company 315 W. Main St., 683-1151 (MW,D,S,PC,WC) 9pm-?

Bookstores & Retail Shops
Regulator Bookshop 720 9th St., 286-2700, 9am-8pm, til 5pm Sun

Erotica
Atlantis Video & News 522 E. Main St., 682-7469

Durham Video & News 502 Lakewood Dr., 489-9945, 24hrs

Elizabethtown (910)

Travel & Tour Operators
North & South Travel 118 W. Broad St., 862-8557/(800) 585-8016

Fayetteville (910)

Bars
Millennium 2540 Gillespie St., 485-2037 (M,D,E,S,PC,WC) 9pm-?, clsd Mon, also sports bar

Spektrum 107 Swain St., 868-4279 (MW,D,S) 5pm-3am, patio

EROTICA
President Video & News 3712 Bragg Blvd., 864-9992, 24hrs
Priscilla's 3800 Sycamore Dairy Rd., 860-1776

Franklin (704)

ACCOMMODATIONS
Honey's Rainbow Acres PO Box 1367, 28734-1367, 369-5162 (W) kitchen privileges, also cabin

Gastonia (704)

TRAVEL & TOUR OPERATORS
Travel By Design 2333 Pine Haven Dr., 864-0631 (IGTA)

EROTICA
321 News & Video 1410 N. Chester St., 866-0075
Gastonia Video & News 414 W. Main, 867-9262, 24hrs

CRUISY AREAS
W. Main St. from Chester St. to Trenton St. (AYOR)

Greensboro (910)

INFO LINES & SERVICES
▲ **Community Real Estate Referrals** (800) 346-5592, gay realtor at your service, no rentals
Gay/Lesbian Hotline PO Box 4442, 27404, 855-8558, 7-10pm Sun, Tue-Th
Lesbian/Gay/Bisexual Resource Center Box 17725 Guilford College, 27410
Live & Let Live AA 2200 N. Elm (St. Pius Catholic Church), 854-4278, 8pm Tue

BARS
Babylon 221 S. Elm St., 275-1006 (★MW,D,A,PC) call for events
The Palms 413 N. Eugene St., 272-6307 (M,D,S,PC) 9pm-2:30am
Warehouse 29 1011 Arnold St., 333-9333 (M,D,E,S,PC) 9pm-3am, clsd Mon-Tue

BOOKSTORES & RETAIL SHOPS
White Rabbit Books 1833 Spring Garden St., 272-7604, 10am-7pm, 1-6pm Sun, lesbigay, gifts

TRAVEL & TOUR OPERATORS
Carolina Travel 2054 Carolina Circle Mall, 621-9000/(800) 289-9009 (IGTA)

SPIRITUAL GROUPS
St. Mary's MCC 6720 W. Friendly Ave., 297-4054, 7pm Sun

EROTICA
Gents Video & News 3722 High Point Rd., 855-9855, 24hrs
New Visions Video 507 Mobile St., 274-6443
Treasure Box Video & News 1203 E. Bessemer, 373-9849, 24hrs

Greenville (919)

BARS
Paddock Club 1008-B Dickinson, 758-0990 (MW,D,A,S,PC,WC) 8pm-2:30am Wed-Sun

Hickory (704)

BARS
Club Cabaret 101 N. Center St., 322-8103 (MW,D,S,PC,WC) 9pm-3am Th-Sun

SPIRITUAL GROUPS
MCC Hickory 109 11th Ave. NW (Unitarian Church), 324-1960, 7pm Sun & Tue

Hot Springs (704)

ACCOMMODATIONS
Deer Park Cabins Hwy. 209, 622-3516 (GF)

The Duckett House Inn Hwy. 209 S., 622-7621 (MW) Victorian farmhouse, vegetarian restaurant

Jacksonville (910)

EROTICA
Priscilla's 113A Western Blvd., 355-0765

Manteo (919)

PUBLICATIONS
Outer Banks GLC PO Box 1444, 27954, 255-2073

Morehead

CRUISY AREAS
Ft. Macon St. Park Beach (AYOR) summers

Raleigh (see also **Chapel Hill** & **Durham** listings) (919)

INFO LINES & SERVICES
AA Gay/Lesbian (Live & Let Live) 1601 Hillsboro St., 783-6144, 8pm

▲ **Community Real Estate Referrals** (800) 346-5592, gay realtor at your service, no rentals

Gay/Lesbian Helpline of Wake County 821-0055, 7-10pm, info, referrals, crisis counseling

ACCOMMODATIONS
Oakwood Inn 411 N. Bloodworth St., 832-9712 (GF) full brkfst

BARS
1622 Club 1622 Glenwood Ave. at Five Points, 832-9082 (MW,D,18+,PC,WC) 8pm-2am, from 5pm Sun, clsd Mon

CC 313 W. Hargett, 755-9599 (M,D,E,18+,PC,WC) 8pm-?, from 4pm Sun, piano bar

▲ **Flex** 2 S. West St., 832-8855 (★M,L) 5pm-?, from 2pm Sun

▲ **Legends** 330 W. Hargett St., 831-8888 (M,D,E,S,YC,PC,WC) 9pm-?, deck, more mixed crowd on wknds

RESTAURANTS & CAFES
Black Dog Cafe 208 E. Martin, 828-1994 (WC) lunch & dinner Wed-Sat, Sun brunch, clsd Mon, American, full bar

Est • Est • Est Trattoria 19 W. Hargett St., 832-8899, 11am-10pm, clsd Sun, pasta, plenty veggie, full bar

Irregardless Cafe 901 W. Morgan St., 833-8898, lunch & dinner, Sun brunch, plenty veggie

Rathskeller 2412 Hillsborough St., 821-5342 (WC) 11am-11pm

BOOKSTORES & RETAIL SHOPS

Innovations 517 Hillsborough St., 833-4833, 11am-7pm, from 1pm Sun, clsd Mon-Tue, leather, fetish wear, piercings

Reader's Corner 3201 Hillsborough St., 828-7024, 10am-9pm, til 6pm Sat, 1-6pm Sun, used books

White Rabbit Books 309 W. Martin St., 856-1429 (WC) 11am-9pm, til 7pm Sat, 1-6pm Sun, lesbigay, gifts

TRAVEL & TOUR OPERATORS

Rainbow Travel 2801 Blue Ridge Rd., 571-9054/(800) 633-9350 (IGTA)

SPIRITUAL GROUPS

Integrity 237-8825, 6pm 2nd Sun, call for location

St. John's MCC 805 Glenwood Ave., 834-2611, 7:15pm Sun

Unitarian Universalist Fellowship 3313 Wade Ave., 781-7635, 9:30am & 11:15am Sun

PUBLICATIONS

▲ **The Front Page** PO Box 27928, Raleigh , 27611, 829-0181

EROTICA

Aphrodite's Adult Entertainment Center 9016 Glenwood Ave., 787- 0016, 24hrs

Capitol Blvd. News 2236 Capitol Blvd., 831-1400

Castle Video & News 1210 Capitol Blvd., 836-9189, 24hrs

Our Place 327 W. Harget, 833-8968

Sanford (919)

EROTICA

Sanford Video & News 667 S. Horner Blvd., 774-9124

Spruce Pine (704)

ACCOMMODATIONS

The Lemon Tree Inn 912 Greenwood Rd., 765-6161 (GF) also Lemon Tree Restaurant

Wilmington (910)

INFO LINES & SERVICES

▲ **Community Real Estate Referrals** (800) 346-5592, gay realtor at your service, no rentals

GROW Switchboard 341-11 S. College Rd. Ste. 182, 28403, 799-7111, 6-10pm, info, counseling, AIDS resource

ACCOMMODATIONS

The Inn on Orange 410 Orange St., 815-0035/(800) 381-4666 (GF,SW,IGTA)

Ocean Princess Inn 824 Ft. Fischer Blvd., South Kure Beach, 458-6712/(800) 762-4863 (GF,SW,WC)

The Taylor House Inn 14 N. 7th St., 763-7581/(800) 382-9982 (GF) full brkfst, romantic 1908 house

BARS

Mickey Ratz 115-117 S. Front St., 251-1289 (MW,D,E,S,PC) 5pm-2:30am

BOOKSTORES & RETAIL SHOPS

Rising Moon Books & Beyond 215-A Princess St., 343-9106 (WC) 10am-6pm, 1pm-5pm Sun, lesbigay & multicultural

CRUISY AREAS
Wrightsville Beach North End (AYOR)

Winston-Salem (910)

INFO LINES & SERVICES
Gay/Lesbian Hotline PO Box 4442, Greensboro, 27404, 855-8558, 7-10pm Sun, Tue-Th

BARS
Bourbon Street 916 Burke St., 724-4644 (MW,D,E,S,PC,WC) 8pm-?, clsd Mon

EROTICA
New Visions Videos 1045 N. Cherry St., 725-8034, also 3061 Kennersville Rd., 788-0020

NORTH DAKOTA

Fargo (218)

INFO LINES & SERVICES
The 10% Society PO Box 266, MSU, Moorhead MN, 56563, (218) 236-2200/236-5859, confidential support group for lesbian/gay/bisexual students

Hotline PO Box 447, 58107, 235-7335, 24hrs, general info hotline (some lesbigay resources)

Prairie Lesbian/Gay Community PO Box 83, Moorhead MN, 56561, 237-0556, info, support & educational network

RESTAURANTS & CAFES
Fargo's Fryn Pan 300 Main St., 293-9952 (★WC) 24hrs

EROTICA
Adult Books & Cinema X 417 NP Ave., 232-9768, 24hrs

CRUISY AREAS
Broadway Broadway (AYOR) nights

Grand Forks (701)

INFO LINES & SERVICES
The UGLC (University Gay/Lesbian Community) Box 8136 University Stn., 58202, 777-4321, educational/social group

EROTICA
Plain Brown Wrapper 102 S. 3rd St., 772-9021, 24hrs

CRUISY AREAS
Island Park nr. pool (AYOR)
South Washington (AYOR)

Mandan (701)

EROTICA
Bookstore of Mandan 116 Main St., 663-9013

Minot (701)

EROTICA
Risque's 1514 S. Broadway, 838-2837

OHIO

Akron (330)

INFO LINES & SERVICES
AA Intergroup 253-8181

▲ **Community Real Estate Referrals** (800) 346-5592, gay realtor at your service, no rentals

BARS
358 Club 358 S. Main, 434-7788 (M) 5pm-2:30am

Adams Street Bar 77 N. Adams St., 434-9794 (★M,D) 4:30pm-2:30am, from 3pm Sat, from 9pm Sun; also Barracks (M,L) 10pm Fri-Sat

Gargoyles 271 S. Main, 384-1447 (MW,D,E) 9pm-3am, clsd Tue, strippers

Interbelt 70 N. Howard St., 253-5700 (M,D,S,V) 9pm-2:30am, clsd Tue & Th

Tear-Ez 360 S. Main, 376-0011 (M,NH,S,WC) 11am-2:30am

RESTAURANTS & CAFES
Cheryl's Daily Grind 1662 Merriman Rd., 869-9980, 6:30am-7pm, til 9pm Th, til 11pm Fri-Sat, 8am-3pm Sun

The Sandwich Board 1667 W. Market St., 867-5442, 11am-8pm, clsd Sun

TRAVEL & TOUR OPERATORS
Parkside Travel 3310 Kent Rd. Ste. 6, Stow, 688-3334/(800) 552-1647 (IGTA)

SPIRITUAL GROUPS
Cascade Community Church 1196 Inman St., 773-5298, 2pm Sun

New Hope Temple 1215 Kenmore Blvd., 745-5757, 10am & 7pm Sun, 7pm Wed

PUBLICATIONS
Gay People's Chronicle PO Box 5426, Cleveland, 44101, 631-8646

MEN'S CLUBS
Akron Steam & Sauna 41 S. Case, 784-0777 (MO,PC)

Amherst (216)

INFO LINES & SERVICES
Gay/Lesbian Info Center 150 Foster Park Rd. (Deca Realty Bldg. lower level), 988-5326/(800) 447-7163, drop-in 6pm-9pm Wed

Athens (614)

INFO LINES & SERVICES
Open Doors (Gay/Lesbian/Bisexual Assoc.) 18 N. College St. OU, 594-2385, mostly students

Canton (216)

BARS
540 Club 540 Walnut Ave. NE, 456-8622 (M,D,S,YC,WC) 9pm-2:30am, clsd Sun-Mon

Boardwalk 1127 W. Tuscarawas, 453-8000 (M,D,S,WC) 5pm-2:30am

Dar's Bar 1120 W. Tuscarawas, 454-9128 (MW,D) 9pm-2:30am

La Casa Lounge 508 Cleveland Ave. NW, 453-7432 (M,NH,WC) 10am-2:30am

EROTICA
Market Street News 440 Market St., 453-1275

Tower Bookstore 219 12th St. NE, 455-1254

Cincinnati (513)

INFO LINES & SERVICES

AA Gay/Lesbian 861-9966

Alternating Currents WAIF FM 88.3, 333-9243/961-8900, 3pm Sat, lesbigay public affairs radio program

Cincinnati Youth Group PO Box 19852, 45219, 684-8405/(800) 347-8336, 24hrs info, mtg 6pm Sun

▲ **Community Real Estate Referrals** (800) 346-5592, gay realtor at your service, no rentals

Gay/Lesbian Community Switchboard 651-0070, 6pm-11pm Sun-Fri, clsd holidays

People of All Colors Together P.O. Box 140856, 45250, 395-7228

ACCOMMODATIONS

Prospect Hill B&B 408 Boal St., 421-4408 (GF,IGTA) gay owned

BARS

Chasers 2640 Glendora, 861-3966 (MW,D,E) 7pm-2:30am, clsd Mon

The Dock 603 W. Pete Rose Wy., 241-5623 (★MW,D,E,S,WC) 4pm-2:30am, from 8pm Mon, volleyball court

Golden Lions 340 Ludlow, 281-4179 (M,NH,D,E,S,OC) 4pm-2:30am

Plum St. Pipeline 241 W. Court, 241-5678 (★M,NH,S,V) 4pm-2:30am

Shooters 927 Race St., 381-9900 (M,D,CW) 4pm-2:30am, lessons 8:30pm Tue & Th

Simon Says 428 Walnut, 381-7577 (★M,NH,WC) 11am-2:30am, from 1pm Sun

Spurs 326 E.8th St., 621-2668 (★M,L,WC) 4pm-2:30am

The Subway 609 Walnut St., 421-1294 (M,NH,D,E,F,S) 6am-2:30am, from noon Sun

RESTAURANTS & CAFES

Carol's Corner Cafe 825 Main St., 651-2667 (★WC) 11am-1am (bar til 2:30am)

Kaldi's Cafe & Books 1204 Main St., 241-3070 (E,WC) 10am-1am, from 10am wknds

Mullane's 723 Race St., 381-1331 (BW,WC) 11:30am-11pm, from 5pm Sat, clsd Sun

BOOKSTORES & RETAIL SHOPS

Fountain Square News 101 E. 5th St., 421-4049, 7:30am-6:30pm

LeftHanded Moon 48 E. Court St., 784-1166, 11:30am-7pm, clsd Sun

Pink Pyramid 36-A W. Court, 621-7465, 11am-10:30pm, til midnight Fri-Sat, clsd Sun, lesbigay

TRAVEL & TOUR OPERATORS

Apache Travel 5017 Cooper Rd., 793-5522, ask for Laura

Victoria Travel 3330 Erie Ave., 871-1100/(800) 626-4932 (IGTA) ask for Dan

SPIRITUAL GROUPS

Integrity /Greater Cincinnati 65 E. Hollister (church), 242-7297, 6:30pm 3rd Mon

PUBLICATIONS

The Ohio Word 225 E. N. St. Tower 1 Ste. 2800, Indianapolis IN, 46204, (317) 579-3075, also publish Kentucky Word

Cleveland (216)

INFO LINES & SERVICES

AA Gay/Lesbian 241-7387

Buckeye Rainbow Society for the Deaf PO Box 6253, 44101

BWMT (Black/White Men Together) PO Box 5144, 44101, 371-4597

Cleveland Lesbian/Gay Community Center 1418 W. 29th St., 522-1999 (WC) 1pm-5pm Mon-Fri

Cleveland Lesbian/Gay Hotline 781-6736, recorded info 24hrs

▲ **Community Real Estate Referrals** (800) 346-5592, gay realtor at your service, no rentals

GLOWS (Gay/Lesbian Older Wiser Seniors) 331-6302, 7:30pm 2nd Tue

BARS

Barnaby Lane 2619 Noble Rd., Cleveland Hts., 382-2033 (MW,F) 3pm-1am, clsd Sun

Club Visions 1229 W.6th , 566-0060 (★M,D,S,WC) 4:30pm-2:30am, til 4am Fri, from 6pm Sat

The Grid 1281 W.9th, 623-0113 (★MW,NH,D) 4pm-2:30am

▲ **Leather Stallion Saloon** 2205 St. Clair Ave., 589-8588 (★MO,L,P,K,V) open 3pm, from 1pm Sun(DJ)

Legends 11719 Detroit, Lakewood, 226-1199 (★M,D,K) 11am-2:30am, from 7pm Sun

Memoirs 11213 Detroit Ave., 221-8576 (★M,NH,D,S) 10am-2:30am

MJ's Place 11633 Lorain Ave., 476-1970 (★M,NH,K,P) 4pm-2:30am Mon-Sat, "the gay Cheers"

Muggs 3194 W.25th St., 661-5365 (MW,NH,F) noon-2:30am

Numbers Nite Club 620 Frankfort, 621-6900 (★M,D,MRC,S,V,YC,WC)

Ohio City Oasis 2909 Detroit Ave. (at 29th St.), 574-2203 (M,L) 8am-2:30am, from noon Sun, CW Sun

Paradise Inn 4488 State Rd. (Rte.94), 741-9819 (MW,NH) 11am-2:30am

▲ **Rockies Bar** 9208 Detroit Rd., 961-3115 (★MO,D,V) 4pm-2:30am, Cleveland's only Sun T-dance

Tomahawk 11217 Detroit Ave., 521-5443 (M,NH) 4pm-2:30am

Too's Attraxxions 6757 W. 130th St., Parma Hts., 842-0020 (MW,D)

U4ia 10630 Berea Rd., 631-7111 (★MW,D,S,WC) 9:30pm-2:30am Fri & Sun, til 4am Sat

Restaurants & Cafes

Billy's on Clifton 11100 Clifton Blvd., 281-7722, 11am-9pm, clsd Mon

Cafe Tandoor 2096 S.Taylor Rd., Cleveland Hts., 371-8500/371-8569, lunch & dinner, Indian

Club Isabella 2025 University Hospital Rd., 229-1177 (E) lunch & dinner, dinner only Sat, clsd Sun, Italian, live jazz

Fulton Ave. Cafe 1835 Fulton Ave., 522-1835 (NH) 4pm-2:30am, from 8pm wknds

The Inn on Coventry 2785 Euclid Heights Blvd., Cleveland Hts., 371-1811, 7am-9pm, 9am-3pm Sun

Lonesome Dove Cafe 3093 Mayfield Rd., 397-9100, 7am-6pm

Patisserie Baroque 1112 Kenilworth Ave., 861-1881, 8am-6pm, til 7pm Fri, from 10am Sat, clsd Sun-Mon

Red Star Cafe 11604 Detroit Ave., 521-7827 (MW,WC) 7am-11pm, til 1am Fri-Sat

Snickers 1261 W. 76th St., 631-7555 (WC) noon-10pm, 4pm-11pm Sat

Bookstores & Retail Shops

Bank News 4025 Clark, 281-8777, 10:30am-8:30pm, clsd Sun

Body Language 3291 W. 115th St. (at Lorian), 251-3330, noon-9pm, til 5pm Sun, "an educational store for adults in alternative lifestyles"

Bookstore on W. 25th St. 1921 W. 25th St., 566-8897, 10am-6pm, noon-5pm Sun, lesbigay section

Borders Bookshop & Espresso Bar 2101 Richmond Rd., Beachwood, 292-2660, 9am-10pm, 11am-midnight Fri-Sat, 11am-9pm Sun

The Clifton Web 11512 Clifton Rd., 961-1120, 10am-9pm, noon-5pm Sun

Daily Planet News 1842 Coventry Rd., 321-9973 (WC) 6:30am-10pm

Travel & Tour Operators

Flite II 23611 Chagrin Blvd., Beachwood, 464-1762/(800) 544-3881

Green Road Travel 2111 S. Green Rd., South Euclid, 381-8060

Playhouse Square Travel 1160 Henna Bldg./1422 Euclid Ave., 575-0813/(800) 575-0813 (IGTA)

Sun Lovers' Cruises & Travel 3860 Rocky River Rd., 252-0900/(800) 323-1362 (IGTA)

University Circle Travel 11322 Euclid Ave., 721-9500/(800) 925-2339

Spiritual Groups

Chevrei Tikva PO Box 18120, Cleveland Hts., 44118, 932-5551, 8pm 1st & 3rd Fri, lesbigay synagogue

Integrity-NE Ohio 18001 Detroit (St. Peter's Church), 671-4946

Publications

Gay People's Chronicle PO Box 5426, 44101, 631-8646

A Traveler's Dream

THE
CLUB
Cleveland

**One Day Memberships • Deluxe Suites
Free Parking • In/Out Privileges
Centrally Located • Tanning
Videos • Steam • Sauna • Whirlpool
Sundeck • Fully Equipped Gym**

**1448 West 32nd Street
Cleveland, Ohio 44113
216-961-2727**

MEN'S CLUBS

▲ **The Club Cleveland** 1448 W. 32nd St., 961-2727 (★MO,PC) 24hrs, steam, sauna, whirlpool, gym

▲ **Flex** 1293 W.9th, 696-0595 (MO,V,PC) 24hrs, lounge, see ad center national section

EROTICA

Brookpark News & Books 16700 Brookport Rd., 267-9019, 24hrs

Hide Park Leather 15521 Detroit Ave., Lakewood, 529-9699, clsd Mon

Laws Leather Shop 11112 Clifton Blvd, 961-0544, 2pm-10pm, clsd Mon-Tue

Park Books 1813 E. 13th St., 621-6545

Rocky's Entertainment & Emporium 13330 Brookpark Rd., 267-4936, 24hrs

Columbus (614)

INFO LINES & SERVICES

AA Gay/Lesbian 253-8501

Columbus Ursine Brotherhood P.O. Box 16822, 43216, 6pm 1st Sat at Tradewinds bar, social group for bears

▲ **Community Real Estate Referrals** (800) 346-5592, gay realtor at your service, no rentals

Crystal Club P.O. Box 287, Reynoldsburg, 4th Sat, transgender social group

Dragon Leather Club P.O. Box 06417, 43206, 258-7100, pansexual leather group

Gay/Lesbian/Bi Alliance of OSU 340 Ohio Union, 1739 N.High St., 292-6200

Nosotros 292-6200, lesbigay Latino social group

Stonewall Union Hotline/Community Ctr. 1160 N. High St., 299-7764 (WC) 10am-7pm, 9am-5pm Fri, clsd wknds

ACCOMMODATIONS

Columbus Bed & Breakfast 769 S. 3rd St., 444-8888 (GF) referral service for German Village district

Five Forty-Two B&B 542 Mohawk St., 621-1741 (GF)

The Gardener's House 556 Frebis Ave., 444-5445 (MW) hot tub, cont'l brkfst

Summit Lodge Resort & Guesthouse PO Box 951-D, Logan, 43138, 385-3521 (★M,F,SW,N) camping available, hot tub & sauna

BARS

Club 20 20 E. Duncan, 261-9111 (M,NH,S) 4pm-2:30am, from 11am Sat, patio

Club Deion 313 S. Fifth St., 221-2804 (MW,D,MRC-AF)

Columbus Eagle Bar 232 N. 3rd St., 228-2804 (★M,D,L,WC) 5pm-2:30am, also 'The Eagle's Nest' inside

Downtown Connection 1126 N. High St., 299-4880 (M,NH) 3pm-2:30am, sports bar

Eagle in Exile (Patrick's) 893 N. 4th St., 294-0069 (M,NH,L,WC) 9pm-2:30am Wed-Sat, strict dress code

The Far Side 1662 W. Mound St., 276-5817 (MW,NH) 5pm-1am, til 2:30am Fri-Sat, from 1pm Sun

Garage Disco (at Trends Bar), 461-0076 (★MW,D,A) 9pm-2:30am

Garrett's Saloon 1071 Parsons Ave., 449-2351 (M,NH) 11am-2:30am

Havana Video Lounge 862 N. High, 421-9697 (MW,NH,V,WC) opens 4pm, 3pm Sun, piano bar

Herby's Tavern 349 Marconi Blvd., 464-2270, 1pm-2:30am

Imagination Too 283 E. Spring St., 224-2407 (GF,D)

A Traveler's Dream

THE
CLUB
Columbus

One Day Memberships · Deluxe Suites
Free Parking · In/Out Privileges
Centrally Located to Nightclubs
Videos · Steam · Sauna · Whirpool
Outdoor Pool & Patio · Tanning
Fully Equipped Gym

777 West River Street
Columbus, OH 43215
Call Info. for Telephone Num

Le Tremont 708 S. High St., 445-9365 (M,NH,S) 10am-2:30pm, 1pm-midnight Sun

Outland 1034 Perry St., 299-0300 (MW,NH) 6am-2:30am

The Red Dog 196-1/2 E. Gay St. (rear), 224-7779 (M,S,WC) 4pm-2:30am

Remo's 1409 S. High St., 443-4224 (MW,NH,F,WC) 10am-2:30am, clsd Sun

Slammers Pizza Pub 202 E. Long St., 469-7526 (MW,K,WC) 11am-2:30am, from 2:30pm wknds

Tradewinds II 117 E. Chestnut, 461-4110 (M,D,WC) 4pm-2:30am, clsd Mon, 3 bars

Trends 40 E. Long St., 461-0076 (★M,D,WC) 5pm-2:30am

Wall Street 144 N. Wall St., 464-2800 (★W,D,S,YC,WC) 6pm-2:30am, clsd Mon, more men Wed

Restaurants & Cafes

Clubhouse Cafe 124 E. Main, 228-5090 (MW) 4pm-1am, clsd Mon

Common Grounds 2549 Indianola Ave., 263-7646, 9am-midnight, til 11pm Sun, from 4pm Mon

Grapevine Cafe 73 E. Gay St., 221-8463 (MW,E,WC) 5pm-1am, clsd Mon

King Ave. Coffeehouse 247 King Ave., 294-8287 (★) 11am-11pm, clsd Mon, funky bohemian crowd, no alcohol

L'Antibes 772 N. High St. (at Warren), 291-1666 (WC) dinner from 5pm, clsd Sun-Mon, French

Out on Main 122 E. Main, 470-1810/(888) 688-6246 (E,WC) 5pm-10pm, til 11pm Fri-Sat, from 1pm Sun, clsd Mon

Gyms & Health Clubs

Ironworks Gym 384 Dublin Ave., 221-4766

Bookstores & Retail Shops

ACME Art Company 737 N. High St., 299-4003, 1pm-7pm Wed-Sat, alternative art space, Cafe Ashtray Fri

An Open Book 749 N. High St., 291-0080 (WC) 11am-10pm, from 10am Sat, til 6pm Sun, lesbigay

The Book Loft of German Village 631 S. 3rd St., 464-1774, 10am-midnight, lesbigay

Hausfrau Haven 769 S. 3rd St., 443-3680, 10am-6:30pm, til 5pm Sun, greetings cards, wine & gifts

Kukala's Tanning & Tees 636 N. High St., 228-8337, 11am-8pm, til 6pm wknds, from noon wknds, lesbigay novelties & gifts

M.J. Originals 745 N. High St., 291-2787, 11am-7pm, til 6pm Sat, 1pm-5pm Sun

Travel & Tour Operators

Just Travel, Inc. 82 S. High St., Dublin, 791-9500/(800) 622-8660 (IGTA) ask for Paul

Ohio Division of Travel & Tourism (800) 282-5393

Travelplex East 555 OffiCenter Pl. Ste. 100, 337-3155/(800) 837-9909 (IGTA)

Spiritual Groups

Integrity/Columbus P.O. Box 292625, 43229, 237-2844

Jewish Group P.O. Box 06119, 43206, informal Shabbat dinners

New Creation MCC 787 E. Broad St., 224-0314, 10:30am Sun

Publications

The Stonewall Union Journal P.O. Box 10814, 43201, 299-7764

MEN'S CLUBS
▲ **The Club Columbus** 777 W. River St. (PC)

EROTICA
Bexley Art Theater & Video 2484 E. Main St., 235-2341

Diablo Body Piercing 636 N. High St., 228-8337, clsd Tue

I.M.R.U. 235 N. Lazelle (above Eagle Bar), 228-9660, 11:30pm-2am Fri-Sat, leather

North Campus Video 2465 High St., 268-4021, 24hrs

Zodiac 1565 Alum Creek Dr., 252-0281, 24hrs

Dayton (513)

INFO LINES & SERVICES
AA Gay/Lesbian 222-2211

▲ **Community Real Estate Referrals** (800) 346-5592, gay realtor at your service, no rentals

Dayton Lesbian/Gay Center & Hotline 1424 W. Dorothy Ln., 274-1776, 7pm-11pm (hotline), center open 6:30pm Wed, coffeehouse 8pm Fri

Youth Quest PO Box 9343, 45409, 275-8336, lesbigay youth group 22 & under

BARS
1470 West 1470 W. Dorothy Ln., Kettering, 293-0066 (★MW,D,S,V,WC) 8:30pm-2:30am, til 5am Fri-Sat, clsd Mon-Tue

Asylum 605 S. Patterson Blvd., 228-8828 (GF,D,A,18+) 9pm-?, clsd Sun-Mon

Dugout 619 Salem Ave., 274-2394 (MW,NH,D,F) 10am-2:30am

The Edge 1227 Wilmington, 294-0713 (M,D,WC) 5pm-2:30am, clsd Sun, CW Tue, HiNRG Fri-Sat

Jessie's After Dark 121 N. Ludlow, 223-2582 (★M,D,F,K,WC) 3pm-2:30am

Right Corner 105 E. 3rd St., 228-1285 (M,NH,WC) noon-2:30am

Rustic Cabin 2320 Wilmington Pike, Kettering, 253-7691 (M,NH,WC) 5pm-2:30am

Stage Door 44 N. Jefferson, 223-7418 (M,MRC-AF) noon-2:30am, from 4pm wknds

BOOKSTORES & RETAIL SHOPS
Books & Co. 350 E. Stroop Rd., 298-6540, 9am-11pm

Q Giftshop 121 N. Ludlow St., 223-4438, 10pm-1am, til 2:30am Fri, til 3am Sat

SPIRITUAL GROUPS
Community Gospel Church 546 Xenia Ave., 252-8855, 10am Sun, 7:30pm Wed

MCC 1630 E. 5th St. (at McClure), 228-4031, 10am & 6:30pm Sun

PUBLICATIONS
The Ohio Word 225 E. N. St. Tower 1 Ste. 2800, Indianapolis IN, 46204, (317) 579-3075

Rightfully Proud PO Box 3032, 45401-3032, 274-1616

Erie (216)

BARS
Leeward Lounge 1022 Bridge St., Ashtabula, (216) 964-9935 (MW,F) 8pm-2:30am

Findlay (419)

EROTICA
Findlay Adult Books & Video 623 Trenton Ave., 422-1301, 24hrs

CRUISY AREAS
Riverside Park (AYOR)

Fremont (419)

BARS
Saloon Bar 531 W. State, 334-9340 (M,NH) 1pm-2:30am, from 4pm wknds, clsd Mon

Glenford (614)

ACCOMMODATIONS
Springhill Farm Resort 5704 Highpoint Rd., 43739-9727, 659-2364 (W,SW) cabins & restored barn

Kent (216)

INFO LINES & SERVICES
Kent Lesbian/Gay/Bisexual Union KSU, 672-2068

RESTAURANTS & CAFES
The Zephyr 106 W. Main St., 678-4848 (E,WC) 8am-9pm, from 9am wknds, clsd Mon

Lima (419)

BARS
Alternatives 138 W. 3rd St., Mansfield, 522-0044, 7pm-2:30am, from 8pm Sun, clsd Mon
Somewhere In Time 804 W. North St., 227-7288 (MW,D,S) 7pm-2:30am, from 8pm Fri-Sat

Logan (614)

ACCOMMODATIONS
Spring Wood Hocking Hills Cabins 15 miles NW of Logan, 385-2042 (MW,WC)

Lorain (216)

BARS
Nite Club 2223 Broadway, 245-6319 (M,NH,D,E,WC) 8pm-2:30am, from 3pm Sun

Mentor (216)

INFO LINES & SERVICES
Hugs East PO Box 253, 44061, 974-8909, 7pm Wed social group, 24hrs referrals

Niles (216)

EROTICA
Niles Books 5970 Youngstown Rd., 544-3755, 24hrs

Oberlin (216)

INFO LINES & SERVICES
Oberlin Lesbian/Gay/Bisexual Union Wilder Rm. 202 (Box 88), 44074, 775-8179

Oxford (513)

INFO LINES & SERVICES
Miami University Gay/Lesbian/Bisexual Alliance 529-3823

Portsmouth (614)

ACCOMMODATIONS
1835 House B&B 353-1856 (MW,SW) cont'l brkfst

Sandusky (419)

BARS
X-Centricities 306 W. Water St., 624-8118 (MW,D,S) 4pm-2:30pm, from 1pm wknds (winter)

BOOKSTORES & RETAIL SHOPS
City News 139 Columbus Ave., 626-1265, 7am-5:30pm

CRUISY AREAS
Boeckling Boat Dock (AYOR)

Springfield (513)

BARS
Chances 1912 Edwards Ave., 324-0383 (GF,D,E) 8:30pm-2:30am, clsd Tue, patio

CRUISY AREAS
Clarence J. Brown Resevoir Beach (AYOR)

Steubenville (614)

EROTICA
Steubenville News 426 Market St., 282-5842

Toledo (419)

INFO LINES & SERVICES
AA Gay/Lesbian 472-8242
▲ **Community Real Estate Referrals** (800) 346-5592, gay realtor at your service, no rentals
Pro Toledo Info Line 472-2364, 4pm-11pm
Silver Owls PO Box 1388, 43603, 242-9057, 8pm last Sat, social group for men

BARS
Blu Jean Cafe 3606 Sylvania Ave., 474-0690 (★MW,F,E,K) 4pm-2:30am
▲ **Bretz** 2012 Adams St., 243-1900 (★MW,D,A,S,V) 4pm-2:30am, til 4:30am Fri-Sat, clsd Mon-Tue
Caesar's Show Bar 133 N. Erie St., 241-5140 (MW,D,S,WC) 8pm-2:30am Th-Sun
Hooterville Station 119 N. Erie St., 241-9050 (M,D,L,WC) 5:30am-2:30am
"R" House 5534 Secor Rd., 474-2929 (M,D) 2pm-2:30am, patio
Rustler Saloon 4023 Monroe St. (rear entrance), 472-8278 (M) 2pm-2:30am

RESTAURANTS & CAFES
Sufficient Grounds 3160 Markway (Cricket West Mall), 537-1988 (WC) 7am-11pm

BOOKSTORES & RETAIL SHOPS
Thackeray's 3301 W. Central Ave., 537-9259 (WC) 9am-9pm, 10am-6pm Sun

TRAVEL & TOUR OPERATORS
Great Ways Travel 4625 W. Bancroft, 536-8000/(800) 729-9297 (IGTA)

Toledo Travel Club 4612 Talmadge Rd., 471-2820/(800) 860-2820 (IGTA)

SPIRITUAL GROUPS
MCC Good Samaritan 720 W. Deleware., 244-2124, 11am Sun, (10am summers)

MEN'S CLUBS
Diplomat Health Club 1313 N.Summit, 255-3700 (PC) 24hrs

EROTICA
Adult Pleasures 4404 N. Detroit, 476-4587, 24hrs

Tremont (216)

BARS
Hi & Dry Inn 2207 W. 11th St., 621-6166 (MW,NH,F) 4pm-2am

Warren (216)

BARS
The Alley 441 E. Market St., 394-9483 (MW,D,S,WC) 2pm-2:30am
The Crazy Duck 121 Pine St. SE, 394-3825 (★MW,D,18+,WC) 4pm-2:30am
The Purple Onion 136 Pine St., 399-2097 (MW,NH,D,S) noon-2:30am, patio

Wooster

INFO LINES & SERVICES
Lambda Wooster Box C-3166, College of Wooster, 44691

Yellow Springs (513)

INFO LINES & SERVICES
Gay/Lesbian Center Antioch College, 767-7331x601

RESTAURANTS & CAFES
Winds Cafe & Bakery 215 Xenia Ave., 767-1144 (WC)

BOOKSTORES & RETAIL SHOPS
Epic Bookshop 232 Xenia Ave., 767-7997, 10am-6pm, til 9pm Fri, noon-6pm Sun

Youngstown

INFO LINES & SERVICES
PACT (People of All Colors Together) P.O. Box 1131, 44501

BARS
Phil's Place 10 E. La Clede, 782-6991 (W,NH,WC) 4pm-2:30am, patio
Sophies 2 E. LaClede, 782-8080 (MW,NH) 4pm-2:30am
Troubadour 2622 Market St. (enter back lot), 788-4379 (MW,D,S,WC) 9pm-2:30am
Uptown Book Store 2597 Market St., 783-2533

OKLAHOMA

Claremore (918)

TRAVEL & TOUR OPERATORS
International Tours of Claremore 608 W. Will Rogers Blvd., 341-6866 (IGTA)

El Reno (405)

ACCOMMODATIONS
The Good Life RV Resort Exit 108 I-40, 1/4 mile S., 884-2994 (GF,SW) campsites & RV hookups

Enid

CRUISY AREAS
Meadowlake Park N. side (AYOR)

Lawton (405)

BARS
Triangles 8-1/2 N 2nd St., 351-0620 (MW,NH,D,S,WC) 9pm-2am, clsd Mon-Tue

CRUISY AREAS
The Strip hitchikers on Ft. Sill Blvd. nr. Cache Rd. (AYOR)

Norman

CRUISY AREAS
Lions & Reavers Parks (AYOR)
White St. nr. OU (AYOR)

Oklahoma City (405)

INFO LINES & SERVICES
AA Live & Let Live 3405 N. Villa, 947-3834, noon, 5:30pm & 8pm
▲ **Community Real Estate Referrals** (800) 346-5592, gay realtor at your service, no rentals
Gay/Lesbian Outreach 4400 N. Lincoln, Oklahoma City , 425-0399, counseling for HIV, substance abuse, support groups for youth, more
Oasis Resource Center 2135 NW 39th St., 525-2437, 7pm-10pm, til midnight Fri-Sat

ACCOMMODATIONS
America's Crossroads B&B PO Box 270642, 73137, 495-1111, reservation service for private homes
▲ **Habana Inn** 2200 NW 39th St., 528-2221 (★MW,SW,WC) also bars & restaurant on premises

BARS
Angles 2117 NW 39th St., 524-3431 (★MW,D,WC) 9pm-2am, clsd Mon-Tue
Bunkhouse 2800 NW 39th St., 943-0843 (★MW,CW,L,E,S,WC) 1pm-2am, til 4am Fri-Sat (restaurant 5-10pm)
▲ **Copa** at Habana Inn Complex, 525-0730 (MW,D,S,WC) 9pm-2am
Coyote Club 2120 NW 39th St., 521-9533 (W,D,WC) 5pm-2am, from 3pm Sun, clsd Mon-Tue
▲ **Finish Line** (at Habana Inn), 525-0730 (MW,D,CW,WC) noon-2am
Hi-Lo Club 1221 NW 50th St., 843-1722 (MW,NH,S) noon-2am
Levi's 2807 NW 36th St., 947-5384 (M,D,L,WC) noon-2am, patio
Park 2125 NW 39th St., 528-4690 (M,D,WC) 5pm-2am, from 3pm Sun, patio
Roadhouse 4801 N. Lincoln Rd., 525-8585/(800) 457-2582 (MW,NH,D,WC) 4pm-2am, 4 bar complex
Tramps 2201 NW 39th St., 521-9080 (★M,D,WC) noon-2am, from 10am wknds
Tropical Heat 2805 NW 36th, 948-0572 (W) 5pm-2am, from 3pm wknds, clsd Mon-Tue, Sun brunch
Wreck Room 2127 NW 39th St., 525-7610 (★MW,D,S,18+) 9pm-? Fri-Sat, juice bar

RESTAURANTS & CAFES
Grateful Bean Cafe 1039 Walker, 236-3503 (E) 8am-5pm, til midnight Fri, 10am-2am Sun

Gusher's Restaurant 2200 NW 39th Expressway, 528-2221 x-411 (WC) 11am-10:30pm, from 7am-3:30am Fri & Sat, at Habana Inn Complex

The Patio Cafe 5100 N. Classen, 842-7273, 7am-2pm

The Pinon Cafe 2124 NW 39th St., 521-9202 (★MW,WC) 5pm-3am, from 11am Th-Sun, clsd Mon

BOOKSTORES & RETAIL SHOPS
Ziggyz 4005 N. Pennsylvania, 521-9999

TRAVEL & TOUR OPERATORS
Oklahoma Traveler Information (800) 652-6552

SPIRITUAL GROUPS
Dignity & Integrity NW 19th & Portland (Lighthouse MCC), 636-4388, 7:30pm 2nd & 4th Tue

Lighthouse MCC 3629 NW 19th, 942-2822, 10:30am Sun, 7:30pm Wed

Oklahoma City Religious Society of Friends (Quakers) 312 SE 25th St., 631-4174, 10am Sun

PUBLICATIONS
Gayly Oklahoman PO Box 60930, 73146, 528-0800

EROTICA
Jungle Red (at Habana Inn), 524-5733 (WC) novelties, leather

Naughty & Nice 3121 SW 29th, 686-1110, 24hrs

CRUISY AREAS
Penn Square (AYOR)

Trosper Park (AYOR)

Shawnee

CRUISY AREAS
Shawnee Reservoir (AYOR)

Stillwater (405)

INFO LINES & SERVICES
Lesbigay Community Assoc. of OSU Student Union 040, Box 601, 74078, 744-5252

BARS
Snuffy's 2106 S. Main St., 743-3659 (M,D) 6pm-2am, from noon wknds, clsd Mon-Tue

Tulsa (918)

INFO LINES & SERVICES
▲ **Community Real Estate Referrals** (800) 346-5592, gay realtor at your service, no rentals

Gay Info Line/TOHR PO Box 52729, 74152, 743-4297, 8pm-10pm

LesBiGay Alliance (at Tulsa University), 583-9780

Rainbow Business Guild 665-5174

T.U.L.S.A. (Tulsa Uniform/Leather Seekers Assoc.) 838-1222

Tulsa Area Prime Timers PO Box 52118, 74128, gay/bisexual men over 40

BARS
Bamboo Lounge 7204 E. Pine, 832-1269 (M,NH,WC) 11am-2am

Concessions 3340 S. Peoria, 744-0896 (★MW,D,S,WC) 9pm-2am, clsd Mon-Wed

Lola's 2630 E. 15th, 749-1563 (MW,NH,S) 4pm-2am, from 2pm wknds

▲ **Renegade/The Rainbow Room** 1649 S. Main St., 585-3405 (★MW,NH,S,WC) 2pm-2am, Rainbow Room from 10pm, clsd Sun-Mon, patio

Silver Star Saloon 1565 S. Sheridan, 834-4234 (MW,D,CW,WC) 7pm-2am, clsd Mon-Tue

The Tool Box 1338 E. 3rd, 584-1308 (M,D,CW,WC) noon-2am

RESTAURANTS & CAFES

Java Dave's 1326 E. 15th St. (Lincoln Plaza), 592-3317, 7am-11pm

Samson & Deliah 10 E. 5th St., 585-2221, 11am-2pm, 5pm-10pm Fri-Sat, French gourmet

Wild Fork 1820 Utica Square, 742-0712 (WC) 7am-10pm, clsd Sun, Novelle American

SPIRITUAL GROUPS

Dignity-Integrity 5635 E.71st St. (church), 298-4648, 5pm 2nd Sat

Family of Faith MCC 5451-E S. Mingo, 622-1441

MCC of Greater Tulsa 1623 N. Maplewood, 838-1715, 10:45am Sun, 7pm Wed

PUBLICATIONS

Tulsa Family News PO Box 4140, 74159, 583-1248

EROTICA

Adult Video Dreamland 8807 E. Admiral, 834-1051, 24hrs

Elite Bookstore 814 S. Sheridan Rd., 838-8503, 24hrs

Midtown Theatre 319 E. 3rd St., 584-3112, 24hrs

Whittier News Stand 1 N. Lewis St., 592-0767, 24hrs)

When Visiting TULSA New Age

RENEGADE

And The

Rainbow Room

Lounge

Shows Saturdays 11pm

17th & Main Downtown Tulsa

(918)585-3405

"Serving Our Community Since 1989"

OREGON

Ashland (503)

ACCOMMODATIONS

Country Willows B&B Inn 1313 Clay St., 488-1590/(800) 945-5697 (GF,SW) full brkfst

Rogues Inn 600 E. Main St., 482-4770/(800) 276-4837 (GF) apts.

Rose Cottage 272 N. 1st St., (805) 684-5963 (MW) open April-Sept

The Royal Carter House 514 Siskiyou Blvd., 482-5623/(800) 460-9053 (GF,SW) full brkfst

Will's Reste 298 Hargadine St., 97520, 482-4394 (MW) spa

BARS

Cook's Playbill Club 66 E. Main St., 488-4626 (GF,D,E,WC) 5pm-2am, more gay Th-Sat

RESTAURANTS & CAFES

Ashland Bakery/Cafe 38 East Main, 482-2117 (WC) 7am-8pm

BOOKSTORES & RETAIL SHOPS

Bloomsbury Books 290 E. Main St., 488-0029, 8am-10pm, from 9am Sat, 10am-9pm Sun

Astoria (503)

ACCOMMODATIONS

Rosebriar Hotel 636 14th St., 325-7427/(800) 487-0224 (GF,WC) upscale classic hotel, full brkfst

Aurora (503)

ACCOMMODATIONS

Eden Gardens B&B 14720 Albers Way NE, 678-5420

Baker City

INFO LINES & SERVICES

Lambda Eastern Oregon Association Box 382, 97814, monthly mtgs.

Bend (541)

INFO LINES & SERVICES

Beyond the Closet PO Box 9174, 97708, 317-8966

Out & About PO Box 8427, 97701, 388-2395, sponsors socials & potlucks, newsletter

RESTAURANTS & CAFES

Cafe Paradiso 945 NW Bond St., 385-5931, 8am-11pm, til midnight wknds

Royal Blend 1075 NW Newport, 383-0873, 7am-7pm

BOOKSTORES & RETAIL SHOPS

Curiosity Shoppe & Juice Bar 140 NW Minnesota, 382-3408

CRUISY AREAS

Sawyer Park (AYOR) evenings

Corvallis (541)

INFO LINES & SERVICES
After 8 Club 101 NW 23rd, 752-8157, mtgs. 7pm 2nd Tue, lesbigay educational & support group

Lesbian/Gay/Bisexual Student Alliance-OSU 249 Snell, Memorial Union East, 737-6360, 7pm Mon at Women's Center

BOOKSTORES & RETAIL SHOPS
Downtown Book Bin 2228 SW 3rd, 752-0040, 7am-8pm, 9:30am-6pm Sat, from noon Sun; also Monroe Ave. Book Bin, 2305 NW Monroe, 753-8398, more text books

Grass Roots Bookstore 227 SW 2nd St., 754-7668 (WC) 9am-7pm, til 9pm Fri, til 5:30pm Sat, 11am-5pm Sun, also full service music section, espresso bar

CRUISY AREAS
Willamette River N. of Willamette Park (N,AYOR)

Eugene (541)

INFO LINES & SERVICES
▲ **Community Real Estate Referrals** (800) 346-5592, gay realtor at your service, no rentals

Gay/Lesbian AA 342-4113, call for hours

Lesbian/Gay/Bisexual Alliance-UO Ste. 319 EMU, 346-3360 (WC) 9am-5pm (office), various drop-in groups, social 4-6pm Th

The Mpowerment Project 775 Monroe St., 97402, 683-4303, 3-9pm Th-Sat (office), many social/support activities for gay & bi men

ACCOMMODATIONS
Campus Cottage B&B 1136 E. 19th Ave., 342-5346 (GF) central location, full brk-fst

River's Edge Inn 91241 Blue River Rd., Blue River, 822-3258/(800) 250-1821 (GF) 40 miles east of Eugene, full brkfst

BARS
Club Arena 959 Pearl St., 683-2360 (★MW,D,S,V,YC) 7pm-2:30am

RESTAURANTS & CAFES
Keystone Cafe 395 W. 5th, 342-2075, 7am-3pm, popular breakfast, plenty veggie

Perry's 959 Pearl St., 683-2360 (WC) 7am-9pm, clsd Sun, also full bar til 2:30am

BOOKSTORES & RETAIL SHOPS
Hungry Head Bookstore 1212 Willamette, 485-0888, 10:30am-6pm, noon-5pm Sun, progressive alternative titles

Peralandra Books & Music 199 E. 5th Ave., Station Square, 485-4848, 10am-6pm, clsd Sun, metaphysical titles

TRAVEL & TOUR OPERATORS
Global Affair 285 E. 5th Ave., 343-8595/(800) 755-2753 (IGTA)

SPIRITUAL GROUPS
MCC 23rd & Harris (1st Congregational Church), 345-5963, 4pm Sun

PUBLICATIONS
View Magazine PO Box 11067, 97440, 302-6523, 'chronicle of gay & lesbian life'

EROTICA
Exclusively Adult 1166 S. 'A' St., Springfield, 726-6969, 24hrs

Gladstone

INFO LINES & SERVICES
G.G.G. (Gorge Gay Group) 269 W. Arlington, 97027, social group for gay men in & around Columbia Gorge

Grants Pass

CRUISY AREAS
Riverside Park nr. Art museum (AYOR)

Klamath Falls (541)

INFO LINES & SERVICES
HIV Resource Center 1112 Pine St., 883-2437, 11am-5pm

KALA (Klamath Area Lambda Association) LesBiGay Hotline PO Box 43, 97601, 883-2437, social/support group

CRUISY AREAS
Moore Park (AYOR) summers

La Grande

INFO LINES & SERVICES
GALA of Eastern Oregon State College Student Activities Office, Hoke College Center EOS, 97850, 7pm 2nd & 4th Mon (Loso Hall #232)

Lincoln City (541)

ACCOMMODATIONS
Lincoln Lodge 2735 NW Inlet, 994-5007
Ocean Gardens Inn 2735 NW Inlet, 994-5007/(800) 866-9925 (GF) Pacific Ocean views

RESTAURANTS & CAFES
Over the Waves 2945 NW Jetty Ave., 994-3877 (E) 8am-10pm, lounge open til 2am wknds

Medford (541)

INFO LINES & SERVICES
AA Gay/Lesbian 773-4848

BOOKSTORES & RETAIL SHOPS
Hands On Books 211 W. Main, 779-6990, 10am-5:30pm, clsd Sun, some lesbigay titles

Newport

CRUISY AREAS
Yaquina Bay State Park (AYOR)

Port Orford

CRUISY AREAS
Battle Rock Wayside Park S. edge of town (AYOR)

Portland (see also Vancouver, WASHINGTON listings) (503)

INFO LINES & SERVICES

Asian/Pacific Islander Lesbian/Gay/Bisexual Info Hotline PO Box 826, 97207, 232-6408, educational/social/support group

BiNet 299-4764, meets 7pm 1st Tue at Laughing Horse Books, call for social schedule

Brother to Brother PO Box 3182, 97208-3182, 227-2453/248-3030, 6:30pm 2nd & 4th Mon, social/political group for African-American gay & bisexual men

Cascade AIDS Project 620 SW 5th Ave. Ste. 300, 223-5907/(800) 777-2437, non-medical services, support groups, counseling

Cascade Bears 625 SW 10th Ave Ste. 125, 97205-2788, group for bears & their admirers, write for membership info

Chaps 321-5139, educational SM group for men

▲ **Community Real Estate Referrals** (800) 346-5592, gay realtor at your service, no rentals

FRIENDS PO Box 3182, 97208, 280-2643, 6-8pm 2nd & 4th Wed, social/support group for African-American gay & bisexual men

Gay Resource Center/Oregon AIDS Hotline 223-2437/(800) 777-2437, 10am-9pm, noon-3pm wknds, statewide info & referrals for gay/lesbian social groups & events, AIDS information

Gay/Lesbian Archives of the Pacific Northwest PO Box 3646, 97208, 1st Mon

Gentle Giants of Oregon PO Box 1844, 97207, 241-4535, social group for heavy-set men & their admirers

Live & Let Live Club 2400 NE Broadway, 2nd flr (MCC Portland), 460-9404, various 12-step meetings

Love Makes a Family PO Box 11694, 97211, 228-3892, many groups, call for locations, also radio show on KKEY 1150 AM, 7am Wed

Metro Club 9961 SW Walnut #17, Tigard, 97223, 4th Sun, social group for gay men 40+ & their admirers

Northwest Gender Alliance P.O. Box 4928, 97208-4928, 646-2802, 3rd Tue & 2nd Sat, transgender support group, newsletter

Phoenix Rising 620 SW 5th Ste. 710, 97204, 223-8299 (WC) sexual minority counseling center

PLM (Portland Leather Men) 1701 Broadway Ste. 273, Vancouver WA, 98663, meets 2nd Sat (potluck)

Pride Line 243-3424, touchtone resource hotline

Reed College Queer Alliance 3203 SE Woodstock Blvd. #718, 97202

ACCOMMODATIONS

Holladay House B&B 1735 NE Wasco St., 282-3172, full brkfst

Hotel Vintage Plaza 422 SW Broadway, 228-1212/(800) 243-0555 (★GF,WC) upscale

The Irvington House 2025 NE 24th, 282-6403 (GF)

MacMaster House 1041 SW Vista Ave., 223-7362/(800) 774-9523 (GF) historic mansion

Sullivan's Gulch B&B 1744 NE Clackamas St., 331-1104 (MW) 1907 Portland home

BARS

Anchors 211 SW Ankeny St., 220-4001 (M,NH,F,BW) 11am-midnight, til 1am Th-Sat, homecookin'

Bar of the Gods 4801 SE Hawthorne, 232-2037 (GF,BW,YC,WC) 4pm-2:30am

Boxx's 1035 SW Stark, 226-4171 (★M,V,WC) 11:30am-2:30am, from noon wknds, also Brig (M,D) 9pm-2:30am

C.C. Slaughter's 1014 SW Stark St., 248-9135 (★M,D,F,V) 11am-2:30am, (CW) on Wed & Sun

Candlelight Room 2032 SW 5th, 222-3378 (GF,F,E) 10am-2:30am, from 11am wknds, hamburgers

Choices Pub 2845 SE Stark St., 236-4321 (MW,D,WC) 1pm-1am, til 2:30am wknds

The City Nightclub 13 NW 13th Ave., 224-2489 (★MW,D,E,18+) 10pm-2am, til 4am Fri-Sat, clsd Mon-Tue, no alcohol

Darcelle XV 208 NW 3rd Ave., 222-5338 (GF,F,S,WC) 5pm-2:30am, clsd Sun

Eagle PDX 1300 W. Burnside, 241-0105 (M,L) 4pm-2:30am

Embers Nightclub 110 NW Broadway, 222-3082 (★GF,D,S,WC) 11am-2:30am

Gail's Dirty Duck Tavern 439 NW 3rd, 224-8446 (M,NH,L,WC) 3pm-2:30am, from noon wknds

▲ **Hobo's** 120 NW 3rd Ave., 224-3285 (GF,E,WC) open from 4pm daily, also full American restaurant, some veggie

J.O.Q.'s Tavern 2512 NE Broadway, 287-4210 (M,NH) 11am-2:30am

La Luna 215 SE 9th Ave., 241-5862 (GF,D,E,18+) 9pm-2am, call for events

Melody Ballroom 615 SE Alder, 232-2759, 24hr msg., special events space - call for events

Panorama 341 SW 10th, 221-7262 (★GF,D,BW,WC) 9pm-4am Fri-Sat, til 2:30am Sun, call for events

Ray's Ordinary Bar & Grille 317 NW Broadway, 222-7297 (★M,WC) 9am-2:30am, also full restaurant, steaks & seafood

Scandal's Tavern 1038 SW Stark St., 227-5887 (M,NH,WC) noon-2:30am

Silverado 1217 SW Stark St., 224-4493 (★M,D,S,WC) 9am-2:30am, also full restaurant, American

Squeezebox 214 SW Broadway (at Saucebox restaurant), 241-3393 (★MW,D,S,WC) 9pm-3am Sun only

Starky's 2913 SE Stark St. (at 29th), 230-7980 (★MW,NH,WC) 11am-2am, patio, also full restaurant

Three Sisters Tavern 1125 SW Stark St., 228-0486 (M,NH,D) 1pm-2:30am, clsd Sun

RESTAURANTS & CAFES

Acapulco's Gold 2610 NW Vaughn, 220-0283 (★) Mexican

The Adobe Rose 1634 SE Bybee Blvd., 235-9114 (BW) 4pm-9pm, clsd Sun, New Mexican cuisine

Assaggio 7742 SE 13th, 232-6151 (BW) 5:30-9:30pm, Italian

B.J.'s Brazilian Restaurant 7019 SE Milwaukie Ave., 236-9629, lunch & dinner, clsd Sun

Bastas Trattoria 410 NW 21st, 274-1572, lunch & dinner, northern Italian, full bar

Bijou Cafe 132 SW 3rd Ave., 222-3187 (★) 7am-3pm

Brasserie Montmartre 626 SW Park, 224-5552, lunch & dinner, Sun brunch, bistro menu, live jazz

Bread & Ink Cafe 3610 SE Hawthorne Blvd., 239-4756 (★WC) 7am-9pm, 8am-10pm Sat, 9am-2pm & 5pm-9pm Sun

Cafe Lena 2239 SE Hawthorne Blvd., 238-7087 (★) 8am-11pm

Caffe Fresco 2387 NW Thurman, 243-3247, 6:30am-4pm, from 8am wknds, til 2pm Sun, Italian

Caribou Cafe & Bar 503 W. Burnside, 227-0245 (WC) noon-1am, from 5pm Sat, from 3pm Sun, diner, full bar

Coffee Cow 5204 NE Sacramento, 282-9910, 7am-7pm, til 10pm Sat, 9am-5pm Sun, open later in summer

Coffee People 533 NW 23rd St., 221-0235 (★)

Cup & Saucer Cafe 3566 SE Hawthorne, 236-6001 (★) 7am-8pm

Esparza's Tex-Mex Cafe 2725 SE Ankeny St., 234-7909 (★) 11:30am-10pm, clsd Sun-Mon

Espress It! 1026 SW Stark, 227-2551 (MW) 5pm-2:30am, also gallery

Fish Grotto 1035 SW Stark (at Boxx's bar), 226-4171 (★) 11:30am-10:30pm, from 4:30pm wknds

Genoa 2832 SE Belmont, 238-1464 (BW) reservations only, clsd Sun, 7-course Italian dinner (prix-fixe)

Gypsy Cafe 625 NW 21st, 796-1859, 11am-1am, from 9am wknds

Hamburger Mary's 3239 SW Broadway, 223-0900 (★) 7am-2am

▲ **Hobo's** 120 NW 3rd Ave., 224-3285 (★E,WC) open from 4pm daily

Majas Tacqueria 1000 SW Morrison, 226-1946, 11am-11pm

Marco's Cafe & Espresso Bar 7910 SW 35th, Multnomah, 245-0199, 7am-9:30pm, from 8am wknds, til 2pm Sun, popular wknd brunch

Old Wives Tales 1300 E. Burnside Ave., 238-0470 (BW,WC) 8am-10pm, til 11pm Fri-Sat, multi-ethnic vegetarian

Pizzacato 505 NW 23rd, 242-0023 (★) 11am-11pm, noon-9pm Sun, plenty veggie

Ron Paul Charcuterie 1441 NE Broadway, 284-5439, 8am-10pm, til midnight Fri & Sat, 9am-4pm Sun, fancy French deli

Santa Fe Taqueria 831 NW 23rd, 220-0406 (★) 11am-midnight Sun-Th, til 1am Fri & Sat, Mexican, patio, full bar

Saucebox 214 SW Broadway, 241-3393 (MW,WC) 11:30am-2am Tue-Sat, multi-ethnic cafe, plenty veggie, full bar

Shakers Cafe 1212 NW Glisan, 221-0011 (BW) 7:30am-4pm, clsd Sun, home-cooking

Swagat Indian Cuisine 4325 SW 109th Ave., Beaverton, 626-3000, 11am-3pm & 5pm-10pm

Vista Spring Cafe 2440 SW Vista, 222-2811, 11am-10pm

Wildwood 1221 NW 21st Ave., 248-9663 (★) 11am-9pm (reservations recommended), also full bar

Zefiro 500 NW 21st, 226-3394, lunch & dinner, clsd Sun, Mediterranean/Southeast Asian, full bar

GYMS & HEALTH CLUBS

Inner City Hot Springs 2927 NE Everett St., 238-4010 (GF) 10am-11pm, 1pm-10pm Sun, wellness center, reservations required

Princeton Athletic Club 614 SW 11th Ave., 222-2639 (GF) 5am-10pm, 7am-7pm wknds, day passes avail.

BOOKSTORES & RETAIL SHOPS

Gai-Pied 2544 NE Broadway, 331-1125, 11am-8pm, til 9pm Th-Sat, til 7pm Sun, gay bookstore

The Jellybean 721 SW 10th Ave., 222-5888 (WC) 10am-6pm, clsd Sun, cards, T-shirts, gifts

Laughing Horse Bookstore 3652 SE Division, 236-2893 (WC) 11am-7pm, clsd Sun, alternative/progressive

Looking Glass Bookstore 318 SW Taylor, 227-4760, 9am-6pm, from 10am Sat, clsd Sun, general, some lesbigay titles

Powell's Books 1005 W. Burnside St., 228-4651 (WC) 9am-11pm, til 9pm Sun, new & used books

Presents of Mind 3633 SE Hawthorne, 230-7740 (WC) 10am-7pm, 11am-5:30pm Sun, jewelry, cards, gifts, candles, unique toys

Twenty-Third Ave. Books 1015 NW 23rd Ave., 224-5097 (WC) 9:30am-9pm, from 10am Sat, 11am-7pm Sun, general, lesbigay section

TRAVEL & TOUR OPERATORS

Advantage Travel Service 812 SW Washington St. Ste. 200, 225-0186 (IGTA)

Gulliver's Travels & Voyages 514 NW 9th Ave., 221-0013/(800) 875-8009 (IGTA)

Hawthorne Travel Company 1939 SE Hawthorne Blvd., 232-5944/(800) 232-5944 (IGTA)

In Touch Travel 121 SW Morrison St. #270, 223-1062/(800) 568-3246 (IGTA)

J&M Travel 4370 NE Halsey Ste. 138, 249-0305/(800) 875-0305 (IGTA)

Mikuni Travel Service 1 SW Columbia St. Ste. 1010, 227-3639/(800) 248-0624 (IGTA)

Oregon Tourism Commission (800) 547-7842, call for a free catalog

Travel Agents International 917 SW Washington St., 223-1100/(800) 357-3194 (IGTA) ask for Rip

Travel Corner 17175 SW T.V. Hwy., Aloha, 649-9867/(800) 327-0840 (IGTA)

Ultimate Travels 621 SW Morrison Ste. 435, 220-8866/(800) 446-4117 (IGTA)

SPIRITUAL GROUPS

Congregation Neve Shalom 246-8831, 8:15pm Fri, 9am Sat

Dignity - Portland 13th & SW Clay (St. Stephen's Episcopal Church), 295-4868, 7:30pm Sat

Integrity Columbia/Willamette 8147 SE Pine St., 288-5949

MCC Portland 2400 NE Broadway, 281-8868 (WC) 10am Sun, 7pm Wed

Pagan Info Line 650-7045, also publishes 'Open Ways' newsletter

Radical Faeries 235-0826, call for events

Reach Out! PO Box 1173, Clackamas, 97015, support group for lesbigay Jehovah's Witnesses & Mormons

Publications

Just Out PO Box 14400, 97214-0400, 236-1252, bi-monthly, extensive resource directory

Men's Clubs

Club Portland 303 SW 12th Ave., 227-9992 (★MO,18+,PC) 24hrs

Olympic Steam Bath-Downtown 509 SW 4th Ave., 227-5718 (MO,V,PC) clsd Sun-Mon

Erotica

The Crimson Phoenix 1876 SW 5th Ave., 228-0129 (WC) 'sexuality bookstore for lovers', condoms, herbs, gifts

Fantasy for Adults 3137 NE Sandy Blvd., 239-6969, 24hrs

Hard Times Video 311 NW Broadway, 223-2398, 24hrs

Hart's Arcade 330 SW 3rd Ave., 224-2338, 24hrs

Leatherworks 2908 SE Belmont St., 234-2697, noon-6pm Tue-Sat

Spartacus Leather 302 SW 12th Ave., 224-2604, 10am-11pm, til 8pm Sun

Tim's Hideaway 4229 SE 82nd Ave., 771-9774

Cruisy Areas

Rooster Rock State Park E. end of beach, 25 mi. E. of Portland (AYOR)

Sauvie's Island Beach 25 mi. NW off US 30, park nr. end of Reeder Park (AYOR)

Washington Park by Lewis & Clark monument Burnside & 25th, also 'Daisy Patch' area (AYOR)

Rockaway Beach (503)

Accommodations

Bear & Penguin Inn 421 N. Miller, 355-8610 (GF)

Rogue River (541)

Accommodations

Whispering Pines B&B/Retreat 9188 W. Evans Creek Rd., 582-1757/(800) 788-1757 (★MW,SW) full brkfst

Roseburg (541)

Info Lines & Services

Gay/Lesbian Switchboard P.O. Box 813, 97470, 672-4126, publishes newsletter

Bars

Roma Cocktail Lounge & Restaurant 5096 Hwy. 99 S., 679-7100 (GF,E) 11am-2am (kitchen closes at 10pm)

Cruisy Areas

Stewart Park river trails & under bridge (AYOR)

Salem (503)

INFO LINES & SERVICES
Mid-Oregon AIDS Support Service 494 State St. Ste. 256, 363-4963 (WC) 9am-2pm

BARS
Sneakers Bar & Dance Club 300 Liberty St. SE, 363-0549 (MW,D,F,E,K,WC) 4pm-2:30am (restaurant clsd Sun-Mon)

RESTAURANTS & CAFES
Off Center Cafe 1741 Center St. NE, 363-9245 (★WC) 7am-2:30pm, from 8am wknds, 6pm-9pm Th-Sat

BOOKSTORES & RETAIL SHOPS
Rosebud & Fish 524 State St., 399-9960, 10am-7pm, noon-5pm Sun, alternative bookstore

SPIRITUAL GROUPS
Dignity 1020 Columbia St. (St. Vincent's Church), 363-0006, 7:30pm 2nd & 4th Sat

Sweet Spirit MCC PO Box 13969, 363-6618, 11am Sun

Unitarian Universalist Congregation of Salem 490 19th St. NE, 364-0932, 9:30am & 11:15am Sun (10am only summers)

PUBLICATIONS
Community News PO Box 663, 97308, 363-0006, monthly

Out & About Entertainer 3470 Donald St. NE, 375-3758

EROTICA
Bob's Adult Bookstore 3655 Portland Rd. NE, 363-3846

Seaside

CRUISY AREAS
Cannon Beach 10 mi. S. (AYOR) summers only

Seaside Beach area beneath turn around (AYOR) summers

Tigard (503)

TRAVEL & TOUR OPERATORS
The Travel Shop 10115 SW Nimbus Ctr. Ste. 600, 684-8533/(800) 285-8835 (IGTA) ask for Mark

Tiller (503)

ACCOMMODATIONS
Kalles Family RV Ranch 233 Jackson Creek Rd., 825-3271 (MW) camping sites & RV hookups, between Medford & Roseburg

Waldport (541)

ACCOMMODATIONS
Cliff House B&B Yaquina John Point at 1450 Adahi St., 97394, 563-2506 (GF) oceanfront

RESTAURANTS & CAFES
Bumps & Grinds 225 SW Maple, 563-5769 (WC) 7:30am-5pm, patio, view

Welches (503)

ACCOMMODATIONS
Cedar Grove Cottage 557-8292 (GF) spa, fireplace, near Sandy River

Wheeler (503)

ACCOMMODATIONS
▲ **The Bay Inn** 294 Hall St., 368-5766/(800) 229-1394 (MW)

Yachats (503)

ACCOMMODATIONS
Morningstar Gallery & B&B 95668 Hwy 101 S., 97498, 547-4412 (GF) ocean-front, full brkfst, hot tub
The Oregon House 94288 Hwy. 101, 547-3329 (GF,WC)
See Vue Motel 95590 Hwy. 101 S., 547-3227 (GF) oceanview

The
Bay Inn
(800) 229-1394
(503) 368-5766
♂♂ G, O-O ♀♀
294 Hall Street
Wheeler, Oregon 97147

PENNSYLVANIA

Allentown (610)

INFO LINES & SERVICES

▲ **Community Real Estate Referrals** (800) 346-5592, gay realtor at your service, no rentals

Gay Men Lehigh Valley 439-8755, 7pm 2nd & 4th Sat

Gays/Lesbians of Reading & Allentown PO Box 1952, 18105, 868-7183

Your Turf 439-8755(MCC#), 7pm Fri, lesbigay youth group

BARS

Candida's 247 N. 12th St., 434-3071 (MW,NH,F,K) 11:30am-2am, from 2pm Fri-Sun

Moose Lounge/Stonewall 28-30 N. 10th St., 432-0706 (★MW,D,F,E,K,S,V,YC) 2pm-2am

SPIRITUAL GROUPS

Grace Covenant Fellowship Church 247 N. 10th St., 740-0247, 10:45am Sun

CRUISY AREAS

The Block 13th & 14th Aves. (AYOR)

Altoona (814)

INFO LINES & SERVICES

Gay/Lesbian/Bisexual Info 944-3583, 8:30am-4:30pm Mon-Fri, ask for Melanie

Beaver Falls

BARS

A.S.S. (Alternative Subway Stop) 1204 7th Ave. (rear entrance) (M,D) 8pm-2am, clsd Sun

Bethlehem (610)

SPIRITUAL GROUPS

MCC of the Lehigh Valley 424 Center St. (Unitarian Church), 439-8755, 6pm Sun

EROTICA

The Green Door/Town Video 1162 Pembroke Rd., 865-5855

Bradford

INFO LINES & SERVICES

University of Pitt-Bradford BiGALA c/o Director of Student Activities 200 Campus Dr./235 Commons, 16701

Bridgeport (610)

BARS

The Lark 302 Dekalb St. (Rte. 202 N.), 275-8136 (MW,D) 8pm-2am, dinner served

Bristol (215)

EROTICA

Bristol News World 576 Bristol Pike (Rte. 13 N.), 785-4770, 24hrs

Variety Adult Books 6909 Rt. 13 S., Levittown, 547-2373, 24hrs

CRUISY AREAS

Silver Lake Park (AYOR)

East Stroudsburg (717)

INFO LINES & SERVICES
▲ **Community Real Estate Referrals** (800) 346-5592, gay realtor at your service, no rentals

ACCOMMODATIONS
▲ **Rainbow Mtn. Resort & Restaurant** RD 8, Box 8174, 223-8484 (★MW,D,TG,E,K,SW,IGTA)

Edgemont

CRUISY AREAS
Ridley Creek State Park W. Chester Pike (AYOR)

Edinboro (814)

INFO LINES & SERVICES
Identity University Center, Edinboro U of P, 16444, 732-2000

Emlenton (412)

ACCOMMODATIONS
Allegheny House 214 River Ave., 867-9636/(800) 547-8499 (GF) full brkfst

Ephrata (717)

TRAVEL & TOUR OPERATORS
Zeller Travel 4213 Oregon Pike, 859-4710/(800) 331-4359 (IGTA)

Come enjoy the freedom to be yourself.

Erie (814)

INFO LINES & SERVICES

Lambda Group AA 7180 New Perry Hwy. (Unitarian Universalist Church), 452-2675 (WC) 8pm Sun

Trigon: Lesbigay Coalition Reed Bldg., Penn State-Behrend, 898-6164

ACCOMMODATIONS

Castle Great House 231 W. 21st St., 454-6465 (MW)

BARS

The Embers 1711 State St., 454-9171 (M,D,F,E) 8pm-2am, clsd Sun

Leeward Lounge 1022 Bridge St., Ashtabula OH, (216) 964-9935 (MW,F) 8pm-2:30am

Lizzy Bordon's Part II 3412 W. 12th St., 833-4059 (★MW,D,WC) 9pm-2am, clsd Sun

RESTAURANTS & CAFES

Cup-A-Ccinos Coffeehouse 18 N. Park Row, 456-1151 (E,WC) 7:30am-9pm, til mid Th-Sat, from 9am Sat, clsd Sun

La Bella Bistro 556 W. 4th, 454-3616 (BYOB) lunch & dinner, dinner only Sat, clsd Sun

Pie in the Sky Cafe 463 W. 8th St., 459-8638 (BYOB,WC) 7:30am-2pm, dinner from 5pm Fri-Sat, clsd Sun

BOOKSTORES & RETAIL SHOPS

Perceptions 328 W. 6th, 454-7364, 11am-7pm, til 5pm Sat, clsd Sun & Wed

TRAVEL & TOUR OPERATORS

Camelot Travel & Tours PO Box 3874, 16508, 835-3434

SPIRITUAL GROUPS

Unitarian Universalist Congregation of Erie 7180 New Perry Hwy., 864-9300, 10:30am Sun

PUBLICATIONS

Erie Gay Community Newsletter 456-9833

Gay Peoples Chronicle PO Box 5426, Cleveland OH, 44101, (216) 631-8646

EROTICA

Eastern Adult Books 1313 State St., 459-7014, 24hrs

Fillmore News 2757 W. 12th, 833-2667

CRUISY AREAS

Presque Isle Park Beach non-guarded area east of Beach 2 (AYOR)

Gettysburg

INFO LINES & SERVICES

Gettysburg College Lambda Alliance Box 2256, Gettysburg College, 17325

Greensburg (412)

BARS

RK's Safari Lounge 108 W. Pittsburgh St., 837-9948 (★M,D,WC) 9pm-2am, clsd Sun, patio

CRUISY AREAS

Harrison Ave. off Otterman St. (AYOR)

Harrisburg (717)

INFO LINES & SERVICES
▲ **Community Real Estate Referrals** (800) 346-5592, gay realtor at your service, no rentals

Gay/Lesbian Switchboard 234-0328, 6pm-10pm

BARS
Neptune's Lounge 268 North St., 233-3078 (★M,NH) 4pm-2am, from 2pm Sun, dinner menu 5pm-9pm

Stallions 706 N. 3rd St. (rear entrance), 233-4681 (★M,D,E,K,YC,WC) 4pm-2am, clsd Sun, also 'Heaven' restaurant

Strawberry Cafe 704 N. 3rd St., 234-4228 (★M,V,YC,WC) 2pm-2am, clsd Sun

RESTAURANTS & CAFES
Colonnade 300 N. 2nd St., 234-8740, 6am-8:30pm, from 7am Sat, clsd Sun

Paper Moon 268 North St., 233-0581 (MW) 5pm-9pm, til 11pm wknds

TRAVEL & TOUR OPERATORS
Pennsylvania Bureau of Travel (800) 847-4872

SPIRITUAL GROUPS
Dignity PO Box 297, 17108, 232-2027

MCC of the Spirit 6th & Herr St. (Friends Meeting House), 236-7387, 7pm Sun

EROTICA
Rural Book & News 315 Market St., 255-9121

CRUISY AREAS
Front & State Sts. (AYOR)

Johnstown (814)

BARS
Lucille's 520 Washington St., 539-4448 (MW,D,E,S) 9pm-2am, clsd Sun-Mon

CRUISY AREAS
Babcock Park (AYOR)

Kutztown (610)

ACCOMMODATIONS
Grim's Manor B&B 10 Kern Rd., 683-7089 (GF) full brkfst

Lancaster (717)

INFO LINES & SERVICES
▲ **Community Real Estate Referrals** (800) 346-5592, gay realtor at your service, no rentals

Gay/ Lesbian Helpline 397-0691, 7pm-10pm Sun,Wed & Th

Pink Triangle Coalition PO Box 176, 17608, 394-6260

ACCOMMODATIONS
Maison Rouge B&B 2236 Marietta Ave., 399-3033 (GF) full brkfst

BARS
Tally Ho 201 W. Orange, 299-0661 (★MW,D,YC) 6pm-2am, from 8pm Sun

RESTAURANTS & CAFES
Loft (above Tally Ho bar), 299-0661, lunch & dinner, clsd Sun, French/American

BOOKSTORES & RETAIL SHOPS
Borders Bookshop 940 Plaza Blvd., 293-8022

SPIRITUAL GROUPS
MCC Vision of Hope 130 E. Main St., Mountville, 285-9070, 10am & 7pm Sun

EROTICA
Den of Pleasure 53 N. Prince St., 299-1779

CRUISY AREAS
Lancaster County Central Park (AYOR)
Long's Park Rte. 30 at Harrisburg Pike (AYOR)

Lebanon
CRUISY AREAS
Coleman's Park (AYOR)

Malvern (610)
ACCOMMODATIONS
Pickering Bend B&B RD 1, Box 121, Church Rd., Charlestown Village, 933-0183 (GF)

Marshalls Creek (717)
ACCOMMODATIONS
Curt & Wally's B&B PO Box 219, 18335, 223-1395 (MO,SW,N)

Monroeville (412)
EROTICA
Monroeville News 2735 Stroschein Rd., 372-5477, 24hrs

Montgomeryville (215)
EROTICA
Adult World Book Store Rtes. 202 & 309, 362-9560

Mt. Pleasant (412)
BARS
Yuppie's 241 E. Main St., 547-0430 (M,NH,F,K) 6pm-2am, from 1pm Sun, gentlemen's bar

New Castle
CRUISY AREAS
McConnell's Mill State Park (AYOR) summers

New Hope (215)
INFO LINES & SERVICES
AA Gay/Lesbian 862-0327/574-6900 (AA#)
▲ **Community Real Estate Referrals** (800) 346-5592, gay realtor at your service, no rentals

ACCOMMODATIONS
The Fox & Hound B&B 246 West Bridge St., 862-5082/(800) 862-5082 (GF)
The Lexington House 6171 Upper York Rd., 794-0811 (MW,SW)
▲ **The Raven** 385 West Bridge St., 862-2081 (★M,SW)

BARS

The Cartwheel 427 York Rd. (US 202), 862-0880 (★MW,D,F,E,S,WC) 5pm-2am

▲ **The Raven Bar & Restaurant** (at Raven accommodations), 862-2081 (MW) 11am-2am

RESTAURANTS & CAFES

Country Host 463 Old York Rd. (Rte. 202), 862-5575 (WC) 7am-10pm

Havana 105 S. Main St., 862-9897 (E) 11am-midnight, bar til 2am

Karla's 5 W. Mechanic St., 862-2612, lunch, dinner & late night breakfast Fri-Sat

Mother's 34 N. Main St., 862-5270, 9am-10pm

Odette's South River Rd., 862-3000 (E,WC) 11am-10pm (piano bar til 1am)

Wildflowers 8 W. Mechanic St., 862-2241, noon-10pm, til 11pm Fri-Sat (summer)

BOOKSTORES & RETAIL SHOPS

Ember'glo Gifts 27 W. Mechanic St., 862-2929, 11am-6pm, wknds only (winter)

TRAVEL & TOUR OPERATORS

Flight of Fancy, Inc. 408 York Rd., 862-9665/(800) 691-1980 (IGTA)

EROTICA

Grown Ups 2 E. Mechanic St., 862-9304, 11am-7pm, til 11pm Fri-Sat

New Milford (717)

ACCOMMODATIONS

Oneida Camp & Lodge PO Box 537, 18834, 465-7011 (M,SW,N) April-Oct, oldest gay-owned campground dedicated to our community

Raven Hall

385 West Bridge St., New Hope, PA 18938
Lodging • Restaurant • Pub • 215-862-2081

Norristown (610)

BARS

Doubleheader/Medusa's 354 W. Elm St., 277-1070 (MW,D,L,V) 8pm-2am, clsd Sun-Mon

Philadelphia (215)

INFO LINES & SERVICES

AA Gay/Lesbian 574-6900

BiUnity 724-3663, bisexual group for men & women

▲ **Community Real Estate Referrals** (800) 346-5592, gay realtor at your service, no rentals

Gay/Lesbian Radio WXPN-FM 88.5, 898-6677, 8pm Sun 'Q Zine'

Gay/Lesbian Switchboard 546-7100, 7pm-10pm

Gay/Lesbian/Bisexual/Transgendered Commmunity Center 201 S. Camac St. (Penquin Place), 732-2220, 6pm-10pm, 11am-5pm Sat, 5pm-9pm Sun, clsd Fri for special events

Gender Transgressors 922-5943, FTM info & referrals, contact Ben

MACT (Men of All Colors Together) PO Box 42257, 19101, (610) 277-6595

Ujima 1207 Chestnut St., 851-1958, 6pm Wed, support group for African American FTMs

Unity Inc. 1207 Chestnut St., 851-1912, 9am-5:30pm Mon-Fri, lesbigay support/social services

ACCOMMODATIONS

Abigal Adams B&B 1208 Walnut St., 546-7336 (GF)

Antique Row B&B 341 S. 12th St., 592-7802 (GF) full brkfst

Bag & Baggage B&B 338 S. 19th St., 546-3807 (GF)

▲ **The Caritas B&B Network** (800) 227-4827, see ad in center National section

Glen Isle Farm Downingtown, 269-9100/(800) 269-1730 (GF,F,IGTA) full brkfst, 30 miles from Philly

Sarah P. Wilson House 155 Main St., Phoenixville, (610) 933-0327 (GF) full brkfst

Travelodge-Stadium 2015 Penrose Ave., 755-6500/(800) 578-7878 (GF,SW,WC) also restaurant & bar

BARS

2-4 Club 1221 St. James St., 735-5772 (M,D,18+,PC) opens midnight, call for info

247 Bar 247 S. 17th St., 545-9779 (★M,F,E,S,V) noon-2am

Bike Stop 204 S. Quince, 627-1662 (★M,D,A,L,F,E) 4pm-2am from 1pm Sat, 3pm Sun

Black Banana 205 N. 3rd, 925-4433 (GF,D,A,WC) 10pm-3am, from midnight wkdays

C.R. Bar 6405 Market St., Upper Darby, (610) 734-1130 (M,NH) 8pm-2am, clsd Sun

Key West 207 S. Juniper, 545-1578 (MW,D,F,E,S,WC) 4pm-2am, from 11am Sun

Milborn Social Club (upstairs at C.R. Bar), (610) 734-1130 (M,D,PC) from midnight Fri-Sat, 4pm-2am Sun

North Beach Resort 829-1500 (MW,D,SW) call for events & info

The Post 1705 Chancellor St., 985-9720 (M,NH,L,WC) noon-2am, Sun brunch

Raffles 243 S. Camac St., 545-6969 (★MW,D,F,E) 4pm-2am, 3 bars

Rodz 1418 Rodman St., 546-1900 (MW,D,F,E) 5pm-11pm, til 2am Fri-Sat, from noon Sun

Stars Too 1315 Samson St., 545-4053 (MW,D,F,V) 3pm-2am

Uncle's 1220 Locust St., 546-6660 (M,NH) 11am-2am, cabaret

Venture Inn 255 S. Camac, 545-8731 (M,F,OC) noon-2am

The Westbury 261 S. 13th, 546-5170 (M,NH,F,WC) 10am-2am, dinner til 10pm, til 11pm wknds

▲ **Woody's** 202 S. 13th St., 545-1893 (★M,D,CW,F,V,YC,WC) 11am-2am, (18+ Wed)

RESTAURANTS & CAFES

10th Street Pour House 262 S. 10th St., 922-5626, 7:30am-11pm, from 9am Sat, 10am-8pm Sun, cafe

16th Street Bar & Grill 264 S. 16th St., 735-3316, 11:30am-11pm, bar til 2am

The Adobe Cafe 4550 Mitchell St., Roxborough, 483-3947 (E) 4:30pm-10:30pm

Astral Plane 1708 Lombard St., 546-6230, 5pm-11pm

Backstage Bar & Restaurant 614 S. 4th St., 627-9887, 4pm-2am, dinner from 6pm-10pm, Sun brunch

Cafe on Quince 202 S. Quince St., 592-1750, 4:30pm-10pm, Sun brunch

Cheap Art Cafe 260 S. 12th St., 735-6650, 24hrs

Circa 1518 Walnut St., 545-6800 (E,WC) lunch, dinner, Sun brunch

Diner on the Square 1839 Spruce St., 735-5787, 24hrs

Galileo's 1701 Spruce St., 735-4611 (MW,E) noon-10pm

The Inn Philadelphia 251 S. Camac St., 732-2339, 4:30pm-10pm, til 9pm Sun

Liberties 705 N. 2nd St., 238-0660 (E) lunch & dinner, Sun brunch

Makam's Kitchen 2401 Lombard, 546-8832, 10am-10pm

Mont Serrat 623 South St., 627-4224, noon-midnight, healthy American

My Thai 2200 South St., 985-1878, 5pm-10pm, til 11pm Fri-Sat

Palladium/Gold Standard 3601 Locust Walk, 387-3463 (WC) dinner, bar til 12:30am

Rhino Coffee Roastery & Cafe 212 South St., 923-2630, 7am-midnight, from 8:30am wknds

Roosevelt's Pub 2222 Walnut, 636-9722, lunch & dinner

Savoy Restaurant 232 S. 11th St., 923-2348 (★) 24hrs

Shing Kee 52 N. 9th St. , 829-8983 (BYOB) lunch & dinner, gay owned

Waldorf Cafe 20th & Lombard Sts., 985-1836 (WC) dinner

GYMS & HEALTH CLUBS

12th St. Gym 204 S. 12th St., 985-4092 (GF) 6am-11pm

BOOKSTORES & RETAIL SHOPS

Afterwords 218 S. 12th St., 735-2393, 10am-midnight

Giovanni's Room 345 S. 12th St., 923-2960 (★) open daily, lesbigay

Thrift for AIDS 633 South St., 592-9014, noon-9pm

Travelers Emporium 210 S. 17th St., 546-2021, 10am-6pm, clsd Sun

Urban Necessities 1506 Spruce St. , 546-6768, 9am-9pm, til 6pm Sat, 'housewares fit for a queen'

TRAVEL & TOUR OPERATORS

Lambda Travel 21 S. 5th St. #545, 925-3011/(800) 551-2240 (IGTA) ask for Scott

Philadelphia Convention & Visitors Bureau 16th St. & JFK Blvd., (800) 225-5745 (IGTA) publishes 'Philadelphia Gay & Lesbian Travel News'

Sigmund Travel 262 S. 12th St., 735-0090

Twin Travel 1101 Spruce St., 923-2995

Will Travel 118 S. Bellevue Ave., Longhorn, 741-4492/(800) 443-7460 (IGTA)

SPIRITUAL GROUPS
Beth Ahavah 8 Letitia St., 923-2003, 8pm 1st, 3rd & 5th Fri
Christ Episcopal Church 2nd above Market, 922-1695, 9am & 11am Sun
Dignity 330 S. 13th St. (church), 546-2093, 7pm Sun
Integrity 1904 Walnut St. (church), 382-0794, 7pm 1st & 3rd Wed
MCC 2125 Chestnut St. (church), 563-6601, 7pm Sun

PUBLICATIONS
Au Courant News Magazine 2124 South St., 790-1179
The Greater Philadelphia Lavender Pages 205 W. Mt. Pleasant Ave. Ste. 1, 247-1018
PGN (Philadelphia Gay News) 505 S.4th St., 625-8501

MEN'S CLUBS
Chancellor Athletic Club 1220 Chancellor St., 545-4098 (MO,PC) 24hrs
Club Body Center 120 S. 13th St., 735-9568 (MO,PC) 24hrs

EROTICA
▲ **Adonis Cinema Complex** 2026 Sansom St., 557-9319, 24hrs
Arch St. Books 1202 Arch St., 854-9546
Both Ways 201 S. 13th St., 985-2344, piercings & leather
Condom Kingdom 441 South St., 829-1668, safer sex materials & toys
▲ **Danny's New Adam & Eve Books** 133 S. 13th St., 925-5041, 24hrs
Infinite Body Piercing 626 S. 4th St., 923-7335
The Pleasure Chest 2039 Walnut, 561-7480, clsd Sun-Mon
Tomcat Bookstore & Cinema 120 S. 13th St., 985-9725, 24hrs

Pine Grove

CRUISY AREAS
Public Park hiking area off I-81 E. (exit 34) (AYOR)

Swatara Falls (AYOR)

Pittsburgh (412)

INFO LINES & SERVICES
AA Gay/Lesbian 471-7472

Asians & Friends PO Box 16455, 15242, 681-1556

'Burgh Bears PO Box 1451, 15230, 521-2327

BWMT (Black & White Men Together) PO Box 101430, 15237, 441-4441

▲ **Community Real Estate Referrals** (800) 346-5592, gay realtor at your service, no rentals

Gay/Lesbian Community Center Phoneline 422-0114, 6:30pm-9:30pm, 3pm-6pm Sat, clsd Sun

ISMIR (International Sexual Minorities Information Resource) P.O. Box 81869, 422-3060

TransFamily c/o Deni Scott 962 Rockdale Rd., Butler, 16001, 758-3578 (ask for Jan), 2nd Tue, call for location

TransPitt P.O. Box 3214, 15230, 224-6015

ACCOMMODATIONS
Brewers Hotel 3315 Liberty Ave., 681-7991 (GF)

Camp Davis 311 Red Brush Rd., Boyers, 637-2402 (MW) 1hr from Pittsburgh, cabin & campsites, variety of events

The Inn on the Mexican War Streets 1606 Buena Vista St., 231-6544 (MW)

The Priory 614 Pressley, 231-3338 (GF,WC)

BARS
Brewery Tavern (at Brewers Hotel), 681-7991 (GF) 10am-2am, from noon Sun

C.J. Deighan's 2506 W. Liberty Ave., Brookline, 561-4044 (MW,D,F,E,S,WC) 9pm-2am, clsd Sun-Mon

Donny's Place 1226 Herron Ave., 682-9869 (★MW,CW,D,F,E) 4pm-2am, from 3pm Sun

Holiday Bar 4620 Forbes Ave., 682-8598 (★M,NH) 4pm-2am, from 2pm wknds

House of Tilden 941 Liberty Ave., 2nd flr., 391-0804 (MW,D,PC) 10pm-3am

Huggs Restaurant & Lounge 704 Thompson Ave., McKees Rocks, 331-9011 (MW,CW,F,K) 4pm-2am, clsd Sun

Images 965 Liberty Ave., 391-9990 (M,K,V) 5pm-2am, from 9pm Sun

Jazi's 1241 Western Ave. N., 231-9395 (M,D,L) 7pm-2am

Metropol 1600 Smallman St., 261-4512 (★GF,D,A,E,WC) 8pm-2am, clsd Mon-Tue, more gay Th

New York, New York 5801 Ellsworth Ave., 661-5600 (★M,F,E,K,WC) 4pm-2am, from 11am Sun

▲ **Pegasus Lounge** 818 Liberty Ave., 281-2131 (★M,D,S,YC) 4pm-2am, from 8pm Sat, clsd Sun

Pittsburgh Eagle 1740 Eckert St., 766-7222 (M,D,L,WC) 8pm-2am, clsd Sun

Real Luck Cafe 1519 Penn Ave., 566-8988 (MW,NH,F,WC) 3pm-2am

RESTAURANTS & CAFES
Common Grounds Coffeehouse 5888 Ellsworth Ave., 362-1190 (MW,WC) 10am-11pm, til 2am Fri-Sat, til 10pm Sun, patio

Rosebud 1650 Smallman St., 261-2221 (E,WC) lunch & dinner, clsd Mon

Sips 238 Shaddy Ave., 361-4478 (E) 10am-midnight, til 4am wknds, Middle Eastern, patio

BOOKSTORES & RETAIL SHOPS

The Bookstall 3604 5th Ave., 683-2644, 9:30am-5:30pm, til 4:40pm Sat, clsd Sun

Iron City Ink Tattoo/Hellion House Body Piercing 1814 Penn Ave., 391-2380

Slacker 1321 E. Carson St., 381-3911 (WC) noon-10pm, til 7pm Sun

St. Elmo's Books & Music 2214 E. Carson St., 431-9100, 9:30am-9:30pm, til 5pm Sun

True Colors P.O. Box 495, Carnegie, 15106, 734-6650/(800) 285-3718, mail order

TRAVEL & TOUR OPERATORS

Alternative Travels 900 Penn Ave., 279-8595

Bon Ami Travel Service 309 1st St., Apollo, 478-2000/(800) 426-6264 (IGTA)

Cruises & Tours McKnight 1319 Boyle St., 366-7678/(800) 992-7678 (IGTA) ask for Frank

Holiday Travel 5832 Library Rd., Bethel Park, 835-8747

Morgan Delfosse Travel 372-1846/(800) 538-2617

Pittsburgh Travel Service Station Square, 321-8511 (IGTA)

SPIRITUAL GROUPS

Bet Tikvah P.O. Box 10140, 15232, 682-2604, 7:30pm 1st Fri

Dignity 100 N. Bellefield (5th Ave), 362-5334, 7:30pm Sun

MCC of Pittsburgh 304 Morewood Ave. (church), 683-2994, 7pm Sun

Radical Faeries c/o Comm. Ctr., 422-0114, 7:30pm 2nd & 4th Tue

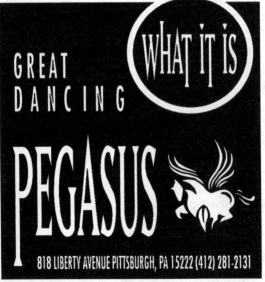

GREAT DANCING

WHAT IT IS

PEGASUS

818 LIBERTY AVENUE PITTSBURGH, PA 15222 (412) 281-2131

PUBLICATIONS
Out 747 South St., 243-3350

MEN'S CLUBS
Arena Health Club 2025 Forbes Ave., 471-8548 (★MO,SW,PC) 24hrs

EROTICA
Boulevard Videos & Magazines 346 Blvd. of the Allies, 261-9119
Golden Triangle News 816 Liberty Ave., 765-3790, 24hrs

Poconos (717)

ACCOMMODATIONS
▲ **Rainbow Mtn. Resort & Restaurant** RD 8, Box 8174, East Stroudsburg, 223-8484 (★MW,D,TG,E,K,SW,IGTA)
Stoney Ridge RD 1, Box 67, Scotrun, 18355, 629-5036 (MW)

Quakerstown (215)

EROTICA
Adult World 80 S. West End Blvd. (Rte.309), 538-1522

Reading (610)

INFO LINES & SERVICES
Berks Gay/ Lesbian Alliance PO Box 417, 19603, 373-0674, meet 2nd Sun
Gays/Lesbians of Reading & Allentown PO Box 1952, Allentown, 18105, 868-7183

BARS
Red Star 11 S. 10th St., 375-4116 (★M,D,F,OC) 5pm-2am, from 8pm Tue, clsd Mon
Scarab 724 Franklin, 375-7878 (★M,D,YC) 8pm-2am, clsd Sun

Rochester

CRUISY AREAS
Brady's Run Park (AYOR)

Scranton (717)

ACCOMMODATIONS
Hillside Campgrounds PO Box 726, Binghamton NY, 13902, 756-2007 (★MO,D,SW,N) campground, cabins & trailers, disco Fri-Sat

BARS
The Buzz 400 Block of Spruce in Forest Ct., 969-0900 (MW,D,E,S,WC) 9pm-2am, clsd Sun-Mon
Silhouette Lounge 523 Linden St., 344-4259 (M,NH,L) 10am-2am, clsd Sun

CRUISY AREAS
Court House Square (AYOR)

State College (814)

INFO LINES & SERVICES
Gay/Lesbian/Bisexual/Transgender Switchboard 237-1950, 6pm-9pm

BARS
Chumley's 108 W. College, 238-4446 (★M,WC) 4pm-2am, from 6pm Sun
Players 112 W. College Ave., 234-1031 (GF,D,V,YC) 8pm-2am

CRUISY AREAS
The Wall 100 block of College Ave. (AYOR)

Sunbury

CRUISY AREAS
Market St. & Park (downtown) (AYOR)
Shikellamy State Park (AYOR)

Valley Forge

CRUISY AREAS
Betzwood Park (AYOR)

West Chester

CRUISY AREAS
Court House Wall (AYOR) late night

West Grove   (610)

BARS
Trib's Waystation 627 W. Baltimore Pike, 869-9067 (GF,F,WC) 11am-2am

Wilkes-Barre

INFO LINES & SERVICES
Coming Home (AA) 97 S. Franklin Blvd. (Pres. Church), noon Th

ACCOMMODATIONS
Grey Oaks Bed & Breakfast 298 E. South St., 829-7097 (MO)

BARS

▲ **Rumors Lounge** 315 Fox Ridge Plaza, 825-7300 (★MW,D,F,WC) 5pm-2am, from 8pm Mon-Tue

▲ **Selections** 45 Public Square, Wilkes-Barre Ctr., 829-4444 (★MW,D,WC) 7pm-2am, clsd Sun

The Vaudvilla (The Vaude) 465 Main St., Kingston, 287-9250 (★MW,D,S,V) 9pm-2am, clsd Sun

Williamsport (717)

INFO LINES & SERVICES

Gay/Lesbian Switchboard of North Central PA PO Box 2510, 17703, 327-1411, 6pm-3am

BARS

Peachie's Court 320 Court St., 326-3611 (MW,NH) 10am-2am, clsd Sun

The Rainbow Room 761 W. 4th St., 320-0230 (★MW,D,F,S,V) 4pm-2am, clsd Sun

CRUISY AREAS

Scenic Overlook 3mi. S. on Rte. 15 N. (AYOR)

York (717)

INFO LINES & SERVICES

York Area Lambda PO Box 2425, 17405, 848-9142, social group, newsletter

EROTICA

Cupid's Connection Adult Boutique 244 N. George St., 846-5029

Swingers Books 226 W. Market St., 845-9803

RHODE ISLAND

Johnston (401)

EROTICA
▲ **Video Expo** 1530 Hartford Ave., 272-0475

Newport (401)

ACCOMMODATIONS
Brinley Victorian Inn 23 Brinley St., 849-7645 (GF)
▲ **Hydrangea House Inn** 16 Bellevue Ave., 846-4435/(800) 945-4667 (★GF) full breakfast, near beach
▲ **The Melville House Inn** 39 Clark St., 847-0640 (MW)

BARS
▲ **David's** 28 Prospect Hill St., 847-9698 (★MW,NH,D) 5pm-1am, from 2pm wknds, Sun T-dance

CRUISY AREAS
First Beach in front of concession stand (AYOR)
Purgatory Chasm-Tuckerman Ave. (middletown) (AYOR)

North Kingstown (401)

EROTICA
▲ **Video Expo** 6774 Post Rd. , 885-0209

Pawtucket (401)

TRAVEL & TOUR OPERATORS
4 Seasons Travel 47 John St., 722-5888

Providence (401)

INFO LINES & SERVICES
AA Gay/Lesbian 438-8860, call for various mtgs.

Enforcers RI PO Box 5770, 02903, women & men into leather/SM/fetish

Gay/Lesbian Helpline of Rhode Island 751-3322, 7pm-11pm (Mon-Fri only during summer)

Gay/Lesbian/Bisexual/Transgender Alliance PO Box 1930, SAO, Brown University, 02912, 863-3062

Rhode Island Gay/Lesbian Youth (RIGLY) PO Box 50, Annex Stn., 02903, 751-3322

Triangle Center 645 Elmwood Ave., 861-4590

BARS
Blinky's 125 Washington, 272-6950 (MW,E,V,WC) noon-1am, til 2am Fri-Sat

Club In Town 95 Eddy St., 751-0020 (★M,E,V) noon-1am, til 2am Fri-Sat

Devilles 10 Davol Square (Simmons Bldg.), 751-7166 (★W,NH,D,WC) 4pm-1am, til 2am Fri-Sat, clsd Mon

Galaxy 123 Empire St., 831-9206 (M,D,K,S,V,WC) noon-1am

Generation X 235 Promenade St., 521-7110 (★MW,D,A) 9pm-2am, clsd Mon-Tue

Gerardo's 1 Franklin Square, 274-5560 (MW,D,E,WC) 4pm-1am, til 2am Fri-Sat

Mirabar 35 Richmond St., 331-6761 (M,D,E,S,WC) 3pm-1am

Skippers 70 Washington St. (at Union), 751-4241 (M,E) noon-1am

Tramps Show Lounge 70 Snow St., 421-8688 (M,S) 4pm-1am, til 2am Fri-Sat

Union Street Station 69 Union St., 331-2291 (M,D,S,WC) noon-1am, til 2am Fri-Sat

Yukon Trading Co. 124 Snow St., 274-6620 (★M,D,L) 5pm-1am, til 2am Fri-Sat, uniform, bear bar

RESTAURANTS & CAFES
Al Forno 577 South Main St., 273-9760 (★) Little Rhody's best dining experience

Down City Diner 151 Weybosset St., 331-9217 (WC) popular Sun brunch (very gay), full bar

Julian's 318 Broadway, 861-1770, 7am-3pm, clsd Mon

Rue de L'Espoir 99 Hope St., 751-8890 (★) 11:30am-2:30pm lunch, 5pm dinner, clsd Mon, full bar

Troye's Southwestern Grill 404 Wickenden St., 861-1430 (BYOB) dinner only, clsd Sun-Mon

Turchetta's 312 Wickenden St., 861-1800, Italian

BOOKSTORES & RETAIL SHOPS
▲ **Airborn for Men** 155 Newport Ave., 438-3070, military-themed & casual clothes, erotica

Books on the Square 471 Angell St., 331-9097, 9am-9pm, til 10pm Fri-Sat, some lesbigay

TRAVEL & TOUR OPERATORS
Travel Concepts 84 Lorimer Ave., 453-6000/(800) 983-6900 (IGTA) ask for Roger

SPIRITUAL GROUPS

Bell St. Chapel (Unitarian Church) 5 Bell St., 831-3794, 10am Sun

Dignity PO Box 2231, Pawtucket, 02861, 727-2657, 2pm 2nd & 4th Sun

Integrity 474 Fruit Hill Ave. (St.James church), 353-2079, 4:30pm 2nd Sun, lesbi-gay Episcopalians

Morning Star MCC 231 Main St., Cherry Valley MA, 553-4320/(508) 892-4320, 11am Sun, 7pm Wed

St. Peter's & Andrew's Episcopal Church 25 Pomona Ave., 272-9649, 8 &10am Sun, 7pm Wed (healing service)

PUBLICATIONS

Options PO Box 6406, 02940, 831-4519, monthly

MEN'S CLUBS

Club Body Center 257 Weybosset, 274-0298 (MO,PC) 24hrs

EROTICA

Corner Book 1954 Westminster, 861-0739

Upstairs Bookshop 206 Washington, 272-3139

▲ **Video Expo** 75 Empire, 274-4477

CRUISY AREAS

State House (AYOR) nights

Smithfield (401)

BARS

The Loft 325 Farnum Pike, 231-3320 (MW,F,SW,WC) 11am-1am, from 10am (wknds & summer), Sun brunch

Warwick (401)

BOOKSTORES & RETAIL SHOPS

Barnes & Noble 1441 Bald Hill Rd., 828-7900, 9am-11pm, 11am-7pm Sun

EROTICA

▲ **Video Expo** 2318 Post Rd., 739-3080

Westerly (401)

ACCOMMODATIONS

The Villa 190 Shore Rd., 596-1054/(800) 722-9240 (GF,SW)

CRUISY AREAS

Misquamicut St. Beach (AYOR)

Woonsocket (401)

BARS

Kings & Queens 285 Front St., 762-9538 (MW,NH,D) 7pm-1am, til 2am Fri-Sat

SOUTH CAROLINA

Anderson (864)

BARS

Europa 116 E. Benson St., 225-6797 (MW,D,S,PC) 9pm-?, clsd Mon-Wed

Charleston (803)

INFO LINES & SERVICES

Acceptance Group (Gay AA) St. Stephen's Episcopal (Anson St.), 762-2433, 8pm Tue & 6:30pm Sat, also meets at MCC 8pm Th

▲ **Community Real Estate Referrals** (800) 346-5592, gay realtor at your service, no rentals

LGLA (Lowcountry Gay/Lesbian Alliance) PO Box 98, 29402, 720-8088, info, referrals

ACCOMMODATIONS

1854 B&B 34 Montagu St., 723-4789 (MW)

65 Radcliff Street 65 Radcliff St, 577-6183 (MW)

▲ **Charleston Columns** 8 Vanderhorst St., 722-7341 (MW)

Happy Landing Folly Beach, 588-6363 (GF,SW) rustic log cabin, sleeps 6, close to beach

BARS

The Arcade 5 Liberty St., 722-5656 (★M,D,A,K,S,YC,WC) 9:30pm-?, clsd Mon-Wed

Deja Vu II 445 Savannah Hwy., 556-5588 (W,D,F,E,PC,WC) 5pm-3am

Dudley's Inc. 346 King St., 723-2784 (M,NH,E,PC) 4pm-3am, from 2pm Sun

RESTAURANTS & CAFES
Bear E. Patch 801 Folly Rd., 762-6555 (WC) 7am-8pm, patio

Cafe Suzanne 4 Center St., 588-2101, 5:30pm-9:30pm, clsd Tue, live jazz

Fanny's Diner 137 Market St., 723-7121 (★) 24hrs, gay-owned

Johns Island Cafe 3406 Maybank Hwy., Johns Island, 559-9090 (★BW) breakfast, lunch Mon-Sat, dinner Wed-Sat

Vickery's of Beaufain Street 15 Beaufain St., 577-5300 (★) 11am-3am, Cuban

SPIRITUAL GROUPS
MCC Charleston 2010 Hawthorne Dr. Ste. 10, 747-6736 (WC) 11am Sun

PUBLICATIONS
The Front Page PO Box 27928, Raleigh NC, 27611, (919) 829-0181

Q Notes PO Box 221841, Charlotte NC, 28222, (704) 531-9988

EROTICA
Excited Video 2070 Harley Ave., N. Charleston, 744-5380, 24hrs

CRUISY AREAS
The Battery Sea wall (AYOR)

Folly Beach (AYOR)

Waterfront Park pier & promenade (AYOR)

Columbia (803)

INFO LINES & SERVICES
AA Gay/Lesbian 254-5301, call for times & locations

Bisexual, Gay & Lesbian Association PO Box 80098, 29225, meet Wed at USC Busn. Admin bldg

▲ **Community Real Estate Referrals** (800) 346-5592, gay realtor at your service, no rentals

South Carolina Gay/Lesbian Community Center/Info Line 1108 Woodrow St., 771-7713, 24hr message, 6pm-10pm, from 2pm Sat, clsd Sun & Mon

BARS
Affairs 712 Huger St., 779-4321 (M,NH) 4pm-2am

Candy Shop 1903 Two Notch Rd. (M,D,MRC-AF,PC)

Capital Club 1002 Gervais St., 256-6464 (M,NH,P,PC,WC) 5pm-2am

Metropolis 1801 Landing, 799-8727 (MW,D,E,S,PC) 10pm-?, from 9pm Fri-Sun, clsd Mon

Pipeline 1109 Assembly, 771-0121 (MW,NH,S,PC) 9pm-6am, clsd Sun-Tue

Traxx 416 Lincoln St., 256-1084 (W,D,E,PC,WC)

BOOKSTORES & RETAIL SHOPS
Intermezzo 2015 Devine St., 799-2276, 10am-midnight

Stardust Books 2805 Devine St., 771-0633, spiritual

TRAVEL & TOUR OPERATORS
B&A Travel Service 2728 Devine St., 256-0547/(800) 968-7658 (IGTA)

South Carolina Division of Tourism 734-0235

Travel Unlimited 612 St. Andrews Rd. #9, 798-8122/(800) 849-2244 (IGTA)

SPIRITUAL GROUPS
MCC Columbia 1111 Belleview, 256-2154, 11am Sun

PUBLICATIONS
▲ **In Unison** PO Box 8024, 29202, 771-0804

EROTICA
Chaser's 3128 Two Notch Rd., 754-6672, 24hrs
Video Magic 5445 Two Notch Rd., 786-8125, clsd Sun

CRUISY AREAS
Lake Murray Dam (AYOR)
Senate Street nr. State House (AYOR)

Florence

CRUISY AREAS
Timrod Park (AYOR)

Folly Beach (803)

ACCOMMODATIONS
Charleston Beach B&B PO Box 41, 29439, 588-9443 (MW,SW,N) spa, Sun BBQ

Greenville (803)

BARS
▲ **The Castle** 8 Le Grand Blvd., 235-9949 (★MW,D,S,V,YC,PC) 10pm-4am, clsd Mon-Wed
Club 621 621 Airport Rd., 234-6767 (★M,D,V,SW,PC) 7pm-4am, from 1pm wknds
New Attitude 706 W. Washington St., 233-1387 (★MW,MRC-AF,D) 10pm-? wknds
South Ramp 404 Airport Rd., 242-0102 (MW,D,CW,WC) 7pm-midnight, til 2am Fri & Sat, clsd Sun-Tue

SPIRITUAL GROUPS
MCC 37 E. Hillcrest Dr. (Unitarian Fellowship), 233-0919, 6:45 Sun

Hilton Head (803)

INFO LINES & SERVICES
▲ **Community Real Estate Referrals** (800) 346-5592, gay realtor at your service, no rentals

BARS
Moon Jammers 11 Heritage Plaza, Pope Ave., 842-9195 (MW,NH,D,A,S,PC,WC) 8pm-2am

Myrtle Beach (803)

BARS
Illusions 1012 S. Kings Hwy., 448-0421 (MW,D,S) 9pm-?
▲ **Time Out** 520 8th Ave. N., 448-1180 (★M,NH,D,PC,WC) 6pm-?, til 2am Sat

EROTICA
Maxwell's (24hr Extra News & Video) 2027 Hwy. 501, 626-3140

CRUISY AREAS
Beach at 82nd Ave. (AYOR)
Hurl Rock Park at 21st Ave S. (south end) (AYOR)

Rock Hill (803)

BARS
Hideaway 405 Baskins Rd., 328-6630 (MW,NH,PC) 8pm-?, clsd Mon-Wed

The NAMES Project Chapters
(USA)

California

Bay Area	415-863-1966
Inland Empire	909-784-2437
Long Beach	310-434-0021
Los Angeles	213-653-6263
Orange County	714-490-3880
Sacramento	916-484-5646
San Diego	619-492-8452
Ventura County	805-650-7382

Connecticut

Central
Connecticut   203-369-9670

District of Columbia

National Capital
Area   202-296-2637

Hawaii

Honolulu   808-948-1481

Iowa

Cedar Valley   319-266-7903

Illinois

Chicago   312-472-4460

Indiana

Indianapolis   317-920-1200

Louisiana

Louisiana
Capital Area   504-753-0864

Massachusetts

Boston   617-262-6263

Maine

Maine   207-774-2198

Michigan

Detroit	313-337-5895
Thumb Area	810-982-6361

Minnesota

Twin Cities   612-373-2468

Missouri

St. Louis   314-995-4638

North Carolina

Charlotte   704-376-2637

New Jersey

New Jersey   908-739-4863

New Mexico

New Mexico   505-466-2211

New York

Buffalo	716-838-4860
Long Island	516-477-2447
New York City	212-226-2292
Syracuse	315-498-4940

Oklahoma

Tulsa   918-748-3111

Oregon

Portland   503-650-7032

Pennsylvania

Philadelphia	215-735-6263
Pittsburgh	412-343-9846
Susquehanna	
Valley	717-234-0629

Rhode Island

Rhode Island   401-847-7637

Texas

Dallas	
Metroplex	214-520-7397
Ft. Worth/Tarrant	
County	817-336-2637
Houston	713-526-2637

Utah

Salt Lake City   801-487-2323

Virginia

Central Virginia   804-346-8047

Washington

Seattle   206-285-2880

West Virginia

Upper Ohio
Valley   304-242-9443

Santee (803)

TRAVEL & TOUR OPERATORS
All Around Travel Network 1568 Village Square Blvd., 854-2475/(800) 395-4255 (IGTA)

Spartanburg (803)

BARS
Cheyenne Cattlemen's Club 995 Asheville Hwy., 573-7304/(800) 428-9808 (M,D,E,S,PC) 8pm-2am, til 4am Fri, from 3pm Sun

CRUISY AREAS
Millikan Park (AYOR)

SOUTH DAKOTA

Pierre

TRAVEL & TOUR OPERATORS
South Dakota Dept. of Tourism 711 Wells Ave., 57501-3335, (800) 952-3625 (in-state only)/(800) 732-5682 (out-of-state only)

Rapid City (605)

ACCOMMODATIONS
Camp Michael 13051 Bogus Jim Rd., 342-5590 (MW)

EROTICA
Heritage Bookstore 912 Main St., 394-9877

CRUISY AREAS
Main & St. Joe Sts. btwn. 6th & 8th (AYOR)

Sioux Falls (605)

INFO LINES & SERVICES
The Coalition PO Box 89803, 57105, 333-0603, 24hrs, info, referrals

RESTAURANTS & CAFES
Touchés 323 S. Phillips Ave., 335-9874 (✷MW,D,F,WC) 8pm-2am

SPIRITUAL GROUPS
St. Francis & St. Clare MCC 1129 E. 9th St., 332-3966, 5:30pm Sun (7pm summers)

EROTICA
Studio One Book Store 311 N. Dakota Ave., 332-9316, 24hrs

CRUISY AREAS
Faywick Park 2nd Ave. & 11th St. (AYOR)

TENNESSEE

Chattanooga (423)

INFO LINES & SERVICES
Gay AA at MCC, 629-2737, 8pm Fri

BARS
Alan Gold's 1100 McCallie Ave., 629-8080 (★MW,D,F,S,WC) 4:30pm-3am
Chuck's II 27-1/2 W. Main, 265-5405 (MW,NH,D,CW,OC) 6pm-1am, til 3am Fri-Sat, patio
Septembers 6005 Lee Hwy., 510-6666 (M,F,E) 4pm-2am, clsd Mon

SPIRITUAL GROUPS
Integrity 20 Belvior Ave. (Grace Church), 629-2871, 6pm 1st & 3rd Sun
MCC Chattanooga 1601 Foust St., 629-2737, 6pm Sun

EROTICA
Rossville News 2437 Rossville Blvd., 266-7639, 24hrs

CRUISY AREAS
Bird Sanctuary Amnocala Hwy. (AYOR)
Chickamauga Dam area Hwy. 153 (AYOR)

Clarksville

CRUISY AREAS
Fairground Park & MacGregor Park (AYOR)

Gatlinburg (423)

ACCOMMODATIONS
River Cove B&B 3559 Emerald Way, Sevierville, 429-0096 (W) full brkfst

Greenville (615)

ACCOMMODATIONS
▲ **Timberfell Lodge** 2240 Van Hill Rd. (exit 36, off I-81), 234-0833/(800) 437-0118 (★MO,F,N,SW) hot tub

Haley (615)

RESTAURANTS & CAFES
Our House 389-6616/(800) 876-6616 (★WC) clsd Mon, fine dining, reservations only

Jackson (901)

BARS
The Other Side 3883 Hwy. 45 N., 668-3749 (MW,S) 5pm-?, from 7pm Sat, clsd Mon-Tue

CRUISY AREAS
Muse Park (AYOR)

Jamestown (615)

ACCOMMODATIONS
Laurel Creek Campground Rock Creek Rte. Box 150, 879-7696 (GF,SW)

Johnson City (423)

INFO LINES & SERVICES
▲ **Community Real Estate Referrals** (800) 346-5592, gay realtor at your service, no rentals

BARS
New Beginnings 2910 N. Bristol Hwy., 282-4446 (★M,D,S,WC) 9pm-2am, 8pm-3am Fri-Sat, clsd Mon

SPIRITUAL GROUPS
MCC of the Tri-Cities Coast Valley Unitarian Church, 926-4393, 7pm Sun

Kingsport

CRUISY AREAS
Broad St. nr. library (AYOR)

Knoxville (423)

INFO LINES & SERVICES
AA Gay/Lesbian 3219 Kingston Pike (Tenn Valley Unitarian Church), 522-9667, 7pm Mon & Fri
▲ **Community Real Estate Referrals** (800) 346-5592, gay realtor at your service, no rentals
Gay/Lesbian Helpline 521-6546, 7pm-11pm
Lambda Student Union PO Box 8529, 37996, 525-2335

BARS
Carousel II 1501 White Ave., 522-6966 (★MW,D,S) 9pm-3am

Old Plantations 837 N. 5th Ave., 637-7132 (MW,NH,S,WC) 8pm-3am, 10pm-6am Fri-Sun, beer/wine & set-ups only

Trumps 4541 Kingston Pike, 584-4884 (MW,D,A,S,WC) 5pm-3am, from 9pm wknds

BOOKSTORES & RETAIL SHOPS

Chelsea Station News 103 W. Jackson Ave., 522-6390, 9am-10pm, til 1am Fri-Sat

Davis Kidd Bookstore The Commons, 113 N. Peters Rd., 690-0136 (WC) 9:30am-10pm, 10am-6pm Sun

Pandora's Books 133 S. Central Ave., 524-1259 (WC) 11am-5pm, from 1pm Sun, alternative

TRAVEL & TOUR OPERATORS

Bryan Travel, Inc. 5614 Kingston Pike, Melrose Place, 588-8166/(800) 234-8166 (IGTA)

SPIRITUAL GROUPS

MCC Knoxville 934 N. Weisgarber Rd. (United Church of Christ), 521-6546, 6pm Sun

CRUISY AREAS

Cumberland Ave. around St. John's church (AYOR)

Downtown btwn. post office & library (AYOR)

Gay St. lower end close to bridge (AYOR)

The Square intersection of Church, Market, Walnut & Union Sts (AYOR)

Liberty (615)

PUBLICATIONS

RFD PO Box 68, 37095, 536-5176, country journal for gay men everywhere

Memphis (901)

INFO LINES & SERVICES

Black & White Men Together Box 42157, 38174, 452-5894

▲ **Community Real Estate Referrals** (800) 346-5592, gay realtor at your service, no rentals

Gay/Lesbian Switchboard 278-4297, 7:30pm-11pm

Memphis Gay/Lesbian Community Center 1486 Madison Ave., 726-5790

Memphis Lambda Center (AA) 1488 Madison, 276-7379, 8pm nightly, meeting place for 12-Step groups

BARS

501 Club 111 N. Claybrook, 274-8655 (M,D,F,S,WC) noon-3am, til 6am Fri-Sat, patio, also cruise bar

Amnesia 2866 Poplar, 454-1366 (★MW,D,A,SW,WC) 8pm-3am, clsd Mon-Wed, dinner nightly, patio

Autumn Street Pub 1349 Autumn St., 274-8010 (MW,NH,D,F,WC) 1pm-3am, from 5pm Mon, clsd Tue, patio

Backstreet 2018 Court Ave., 276-5522 (MW,D,WC) 8pm-3am, til 6am wknds, beer & setups only

Crossroads 102 N. Cleveland, 725-8156 (MW,NH) noon-3am

David's 1474 Madison, 278-4313 (M,NH) 3pm-3am, from noon Sat, beer & setups only

The Edge 532 S. Cooper, 272-3036 (M) 5pm-1am

J. Wags Bar 1268 Madison, 725-1909 (M,D,F,S) 24hrs, beer & set-up only, patio

One More 2117 Peabody Ave., 278-8015 (GF,NH,MRC,F) 10am-3am, from noon Sun

Pipeline 1382 Poplar, 726-5263 (M,L,WC) 2pm-3am, beer & setup only, courtyard

Sunshine Lounge 1379 Lamar, 272-9843 (GF,NH,WC) 7am-midnight, til 3am Fri-Sat, beer & setups only

X-scape 227 Monroe, 528-8344 (M,D,A,S) 10pm-3am, clsd Mon-Wed

RESTAURANTS & CAFES

Alternative Restaurant 553 S. Cooper, 725-7922 (BYOB) 11am-8pm, til midnight Fri-Sat, clsd Sun, homecooking

Coffee Cellar 3573 Southern, 320-7853 (WC) 7am-midnight, 8am-8pm Sat, patio

P&H Cafe 1532 Madison, 726-0906 (BW,WC) 11am-3am, from 5pm Sat, clsd Sun

BOOKSTORES & RETAIL SHOPS

Davis Kidd Booksellers 397 Perkins Rd. Ext., 683-9801, 9:30am-10pm, 10am-6pm Sun, lesbigay titles

Meristem Women's Bookstore 930 S. Cooper, 276-0282 (WC) 10am-8pm, til 6pm Th & Sat, 1pm Sun, clsd Mon-Tue, some gay men's titles

SPIRITUAL GROUPS

First Congregational Church 234 S. Watkins, 278-6786, 11am Sun

Holy Trinity Community Church 1559 Madison, 726-9443, 11am & 7pm Sun, 7:30pm Wed

Integrity 102 N. Second St. (Calvary Episcopal Church), 525-6602, 3rd Tue 6pm

PUBLICATIONS

Triangle Journal News Box 11485, 38111-0485, 454-1411

EROTICA

Airport Books 2214 Brooks Rd. E., 345-0657, 24hrs

Cherokee Adult Book Store 2947 Lamar, 744-7494, 24hrs

Getwell Book Mart 1275 Getwell, 454-7765, 24hrs

Paris Theater 2432 Summer Ave., 323-2665, 24hrs

CRUISY AREAS

Overton Square nr. Playhouse (AYOR)

Nashville (615)

INFO LINES & SERVICES

AA Gay/Lesbian 831-1050

Center for Lesbian/Gay Community Services 703 Berry Rd., 297-0008, 5pm-10pm

▲ **Community Real Estate Referrals** (800) 346-5592, gay realtor at your service, no rentals

Gay Cable Network Channel 19, 9pm Tue & 10pm Sat

ACCOMMODATIONS

IDA 904 Vikkers Hollow Rd., Dowelltown, 597-4409 (MW) camping avail May-Sept, a private community "commune" located in the hills 1hr SE of Nashville

Savage House 167 8th Ave. N., 244-2229 (GF) full brkfst

BARS

Boots 301 S. Second St., 254-8037 (M,NH) 5pm-1am, til 3am Fri & Sat, clsd Mon

Chez Collette 300 Hermitage Ave., 256-9134 (W,NH) 4pm-3am

Chute Complex 2535 Franklin Rd., 297-4571 (★M,D,CW,L,F,E,WC) 5pm-3am, 5 bars, patio, also full restaurant

Connection Nashville 901 Cowan, 742-1166 (M,D,F,E,WC) opens 8pm, gift shop from 10pm, patio

Crazy Cowboy 2311 Franklin Rd., 269-5318 (M,NH) 3pm-3am, beer only

Gas Lite 167-1/2 8th Ave. N., 254-1278 (MW,F,E) 4:30pm-1am, til 3am Fri-Sat, from 3pm wknds

Jungle Lounge & Restaurant 306 4th Ave. S., 256-9411 (M,D,F,S) 11am-3am, patio

KC's Club 909 909 Church St., 251-1613 (W,D,F,E,WC) 6pm-3am, clsd Tue

The Triangle 1401 4th Ave. S., 242-8131 (MW,NH,F,WC) 8am-3am, from noon Sun

Underground 176 2nd Ave. N., 742-8909 (GF,D,A) 9pm-3am

Victor Victoria's 111 8th Ave. N., 244-7256 (M,D,S,WC) 11am-3am, from noon-3am Sun

Warehouse 2 2529 Franklin Pike, 385-9689 (★M,D,S) 8pm-3am

Ynonah's Saloon 1700 4th Ave. S., 251-0980 (M,NH,WC) 10am-3am, from noon wknds

RESTAURANTS & CAFES

Garden Allegro 1805 Church St., 327-3834, 8am-9pm, from 10am wknds, juice bar

The Mad Platter 1239 6th Ave. N., 242-2563 (WC) lunch, dinner by reservation only, clsd Sun-Mon

Towne House Tea Room 165 8th Ave. N. (next to Gas Lite bar), 254-1277, lunch wkdays

World's End 1713 Church St., 329-3480 (MW) 4pm-1am, clsd Mon

BOOKSTORES & RETAIL SHOPS

Davis-Kidd Booksellers 4007 Hillsboro Rd., 385-2645, 9:30am-10pm, lesbigay section

Tower Books 2404 West End Ave., 327-8085, 9am-midnight, large lesbigay section

TRAVEL & TOUR OPERATORS

Tennessee Tourist Development 741-2158

SPIRITUAL GROUPS

Integrity 419 Woodland St. (St. Ann's Church), 383-6608, 4th Tue 6:30pm

MCC 1808 Woodmont Blvd., 262-0922, 7pm Sun

PUBLICATIONS

Etc. PO Box 8916, Atlanta GA, 30306, (404) 525-3821, weekly

Query PO Box 24241, 37202-4241, 259-4135, weekly

Xenogeny PO Box 60716, 37206

EROTICA

Carousel Book Store 5606 Charlotte, 352-0855

Metro News 822 5th Ave. S., 256-1310, 24hrs

Odyssey Adult Bookstore 700 Division St., 726-0243

Purple Onion 2807 Nolansville Rd., 259-9229, 24hrs; also 2702 Dickerson Rd. location 226-9192

The Wheel 421 Broadway, 256-4597

CRUISY AREAS

Cedar Hill Park (AYOR)

Percy Priest Dam (AYOR)

Newport (423)

ACCOMMODATIONS
Christopher Place 1500 Pinnacles Way, 623-6555/(800) 595-9441 (GF,IGTA)

Rogersville (615)

ACCOMMODATIONS
Lee Valley Farm 142 Drinnon Ln., 272-4068 (M) private retreat

Saltillo (901)

ACCOMMODATIONS
Parker House 1956 Tutwiller Ave., 278-5844 (MW,F,SW) full brkfst, 2 hrs outside Memphis

Sewanee (615)

ACCOMMODATIONS
Boxwood Cottage B&B 333 Anderson Cemetery Rd., 598-5012 (MW) seasonal, full brkfst

TEXAS

Abilene (915)

BARS
Just Friends 201 S. 14th St., 672-9318 (MW,D,S,WC) 7pm-midnight, til 1am Fri, til 2am Sat, clsd Mon

SPIRITUAL GROUPS
Exodus MCC 904 Walnut, 672-7922, 10:45am & 6pm Sun

CRUISY AREAS
Kirby Park (AYOR)

Amarillo (806)

INFO LINES & SERVICES
Amarillo Lesbian/Gay Alliance Info Line 373-5725, 7:30pm 1st Tue

BARS
Classifieds 519 E. 10th St., 374-2435 (MW,D,E,WC) noon-2am, clsd Mon
The Ritz 323 W. 10th Ave., 372-9382 (MW,CW,D,S) 2pm-2am
Sassy's 309 W. 6th St., 374-3029 (MW,D,A) 5pm-2am

RESTAURANTS & CAFES
Italian Delight 2710 W. 10th, 372-5444 (BW,WC) lunch & dinner, clsd Sun

SPIRITUAL GROUPS
MCC 2123 S. Polk St., 372-4557, 10:30am & 6pm Sun

EROTICA
Boulevard Book Store & Video 601 N. Eastern, 379-9002, 24hrs
Studio One 9000 Triangle Dr., 372-0648, 24hrs

Arlington (see also Fort Worth) (817)

INFO LINES & SERVICES
▲ **Community Real Estate Referrals** (800) 346-5592, gay realtor at your service, no rentals

Tarrant County Lesbian/Gay Alliance 1219 6th Ave., Fort Worth, 877-5544, info line & newsletter

Bars
Arlington 651 1851 W. Division, 275-9651 (★M,D,E,K,S,WC) 4pm-2am

Spiritual Groups
Trinity MCC 609 Truman, 265-5454, 9:30am Sun, 7:30pm Wed

Austin   (512)

Info Lines & Services
Adventuring Outdoors 445-7216

ALLGO (Austin Latino/a Lesbian/Gay Organization) PO Box 13501, 78711, 472-2001, 6:30pm 3rd Th

▲ **Community Real Estate Referrals** (800) 346-5592, gay realtor at your service, no rentals

Hotline 472-4357, 24hrs

Accommodations
Driskill Hotel 604 Brazos St., 474-5911/(800) 527-2008 (GF,WC)

Omni Hotel 700 San Jacinto, 476-3700/(800) 843-6664 (GF,F,SW,WC)

Summit House B&B 1204 Summit St., 445-5304 (GF) full brkfst, centrally located

Bars
5th St. Station Saloon/Auntie Mame's 505 E. 5th St., 478-6065 (MW,D,CW,E,S,WC) 2pm-2am

Area 52 404 Colorado, 476-8297 (★MW,D,A,S,18+,WC) 9pm-?, clsd Mon-Tue

Blue Flamingo 617 Red River, 469-0014 (GF,NH,S) noon-2am, strong coffee served

'Bout Time 9601 N. 1H-35, 832-5339 (★MW,NH,S) 2pm-2am

Casino El Camino 517 E. 6th St., 469-9330 (GF,NH,F) 4pm-2am, from 11am Sun, psychedelic punk jazz lounge

Chain Drive 504 Willow St., 480-9017 (M,L,WC) 2pm-2am, Sun buffet 4pm

Charlie's 1301 Lavaca, 474-6481 (★M,D,S,YC,WC) 2pm-2am, patio

Kansas 213 W. 4th, 480-8686 (MW,NH,D,WC) noon-4am

The Naked Grape 611 Red River, 476-3611 (M,D,S,WC) 10am-2am, patio

O.H.M.S. 611 E. 7th, 472-7136 (GF,D,A,18+) 10pm-?, clsd Sun-Mon

Oil Can Harry's 211 W. 4th, 320-8823 (★M,D,A,YC,WC) 2pm-2am, patio

Proteus 501 6th St., 472-8922 (GF,D,A,V) 10pm-4am, clsd Sun-Tue

Restaurants & Cafes
Bitter End Bistro & Brewery 311 Colorado St., 478-2337, wood baked pizza

Common Market Cafe 1600 S. Congress Ave., 416-1940, 8am-10pm, 10am-3pm Sun

Eastside Cafe 2113 Manor Rd., 476-5858 (BW,WC) lunch & dinner

Katz's 618 W. 6th St., 472-2037 (WC) 24hrs, NY deli food, full bar

Momma's Diner 314 Congress, 474-5730, 24hrs

Romeo's 1500 Barton Springs Rd., 476-1090 (BW,WC)

Soma 212 W. 4th St., 474-7662, 7am-midnight, til 4am Fri-Sat, espresso bar & cafe

West Lynn Cafe 1110 W. Lynn, 482-0950 (BW) vegetarian

BOOKSTORES & RETAIL SHOPS
Congress Avenue Booksellers 716 Congress Ave., 478-1157, 7:45am-8pm, 9am-6pm Sat, til 4pm Sun

Lobo 3204-A Guadalupe, 454-5406 (WC) 10am-10pm, lesbigay

TRAVEL & TOUR OPERATORS
Capital of Texas Travel, Inc. 3006 Medical Arts St., 478-2468/(800) 880-0068 (IGTA)

Creative Travel Center 8650 Spicewood Springs Ste. 210, 331-9560 (IGTA)

Texas Tourist Division PO Box 5064, 78763-5064, 462-9191/(800) 888-8TEX

West Austin Travel 2737 Exposition Blvd., 482-8197/(800) 541-8583 (IGTA)

SPIRITUAL GROUPS
Affirmation (Methodist) 7403 Shoal Creek Blvd., 451-2329, meets every other month

First Unitarian Church 4700 Grover Ave., 452-6168 (WC) 9:15, 10:30 & 11:15am Sun

Integrity 27th & University Ave.(church), 445-6164, 8pm 3rd Sun

MCC Austin 425 Woodward St., 416-1170 (WC) 9am, 11am & 7pm Sun

Mishpachat Am Echad PO Box 9591, 78766, 451-7018, social group for Jewish lesbians/gays

PUBLICATIONS
Fag Rag PO Box 1034, 78767, 479-9800, gay boy party paper

Texas Triangle 1615 W. 6th St., 476-0576

MEN'S CLUBS
▲ **Midtowne Spa-Austin** 5815 Airport Blvd., 302-9696 (MO,PC) 24hrs

EROTICA

Austin Six 521 Thompson Ln., 385-5329, 24hrs

Forbidden Fruit 512 Neches, 478-8358; also 2001-A Guadalupe, 478-8542

Oasis Bookstore 9601 N. IH-35, 835-7208, 24hrs

Pleasureland Adult Video Center 613 W. 29th St., 478-2339, 24hrs

CRUISY AREAS

Hippy Hollow-Lake Travis (AYOR)

Beaumont (409)

INFO LINES & SERVICES

Lambda AA 6300 College, 835-1508

BARS

Copa 304 Orleans St., 832-4206 (★MW,D,S,WC) 9pm-2am

Sundowner 497 Crockett St., 833-3989 (MW,D,S,BW,BYOB) 4pm-2am

SPIRITUAL GROUPS

Spindletop Unitarian Church 1575 Spindletop Rd., 833-6883, 10:30am Sun

College Station (409)

INFO LINES & SERVICES

Gayline 847-0321, Texas A&M Gay/Lesbian/Bisexual Student Services

BARS

Club 308 S. Bryan St., Bryan, 823-6767 (★MW,D,S) 9pm-2am

Dudley's Draw 311 University, 846-3030 (GF,NH,WC) 11am-1am

Corpus Christi (512)

INFO LINES & SERVICES

▲ **Community Real Estate Referrals** (800) 346-5592, gay realtor at your service, no rentals

Lambda AA (at Christ's Temple MCC), 882-8255

ACCOMMODATIONS

The Anthony's By The Sea 732 Pearl, Rockport, 729-6100/(800) 460-2557 (GF,SW) full brkfst

The Sea Horse Inn 1423 11th St., PO Box 426, Port Aransas, 78373, 749-5221 (MW,SW)

BARS

Club Unity 4125 Gollihar, 851-1178 (W,D) 3pm-2am, from noon Sun

The Hidden Door 802 S. Staples St., 882-5002 (M,L,WC) 3pm-2am, from noon Sun

The Hideout Leopard St. (M,NH,MRC-L) 8pm-2am, clsd Mon, inquire locally

Mingles 512 S. Staples, 884-8022 (W,D)

Numbers 1214 Leopard, 887-8445 (M,D) 4pm-2am

UBU 511 Starr, 882-9693 (GF,D,S,WC) 9pm-2am Wed-Sun

SPIRITUAL GROUPS

Christ's Temple MCC 1315 Craig St., 882-8255, 11am Sun

CRUISY AREAS

Seawall (AYOR)

Dallas (214)

INFO LINES & SERVICES

Asians & Friends PO Box 9142, 75209, 480-5906

▲ **Community Real Estate Referrals** (800) 346-5592, gay realtor at your service, no rentals

Couples-Metro-Dallas PO Box 803156, 75380-3156, 504-6775

Crossdressers/TV Helpline 264-7103

Crossroads Bar Hotline 380-3808, 24hrs

Dallas Gay Historic Archives (at Gay/Lesbian Center)

Gay/Lesbian Community Center 2701 Reagan St., 528-9254 (WC) 9am-9pm, 10am-6pm Sat, from noon Sun

Gay/Lesbian Information Line 520-8781, 7pm-9pm, 8pm-midnight Fri-Sat

Lambda AA 2727 Oaklawn, 522-6259, noon, 6pm, 8pm daily

Lesbian/Gay Welcome Wagon 2612 Bell St., 979-0017, community info for new arrivals

MACT (Men of All Colors Together) PO Box 190611, 75219, 521-4765

Metroplex Prime Timers (at Gay Center), 3pm 3rd Sun, social group for mature men

ACCOMMODATIONS

The Courtyard on the Trail 8045 Forest Trail, 553-9700 (MW,SW) full brkfst

▲ **The Inn on Fairmount** 3701 Fairmount, 522-2800 (MW) hot tub

Melrose Hotel 3015 Oaklawn Dr., 521-5151/(800) 635-7673 (GF) piano bar & restaurant

BARS

Anchor Inn 4024 Cedar Springs, 526-4098 (M,E) 4pm-2am, also 'Numbers' 521-7861, from 7am

Another Bar 4020 Maple Ave., 520-1366 (M,NH,WC) noon-2am, patio

Bamboleo's 5027 Lemmon St., 520-1124 (MW,MRC-L,WC) 9pm-2am Fri-Sun

Big Daddy's 4024 Cedar Springs Rd., 528-4098 (M,V,S) 6pm-2am

Boxx Office/Las Mariposas 2515 N. Fitzhugh, 828-2665 (M,D,MRC,S,WC) 6pm-2am

The Brick 4117 Maple, 521-3154 (M,D,L) 2pm-2am, til 4am Fri-Sat

Buddies 3415 Mahanna, 526-8720 (MW,D,S) 11am-2am, from noon Sun

Club Escape 2525 Wycliff #130, 521-7255 (GF,S) 9pm-?, from 7pm Sun, clsd Mon-Tue

Crews Inn 3215 N. Fitzhugh, 526-9510 (★M,D,S,WC) noon-2am, popular Tue nights, patio

Dallas Eagle 2515 Inwood #107 (entrance in rear), 357-4375 (M,L) 4pm-2am, til 4am Fri-Sat, clsd Mon-Tue.

The Headquarters 4117 Maple Ave., 521-1193 (M,NH,WC) 7am-2am, patio

Hidden Door 5025 Bowser, 526-9211 (M,NH,L) 7am-2am, from noon Sun

Hideaway Club 4144 Buena Vista, 599-2966 (MW,P,E,OC) 8am-2am, from noon Sun

▲ **J.R.'s** 3923 Cedar Springs Rd., 528-1004 (★M,F,WC) 11am-2am

John L.'s 2525 Wycliff #120, 520-2525 (MW,S,WC) 4pm-2am

The Metro 2204 Elm, 742-2101 (M,D,MRC-AF,S,WC) 9pm-2am, from 7pm Sun, clsd Mon-Tue, 18+ Wed & Sun

A Traveler's Dream

THE
CLUB
Dallas

One Day Memberships • Deluxe Suites
Free Parking • In/Out Privileges
Centrally Located
Videos • Steam • Sauna • Whirpool
Outdoor Pool & Patio • Tanning
Fully Equipped Gym

2616 Swiss Avenue
Dallas, Texas 75204
214-821-1990

When you come to

DALLAS

come to us.

Moby Dick 4011 Cedar Springs Rd., 520-6629 (M,V,WC) noon-2am

Pub Pegasus 3326 N. Fitzhugh, 559-4663 (M,NH,WC) 10am-2am, from 8am Sat, from noon Sun

Round-Up Saloon 3912-14 Cedar Springs Rd., 522-9611 (★M,D,CW,WC) 8pm-2am, clsd Mon-Tue

Side 2 Bar 4006 Cedar Springs Rd., 528-2026 (MW,NH,WC) 10am-2am

▲ **Sue Ellen's** 3903 Cedar Springs, 559-0707 (W,D,E,WC) 3pm-2am, from noon wknds

▲ **Throckmorton Mining Co.** 3014 Throckmorton, 521-4205 (★M,L) 1pm-2am, Wed-Sun Beer Bust

Trestle 412 S. Haskell, 826-9988 (M,NH,L) 8pm-2am

▲ **Village Station** 3911 Cedar Springs Rd., 526-7171 (★M,D,S,V) 9pm-3am, from 5pm Sun

Zippers 3333 N. Fitzhugh, 526-9519 (M,NH,S) noon-2am

RESTAURANTS & CAFES
Black-Eyed Pea 3857 Cedar Springs Rd., 521-4580 (WC) 11am-10:30pm

The Bronx Restaurant & Bar 3835 Cedar Springs Rd., 521-5821 (WC) lunch & dinner, Sun brunch, clsd Mon

Hunky's 4000 Cedar Springs Rd., 522-1212 (★BW,WC) 11am-10pm

The Natura Cafe 2909 McKinney Ave., 855-5483, lunch & dinner

Panda's 3917 Cedar Springs Rd., 528-3818 (★) til 3am, Chinese

The Wok 4006 Cedar Springs Rd., 528-0000, 10am-3am

GYMS & HEALTH CLUBS
Centrum Sports Club 3102 Oak Lawn, 522-4100 (GF,SW)

BOOKSTORES & RETAIL SHOPS

Crossroads Market 3930 Cedar Springs Rd., 521-8919 (WC) 10am-10pm, noon-9pm Sun, lesbigay bookstore

Shocking Gray 2851 Anode Ln., 75220, 353-0882/(800) 344-4729

TapeLenders 3926 Cedar Springs Rd., 528-6344, 9am-midnight

TRAVEL & TOUR OPERATORS

Strong Travel 8201 Preston Rd. Ste. 160, 361-0027/(800) 747-5670 (IGTA)

Travel Friends 8080 N. Central Expwy. Ste.320, 891-8833/(800) 862-8833 (IGTA)

Travel With Us 6116 N. Central Expressway Ste. 175, 987-2563/(800) 856-2563 (IGTA)

SPIRITUAL GROUPS

Affirmation (Methodist) at North Haven United Methodist, 528-4913, 7:30pm 4th Mon

Cathedral of Hope MCC 5910 Cedar Springs, 351-1901 (WC) 9am, 11am & 6:30pm Sun, 6:30pm Wed & Sat

Congregation Beth El Binah 497-1591

Dignity/Dallas 6525 Inwood Rd. (St. Thomas the Apostle), 521-5342x832 (WC) 5:30pm Sun (6:30pm summers)

First Unitarian Church of Dallas 4015 Normandy , 528-3990, 9am & 11am Sun (only 10am Sun summers)

Holy Trinity Community Church 4402 Roseland, 827-5088, 11am Sun

Integrity PO Box 190351, 75219, 520-0912

White Rock Community Church 722 Tennison Memorial Rd., 320-0043, 9am, 10:30am & 7:30pm Sun, 7pm Wed

PUBLICATIONS
TWT (This Week in Texas) 3300 Regan Ave., 521-0622, weekly

MEN'S CLUBS
▲ **Club Dallas** 2616 Swiss, 821-1990 (★MO,PC,SW) 24hrs
▲ **Midtowne Spa** 2509 Pacific, 821-8989 (★MO,PC) 24hrs

EROTICA
▲ **Alternatives** 1720 W. Mockingbird Ln., 630-7071, 8am-6pm
Leather by Boots 2525 Wycliff Ste.124, 528-3865, noon-8pm, clsd Sun
Shades of Grey Leather 3928 Cedar Springs Rd., 521-4739

Denison (903)

BARS
Goodtime Lounge 2520 N. Hwy. 91 N., 463-9944 (MW,PC) 6pm-2am, from 2pm Sun

Denton (817)

INFO LINES & SERVICES
Denton County Lambda AA (at Harvest MCC), 321-2332

BARS
Bedo's 1215 E. University Dr. , 566-9910 (MW,D,S,PC,WC) 8pm-midnight, from 6pm Fri, til 1am Sat, from 5pm Sun

SPIRITUAL GROUPS
Harvest MCC 5900 S. Stemmons, 321-2332, 10:30am Sun

CRUISY AREAS
Lake Lewisville-Queens Pt. (AYOR)

El Paso (915)

INFO LINES & SERVICES
Lambda AA 833-9544(private home), 7:30pm Mon
Lambda Line/Lambda Services PO Box 31321, 79931, 562-4297, 24hrs
Youth OUTreach (contact Lambda Line), 562-4297

BARS
Briar Patch 204 E. Rio Grande St., 546-9100 (MW,NH,OC) noon-2am
The Hawaiian 919 Paisano St., 541-7009, unverified '97
The Old Plantation 301-309 S. Ochoa St., 533-6055 (★MW,D,S,V,WC) 8pm-2am, til 4am Th-Sat, clsd Mon-Wed
San Antonio Mining Co. 800 E. San Antonio Ave., 533-9516 (★MW,D,S,V,WC) 3pm-2am
U-Got-It 216 S. Ochoa, 533-9510 (M,D,A,S,WC) 8pm-2am, clsd Sun-Tue
The Whatever Lounge 701 E. Paisano St., 533-0215 (M,MRC-L,BW,BYOB,WC) 3pm-2am

RESTAURANTS & CAFES
The Little Diner 7209 7th St., Canutillo, 877-2176, true Texas fare

SPIRITUAL GROUPS
MCC 916 E. Yandell, 591-4155, 6pm Sun, 7pm Wed

PUBLICATIONS
Lambda News PO Box 31321, 79931, 562-4297

EROTICA
Eros Adult Book Store 4828 Montana, 565-2929

Trixx Adult Cinema 2230 Texas St., 532-6171

Venus Adult Theatre & Books 4812 Montana, 566-8061

Fort Worth (817)

INFO LINES & SERVICES
▲ **Community Real Estate Referrals** (800) 346-5592, gay realtor at your service, no rentals

Lambda AA 3144 Ryan Ave., 921-2871, 8pm daily

Tarrant County Lesbian/Gay Alliance 1219 6th Ave., 763-5544, info line & newsletter

ACCOMMODATIONS
Two Pearls B&B 804 S. Alamo St., Weatherford, 596-9316 (MW)

BARS
651 Club Fort Worth 651 S. Jennings Ave., 332-0745 (M,D,CW,WC) noon-2am

Copa Cabana 1002 S. Main, 336-8911 (M)

The Corral 621 Hemphill St., 335-0196 (M,D,V,WC) 11am-2am, from noon Sun

D.J.'s 1308 St. Louis St., 927-7321 (★MW,D,F,S) 7pm-2am, til 3am Fri-Sat, clsd Mon-Tue

Magnolia Station 600 W. Magnolia, 332-0415 (M,S) 8pm-2am, clsd Mon-Tue

Neon Nights 1408 W. Magnolia, 870-0022 (M,NH,WC) 3pm-2am, clsd Mon

TRAVEL & TOUR OPERATORS
Country Day Travel 6022 Southwest Blvd., 731-8551 (IGTA)

SPIRITUAL GROUPS
Agape MCC 4516 SE Loop 820, 535-5002 (WC) 9am & 11am Sun

First Jefferson Unitarian Universalist 1959 Sandy Ln., 451-1505 (WC) 11am Sun, lesbigay group 7pm 1st Th

PUBLICATIONS
Alliance News 1219 6th Ave., 877-5544, monthly

Galveston (409)

INFO LINES & SERVICES
Lambda AA ACCT office (23rd & Ursula), 684-2140, 8pm Th & 5pm Sun

BARS
Evolution 2214 Ships Mechanic Rd., 763-4212 (★MW,D,V) 4pm-2am, til 4am Fri-Sat

Kon Tiki Club 312 23rd St., 763-6264 (★MW,D,S) 4pm-2am, from 2pm wknds

Robert's Lafitte 2501 'Q' Ave., 765-9092 (M,S,WC) 10am-2am, from noon Sun

EROTICA
The Dunes (AYOR)

Groesbeck (817)

ACCOMMODATIONS
Rainbow Ranch Rte. 2, Box 165, 729-5847 (GF) campsites & RV, on Lake Limestone (halfway between Houston & Dallas)

Gun Barrel City (903)

BARS

231 Club 231 W. Main St. (Hwy. 85), 887-2061 (GF,NH,WC) 6pm-midnight, til 1am Sat

Harlingen (210)

BARS

Colors 703 N. Ed Carey, 440-8663 (MW,D,S,WC) 8pm-2am, til 3am Fri-Sat, clsd Mon-Tue

Zippers 319 W. Harrison, 412-9708 (MW,E,WC) 8pm-2am

Houston (713)

INFO LINES & SERVICES

▲ **Community Real Estate Referrals** (800) 346-5592, gay realtor at your service, no rentals

Gay/Lesbian Hispanics Unidos PO Box 70153, 77270, 813-3769, 7pm 2nd Wed

Gay/Lesbian Radio KPFT-FM 90.1, 526-4000, mid-4am Sat 'After Hours', 6pm Fri 'Lesbian/Gay Voices'

Gay/Lesbian Switchboard PO Box 66469, 77266, 529-3211, 3pm-midnight

Houston Outdoor Group PO Box 980893, 77098, 526-7688

Lambda AA Center 1201 W. Clay, 521-1243 (WC) noon-11pm, til 1am Fri-Sat

ACCOMMODATIONS

▲ **The Lovett Inn** 501 Lovett Blvd., Montrose, 522-5224/(800) 779-5224 (GF,SW)

Montrose Inn 408 Avondale, 520-0206/(800) 357-1228 (MO) basic & butch, full brkfst

BARS

The 611 Club 611 Hyde Park, 526-7070 (★M,NH) noon-2am

Backyard Bar & Grill 10200 S. Main, 660-6285 (GF,F,WC) 5pm-2am, from noon wknds

The Berryhill II 12726 North Freeway, 873-8810 (MW,NH,D,E,WC) 6pm-2am

Brazos River Bottom (B.R.B.) 2400 Brazos, 528-9192 (★M,D,CW) 7am-2am, from noon Sun

Briar Patch 2294 W. Holcombe, 665-9678 (M,NH,E) 2pm-2am

Chances 1100 Westheimer, 523-7217 (W,D,E,WC) 10am-2am

Cousins 817 Fairview, 528-9204 (MW,NH,S,WC) 7am-2am

E.J.'s 2517 Ralph, 527-9071 (★M,NH,E) 7am-2am, from noon Sun

Gentry 2303 Richmond, 520-1861 (★M,NH,S,WC) 2pm-2am, from noon wknds

Heaven 810 Pacific, 521-9123 (★M,D,V,S,YC) 9pm-2am Wed-Sat, from 7pm Sun

Incognito 2524 McKinney, 237-9431 (MW,MRC,S) 9pm-2am, from 6pm Sun, clsd Mon-Tue

Inergy 5750 Chimney Rock, 666-7310 (★MW,D,MRC-L,E) 8pm-2am

J.R.'s 808 Pacific, 521-2519 (★M,S,V,WC) 11am-2am, from noon Sun

Jo's Outpost 1419 Richmond, 520-8446 (M,NH) 11am-2am

Lazy J. 312 E. Tuam, 528-9343 (M,S,OC,WC) 10am-midnight, til 2am Fri-Sat

Mary's 1022 Westheimer, 527-9669 (★M,L,WC) 7am-2am, from 10am Sun for brunch, patio

Melas Tejano Country 1016 W. 19th St., 880-1770 (M,MRC-L) 5pm-2am, clsd Mon-Tue

Montrose Mining Co. 805 Pacific, 529-7488 (★M,L,S) 1pm-2am, patio

Numbers 300 Westheimer, 526-6551 (GF,D,YC)

▲ **Pacific Street** 710 Pacific St., 523-0213 (★M,D,L,S,V,WC) 9pm-2am, from 7pm Fri & Sun, patio

Palm Beach Club (at West Houston Hilton) 12401 Katy Fwy. (I-10), 496-9090 (GF,D,TG) Sat night 'Fantasy BBS' party

Past Time 617 Fairview, 529-4669 (MW,NH) 7am-2am

Q.T.'s 534 Westheimer, 529-8813 (M,NH,S,WC) 8am-2am, from noon Sun

The Ranch 9218 Buffalo Speedwy., 666-3464 (W,D,CW,WC) 4pm-2am, clsd Mon

Rich's 2401 San Jacinto, 759-9606 (★M,D,A,E,V,YC,18+) 9pm-2am Th-Sat, from 7pm Sun

Ripcord 715 Fairview, 521-2792 (M,L,WC) 1pm-2am, from noon Sun

Steam 402 Lovett, 521-1450 (M) 1:30am-dawn, clsd Mon-Tue

Trading Post Ice House 11410 S. Post Oak Dr., 726-1963 (MW,BW,WC) 11am-midnight, til 1am Sat, clsd Sun, sports bar

Venture-N 2923 S. Main, 522-0000 (M,NH,L) noon-2am

RESTAURANTS & CAFES

A Moveable Feast 2202 W. Alabama, 528-3585 (WC) 9am-10pm

Baba Yega's 2607 Grant, 522-0042, 10am-10pm, patio

Barnaby's Cafe 604 Fairview, 522-0106 (★BW,WC) 11am-10pm, til 11pm Fri-Sat

Black-Eyed Pea 2048 W. Grey, 523-0200

Brasil 2604 Dunlavy, 528-1993, 9am-2am, bistro

Chapultepec 813 Richmond, 522-2365 (E) 24hrs

Charlie's 1102 Westheimer, 522-3332 (MW,WC) 24hrs

House of Pies 3112 Kirby, 528-3816, 24hrs

Jack Laurenzo's 5589 Richmond Ave., 266-4191, lunch & dinner

Java Java Cafe 911 W. 11th, 880-5282 (★)

Ninfa's 2704 Navigation, 228-1175, 11am-10pm, Mexican

Ninos 2817 W. Dallas, 522-5120 (WC) lunch & dinner, clsd Sun

Pot Pie Pizzeria 1525 Westheimer, 528-4350 (BW) 11am-11pm, clsd Mon

Q Cafe 2205 Richmond Ave., 524-9696, 4pm-2am, full bar

Rocky Java 220 Avondale, 521-7095 (WC) 24hrs, patio

Spanish Flower 4701 N. Main, 869-1706, 24hrs

Toopes Coffeehouse 1830 W. Alabama , 522-7662 (BW,WC) 6am-11pm, from 7am wknds, patio

GYMS & HEALTH CLUBS

Fitness Exchange 3930 Kirby Dr. Ste. 300, 524-9932 (GF) 6am-10pm, 10am-8pm wknds

YMCA Downtown 1600 Louisiana St., 659-8501 (GF,SW) 5am-10pm, 8am-6pm Sat, from 10am Sun

BOOKSTORES & RETAIL SHOPS

Basic Brothers 1232 Westheimer , 522-1626, 10am-9pm, noon-6pm Sun, lesbigay merchandise

Crossroads Market Bookstore/Cafe 1111 Westheimer, 942-0147 (F,WC) 9am-10pm, til 11pm Fri-Sat, lesbigay

Hyde Park Gallery 711 Hyde Park, 526-2744, lesbigay art gallery

A Traveler's Dream

 THE
CLUB
Houston

One Day Memberships • Deluxe Suites
Free Parking • In/Out Privileges
Centrally Located to Nightclubs
Videos • Steam • Sauna • Whirpool
Outdoor Pool & Patio • Tanning
Fully Equipped Gym

2205 Fannin Street
Houston, Texas 77002
713-659-4998

Inklings: An Alternative Bookstore 1846 Richmond Ave., 521-3369/(800) 931-3369, 10:30am-6:30pm, noon-5pm Sun, clsd Mon

Lobo-Houston 3939 S. Montrose Blvd., 522-5156, 10am-10pm, lesbigay bookstore

Lucia's Garden 2942 Virginia, 523-6494, 10am-6pm, spiritual herb center

TRAVEL & TOUR OPERATORS

▲ **Advance Travel** 10700 NW Freeway Ste. 160, 682-2002/(800) 292-0500 (★IGTA)

DCA Travel 1535 W. Loop S. Ste. 115, 629-5377/(800) 321-9539

Woodlake Travel 1704 Post Oak Rd., 942-0664/(800) 245-6180 (IGTA)

SPIRITUAL GROUPS

Dignity/Houston 1307 Yale Ste. 8, 880-2872, 7:30pm Sat, 5:30pm Sun

Integrity 6265 S. Main (Autry House), 432-0414, 7pm 2nd & 4th Mon

Maranatha Fellowship MCC 3400 Montrose Ste. 600, 528-6756, 11am Sun

MCC of the Resurrection 1919 Decatur St., 861-9149, 9am & 11am Sun

Mishpachat Alizim PO Box 980136, 77298-0136, 748-7079, worship & social/support for lesbian/gay Jews

PUBLICATIONS

Houston Voice 811 Westheimer Ste. 105, 529-8490

Out Smart 3406 Audubon Pl., 520-7237

TWT (This Week in Texas) 811 Westheimer St., 527-9111

MEN'S CLUBS

▲ **Club Houston** 2205 Fannin, 659-4998 (★MO,SW,PC) 24hrs

▲ **Midtowne Spa** 3100 Fannin, 522-2379 (★MO,SW,PC) 24hrs

EROTICA
Diners News 240 Westheimer, 522-9679, 24hrs
French Quarter All Male Theater 3201 Louisiana, 527-0782 (MO,PC)
Leather by Boots 2424 Montrose, 526-2668, noon-8pm
Leather Forever 711 Fairview, 526-6940, noon-8pm

Katy (713)

TRAVEL & TOUR OPERATORS
In Touch Travel 1814 Powderhorn, 347-3596 (IGTA)

Lampasas

CRUISY AREAS
William Brook Park at Sulpher Creek (AYOR)

Laredo (210)

BARS
Discovery 2019 Farragut, 722-9032 (M,D,S,BW) 6pm-2am Wed-Sun

Longview (903)

BARS
Decisions 2103 E. Marshall, 757-4884 (MW,D) 3pm-2am, patio
Lifestyles 446 Eastman Rd., 758-8082 (MW,D,S) 11am-2am

BOOKSTORES & RETAIL SHOPS
Newsland 301 E. Marshall, 753-4167, 9am-6pm, clsd Sun

SPIRITUAL GROUPS
Church With A Vision MCC 420 E. Cotton St., 753-1501 (WC) 10am Sun

Lubbock (806)

INFO LINES & SERVICES
AA Lambda 828-3316, 8pm Mon at MCC
LLGA (Lubbock Lesbian/Gay Alliance) PO Box 64746, 79464, 766-7184, 7:30pm
2nd Wed

BARS
The Captain Hollywood Main St. at Ave. X, 797-1808 (MW,D,S) 8pm-2am
Metro 1806 Clovis Rd., 740-0006 (MW,D,A) 7pm-2am

SPIRITUAL GROUPS
The MCC 4501 University Ave., 792-5562 (WC) 11am & 6pm Sun, & 7:30 Wed

CRUISY AREAS
McKenzie Park (AYOR)

McAllen (210)

BARS
Austin St. Inn 1110 Austin St., 687-7703 (MW,D,S) 8pm-2am, clsd Mon-Tue
P.B.D.'s 2908 Ware Rd. (at Daffodil), 682-8019 (M,NH,WC) 8pm-2am
Tenth Avenue 1820 N. 10th St., 682-7131 (MW,D,MRC-L,S) 8pm-2am Wed-Sun

Odessa/Midland (915)

INFO LINES & SERVICES
Free & Clean Lambda Group (Gay AA/AlAnon) 2535 E. Roper (The Basin), 337-1436, 7pm Fri & Sun

BARS
Mining Co. 409 N. Hancock, 580-6161 (MW,D,S,BW,BYOB,WC) 9pm-2am , clsd Mon-Tue

Nite Spot 8401 Andrews Hwy., 366-6799 (★MW,D,E,S,V,WC) 8pm-2am, clsd Mon

SPIRITUAL GROUPS
Holy Trinity Community Church 402 E. Gist, Midland, 570-4822, 11am Sun

Prodigal Ministries Community Church 1500 E. Murphy, 563-8880, 10:30am Sun

EROTICA
B&L Adult Bookstore 5890 W. Univ. Blvd., 381-6855

Club Fifty-One 4721 Andrews Hwy., 362-9018

Port Aransas (512)

ACCOMMODATIONS
Port Aransas Inn 1500 11th St., 749-5937 (GF,SW) full brkfst

San Angelo (915)

BARS
Silent Partners 3320 Sherwood Wy., 949-9041 (W,D,CW,S) 6pm-2am, clsd Mon

CRUISY AREAS
Downtown River (AYOR)

San Antonio (210)

INFO LINES & SERVICES
▲ **Community Real Estate Referrals** (800) 346-5592, gay realtor at your service, no rentals

Gay & Lesbian Community Center 923 E. Mistletoe, 732-4300 (WC) noon-8pm, til 11pm Fri (movie night)

The Happy Foundation 411 Bonham, 227-6451, lesbian/gay archives

Lambda Club AA 8546 Broadway Ste. 255, 824-2027, 8:15pm daily

San Antonio Gay/Lesbian Switchboard 733-7300, 7pm-11pm

ACCOMMODATIONS
Adelynne Summit Haus I & II 427 W. Summit Ave., 736-6272/(800) 972-7266 (GF) full brkfst

Arbor House Hotel 339 S. Presa St., 472-2005/(800) 272-6700 (GF,IGTA) gay owned

Elmira Motor Inn 1123 E. Elmira, 222-9463 (GF)

The Garden Cottage PO Box 12915, 78212, (800) 235-7215 (GF) private cottage

The Painted Lady B&B 620 Broadway, 220-1092 (★MW)

San Antonio B&B 510 E. Guenther, 222-1828 (GF)

BARS
2015 Place 2015 San Pedro, 733-3365 (M,NH,S) 2pm-2am

8th St. Restaurant & Bar 416 8th St., 271-3227 (GF) 4:30pm-midnight, til 2am Fri-Sat

B.B.'s Pub 5307 McCullough, 828-4222 (MW,NH,D) 2pm-?

Bamboleo's Latin Fever 2022 McCullough, 738-3118 (M,D,MRC-L,S)

The Bonham Exchange 411 Bonham St., 271-3811 (★GF,D,A,V,18+) 4pm-2am, from 8pm wknds, til 4am Fri-Sat

Cameo 1123 E. Commerce, 226-7055 (GF,D,BW) 10pm-4am Fri-Sun, underground mini-rave

Cowboy's 622 Roosevelt, 532-9194 (MW,CW) 4pm-2am, clsd Mon

Eagle Mountain Saloon 1902 McCullough Ave., 733-1516 (M,D,CW,WC) 4pm-2am

El Jardin 106 Navarro, 223-7177 (M,NH,P,S) 10am-2am

Lorraine's South Presa (at Military), 532-8911 (GF,D,A) 6pm-2am

Mick's Hideaway 5307 McCullough, 828-4222 (MW,NH,WC) 3pm-2am, patio

Miriam's 115 General Krueger, 308-7354 (MW,NH,D) 2pm-2am

The New Crew 309 W. Market St., 222-0310 (M,NH,WC) 11am-2am

New Ponderosa 5007 S. Flores, 924-6322 (MW,D,MRC-L,S) 6pm-2am, from 3pm wknds

Nite Owl 330 San Pedro Ave., 223-6957 (M,NH) 4pm-2am, from noon Sun

One-Oh-Six Off Broadway 106 Pershing St., 820-0906 (M,NH,OC,WC) noon-2am

Pegasus 1402 N. Main, 299-4222 (M,E) 2pm-2am

Rebar 826 San Pedro, 226-2620 (M) 9pm-2am, bear bar

Red Hot & Blues 450 Soledad, 227-0484 (GF,D,E,V,WC) 4pm-2am

The Saint 1430 N. Main, 225-7330 (M,D,A,S,18+) 9pm-2am Fri, til 4am Sat only

Showcase 3625 West Ave., 690-7727 (MW,D,A,18+) 10pm-3am

Silver Dollar Saloon 1418 N. Main Ave., 227-2623 (M,D,CW,V) 2pm-2am

Sparks 8011 Webbles St., 653-9941 (M,V,S) 3pm-2am

Stallion 2003 McCullough, 734-7977 (M,NH,L,WC) 8am-2am, from noon Sun

Wild Club (Wild Corner) 820 San Pedro, 226-2620 (M,D,A,S,18+) 9pm-2am, til 4am Fri-Sat

Woody's 826 San Pedro, 271-9663 (M,V) 2pm-2am

RESTAURANTS & CAFES

Giovanni's Pizza & Italian Restaurant 1410 Guadalupe, 212-6626, 10am-7pm, clsd Sun

North St. Mary's Brewing Co. Pub & Deli 2734 N. St. Mary's, 737-6255 (E) 7pm-2am

BOOKSTORES & RETAIL SHOPS

On Main 2514 N. Main, 737-2323, 10am-6pm, clsd Sun

Over the Rainbow CD's & Gifts 5301 McCullough, 822-6965, 10am-6:30pm

Q Bookstore 2803 N. St. Mary's, 734-4299, 10am-9pm, noon-6pm Sun, lesbigay

TRAVEL & TOUR OPERATORS

Advantage Plus Travel 800 NW Loop 410 Ste. 306 S., 366-1955/(800) 460-3755 (IGTA)

SPIRITUAL GROUPS

Dignity St. Anne's St. & Ashby Pl. (St. Anne's Convent), 558-3287, 5:15pm Sun

MCC San Antonio 1136 W. Woodlawn, 734-0048, 10:30am & 7pm Sun

River City Living MCC 202 Holland, 822-1121, 11am Sun

PUBLICATIONS

Bar Talk PO Box 15568, 78291, 737-7157

The Marquise PO Box 701204, 78232, 545-3511

MEN'S CLUBS
▲ **Alternative Clubs Inc.** 827 E. Elmira St, 223-2177 (★MO,SW,PC) 24hrs
Executive Spa 703 Ave. 'B', 225-8807 (PC) 24hrs

EROTICA
Apollo News 2376 Austin Hwy., 653-3538, 24hrs
Encore Video 8888 Broadway St., 821-5345
FleshWorks 2423 W. Wildwood, 731-8185, clsd Sun & Tue, body piercing & alterations
Minx 1621 N. Main Ave. #2, 225-2639, piercing studio
Video Exchange 2122 Broadway, 223-2034

Sherman (903)

TRAVEL & TOUR OPERATORS
About Travel 5637 Texoma Pkwy., 893-6888/(800) 783-6481

South Padre Island (512)

ACCOMMODATIONS
▲ **Upper Deck - A Guesthouse** 120 E. Atol, 761-5953 (★M,SW,N)

CRUISY AREAS
Andy Bowie Beach (AYOR)
Atol Beach (AYOR)
The Jetties County Park at S. end (AYOR)

Temple (817)

BARS
Hard Tymes 313 S. 1st. St., 778-9604 (M) 9pm-2am, military clientele

Texarkana (501)

BARS
The Gig 201 East St. (Hwy. 71 S.), 773-6900 (M,D,S,PC) 8pm-5am, from 3pm Sun, clsd Mon-Tue

Tyler (903)

BARS
Outlaws Hwy. 110 (4 miles S. of Loop 323), 509-2248 (GF,D,18+)

SPIRITUAL GROUPS
St. Gabriel's Community Church 13904 Country Rd. 193, 581-6923, 10:30am Sun

CRUISY AREAS
Bergfield Park (AYOR)
Fun Forest Park (AYOR)

Waco (817)

INFO LINES & SERVICES
Gay/Lesbian Alliance of Central Texas PO Box 9081, 76714, 752-7727/(800) 735-1122 (in state only)

BARS
David's Place 507 Jefferson, 753-9189 (MW,D,S,WC) 7pm-2am

SPIRITUAL GROUPS
Central Texas MCC From the Heart 1601 Clay, 752-5331, 10:45am Sun, 7:30pm Wed

Unitarian Universalist Fellowship of Waco 4209 N. 27th St. , 754-0599, 10:45am Sun

Unity Church of the Living Christ 400 S. 1st , Hewitt, 666-9102, 11am Sun

CRUISY AREAS
Cameron Park (AYOR)
Midway Park (AYOR)

Wichita Falls (817)

BARS
Rascals 811 Indiana, 723-1629 (MW,D,S,BYOB) noon-2am

SPIRITUAL GROUPS
MCC 1407 26th St., 322-4100, 11am Sun, 7pm Wed

UTAH

Bicknell (801)

TRAVEL & TOUR OPERATORS
CowPie Adventures Boulder Mtn., 297-2140, camping trips

Escalante (801)

ACCOMMODATIONS
Rainbow Country B&B & Tours PO Box 333, 84726, 826-4567/(800) 252-8824 (GF)

La Sal (801)

ACCOMMODATIONS
Mt. Peale Resort B&B PO Box 366, 84530, 686-2284, hot tub

Logan (801)

SPIRITUAL GROUPS
MCC Briderland 1315 E. 700 N., 750-5026, 11am Sun

Ogden (801)

BARS
Brass Rail 103 27th St., 399-1543 (★MW,D,F,PC) 3pm-1am

SPIRITUAL GROUPS
Unitarian Universalist Society of Ogden 2261 Adams Ave., 394-3338, 10:30am Sun

CRUISY AREAS
Mount Ogden Park (AYOR)
Pine View Reservoir Cemetery Point (AYOR)

Park City

TRAVEL & TOUR OPERATORS
Resort Property Management PO Box 3808, 84060, (800) 243-2932 (IGTA)

Salt Lake City (801)

INFO LINES & SERVICES
AA Gay/Lesbian 539-8800, call for times & locations

Bisexual Group Stonewall Center, 350-3915, 7pm Fri, contact Brenda

▲ **Community Real Estate Referrals** (800) 346-5592, gay realtor at your service, no rentals

Concerning Gays & Lesbians KRCL 91 FM, 363-1818, 12:30pm-1pm Wed

Gay and Lesbian Youth of Utah at Stonewall Center, 539-8800, 7pm Wed

Gay Helpline 243 W. 400 S., 533-0927

S/M Social and Support Group Stonewall Center, 7pm Th, pansexual

Utah Stonewall Center 770 S. 300 W., 539-8800, 1pm-9pm, til 6pm Sat clsd Sun, info, referrals, mtgs

ACCOMMODATIONS
Aardvark B&B 249 W. 400 S., 533-0927/(800) 533-4357 (M,WC) call for reservations & info

Anton Boxrud B&B 57 S. 600 E., 363-8035/(800) 524-5511 (GF)

Peery Hotel 110 W. 300 S., 521-4300 (★GF,F,WC)

Saltair B&B/Alpine Cottages 164 S. 900 E., 533-8184/(800) 733-8184 (★GF) oldest continuously operating B&B in Utah, cottages from 1870s

BARS
Bricks Tavern 579 W. 200 S., 328-0255 (★M,D,S,YC) 9:30pm-2am, clsd Sun-Mon

Deer Hunter 636 S. 300 W., 363-1802 (M,D,L,PC) 4pm-1am, from 2pm wknds

Kings 108 S. 500 W., 521-5464 (MW,D,PC,WC) 10am-1am

Radio City 147 S. State St., 532-9327 (M,WC) 11am-1am

The Sun 702 W. 200 S., 531-0833 (★MW,D,YC,PC) noon-2am

The Trapp 102 S. 600 W., 531-8727 (MW,D,CW,PC,WC) 11am-1am

The Vortex 32 Exchange Pl., 521-9292 (GF,D,A) 9pm-2am, clsd Sun-Tue

RESTAURANTS & CAFES
Baci Trattoria 134 W. Pierport Ave., 328-1333 (WC) lunch & dinner, clsd Sun, Italian, also full bar

Bill & Nadas Cafe 479 S. 600 E., 359-6984, 24hrs

Coffee Garden 898 E. 900 S., 355-3425 (WC) 7am-10pm

Market St. Grill 50 Market St., 322-4668 (WC) lunch, dinner, Sun brunch, seafood/steak, full bar

Rio Grande Cafe 270 S. Rio Grande, 364-3302 (★) lunch & dinner, Mexican, full bar

Sante Fe 2100 Emigration Canyon, 582-5888, lunch & dinner, Sun brunch

BOOKSTORES & RETAIL SHOPS
Cahoots 878 E. 900 S., 538-0606 (WC) 10am-7pm, noon-5pm Sun

Gypsy Moon Emporium 1011 E. 900 S., 521-9100, 11am-6pm, clsd Sun, metaphysical

TRAVEL & TOUR OPERATORS
Olympus Tours & Travel 311 S. State St. Ste. 110, 521-5232/(800) 338-9661

SPIRITUAL GROUPS
Restoration Church (Mormon) (800) 677-7252, call for info

Sacred Light of Christ MCC 823 S. 600 E., 595-0052, 11am Sun

South Valley Unitarian Universalist Society 6876 S. 2000 E., 944-9723, 4pm Sun

Wasatch Affirmation (Mormon) PO Box 1152 (at Utah Stonewall Center), 84110, 534-8693, 5pm Sun

MEN'S CLUBS

14th St. Gym 1414 W. 200 S., 363-2023, 6pm-4am

EROTICA

Blue Boutique 2106 S. 1100 E., 485-2072

Hayat's Magazines & Gifts 228 S. Main, 531-6531

Mischievous 559 S. 300 W., 530-3100, 10am-8pm

Video One 484 S. 900 W., 539-0300, also cult & art films

Spring City

ACCOMMODATIONS

▲ **The Caritas B&B Network** (800) CARITAS (227-4827), see ad in center National section

Springdale (801)

ACCOMMODATIONS

Red Rock Inn 998 Zion Park Blvd., 772-3836 (GF,WC) full brkfst

Torrey (801)

ACCOMMODATIONS

Sky Ridge B&B Inn PO Box 750220, 84775, 425-3222 (GF) full brkfst, hot tub, near Capitol Reef National Park

VERMONT

Andover (802)

ACCOMMODATIONS

The Inn At High View East Hill Rd., 875-2724 (GF,F,SW,IGTA)

Arlington (802)

ACCOMMODATIONS

Candlelight Motel Rte. 7A PO Box 97, 05250, 375-6647/(800) 348-5294 (GF,SW,IGTA)

Hill Farm Inn RR #2, Box 2015, 375-2269/(800) 882-2545 (GF) full brkfst, dinner avail. Th-Sat

Bennington (802)

ACCOMMODATIONS

Country Cousin B&B Rte. 1B, Box 212, Shaftsbury, 05262, 375-6985/(800) 479-6985 (MW,IGTA)

Brattleboro (802)

INFO LINES & SERVICES

BAGL (Brattleboro Area Gays/Lesbians) PO Box 875, 05302, 254-5947

ACCOMMODATIONS

Mapleton Farm B&B RD 2 Box 510, Putney, 257-5252

BARS

Rainbow Cattle Company Rte. 5, Dummerston, 254-9830 (D,CW) 11am-2am, 2 bars

RESTAURANTS & CAFES

Common Ground 25 Elliott St., 257-0855 (★BW) lunch & dinner, vegetarian/local fish

Peter Haven's 32 Elliott St., 257-3333 (★) 6pm-10pm clsd Sun-Mon

BOOKSTORES & RETAIL SHOPS

Everyone's Books 23 Elliott St., 254-8160, 10am-6pm, til 8pm Fri, 11am-4pm Sun

Burlington (802)

INFO LINES & SERVICES

AA Gay/Lesbian St. Paul's Church on Cherry St., 658-4221, 7pm Th

Outright Vermont PO Box 5235, 05401, 865-9677, support/educational group for lesbigay youth

SAGE (Senior Action in a Gay Environment) PO Box 863, 05402, 860-1810, gay men over 40

Univ. of VT Gay/Lesbian/Bisexual Alliance B-163 Billings, UVM, 05405, 656-0699, 7pm Mon

Vermont Bisexual Network PO Box 8124, 05402

Vermont Gay Social Alternatives PO Box 237, 05402, 865-3734

ACCOMMODATIONS

Allyn House B&B 16 Orchard Terr., 863-0379 (GF) full brkfst

Howden Cottage B&B 32 N. Champlain St., 864-7198 (MW)

BARS

135 Pearl 135 Pearl St., 863-2343 (MW,D,WC) noon-2am, also juice bar, 18+ Fri

RESTAURANTS & CAFES

Alfredo's 79 Mechanics Ln., 864-0854 (WC) 4:30pm-10pm, from 3pm Sun

Daily Planet 15 Center St., 862-9647, 11:30am-10:30pm

Silver Palace 1216 Williston Rd., 864-0125, 11:30am-9:30pm, Chinese

BOOKSTORES & RETAIL SHOPS

Chassman & Bem Booksellers 81 Church St. Market Place, 862-4332, 9am-9pm, til 5pm Sun

SPIRITUAL GROUPS

Dignity/Vermont PO Box 782, 05402, 863-1377

Interweave G/L/B/T/S Unitarian Church 152 Pearl St., 05401

PUBLICATIONS

Out in the Mountains PO Box 177, 05402

CRUISY AREAS

Battery Park N. Public Beach (AYOR)

The Fruit Loop downtown Bank, College & St. Pauls Sts. (AYOR)

Dorset

CRUISY AREAS

Dorset Quarry on Rte. 30 & Kelly Rd. (AYOR)

Hartland Four Corners (802)

ACCOMMODATIONS
Twin Gables PO Box 101, 05049, 463-3070 (GF)

Hyde Park (802)

ACCOMMODATIONS
Arcadia House PO Box 520, 05655, 888-9147

Killington (802)

ACCOMMODATIONS
Cortina Inn Rte. 4, 773-3333/(800) 451-6108 (GF,F,WC) also a tavern

Ludlow

CRUISY AREAS
Buttermilk Falls off Rte. 103 toward Rutland (AYOR)

Manchester Center (802)

BOOKSTORES & RETAIL SHOPS
Northshire Bookstore Main St., 362-2200, 10am-5:30pm, til 9pm Fri, til 7pm Sat, clsd Sun

Middlebury

INFO LINES & SERVICES
MGLBA (Middlebury Gay/Lesbian/Bisexual Alliance) Drawer 8, Middlebury College, 05753

Montgomery Center (802)

ACCOMMODATIONS
Phineas Swann B&B PO Box 43, 05471, 326-4306 (GF) full brkfst

Montpelier

INFO LINES & SERVICES
Vermont Coalition of Lesbians/Gays PO Box 1125, 05602, political group

RESTAURANTS & CAFES
Julio's 44 Main St., 229-9348, lunch & dinner, from 4pm wknds, Mexican
Sarducci's 3 Main St., 223-0229 (WC) 11:30am-10pm, Italian

BOOKSTORES & RETAIL SHOPS
Phoenix Rising 104 Main St 2nd flr, 229-0522, 10am-5pm, 11am-3pm wknds

SPIRITUAL GROUPS
Radical Faeries of Vermont RR 2, Box 1640, Plainfield, 05667, 454-1635, Destiny Lodge faerie group for central Vermont, monthly moon rituals

Norwich (802)

INFO LINES & SERVICES
SAM (Social Alternative for Gay Men) Box 479, 05055, 649-3133, 7:30pm Tue, call for location

Plainfield

INFO LINES & SERVICES
Lesbian/Gay/Bisexual Alliance Goddard College, 05667

Rutland (802)

EROTICA
AA Video & Books 156 West St., 773-8990, clsd Sun

St. Johnsbury (802)

INFO LINES & SERVICES
Game Ends 23 North Ave., 05819, 748-5849, social activities group

Stowe (802)

ACCOMMODATIONS
Buccaneer Country Lodge 3214 Mountain Rd., 253-4772/(800) 543-1293 (★GF,SW) full brkfst
Fitch Hill Inn RFD Box 1879, Hyde Park, 888-3834/(800) 639-2903 (GF,F) full brkfst

Waterbury (802)

ACCOMMODATIONS
Grünberg House B&B RR 2, Box 1595, Rte. 100 S., 05676-9621, 244-7726/(800) 800-7760 (GF) full bkfst

EROTICA
Video Exchange 21 Stowe St., 244-7004, clsd Sun

West Dover (802)

TRAVEL & TOUR OPERATORS
New England Vacation Tours Rte. 100 Mt. Snow Village, 464-2076/(800) 742-7669 (IGTA)

Woodstock (802)

ACCOMMODATIONS
Country Garden Inn B&B 37 Main St., Quechee, 295-3023 (GF,SW) full brkfst
Maitland-Swan House PO Box 72, Taftsville, 05073, 457-5181/(800) 959-1404 (GF)
Rosewood Inn 457-4485/(203) 829-1499, full brkfst
South View B&B PO Box 579 Rowe Hill Rd., Brownsville, 05037, 484-7934 (GF) classic Vermont log home

VIRGINIA

Alexandria (703)

INFO LINES & SERVICES
▲ **Community Real Estate Referrals** (800) 346-5592, gay realtor at your service, no rentals

TRAVEL & TOUR OPERATORS
Just Vacations, Inc. 501 King St., 838-0040
Uniglobe Direct Travel 1800 Diagonal Rd. Plaza D, 684-8824 (IGTA)

Arlington (703)

INFO LINES & SERVICES
Arlington Gay/Lesbian Alliance PO Box 324, 22210, 522-7660

▲ **Community Real Estate Referrals** (800) 346-5592, gay realtor at your service, no rentals

ACCOMMODATIONS
Highgate House B&B 1594 Colonial Terr., 524-8431 (GF) full brkfst

CRUISY AREAS
Columbia Island Marina (AYOR)
Iwo Jima Memorial wooded area (AYOR)

Cape Charles (804)

ACCOMMODATIONS
Sea Gate B&B 9 Tazewell Ave., 331-2206 (GF) full brkfst

Charlottesville (804)

INFO LINES & SERVICES
▲ **Community Real Estate Referrals** (800) 346-5592, gay realtor at your service, no rentals
Gay AA (at Unitarian Church on Rugby Rd.), 971-7720, 7:30pm Th
Gay/Lesbian Information Service PO Box 2368, 22902, 296-8783

ACCOMMODATIONS
The Mark Addy Rte. 1, Box 375, Nellysford, 22958, 361-1101/(800) 278-2154 (GF,SW,WC) full brkfst

BARS
Club 216 216 W. Water St. (rear entrance), 296-8783 (★MW,D,S,PC,WC) 9pm-2am, til 4am Fri-Sat, clsd Mon-Wed

RESTAURANTS & CAFES
Brasa 215 W. Water, 296-4343 (★) lunch & dinner, seafood, full bar
Eastern Standard/Escafe 102 Old Preston Ave. (W. end downtown mall), 295-8668 (MW,E) 5pm-midnight, til 2am Th-Sat, clsd Sun-Mon, full bar

SPIRITUAL GROUPS
Chavurah 982-2361, lesbigay Jewish study group
MCC 717 Rugby Rd. (church), 979-5206, 6pm Sun

PUBLICATIONS
Lambda Letter PO Box 2191, 22902

CRUISY AREAS
Lee Park (AYOR)

Chesterfield (804)

ACCOMMODATIONS
Historic Bellmont Manor 6600 Belmont Rd., 745-0106/(800) 809-9041x69 (GF,WC) full brkfst

Colonial Beach (804)

ACCOMMODATIONS
Tucker Inn 21 Weems St., 224-2031 (W) full brkfst, seasonal

Culpepper (703)

TRAVEL & TOUR OPERATORS
Culpepper Travel 763 Madison Rd. Ste. 208-B, 825-1258/(800) 542-4881 (IGTA)

Danville

CRUISY AREAS
Ballou Park (AYOR)

Fairfax

CRUISY AREAS
Turkey Run Park off G.W. Parkway. (AYOR)

Falls Church (703)

SPIRITUAL GROUPS
MCC of Northern VA Fairfax Unitarian Church, 532-0992, 6pm Sun

Fredericksburg (540)

RESTAURANTS & CAFES
Merrimans 715 Caroline St., 371-7723 (★MW,D,WC) lunch & dinner, lounge til 2am, clsd Mon

Hampton

CRUISY AREAS
Grandview Shores Beach Park walk past rock mounds to nude beach (AYOR)

Luray (540)

ACCOMMODATIONS
Ruffner House Rte. 4 Box 620, 22835, 743-7855 (MW,SW) full brkfst, hot tub

Lynchburg (804)

INFO LINES & SERVICES
Lesbian/Gay Helpline PO Box 10511, 24506, 847-5242

CRUISY AREAS
Blackwater Creek area (AYOR)
Court Street area (AYOR)

New Market (540)

ACCOMMODATIONS
A Touch of Country B&B 9329 Congress St., 740-8030 (GF) full brkfst

Newport News (804)

INFO LINES & SERVICES
▲ **Community Real Estate Referrals** (800) 346-5592, gay realtor at your service, no rentals

BARS
Frank Corner Pocket 3516 Washington Ave., 380-9875 (M,NH)

BOOKSTORES & RETAIL SHOPS
Just For Us 9902-B Warwick Blvd., 599-4070 (WC) 11am-7pm, 10am-9pm Fri-Sat, clsd Sun (seasonal), lesbigay
Mr. D's Leather & Novelties 9902-A Warwick Blvd., 599-4070, 11am-7pm, til 8pm Fri-Sat, clsd Sun
Out of the Dark 530 Randolph Rd., , 596-6220, 10am-6pm, til 8pm Fri-Sat, clsd Sun-Mon, Wiccan/pagan

Norfolk (804)

INFO LINES & SERVICES
AA Gay/Lesbian 1610 Meadow Lake Dr. (Triangle Services Center), 622-3701

▲ **Community Real Estate Referrals** (800) 346-5592, gay realtor at your service, no rentals

Mandamus Society PO Box 1325, 23501, 625-6220

BARS
Charlotte's Web 6425 Tidewater Dr. (Roland Park Shopping Center), 853-5021 (W,D,WC) 10am-2am, men's night Wed

Club Rumours 4107 Colley Ave., 440-7780 (MW,D) 11am-2am, clsd Mon-Wed

The Garage 731 Granby St., 623-0303 (M,NH,F,WC) 8am-2am, from 10am Sun; also 'Otherside' dance bar from 9pm

Late Show 114 E. 11th St., 623-3854 (★MW,D,PC) midnight til dawn

Nutty Buddys 143 E. Little Creek Rd., 588-6474 (★MW,D,F,S,WC) 4pm-2am

RESTAURANTS & CAFES
Charlie's Cafe 1800 Granby St., 625-0824 (BW,WC) 7am-3pm

Mom's Diner 119 W. Charlotte St., 627-4491, 6:30am-6pm, 7am-2pm wknds

Uncle Louie's 132 E. Little Creek Rd., 480-1225 (E,WC) 11am-11pm, bar til 2am, Jewish fine dining

White House Cafe/Private Eyes 249 W. York St., 533-9290 (S,WC) 11am-2am, grand buffet Sun, full bar

BOOKSTORES & RETAIL SHOPS
Lambda Rising 9229 Granby St., 480-6969, 10am-10pm, lesbigay

Leather & Lace 149 E. Little Creek Rd., 583-4334, 11am-9pm, clsd Sun

Phoenix Rising East 808 Spotswood Ave., 622-3701/(800) 719-1690, 11am-9pm, til 7pm Sun, lesbigay

Two of a Kind 6123 Sewells Pt. Rd., 857-0223 (WC) 11am-9pm, til 11pm Wed-Th, til 2am Fri-Sat, 2pm-7pm Sun, lesbigay

TRAVEL & TOUR OPERATORS
Moore Travel Inc. 7516 Granby St., 583-2361 (IGTA)

SPIRITUAL GROUPS
All God's Children Community Church 9229 Granby St., 480-0911, 10:30am Sun, 7:30pm Wed

Dignity 600 Tabbot Hall Rd. , 625-5337, 6:30pm Sun

MCC New Life 1530 Johnston Rd., 855-8450, 10:30am Sun

PUBLICATIONS
Our Own Community Press 739 Yarmouth St., 625-0700

EROTICA
Ghent Video & Newsstand 801 E. Boush St., 627-1277

CRUISY AREAS
Northside Park nr. baseball diamond (AYOR)

Petersburg (804)

EROTICA
Thriller Books 1919 E. Washington, 733-0064

Richmond (804)

INFO LINES & SERVICES
AA Gay/Lesbian 355-1212

▲ **Community Real Estate Referrals** (800) 346-5592, gay realtor at your service, no rentals

Gay Info Line 967-9311

Richmond Organization for Sexual Minority Youth PO Box 5542, 23220, 353-2077, 3pm-8pm Mon & Wed

Virginians for Justice PO Box 342 Capital Stn., 23202, 643-4816

BARS
Babe's of Carytown 3166 W. Cary St., 355-9330 (W,D,F,WC) 11am-midnight, til 2am Fri-Sat, 9am-5pm Sun

Chaplin's Grill/Sanctuary Dance Club 2001 E. Franklin St., 643-7520 (MW,D,F) 6pm-2am, from 9pm Sun, clsd Mon-Th

Club Colors 536 N. Harrison St., 353-9776 (MW,D,MRC,F,WC) 10pm-3am Fri-Sat

Fielden's 2033 W. Broad St., 359-1963 (★M,D,BYOB,PC,WC) midnight-6am, clsd Mon-Wed

RESTAURANTS & CAFES
Broadway Cafe & Bar 1624 W. Broad St., 355-9931 (WC) 5pm-2am, from 6pm wknds

Casablanca 6 E. Grace St., 648-2040 (MW,WC) 11am-2am, from 3pm Sat, full bar

BOOKSTORES & RETAIL SHOPS
Biff's Carytown Bookstore 2930 W. Cary St., 359-4831 (WC) 9am-7pm, til 5pm Sun

Phoenix Rising 19 N. Belmont Ave., 355-7939/(800) 719-1690 (WC) 11am-7pm, lesbigay

TRAVEL & TOUR OPERATORS
Covington International Travel 4401 Dominion Blvd., Glen Allen, 747-4126/(800) 922-9238 (IGTA) ask for Roy

Virginia Division of Tourism (800) 847-4882

SPIRITUAL GROUPS
Dignity-Integrity 815 E. Grace (St. Paul's Episcopal Church), 355-0584, 6:30pm Sun

MCC Richmond 2501 Park Ave., 353-9477, 9am,10:45am & 6:30pm Sun

CRUISY AREAS
Bryan Park James River Park, N. bank nr. S. end of Meadow St. (AYOR)

Byrd Park (AYOR)

Forest Hill Park (AYOR)

Roanoke (540)

INFO LINES & SERVICES
▲ **Community Real Estate Referrals** (800) 346-5592, gay realtor at your service, no rentals

BARS
The Alternative Complex(Edge) 3348 Salem Trnpk., 344-4445 (MW,D,F,S) 9pm-? Fri-Sat

Back Street Cafe 356 Salem Ave., 345-1542 (MW,NH,F) 7pm-2am, til midnight Sun

The Park 615 Salem Ave., 342-0946 (★MW,D,S,V,YC,PC,WC) 9pm-2am, clsd Mon-Tue & Th

The Stag 9 W. Salem Ave., 982-1668 (MW,NH) 2pm-2am, from 7pm Sun-Mon

BOOKSTORES & RETAIL SHOPS
Out Word Connections 114 Kirk Ave. SW, 985-6886, noon-8pm, til 9pm Fri-Sat, lesbigay

SPIRITUAL GROUPS
MCC of the Blue Ridge 2015 Grandin Rd. SW (Unitarian Church), 344-4444, 7pm Sun

Unitarian Universalist Church 2015 Grandin Rd. SW, 342-8888, 11am Sun (10am summer)

PUBLICATIONS
Blue Ridge Lambda Press PO Box 237, 24002, 890-6612

Buddies PO Box 21201, 24018, 989-1579, monthly, entertainment & personals

Stanley (540)

ACCOMMODATIONS
The Ruby Rose Inn Rte. 2 Box 147, 778-4680 (GF) full brkfst

Virginia Beach (804)

INFO LINES & SERVICES
▲ **Community Real Estate Referrals** (800) 346-5592, gay realtor at your service, no rentals

ACCOMMODATIONS
▲ **Coral Sands Motel** 2307 Pacific Ave., 425-0872/(800) 828-0872 (GF)

BARS
Ambush 2838 Virginia Beach Blvd., 498-4301 (M,NH) 4pm-2am

The Birdcage 4801 Shore Dr. (Bayside Shopping Ctr.), 460-6336 (M,D,F,S) 4pm-2am

Danny's Place 2901 Baltic Ave., 428-4016 (M,D,F,WC) 5pm-2am

TRAVEL & TOUR OPERATORS
Alternative Adventures in Travel 6529 Auburn Dr., 424-6362 (IGTA) call collect

Travel Merchants, Inc. 2232 Virginia Beach Blvd. #112, 463-0014

PUBLICATIONS
Lambda Directory 198 S. Rosemont Rd., 486-3546

WASHINGTON

Anacortes (360)

ACCOMMODATIONS
Blue Rose B&B 1811 9th St., 293-5175 (GF) full brkfst

Auburn

CRUISY AREAS
Lesgrove Park (AYOR)

Bellevue (206)

SPIRITUAL GROUPS
East Shore Unitarian Church 12700 SE 32nd St., 747-3780 (WC) 9:15am & 11:15am Sun (10am summer)

Bellingham (360)

INFO LINES & SERVICES
▲ **Community Real Estate Referrals** (800) 346-5592, gay realtor at your service, no rentals

Lesbian/Gay/Bisexual Alliance Western Washington University, 650-6120, social/political group

BARS
Rumors 1317 N. State St., 671-1849 (MW,BW,D) noon-2am

Tony's Coffee 1101 Harris Ave., 738-4710 (WC) 7am-10pm, patio

BOOKSTORES & RETAIL SHOPS
Village Books 1210 11th St., 671-2626, 9am-10pm, til 8pm Sun

SPIRITUAL GROUPS
Song of Messiah MCC 929 N. State St. Ste. B, 671-1172 (WC) 6pm Sun

EROTICA
Great Northern Bookstore 1308 Railroad Ave., 733-1650

CRUISY AREAS
Cornwall Park (AYOR)

Teddy Bear Cove (AYOR)

Whatcom Falls Park (AYOR)

Blaine (206)

EROTICA
Blaine Books 715 Peace Portal Wy., 332-6964

Bremerton (360)

INFO LINES & SERVICES
West Sound Family 792-3960, lesbigay social/support group

BARS
Brewski's 2810 Kitsap Wy. (enter off Wycuff St.), 479-9100 (GF,NH,F,WC) 11am-2am
Fandango Tavern 2711 6th St., 373-9229 (GF,NH,BW) 11am-2am, Wed & Sun 'family nights'

EROTICA
Turf News 321 N. Callow Ave., 479-0111

CRUISY AREAS
Waterfront Boardwalk/Pier across from ferry terminal (AYOR)

Chelan (509)

ACCOMMODATIONS
Whaley Mansion 415 3rd St., 682-5735/(800) 729-2408 (GF) full brkfst

Columbia River (509)

ACCOMMODATIONS
Sojourner Inn 142 Lyons Rd., Home Valley, 427-7070 (GF,F)

Edmonds

CRUISY AREAS
Edmonds Beach Park by ferry dock (AYOR)

Ellensburg (509)

INFO LINES & SERVICES
Central Gay/Lesbian Alliance (CWU) 963-1391, contact Sally Thelen for more info

Everett (206)

INFO LINES & SERVICES
AA Gay/Lesbian 2324 Lombard (church basement), 252-2525, 7pm Mon

BARS
Everett Underground 1212 California Ave., 339-0807 (MW,D,F) 4pm-2am

BOOKSTORES & RETAIL SHOPS
Orion at Twilight/Highlights 2934-B Colby Ave., 303-8624, metaphysical store, also publishes pagan newsletter

CRUISY AREAS
Forest Park (AYOR)

Index (206

ACCOMMODATIONS
Bush House Country Inn 300 5th St., 793-2312/(800) 428-2874 (GF) restaurant & cocktail lounge

Wild Lily Ranch B&B PO Box 313, 98256, 793-2103 (★MW,SW,N,IGTA)

Kennewick (509)

SPIRITUAL GROUPS
River of Life MCC 619 W. Albany (Unitarian Church), 946-5250 (WC) 6:30pm Sun

Kirkland (206)

BOOKSTORES & RETAIL SHOPS
Magazine City 12063 124th Ave. NE, 820-9264

Langley (360)

ACCOMMODATIONS
The Gallery Suite B&B 302 First St., 221-2978 (GF) art gallery
The Sea Haven II 3766 S. Bells Rd., 730-3766 (GF) cottage on Whidbey Island
The Whidbey Inn 106 1st St., 221-7115 (GF) full brkfst

Lopez Island (360)

ACCOMMODATIONS
The Inn at Swifts Bay Rte. 2 Box 3402 , 98261, 468-3636 (★GF,IGTA) spa

Lynnewood

CRUISY AREAS
Flag Pavilion Park (AYOR)

Mt. Vernon (360)

ACCOMMODATIONS
The Heron 117 Maple Ave., 466-4626 (GF,WC) hot tub, smokefree
The White Swan Guesthouse 1388 Moore Rd., 445-6805 (GF) farmhouse B&B; also cabin

RESTAURANTS & CAFES
Deli Next Door 202 S. 1st St., 336-3886, 9am-7pm, til 4pm Sun

BOOKSTORES & RETAIL SHOPS
Scott's Bookstore 121 Freeway Dr., 336-6181

PUBLICATIONS
Northwest Gay Times 1500-A E. College Wy. #458, 416-0498

CRUISY AREAS
Hillcrest Park just off Blackburn Rd. (AYOR)

Ocean Park (360)

ACCOMMODATIONS
Shakti Cove PO Box 385, 98640, 665-4000 (MW)

Olympia (360)

INFO LINES & SERVICES
Free at Last AA 11th & Washington (church), 352-7344, 7pm Th
Gay Men's Social Network PO Box 11032, 98508
Lesbian/Gay/Bisexual Support Services 943-4662, 24hr info & referrals
Queer Alliance Evergreen State College, 866-6000x6544, social/support group

BARS
Thekla 116 E. 5th Ave., 352-1855 (GF,D,E,WC) 6pm-2am

RESTAURANTS & CAFES
Smithfield Cafe 212 W. 4th Ave., 786-1725 (★WC) 7am-8pm

BOOKSTORES & RETAIL SHOPS
Bulldog News 116 E. 4th Ave., 357-6397, 7am-9pm

SPIRITUAL GROUPS
Eternal Light MCC 219 'B' St., 352-8157, 7pm Sun

Port Townsend (206)

ACCOMMODATIONS
Bella Vista c/o L. Silverman 5590 Taft, Oakland CA, 94618, (510) 655-5495, vacation rental

Gaia's Getaway 4343 Haines St., 385-1194 (MW) large studio apt.

The James House 1238 Washington St., 385-1238 (GF)

Ravenscroft Inn 533 Quincy St., 385-2784 (GF) full brkfst

Pullman (509)

INFO LINES & SERVICES
Washington State U. LesBiGay Group 335-6388

Seattle (206)

INFO LINES & SERVICES
Capitol Hill Alano 123 E. Boylston, 587-2838 (AA#) / 322-9590 (club), noon, 5:30pm, 8pm

▲ **Community Real Estate Referrals** (800) 346-5592, gay realtor at your service, no rentals

Counseling Service for Sexual Minorities 1820 E. Pine, 323-0220, noon-9pm Mon-Fri

GSBA (Greater Seattle Business Association) 2033 6th Ave. #804, 98121, 443-4722, publishes extensive directory

Lambert House 1818 15th Ave., 322-2735, 4pm-10pm, til mid Fri-Sat, drop-in center for sexual minority youth

Men of All Colors & Cultures Together (MACCT) 1202 E. Pike St. #936, 98122

Partners Task Force for Gay/Lesbian Couples PO Box 9685, 98109, 935-1206

The TEN (The Eastside Network) 450-4890

ACCOMMODATIONS
Bacon Mansion/Broadway Guesthouse 959 Broadway E., 329-1864/(800) 240-1864 (GF,IGTA)

Capitol Hill Inn B&B 1713 Belmont Ave., 323-1955 (GF) full brkfst

Chambered Nautilus B&B 5005 22nd Ave. NE, 522-2536 (GF)

The Country Inn 685 NW Juniper St., Issaquah, 392-1010 (GF) full brkfst, private estate

▲ **Gaslight Inn** 1727 15th Ave., 325-3654 (★GF,SW)

Hill House B&B 1113 E. John St., 720-7161/(800) 720-7161 (★MW) full brkfst

The Island Within B&B PO Box 2241, Vashon Island, 98070, (360) 567-4177 (GF) private cottage

▲ **Landes House B&B** 712 11th Ave. E., 329-8781 (MW)

Poineer Square Hotel 77 Yesler Way, 340-1234 (GF)

Scandia House 2028 34th Ave. S., 722-6216 (GF)

The Shafer-Baillie Mansion 907 14th Ave. E., 322-4654 (GF)

Wild Lily Ranch B&B PO Box 313, Index, 98256, 793-2103 (★MW,SW,N,IGTA)

BARS

C.C. Attle's 1501 E. Madison, 726-0565 (★M,NH,V,WC) 6am-2am, also 'Cadillac Grill Diner,' 323-4017, 7am-4am, 24hrs wknds

Changes 2103 N. 45th St., 545-8363 (M,NH,BW,WC) noon-2am

Crescent Tavern 1413 E. Olive Wy., 720-8188 (M,NH,WC) noon-2am, from 2pm wknds, piano bar Sun

▲ **The Cuff** 1533 13th Ave., 323-1525 (★M,L,WC) 2pm-2am, uniform bar

Double Header 407 2nd Ave., 624-8439 (M,NH) 10am-1am, one of the oldest gay bars in the US

The Easy 916 E. Pike, 323-8343 (W,D,F,E,WC) 11am-2am, from 9am wknds

Elite Tavern 622 Broadway Ave. E., 324-4470 (MW,NH,BW,WC) 10am-2am

Elite Two 1658 E. Olive Wy., 322-7334 (MW,NH,BW) noon-2am, from 10am wknds

Encore Restaurant & Lounge 1518 11th Ave., 324-6617 (MW,WC) 11am-2am, from 8am wknds, American

Hana Restaurant & Lounge 1914 8th Ave., 340-1536 (M,WC) noon-2am, Japanese

HopScotch 332 15th Ave. E., 322-4191 (GF,F) over 75 single malts

Jade Pagoda 606 Broadway E., 322-5900 (M,NH,F,WC) 5pm-2am, from noon Th-Fri, Chinese/American

Kid Mohair 1207 Pine St., 625-4444 (GF,D,E,BW) 4pm-2am

THE Cuff

A MEN'S LEATHER/ UNIFORM BAR

1533 13TH AVE
SEATTLE, WA
(206) 323-1525

Madison Pub 1315 E. Madison St., 325-6537 (★M,NH,OC,BW,WC) 2pm-2am

Neighbors Restaurant & Lounge 1509 Broadway (entrance on alley), 324-5358 (★M,D,S,YC,WC) 3pm-2am, til 4am Fri-Sat, clsd Mon

Nitelite Cafe & Lounge 1920 2nd Ave., 448-4852 (GF,WC) 10am-2am, restaurant 24hrs

The Palms Bar & Grill 420 E. Denny, 322-2555 (MW,E,WC) 11am-2am, upscale American/cont'l

R Place 619 E. Pine, 322-8828 (M,NH,V,WC) 2pm-2am, 3 flrs

Re-bar 1114 Howell (at Boren Ave.), 233-9873 (★GF,D,E,YC) 9pm-2am, 'Queer Disco' Th

Romper Room 106 1st Ave. N., 284-5003 (GF,D,BW) 11am-2am

Sea Wolf 1413 14th Ave., 323-2158 (M,NH,WC) 2pm-2am

The Seattle Eagle 314 E. Pike St., 621-7591 (M,L,WC) 2pm-2am, patio

Six Eleven Tavern 611 2nd Ave., 345-9430 (MW,NH) noon-2am

Sonya's Bar & Grill 1532 7th Ave., 624-5377 (M,NH) 6am-2am

Spag's Tavern 1118 E. Pike, 322-3232 (M,NH,OC) 2pm-2am, from noon wknds, bear bar

Tacky Tavern 1706 Bellevue Ave., 322-9744 (MW,NH,TG) 11am-2am, from 6am wknds, TV/TS night Wed

Thumpers 1500 E. Madison St., 328-3800 (★M,F,WC) 11am-2am

Timberline Tavern 2015 Boren Ave., 622-6220 (MW,D,CW,BW) 6pm-2am, from 4pm Sun, clsd Mon

The Vogue 2018 1st Ave., 443-0673 (GF,D,E) 9pm-2am

Wildrose Tavern & Restaurant 1021 E. Pike St., 324-9210 (W,F,E,BW,WC) 11am-midnight, til 2am Fri-Sat

RESTAURANTS & CAFES

Addis Cafe 61224 E. Jefferson, 325-7805 (★) 8am-midnight, Ethiopian

Beyond the Edge Cafe 703 E. Pike St., 325-6829 (E) 7am-10pm, til 3am Fri-Sat

Black Cat Cafe 4110 Roosevelt Wy NE, 547-3887, 10am-10pm, til 7pm Sun, clsd Mon, vegetarian

Cafe Illiterati 5327 Ballard NW, 782-0191 (WC) 9am-5pm

Cafe Paradiso 1005 E. Pike, 322-6960 (★) 6am-1am, til 4am Fri-Sat

Cafe Septieme 214 Broadway Ave. E., 860-8858 (★MW)

Cafe Vivace 901 E. Denny Wy. #100, 860-5869

Dahlia Lounge 1904 4th Ave., 682-4142, lunch & dinner, New American, full bar

Frontier Restaurant & Bar 2203 1st Ave., 441-3377 (WC) 10am-2am

Giorgina's Pizza 131 15th Ave. E., 329-8118, 11am-9pm, from 4pm Sat, clsd Sun

Gravity Bar 415 E. Broadway, 325-7186 (WC) 9am-10pm, vegetarian/juice bar

Jack's Bistro 405 15th Ave. E., 324-9625 (WC) lunch & dinner, cont'l, full bar

Kokeb 9261 12th Ave., 322-0485, lunch & dinner, Ethiopian

Mae's Phinney Ridge Cafe 6410 Phinney Ridge N. (at 65th), 782-1222 (★WC) 7am-3pm, Mud Room Cafe til 5pm

Plaza Mexico 4116 University Wy. NE, 633-4054, full bar

Queen City Grill 2201 1st Ave., 443-0975 (★WC) noon-11pm, from 5pm wknds, fresh seafood

Sunlight Cafe 6403 Roosevelt Wy. NE, 522-9060 (BW,WC) 8am-3pm, vegetarian

Landes

House

BED & BREAKFAST

712 11th Ave. East   Seattle, WA 98102

(206) 329-8781

GYMS & HEALTH CLUBS

BQ Workout (in the Broadway Market), 860-3070 (GF) 6am-11pm, 9am-7pm Sun

BOOKSTORES & RETAIL SHOPS

Bailey/Coy Books 414 Broadway Ave. E., 323-8842 (WC) 10am-10pm, til 11pm Fri-Sat, 11am-8pm Sun

Beyond the Closet Bookstore 518 E. Pike, 322-4609, 10am-10pm, til 11pm Fri-Sat, lesbigay

Broadway Market 401 E. Broadway (★) queer- friendly mall

Edge of the Circle 701 E. Pike, 726-1999, 10am-8pm, alternative spirituality store

Fremont Place Book Company 621 N. 35th, 547-5970, 11am-6pm, til 8pm Fri-Sat

Metropolis 7220 Greenwood Ave. N., 782-7002, cards & gifts

The Pink Zone 401 Broadway E. (B'way Mkt.), 325-0050, tattoos & piercing

Pistil Books & News 1013 E. Pike St., 325-5401

Red & Black Books 432 15th Ave. E., 322-7323, 10am-8pm

The Rubber Tree 4426 Burke Ave. N., 633-4750, 10am-7pm, clsd Sun, non-profit safer sex supplies & referrals

Sin 616 E. Pine, 329-0324 (WC) noon-8pm, leather & piercings

Sunshine Thrift Shops 1605 12th Ave. #25, 324-9774 (WC) noon-6pm, 10am-7pm Sat, non-profit for AIDS

TRAVEL & TOUR OPERATORS

Capitol Hill Travel Broadway Market 2nd Flr., 726-8996/(800) 726-8996 (IGTA)

It's Your World Travel 1411 E. Olive Wy., 328-0616/(800) 955-6077 (IGTA)

Passport Travel 6720 NE Bothell Way, 365-6755/(800) 373-6160 (IGTA)

Progressive Travels 224 W. Galer Ste. C, 285-1987/(800) 245-2229 (IGTA)

Sunshine Travel 519 N. 85th St., 784-8141 (IGTA)

Travel Solutions 4009 Gilman W., 281-7202/(800) 727-1616 (IGTA)

SPIRITUAL GROUPS

Affirmation (Mormon) PO Box 23223, 98102, 820-5729

Congregation Tikvah Chadashah 20th Ave. E. & E. Prospect (Prospect Cong. Church), 329-2590, 2nd & 4th Fri 8:15pm, lesbigay Shabbat services

Dignity Seattle 723 18th Ave E. (St. Joseph's Church), 325-7314, 7:30pm Sun

Grace Gospel Chapel 2052 NW 64th St., Ballard, 784-8495, 11am Sun

Integrity 1245 10th Ave. E. (Chapel of St. Mark's), 525-4668, 7pm Sun

The MCC 2101 14th Ave. S., 325-2421, 11am Sun

PUBLICATIONS

The 2002 85 S. Washington, 622-2002, 11am Sun

Seattle's Alternative Guidebook 229 Broadway E. #22, 726-9936

SGN (Seattle Gay News) 1605 12th Ave. Ste. 31, 324-4297

The Stranger 1202 E. Pike, 323-7101, weekly alternative

MEN'S CLUBS

Basic Plumbing 1104 Pike St., 682-8441 (MO)

Club Seattle 1520 Summit Ave., 329-2334 (★MO,PC) 24hrs

Club Z 1117 Pike St., 622-9958 (MO,PC) 4pm-9:30am, 24hrs Fri-Mon

Seattle Jacks 1115 Pike St. (nr. Boren) (MO) every Tue, door 7:30pm-8pm

South End Steam Baths 115-1/2 1st Ave. S. (Pioneer Square), 223-9091 (MO,PC) 24hrs

EROTICA
Champ Arcade 1510 1st Ave., 624-1784, 24hrs

The Crypt 1310 E. Union St., 325-3882, 10am-midnight, til 1am Fri-Sat

Fantasy Unlimited 102 Pike St., 682-0167

Onyx Leather 328-1965, by appt. only

CRUISY AREAS
Arboretum (AYOR) days

Beach 1 mi. N. Carkeek Park along RR tracks (N,AYOR)

Edmonds Ferry Pier bluffs above parking lot & beach (AYOR)

Madison Beach 43rd & Madison (AYOR)

Seaview (360)

ACCOMMODATIONS
Sou'wester Lodge Beach Access Rd. (38th Place), 642-2542 (GF)

Spokane (509)

INFO LINES & SERVICES
AA Gay/Lesbian 224 S. Howard (upstairs), 624-1442, 6:30pm Mon

▲ **Community Real Estate Referrals** (800) 346-5592, gay realtor at your service, no rentals

Lesbian/Gay Community Services Hotline 489-2266, 24hrs

BARS
Dempsey's Brass Rail 909 W. 1st St., 747-5362 (★MW,D,F,BW,WC) 3pm-2am, til 3:30am Fri-Sat, American

Hour Place 415 W. Sprague, 838-6947 (MW,D,F) 11am-2am

Pumps II W. 4 Main St., 747-8940 (MW,D,F,S) 3pm-2am, from noon Sun

BOOKSTORES & RETAIL SHOPS
Auntie's Bookstore & Cafe W. 402 Main St., 838-0206 (WC) 9am-9pm, 11am-5pm Sun

Boo Radley's 5 N. Post, 456-7479 (WC) 10am-6pm, noon-5pm Sun, gift shop

TRAVEL & TOUR OPERATORS
Edwards LaLone Travel S. 5 Washington, 747-3000/(800) 288-3788 (IGTA)

The Travel Place W. 505 Parkade Plaza, 624-7434/(800) 727-9114

SPIRITUAL GROUPS
Emmanuel MCC 307 W. 4th, 838-0085, 10:30am Sun & 7pm Wed (412 S. Bernard)

PUBLICATIONS
Stonewall News Spokane PO Box 3994, 99220, 456-8011

EROTICA
Paradise E. 12122 Sprague Ave., 926-7931

Spokane Arcade 1125 W. 1st, 747-1621, 24hrs

CRUISY AREAS
High Bridge Peoples Park (AYOR)

Manito Park (AYOR)

Mission Park (AYOR)

Tacoma (206)

Info Lines & Services
AA Gay/Lesbian 209 S. 'J' St. (church), 474-8897, 7:30pm Mon & Fri

▲ **Community Real Estate Referrals** (800) 346-5592, gay realtor at your service, no rentals

Oasis 596-2860, lesbigay youth group run by Health Dept.

South Sound Alliance 924-1459

Accommodations
Chinaberry Hill 302 Tacoma Ave. N., 272-1282 (GF) full brkfst

Commencement Bay B&B 3312 N. Union Ave., 272-1282 (GF) full brkfst, hot tub

Bars
24th Street Tavern 2409 Pacific Ave., 572-3748 (MW,D,TG,S,BW,WC) 2pm-2am, from noon Fri-Sun

733 Restaurant & Lounge 733 Commerce St. (MW,D,TG,V,S) 6pm-2am, clsd Sun-Mon

The Gold Ball Grill & Spirits 2708 6th Ave., 305-9861/627-0430 (MW,NH,TG,S,WC) 8am-2am, beer garden & gambling

Goodfellows 5811 N. 51st., 761-9802 (M,NH,F,K) 4pm-2am

Reflections 2405 Pacific Ave., 593-4445 (M,NH) 5pm-2am

Spiritual Groups
New Heart MCC 2150 S. Cushman, 272-2382, 11am Sun, 7pm Wed

Publications
Tacoma Sounds PO Box 110816, 98411-0816, 460-1308

Erotica
Jerry's Mecca Theater 755 Broadway, 272-4700

Cruisy Areas
Nude Beach follow RR tracks 1mi. N. of Chambers Creek (AYOR)

Vancouver (see also **Portland, Oregon** listings) (206)

Bars
North Bank Tavern 106 W. 6th St., 695-3862 (MW,F,BW,WC) noon-2am

Travel & Tour Operators
First Discount Travel 11700 NE 95th St. Ste. 110, 896-6200/(800) 848-1926, ask for Carl

Spiritual Groups
MCC of the Gentle Shepherd 4505 E. 18th St. (church), 695-1480 (WC) 6pm Sun

Walla Walla

Cruisy Areas
Fort Walla Walla Park (AYOR)

Pioneer Park (AYOR)

Wildwood Park (AYOR)

Wenatchee

Info Lines & Services
North Central Washington Lesbian/Gay Alliance PO Box 234, 98807

CRUISY AREAS
Washington & Miller Sts. (AYOR)

Yakima (509)

EROTICA
Yakima Magazine Ctr. 18 S. 1st St., 248-8598

WEST VIRGINIA

Berkeley (304)

EROTICA
Adam & Eve Adult Bookstore 2301 S. Fayette, 252-6733

Berkeley Springs (304)

EROTICA
Action Books & Video Rte. 522 S., 258-2529

Bluefield

CRUISY AREAS
Kee Dam (Cattail Hollow) State Rte. 123, 3 mi. E. of airport (AYOR)
Raleigh St. nr. Norfolk & Sou. RR (AYOR)

Charleston (304)

INFO LINES & SERVICES
Community Oriented Gay/Lesbian Evnts/Svcs (COGLES) 1517 Jackson St., 345-0491
West Virginia Lesbian/Gay Coalition PO Box 11033, 25339, 343-7305

BARS
Broadway 210 Broad St., 343-2162 (M,D,PC,WC) 4pm-3am, from 1pm wknds
Grand Palace 617 Brooks St., 342-9532 (M,D,V,S,PC) noon-2:30am
Tap Room 1022 Quarrier St. (rear entrance), 342-9563 (M,NH,PC) 5pm-midnight, later on weekends

RESTAURANTS & CAFES
Lee Street Deli 1111 Lee St. E., 343-3354, 11am-3pm, bar til 1am

TRAVEL & TOUR OPERATORS
West Virginia Tourism Division (800) 225-5982
Wild Wonderful Travel 1517 Jackson St., 345-0491 (IGTA)

PUBLICATIONS
Graffiti 1505 Lee St., 342-4412, mostly straight alternative entertainment guide

CRUISY AREAS
The Block Summers, Donnally, Capitol & Christopher Sts. (AYOR)
Daniel Boone Park Rte. 60 E. (AYOR) evenings

Elkins (304)

ACCOMMODATIONS
Retreat at Buffalo Run B&B 214 Harpertown Rd., 636-2960 (GF)

Huntington (304)

BARS
Driftwood Lounge 1121 7th Ave., 696-9858 (MW,D,V,YC,WC) 5pm-3am, also Beehive upstairs

Polo Club 733 7th Ave. (rear), 522-3146 (M,D,S,PC,WC) 3pm-3:30am

The Stonewall 820 7th Ave. (rear), 528-9317 (★MW,D) 5pm-3:30am

RESTAURANTS & CAFES
Calamity Cafe 1555 3rd Ave., 525-4171 (E,WC) 11am-10pm, til 3am wknds

EROTICA
Bookmark Video 1119 4th Ave., 525-6861

House of Video 1109 4th Ave., 525-2194

Lost River (304)

ACCOMMODATIONS
The Guesthouse Settlers Valley Way, 897-5707 (MW,SW) full brkfst, spa

Martinsburg (304)

EROTICA
Variety Books & Video 255 N. Queen St., 263-4334, 24hrs

Morgantown (304)

INFO LINES & SERVICES
Gay/Lesbian Switchboard PO Box 576, 26505, 292-4292

BARS
Class Act 335 High St. (rear entrance), 292-2010 (MW,D,E,S,PC) 8pm-3am, from 8pm Th-Sat, clsd Mon

EROTICA
Select Books & Videos 237 Walnut St., 292-7714, 24hrs

Parkersburg (304)

BARS
Different Strokes 604 Market St., 485-5113 (D) 8pm-3am

CRUISY AREAS
The Boat Ramp (AYOR)

Summersville

CRUISY AREAS
Roadside Park Rte. 19 S. N. of Summersville Lake (AYOR)

Wheeling (304)

ACCOMMODATIONS
Row House Guest Quarters 718 Main St., 232-5252/(800) 371-3020 (GF) apt w/ kitchen

BARS
The Tricks 1429 Market St. (behind Market St. News), 232-1267 (MW,D,S) 9pm-2am, til 3am Fri, clsd Mon-Tue

EROTICA
Market St. News 1437 Market St., 232-2414, 24hrs

WISCONSIN

Appleton (414)

BARS
Pivot Club 4815 W. Prospect Ave., 730-0440 (MW,D,S,V,WC) 5pm-2am, from 7pm Sat, from 2pm Sun

Rascals Bar & Grill 702 E. Wisconsin Ave., 954-9262 (MW,F) 5pm-2am, from noon Sun

CRUISY AREAS
Lutz Park (AYOR)

Ashland

CRUISY AREAS
Prentice Park (AYOR)

Aztalan (414)

BARS
Crossroads Bar W. 6642 Hwy. B., Lake Mills, 648-8457 (GF) 1pm-2am, clsd Mon

Baileys Harbor (414)

ACCOMMODATIONS
Blacksmith Inn B&B PO Box 220, 54202, 839-9222 (GF) fireplaces

Eagle River (715)

ACCOMMODATIONS
Edgewater Inn 5054 Highway 70 West, 479-4011 (GF) cont'l brkfst

Eau Claire (715)

BARS
Scruples 411 Galloway (behind adult bookstore), 839-9606 (MW,D,S,WC) 5pm-2am, from 3pm wknds

The Trading Company 304 Eau Claire St., 838-9494 (M,S)

Wolf's Den 302 E. Madison, 832-9237 (M,NH) 3:30pm-2:30am

EROTICA
Adult Book & Novelty 129 N. Barstow, 835-7292

Adult Video Unlimited 1518 Bellinger St., 834-3393

Green Bay (414)

INFO LINES & SERVICES
Gay AA/Al-Anon 494-9904/469-9999, call for schedule

BARS
Brandy's II 1126 Main St., 437-3917 (M) 1pm-2am

Java's/Za's 1106 Main St., 435-5476 (MW,D,V) 8pm-2:30am, 18+ Sun

Napalese Lounge 515 S. Broadway, 432-9646 (M,D,WC) 3pm-2am

Sass 840 S. Broadway, 437-7277 (MW,D) 5pm-2am, from noon Sun (winters)

SPIRITUAL GROUPS
Angel of Hope MCC PO Box 672, 54305, 432-0830, 11am Sun, services held at 614 Forest St.

PUBLICATIONS
Quest PO Box 1961, 54301, bi-weekly

EROTICA
Adult Movieland 836 S. Broadway, 433-9640, 24hrs

Main Attraction Book & Video/Nite Owl Motel 1614 Main, 465-6969, 24hrs

Hayward (715)

ACCOMMODATIONS
The Lake House 5793 Division on the Lake, Stone Lake, 865-6803 (GF,SW) full brkfst

Hazelhurst (715)

BARS
Willow Haven Resort/Supper Club 4877 Haven Dr., 453-3807 (GF) full bar, cabin rentals

Kenosha (414)

BARS
Club 94 9001 120th Ave., 857-9958 (★MW,D,E,S,V) 7pm-2am, from 3pm Sun, clsd Mon

Kimberly (414)

RESTAURANTS & CAFES
Grand American Restaurant & Bar 800 Eisenhower Dr., 731-0164 (WC) 11:30am-2pm, 10:30am-2:30pm Sun (brunch)

La Crosse (608)

INFO LINES & SERVICES
Gay/Lesbian AA 126 N. 17th St., 784-7560, call for schedule

Gay/Lesbian Support Group 126 N. 17th St., 784-7600, 7:30pm Sun

BARS
Cavalier 114 N. 5th, 782-9061 (GF,WC) 2pm-2am, gay evenings only

Rainbow's End 417 Jay St., 782-9802 (MW,NH) opens 11am

BOOKSTORES & RETAIL SHOPS
Rainbow Revolution 122 5th Ave. S., 796-0383 (WC) 10am-5:30pm, til 5pm Sat, noon-4pm Sun, progressive

Red Oaks Books 323 Pearl St., 782-3424, 9am-8pm, til 9pm Fri, 10am-5pm wknds, general, lesbigay section

PUBLICATIONS
New Beginnings Penpals PO Box 25, Westby, 54667, pen-pal publication

EROTICA
Best Buy Books 314 Jay St., 784-6350

Pure Pleasure Books 407 S. 3rd St., 785-1912

La Farge (608)

ACCOMMODATIONS
Trillium Rt 2, Box 121, 54639, 625-4492 (GF) 35 mi. from La Crosse

Lake Geneva (414)

ACCOMMODATIONS
Eleven Gables Inn on the Lake 493 Wrigley Dr., 248-8393 (GF,WC) full brkfst wknds

CRUISY AREAS
Riviera Beach (AYOR)
Waterfront & Flat Iron Park (AYOR)

Laona (715)

ACCOMMODATIONS
Alexander's Guest House 5371 Beech, 674-2615 (GF,SW) dorm-style/youth hostel rooms

Madison (608)

INFO LINES & SERVICES
AA Gay/Lesbian 255-4297
Gay Line 255-4297, 9am-9pm Mon-Fri
LesBiGay Campus Center 510 Memorial Union, 265-3344, drop-in 9am-4pm, Video Night 7:30pm Th
Nothing to Hide cable Ch. 4, 241-2500, 8:30pm Wed, lesbigay TV
The United 14 West Mifflin St. Ste. 103, 255-8582, 9am-5pm, 7pm-10pm Mon-Fri, drop-in center, library, newsletter, counseling service (call ahead)

ACCOMMODATIONS
Prairie Garden B&B W. 13172 Hwy. 188, Lodi, 592-5187/(800) 380-8427 (MW) full brkfst

BARS
Cardinal 418 E. Wilson St., 251-0080 (GF,D) 8pm-2am, clsd Mon
Flamingo 636 State, 257-3330 (GF,F) 11am-2pm (lunch), 8pm-2am (bar)
Geraldine's 3052 E. Washington Ave., 241-9335 (MW,D) 4pm-2am
Green Bush 914 Regent St., 257-2874 (GF,F) 4pm-2am
Manoeuvres 150 S. Blair, 258-9918 (M,D,V) 4pm-2am
R Place 121 West Main St., 257-5455 (D) 4pm-2am, til 2:30am Fri-Sat, fireplace
Shamrock 117 W. Main St., 255-5029 (MW,D,F,WC) 2pm-2am, from 11am Fri-Sat, from 5pm Sun, also a grill

RESTAURANTS & CAFES
Monty's Blue Plate Diner 2089 Atwood Ave., 244-8505 (BW,WC) 7am-10pm, til 9pm Sun-Tue, from 7:30am Sat-Sun
Wild Iris 1225 Regent St., 257-4747 (BW) 11:45am-10pm, from 9am wknds, Italian/Cajun

BOOKSTORES & RETAIL SHOPS
Borders Book Shop 3416 University Ave., 232-2600, 9am-11pm, til 8pm Sun, general, lesbigay section, also espresso bar
Going Places 2860 University Ave., 233-1920, travel-oriented books
Mimosa 212 N. Henry, 256-5432, 9:30am-6pm, noon-5pm Sun, progressive
Pic-A-Book 506 State St., 256-1125, 9am-8pm, til 5pm Sun

TRAVEL & TOUR OPERATORS
Dan's Travel The Gateway, 600 Williamson St., 251-1110/(800) 476-0305 (IGTA)
Wisconsin Division of Tourism (800) 432-8747

SPIRITUAL GROUPS

Affirmation Methodist 1127 University Ave. (United Methodist Church), 256-2353, 10am Sun, also social group, call for details

Integrity & Dignity 1001 University Ave. (St. Francis Episcopal), 7:30pm 2nd & 4th Sun (Sept-May)

James Reeb Unitarian Universalist Church 2146 E. Johnson St., 242-8887, 10am Sun (summer), call for winter hours

EROTICA

Piercing Lounge 520 University Ave. #120, 284-0870

Red Letter News 2528 E. Washington, 241-9958, 24hrs

CRUISY AREAS

Burrows Park (AYOR)

Nude beach (Mazomanie) (AYOR) 30 mi. NW on Hwy. 4, then 4mi. N. to Laws Rd., turn left 1/2mi. to gravel rd.

Olin Park E. of Coliseum (AYOR)

Maiden Rock (715)

ACCOMMODATIONS

Eagle Cove B&B W 4387 120th Ave., 448-4302/(800) 467-0279 (GF,WC) country retreat, expanded cont'l brkfst

Milton

ACCOMMODATIONS

▲ **The Caritas B&B Network** (800) CARITAS (227-4827), see ad in center National section

Milwaukee (414)

INFO LINES & SERVICES

AA Galano Club 2408 N. Farwell Ave., 276-6936, 12-step social group, call after 5pm for extensive mtg. schedule

AA Gay/Lesbian 771-9119

Baron's - Milwaukee PO Box 166, 53201, levi/leather social club

Black Gay Conciousness Raising 933-2136, 7:30pm 3rd Mon

▲ **Community Real Estate Referrals** (800) 346-5592, gay realtor at your service, no rentals

Gay Information & Services 444-7331, 24hr referral service

Gay People's Union Hotline 562-7010, 7pm-10pm

Gemini Gender Group PO Box 44211, 297-9328, 2nd Sat, call for location, TV/TS/TG support

Girth & Mirth PO Box 862, 53201-0862, for big men & their admirers

People of All Colors Together PO Box 93127, 53203, 871-3048, 3rd Sun, newsletter

SAGE Milwaukee PO Box 92482, 53202, 271-0378, for older lesbigays, call after 4pm

Ujima PO Box 92183, 53202, 272-3009, African-American social/support group

ACCOMMODATIONS

▲ **The Caritas B&B Network** (800) CARITAS (227-4827), see ad in center National section

Park East Hotel 916 E. State St., 276-8800/(800) 328-7275 (GF,F,WC)

BARS

1100 Club 1100 S. 1st St., 647-9950 (M,D,F) 7am-2am

The 3B Bar 1579 S. 2nd St., 672-5580 (MW,CW,D) 3pm-2am, from noon wknds

Ballgame 196 S. 2nd St., 273-7474 (★M,NH) 2pm-2am, from 11am wknds

Boot Camp Saloon 209 E. National Ave., 643-6900 (M,L) 4pm-2am

C'est La Vie 231 S. 2nd St., 291-9600 (M) noon-2am

Cafe Melange 720 N. 3rd St., 291-9889 (GF,D,F,E,WC) 11am-2am

Club 219 219 S. 2nd St., 271-3732 (MW,D,MRC,S) 4pm-2am

Gargoyles 354 E. National, 225-9676 (M,L,S,WC) 2pm-2am

Grubb's Pub & Le Grill 807 S. 2nd St., 384-8330 (MW) 9pm-3:30am

In Between 625 S. 2nd St., 273-2693 (M,NH,WC) 5pm-2am, from 3pm wknds

Just Us 807 S. 5th St., 383-2233 (MW,D,TG) 4pm-2am, from 1pm Sun

La Cage (Dance, Dance, Dance) 801 S. 2nd St., 383-8330 (★M,D,F,E,S,YC,WC) 9pm-2am, 2 bar complex

M&M Club 124 N. Water St., 347-1962 (M,F,E,WC) 11am-2am

The Nomad 1401 E. Brady St., 224-8111 (GF) noon-2am

This Is It 418 E. Wells St., 278-9192 (★M) 3pm-2am

Triangle Bar 135 E. National Ave., 643-9758 (★M,NH,WC) 5pm-2am, from 3pm wknds

Walker's Point Marble Arcade 1101 S. 2nd St., 647-9430 (MW,F,E,WC) bowling alley

Wreck Room 266 E. Erie St., 273-6900 (★M,L) 3:30pm-2am, til 2:30am wknds

Zippers 819 S. 2nd St., 645-8330 (M,NH) 3pm-2am, 2pm-2:30am Fri-Sat

RESTAURANTS & CAFES

Cafe Knickerbocker 1030 E. Juneau Ave., 272-0011 (★WC) 6:30am-10pm, til 11pm Sat-Sun

La Perla 734 S. 5th St., 645-9888, 10:30am-10pm, til 11:30pm Fri-Sat, Mexican

Mama Roux 1875 N. Humboldt, 347-0344 (WC) 3pm-2am, Cajun, full bar

Walkers Point Cafe 1106 S. 1st St., 384-7999, opens 10pm

BOOKSTORES & RETAIL SHOPS

AfterWords Bookstore & Espresso Bar 2710 N. Murray, 963-9089 (WC) 10am-10pm, til 11pm Fri-Sat, noon-6pm Sun

Designing Men 1200 S. 1st St., 389-1200, noon-7pm, from 3pm Mon-Tue, til 10pm Fri-Sat, til 6pm Sun, jewelry, cards, leather

Peoples' Books 3512 N. Oakland Ave., 962-0575, 10am-7pm, til 6pm Sat, noon-5pm Sun

Schwartz Bookstore 209 E. Wisconsin Ave., 274-6400, 9:30am-5:30pm, clsd Sun

TRAVEL & TOUR OPERATORS

Horizon Travel N. 81 W. 15028 Appleton Ave., Menomonee Falls, 255-0704/(800) 562-0219 (IGTA)

Trio Travel 2812 W. Forest Home Ave., 384-8746/(800) 417-4159 (IGTA)

SPIRITUAL GROUPS

Dignity 2506 Wauwatosa Ave. (St. Pius X Church), 444-7177, 6pm Sun

First Unitarian Society 1342 N. Astor, 273-5257, 9:30am Sun

Integrity 914 E. Knapp, 53211, 276-6277, lesbigay Episcopalians

Lutherans Concerned 2460-A S. Kinnickinnic Ave., 5pm 3rd Sun

Milwaukee MCC 924 E. Juneau (Astor Hotel), 332-9995, 11am & 7pm Sun

St. James Episcopal Church 833 W. Wisconsin Ave., 271-1340, 10:30am Sun, call for schedule of weekday masses

PUBLICATIONS
In Step 225 S. 2nd St., 278-7840, bi-monthly
Quest PO Box 1961, Green Bay, 54301, bi-weekly
Wisconsin Light 1843 N. Palmer St., 372-2773, bi-monthly

EROTICA
Popular News 225 N. Water St., 278-0636, toys, videos

CRUISY AREAS
Juneau Park (AYOR)
Underwood Parkwy. (AYOR)
Warnimont Park (N,AYOR) beach

Mineral Point (608)

ACCOMMODATIONS
The Cothren House 320 Tower St., 987-2612 (GF) full brkfst

RESTAURANTS & CAFES
Chesterfield Inn/Ovens of Brittany 20 Commerce St., 987-3682, Cornish/American

Oconto

ACCOMMODATIONS
▲ **The Caritas B&B Network** (800) CARITAS (227-4827), see ad in center National section

Oshkosh (414)

EROTICA
Pure Pleasure 1212 Oshkosh Ave., 235-9727

CRUISY AREAS
Menomonee Park (AYOR)

Racine (414)

INFO LINES & SERVICES
Gay/Lesbian Union 625 College, 54303

BARS
JoDee's International 2139 Racine St. (S. Hwy. 32), 634-9804 (MW,D,S) 7pm-2am
What About Me? 600 6th St., 632-0171 (MW,NH) 7pm-2am, from 3pm Tue & Fri

EROTICA
Racine News & Video 316 Main St., 634-9827

Shawano (715)

ACCOMMODATIONS
Prince Edward B&B 203 W. 5th St., 526-2805, full brkfst

Sheboygan (414)

BARS
▲ **The Blue Lite** 1029 N. 8th St., 457-1636 (MW,NH) 2pm-2am, til 2:30am Fri-Sat
Sherlock's Home 733 Pennsylvania Ave. (GF)

CRUISY AREAS
Fountain Park (AYOR)
North Beach (AYOR) summers

Stevens Point (715)

BARS
Platwood Club 701 Hwy. 10 W., 341-8862 (MW,D,WC) 9pm-? Th-Sat

Sturgeon Bay (414)

ACCOMMODATIONS
Chadwick Inn B&B 25 N. 8th Ave., 743-2771 (GF) cont'l brkfst, fireplaces
The Chanticleer 4072 Cherry Rd., 746-0334 (GF,SW) cont'l brkfst

Superior (715)

INFO LINES & SERVICES
Backwoods Bears PO Box 264, 54880, SASE for info

BARS
The Main Club 1813 N. 3rd St., 392-1756 (★MW,D) 3pm-2am, til 2:30am Fri-Sat
Molly & Oscar's 405 Tower Ave., 394-7423 (GF,NH) 3pm-2am, til 2:30am Fri-Sat
Trio 820 Tower Ave., 392-5373 (W,NH,F,WC) 1pm-2am, also a grill

Wausau (715)

ACCOMMODATIONS
▲ **The Caritas B&B Network** (800) CARITAS (227-4827), see ad in center National
section

BARS
Mad Hatter 320 Washington, 842-3225 (MW,D,WC) 7pm-2am, from 3pm Sun

West Allis (414)

EROTICA
Booked Solid 7035 W. Greenfield Ave., 774-7210

Willard (715)

ACCOMMODATIONS
The Barn B&B N 7890 Bachelors Ave., 267-3215 (WC) cont'l brkfst, hot tub

Winter (715)

ACCOMMODATIONS
Flambeau Forest Resort Star Rt. 67, Box 65, 54896, 332-5236 (GF,WC)

WYOMING

Casper (307)

INFO LINES & SERVICES
Central Wyoming Gender Support Group PO Box 1301, Evansville, 82636, 265-3123, contact Bernadette

EROTICA
Emporium 1210 East 'F' St., 265-9726

Cheyenne (307)

INFO LINES & SERVICES
United Gay/Lesbians of Wyoming PO Box 2037, Laramie, 82070, 632-5362, info, referrals, also newsletter

EROTICA
Cupid's 511 W. 17th, 635-3837

CRUISY AREAS
Holiday Park nr. bandstand (AYOR)
Lions Park nr. skating pond (AYOR)

Etna (307)

BOOKSTORES & RETAIL SHOPS
Blue Fox Studio & Gallery 107452 Hwy 89, 883-3310, open 7 days, hours vary, pottery & jewelry studio, local travel info

Jackson (208)

ACCOMMODATIONS
Bar H Ranch P.O. Box 297, Driggs ID, 83422, (208) 354-2906 (GF) seasonal
Redmond Guest House 110 Redmond St., 733-4003 (MW) seasonal, house rental
Spring Creek Resort 733-8833/(800) 443-6139 (★GF,F,SW,WC)
Three Peaks Inn 53 S. Hwy. 33, Driggs ID, (208) 354-8912 (GF) full brkfst

RESTAURANTS & CAFES
Sweetwater 85 King St., 733-3553, lunch & dinner

BOOKSTORES & RETAIL SHOPS
Valley Books 125 N. Cache, 733-4533

Riverton (307)

RESTAURANTS & CAFES
Country Cove 301 E. Main, 856-9813 (WC) 6am-4pm, clsd Sun

Thermopolis (307)

ACCOMMODATIONS
Out West B&B 1344 Broadway, 864-2700 (GF) nr. world's largest natural hot spring, gift shop, gay-owned

KEY
TO THE CODES

▲	Advertiser	*please mention Damron when patronizing businesses that support us with advertising*
★	Very Popular	
MO	Men Only	
GF	Gay Friendly (mostly straight)	
MW	gay men & lesbians (Men & Women)	
M	mostly gay Men	
W	mostly Women / lesbians	
NH	NeighborHood bar	
D	Dancing (DJ spinning)	
A	Alternative music (modern rock)	
CW	Country / Western	
L	Leather / fetish	
P	Professional	
MRC	Multi-Racial Clientele	
MRC-A	mostly Asian-American	
MRC-AF	mostly African-American	
MRC-L	mostly Latino-American	
TG	TransGender friendly	
F	Food served	
E	Live Entertainment (bands, piano, comedy, etc.)	
K	Karaoke	
S	Shows (drag, strippers)	
V	Videos	
18+	must be 18 years or older	
YC	Young / Collegiate types	
OC	Older / more mature Crowd	
BW	Beer and/or Wine only	
BYOB	Bring Your Own Bottle	
SW	SWimming onsite or nearby	
N	Nudity permitted in some areas	
PC	Private Club	
WC	WheelChair accessible (bathrooms too)	
IGTA	International Gay Travel Association	
AYOR	At Your Own Risk (use caution)	

INTERNATIONAL LISTINGS

Canada

Caribbean

Mexico
is listed by city

ALBERTA

Calgary (403)

INFO LINES & SERVICES

Bearback Calgary 1400 12th Ave. SW, 234-8458, for hirsute guys & their admirers

CLUB (Cowboys/Leather/Uniform Buddies) 234-8973, 2nd Fri, 4th Sat

Front Runners AA 777-1212, 7:30pm Fri-Sat, 8:30pm Mon-Th

Gay Line & Center 223 12th Ave. SW #206, 234-8973, 7pm-10pm, many groups; including 'Of Color' & 'Queer Youth'

Illusions Social Club Box 2000, 6802 Ogden Rd. SE, T2C 1 B4, 236-7072, TV/TS club

Southern Alberta Assoc. for Fetish/Fantasy Exploration 42014 Acadia PO, T2J 7A6

ACCOMMODATIONS

Black Orchid Manor B&B 1401 2nd St. NW, 276-2471 (MW) leather-friendly

Westways Guest House 216 25th Ave. SW, 229-1758 (MW) full brkfst, hot tub

BARS

Arena 310 17th Ave. SW, 244-8537 (GF,D) 9pm-3am Th-Sat

Boystown: Metro 213 10th Ave. SW, 265-2028 (MO,D,S,PC) 9pm-3am

Loading Dock/Detour 318 17th Ave. SW, 244-8537 (M,NH,D) 3pm-3am

The Rekroom 213-A 10th Ave. SW, 265-4749 (MO,PC) 4pm-3am

Rooks 112 16th Ave. NW, 277-1922 (W,D) 11am-2am

Trax 1130 10th Ave. SW, 245-8477 (M,D,CW,S,V,PC) 4pm-2am

The Warehouse 731 10th Ave. SW (alley entrance), 264-0535 (GF,D,YC,PC) 9pm-3am, clsd Sun & Tue

RESTAURANTS & CAFES

Andrews Pizza 719 Edmonton Trail NE, 230-4202 (WC) 11am-1am, full bar, more gay weeknights

Cafe Beano 1613 9th St. SW, 229-1232 (WC) 7am-midnight

Folks Like Us 110 10th St. NW, 270-2241 (MW,BW) 11am-10pm, til 8pm Sat, til 5pm Sun, clsd Mon

Grabbajabba 1610 10th St. SW, 244-7750 (WC) 7am-11pm

The Koop Cafe 211-B 12th Ave. SW, 269-4616, 11am-1am

Max Beanie's Coffee Bar 1410 4th St. SW, 237-6185 (F,WC) 9am-10pm, clsd Sun

Victoria's 306 17th Ave. SW, 244-9991 (WC) lunch, dinner, wknd brunch

The Wicked Wedge Pizza 618 17th Ave. SW, 228-1024

BOOKSTORES & RETAIL SHOPS

A Woman's Place 1412 Centre St. S., 263-5256 (WC) 10am-6pm, clsd Sun, many gay titles

B&B Leatherworks 6802 Ogden Rd. SE, 236-7072, 10am-6pm Tue-Sat

Books 'n Books 738-A 17th Ave. SW, 228-3337 (WC) 10am-6pm, til 9pm Th-Fri

Daily Globe 1004 17th Ave. SW, 244-2060

With the Times 2212-A 4th St. SW, 244-8020, 8:30am-11pm

TRAVEL & TOUR OPERATORS

Fletcher/Scott Travel 803 8th Ave. SW, 232-1180/(800) 567-2467 (IGTA)

Leisure Life Vacations 333 11th Ave. SW Ste. 1100, 264-2604

Let's Talk Travel Worldwide Ltd. 4428 16th Ave. NW, 247-0600 (IGTA)

Uniglobe Swift Travel 932 17th Ave. SW #220, 244-7887

SPIRITUAL GROUPS

Integrity/Calgary Box 23093 Connaught PO, T2S 3B1

PUBLICATIONS

Perceptions Box 8581, Saskatoon SK, S7K 6K7, (306) 244-1930, covers the Canadian prairies

MEN'S CLUBS

Goliath's Saunatel 308 17th Ave. SW (rear), 229-0911 (F,PC) 24hrs, cocktails

EROTICA

The Angelheart Tattoo Studio 6130 1A St. SW #52, 259-5662

Tad's Bookstore 1217-A 9th Ave. SE, 237-8237 (WC)

CRUISY AREAS

Glenmore Park (AYOR)

Prince's Island at 4th St. (AYOR)

Edmonton (403)

INFO LINES & SERVICES

AA Gay/Lesbian 424-5900

The B.E.A.R.S. (The AlBEARta Club) 12718 93rd St., 486-9661 x5

The Gay Line 486-9661

Gay/Lesbian Community Centre 10112 124th St., 488-3234, 7pm-10pm Mon-Fri, info, referrals, youth group

Gay/Lesbian Info Line 988-4018, 24hrs

Northern Chaps 10342 107th St. #216, T5J 1K2, 486-9661x2, 9pm 1st & 3rd Fri at Boots, mixed SM group

ACCOMMODATIONS

Northern Lights B&B 8216 151st St., 483-1572 (MW,SW) full brkfst

BARS

The Bar at the Crockery 4005 Calgary Trail N., 435-4877 (W) 7pm-2am

Boots 'N Saddle 10242 106th St., 423-5014 (M,PC,WC) 3pm-2am

Rebar 10551 Whyte Ave., 433-3600 (GF,D,WC) 8pm-3am

The Roost 10345 104th St., 426-3150 (MW,D,S) 8pm-3am

RESTAURANTS & CAFES

Boystown Cafe 10116 124th St., 488-6636 (MW,BW,WC) 11am-midnight; also 'Buddy's' bar upstairs

Jazzberry's 9965 82nd Ave., 433-2039

BOOKSTORES & RETAIL SHOPS

Audrey's Books 10702 Jasper Ave., 423-3487, 9am-9:30pm, til 5:30pm Sat, noon-5pm Sun

Divine Decadence 10441 82nd Ave., 439-2977, 10am-9pm, hip fashions, accessories

The Front Page 10846 Jasper Ave., 426-1206, 8am-6pm

Greenwood's Bookshoppe 10355 82nd Ave., 439-2005, 9:30am-9pm, til 5:30pm Sat, clsd Sun

The Orlando Books 10640 Whyte Ave., 432-7633 (WC) 10am-6pm, til 9pm Th-Fri, noon-4pm Sun, women's bookstore w/gay section

Varscona Books 10309 Whyte Ave., 439-4195, 10am-6pm, til 9pm Th, clsd Sun

SPIRITUAL GROUPS
Dignity PO Box 55, T5J 2G9, 469-4286
MCC - Edmonton 10086 MacDonald Dr., 429-2321, 7:15pm Sun

CRUISY AREAS
River Road nr. Victoria Golf Course (AYOR)

Grand Prairie (403)

INFO LINES & SERVICES
Peace Gay/Lesbian Association Box 1492, T8V 4Z3, 539-3325, 7:30-9:30pm Tue-Sat

BARS
The Touché 8502 112th St. #201, Grande Prairie, 538-9998 (MW,NH,D,PC) 9pm-3am, from 2pm Sun

Lethbridge (403)

INFO LINES & SERVICES
GALA (Gay/Lesbian Association of Lethbridge) Box 2081, T1J 4K6, 329-4666, 7-10pm Wed
Lighthouse Social Club PO Box 24003, T1J 1T7, 380-4257, dances & weekly events

Millet (403)

ACCOMMODATIONS
Labyrinth Lake Lodge RR 1 Site 2, Box 3, 878-3301 (W,SW) retreat

Red Deer (403)

INFO LINES & SERVICES
Gay/Lesbian Association of Central Alberta PO Box 1078, T4W 5E9, 340-2198, 7-9pm Wed

BARS
The Other Place Bay #3-4, 5579 47th St., T4N 1A1, 342-6440 (MW,D,WC) 4pm-3am, 3-11pm Sun

CRUISY AREAS
Kin Canyon (AYOR)

Rocky Mtn. House (403)

ACCOMMODATIONS
Country Cabin B&B Box 1916, 845-4834 (GF,SW) hot tub

BRITISH COLUMBIA

Birken (604)

ACCOMMODATIONS
Birkenhead Resort Box 369, Pemberton, V0N 2L0, 452-3255 (GF,SW) cabins & campsites, hot tub; also a restaurant, full bar

Blind Bay (604)

ACCOMMODATIONS
The Sunset B&B 3434 McBride Rd., Box 168, 675-4803 (GF)

Campbell River

CRUISY AREAS
Quadra Ferry Landing (AYOR) wknds & evenings

Duncan (604)

INFO LINES & SERVICES
Island Gay/Lesbian Society of Duncan 748-7689

Kelowna (604)

INFO LINES & SERVICES
Okanagan Rainbow Coalition PO Box 711 Stn. A, V1Y 7P4, 860-8555, info line & events

ACCOMMODATIONS
The Flags B&B 2295 McKinley Rd., RR1 Site10 C2, 868-2416 (MW,SW,N) full brk-fst

Nanaimo (604)

RESTAURANTS & CAFES
Olde Firehall Coffee Roastery 34 Nichol St. Ste. 2, 754-7733, 9am-midnight, til 1am Fri-Sat, vegetarian

CRUISY AREAS
Bowen Park (AYOR)
Maffeo Sutton Park (AYOR)

Nelson (604)

INFO LINES & SERVICES
West Kootaney Gay/Lesbian Line Box 725, V1C 4C7, 354-4297

Port Alberni

CRUISY AREAS
Harbor Quay Promenade (AYOR)

Prince George (604)

INFO LINES & SERVICES
GALA North 562-6253, 24hr taped message
Teen Crisis Line 564-8336, 4pm-11pm

ACCOMMODATIONS
Hawthorne B&B 829 P.G. Pulp Mill Rd., 563-8299

Prince Rupert (604)

INFO LINES & SERVICES
Prince Rupert Gay Info Line PO Box 881, V8J 3Y1, 627-8900

Revelstoke

INFO LINES & SERVICES
Lothlorien Box 8557, V0E 3G0, info & referrals

Richmond

CRUISY AREAS
Richmond Nature Park (AYOR)

Saltspring Island (604)

ACCOMMODATIONS

The Blue Ewe 1207 Beddis Rd., 537-9344 (MW,N) full brkfst, hot tub

Green Rose Farm B&B 346 Robinson Rd., Ganges, 537-9927 (GF) full brkfst

Saltspring Driftwood Bed & Brunch 1982 N. End Rd., 537-4137 (GF) miniature farm for art & animal lovers

Summerhill Guesthouse 209 Chu-An Dr., 537-2727 (MW) full brkfst, on the water

Sunnyside Up B&B 120 Andrew Pl., 653-4889 (MW) full brkfst, hot tub

Tofino (604)

ACCOMMODATIONS

West Wind Guest House 1321 Pacific Rim Hwy., 725-2224 (MW) hot tub, nr. the beach

Vancouver (604)

INFO LINES & SERVICES

AA Gay/Lesbian 434-3933/434-2553 (TDD)

Gay Asians of Vancouver Area (GAVA) 683-3825/684-6869, social group

Vancouver Gay/Lesbian Center 1170 Bute St., 684-6869, 11am-5pm, 7pm-10pm

ACCOMMODATIONS

▲ **The Albion Guest House** 592 W. 19th Ave., 873-2287 (MW) full brkfst, hot tub

Beach House 5834 Morgan Rd., Mirror Lake, 353-7676 (GF) private rental house on Lake Kootenay

The Buchan Hotel 1906 Haro St., 685-5354/(800) 668-6654 (GF)

Colibri B&B 1101 Thurlow St., 689-5100 (GF) full brkfst

Columbia Cottage 205 W. 14th Ave., 874-5327 (GF,IGTA)

Dufferin Hotel 900 Seymour St., 683-4251 (GF,F,WC)

French Quarter B&B 2051 W.19th Ave., 737-0973 (GF,SW) full brkfst, gym, French spoken

Heritage House Hotel 455 Abbott St., 685-7777 (MW,E,WC) 3 bars on premises

The Johnson House 2278 W. 34th Ave., 266-4175 (GF) full brkfst

Mountain B&B 258 E. Balmoral Rd., 987-2725 (GF) full brkfst

Nelson House 977 Broughton St., 684-9793 (MW,IGTA)

River Run Cottages 4551 River Rd. W., Ladner, 946-7778 (GF) on the Fraser River

Rural Roots 4939 Ross Rd., 856-2380 (M,SW,WC) full brkfst

▲ **The West End Guest House** 1362 Haro St., 681-2889 (GF) full brkfst

BARS

Avenue Lounge 900 Seymour St. (at Dufferin Hotel), 683-4251 (M,NH) 2:30pm-2:30am; also Back Alley 3pm-2am, 4pm-midnight Sun, Streets (M,D,E) noon-2am

Celebrities 1022 Davie St., 689-3180 (M,D) 9pm-2am, til midnight Sun

Chuck's Pub (at Heritage House Hotel), 685-7777 (MW,D,S) 11am-1:30am; also 'Uncle Charlie's'

Denman Station 860 Denman, 669-3448 (M,NH,D,K,S,V) 7pm-2am, til midnight Sun

Lotus Club (at Heritage House Hotel), 685-7777 (MW,D)

Ms. T's Cabaret 339 W. Pender St., 682-8096 (MW,D,TG,K) 8pm-2am

Numbers 1042 Davie, 685-4077 (M,D,S,V) 8pm-2am, til midnight Sun

The Odyssey 1251 Howe St., 689-5256 (★M,D,A,YC) 9pm-2am

Papa's Place 1025 Granville St. (at Royal Hotel), 685-5335 (M,NH,E) 11am-11pm

Shaggy Horse 818 Richards St., 688-2923 (MW,D) 8pm-2am, clsd Sun-Mon

Twilite Zone 7 Alexander St., 682-8550 (GF,D,A,L) more gay Tue & Sat

The Underground 1082 Granville St., 681-3020 (M,D,L,S) 9pm-2am, 7pm-midnight Sun

RESTAURANTS & CAFES

The Alabaster 1168 Hamilton St., Yaletown, 687-1758, Italian

Cafe S'il Vous Plaît 500 Robson St., 688-7216 (WC) 9am-10pm, clsd Sun

D.D.'s on Denman 1030 Denman, 688-6264 (BW) noon-10pm, from 10am wknds, vegetarian

Delilah's 1906 Haro St., 687-3424 (WC) 5:30pm-midnight

Friends Cafe 1221 Thurlow St., 685-0995 (★MW) 11am-11pm, full bar, patio

Hamburger Mary's 1202 Davie St., 687-1293 (NH) 6am-4am

Isadora's 1540 Old Bridge St., Granville Island, 681-8816, 9am-9pm

La Quena 1111 Commercial Dr., 251-6626 (WC) 11am-11pm, vegetarian

Lola's at the Century House 432 Richards St., 684-5652, great menu & atmosphere, full bar

Luxy Bistro 1235 Davie St., 681-9976 (WC) 9am-11pm

O-Tooz 1068 Davie St., 689-0208, 7am-midnight, lowfat veggie fast food

The Oasis 1240 Thurlow St. (upstairs), 685-1724 (E) dinner, wknd brunch, patio

Riley Cafe 1661 Granville St., 684-3666 (WC) 10:30am-11pm; also 'Riley T', alternative social night for lesbians/gays, 1st & 3rd Sun

The Second Cup 1184 Denman, 669-2068 (WC) 7am-midnight

BOOKSTORES & RETAIL SHOPS
D&R Clothing 1112 Davie St., 687-0937, clubwear & underwear
Little Sister's 1238 Davie St., 669-1753/(800) 567-1662, 10am-11pm, lesbigay
Return to Sender 1076 Davie St., 683-6363 (WC) 11am-9pm, noon-6pm Sun
Spartacus Books 311 W. Hastings, 688-6138, 10am-8:30pm, noon-6pm wknds, progressive
State of Mind 1100 Davie St., 682-7116, designer queer clothes

TRAVEL & TOUR OPERATORS
English Bay Travel 1267 Davie St., 687-8785 (IGTA)
Progressive Travel Inc. 1120 Davie St., 687-3837 (IGTA)
Travel Clinic 669-3321/(800) 705-7454

SPIRITUAL GROUPS
Dignity PO Box 3016, V6B 3X5, 432-1230
Integrity PO Box 2797, V6B 3X2, 432-1230
MCC 3214 W. 10th (St. James), 739-7959, 7:15pm Sun

PUBLICATIONS
Angles 1170 Bute St. Ste. 4-B, 688-0265
Diversity Magazine PO Box 47558, Coquitlam, V3K 6T3, 937-7447, fetish/fantasy
Xtra! West 1033 Davie St. Ste. 501, 684-9696

MEN'S CLUBS
Club Vancouver 339 W. Pender St., 681-5719 (★MO,PC),24hrs
Fahrenheit 212° 971 Richards St., 689-9719 (MO) 24hrs
Hastings Steam & Sauna 766 E. Hastings, 251-5455
Richards St. Service Club 1169 Richards St., 684-6010 (PC) 24hrs

EROTICA
Love's Touch 1069 Davie St., 681-7024
Mack's Leathers 1043 Granville, 688-6225, 11am-7pm
Next Body Piercing 1068 Granville St., 684-6398

CRUISY AREAS
Wreck Beach below UBC (AYOR) great beach adventure

Vernon (604)

ACCOMMODATIONS
Rainbows End RR 3, Site 11, Box 178, V1T 6L6, 542-4842 (MW,WC) full brkfst, hot tub

CRUISY AREAS
White Rock Beach on Kalamalka Lake (AYOR)

Victoria (604)

INFO LINES & SERVICES
Gay/Lesbian AA 383-7744
Island Gay/Lesbian Association Phone Line 598-4900, 6pm-10:30pm
Prime Timers Victoria PO Box 45030, Mayfair PO, V8Z 7G9, 727-6669, 3pm 3rd Sun

ACCOMMODATIONS
Claddagh House B&B 1761 Lee Ave., 370-2816 (GF) full brkfst
Hospitality Exchange 562 Simcoe St. Apt. 205, V8V 1L8, 385-4945

altitude 97

Taking You Higher

February 2 - 9, 1997

The 5th Annual Gay Ski Week
at Whistler Resort, B.C., Canada

SPONSORED BY DAMRON COMPANY
PRODUCED BY OUT ON THE SLOPES PRODUCTIONS
1238 MELVILLE ST, SUITE 204,
VANCOUVER, BC, CANADA, V6E 4N2

FOR MORE INFO
TEL: 604-688-5079   FAX: 604-688-5033
TOLL FREE: 1-888-ALTITUDE
(258-4883)

PHOTO: KLAUS GERHART

Lavender Link 136 Medana St., 380-7098 (GF,WC)

Oak Bay Guest House 1052 Newport Ave., 598-3812 (GF) full brkfst

The Weekender 10 Eberts St., 389-1688 (MW) June-Sept (wknds only Nov-May)

BARS

BJ's Lounge 642 Johnson (enter on Broad), 388-0505 (MW) noon-1am, lunch daily

CRUISY AREAS

Gay Beach Dallas Rd. W. of stairway at Cook (AYOR)

Whistler (604)

ACCOMMODATIONS

The Whistler Retreat 8561 Drifter Wy., 938-9245 (MW) hot tub

White Rock

CRUISY AREAS

Marine Dr. at Balsam & Kent (AYOR)

Winfield (604)

ACCOMMODATIONS

Willow Lane 11571 Turtle Bay Ct., 766-4807 (MW) full brkfst

MANITOBA

Brandon (204)

INFO LINES & SERVICES

Gays/Lesbians of Western Manitoba PO Box 22039, R7A 6Y9, 727-4297, 7pm-9pm Fri

Winnipeg (204)

INFO LINES & SERVICES

Coming Out cable channel 11, 9pm Fri

Gay/Lesbian Resource Center 1-222 Osborne St., 284-5208, office 1-4:30pm, info line 7:30-10pm Mon-Fri, Wed info in French

New Freedom AA Group 300 Hugo at Mulvey (St. Michael & All Angels), 942-0126, 8:30pm Th, 3:30pm Sun

Prairie Rose Gender Group Box 3, Group 4, RR#1, Dugald, R0E 0K0, (204) 257-2759, TG support/social

ACCOMMODATIONS

Winged Ox Guest House 82 Spence St., 783-7408 (GF) full brkfst

BARS

Club 200 190 Garry St., 943-6045 (MW,D,F,E,S) 4pm-2am, clsd Sun

Gio's 272 Sherbrooke St., 786-1236 (M,D,S,PC) 9pm-2am, clsd Sun

Happenings 274 Sherbrooke St. (upstairs), 774-3576 (MW,D,S,PC) 9pm-2am, til 3am Sat, clsd Sun

Heartland Social Club 298 Fort St., 957-0591 (M,F,PC)

RESTAURANTS & CAFES

Times Change Blues Cafe 234 Main, 957-0982 (E) from 8pm

BOOKSTORES & RETAIL SHOPS

Dominion News 263 Portage Ave., 942-6563, 8am-9pm, noon-6pm Sun

McNally Robinson 100 Osborne St. S. (at River), 453-2644, 9:30am-9:30pm, til 6pm Sat, noon-5pm Sun

SPIRITUAL GROUPS
Affirm 452-2853

Dignity PO Box 1912, R3C 3R2, 772-4322, 7:30pm 1st & 3rd Th

MCC St. Stephen's on B'way & Kennedy, Winnipeg, 661-2219, 7:30 Sun

PUBLICATIONS
Perceptions PO Box 8581, Saskatoon SK, S7K 6K7, (306) 244-1930, covers the Canadian prairies

MEN'S CLUBS
Office Sauna Baths 1060 Main St., 589-6133 (PC) 24hrs

EROTICA
Newsstand 561 Portage Ave., 775-5435

Unique Boutique 561 Portage Ave. (may be moving), 775-5435, 10am-midnight, til 10pm wknds

CRUISY AREAS
Osbourne St. Village (AYOR)

Parliament Grounds - The Hill (AYOR)

NEW BRUNSWICK

Fredericton (506)

INFO LINES & SERVICES
Fredericton Gay Line 457-2156, 6-9pm Mon & Th

BARS
Kurt's Dance Warehouse/Phoenix Rising 377 King St. 3rd flr, 453-0740 (MW,D,WC) 8pm-1am

SPIRITUAL GROUPS
New Hope MCC 749 Charlotte St.(Unitarian Fellowship House), 455-4622, 7pm Sun

CRUISY AREAS
The Green (AYOR)

Moncton (506)

BARS
La Cave/Dans L'Fond 234 St. George St./Alexander (MW,D)

Triangles 234 St. George St., 857-8779 (MW,D) clsd Mon

CRUISY AREAS
The Block Main St. btwn. Highland & Fleet Sts. (AYOR)

Champlain Place (AYOR)

Sackville (506)

ACCOMMODATIONS
Georgian House RR #3, 536-1481 (GF) full brkfst

St. John (506)

ACCOMMODATIONS
Mahogany Manor 220 Germain St., 636-8000 (GF) full brkfst

BARS
Bogarts 9 Sydney St., 652-2004 (MW,D) 8pm-2am, clsd Sun-Tue

CRUISY AREAS
Carlton St. (AYOR)
City Market (AYOR)
Princess St. nr. Union (AYOR)

NEWFOUNDLAND

St. John's   (709)

INFO LINES & SERVICES
Gay/Lesbian Info Line 753-4297, 7-10pm Th

BARS
Schroders Piano Bar 10 Bates Hill, 753-0807 (GF,F,E) 4pm-1am, til 2am Fri-Sat, til midnight Sun; also Zapata's Mexican restaurant

Zone 216 216 Duckworth St., 754-2492 (MW,D,WC) 8pm-2am, til midnight Sun

NOVA SCOTIA

Bear River   (902)

ACCOMMODATIONS
Lovett Lodge Inn PO Box 119, B0S 1B0, 467-3917/(800) 341-6096 (Canada only) (GF,SW) open May-Oct, full brkfst

Halifax   (902)

INFO LINES & SERVICES
Lesbigay Line (902) 423-7129, 7-10pm Th-Sat, AA info
The Queer News CKDU (97.5FM), 494-6479

ACCOMMODATIONS
Centretown B&B 2016 Oxford St., 422-2380 (MW)
Fresh Start B&B 2720 Gottingen St., 453-6616 (GF)

BARS
Reflections Cabaret 5184 Sackville St., 422-2957 (MW,D,F,E,WC) noon-3:30am, from 4pm Sun

The Stonewall Inn 1566 Hollis St., 425-2166 (MW,NH,F) 11:30am-2am

The Studio Lounge 1537 Barrington St., 423-6866 (M,D) 4pm-2am, 6pm-1am Sun

RESTAURANTS & CAFES
The Daily Grind 5686 Spring Garden Rd., 429-6397, 7am-11pm, also newsstand
Le Bistro 1333 South Park, 423-8428 (WC) lunch & dinner

GYMS & HEALTH CLUBS
Apollo Sauna Bath 1547 Barrington, 423-6549, 7pm-midnight

BOOKSTORES & RETAIL SHOPS
Entitlement Book Sellers Lord Nelson Arcade, 420-0565, 9:30am-10pm, noon-6pm Sun

Frog Hollow Books 5640 Spring Garden Rd. 2nd Flr., 429-3318

Red Herring Book Store 1578 Argyle St., 422-5087, 10am-6pm, til 9pm Th-Fri

Schooner Books 5378 Inglis St., 423-8419, 9:30pm-6pm, til 9pm Fri, til 5:30pm Sat, clsd Sun

Smith Books 5201 Duke St. (Scotia Sq.), 423-6438, 9:30am-6pm, til 9pm Fri-Sat
Trident Booksellers & Cafe 1570 Argyle St., 423-7100, 8:30am-9pm

SPIRITUAL GROUPS
Safe Harbor MCC 550 Inglis St. (church), 453-9249, 7:30pm Sun

PUBLICATIONS
Wayves PO Box 34090 Scotia Sq., B3J 3S1, 429-2661

EROTICA
Atlantic News 5560 Morris St., 429-5468

CRUISY AREAS
Citadel Hill (AYOR) evenings
Crystal Crescent Beach (N,AYOR)
Public Gardens (AYOR) summers

Lunenburg (902)

ACCOMMODATIONS
Brook House 3 Old Blue Rocks Rd., 634-3826 (GF)

Shelburne (902)

ACCOMMODATIONS
The Toddle Inn 163 Water St., 875-3229/(800) 565-0000 (GF) seasonal April-Dec, restaurant & bar on premises

Yarmouth (902)

ACCOMMODATIONS
Murray Manor B&B 225 Main St., 742-9625 (GF) full brkfst

ONTARIO

Brighton (613)

ACCOMMODATIONS
Butler Creek B&B RR 7, Hwy. 30, 475-1248 (GF)

Cambridge (519)

BARS
Robin's Nest 26 Hobston St. (in Farmers Bldg., Galt St. entrance), 621-2688, Tue, Fri-Sat only

Dutton (519)

ACCOMMODATIONS
Victorian Court B&B 235 Main St., 762-2244 (MW,WC)

Fort Erie (905)

MEN'S CLUBS
▲ **Fort Erie Steam Baths** 216 Jarvis St. (next to laundromat), 871-0023, 24hrs, 25 min. from Niagara Falls

Grand Valley (519)

ACCOMMODATIONS
Manfred's Meadow Guest House RR #1, 925-5306 (MW,SW) all meals included, sauna & spa

Guelph (519)

INFO LINES & SERVICES
Gay Line 836-4550
Guelph Queer Equality Box 773, N1H 6L8, 824-4120x8575, info, social group

BOOKSTORES & RETAIL SHOPS
Bookshelf Cafe 41 Quebec St., 821-3311 (★) 9am-9pm, til 10pm Fri-Sat, 10:30am-3pm Sun, cinema, restaurant & full bar til 1am

Hamilton (905)

ACCOMMODATIONS
The Cedars Tent & Trailer Park 1039 5th Concession Rd. RR2, Waterdown, 659-3655/7342 (MW,F,D,K,SW)

BARS
Cafe 121 121 Hughson St. N., 546-5258 (MW,D,F) noon-1am
The Embassy Club 54 King St. E., 522-7783 (M,D) 9pm-3am Fri-Sat
Windsor Hotel 31 John St. N., 522-5990 (GF,F,K) 11am-1am

CRUISY AREAS
Dundern Park nr. bridge (AYOR)
Jackson St. from Catherine to City Hall (AYOR)

Jasper (613)

ACCOMMODATIONS
Starr Easton Hall PO Box 215 RR #3, K0G 1G0, 283-7497 (GF) also a restaurant, fine dining, full bar

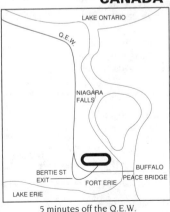

Kingston (613)

INFO LINES & SERVICES
Lesbian/Gay/Bisexual Phoneline & Directory 531-8981, 7-9pm Mon-Fri

BARS
Robert's Club Vogue 477 Princess St., 547-2923 (★MW,D,A,F) 4pm-1am, til 3am Fri-Sat

RESTAURANTS & CAFES
Chinese Laundry Cafe 291 Princess St., 542-2282 (★) 10am-midnight, til 2am Fri-Sat

CRUISY AREAS
City Park nr. Bagot St. (AYOR)
MacDonald Park (AYOR)

Kitchener (519)

BARS
Club Renaissance 24 Charles St. N., 570-2406 (MW,D,F,S) 9pm-3am
Club XTC 1 Queen St. N, 743-3016 (MW,D,WC) 9pm-1am

TRAVEL & TOUR OPERATORS
TCB Travel 600 Doon Village Rd., 748-0850, ask for Linda

London (519)

INFO LINES & SERVICES
AA Gay/Lesbian 649 Colborne (at Halo Club), 7pm Mon & Wed
Gay Line 433-3551, live 7-10pm Mon, Tue & Th
UW Out 432-3078, 7-10pm Mon, lesbigay student group

BARS
52nd Street 347 Clarence St., 679-4015 (MW,D,WC) 2pm-2am, patio
Halo Club (Gay/Lesbian Community Center) 649 Colborne St., 433-3762 (MW,D,E,PC,WC) 7pm-midnight, 9pm-2am wknds
The Junction 722 York St., 438-2625 (M,S) 24hrs, cabaret

RESTAURANTS & CAFES
Blackfriars Cafe 46 Blackfriars, 667-4930 (★) 10am-10pm

BOOKSTORES & RETAIL SHOPS
Mystic Book Shop 616 Dundas St., 673-5440, 11am-6pm, clsd Sun

SPIRITUAL GROUPS
Dignity London PO Box 1884 Stn. A, N6A 5J4, 686-8809 (evenings), 7.30pm 2nd Mon (at HALO 2nd Flr.)
Holy Fellowship MCC 442 Williams St., 645-0744, 7:20 Sun

MEN'S CLUBS
Club London Health Club 722 York St., 438-2625

Maynooth (613)

ACCOMMODATIONS
Wildewood Guesthouse Box 121, K0L 2S0, 338-3134 (MW,SW,WC) all meals included

Niagara Falls

CRUISY AREAS
Clifton Hill (AYOR)
Dufferin Islands (AYOR)
Queen Victoria Park (AYOR)

Niagara on the Lake

CRUISY AREAS
Simcoe Park (AYOR)

North Bay (705)

INFO LINES & SERVICES
Gay/Lesbian/Bisexual North Bay Area Box 1362, P1B 8K5, 495-4545, 7-9pm Mon

BARS
The East End 550 Main St. E. (MW) 7pm-? Wed-Sat, unverified for '97

Oshawa (905)

BARS
Club 717 7-717 Wilson Rd. S., 434-4297, 2pm-2am Sat only

MEN'S CLUBS
Continental Spa/Sauna 16-A Ontario St., 728-0545, 3pm-1am, clsd Sun

Ottawa (see also **Hull, PROVINCE OF QUEBEC**) (613)

INFO LINES & SERVICES
237-XTRA 237-9872, touch-tone lesbigay visitor's info
Gayline/Télégai 238-1717, 7-10pm
Lambda Line 233-8212, business/professional group
Pink Triangle Services 71 Back St. (above McD's), 563-4818

ACCOMMODATIONS
Rideau View Inn 177 Frank St., 236-9309/(800) 268-2082 (GF) full brkfst
The Stonehouse B&B 2605 Yorks Corners, 821-3822 (MW) full brkfst

BARS
Camp B Taverne/Pride Disco 363 Bark St., 237-0708 (MW,NH,D,F) 11am-2am, disco from 9pm
Centretown Pub 340 Somerset St. W, 594-0233 (MW,D,F,V) 2pm-1am; also leather bar & piano bar
Coral Reef Club 30 Nicholas, 234-5118 (MW,D) Fri & Sat only
Le Club 77 Wellington, Hull PQ, (819) 777-1411 (★MW,D) 10pm-3am
Market Station 15 George St. (downstairs), 562-3540 (GF,F) noon-1am, from 11am Sun (brunch)

RESTAURANTS & CAFES
Alfonsetti's 5830 Hazeldern, Stittsville, 831-3008, noon-11pm, from 5pm Sat, clsd Sun
Blue Moon Cafe 311 Bank, 230-1199 (MW) 10am-midnight, French
Cafe Deluxe 283 Dalhousie St., 241-4279, 4pm-1am, from noon wknds
Manfred's 2280 Carling Ave., 829-5715, 5-10pm, full bar
The News 284 Elgin, 567-6397 (WC) noon-midnight

BOOKSTORES & RETAIL SHOPS

After Stonewall 105 4th Ave., 2nd flr., 567-2221, 10am-6pm, til 7pm Fri, noon-4pm Sun, lesbigay bookstore

Food for Thought Books 103 Clarence St., 562-4599, 10am-10pm

Mags & Fags 286 Elgin St., 233-9651, gay magazines

Octopus Books 798 Bank St., 235-2589, 10am-6pm, til 9pm Th-Fri, noon-5pm Sun

SPIRITUAL GROUPS

Dignity Ottawa Dignité 386 Bank St., 746-7279

MCC of Ottawa Somerset & Elgin (St. John's Anglican Church), (800) 786-6622, 4pm Sun

PUBLICATIONS

Capital Xtra! 303-177 Nepean St., 237-7133

MEN'S CLUBS

Club Ottawa Health Club 1069 Wellington St., 722-8978 (★MO,PC) 24hrs

Steamworks 487 Lewis, 230-8431

CRUISY AREAS

Elgin St. (AYOR)

Peterborough   (705)

ACCOMMODATIONS

Windmere Selwyn RR#3, Lakefield, 652-6290/(800) 465-6327 (GF) full brkfst, sauna

Port Sydney   (705)

ACCOMMODATIONS

Divine Lake Resort RR1, Box XD3, 385-1212/(800) 263-6600 (MW,D,E,SW,N) resort & cottages, breakfast & dinner included

Sault Ste. Marie   (705)

BARS

The Warehouse 196 James St., 759-1903 (MW,D,S) 4pm-2:30am

Stratford   (519)

ACCOMMODATIONS

Anything Goes B&B 107 Huron St., 273-6557 (GF) full veggie brkfst

Burnside Guest Home 139 William St., 271-7076 (GF) full brkfst, hot tub, on Lake Victoria

The Maples of Stratford 220 Church St., 273-0810 (GF)

BARS

Old English Parlour 101 Wellington St., 271-2772 (GF,WC) 11:30-1am, from 10:30am Sun brunch

RESTAURANTS & CAFES

Down the Street 30 Ontario St., 273-5886 (E) noon-11pm, Mediterranean/Mexican, full bar

BOOKSTORES & RETAIL SHOPS

Fanfare Books 92 Ontario St., 273-1010, 9:30am-8pm, til 5pm Sun-Mon

CRUISY AREAS

Shakespeare Memorial Gardens (AYOR)

Tom Patterson Island (AYOR)

Sudbury (705)

BARS

D-Bar 83 Cedar St., 670-1189 (MW,D,E) 8pm-1am

Toronto (416)

INFO LINES & SERVICES

2-Spirited People of the 1st Nations 2 Carlton St. Ste. 1006, 944-9300, lesbigay native group

519 Church St. Community Center 519 Church St., 392-6874 (WC) 9:30am-10:30pm, noon-5pm wknds

925-XTRA 925-9872, touch-tone lesbigay visitors info

AA Gay/Lesbian 487-5591

Canadian Lesbian/Gay Archives 86 Temperance St., 777-2755, 7-10pm Tue-Th

Durham Alliance Association PO Box 914, Oshawa, L1H 7H1, 434-4297, info & social group

¡Hola! (Grupo Gay Latino) 925-9872 x2850, 8-10pm 1st & 3rd Th at '519 Center'

Toronto Area Gay/Lesbian Phone Line 964-6600, 7-10pm, clsd Sun

ACCOMMODATIONS

Acorn House B&B 255 Donlands Ave., 463-8274 (M)

Allenby B&B 223 Strathmore Blvd., 461-7095 (GF)

Amblecote B&B 109 Walmer Rd., 927-1713 (MW,IGTA) full brkfst

Burken Guest House 322 Palmerston Blvd., 920-7842 (GF,IGTA)

▲ **The Caritas B&B Network** (800) CARITAS (227-4827), see ad in center National section

Catnaps Guesthouse 246 Sherbourne St., 968-2323/(800) 205-3694 (MW)

▲ **Dundonald House** 35 Dundonald St., 961-9888/(800) 260-7227 (MW) full brkfst, hot tub

▲ **Hotel Selby** 592 Sherbourne St., 921-3142/(800) 387-4788 (★MW,SW,IGTA)

Mike's on Mutual 333 Mutual St., 944-2611 (M) full brkfst

Muther's (at Tool Box bar), 466-8616 (M,N)

Seaton Pretty 327 Seaton St., 972-1485 (GF) full brkfst

Toronto Bed & Breakfast 588-8800 (GF) contact for various B&Bs

Winchester Guesthouse 35 Winchester St., 929-7949 (MW) hot tub

BARS

Aztec/Tango 2 Gloucester St., 975-8612 (MW,D,F) 11am-2am

Bar 501 501 Church, 944-3163 (MW,NH) 11am-1am

Barn 83 Granby, 977-4684 (★M,D,L) 9pm-1am, til 4am Fri-Sat; also 'Stables' 977-4702

The Bijou Bar 370 Church St., 960-1272 (MO,F) 9pm-4am, "Canada's only porno bar"

The Black Eagle 459 Church St. (upstairs), 413-1219 (M,L,F) 4pm-1am, from 2pm Sat, from noon Sun brunch

Blue Atlantis Bar & Cafe 2318 Danforth Ave., 422-0766 (MW) 4pm-1am

Boots Warehouse/Kurbash (at Hotel Selby), 921-0665 (★M,D,L,E,K,V,WC) noon-1am

Bulldog Cafe 457 Church St., 923-3469 (MW,NH,F) noon-2am

Catch 22 379 Adelaide St. W., 703-1583 (GF,D) 9pm-3am, clsd Sun-Tue

Colby's 5 St. Joseph St., 961-0777 (★M,D,K,S,V) 11am-1am

Crews/Ghetto Fag 508 Church, 972-1662 (M,F,YC,WC) noon-3am

El Convento Rico 750 College St., 588-7800 (M,D,MRC-L,S) 8pm-4am Wed-Sun, clsd Mon

Jax 619 Yonge St., 2nd flr., 922-3068 (M,NH) 11am-1am

Oz/Emerald City 15 Mercer St., 506-8686 (MW,D,18+)

Pegasus 491 Church St., 2nd flr., 927-8832 (M,NH) 11am-1am

The Playground 11-A St. Joseph St., 923-2595 (MW,D) 12:30am-4am, from 11pm Fri-Sat, clsd Mon

Queen's Head Pub 263 Gerrard St. E., 929-9525 (GF,NH,F,WC) 3pm-1am, patio

Remington's Men of Steel 379 Yonge St., 977-2160 (MO,S) 11am-1am, strip bar

Sneakers 502 Yonge St., 961-5808 (M,NH,F) 11am-3am, cruise bar

Tool Box 508 Eastern Ave., 466-8616 (★M,L,F) 5pm-1am, noon-3am Fri-Sat, from noon Sun, patio

Trax V 529 Yonge St., 963-5196 (★M,D,F,E,OC,WC) 11am-1am

Whiskey Saigon 250 Richmond, 593-4646 (GF,D,S) 10pm-2am Th-Sun

Woody's 467 Church, 972-0887 (★M,NH,F,WC) noon-2am

RESTAURANTS & CAFES

Archer's 796 St. Clair Ave. W., 656-7335, 5:30-10pm, clsd Mon, fixed cont'l menu

The Babylon 553 Church St., 923-2626, til 4am, 11am-4pm Sun brunch

Bistro 422 422 College St., 963-9416, 4pm-midnight

Byzantium 499 Church St., 922-3859, 5:30pm-1am

Cafe Diplomatico 594 College, 534-4637 (★) 8am-1am, in Little Italy, patio

Cafe Volo 587 Yonge St., 928-0008, 11am-10pm, bar til 1am

The Courtyard (at Hotel Selby), 921-0665, seasonal, BBQ, full bar, patio

Il Fornello 1560 Yonge, 920-8291, also 486 Bloor W. 588-9358, 576 Danforth Ave. 466-2931

La Hacienda 640 Queen W., 703-3377, lunch & dinner, sleazy, loud & fun Mexican

The Living Well 692 Yonge St., 922-6770, noon-1am, til 3am Fri-Sat

The Mango 580 Church St., 922-6525 (★MW) 11am-1am, also Sun brunch

Pints 518 Church St., 921-8142 (NH) 11:30am-1am

PJ Mellon's 489 Church St., 966-3241 (WC) 11am-11pm, Thai/cont'l

Rivoli Cafe 332 Queen St. W., 597-0794, 11am-11pm, bar til 1am

The Second Cup 548 Church St. (Wellesley), 964-2457 (★) 24hrs

Trattoria Al Forno 459 Church St., 944-8852

BOOKSTORES & RETAIL SHOPS

Ex Libris 467 Church St., 2nd flr., 975-0580, 11am-9pm, til 6pm Wed, from 10am Sat, noon Sun, new & used lesbigay books

Glad Day Bookshop 598-A Yonge St., 961-4161, 10am-9pm, noon-8pm Sun, lesbigay

The Omega Centre 29 Yorkville Ave., 975-9086/(888) 663-6377 (Canada only), 10am-9pm, til 5pm wknds, spiritual books

Out in the Street 551 Church St., 967-2759/(800) 263-5747, lesbigay accessories

This Ain't The Rosedale Library 483 Church St., 929-9912, 10am-7pm

Volumes 74 Front St. E., 366-9522

TRAVEL & TOUR OPERATORS

La Fabula Travel & Tours Inc. 551 Church St., 920-3229/(800) 667-2475 (IGTA)

Talk of the Town Travel 565 Sherbourne St., 960-1393 (IGTA)

Toronto Convention & Visitors Association PO Box 126, 207 Queen's Quay W., M5J 1A7, (800) 363-1990

SPIRITUAL GROUPS

Christos MCC 353 Sherbourne St. (church), 925-7924, 7pm Sun

MCC Toronto 115 Simpson Ave., 406-6228, 9am, 11am & 7pm Sun

PUBLICATIONS

Fab 25 Wood St. Ste. 104, 599-9273, good gay rag

The Pink Pages 392 King St. E., 864-9132, annual lesbigay directory

Xtra! 100 Wellesley St. E. #104, 925-6665, monthly

MEN'S CLUBS

The Barracks 56 Widmer St., 593-0499 (MO,L) 24hrs, spa

The Cellar 78 Wellesley St. E. (black door no sign), 944-3779 (MO) 24hrs

Club Toronto Baths & Health Club 231 Mutual St., 977-4629 (MO,SW,PC) 24hrs

Kurbash 17 Selby St., 921-0665 (MO,L) 9pm-3am

The Spa on Maitland 66 Maitland, 925-1571 (MO) 24hrs, sauna & full gym

St. Marc Sauna 543 Yonge St., 4th flr., 927-0210 (★MO,WC) 24hrs

EROTICA

Doc's Leather & Latex 726 Queen, 324-8686

Fantasies 699 Yonge St., 968-2832 (E) gay Sun night, strippers

North Bound Leather 19 St. Nicholas St., 972-1037 (WC) 10am-7:30pm, noon-5pm Sun

Passage Body Piercing 473 Church St., 929-7330, 11am-7pm, tattoos & scarification too

▲ **Priape** 465 Church St., 586-9914, 11am-7pm, til 9pm Th-Sat

Studio Auroboros 580 Yonge St., 962-7499, noon-8pm, body ornaments & piercing

CRUISY AREAS

Canthra Parkette Church St. (AYOR) summer sunbathing

Hanlan's Pt. Beach Toronto Islands (AYOR) summers

Yonge Street Walkway E. of Yonge from Charles to Alexander (AYOR)

Trenton (613)

ACCOMMODATIONS

Devonshire House B&B RR #4 (Hwy. 2 West), 399-1851 (GF) full brkfst

Whitby (905)

BARS

The Bar 110 Dundas St. W., 666-3121 (MW,D) 8pm-3am, clsd Mon-Wed

Windsor (519)

INFO LINES & SERVICES

Lesbian/Gay/Bisexual Phone Line 973-4951, 8-10pm Th-Fri

BARS

Club Happy Tap Tavern 1056 Wyandotte St. E., 256-8998/2737 (MW,D,S) 2pm-1am, from 4pm Sun

Silhouettes 1880 Wyandotte St. E., 252-0887 (M,NH,F) 4pm-1am, from 11am wknds

SPIRITUAL GROUPS

MCC Windsor 977-6897, 7pm Sun

MEN'S CLUBS

Vesuvio Steam Bath 563 Brant St., 977-8578 (PC) 24hrs

CRUISY AREAS

Jackson Park area at Ouelette Overpass (AYOR)

River Front Park at foot of Ouelette St. (AYOR) evenings

PRINCE EDWARD ISLAND

Charlottetown (902)

ACCOMMODATIONS

Blair Hall Vernon Bridge, 651-2202/(800) 268-7005 (GF) full brkfst

Charlottetown Hotel PO Box 159, C1A 7K4, 894-7371 (GF,F,SW)

BARS

Baba's Lounge 81 University Ave., 892-7377 (GF,F) 5pm-2am

Doc's Corner 185 Kent St., 566-1069 (GF,E,WC) 11am-2am; also Hillard's Dining Room

BOOKSTORES & RETAIL SHOPS

Book Mark 172 Queen St. (in mall), 566-4888, 8:30am-9pm

PROVINCE OF QUEBEC

Acton Vale (514)

ACCOMMODATIONS
Domaine Plein Vent Inc. 130 Principal, Upton, 549-5831 (MO,D,F,E,SW) May-Sept

Alma

CRUISY AREAS
Carcajou Bridge (AYOR)
Parc de la Falaise beach of Dam-en-terre (AYOR)

Chicoutimi (418)

BARS
Bar Rosco 70 W. rue Racine, 698-5811 (M) 3pm-3am

Drummondville (819)

ACCOMMODATIONS
Motel Alouette 1975 Boul. Mercure, 478-4166 (GF)

CRUISY AREAS
Woodyat Park (AYOR)

Hull (see also **Ottawa, ONTARIO**) (613)

BARS
Le Pub de Promenade 175 Promenade de Portage, 771-8810 (MW,NH,D,F) 11am-3am

CRUISY AREAS
Meach Lake Beach (AYOR)
Place du Centre (AYOR)

Joliette (514)

ACCOMMODATIONS
L'Oasis des Pins 381 boul. Brassard, St. Paul de Joliette, 754-3819 (GF,F,SW) camping April-Sept., restaurant open year-round

Jonquiere

CRUISY AREAS
rue St-Aime & rue St-Dominique (AYOR)

Laval

INFO LINES & SERVICES
Comité des Gaies/Lesbiennes Montmorency 475 boul. de L'Avenir, N74 5H9

MEN'S CLUBS
Sauna Pont Viau 15-A des Laurentides, 663-3386, 24hrs

EROTICA
Boutique Carrefour du Sexe 1735 Blvd. Labelle, 688-6969

Longueuil (514)

MEN'S CLUBS
Sauna 1286 1286 Chemin Chambly, 677-1286, 24hrs

Mont-Tremblant (819)

ACCOMMODATIONS

Versant Ouest B&B 110 Chemin Labelle, Mont-Tremblant, 425-6615/(800) 425-6615 (MW) full brkfst

Montréal (514)

INFO LINES & SERVICES

AA Gay/Lesbian 4024 Hingston Ave. (church), 376-9230, 7pm Tue, 7:30pm Th

FACT (Federation of American & Canadian Transsexuals) C.P. 293 Succ. Cote des Neiges, H3S 2S6

Gai Ecoute 521-1508, 7pm-11pm

Gay Line 990-1414, 6:30pm-10pm

Gay/Lesbian Community Center of Montréal 2035 Amherst St., 528-8424, 9am-9pm, clsd wknds

ACCOMMODATIONS

Angelica B&B 1074 St-Dominique, 875-5270 (GF)

Au Bon Vivant Guest House 1648 Amherst, 525-7744 (★MW,IGTA)

Auberge de la Fontaine 1301 Rachel St. est, 597-0166/(800) 597-0597 (GF,WC) full brkfst

▲ **Auberge du Centre-Ville** 1070 rue Mackay, 938-9393/(800) 668-6253 (★MO) sauna

Auberge Encore 53 rue Milton, 483-0834 (MW)

Canadian Accommodations Network Box 42-A Stn. M, H1Z 3L6, 254-1250

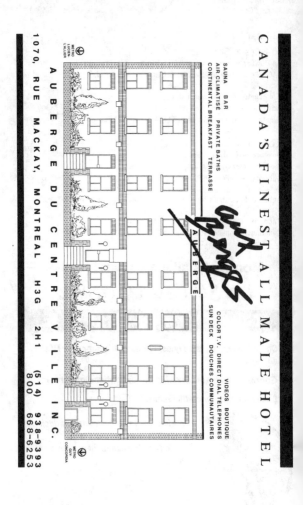

CANADA'S FINEST ALL MALE HOTEL

SAUNA BAR
AIR CLIMATISÉ PRIVATE BATHS
CONTINENTAL BREAKFAST TERRASSE

VIDÉOS BOUTIQUE
COLOR T.V. DIRECT DIAL TELEPHONES
SUN DECK DOUCHES COMMUNAUTAIRES

METRO
LUCIEN
L'ALLIER

METRO
GUY
CONCORDIA

1070, RUE MACKAY, MONTREAL H3G 2H1

AUBERGE DU CENTRE VILLE INC.

(514) 938-9393
800 668-6253

Chateau Cherrier 550 Cherrier St., 844-0055/(800) 816-0055 (MW) April-Nov, full brkfst

Ginger Bread House 1628 St-Christophe, 597-2804 (M,IGTA)

Hébergement touristique du Plateau Mont-Royal 1301 rue Rachel est, 597-0166/(800) 597-0597 (GF) reservation service

Home Suite Hom PO Box 762 Succ. C, H2L 4L6, 523-4642, home exchange

Hotel Bourbon 1574 Ste. Catherine est, 523-4679/(800) 268-4679 (M) also Bar Cajun, 3pm-3am & 'Club Sandwich' 24hrs

Hotel du Parc 3625 Parc Ave., 288-6666 (GF,IGTA)

Hotel Kent 1216 rue St-Hubert, 845-9835 (GF)

Hotel Le St-Andre 1285 rue St-Andre, 849-7070 (MW)

Hotel Lord Berri 1199 rue Berri, 845-9236 (GF,WC) also Italian restaurant

Hotel Manoir des Alpes 1245 rue St-André, 845-9803 (GF)

Hotel Pierre 169 Sherbrooke est, 288-8519 (GF)

Hotel Vogue 1425 rue de la Montagne, 285-5555/(800) 465-6654 (★GF,F) full service upscale hotel

▲ **La Conciergerie Guest House** 1019 rue St-Hubert, 289-9297 (★MO,N,IGTA) brkfst, gym & sundeck

Le Chasseur Guest House 1567 rue St-André, 521-2238, summer terrace

Le Dortoir 2042 rue de la Visitation, 597-2688 (M)

▲ **Le St-Christophe** 1597 St-Christophe, 527-7836 (MO,N) full brkfst, sundeck & hot tub

Lesbian/Gay Hospitality Exchange International PO Box 612, Stn. C, H2L 4K5, 523-1559

la **Conciergerie**
GUEST HOUSE
Your resort in the city!

1019, rue Saint Hubert
Montréal, (Québec) H2L 3Y3 Canada
Tel: (514) 289-9297 Fax: (514) 289-0845

Maison Chablis 1641 St-Hubert, 527-8346 (MO,F)

Turquoise B&B 1576 rue Alexandre de Sève, 523-9943 (GF)

BARS

Agora 1160 Mackay, 934-1428 (M) 4pm-3am

Bistro 4 4040 St-Laurent (Duluth), 844-6246 (MW,F) 9am-mid, til 2am wknds

Black Eagle Bar 1315 Ste-Catherine est, 529-0040 (M,L) 8am-3am

Cabaret L'Entre Peau 1115 Ste-Catherine est (below Le Campus), 525-7566 (★M,S) noon-3am

Cafe Fetiche 1426 Beaudry, 523-3013 (M) noon-3am

Campus 1111 Ste-Catherine est, 2nd flr., 526-9867 (M,S) 7pm-3am

Chez Jean Pierre 1071 Beaver Hall, 878-3570 (M,D,S) 3pm-3am, nude go-go boys

Citibar 1603 Ontario est, 525-4251 (MW,NH) 11am-3am

City Pub 3820 St-Laurent, 499-8519 (GF,F,BW) 11am-3am

Club Date 1218 Ste-Catherine est, 521-1242 (GF,NH) 3pm-3am

Disco Pyramide 1230 boul. St-Laurent, 871-8066 (M,D) 8pm-1am

K.O.X. 1450 Ste-Catherine est, 523-0064 (★MW,D,E) 3pm-3am

L' Adonis 1681 Ste-Catherine est, 521-1355 (MO,D,S) 7pm-3am

La Boîte En Haut 1320 Alexandre de Sève, 527-2237 (★M,D,E)

La California 1412 Ste-Elizabeth, 843-8533 (★MW,NH) 3pm-1am

La Track 1584 Ste-Catherine, 521-1419 (★M,D,L) 3pm-3am

Le Mystique 1424 rue Stanley, 844-5711 (M,NH) 3pm-3am

Le St-Sulpice 1680 St-Denis, 844-9458 (GF,D) noon-3am, patio

Lézard 4177 St-Denis & Rachel, 2nd flr., 289-9819 (GF,D,A) 11pm-3am, more gay Tue

Max 1166 Ste-Catherine est, 598-5244 (★M,D,YC) 3pm-3am

Meteor 1661 Ste. Catherine est, 523-1481 (MW,D,F) 11am-3am

Paco Paco 451 Rachel est, 499-0210 (★MW,NH) 4pm-3am

Playground/Groove Society 1296 rue Amherst, 284-2266 (M,D) 2am-10am Sun/'Groove' 10pm Th

Pub du Village 1366 Ste-Catherine est, 524-1960 (★MW,F,BW) pam-3am

Rocky 1673 Ste Catherine est (at DeChamplain), 521-7865 (M,NH,V) 3pm-3am

Sky 1474 Ste-Catherine est (★MW,D,A) 10pm-3am

Stud Bar 1812 Ste. Catherine est (M,L)

Tabu 1950 boul. de Maisonneuve est, 597-0010 (MO,NH) 7pm-3am, nude go-go boys

Taverne Gambrinus 1151 Ontario, 522-0416 (M) noon-midnight

Taverne Normandie 1295 Amherst, 522-2766 (M,V) 11am-midnight

Taverne Plateau 71 Ste-Catherine est, 843-6276 (GF) 9am-midnight

RESTAURANTS & CAFES

Après le Jour 901 Rachel est, 527-4141

Cafe Titanic 445 St-Pierre, 849-0894, 7am-5pm, clsd wknds

Callipyge 1493 Amherst, 522-6144 (★) 5pm-11pm, clsd Mon-Tue, Sun brunch

Cantarelli 2181 Ste-Caterine est, 521-1817, Italian

Chablis 1639 St-Hubert, 523-0053, Spanish/French, patio

Chez Better 1310 De Maisonneuve, 525-9832 (BW) European sausages, french fries

Commensal 400 Sherbrooke est (St-Denis), vegetarian

Da Salossi 3441 St-Denis, 843-8995 (BW)

Jardin du Me-Kong 1330 Ste-Catherine, 523-6635

L'Ambiance (Salon De Thé) 1874 Notre-Dame ouest, 939-2609 (W)

L'Anecdote I 801 Rachel est, 526-7967 (MW) 8am-10pm

L'Exception 1200 St-Hubert, 282-1282, vegetarian

L'Express 3927 St-Denis, 845-5333 (★) 8am-3am, French bistro & bar, great pâté

L'Un & L'Autre 1641 rue Amherst, 597-0878, 11am-1am, from 5pm wknds, bistro, also full bar

La Campagnola 1229 rue de la Montagne, 866-3234 (★BW) great eggplant!

La Paryse 302 Ontario est, 842-2040 (MW) 11am-11pm

Le Crystal 1140 Ste-Catherine est, 525-9831 (★) 7pm-5am

Napoléon 1694 Ste-Catherine est, 523-2105

Paganini 1819 Ste-Catherine, 844-3031 (★) 11:30am-midnight, fine Italian

Piccolo Diavolo 1336 Ste-Catherine est, 526-1336

Pizzédélic 1329 rue Ste-Catherine est, 526-6011, noon-midnight, also 3509 boul. St-Laurent, 282-6784, also 370 Laurier ouest, 948-6290

Saloon Cafe 1333 Ste-Catherine est, 522-1333 (★) 11am-1am, til 3am Fri-Sat, full bar

GYMS & HEALTH CLUBS

Physotech 1657 Amherst, 527-7587 (MW)

Stone Gym 1440 Ste-Catherine ouest, 397-8663, 7am-10pm

BOOKSTORES & RETAIL SHOPS

L'Androgyne 3636 boul. St-Laurent, 842-4765 (★WC) 9am-6pm, til 9pm Th-Fri, lesbigay bookstore

TRAVEL & TOUR OPERATORS

Gayroute CP 1036-G, Stn. C, H2L 4V3, ours of 'Gay Canada,' send $2 + SASE for more info

M.A.P. Travel 410 St-Nicholas Ste. 118, 287-7446/(800) 661-6627 (IGTA)

Voyages Alternative 42 Pine Ave. W. Ste. 2, 845-7769 (IGTA)

PUBLICATIONS

Fugues/Gazelle/Village 1212 St-Hubert, 848-1854

Homo Sapiens C.P. 8888 succ.A (U du Q), H3C 3P8, 987-3000

Le Guide Gai du Québec/Insiders Guide to Gay Quebec 915 Stn. C., H2L 4Z2, 523-9463

MEN'S CLUBS

5018 Sauna 5018 boul. St-Laurent, 277-3555, 24hrs

Colonial Bath 3963 Colonial, 285-0132 (MO) clsd Tue

L'Oasis 1390 Ste-Catherine est, 521-0785 (★M,PC) 24hrs

Sauna 226 226 boul. des Laurentides Pont-Viau, 975-4556 (MO) 24hrs

Sauna 456 456 La Gauchetière ouest, 871-8341 (★PC) 24hrs

Sauna Centre-Ville 1465 Ste-Catherine est, 524-3486, 24hrs

Sauna St-Hubert 6527 St-Hubert, 277-0176, 24hrs wknds

Sauna St-Marc 1168 Ste-Catherine est (above Max bar), 525-8404 (★M,E,PC) 24hrs

EROTICA

Cuir Plus 1321 Ste-Catherine est, 521-7587 (WC) 11am-6pm, leather, sex toys

Erotim 818 Ste-Catherine, 982-2534, 10am-midnight

▲ **Priape** 1311 Ste-Catherine est, 521-8451 (★) open 10am, from noon Sun, erotic gay material

CRUISY AREAS

Angrignon Park (AYOR)

De Maisonneuve Park (AYOR)

Mont Royal (AYOR) summer nights on Park Ave.

Phillips Square (AYOR)

Place Dupuis (AYOR)

Pointe au Pic (418)

ACCOMMODATIONS

Auberge Mona 212 rue du Quai, 665-6793 (MW) full brkfst

Prevost (514)

BARS

Le Secret 3029 boul. Labelle (at Hotel Up North, Rte. 117 N.), 224-7350 (M,D,E) 9pm-3am

Québec (418)

ACCOMMODATIONS

727 Guest House 727 rue d'Aquillon, 648-6766 (MW)

Auberge Montmorency Inn 6810 boul. Ste-Anne, L'Ange-Gardien, 822-0568 (GF)

Bed & Breakfast in Old Québec City 35 rue des Ramparts, 655-7685 (GF)

Hotel la Maison Doyon 109 rue Ste-Anne, 694-1720 (GF)

L'Auberge Du Quarter 170 Grande Allée ouest, 525-9726 (GF)

Le Coureur des Bois Guest House 15 rue Ste-Ursule, 692-1117 (MW)

BARS

Bar de la Couronne 310 de la Couronne, 525-6593 (★M,S) 2pm-3am, nude go-go boys

Bar L' Eveil 710 rue Bouvier Ste. 120, 628-0610 (MW,NH) 11am-3am, patio

Bar Male 770 rue Ste-Genevieve, 522-6976 (M,CW,L,V)

Fausse Alarme 161 rue St-Jean, 529-0277 (M,NH) 4pm-3am (from 11am summers)

L'Amour Sorcier 789 Côte Ste-Genevieve, 523-3395 (★MW,NH,V) 11:30am-3am

La Ballon Rouge 811 rue St-Jean, 647-9227 (★M,D,YC) 9pm-3am

Le Bol Vert 2470 Chemin Ste-Foy, 650-6525 (W,D)

Pub du Carré 945 rue d' Aiguillon, 692-9952 (M,NH) 8am-midnight, clsd Sun

Studio 157 157 Chemin Ste-Foy, 529-9958 (★W,D,E,YC) 10pm-3am Wed-Sat, call for men's nights

Taverne 321 321 de la Couronne, 525-5107 (M,V) 8am-3am

Taverne Le Draque 815 rue St-Augustin, 649-7212 (★M,S,BW,YC) 8am-3am

RESTAURANTS & CAFES

Kookening Kafe 565 rue St-Jean, 521-2121

Le Commensal 860 rue St-Jean, 647-3733, vegetarian

Le Hobbit 700 rue St-Jean, 647-2677, opens 7:30am

Restaurant Diana 849 rue St-Jean, 524-5794 (★) 8am-1am, 24hrs Fri-Sat

Zorba Grec 853 St-Jean, 525-5509, 8am-5pm, Greek

BOOKSTORES & RETAIL SHOPS

L'Accro Librairie 845 rue St-Jean, 522-9920, lesbigay

MEN'S CLUBS

Bloc 225 225 St-Jean, 523-2562 (MO,PC) 24hrs

Le Bain Sauna 920 rue St-Jean, 694-9724 (★MO,PC) 24hrs

Le Sauna Hippocampe 31 rue McMahon, 692-1521 (MO,PC★) 24hrs

EROTICA

Importation André Dubois 46 Côte de la Montagne, 692-0264

Importation Delta 387 St-Jean, 647-6808

CRUISY AREAS

Boardwalk by Chateau Frontenac (AYOR)

Rue Grande Allée btwn. rue Montcalm & Place George V (AYOR) summers only, at the outdoor cafes

Rue St-Denis (AYOR)

Rivière Du Loupe (418)

BARS

Disco Jet rue Lafontaine, 862-6308 (MW,D) 3pm-3am, clsd Mon-Tue

Sherbrooke (819)

BARS

Les Dames de Coeur 54 rue King est, 821-2217 (MW) 4pm-2am, clsd Mon-Tue

RESTAURANTS & CAFES

Au Pot au Vin 40 rue King est, 562-8882, lunch & dinner

CRUISY AREAS
Wellington St. downtown (AYOR)

St-Alphonse-de-Granby (514)

ACCOMMODATIONS
Bain Gai de Nature 125 Lussier St., 375-4765 (MO,SW)

St-Donat (819)

ACCOMMODATIONS
Havre du Parc Auberge 2788 Rte. 125 N., St. Donat, 424-7686 (GF,F)

St-François-du-Lac (514)

ACCOMMODATIONS
Domaine Gay Luron 263 Rte. Grande Terre, 568-3634 (MO,F,N)

St-Hyacinthe (514)

BARS
Bistrot Mondor 1400 Cascades ouest, 773-1695

Ste-Marthe (514)

ACCOMMODATIONS
Camping du Plein Bois 550 Chemin St-Henri, Ste. Marthe, 459-4646 (MO,D,SW,N)

Trois Rivières (819)

INFO LINES & SERVICES
Gay Ami CP 1152, G9A 5K1, 373-0771, lesbigay social contacts

BARS
La Maison Blanche #3 767 St-Maurice, 379-4233 (MW,D,E) 9pm-3am
Le Gité Du Huard 42 rue St-Louis, 375-8771 (MW)
Le Lien 1572 rue Royal, 370-6492 (W)

SASKATCHEWAN

Moose Jaw (306)

INFO LINES & SERVICES
Lesbian/Gay Committee 692-2418, social/support group

Ravenscrag (306)

ACCOMMODATIONS
Spring Valley Guest Ranch Box 10, 295-4124 (★GF,F)

Regina (306)

INFO LINES & SERVICES
Gay Men's AA Group 585-3238, 7:30pm Fri
Pink Triangle Community Services 24031 Broad St., 525-6046, 8:30pm-11pm Tue & Fri

BARS
Oscar's 1422 Scarth St., 522-7343 (MW,S,YC) 8:30pm-2am

SPIRITUAL GROUPS
Dignity Regina Box 3181, S4P 3G7, 569-3666, 6:30pm 3rd Sun
Koinonia 3913 Hillsdale Ave., 525-8542, 7pm 2nd & 4th Sun, interfaith worship

CRUISY AREAS
Victoria Park (AYOR)
Wascana Park (AYOR)

Saskatoon (306)

INFO LINES & SERVICES
Gay/Lesbian AA 665-6727, also call Gay/Lesbian Line for schedule
Gay/Lesbian Line 665-1224, noon-4:30pm & 7:30pm-10:30pm, til 5:30pm Sat

ACCOMMODATIONS
Brighton House 1308 5th Ave. N., 664-3278 (GF,WC)

BARS
Diva's 220 3rd Ave. S. Ste. 110 (alley entrance), 665-0100 (MW,D,PC) 8pm-2am, clsd Mon

BOOKSTORES & RETAIL SHOPS
Cafe Browse 269-B 3rd Ave. S., 664-2665, 10am-11pm, from 12:30pm Sun
Out of the Closet 241 2nd Ave S., 3rd flr., 665-1224

TRAVEL & TOUR OPERATORS
Jubilee Travel 108-3120 8th St. E., 373-9633 (IGTA) ask for Mike

SPIRITUAL GROUPS
Affirm PO Box 7518, S7K 6K7, 653-1475, 1st Sun
Dignity Saskatoon PO Box 7283, S7K 4S2

PUBLICATIONS
Perceptions Box 8581, S7K 6K7, 244-1930, covers the Canadian prairies

CRUISY AREAS
Kiwanis Park along river bank (AYOR)

YUKON

Whitehorse (403)

INFO LINES & SERVICES
Gay/Lesbian Alliance of the Yukon Territory PO Box 5604, Y1A 5H4, 667-7857
Yukon Gays/Lesbians PO Box 5604, Y1A 5H4, 667-7857

COSTA RICA

Manuel Antonio (506)

ACCOMMODATIONS

El Parador (800) 451-4398 (GF,SW) large resort

▲ **Hotel Casa Blanca** apdo. 194 Entrada La Mariposas, Quepos, 777-0253 (MW,SW) walking distance to gay beach

Makanda by the Sea 777-8201 (GF,SW) private oasis

Si Como No (800) 237-8207 (★GF,SW)

Villas Mar y Sol Inn PO Box 256-6350, Quepos, 777-0307 (GF,F)

BARS

Arco Iris behind iron bridge at the waterfront, Quepos (GF,D) clsd Mon

Kamuk Pub at Katuk Hotel, downtown, Quepos (GF,E) open til 4am

Mar y Sombra 1st Beach (★MW,D,F)

The Vela Bar 1st Beach, 777-0413

RESTAURANTS & CAFES

El Barba Roja Quepos (★) great sunset location

El Gran Escape Quepos, clsd Tue, Tex-Mex

Karola's Quepos, clsd Wed, great brkfst with a view

The Plinio located in the Hotel Plinio, 777-0055, Italian

Tico Rico paved road to national park, Quepos, lunch & dinner, includes use of pool bar

TRAVEL & TOUR OPERATORS
Costa Rica Connnection 975 Osos St., San Luis Obispos CA, 93401, (805) 543-8823/(800) 345-7422

CRUISY AREAS
La Playita (N,AYOR)

Puntarenas

BARS
La Deriva (GF)

CRUISY AREAS
Beach from the port to the jetties (Malecones) (AYOR)
Calle el Paseo de los Turistas (AYOR)

San Jose (506)

ACCOMMODATIONS
Amstel Amon (800) 575-1253 (GF) modern hotel, quiet location
Cariari Hotel & Country Club (800) 227-4274 (GF,SW) luxury resort, great golfing
▲ **Colours - The Guest Residence** El Triangulo, Blvd. Rohrmoser, 32-35-04/(800) 934-5622/(305) 532-9341 (★MW,SW,IGTA) brkfst & complementary cocktails
Don Carlos B&B 221-6707 (★GF)
Hotel L'Ambiance 949 Calle 27, 23-15-98 (GF,F) also bar
Joluva Guesthouse Calle 3 B, Aves. 9 & 11 #936, 223-7961/(800) 298-2418 (MW)
Scotland Apartments Ave. 1 Calle 27, 23-08-33 (GF)

Bars

Antros Ave. 14 btwn Calle 7 & 9 (GF)

Cantabrico Ave. 6 btwn. Calles Central & 2nd (MW)

De Ja Vu Calle 2 btwn Ave. 14 & 16 (★MW,D,S) 8pm-?, clsd Mon-Th, take taxi to avoid bad area

El Churro Español Calle 11 btwn 8 & 10 (knock on the door) (MW)

La Avispa Calle 1 btwn Ave. 8 & 10, #834 (no name outside, pink house) (MW) clsd Mon & Th

La Esmeralda Ave. Segunda btwn Calles 5 & 7 (GF,F,E)

La Taberna Calle 1, btwn Ave. 7 & 9 (no sign) (M) 6pm-midnight, 1st & 2nd flr

Los Cucharones Ave. 6 btwn Calles Central & 1st (no name outside, listen for music) (M) opens 8pm, clsd Mon-Tue

Monte Carlo Ave. 4 & Calle 2 (on corner) (GF)

Restaurants & Cafes

Cafe de Teatro National National Theatre, 223-4488, lunch

La Cocina de Lena El Pueblo area (★) Costa Rican foods, 5 min. from downtown

La Perla Calle Central Ave. 2 (on corner)

La Piazetta Paseo Colon, Italian

Machu Pichu off Paseo Colon, just out of downtown

Nimbe suburb of Escazu, 281-1739

Vishnu Vegetarian Restaurant Ave. 1 btw Calle 3 & 1 (★)

Gyms & Health Clubs

Exclusives Gym La Sabana Norte

Leblon Calle 9 btwn. Aves. 1 & 3

Travel & Tour Operators

Amatirasu Tours 257-8529

Men's Clubs

Decameron Ave. 10 btwn. Calles 7 & 9

Cruisy Areas

Plaza de la Democracia Central Ave. in front of Museo (AYOR)

Dominican Republic

El Huacal (787)

Info Lines & Services

Amigos Siempre Amigos Apartado Postal 2231, 681-6366, social group

Santo Domingo (787)

Accommodations

Hotel David Arzobispo Novel 308, Zona Colonial, 688-8538 (GF)

Bars

Freddy's Bar Polvorin #10, 688-7505 (M,OC)

The Malecon btwn. Sheraton & Hotel Jaragua

Pariguayso Calle Padre Billini #412, 682-2735 (MW)

The Penthouse Calle Saibo & 20th St. (difficult to find) (★MW,D) Th-Sat

RESTAURANTS & CAFES
Cafe Coco Calle Sanchez 153, 687-9624 (E) noon-10pm, small English restaurant, full bar
Le Pousse Cafe 107 19 de Marzo (★MW,D)

DUTCH WEST INDIES

Aruba (297)

BARS
Cafe the Paddock 94 L.G. Smith Blvd., Oranjestad, 83-23-34 (GF,NH)
The Cellar 2 Klipstraat, Oranjestad, 82-64-90 (★GF,NH) 3pm-5am; also 'The Penthouse' (MW,D,A) from 11pm Wed-Sat
Jewel Box Revue La Cabana Resort & Casino, Oranjestad, 87-90-00 (GF,E,S)
Jimmy's Waterweg & Middenweg, Oranjestad, 82-25-50 (★GF,NH,F) afterhours
Paradiso 16 Wilhelminastraat, Oranjestad, opening fall '96, inquire locally

RESTAURANTS & CAFES
Grand Cafe Cobra 60 L.G. Smith Blvd. (Marisol Bldg.), Oranjestad, 83-31-03

EROTICA
Hot Spot Waterweg & Steenweg, Oranjestad, 82-69-32, 2pm-10pm, clsd Sun

CRUISY AREAS
California Dunes behind lighthouse at the rocks, Oranjestad (N,AYOR)
Caya G.F. Croes Main St., Oranjestad (AYOR) afterhours
Eagle Beach Oranjestad
Manchebo Beach Oranjestad
Sonesta Island European (topless) side, Oranjestad

FRENCH WEST INDIES

St. Barthelemy (596)

ACCOMMODATIONS
Hostellerie des 3 Forces Vitet, 27-61-25/(800) 932-3222 (★GF,F,SW,IGTA) metaphysical retreat/inn
Hotel Normandie 27-62-37 (GF)
St. Bart's Beach Hotel Grand Cul de Sac, 27-60-70 (GF)
Village St. Jean 27-61-39/(800) 633-7411 (GF)

BARS
American Bar Gustavia (GF,F)
Le Sélect Gustavia, 27-86-87 (GF) more gay after 11pm

RESTAURANTS & CAFES
Eddie's Ghetto Gustavia, Creole
Newborn Restaurant Anse de Caye, 27-67-07, French Creole

CRUISY AREAS
Anse Grande Saline Beach gay section on the right side of Saline (AYOR)

St. Martin (590)

BARS
Pink Mango at Laguna Beach Hotel, Nettle Bay, 87-59-99 (★MW,D) 6pm-3am

PUERTO RICO

Aguada
(787)

ACCOMMODATIONS

San Max PO Box 1294, 00602, 868-2931 (MW) guesthouse & studio apt on beach

BARS

Johnny's Bar Carretera 115 (MW) inquire at San Max accommodations

Aguadilla
(787)

BARS

Carl's by the Sea Carretera Parque Colon, 882-2888 (M,D,S,WC) opens 7pm, clsd Mon, hustlers

Bayamón
(787)

BARS

Gilligan's Betances D-18 Hnas. Davila, 786-5065 (MW,E,PC)

Yabba Dabba Pub Rd. 110 (GF) open daily

Cabo Rojo
(787)

BARS

Village Pub Cafe HCO 1 Box 13819, 851-6783 (GF)

Caguas

BARS

Villa Camito Country Club off old Hwy. 3 (turn right at Cafe de los Pisos) (★MW,F,S) opens 6pm Sat

Coamo
(787)

ACCOMMODATIONS

Parador Banos de Coamo PO Box 540, 825-2186/825-2239 (GF,F) resort w/ mineral baths, public baths open 24hrs (MO late night)

Corozal
(787)

BARS

Excape Calle O'Neil #5, 759-1111 (M,E)

Eujasco

BARS

El Quinque de Conce Jr. B.O. Carreritas, 4.0 interior (M,NH) open daily, pool tables

Hato Rey

BARS

Choices 70 Eñasco (M,D) open wknds

Isabela

BARS

Paradise Cocktail Lounge Hacia La Playa de Jobos, Carr. 466, KM.06.3 (M) 9pm-?, clsd Mon-Tue

Villa Ricomar 8 Calle Paz, Carretera 459, Barrio Jobos (MW,D,S) opens 9pm Fri-Sat, from 6pm Sun

Mayaguez

BARS
Roma Calle de Diego 151 (MW,D,PC) open Th-Sun

CRUISY AREAS
Plaza Colon by City Hall (AYOR)

Ponce

BARS
The Cave Barrio Teneria #115 (M,E)

CRUISY AREAS
Off Main Plaza nr. the Cathedral (AYOR)

San German (787)

BARS
Norman's Bar Carretera 318, Barrio Maresúa (MW,NH,D) 6pm-1am, salsa & merengue

The World Road 360 km. 1, 892-7067 (GF,D,YC) 10pm-7am Wed, Fri-Sat

San Juan (787)

INFO LINES & SERVICES
CONCRA 112 Ave. Universidad, Santa Rita, Rio Piedras, 753-9443, STD/HIV clinic, health care & referrals

Telefino Gay PO Box 11003, Estación Viejo San Juan, 722-4838/(800) 981-9179

Ocean Walk
Guest House

**Puerto Rico's largest gay accommodations facility.
40 rooms in a beautiful courtyard setting directly on the
best beach. Pool, bar and grill, large sundeck. Very casual.**

(809) 728-0855   **ATLANTIC PLACE 1**
(809) 726-0445   **SAN JUAN, PR 00911**
(800) 468-0615
FAX: (809) 728-6434

ACCOMMODATIONS

Atlantic Beach Hotel 1 Calle Vendig, Condado, 721-6900 (★MW,SW,IGTA)

Casablanca Guest House 57 Caribe St., Condado, 722-7139 (★GF)

Condado Inn 6 Condado Ave., 724-7145 (MW,F) also lounge

El Canario Inn 1317 Ashford Ave., Condado, 722-3861/(800) 742-4276 (GF)

▲ **Embassy Guest House** 1126 Seaview, Condado, 725-8284

Glorimar Guesthouse 111 University Ave., Rio Piedras (GF)

Gran Hotel El Convento 100 Christo St., Old San Juan, 723-9020/(800) 468-2779 (★GF,SW)

Hotel Iberia 1464 Wilson Ave., Condado, 722-5380 (MW,F)

L' Habitation Beach Guesthouse 1957 Calle Italia, Ocean Park, 727-2499 (GF,F)

Numero Uno on the Beach 1 Calle Santa Ana, Ocean Park, 726-5010 (GF,SW,WC) also bar & grill

▲ **Ocean Park Beach Inn** Calle Elena # 3, Ocean Park, 728-7418/(800) 292-9208 (★MW,F,SW,IGTA)

▲ **Ocean Walk** 1 Atlantic Place, Ocean Park, 728-0855/(800) 468-0615 (GF,SW,IGTA)

BARS

Abbey Disco Calle Cruz #251 (Lazer Bar), 725-7581 (GF,D) gay Sun & Th

Barefoot Bar 2 Calle Vendig, Condado, 724-7230 (★M,F) 9am-3am, hustlers, brkfst & lunch

Bebo's Playa Pinones, 253-3143/269-3429 (MW,D,S) 3pm-?, clsd Sun-Tue

Boccacio Muñoz Rivera, Hato Rey (across from Fire Dept.) (★MW,D) on dead end st.

Cups Calle San Mateo #1708, Santurce, 268-3570 (MW) clsd Mon

El Danuvio Azul Calle San Juan #613, Santurce (MW) 8pm-4am, clsd Sun

Junior's Bar 602 Calle Condado, Santurce (MW,NH,D) 6pm-2am, til 4am Fri-Sat

Kenny's Carretera de Rio Piedras a Caguas (GF,F,SW) from 8pm Fri-Sun

Krash 1257 Ponce de Leon, Santurce, 722-1131 (★MW,D,E,V) 9pm-4am, clsd Mon

La Laguna Night Club 53 Calle Barranquitas, Condado (★M,D,S,PC) from 10pm

Taboo Calle Loiza #1753, Santurce, 728-5906 (MW,PC) 8pm-?, clsd Sun

Tia Maria's Jose de Diego, Stop 22, Ponce de Leon, Santurce (★GF) liquor shop & bar

Vibration 51 Ave. Barranquitas, Condado (★MO,S) 10pm-5am

RESTAURANTS & CAFES

809 Cafe 1 Vendig St., Condado, 721-6900

Amanda's Cafe 424 Norzagaray, Old San Juan, 722-1682, 11am-2am, til 4am Fri-Sat

Cafe Amadeus Calle San Sebastian, 722-8635 (★)

Cafe Berlin 407 Calle San Francisco, Old San Juan, 722-5205, espresso bar

Golden Unicorn 2415 Calle Laurel, 728-4066, 11am-11pm

La Bombonera 259 San Francisco St., Old San Juan, 722-0658 (★)

Panache 1127 Calle Seaview, Condado, 725-2400 (★) dinner only, French

Sam's Patio 102 San Sebastian, Old San Juan

The Terrace Restaurant 6 Condado Ave., 724-7145, dinner, clsd Tue

PUERTO RICO

Breeze

The Only Party Guide,
Information & News Source
For Puerto Rico's Gay, Lesbian,
Bi-Sexual & Transgender Community.

#56 CALLE BETANCES
FLORAL PARK, P.R. 00917
TEL.: (787)282-7184

*Subscriptions & Travel Information Available.

TRAVEL & TOUR OPERATORS
Travel Maker International Tours San Claudio Mail Stations, Box 224, Rio Piedras, 00926, 755-5878 (IGTA) ask for Ruben

PUBLICATIONS
▲ **Puerto Rico Breeze** Castillo del Mar #1397, Isla Verde, 00979, 282-7184

MEN'S CLUBS
▲ **Steam Works** 205 Calle Luna, 725-4993 (PC) 24hrs wknds

EROTICA
The Condom Mania 353 San Francisco St., Old San Juan, 722-5348, toys

CRUISY AREAS
Condado Beach (AYOR)
Ocean Park Beach (AYOR)

VIRGIN ISLANDS

St. Croix (787)

ACCOMMODATIONS
King Christian Hotel 59 Kings Wharf, Christiansted, 773-2285 (GF,F,SW)

▲ **The On The Beach Resort** 127 Smithfield Rd., Frederiksted, 772-1205/(800) 524-2018 (★MW,F,SW) beachfront resort, full bar

Prince Street Inn 402 Prince St., Frederiksted, 772-9550 (GF) apts, near beach

BARS
The Last Hurrah King St., Frederiksted, 772-5225 (GF)

CRUISY AREAS
Old Fortress Christiansted (AYOR)

Park along waterfront Frederiksted (AYOR) nights

St. John (787)

ACCOMMODATIONS
Gallows Point Suite Resort Cruz Bay, 776-6434 (GF,F,SW,WC) beachfront resort

Maho Bay & Harmony V.I. National Park, 776-6240/(800) 392-9004 (GF) camping & an environmentally aware resort

Oscar's Guest House Estate Pastory #27, 776-6193/(800) 854-1843 (GF)

Sunset Pointe 773-8100, rental residences

TRAVEL & TOUR OPERATORS
Sail Ananda Cruz Bay, 776-6922, private charters

CRUISY AREAS
Solomon Bay gay beach & scene (AYOR)

St. Thomas (787)

ACCOMMODATIONS
Blackbeard's Castle PO Box 6041, 00801, 776-1234/(800) 344-5771 (★GF,F,SW) atop Blackbeard's Hill

Danish Chalet Guest House PO Box 4319, 00803, 774-5764/(800) 635-1531 (GF)

Hotel 1829 PO Box 1567, St.Thomas, 00804, 776-1829/(800) 524-2002 (GF,F,SW)

Pavilions & Pools Hotel 6400 Estate Smith Bay, 775-6110/(800) 524-2001 (GF,WC)

RESTAURANTS & CAFES
Fiddle Leaf Restaurant Government Hill (★) dinner only, clsd Sun

TRAVEL & TOUR OPERATORS
Journeys by the Sea, Inc. 6501 Redhook Plaza, Ste. 201, 775-3660/(800) 825-3632 (IGTA)

CRUISY AREAS
Morning Star Beach nr. the Marriott (AYOR) popular gay beach

Tortola (787)

ACCOMMODATIONS
Fort Recovery Estate Village Box 239, Road Town, British VI, 495-4354/(800) 367-8455 (GF,SW)

MEXICO

Acapulco, Gro. (748)

ACCOMMODATIONS

Caracol 90 Calle Caracol 90, 4-0139 (★MO,SW)

Casa Condesa 125 Bella Vista, 4-1616 (M)

Casa Le Mar Lomas Del Mar 32B, 4-1022 (M,SW) full brkfst

Fiesta American Condessa Costera Miguel Aleman, 4-2355/(800) 223-2332 (GF,SW)

Las Brisas 4-1580/(800) 223-6800 (GF) luxury resort, rooms w/private pools

▲ **Las Palmas** 155 Ave. Las Conchas, 7-0843 (MO,F,SW) private villas

Royale De Acapulco & Beach Club Calle Caracol 70, Fraccion Amiento Farallón, 4-3707 (GF,F,SW)

Villa Costa Azul 555 Fdo. Magallanes, 4-5462 (MW,SW,IGTA)

BARS

Demas Privada Piedra Picuda #17 (behind Carlos & Charlie's) (★MW,D) opens 10pm

La Melinche Picuda 216 behind Plaza Condesa (M,S)

Open House Bar Condesa Plaza (across from gay beach & Betos), 4-7285 (M,NH,D,V)

Relax Calle Lomas de Mar 7, 4-04-21 (M,D,S) 9pm-5am, clsd Mon-Wed

RESTAURANTS & CAFES

Beto's Beach Restaurant Condessa Beach (MW)

Chicken Choza Benito Juárez St. (1/2 blk off Zócalo) (MW) full bar

Jovitos Costera across from the Fiesta Americana Condesa, traditional fare

Kookaburra Carretera Escénica (at Marina Las Brisas), 84-1448 (★) International

La Guera de Condesa Condesa Beach

La Tortuga Calle Lomas del Mar 5-A, noon-2am, full bar

Le Bistrquet Andrea Doria #5, Fracc. Costa Azul, 4-6860 (★MW) turn off the costera at the Oceanic Park

Su Casa/La Margarita Ave. Anahuac 110, 4-4350, great views

CRUISY AREAS

Condesa Beach by umbrellas & rocks (AYOR)

Plaza Alvarez/Zócalo (AYOR) hustlers-chichifos

Aguascalientes, Ags.

BARS

Merendero Kikos Calle Arturo J. Pani 132 (GF,F) closes at 11pm

RESTAURANTS & CAFES

Restaurant Mitla Calle Madero 220

Restaurant San Francisco Plaza Principal

CRUISY AREAS

Jardin de San Marcos Calle Carraza & Calle Arturo J. Pani (AYOR)

Plaza Principal (AYOR)

Cabo San Lucas

Bars
The Rainbow Bar far east side of the Marina (★MW) from 8pm, from 4pm wknds, clsd Mon

Campeche, Camp.

Restaurants & Cafes
Restaurant del Parque Calle 570 (opposite Plaza Principal)

Cruisy Areas
Plaza Principal/Plaza de Independencia (AYOR)

Cancun, Q.R. (988)

Accommodations
Caribbean Reef Club 20 mi. S. in Puerto Morelos, (800) 322-6286 (★GF,F,SW)

Bars
Caramba Ave. Tulum 87, 4-0032 (GF,D) 10pm-?

Picante Bar Avenida Tulum 20, east of Ave. Uxmal (★M,YC) 9:30pm-4am

Ta' Qüeno Ave. Yaxachilián 15 (M,D,S) 9pm-4am

Gyms & Health Clubs
Shape Calle Conoco, 1 blk from San Yaxchen (GF)

Cruisy Areas
Avenida Tulum Centro (AYOR) late

Beach btwn. Camino Real & The Beach Club (AYOR)

Gay Dunes at Beach nr. Holiday Inn (AYOR)

Palapa Park opposite Cinema Blanquita (AYOR) nights

Chihuahua, Chih. (141)

Bars
Chindos Calle 6 #30, Centro (M) closes at 11pm, door to the right of Hotel Maceyra

Cruisy Areas
Plaza de la Constitución Plaza Hidalgo (AYOR)

Ciudad Juárez, Chih. (161)

Accommodations
Hotel de Luxe 300 S. Lerdo Ave., PO Box 1061, El Paso TX, 79946, 5-0202 (GF,F) not quite deluxe (cheap)

Plaza Continental Ave. S. Lerdo de Tejada 112, 2-2610 (★GF,F)

Bars
Bar Omare Calle Corona & Calle Ignacio de la Peña, 2-7300 (GF) closes at midnight

The Club Madelon Calle Santos Degollado 771 N. (MW,D,E)

Club Olympico Ave. Lerdo 210, 2-5742 (★M,NH) noon-2am

Nebraska Mariscal #251 Centro (MW) closes at midnight

Ritz 1/2 block N. & 1/2 block E. of Hotel de Luxe, 4-2291 (M,YC)

Restaurants & Cafes
El Coyote Invalido Ave. Lerdo Sur, 24hrs

GYMS & HEALTH CLUBS
Jordan Baños Ave. 16 de Septiembre (AYOR)

CRUISY AREAS
Monument to Bonito Juárez Lerdo Ave. & V. Guerrero Ave. (AYOR)

Cordoba, Ver.

BARS
Salon Bar El Metro Ave. 7 No. 117-C, 1&3 (MW,D)

CRUISY AREAS
Mercado Juárez, btwn. Calles 7&9 (AYOR)
Sidewalk Cafes (AYOR) El Portal Zevallos

Cozumel, Q.R. (987)

ACCOMMODATIONS
La Perla Beach & Diving Resort Playa Paraiso, 2-0188/(800) 852-6404 (GF,SW)
Sol Cabañas del Caribe beachfront, 2-0017/0072/(800) 336-3542 (GF,F)

BARS
Scaramouche (GF,D)

CRUISY AREAS
Zócalo (AYOR)

Cuernavaca, Mor. (73)

ACCOMMODATIONS
Aurora B&B Calle Arista 303, 18-6394 (GF)
Hotel Narajeva Sonora 1000 Col. Vista Hermosa (GF)

BARS
Shadee Avenida Adolfo Lopez Mateos, 12-4367 (★M,F,S) 9pm-4am , clsd Mon-Tue, expensive cover

CRUISY AREAS
Jardin Juárez (AYOR)
Mercado (AYOR)
Plaza Morelos (AYOR)
Zócalo & adj. bar (AYOR) Fri-Sat only

Durango, Dgo. (181)

BARS
Arthur's 134 Bruno Martínez Sur (GF,D)
Bar Country 122 Constitución Norte (MW,F)
Buhós Restaurant & Bar 615 5 de Febero, 2-5811 (GF)
Eduardos 805 20 de Noviembre Pte. (MW)

Enseñada, B.C.N. (684)

BARS
Club 74 Calle 2 N. 461 (GF)
Club Ibis Blvd. Costero at Ave. Sangines, 6-1440 (GF,D) Fri & Sat only
Coyote Club 1000 Blvd. Costero #4 & 5 at Diamante, 7-3691 (★M,D) 9pm-3am, from 6pm Sun, clsd Mon-Tue, patio
Ola Verde Calle Segunda 459-A (MW,F) popular late

Guadalajara • Mexico

Restaurants & Cafes
Mariscos California Calle Ruiz & Segunda, 9am-9pm, clsd Mon, seafood

Travel & Tour Operators
Gay Baja Tours Alvarado 143, Local 7J, 8-3676/(888) 225-2429

Men's Clubs
Banos Floresta Calle Segunda 1357 (AYOR)

Cruisy Areas
Gay Beach past the Corona Beer Distrib., turn right on dirt road(Farmacia San Jorge) before pedestrian bridge (AYOR) "do not swim in the water"

Guadalajara, Jal. (36)

Accommodations
Hotel Calinda Roma Ave. Juarez 170, (800) 228-5151 (GF,F)
Travel Recreation International 1875 Ave. Libertad, Local-C, Sec Juárez, 26-3398 (GF,IGTA)

Bars
Candilejas 961 Ave. Niños Héroes (Hotel Carlton) (GF,D,S) 8pm-4am, clsd Mon
Chivas López Cotilla at Calle Degollado, 13-1617 (M) 6am-2am
El Botanero Javier Mina Ave., at 54th St. (M,S,YC)
El Taller 30 Calle 66, Reforma District (★M0,S) 9pm-3am, clsd Mon-Tues
La Malinche 1230 Alvaro Obregón St. at Calle 50, Libertad District (M,D,F,S,YC) 8pm-3am
Monica's Disco Bar 1713 Alvaro Obregón St., Libertad District, 43-9544 (★M,D,S,YC) 9pm-3am, clsd Mon
Pancho's 179 Calle Maestranza Centro (GF,F) 11am-midnight
SOS Club 1413 Ave. La Paz, Hidalgo District (★MW,D,S) 11pm-3am, clsd Mon

Restaurants & Cafes
Brasserie 1171 Prisciliano Sanchez St., downtown Juárez District
Copa de Leche 414 Juárez Ave., Juárez District, 14-5347 (E) 7am-10pm
Sanborn's Juárez Ave. at 16 de Septiembre St.
Sanborn's Vallarta 1600 Vallarta Ave., downtown Juárez District

Men's Clubs
Baños Galeana 167 Galeana St., 13-6286 (★GF,YC) 7am-8pm
Baños Guadalajara 634 Federalismo Sur Ave. (GF,YC)

Erotica
Paris 155 Juárez Ave., at Degollado (AYOR) theater

Cruisy Areas
Plaza Tapatia nr. Delgollado Theater (AYOR) days

Guanajuato, Gto. (473)

Accommodations
Castillo Santa Cecilia Camino a La Valenciana, 2-0477 (★GF,F)
Hotel Museo Posada Sante Fe downtown, 2-0084 (GF)

Bars
El Incendio Calle Cantarranas 15, 2-1372 (GF)

Jalapa, Ver.

BARS
La Mansion Sobre la carretera (MW,S)
La Mansions take a cab towards Bandarilla, 20min. NW of town (MW,D,S) Fri-Sat only

CRUISY AREAS
Parque Juárez/Zócalo Enriquez & Zaragoza (AYOR)

La Paz, B.C.S. (112)

ACCOMMODATIONS
Casa La Paceña Calle Bravo 106 , 5-2748/(707) 869-2374(off-season) (GF) open Nov-June
Gran Baja near harbor Mariano Abasolo (GF)
Hotel Perla 1570 Ave., Alvaro Obregón, 2-0777 x131 (GF)

BARS
Bar Intimo Calle 16 de Septiembre (MW)

CRUISY AREAS
Malecón (the Seawall) afternoon & early evening (AYOR)

Manzanillo, Col. (333)

ACCOMMODATIONS
Pepe's c/o 2698 Pacific Ave., San Francisco CA, 94115, 3-0616/(415) 346-4734 (GF,F)

Matamoros, Tamps.

BARS
Moutezuma Lounge St. 6 Gonzalez (GF)
Mr. Lee Disco Ave. de las Rosas, Col. Jardin (GF,D)

CRUISY AREAS
Mercado & Zócalo (AYOR)

Mazatlan, Sin. (678)

BARS
Panama Restaurant Pasteleria Ave. del las Garzas & Cammarron Sabalo (MW) cafe
Pepe Toro Ave. de las Garzas 18, Zona Dorado, 14-4167 (MW,D) 8pm-4am, lunch daily
Senor Frogs Ave. del Mar, Zona Costera (GF,D,F) noon-midnight, expensive menu
Valentino's Ave. Camarón Sabalo (GF,D)

RESTAURANTS & CAFES
Restaurante Rocamar Ave. del Mar, Zona Costera, 81-6008 (★)

CRUISY AREAS
Avenida Del Mar along Malecon (AYOR)

Merida, Yuc. (992)

ACCOMMODATIONS
Casa Exilio B&B Calle 68, N. 495 between. 57 & 59, 8-2505 (GF,SW)
Gran Hotel Parque Hidalgo, Calle 60 #496 , 4-7622 (GF,F)

BARS
Ciudad Maya Calle 84 #506, 4-3313 (MW)
Kabuki's Calle 60 & 53 (MW,D) many bars come & go in the area- follow the crowd
Romanticos Piano Bar Calle 60 #461 (MW,S) 9pm-3am

RESTAURANTS & CAFES
Bar La Ruina Calle 69 & 72 (MO)
Cafe Express Calle 60 across from Hidalgo Park
La Bella Epoca Calle 69 #447 (Hotel de Parque), 28-1928, 6pm-1am, Yucatan

MEN'S CLUBS
Hotel Colon Calle 58

CRUISY AREAS
Hidalgo Park (AYOR)
Santa Lucia Park (AYOR)

Mexicali, B.C.N.

BARS
El Taurino Calle Zuazua 480 (at Ave. José Maria Morelos) (★MW)
Jardin Tecate Ave. José Maria Morales (M,NH)
Los Panchos Ave. Juárez 33 (★MW) oldest gay bar in Mexicali
Shaflarelo's Bar Ave. de la Reforma at Calle Mexico (GF,S) open late
Tare Calle Uxmal & Ave. Jalisco (M)

EROTICA
Variedades 500 Ave. Francisco

México City, D.F. (905)

INFO LINES & SERVICES
Calamo Gay Center 118 Culiacán (3rd flr.), support & social group
Casa de la Sal A.C. Córdoba 76, Roma Sur, 207-8042
Gay/Lesbian AA 123 Culiacán Atlas, Colonia Hipodromo Condessa, 8pm Mon-Sat, 6pm Sun
Voz Humana A.C. 530-2873/2592

ACCOMMODATIONS
Aristos Paseo de la Reforma #276, 211-0112/(800) 527-4786 (GF,SW)
Hotel Casa Blanca Lafragua #7, 566-3211/(800) 448-8355 (GF,F,SW)
Hotel Krystal Rosa Liverpool #155, 221-3460/(800) 231-9860 (GF,F,SW)
Marco Polo 27 Amberes, Pink Zone, 207-1893/(800) 223-0888 (GF) upscale hotel
Westin Galeria Plaza Hamburgo #195, 211-0014/(800) 228-3000 (GF,F,SW)

BARS

33 Ave. Lázaro Cárdenas & Republica del Perú (M,NH) 7pm-7am, hustlers

Butterfly Disco Calle Izazaga 9 at Ave. Lazaro Cárdenas Sur (★MW,S) 9pm-4am, clsd Mon

Caztzi Calle Carlos Arellano 4, Ciudad Satélite (MW,D,S)

Dandy's Le Club 118 Martin del Campo (★M,D,S) 9pm-4am

Dark Room Calle Bajio 339 (M,S,V,YC) 7pm-4am

El Don 79 Tonalá St. (MW,D,S) 9pm-4am

El Paseo 148 Paseo de la Reforma, Col. Juárez (★M,OC)

El Taller Ave. Florencia 37-A (MW,D,S)

Enigma Calle Morelia 111 (MW,S) 9pm-5am

L' Baron Ave. Insurgentes Sur 1231 (★M,D)

La Cantina Del Vaquero Ave. Insurgentes Sur 1231 (M,L,S) leather/gift shop inside

Los Rosales Calle Pensador Mexicano 11 (M,D,S)

Privata Ave. Universidad 1901 Col. Copilco, 661-5939 (M,D,S)

Spartacus 8 Cuauhtémoc Ave., Nezahualcóyotl City (★M,S) 9pm-5am wknds

Tom's Leather Bar Ave. Insurgentes Sur 357 (M,L)

Viena Bar República de Cuba 3 (M) noon-midnight

RESTAURANTS & CAFES

El Hábito 13 Madrid St., Coyoacan District (GF,E,S) avante-garde theater

La Fonda San Francisco Calle Velázquez de Leon 126, 546-4060 (MW,E,S) noon-1am

La Opera Calle 5 de Mayo 10, 1pm-midnight, clsd Sun

Vip's Hamburgo 126 Calle Hamburgo, Zona Rosa, also at Paseo de la Reforma & Florencia, nr. Independence Angel Statue; also Niza & Hamburgo

BOOKSTORES & RETAIL SHOPS

El Angel Azul 64 Londres A&B, periodicals & clothing

Sueños Salvajes 177 E. Zapata, Col. Portales

TRAVEL & TOUR OPERATORS

The Gay Travel Club Ave. Mexico 99-PB Col. Hipodromo, 06170, unverified '97

Stag Travel & Tours Hamburgo 214-31 Col. Juárez, 06600, 525-4658 (IGTA)

PUBLICATIONS

41 Soñar Fantasmas/Del Otro Lado Apartado Postal 13-424, 03500

Hermes Febo Editores Apartado Postal 73-025 CP, 03311

Ser Gay 534-3804, covers all Mexico nightlife, limited resources

MEN'S CLUBS

Baños Finisterre 11 Calle Manuel Maria

Baños Riviera Calzada de Tlalpan 634

Baños San Christobal Ave. Nacional 366, Col. Hogares, 787-2770, 6am-8:30pm, til 6pm Sun

Baños Senorial Calle Isabel La Católica 92

Baños Torre Nueva Ave. Alvaro Obregón 42, 7am-10pm, best to go at 6pm

Club San Francisco Calle Rio Panuco 207, Col. Cuauhtemoc, 519-8682

Monterey, N.L. (83)

BARS
Charaos Calle Isacc Garza Oriente (at Zaragoza) (GF,D) open late, clsd Sun
Fridas Calle Padre Mier Poniente (MW,E)
La Opera Calles Colegio Civil Poniente & Aramberri (M,NH)
Napoleón Calle Garibaldi Sur 727 (M,V) 24hrs
Obelisco Ave. Juán Ignacio Ramón 333 Pte. 3rd Flr. (MW,D,S) 10pm-2am, clsd Sun-Tue
Vongole Blvd. Pedrera 300, 336-0335 (M,D,S) 10pm-3am, clsd Sun-Tue, may be closing

GYMS & HEALTH CLUBS
Human Band Gym 832 Calle Escobado Sur (GF)

BOOKSTORES & RETAIL SHOPS
Revisteria Johnny Calle Aramberri 807 Poniente

MEN'S CLUBS
Baños Orientales Calle Hidalgo Oriente 310, 67-2843

CRUISY AREAS
Calle Morelos (AYOR)
Calle Zaragoza (AYOR)
Plaza Hidalgo (AYOR)

Morelia, Mich. (43)

ACCOMMODATIONS
Casa Camelinas 2-1/2 hours from Mexico City in Camelinas, 14-0963/(415) 661-5745 (GF)

BARS
Los Ebines Ave. Madero Pte. at Guadalajara 5039 (GF,D,S)
No Que No Ave. Campestre at Rincón de los Compadres (M,D,S) 10pm-3am, clsd Mon

RESTAURANTS & CAFES
Cafe Bizare 90 Ignacio Zaragoza, inside Posada dela Soledad Ho, 12-1818
Cafe Catedral Portal Hidalgo 23
Las Mercedes Calle Leon Guzmán 47, 12-6113 (★)

MEN'S CLUBS
Baños Mintzicuri Calle Vasco de Quiroga 227, 12-0664

Nuevo Laredo, Tamps.

BARS
El Cielo Del Muerto enter Boys Town turn right (M,D) 10pm-8am, patio
Gusano Bar Calle Dr. Mier 2908 (M)
La Herradura Bar Calle Hidalgo at Ave. Ocampo (GF,S)

Oaxaca, Oax. (951)

ACCOMMODATIONS
Mission de los Angeles Hotel Calzada Porfirio Diaz 102, 5-1500/1000/(800) 221-6509 (GF,F,SW)

Stouffer Presidente 300 Ave. 5 de Mayo, (800) 468-3571 (GF,F,SW) four star hotel

BARS
Bar Jardin Portal de Flores, 6-2092 (MW,F)

Coronita Bustamante at Xochitc (GF,D)

La Cascada Bustamente, N. of Periferico (★M,F)

RESTAURANTS & CAFES
El Asador Vasco Portal de Flores (upstairs), 6-9719, great views

CRUISY AREAS
Alemeda (AYOR) early evenings

Bustamante Zaragoza to Periferico (AYOR) late evenings

Zócalo/Plaza de Armas (AYOR) early evenings

Orizaba, Ver.

CRUISY AREAS
Parque del Castillo (AYOR)

Pachuca, Hgo.

CRUISY AREAS
Zócalo (AYOR)

Pátzcuaro, Mich. (454)

ACCOMMODATIONS
Hotel Posada San Rafael Plaza Vasco de Quiroga, 2-0770 (GF,F)

RESTAURANTS & CAFES
Doña Pala Calle Quiroga

CRUISY AREAS
Mercado (AYOR)

Plaza Principal/Plaza Grande (AYOR)

Puebla, Pue.

BARS
Keops Disco Calle 14 Poniente 101, Cholula (★MW,D,S,YC) 10pm-3am Fri-Sat only

La Cigarra 5 Poniente & 7 Sur, Centro (★MW)

La Fuente Hermanos Serdán 343 (GF,D)

MEN'S CLUBS
Baños La Limpia 3 Sur, btwn. 7th & 9th Poniente (GF)

CRUISY AREAS
Mercado Garibaldi Calle 14 Oriente (AYOR)

Zócalo/Main Park at Cathedral (AYOR) late evenings

Villa Felíz

A luxury hillside vacation villa in
Puerto Vallarta

- Picturesque, old town location
- 5 air-conditioned guestrooms with private baths
- Full bay and city views
- Pool, wet bar, spacious sunning terraces
- Minutes to beach, bars, shopping and restaurants
- Fully staffed with daily maid services
- Full breakfast included

For further information contact:

USA
(714) 752-5456 ext. #277
Mr. Ron Oyer

Canada
(416) 925-9621

Mexico
011 (52322) 2-07-98

Puerto Vallarta, Jal. (322)

ACCOMMODATIONS

Casa de los Arcos Apto 239-B, 48300, 2-5990 (GF) vacation rental near beach

Casa dos Comales Calle Aldama 274, 3-2042 (GF)

▲ **Casa Panoramica Bed & Breakfast** Carratera a Mismaloya, 2-3656/(800) 745-7805 (GF,SW,IGTA) full brkfst

● **Paco Paco Descanso del Sol** 583 Pino Suarez, 3-2077/(800) 936-3646 (★MW)

Vallarta Cora 174 Pilitas, 3-2815 (GF,SW) apts.

▲ **Villa Felíz** PO Box 553, 48300, 2-0798/(714) 752-5456 x277 (MW) (416) 925-9621 (Canada only)

BARS

Blue Chairs (Tito's) southern Los Muertos Beach (MW,F)

Club Paco Paco Ignacio L. Vallarta 278, 2-1899 (★MW,D) 3pm-4am

Gerardo's Party Pad Calle Venustiano 268 (MW,E)

Los Balcones 182 Juárez, upstairs (at Libertad) (M,D) 10pm-3am

Studio 33 Avenida Juárez 728 (GF,D,S) clsd Mon

▲ **Xanadu** (opens Oct 1996) 1-5201 (GF,D,S,E,SW) 4pm-6am, patio

Zotano 101 Morelos by Plaza Rio (GF,D)

RESTAURANTS & CAFES

Adobe Cafe 252 Basilio Badillo

Bombo's 327 Corona

Cafe Sierra Insurgentes 109, 2 -2748 (MW) 9am-11pm

Cuiza Isla Rio Cuale, West Bridge, 2-5646 (MW)

De Claire's 269 Basilio Badillo

La Palada Los Muertos Beach, nr. Pier

Le Bistro Jazz Cafe Isla Ria Cuale #16-A (★) expensive & touristy

Marilyn's Isla Rio Cuale

Memo's Casa de los Hotcakes 289 Basilio Badillo (★)

Papaya 3 169 Abasalo

Santos Francisca Rodriquez 136, 2-5670 (MW) clsd Mon, full bar

Sego's 625 Aguiles Serdán (★)

BOOKSTORES & RETAIL SHOPS
Safari Accents 244 Olas Altas

Studio Rustiko Basilo Badillo 300

TRAVEL & TOUR OPERATORS
Amadeus Tours 3-2815

Doin' It Right Travel (415) 621-3576/(800) 936-3646 (IGTA) Puerto Vallarta gay travel specialist

CRUISY AREAS
Playa del Sol Beach (AYOR)

Playa Los Muertos nr. blue chairs (AYOR)

Plaza Caracol Mall (AYOR)

Queretaro, Qro. (463)

BARS
Gyros Blvd. Venustiano Carranza (M)
La Iguana at Hotel Maria Teresa, Ave. Universidad 308 (GF,D,S)

CRUISY AREAS
Alameda Parque (AYOR)
Plaza de Armas (AYOR)
Zócalo/Obregón Plaza (AYOR)

Reynosa

CRUISY AREAS
Plaza Main Square (opposite American Hotel) (The Circuit) (AYOR)

San Cristobal de las Casas

CRUISY AREAS
Zócalo (AYOR)

San Luis Potosí (481)

BARS
Carretera Ladies Bar Calle 20 de Noviembre 1453 (MO) 8am-midnight
La Laqunita Calle Manuel José Othon 435 (MO)
Sheik Calle Prolongación Zacatecas 347, 2-7457 (MW,D,S) 10pm-4am Fri-Sat

San Miguel De Allende (465)

ACCOMMODATIONS
Aristos San Miguel De Allende 30 Calle Ancha de Santonio, 2-0149/(800) 223-0880 (GF,SW) full service hotel
Casa de Sierra Nevada 35 Calle Hospicio, 2-0415/(800) 223-6510 (GF)

BARS
El Ring 25 Calle Hidalgo (GF,D) 10pm-4am Fri-Sat

Tampico, Tamps.

BARS
Bilbao W. of Calle Francisco I. Madero Oriente & A. Serdan Sur (MW)
Tropicana Bar Calle de General López de Lar (MW)

CRUISY AREAS
Zócalo/Plaza de Armas (AYOR)

Tapachula, Chi.

CRUISY AREAS
Zócalo (AYOR)

Tepic, Nay. (321)

BARS
Bar Club Tepic Calle Veracruz Norte 131 (MO) more gay after 11pm

RESTAURANTS & CAFES
Cafe La Parroquia Calle Amado Nerro 18 (upstairs), 2-6772
Wendy's Ave. México, Norte 178, (not burgers)

Tijuana, B.C.N. (66)

INFO LINES & SERVICES
Gay/Lesbian Info Line 88-0267

ACCOMMODATIONS
Fiesta Americana Hotel 4558 Blvd. Agua Caliente, 81-7000/(800) 343-7821 (GF)
La Villa De Zaragoza 1120 Ave. Madero, 85-1832 (GF)
Palacio Azteca Hotel Ave. 16 de Septiembre, 86-5401 (GF)
Plaza De Oro Hotel 2nd St. at Ave. 'D', 85-1437 (GF)

BARS
D.F. 1910 Plaza Santa Cecilia nr. 3rd St. (M,NH)
El Ranchero Bar 1914 Plaza Santa Cecilia btwn. 1st & 2nd St. (M,NH,F,AYOR)
opens 10am, caution in bathrooms
El Taurino Bar 198 Niños Héroes Ave. between 1st St. & Coahuila, 85-2478
(★MW,S,YC) 10am-3am, til 6am wknds
Emilio's Cafe Musical 1810-11 Calle Tercera (3rd St.), downtown, 88-0267
(★GF,F,E,BW) from dusk til 3am
Jardin de Alá btw. Calle 4 & 5, 2nd Flr. (MW,F,E)
Los Equipales 2024 7th St. (opposite Jai Alai Palace), 88-3006 (★MW,D,S,YC)
opens 9pm, clsd Mon-Tue
Mi Kasa Calle 4 #1923 (GF,D,S,YC) noon-3am
Mike's 1220 Revolución Ave. & 6th St., 85-3534 (★MW,D,S) 9pm-6am Mon-Tue
Noa Noa Calle Primera & 154 'D' Miguel F. Martinez Ave., 81-7901 (★MW,D,S)
clsd Mon, opens 9pm
Terraza 9 Calle 5 at Ave. Revolución, 85-3534 (MW) 8pm-2am

PUBLICATIONS
Frontera Gay A.P. 3302, 22000, 88-0267

MEN'S CLUBS
Baños San José SW corner of Negrete & 8th St. (AYOR)

Toluca, Edo de Méx

BARS
Bar El Conde 201-E Passaje Curi Norte (GF,F)
Bar El Jardin 100-D Ave. Hildalgo Ote. (GF)
Cafe del Rey Portal 20 de Noviembre (GF,F)
Vip's Toluca Paseo Tollocán y Boulevard Isidoro Fabela (MW)

CRUISY AREAS
Mercado (AYOR)
Zócalo/Plaza de Los Martires (AYOR)

Tuxpan

CRUISY AREAS
Ave. Juárez nr. hotels (AYOR)

Tuxtla Guiterrez, Chis. (961)

BARS
Olas Calle 9 Sur Oriente 1498 (M,NH)
Sandy's Bar Calle 9 Sur at 8 Poniente (inquire in 'Via Fontana') (GF,TG)

CRUISY AREAS
Cristobal Colón (AYOR)
Plaza Belisario Dominguez (AYOR)

Veracruz, Ver. (29)

ACCOMMODATIONS
Hotel Imperial Plaza de Armas, 32-8788 (GF,F) expensive

BARS
Deeper Calle Icazo 1005 (Victoria & Revillagigedo), 35-0265 (M,S)
Hippopotamos Fracc. Costa Verde (GF,D,S,YC) 9pm-6am, clsd Mon-Wed
Sotano's Bar Calle 1 (corner of Olmedo), 37-04-44 (M,D) 10pm-5am Th-Sat

MEN'S CLUBS
Baños El Edén Calle Hidalgo 1113 (GF)

CRUISY AREAS
Plaza de Armas/Zócalo (AYOR)
Waterfront & Ave. República (AYOR)

Villahermosa, Tab. (931)

ACCOMMODATIONS
Hotel Don Carlos Ave. Madero 418 centro, 2-2499 (GF,F)
Hyatt Villahermosa 106 Juarez Ave., 3-4444/(800) 233-1234 (GF)

BARS
Yardas 1318 Ave. 27 de Febrero, 3-4362 (MW)

Zacatecas, Zac. (492)

ACCOMMODATIONS
Quinta Real Zacatecas Ave. Rayon 434, 2-9104/(800) 878-4484 (GF) five star hotel

BARS
La Toma Calle Juárez 116 (GF,D) clsd Sun-Tue

RESTAURANTS & CAFES
Cafe Acropolis Ave. Hidalgo

CRUISY AREAS
Ave. Juárez east from Ave. Hidalgo for 2 blocks (AYOR)

Zihuatanejo, Jal.

BARS
La Cambina del Captain Calle Vincente Guerrero at Nicolas Bravo 2nd Flr. (GF)
La Casita Camino escenico a Playa 'La Ropa', across from 'Kontiki' restaurant (GF)
Roca Rock Calle 5 de Mayo (GF,D)

RESTAURANTS & CAFES
Splash Calle Ejido and Calle Vincente Guerrero (★MW)

EVENTS CALENDAR

TOURS & TOUR OPERATORS

JANUARY

25-Feb 1: **Aspen Gay Ski Week**   Aspen, CO
gay/lesbian, 2000+ attendees • (970) 925-9249 • c/o Aspen Gay/Lesbian Community, Box 3143, Aspen, CO 81612

31-Feb 2: **Pantheon of Leather**   New Orleans, LA
annual SM community service awards, at the Radisson Hotel (800) 824-3359, mixed gay/straight • (213) 656-5073 • c/o The Leather Journal, 7985 Santa Monica Blvc. 109-368, W. Hollywood, CA 90046

FEBRUARY

Jan 31-Feb 2: **Blue Ball**   Philadelphia, PA
AIDS benefit weekend highlighted by Saturday night dance, mostly men, $35-100 • (215) 575-1110 • c/o AIDS Information Network, 1211 Chesnut St., 7th flr, Philadelphia, PA 19107

2-9: **Whistler Gay Ski Week:Altitude '97**   Whistler, BC
popular ski destination 75 mi. north of Vancouver, gay/lesbian • (604) 938-0772 / (604) 816-6710 • c/o Out On The Slopes Productions, PO Box 1370, Whistler, BC V0N 1B0

11: **Mardi Gras**   New Orleans, LA
North America's rowdiest block party, mixed gay/straight • (504) 566-5011 • c/o New Orleans Convention & Visitors Bureau, 1520 Sugarbowl Dr., New Orleans, LA 70112

13-17: **Black Gay/Lesbian Conference**   Dallas, TX
gay/lesbian • (213) 964-7820 • c/o Nat'l Black Gay/Lesbian Leadership Forum, 1219 S. La Brea Ave., Los Angeles, CA 90019

14-15: **Hearts Party**   Chicago, IL
AIDS benefit, mostly men • (312) 404-8726 • c/o Test Positive Aware (TPA), 1258 W. Belmont Ave., Chicago, IL 60657-3292

14-17: **Pantheacon**   Oakland, CA
Pagan convention at the Red Lion Hotel, Starhawk ritual, Reclaiming collective, mixed gay/straight • (510) 653-3244 • c/o Ancient Ways, 4075 Telegraph Ave, Oakland, CA 94609

15: **Saint-at-Large White Party**   New York, NY
$30-50 • (212) 674-8541 • c/o Saint-at-Large, 8 St. Mark's Place, Ste. 1A, New York, NY 10003

TBA: **Outwrite**   Boston, MA
annual national lesbian/gay writers & publishers conference, gay/lesbian, 1500+ attendees, $55-65 • (617) 426-4469 • c/o Bromfield St. Educational Foundation, 25 West St., Boston, MA 02111

March 1: **Sydney Gay Mardi Gras**   Sydney, Australia
huge international month-long festival in February, including the Int'l Lesbian/Gay Comedy Festival, culminates in the Mardi Gras parade • (011-61-2) 557-4332 • c/o Sydney Gay/Lesbian Mardi Gras Committee

MARCH

7-10: Gay Ski East '97: The Winter Games · Lake Placid, NY
gay/lesbian, 200+ attendees • (813) 734-1111 • c/o Eclectic Excursions, 2045 Hunters Glen Dr. Ste. 502, Duneden, FL 34698

9: Winter Party · Miami Beach, FL
AIDS benefit dance on the beach, 3500+ attendees, $50 • (305) 593-6666 • c/o Dade Human Rights Foundation, c/o SS, 1541 Brickell Ave. #1105, Miami, FL 33129

22: Saint-at-Large Black Party · New York, NY
gay/lesbian, $30-50 • (212) 674-8541 • c/o Saint-at-Large, 8 St. Mark's Place, Ste. 1A, New York, NY 10003

28-30: White Party · Palm Springs, CA
weekend of buffed, tan & beautiful party circuit queens, benefits Desert AIDS Project & Aides for AIDS etc., mostly men, $75 weekend pass • (213) 653-2699 / (213) 874-4007 • c/o JeffreySanker Enterprises, PO Box 691745, W. Hollywood, CA 90069

APRIL

9: AIDS Dance-a-thon San Francisco · San Francisco, CA
AIDS benefit dance at the Moscone Center, mixed gay/straight, 7000+ attendees, $75+ pledges • (415) 392-9255 • c/o Miller Zeitchik Publicity, PO Box 193920, San Francisco, CA 94119

25-May 4: May Day on Short Mtn. · Liberty, TN
radical faerie gathering, 200+ attendees • (615) 536-5176 • c/o RFD, PO Box 68, Liberty, TN 37095

TBA: AIDS Dance-a-thon L.A. · Los Angeles, CA
AIDS benefit at Universal Studios, mixed gay/straight, $75+ pledges • (213) 466-9255 • c/o AIDS Walk LA, PO Box 933005, Los Angeles, CA 90093

TBA: Readers/Writers Conference · San Francisco, CA
3rd annual weekend of workshops & roundtables with queer writer & readers, at the Women's Building • (415) 431-0891 • c/o A Different Light, 489 Castro St., San Francisco, CA

MAY

2-4: Splash Days · Austin, TX
weekend of parties in clothing-optional Hippie Hollow, highlighted by the beer barge on Sunday • (512) 320-8823 • c/o Tavern Guild, 611 Red River, Austin, TX 78701

9-11: Pridefest Philadelphia · Philadelphia, PA
70 events capped by Saturday night party, gay/lesbian • (215) 732-3378 • c/o Pridefest, 200 S. Broad St., Philadelphia, PA 19102

22-26: Pensacola Memorial Day Weekend · Pensacola, FL
many parties on beaches & bars, 35,000+ attendees • (904) 433-0353 / (904) 432-5777 • c/o Christopher St. South, 2550 Hallmark Dr., Pensacola, FL 32503-4240

23-26: Armory Sports Classic · Atlanta, GA
softball & many other sports competitions, mostly men • (404) 874-2710 •

23-26: Bear Pride · Chicago, IL
1000+ attendees • (312) 509-5135 • c/o Great Lakes Bears

23-26: International Mr. Leather   Chicago, IL
weekend of leather events, capped by contest Sunday, Black and Blue Ball on
Monday • (800) 545-6753 • c/o *International Mr. Leather*, 5015 N. Clark St.,
Chicago, IL 60640

23-25: LesBiGay Gathering   Pahoa, HI
healing & celebration of lesbian/gay natures & creativity, $490-990 • (800) 800-
6886 / (808) 965-7838 • c/o *Pacific Men*, RR2 Box 4500, Pahoa, HI 96778

23-June 8: Spoleto Festival   Charleston, SC
one of the continent's premier avant-garde culture festivals, in late May • (803)
722-2764 • c/o *Spoleto Festival*, PO Box 157, Charleston, SC 29402-0157

25: Beach Maneuvers   Pensacola, FL
mostly men, 5000 attendees, $30-35 • (213) 653-2699 / (213) 874-4007 • c/o
JeffreySanker Enterprises, PO Box 691745, W. Hollywood, CA 90069

30: Lambda Literary Awards   Chicago, IL
the 'Lammies' are the Oscars of lesbigay writing & publishing, gay/lesbian •
(202) 462-7924 • c/o *Lambda Book Report*, 1625 Connecticut Ave. NW,
Washington, DC` 20009

TBA: Ancient Ways Festival   Harbin Hot Springs, CA
annual 4-day mixed gender/orientation spring festival in May or June of pan-
pagan rituals, workshops and music w/ lesbian/gay campsite, mixed
gay/straight • (510) 653-3244 • c/o *Ancient Ways*, 4075 Telegraph Ave., Oakland,
CA 94609

TBA: Geared for Life   Detroit, MI
3rd annual AIDS fundraising art auction & parties in Motor City, topped off by
Gear Party Saturday, 2000+ attendees • (810) 358-9849 / (800) 359-6697
(OurWorld Travel) • c/o *Gear Party*, PO Box 25138, Harper Woods, MI 48225

JUNE

15-22: Pagan Spirit Gathering   Mt. Horeb, WI
summer solstice celebration in Wisconsin, primitive camping, workshops, rituals, mixed gay/straight • (608) 924-2216 • c/o *Circle Sanctuary*, PO Box 219, Mt.
Horeb, WI 53572

20-30: S.F. Int'l Lesbian/Gay Film Festival   San Francisco, CA
get your tickets early for a slew of films about us, 53,000+ attendees • (415)
703-8650 • c/o *Frameline*, 346 9th St., San Francisco, CA 94103

TBA: JeffreySanker L.A. Pride Party   Los Angeles, CA
mostly men, 5000 attendees • (310) 659-3555 / (213) 874-4007 • c/o *JeffreySanker
Enterprises*, PO Box 691745, W. Hollywood, CA 90069

TBA: Lesbian/Gay Pride   Everywhere, USA
Parades, parties and rainbow flags across the country. If you love a spectacle
with a cast of thousands, go to one or all of the events in New York, Los
Angeles or San Francisco or other metropolitan cities. Usually held the last or
next-to-last Sunday in June

5: Wet Party Tampa Bay, FL

dance party benefiting Tampa Bay Gay Men's Chorus, mostly men • (813) 837-4485

26: Up Your Alley Fair San Francisco, CA

local SM/leather street fair held in Dore Alley, South-of-Market, hundreds of local kinky men & women attendees, free • (415) 861-3247 • c/o SMMILE, 1072 Folsom St. #272, San Francisco, CA 94103

TBA: OutFest 97 Los Angeles, CA

gay/lesbian • (213) 951-1247 • c/o *Out on the Screen*, 8455 Beverly Blvd. Ste. 309, Los Angeles, CA 90048

TBA: Take-Off Flight 97 Party East Hampton, NY

AIDS benefit party in late July, 2000+ attendees • (516) 385-2451 • c/o *Long Island Association for* AIDS Care, PO Box 2859, Huntington Stn., NY 11746

2-9: Pacific Men's Conference Pahoa, HI

gay spirituality conference, $490-990 • (800) 800-6886 / (808) 965-7838 • c/o *Pacific Men*, RR2 Box 4500, Pahoa, HI 96778

7-10: Hotlanta River Expo Atlanta, GA

mostly gay men • parties, events & river-rafting parade, mostly men, $130-150+ • (404) 874-3976 • c/o *Hotlanta River Expo*, PO Box 8375, 31106

8-10: Guys & Gals Kent's Store, VA

live country/western music & dancing, gay/lesbian, 80 attendees, $40 • (804) 589-6542 • c/o *Intouch*, Rte. 2, Box 1096, Kent's Store, VA 23084

22-27: Provincetown Carnival Provincetown, MA

mixed gay/straight • (800) 637-8696 / (508) 487-2313 • c/o *Provincetown Business Guild*, PO Box 421, Provincetown, MA 02657

23-24: Sunset Junction Fair Los Angeles, CA

carnival, arts & information fair on Sunset Blvd. in Silverlake benefits Sunset Junction Youth Center, 7500+ attendees, $2+ • (213) 661-7771 • c/o *Sunset Jct. Fair*, PO Box 26565, Los Angeles, CA 90026

30-Sept 2: Labor Day L.A. Los Angeles, CA

weekend-long AIDS fundraising celebration with many events, gay/lesbian • (800) 522-7329 • c/o *Foundation for Educational Research*, PO Box 69504, Los Angeles, CA 90069-9504

TBA: GMHC Morning Party Fire Island, NY

AIDS fundraiser in mid-August • (212) 337-1913 • c/o *Gay Men's Health Crisis*, 129 W. 20th St., New York, NY 10011

TBA: National Gay Softball World Series San Diego, CA

gay/lesbian • (412) 362-1247 • c/o NAGAAA, 1014 King Ave., Pittsburgh, PA 15206

TBA: Wigstock New York, NY

outrageous wig/drag/performance festival in the East Village, gay/lesbian • (212) 620-7310 • c/o *Lesbian/Gay Community Services Center*, 208 W. 13th St., New York, NY

SEPTEMBER

Aug 29-Sept 11: Austin Gay/Lesbian Film Festival   Austin, TX
gay/lesbian • (512) 472-3240 / (512) 476-2454

Sept. 5-7: Last Splash   Austin, TX
weekend of parties in clothing-optional Hippie Hollow, highlighted by the beer barge on Sunday • (512) 476-3611 • c/o *Tavern Guild*, 611 Red River, Austin, TX 78701

13-15: PFLAG Convention   Washington, DC
annual convention of Parents, Friends and Family of Lesbians and Gays, 1000+ attendees • (415) 328-0852 / (202) 638-4200 • c/o PFLAG, 1101 14th St. NW, Ste. 1030, Washington, DC 20005

27: Red Party   Columbus, OH
19th annual, 2500+ attendees, $25 • (614) 294-8309 • c/o *Rudely Elegant*, 1153 Neil Ave., Columbus, OH 43201

28: Mr. Drummer Contest   San Francisco, CA
international leather title contest & vendors • (415) 252-1195 • c/o *Desmodus*, PO Box 410390, San Francisco, CA 94141-0390

TBA: Cruise with Pride   San Juan, PR
Pride Foundation fundraiser in the Greek Islands, 6 days, gay/lesbian, 50+ cabins attendees • (800) 340-0221 • c/o *Cruiseworld*, 901 Fairview Ave. N. #A150, Seattle, WA 98126

TBA: Fall Gathering   Liberty, TN
radical faerie gathering for 9 days, mostly men, 200+ attendees • (615) 536-5176 • c/o RFD, PO Box 68, Liberty, TN 37095

OCTOBER

3-5: Black & Blue Party   Montreal, Quebec
AIDS benefit dance, mostly men, 5000+ attendees, $25-35+ • (514) 875-7026 • c/o *Bad Boy Club Montreal*, 800 Rene-Levesque W. Ste. 450, Montreal, Quebec H3B 1X9

3-12: Pride Film Festival Tampa   Tampa, FL
gay/lesbian • (813) 837-4485 • c/o *Lesbian/Gay Film Festival*, 1222 Dale Mabry Ste. 602, Tampa, FL 33629

10-13: Love Ball   Vancouver, BC
benefits Vancouver Gay/Lesbian Center, mostly men, 5000 attendees, $25-30 • (310) 659-3555 / (213) 874-4007 • c/o *JeffreySanker Enterprises*, PO Box 691745, W. Hollywood, CA 90069

11: National Coming Out Day
gay/lesbian • (800) 866-6263 • c/o *National Coming Out Day*, PO Box 34640, Washington, DC 20043-4640

14: Native Peoples' Day (formerly Columbus Day)
Celebrate the many cultures of native people displaced by invasions, slavery, wars, and territorial conflicts., mixed gay/straight

17-25: Fantasy Fest   Key West, FL
week-long Halloween celebration with parties, masquerade balls & parades, 55,000+ attendees • (800) 535-7797 / (305) 294-4603 • c/o *Key West Business Guild*, PO Box 1208, Key West, FL 33041

24-26: International Gay Rodeo Finals Albuquerque, NM
gay/lesbian • (303) 832-4472 • c/o *International Gay Rodeo*, 900 E. Colfax, Denver, CO 80218

TBA: AIDS Dance-a-thon New York New York, NY
AIDS benefit, mixed gay/straight, 6000+ attendees, $75+ pledges • (212) 807-9255 • c/o *Gay Men's Health Crisis*, PO Box 10, Old Chelsea Stn. , New York, NY 10113-0010

TBA: Film Festival Chicago, IL
gay/lesbian, 7-10,000 attendees, 75 • (312) 384-5533 • c/o *Chicago Filmmakers*, 1543 W. Division, Chicago, IL 60622

NOVEMBER

28: Snow Ball Miami Beach, FL
benefits local charities, mostly men, 6000 attendees, $40-45 • (310) 659-3555 / (213) 874-4007 • c/o *JeffreySanker Enterprises*, PO Box 691745, W. Hollywood, CA 90069

30: White Party Week Vizcaya Miami, FL
Six days of festivities capped by the 11th annual White Party Vizcaya, benefitting the Health Crisis Network, mostly men, $100+ • (305) 757-4444 / (305) 751-7775 • c/o *Health Crisis Network*, PO Box 37-0098, Miami, FL

TBA: Santa Barbara Lesbian/Gay Film Fest Santa Barbara, CA
gay/lesbian • (805) 963-3636 • c/o *Gay/Lesbian Resource Center*, 126 E. Haley Ste. A-17, Santa Barbara, CA 93101

DECEMBER

6-13: International Gay Arts Fest Key West, FL
cultural festival of film, theatre, art, concerts, seminars, parties and a parade • (800) 535-7797 / (305) 294-4603 • c/o *Key West Business Guild*, PO Box 1208, Key West, FL 33041

20-27: Gay Spirit Gathering Pahoa, HI
exploration of myth & meaning in gay spirituality in the Aikane tradition, $490-990 • (800) 800-6886 / (808) 965-7828 • c/o *Pacific Men*, RR2 Box 4500, Pahoa, HI 96778

TBA: Gay Day at Disneyland Anaheim, CA
gay/lesbian, 32-37 • (818) 893-2777 • c/o *Odyssey Adventures*, PO Box 923094, Sylmar, CA 91392

A Friend in New York
Gay/Lesbian
260 7th St., Hoboken, NJ 07030 • (201) 656-7282 • Personalized excursions tailored to your budget and schedule.

Above & Beyond Tours
Mostly Men
(415) 284-1666, (800) 397-2681, Fax: (415) 284-1660 • 13 departures/year to South Pacific, Brazil, Europe

Advance Damron Vacations
Mostly Men
10700 NW Freeway, Ste. 160, Houston, TX 77092 • (713) 682-2002, (800) 695-0880, Fax: (713) 680-3200 • cruises and tours • member IGTA
February -- Whistler Gay Ski Week
April 20-26 -- Windjammer Cruise
October -- Star Clipper Yacht Caribbean Cruise

Adventure Bound Expeditions
Men Only
711 Walnut St., Boulder, CO 80302 • (303) 449-0990, Fax: (303) 449-9038 • mountain tours and hiking excursions

African Pride Safaris
Gay/Lesbian
673 NE 73rd St., Miami, FL 33138 • (305) 751-5216, (800) 237-4225, Fax: (305) 751-6362 • Group and individual tours to Africa • member IGTA
March 29 — Out in Africa
September 27 — Out in Africa
December 27 — Out in Africa (New Year's Party)
March 14 — Kenya Explorer
April 22 — Kenya Explorer
August 22 — Kenya Explorer
September 26 — Kenya Explorer
November 14 — Kenya Explorer
March 14 — African Pride
August 22 — African Pride
December 5 — African Pride
May 10 — Okavango
August 9 — Okavango
March 19 — Pride of Africa
August 23 — Pride of Africa
July 19 — Camp Tanzania
October 24 — Gambia Roots

Ahwahnee Whitewater Expeditions
Mixed Gay/Straight
PO Box 1161, Columbia, CA 95310 • (209) 533-1401 • women-only, co-ed & charter rafting • member IGTA

All About Destinations
Gay/Lesbian
Gallery 3 Plaza, 3819 N. 3rd St., Phoenix, AZ 85012-2074 • (602) 277-2703, (800) 375-2703 • member IGTA
January 10-17 — Cruise Los Angeles to Acapulco
May 12-19 — Cruise Acapulco to San Francisco
July 3-6 — "Homo-on-the-Range" Southwest adventure & circuit party
July 3-13 — "Homo-on-the-Range" Southwest adventure & circuit party
August 29-Sept 1 — Labor Day Community Cruise to Baja, Mexico

Allegro Travel
Gay/Lesbian
900 West End Ave. #12C, New York, NY 10025 • (212) 666-6700, (800) 666-3553, Fax: (212) 666-7451 • 22 departures yearly to Russia, Italy, Egypt & Scandinavia

Alyson Adventures
Mostly Gay/Lesbian
PO Box 181223, Boston, MA 02118 • (617) 247-8170, (800) 825-9766, Fax: (617) 542-9189 • member IGTA

Atlantis Events
Mostly Men
9060 Santa Monica Blvd. Ste. 310, W. Hollywood, CA 90069 • (310) 281-5450, (800) 628-5268, Fax: (310) 281-5455 • all-inclusive resorts 5 times a year • member IGTA
    February 26-March 3 — Sydney Mardi Gras, Club Med Lindeman Island
    April 26-May 3 — Club Atlantis

Atlas Travel Service
Straight/Gay
8923 S. Sepulveda Blvd., Los Angeles, CA 90045 • (310) 670-3574, (800) 952-0120, Fax: (310) 670-0725 • member IGTA

Connections Tours
Gay/Lesbian
169 Lincoln Rd., Ste. 302, Miami Beach, FL 33139 • (305) 673-3153, (800) 688-8463 (OUT-TIME), Fax: (305) 673-6501 • Local arrangements in Florida • member IGTA

Cruise Express
Gay/Lesbian
1904 3rd Ave., Ste. 900, Seattle, WA 98101 • (206) 467-0467, (800) 682-1988, Fax: (206) 467-6255 • cruises & tours • member IGTA

Cruisin' the Castro
Gay/Lesbian
375 Lexington St., San Francisco, CA • (415) 550-8110 • guided walking tour of the Castro • member IGTA

Custom Cruises International
482 Great House Dr., Milpitas, CA 95035 • (408) 945-8286, Fax: (408) 945-8989

Destination Discovery
Mostly Men
PO Drawer 659, Rutherford, CA 94573 • (707) 963-0543, (800) 954-5543, Fax: (707) 963-4160 • Wellness Vacations for HIV+ gay men • member IGTA
    February 23-March 2 — Hawaii
    May 25-June 1 — Hawaii
    October 12-19 — Hawaii

Different Drummer Tours
Men Only
PO Box 528, Glen Ellyn, IL 60137 • (708) 993-1716, (800) 645-1275, Fax: (708) 530-0059 • upscale foreign tours • member IGTA

Different Strokes Tours
Gay/Lesbian
1841 Broadway Ste. 607, New York, 10023 • (212) 262-3860, (800) 688-3301, Fax: (212) 262-3865 • gay cultural safaris to worldwide destinations • member IGTA

Doin' It Right Tours & Travel
Gay/Lesbian
1 St. Francis Pl. Ste. 2106, San Francisco, CA 94107 • (415) 621-3576 • gay cultural exchange tours & SF accommodations • member IGTA

Earth Walks
Straight/Gay
(505) 988-4157 • guided tour of American Southwest & Mexico
    December 27-Jan 3 — New Year's Journey for Men Who Love Men, Mexico
    February 9-16 — Yoga Retreat, Oaxaca, Mexico

Executive Tour Associates
Gay/Lesbian
PO Box 42151, Mesa, AZ 85274 • (602) 898-8853, (800) 382-1113 • Deluxe motor-coach tours of the Southwest • member IGTA

GAYVentures
Gay/Lesbian
2009 SW 9th St., Miami, FL 33135 • (305) 541-6141, (800) 940-7757, Fax: (305) 388-5259 • Puerto Rico tours • member IGTA

Great Canadian Ecoventures
Mixed Gay/Straight
PO Box 155, 1896 W. Broadway
Vancouver, BC V6J-1Y9 • (604) 730-0704, (800) 667-9453 • wildlife photography tours

Hanns Ebensten Travel
Mostly Men
513 Fleming St., Key West, FL 33040 • (305) 294-8174, Fax: (305) 292-9665 • Luxury and adventure star in Mr. Ebensten's unique worldwide tours for 10-24 gentlemen.
- January 30-Feb 8 — Cruise the Galapagos Islands in Style
- March 24-April 4 — Expedition to Easter Island
- April 7-21 — The Thai Experience
- April 30-May 13 — Cruise the Nile in Style (25th Anniversary Cruise)
- May 31-June 14 — Islands of Indonesia
- June 26-July 5 — Great Amazon Adventure Cruise
- August 31-September 14 — Sailing Cruise in Turkey
- September 14-28 — Expedition to Vilcabamba

Happy People Tours
Mostly Men
PO Box 620219, San Diego, CA 92162 • (619) 236-0984, (800) 227-9858, Fax: (619) 239-8700

International Gay Rodeo Association
Gay/Lesbian
(303) 832-4472

L'Arc en Ciel Voyages
Gay/Lesbian
PO Box 234, Wayne, PA 19087-0254 • (610) 964-7888, (800) 965-LARC (5272), Fax: (610) 964-8220 • Custom-Designed Tour Programs for the Gay & Lesbian Community

Lotus Land Tours
Straight/Gay
1251 Cardero St., Ste. 1251, Vancouver, Canada, BC V6G 2H9 • (604) 684-4922, Fax: (604) 684-4921 • Day paddle trips, no experience necessary.

New England Vacation Tours
Gay/Lesbian
PO Box 571 - Rte. 100, West Dover, VT 05356 • (802) 464-2076, (800) 742-7669, Fax: (802) 464-2629 • Fall foliage and party weekend gay/lesbian tours conducted by a mainstream tour operator.

Ocean Voyager
Gay/Lesbian
404 1/2 Henry St., Brooklyn, NY 11201 • (718) 624-3063, (800) 435-2531, Fax: (718) 624-5437 • Cruise Consultants, LTD
- December 21-Jan 4 1997 — Christmas Cruise
- February 14-17 — Key West Cruise
- March 15-22 — East Caribbean Cruise
- April 19-27 — Transatlantic Crossing
- May 24-June 1 — Grandeur of the Seas, East Caribbean Cruise
- July 11-18 — Alaska Cruise

Our Family Abroad
Gay/Lesbian
40 W. 57th St., New York, NY 10019 • (212) 459-1800, (800) 999-5500, Fax: (212) 581-3756 • All-inclusive package and guided motorcoach tours for lesbians and gay men to Europe, Asia, Africa and South America.

Outland Adventures
Straight/Gay
PO Box 16343, Seattle, WA 98116 • (206) 932-7012, Fax same as voice • ecologically sensitive cultural tours, snorkeling and biking adventures in Central America, Canada, Alaska and Washington State

OutWest Adventures
Gay/Lesbian

PO Box 8451, Missoula, MT 59807 • (406) 543-0262, (800) 743-0458 • Specializing in active Western vacations.

January 25-Feb 1 — Big Sky Gay Ski Tour
February 22-Mar 1 — Big Sky Gay Ski Tour
March 15-22 — Big Sky Gay Ski Tour

Pied Piper Tours
Mostly Men

330 W. 42nd St. Ste. 1804, New York, NY 10036 • (212) 239-2412, (800) 874-7312, Fax: (212) 643-1598 • QE2 cruises and more

January 18 — QE2 Hawaiian Cruise, 5 days
May 3 — QE2 Transatlantic Cruise, 6 days
May 9 — QE2 Weekender Cruise, 3 days
May 24-31 — Caribbean Cruise on the Norway
June 3 — QE2 Paris Sampler Cruise, 3 days
August 13 — QE2 Jazz Festival Cruise, 5 days
August 18 — QE2 Transatlantic Cruise, 6 days
August 30 — QE2 Bermuda Cruise, 5 days
October 7 — QE2 Fall Foliage Cruise, 13 days
November 26 — QE2 TransCanal Cruise, 13 days
December 21 — QE2 Caribbean Cruise, 15 days

Pink Triangle
Mostly Gay/Lesbian

743-A Addison St., Berkeley, CA 94710 • (510) 843-0181, Fax: (510) 843-4066 • Once-yearly worldwide country/western and square-dancing oriented tours.

February 17-March 3 — Pink Triangles Down Under — Australia
July 15-26 — Pink Triangles in Green & Plaid — Ireland & Scotland

Progressive Travels
Mostly Gay/Lesbian

224 W. Galer Ste. C, Seattle, WA 98119 • (206) 285-1987, (800) 245-2229, Fax: (206) 285-1988 • Luxury and standard walking and biking tours of Europe and the Pacific Northwest. • member IGTA

Rainbow Tours
Gay/Lesbian

87-3203 Road Guava, Kona Paradise, Captain Hook, HI 96704 • (808) 328-8406, Fax: (808) 328-8406 • Kayaking & snorkeling off black sand beaches of Kona Coast.

Rockwood Adventures
Straight/Gay

1330 Fulton Ave., West Vancouver, Canada, BC V7T 1N8 • (604) 926-7705, Fax: (604) 926-4139 • Rain Forest Walks, all levels, free hotel pick up.

RSVP
Mostly Men

2800 University Ave. SE, Minneapolis, MN 55414 • (612) 379-4697, (800) 328-7787, Fax: (612) 379-0484 • Cruises and all-gay resorts in the Caribbean, Mexico and the Mediterranean • member IGTA

February 8-15 — Mardi Gras Cruise
March 1-8 — Caribbean Cruise
March 21-29 — South American Cruise
June TBA — London, Paris, Amsterdam Europride '97 Cruises

T.R.I.P. Tours LTD.
Gay/Lesbian

11 Grace Ave., Great Neck , NY 11021 • (516) 487-9400, (800) 553-7494, Fax: (516) 487-5994 • Holidays at Sea: Cruise with Congenial Companions • member IGTA

February 14-17 — Valentine's Day: South Caribbean on the Nordic Empress
February 15-22 — Presidents' Week: West Caribbean on the Sun Princess
February 15-22 — Presidents' Week: South Caribbean on the Windward

Toto Tours *Mostly Men*
1326 W. Albion Ave. #3, Chicago, IL 60626 • (773) 274-8686, (800) 565-1241, Fax: (312) 274-8695 • Unique worldwide adventures

Tours to Paradise *Men Only*
PO Box 3656 , Los Angeles, CA 90078 • (213) 962-9169, Fax: (213) 962-3236 • Tours to Thailand • member IGTA

Underseas Expeditions *Gay/Lesbian*
PO Box 9455, Pacific Beach, CA 92169 • (619) 270-2900, (800) 669-0310, Fax: (619) 490-1002 • Warm water diving and scuba trips worldwide • member IGTA
   February 15-22 — Dive Saba aboard Caribbean Explorer
   March 12-22 — Dive Palau aboard Sun Dancer
   March 23-30 — Dive Truk, wrecks from WWII Japanese fleet
   August TBA — Dive Fiji aboard Fiji Aggressor

Please take a few minutes to fill out this survey and mail it back to us. *We want our Damron books to remain the best travelling guides for the gay and lesbian community for many years to come – and we need your input! Thanks for your time.*

1. Gender: ❑ Male ❑ Female

2. Race: ❑ Asian ❑ African-American ❑ Latino
❑ Native American ❑ Euro-American/White ❑ Other

3. Age: ❑ under 21 ❑ 21-25 ❑ 26-32
❑ 33-39 ❑ 40-49 ❑ 50+

4. Sexual Identity: ❑ Gay Male ❑ Bisexual
❑ Heterosexual ❑ Lesbian

5. Personal Income:
❑ under $15K ❑ $15-20K ❑ $20-25K
❑ $25-35K ❑ $35-50K ❑ $50-75K or more

6. Total Household Income:
❑ under $15K ❑ $15-20K ❑ $20-25K
❑ $25-35K ❑ $35-50K ❑ $50-75K
❑ $75-100K ❑ $100-150K ❑ $150K or more

7. Type of Residence:
❑ Own Home ❑ Rent Home
❑ Rent Apt/Flat ❑ Live with Family

8. Where do you live? (City, State, Country)

_____

9. Education:
❑ High School Graduate ❑ Some College
❑ Associate Degree ❑ Technical Certificate
❑ College Graduate ❑ Post-Graduate Studies
❑ Master's/Doctorate ❑ None of above

10. Employment Status:
❑ Unemployed ❑ Employed
❑ Retail Sales/Service ❑ Artist/Craftperson
❑ Skilled Labor ❑ Clerical
❑ Military ❑ Not Employed

11. Events you plan to attend in the future:
❑ Gay Ski Trip _____
❑ Gay Pride Parade _____
❑ Gay Cruises _____
❑ Circuit Party _____
❑ Other_____

READER SURVEY

12. Own or Use a Computer: ❑ Yes ❑ No (skip to 19)

13. What Make & Model: _____

14. How Much Memory: RAM _____ Hard Drive _____

15. Peripherals You Use: ❑ Modem: Speed: _____
                      ❑ CD-Rom: Speed: _____
                      ❑ Newton/PDA

16. Online Services You Use:
    ❑ America Online   ❑ Compuserve
    ❑ Prodigy   ❑ GayNet
    ❑ Other:_____

17. Internet Access:
   ❑ Email Only   ❑ Web   ❑ Full Access   ❑ None

18. Services You Would Use for Gay Travel Info:
    ❑ CD-Rom   ❑ Floppy Disks
    ❑ Website   ❑ Bulletin Board
    ❑ Mailing List   ❑ Chat Forum
    ❑ Newton/PDA program
    ❑ Other:_____

19. Familiarity with the Damron Address Book:
    ❑ This is the first copy I've looked at
    ❑ I've used previous editions

20. Other Damron Publications You Have Used:
    ❑ Damron Road Atlas
    ❑ Damron Accommodations
    ❑ Damron Women's Traveller
    ❑ None

21. Please Comment on the Damron Address Book
(compared to other travel guides):

_____

_____

_____

_____

To get on our mailing list, please fill in:

Name _____

Address _____

City/State/Zip _____

Please Mail To: Damron Survey, PO Box 422458
                       San Francisco, CA 94142

Male Order

1997 Damron Address Book

1997 Damron Address Book

1997 Damron Address Book

1997 Damron Address Book

USE YOUR HEAD.

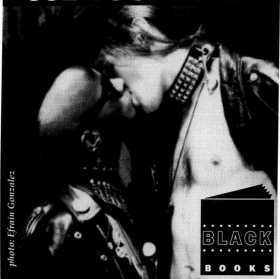

photo: Efrain Gonzalez

BLACK BOOKS

Sex for smart folks? You betcha. We publish and distribute books, zines, and other media on sex. Our best sellers:

The Black Book is a resource guide for the erotic explorer! It lists publications, clubs, groups, fetish wear, videos, adult toys, and much more throughout US/Canada. Fun to read! 4th edition is $18 postpaid, $19.30 to Calif., $20 to Canada/Mexico, $24 overseas.

Black Sheets is our hot zine of humor and sex. Kinky, queer, intelligent, and irreverent. For thinking sex maniacs everywhere! $20/4 issues, $6/sample. Add $1/issue to Can/Mex, $3/issue overseas.

Age statement to: PO Box 31155-D7, San Francisco CA 94131-0155 USA. Send $1 for our complete catalog, $2 outside USA, or included FREE with an order from this ad! Credit card orders: (800) 818-8823.